Research Methods and Data Analysis for Psychology

Stuart Wilson and Rory MacLean

McGraw-Hill Higher Education

London Boston Burr Ridge, IL Dubuque, IA Madison, WI New York San Francisco
St. Louis Bangkok Bogotá Caracas Kuala Lumpur Lisbon Madrid Mexico City
Milan Montreal New Delhi Santiago Seoul Singapore Sydney Taipei Toronto

Research Methods and Data Analysis for Psychology
Stuart Wilson and Rory MacLean
ISBN-13 9780077121655
ISBN-10 0077121651

Published by McGraw-Hill Education
Shoppenhangers Road
Maidenhead
Berkshire
SL6 2QL
Telephone: 44 (0) 1628 502 500
Fax: 44 (0) 1628 770 224
Website: www.mcgraw-hill.co.uk

British Library Cataloguing in Publication Data
A catalogue record for this book is available from the British Library

Library of Congress Cataloguing in Publication Data
The Library of Congress data for this book has been applied for from the Library of Congress

Acquisitions Editor: Natalie Jacobs/Ruben Hale
Development Editor: Jennifer Rotherham/Hannah Cooper
Senior Production Editor: James Bishop
Marketing Manager: Mark Barratt

Cover design by Adam Renvoize
Printed and bound in Great Britain by Bell & Bain Ltd., Glasgow

ISBN-13 9780077121655
ISBN-10 0077121651

Dedication

SW – To my parents, Kathleen and Joe, who taught me how to read and write.
RM – For Claire, Ailsa, Megan and Martha

Brief Table of Contents

Detailed Table of Contents

Preface

This text started out as an adaptation of four existing American texts,[1] but soon took on a life of its own. Although there is much material that we have used from each of these excellent texts, the resulting book is distinct from all of them in terms of its organization and focus. Our main aim when starting this project was to make a text that undergraduates would find accessible. This may sound obvious, but getting new students enthused about research methods and data analysis is no easy task. We have done our best to keep the language straightforward and to avoid long-winded technical explanations wherever possible. By the time we get to the statistics, we should hopefully have built up enough trust in the reader that they stick with us whenever they find the technical material challenging. More than anything, however, we hope that our genuine enthusiasm for the subject has come across in the text, and that students will appreciate from this just how interesting, engaging and useful the ideas presented are.

Features

There are a number of pedagogical features that we have used. Most of them are obvious and straightforward. Within the chapters, we have tried to include as many illustrations as we could get away with, in order to help illustrate the concepts that we are trying to explain. There are "Stop and Think" boxes at various points, which should allow students to reflect upon the material, and "Test Yourself" boxes that are intended to consolidate learning. We also have "In the Know" boxes. These serve a number of functions. They will sometimes provide a more in-depth explanation for some ideas, while at other times they give historical context. We have also used them in order to highlight instances from the research literature that help bring to life the concepts in the text. As well as these features, each chapter has an overview, a set of objectives, a summary, questions and activities. A list of key terms is provided on the accompanying website (see below). Combined with the features in the main body of the text, these features should provide students with a wide variety of learning tools.

Resources for students and instructors

We had originally planned to include step-by-step instructions for conducting statistical tests on SPSS. It quickly became clear that this would only add clutter to the text, and so we have decided to put this material on to the book's supporting website (www.mcgraw-hill.co.uk/textbooks/wilsonandmaclean). The website can be used in conjunction with the book (or on its own) and provides information on how to perform the many statistical tests we describe in the text. Between the text and the website, we believe that there is adequate material for most undergraduate research methods and data analysis courses in psychology.

---

1 Bordens and Abbott's *Research Design and Methods: A Process Approach* (2008), Cozby's *Methods in Behavioural Research* (2007), Shaughnessy, Zechmeister and Zechmeister's *Research Methods in Psychology* (2006), and Spatz and Kardas's *Research Methods: Ideas, Techniques and Reports* (2008).

Learning Outcomes

At the beginning of each chapter, this feature outlines the key topics that will be presented to you.

Key terms

These are highlighted and defined in the margins. An ideal tool for last-minute revision or to check definitions as you read.

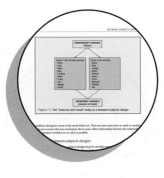

Figures and tables

Each chapter provides a number of figures, illustrations and photos to help you to visualize key methods.

Stop and Think boxes

These appear throughout the chapters and provide an opportunity for you to reflect upon the topics being discussed.

In the Know boxes

These serve a number of functions. They will sometimes provide a more in-depth explanation for some ideas, while at times they give historical context.

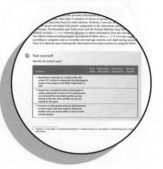

Test yourself

This feature provides you with additional opportunity to consolidate your learning by testing yourself on what you have just read.

Summary

At the end of each chapter, this section pulls together the threads of the discussion. An ideal tool for recapping and revision.

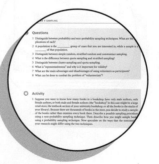

Activities and questions

Discussion questions and activities encourage you to review and apply the knowledge you have acquired from each chapter. They are a useful revision tool.

Technology to Enhance Learning and Teaching

After completing each chapter, log on to the supporting Online Learning Centre website. Take advantage of the study tools offered to reinforce the material you have read in the text, and to develop your knowledge of research methods and data analysis for psychology in a fun and effective way.

Resources for students include:

- Glossary
- Weblinks
- Self-test multiple choice, true/false and essay questions
- Datasets
- Additional questions

Resources for lecturers:

- Instructor's Manual
- PowerPoint presentations
- Image Bank
- Case studies with teaching notes
- Solutions to questions in the book

Visit www.mcgraw-hill.co.uk/textbooks/wilsonandmaclean today

Test Bank available in McGraw-Hill EZ Test Online

A test bank of hundreds of questions is available to lecturers adopting this book for their module. A range of questions is provided for each chapter, including multiple choice, true or false, and short answer or essay questions. The questions are identified by type, difficulty and topic to help you to select questions that best suit your needs and are accessible through an easy-to-use online testing tool, **McGraw-Hill EZ Test Online**.

McGraw-Hill EZ Test Online is accessible to busy academics virtually anywhere – in their office, at home or while travelling – and eliminates the need for software installation. Lecturers can choose from question banks associated with their adopted textbook or easily create their own questions. They also have access to hundreds of banks and thousands of questions created for other McGraw-Hill titles. Multiple versions of tests can be saved for delivery on paper or online through WebCT, Blackboard and other course management systems. When created and delivered though EZ Test Online, students' tests can be immediately marked, saving lecturers time and providing prompt results to students.

To register for this FREE resource, visit www.eztestonline.com

Custom Publishing Solutions: Let us help make our **content** your **solution**

At McGraw-Hill Education our aim is to help lecturers to find the most suitable content for their needs delivered to their students in the most appropriate way. Our **custom publishing solutions** offer the ideal combination of content delivered in the way that best suits lecturer and students.

Our custom publishing programme offers lecturers the opportunity to select just the chapters or sections of material they wish to deliver to their students from a database called CREATE™ at www.mcgrawhillcreate.com

CREATE™ contains over two million pages of content from:

- textbooks
- professional books
- case books – Harvard Articles, Insead, Ivey, Darden, Thunderbird and BusinessWeek
- Taking Sides – debate materials

across the following imprints:

- McGraw-Hill Education
- Open University Press
- Harvard Business Publishing
- US and European material

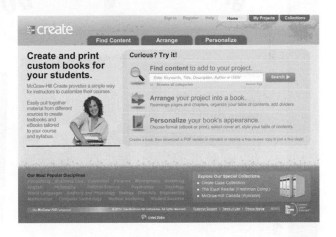

There is also the option to include additional material authored by lecturers in the custom product – this does not necessarily have to be in English.

We will take care of everything from start to finish in the process of developing and delivering a custom product to ensure that lecturers and students receive exactly the material needed in the most suitable way.

With a custom publishing solution, students enjoy the best selection of material deemed to be the most suitable for learning everything they need for their courses – something of real value to support their learning. Teachers are able to use exactly the material they want, in the way they want, to support their teaching on the course.

Please contact your local McGraw-Hill representative with any questions, or alternatively contact Warren Eels e: warren_eels@mcgraw-hill.com.

Acknowledgements

Authors' acknowledgements

First, we would both like to thank Ruben Hale, who was the commissioning editor who got us both involved in this project and who was so enthusiastic about it at the outset. Hannah Cooper was our initial development editor at the point where were trying to get the project off the ground, so thanks to her for her support. After Ruben and Hannah left McGraw-Hill we were lucky enough to work with Natalie Jacobs and Jennifer Rotherham, who have both been a joy to work with, and who have shown great patience and professionalism.

SW would like to thank: Everyone whose name appears in Table 4.1. Everyone who read and commented on a chapter, especially Maria Canos, Jill Domoney, Melissa Llano, Jennifer McGhie, Trudi Slater, and one Speech and Language Therapy student at QMU whose name I have forgotten (sorry). Also, thanks to Stuart, Lynette, Ruaridh and Owen; to Jackie and Zack; and to Duncan Robb, Karen Goodall, Chris McVittie, and all other colleagues and students in the School of Arts and Social Sciences, Queen Margaret University, Edinburgh. Thanks to Rahul Sambaraju for his efforts in creating the online content.

RM would like to thank colleagues and students at the School of Health and Social Sciences, Edinburgh Napier University.

Publisher's acknowledgements

Our thanks go to the following reviewers for their comments at various stages in the text's development:

Michael Price	Brunel University
Mike Cox	Newcastle University
Kiran Sarma	NUI Galway
Phil Gee	Plymouth University
Chris McVittie	Queen Margaret University
Barbara Kingsley	Roehampton University
Annette Steer	Surrey University
Elizabeth Attree	University of East London
Peter Gardner	University of Leeds
Bonaventura Majolo	Lincoln
Peter Theuns	Vrije Universiteit Brussels
Simon Cooper	Liverpool John Moores

Jurek Kirakowski	University College Cork
Magnus Lindgren	Lund
Angela Nananidou	Liverpool John Moores
Kamilla Johannsdottir	University of Akureyri
Michael Waldmann	University of Gottingen
Paul Redford	UWE
Suzanne Guerin	UCD
Werner Bohmke	Rhodes University
Terry Dowdall	University of Cape Town
Richard Rowe	Sheffield
Sibe Doosje	Utrecht
Iain Williamson	De Montfort
Jo Horne	Hull
Frederik van Acker	Vrije Universiteit Brussels
Denny Borsboom	University of Amsterdam
Magnus Lindgren	Lund
Eric Hansen	Mälardalen University

About the Authors

Stuart Wilson I am a graduate of University of Glasgow, and completed a PhD at University of Edinburgh in 2003. I have been teaching research methods and data analysis since 1999. As strange as it may sound, I have always had a vague notion that I'd like to be involved in authoring a research methods and data analysis textbook. I have a wide range of interests, from consciousness and philosophy of mind to understanding anomalous experiences and strange beliefs. I have been a member of the Psychology department at Queen Margaret University, Edinburgh, since 2003.

Rory MacLean is a Lecturer at Napier University, Edinburgh, and has seven years' experience of teaching research methods and data analysis.

Chapter 1

Why Do I Have to Study *This*?

OVERVIEW

This is a general introductory chapter, but please do not skip it! We try to set the context for everything that follows in this book, and we try to give a few handy survival tips as well. The chapter will discuss why knowledge of research methods and data analysis is important, and will try to address some of the common concerns that students have when embarking on a research methods and data analysis course. We also provide short summaries for the rest of the chapters in this book.

Introduction

"Why do we have to study *this*?" It is a simple question. It has a (fairly) simple answer. But it is still the most common question that we hear from students when they find out for the first time that they will have to study research methods and data analysis as part of their psychology degree. Other things that we hear include: "but I can't do maths", "I'm rubbish with numbers" and "what does this have to do with psychology?" These are all valid comments and they are common to many students when starting a course on psychology without having much previous knowledge about the subject. For many students, studying research methods and data analysis is a chore. These things do not immediately seem relevant when you start studying psychology and are eager to find out lots of interesting and exciting facts about the mind and behaviour. To many, the research methods part of their course is viewed as an irritant and a distraction from the "real" psychology. Unfortunately, this negativity is often left to linger. This is not the case with all degrees or all research methods and data analysis courses. There are many excellent teachers and lecturers who do a great job in making research methods and data analysis relevant to the rest of psychology and less painful for their students. However, there will always be some students who never fully understand why research methods and data analysis are important.

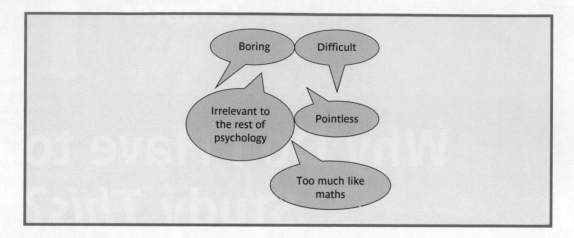

When studied out of context, it is not difficult to see why people think like this. In isolation, many of the topics *are* dry and it is sometimes hard to see the links with psychology. But when you scratch the surface, you will find that research methods and data analysis are at the very core of psychology, and a good working knowledge of these areas is indispensable to all psychologists and students of psychology. Not only that, the subjects can even be fun once you get to grips with them, and understanding methods will allow you to unleash your imagination in your quest to discover more about mind and behaviour. Let's see why.

So why do *you* have to study this?

Regardless of whether you are studying psychology or some other subject, research is likely to play an important role in it. The reason for this is simple. Flick through any textbook on any subject[1] and you will find lots of facts, ideas, theories, discoveries, debates and descriptions of phenomena. Where does all of this come from? The knowledge that fills your textbooks does not arrive fully formed out of nowhere. Smart people can (and do) have great ideas, but it is very unusual for the ideas to go straight from someone's head and into a textbook. They have to be checked. Most of the facts that you find in your textbooks are a product of research. A good idea is one thing, but for the idea to have any influence or to be accepted by other people in the area it has to be supported with evidence, and that evidence is a result of research.

In the Know

What do we mean by "research"?
We have used the word "research" a few times already, and it is in the title of this book, so we think we should say a bit about what we mean when we use it. To many people (students included) "research" means looking for books, articles and reports that people have already written on a specific topic. This is one meaning of "research" but it is not what we're talking about. In psychology (and in most

---

1   Probably the only exceptions to this are "pure" philosophy and mathematics.

other areas) research is the process of finding out facts that relate to a question that you have asked. So, if you have asked a question about whether drinking alcohol influences our ability to make rational decisions, then research is the process that you will go through to help you investigate that question directly. You can search for books or articles that have already looked at this question, but we are using the word "research" to describe a more "hands on" approach. This might involve actually doing a study that (for example) would look at the effect that alcohol has on people's decision making. How you do this will depend on the method of research that you decide to use. There are many, and the first part of this book will introduce you to some of them. The second part explains what you do with the information that you collect from your research and how you can draw conclusions from it.

Part of your job as a student in your area is to learn the facts, ideas, theories and concepts associated with the discipline that you have chosen to study. This is not enough, however. Knowing these things is only one part of learning about a subject like psychology.

Evaluating research

As well as learning all the "facts" that you read in textbooks, you also need to have an understanding of the ways in which these facts were generated. This is important for two reasons. First, knowing the process of research that has led to certain things being accepted[2] will allow you to look at them with a critical eye. Just because you read about things in a textbook does not necessarily mean that you have to accept them as being true. But if you are going to criticize them, then you will need a good reason to do so. You cannot just base a criticism on your gut instinct or because something does not sit well with your prior beliefs. If you want to critically evaluate something in your area of study, then you will need to fully understand the process that led to this fact being accepted in the first place. In most cases, this process will involve research. If you can understand the method of research used to investigate a phenomenon, then you are in a powerful position because you can then evaluate it and assess whether, in your opinion, it is a legitimate finding. You may spot a potential problem with some part of the research process and this might lead you to think that the conclusions are invalid. If you decided that a finding is not legitimate, then an understanding about how to do research will allow you to investigate it for yourself. This is the second reason why knowledge of research methods is important.

Doing your own research

Another feature of being a student of a given subject is learning how to conduct your own research. Learning all the facts in a textbook is fine, but sooner or later you will also have to become an active participant in your chosen area of study. This means that you should become familiar with the various ways in which research is conducted so that you can then do your own. This is a feature of most courses, but it is often overlooked by students (as well as some teachers and lecturers) and is sometimes seen as being secondary to the learning of all the "facts" that already exist. In truth, the learning of the "facts" should never be completely divorced from understanding the research process that gave rise to those facts, but this is what sometimes happens. Most courses

---

2   We use the term "accepted" very loosely – most "facts" are only tentatively accepted and are always under scrutiny.

in psychology will require you to become an active researcher, posing meaningful psychological questions and then conducting research to address them. All of this requires an understanding of research methods (and, inevitably, methods of data analysis). Convinced? We hope so. Let's look at one other way in which an understanding of these things can be valuable.

Research methods in the real world

Knowledge of research methods is a powerful tool to have at your disposal. If you understand the principles of good research, and then add to the mix some logical and critical thinking skills, then you have a set of intellectual tools with which to think about the world around you. What do we mean by that? Table 1.1 has some questions that you may have asked at some point.

It is likely that you will have pondered some of these questions at some point in the past. Every day we are faced with claims about the world. People try to sell us a new "miracle cure"; politicians warn us about environmental catastrophe; a friend tries to convince us to take a rabbit's foot on a long journey to bring good luck. Nobody can be an expert on all of these things, but these are all claims that we can investigate, and an understanding of the research process and how we gather and evaluate evidence will help us think about such things in a new way. If someone tries to sell you a vitamin that they say will make you more intelligent, you have a right to ask about the evidence for this claim. A working knowledge of research methods and data analysis will allow you to either conduct your own research into the claim, or at least evaluate any evidence (or otherwise) that is already out there. This is why knowledge of these things is useful in the real world. Yes, these things can sometimes be a bit dry but they will help you to understand the world. Is that not worth knowing? It doesn't matter what course you happen to be on or what you are studying: you will most likely have experienced at least some curiosity about *something* that has caused you to embark on your chosen path. If it is a psychology course that you are doing, then you will undoubtedly have an interest in the mind and in behaviour. If this is the case then you will have to know about research to understand *how* we come to know what we do, and to pursue your own interests in the field. *That's* why you have study this and *that's* why it is so important.

Is "doing statistics" as painful as it sounds?

Before we answer that question, we need to quickly convince you that statistics are necessary. Let's take the question of whether "telepathy" exists or not from Table 1.1. It is a controversial

Table 1.1 Questions we could ask

Can people learn while sleeping?	Does telepathy (mind-reading) really exist?
Is astrology valid?	Do people behave differently when there is a full moon?
Does hypnosis help people give up smoking?	Can we spot the signs that give away a liar?
Does eating fish make us more intelligent?	Does the MMR vaccine increase the risk of autism?
Are men better drivers than women?	Is global warming a result of humans and how much of a risk does it really pose?

subject, but we can test it. Suppose you decide to look into this, and you design a research study in which two people are physically separated by a large enough distance that normal communication between them should be impossible (and mobile phones are confiscated at the door). You get one of these people (the "sender") to look at a picture and try to telepathically "send" it to the other person (the "receiver"). Once they have done this for a while, the "receiver" looks at four pictures, one of which was the one that the "sender" was looking at, and tries to tell which of the four pictures it was. You do this with 100 different "senders" and "receivers" and at the end you find that the "receivers" managed to correctly guess which picture was being sent 28% of the time. Does this mean that telepathy was working in your study? You will have to understand statistics to be able to draw a conclusion. If each "receiver" looks at four pictures, then you would expect them to choose the correct picture *by chance* 1 in 4 times. That is, if they were purely guessing (and there was no telepathy) then you would expect them to be correct 25% of the time (25% being the same as 1 in 4). But you found they were correct on 28% of the trials. This is higher than 25%, but is it high enough to allow us to conclude that telepathy may have been working, or is this just a statistical "wobble" that can be explained by chance? What if their average score was 30%? Or 22%? Knowledge of statistics will help you make decisions about what the outcome of your study might mean. In **Chapter 15** we discuss why we need to know about statistics – they allow us to make decisions about whether or not the information that we collect from our research is actually telling us anything interesting or meaningful.

ch. 15

Which, of course, brings us to the question above; is "doing statistics" as painful as it sounds? We will not lie to you. There are numbers involved. And calculations. But that doesn't mean that it is the same as mathematics. It is similar, but it's not the same. Usually, the most important thing for you to understand is what a statistical test does and how it does it. You do not have to understand the mathematics behind each test and you *will not* have to work from "first principles" and be able to derive statistical equations from mathematical theory. What you will have to do is be able to "plug" data into statistical formulae, which you probably can do already (for example, working out an average – if you can do this, then you can plug numbers into a formula, because that is what you are doing when you work out an average). The most important part of learning about statistics is gaining an understanding of the concepts involved. Statistics can sometimes look quite frightening, but do not let that put you off. If you can get your head around *what* a particular statistical test is doing and *how* it does it, then you will be better prepared for the parts that actually involve playing with numbers.

Doing stats

When it comes to doing statistical calculations, there are two ways of approaching them. The first way of approaching statistical calculations is to do them "by hand". This involves using the data that you obtain from your research and plugging it into statistical formulae. It is a long, slow, boring and often painful process. In reality, few psychologists these days actually do their analyses in this way, because it is far easier to use a computer program. Despite this, we will be running through many of the less painful tests by hand. We do not do this because we are sadists, but because it will help you to gain an understanding of what the statistical test is actually doing to the numbers (honestly). Some readers will be tempted to avoid doing this. We would advise against this (partly because it is the type of thing you might be asked to do in a statistics examination), but if you do avoid it, then at least try to understand the conceptual explanation for what the statistical test does to the numbers. As for doing statistics by hand, it really is a matter of being patient, fighting off the creeping panic and working through the equations in a sensible and ordered way.

The second way to approach statistical calculations is to use statistical software such as SPSS (Statistical Package for the Social Sciences). These programs are powerful tools with many applications. Using them can be quite frustrating at first, because they require you to become familiar with their many menus and features. This takes a bit of getting used to, but no more so than any other new software that you use for the first time. It is also the case that to be able to successfully navigate your way around the software you will have to be familiar with many of the terms introduced in this text and have an understanding of the principles of research methods and data analysis. You should see statistical software as a tool that can be used to do complex statistical analyses very quickly. You should not see it as an excuse not to learn statistics because "the computer will do it for me". Unfortunately, it doesn't work like that, and you will require a decent working knowledge of the statistics you are using to be able to efficiently use SPSS. If you do not have this basic working knowledge, then you will find it very difficult to understand the menus in SPSS, will find it extremely hard to decide which features are best suited to the data that you are trying to analyse, and will find it practically impossible to make sense of the output that SPSS gives you. Statistical software like SPSS should *not* be seen as a "crutch" for people who do not understand or cannot be bothered learning statistics, because if you view it this way you will end up even more confused! When it comes to statistics, there are very few short cuts to understanding, and using SPSS as a substitute for learning the "hard" stuff is not one of them. As we mentioned above, one of the skills required in using programs like SPSS is being able to interpret the results of the tests that you conduct. You will find that these programmes give you a lot of output, not all of which is directly relevant to the question that you are asking. You will have to develop the skill of identifying what is important and what it is telling you.

Survival tips

One thing that we have noticed over the years is that the way people learn about research methods and data analysis is different to the way they learn about things in their course. Knowledge about research methods and data analysis tends to be cumulative. What this means is that much of the material that you will be taught later in a course (or later in this book) will build upon concepts that were introduced earlier. The assumption is that you already know and understand these concepts and can use them when more difficult or advanced material is being introduced. This tends to be a bit different to other things you might be learning. When learning other things, it is sometimes possible for you to "dip in and out" of material without too much difficulty. If you miss a few lectures (or a few chapters in a textbook) in another area, you might find that it is fairly easy to understand what is going on despite having missed some previous information. In research methods and data analysis courses, it is far more difficult to dip in and out. If you do miss a few classes or skip a few chapters, you might find yourself a bit lost. This is one of the main reasons why students lose their way in these courses. Now, we do not want to sound like strict schoolteachers, telling you that "you must attend all classes and read this book from cover to cover". We appreciate that this is not always possible and acknowledge that there are other reasons why students miss classes and skip chapters. However, if you do find yourself in that position, then you should be aware that it is in your interests to cover the material that you have missed. Again, we are not saying this to be strict. We are saying it because it will prevent you from finding yourself adrift. The "take home" message is that knowledge in research methods and data analysis builds upon what came before. If you keep this in mind then you will be more likely to tailor the way you learn to suit your own needs.

Another way in which research methods and data analysis classes are different in comparison to other subjects is in the way that people learn the material. The way that you learn is likely to change and develop during your time as a student. At first, you will probably find yourself learning "facts". Names/dates/ideas in textbooks are all facts to be learned, and you will try very hard to cram them all into your head. Learning research methods and data analysis is, once again, different. If you start the research methods and data analysis component of your course at the same time as other topics, then it is natural that you will employ a similar learning strategy, which generally involves squeezing as many facts as possible into your brain. Unfortunately, this will only get you so far. Suppose you learn about a particular type of experimental design. You might learn that "a **within subjects design** is one in which all participants are tested under all conditions". Learning that fact will serve you well if the question you are asked in an examination is "What is a within-subjects design?" However, what is more likely is that you will be asked something like, "Jane wants to study the effect of alcohol on decision making. How can she do this using a within-subjects design?" In other words, you should have an understanding of the concepts involved and how to apply them rather than having a list of facts in your head. This discrepancy will reduce as you progress, because it is likely that you will be increasingly asked to understand concepts and apply them, but your approach to learning research methods and data analysis may be of a different type to how you will learn other things at the start of your course. This may not apply to absolutely everyone, but we mention it so that you are aware of it and know that cramming your head full of facts can only get you so far in this topic.

ch. 7
p.125

Related to this is the way that you might learn statistical tests. There is no substitute for experience, so as well as learning about the concepts behind the statistics you should also try to complete as many practical examples as possible. This will serve you well and you may well find that it becomes easier the more you do it. It is time for us to stop sounding like schoolteachers.

Using this book

We have included several features in this text to help you through. We understand that most people will not necessarily read chapters in the order that we have included them, so we have included "signposts" (like this one ◀━━) to other chapters and other sections within chapters to help you navigate your way through the concepts. Sometimes, you will be reading a chapter and we will refer to something in a previous chapter (or a later chapter). Rather than having to look up the index and then find the relevant page, the signposts should allow you to quickly refer backwards (or forwards). This is particularly useful when we use bits of jargon or technical terms, the meaning of which you may have forgotten. As technical terms and jargon are introduced, we will also include a margin box containing a definition.

Each chapter begins with a summary and a list of "learning outcomes". The learning outcomes are an indication of what you should have achieved by the end of the chapter. At various points in each chapter you will find visual aids. Rather than clutter up the text and distract your attention, we have tried to include these at points when they are most useful to you. The "In the Know" boxes (like the one on research in this chapter) serve several purposes. Sometimes we will use them to describe bits of research or put certain concepts into context; at other times we will use them to clarify certain things (which is what the one above does). Other features are fairly self-explanatory and we will leave you to discover them for yourselves.

We have also included end-of-chapter questions and activities for you to test your knowledge and further your understanding. It is very tempting just to skip these things once you finish reading the text, but they can be useful as they allow you to assess your own progress.

Stylistically, we have tried to make the text as easy to read as possible. Books on this topic can be quite dense and impenetrable. Where possible, we have tried to avoid this, although difficult material is difficult material and there will be points where you will have to stick with us and get through it.

Chapter summaries

Section 1: Conceptual issues – getting started in research

Chapter 2: Science and knowledge

Where does knowledge come from? How do we know what we know? What is "science"? How does science work? This chapter will introduce you to these questions. After looking at various ways of acquiring "knowledge" we will then dive head-first into science – what it is, what it is for, who does it and how they do it. Hopefully, you will learn something you did not know already and we may even be able to shatter a few preconceptions about science in the process.

Chapter 3: Psychology as a science

Is psychology a science? This is a question that is still being debated by psychologists and other scientists. If it is a science, then it seems quite unlike physics, biology and chemistry. Can psychologists measure things in the same way as other scientists? What does "measurement" mean to a psychologist? What are the similarities and differences between psychology and other sciences? In this chapter, we will explore the issues surrounding treating psychology as a science.

Section 2: Methods and issues in research

Chapter 4: The language of research

The previous chapters should have started you thinking about psychology and how it is conducted. Chapter 4 will introduce you to the language of research. We will introduce the basic terms and concepts that will reappear throughout the rest of the book and are central to understanding research methods.

Chapter 5: Introduction to methods

Psychologists have a variety of ways to find out about the mind and behaviour. The methods that are used to answer psychological questions are many and varied. This chapter will cover what methods are, as well as serving as a brief introduction to the methods that will be described in more detail in later chapters. The chapter ends with a discussion of validity and how it applies to methodology.

Chapter 6: Introduction to experimental methods

Experiments are one of the most common and powerful methods used in psychology. Chapter 6 outlines the basic features of experiments and will cover the concepts and terminology associated with them. This short chapter concludes with a discussion on how researchers control their experiments in order to reduce the likelihood that their conclusions are mistaken.

Chapter 7: Experimental designs

Having laid the groundwork in Chapter 6, we now go on to describe the various types of experimental design that a researcher can use. Basic experimental designs such as within- and between-subjects will be covered, along with their strengths and weaknesses. The second half of the chapter will expand upon these and will cover more complex designs.

Chapter 8: Quasi-experimental and developmental designs

Chapter 8 begins by covering designs used by researchers when the strict conditions of "experimental" research cannot be met. These designs are known as "quasi-experiments", and we will discuss some of the issues associated with using such techniques. The second half of the chapter focuses on developmental designs, which are used whenever we want to look at the way in which something changes over a period of time.

Chapter 9: Sampling

Who do you get to take part in your research? It might seem like a simple question, but there are many issues associated with obtaining a "sample", and this is the chapter in which we will introduce you to the perils, pitfalls and methods of sampling from a population.

Chapter 10: Introduction to qualitative research

In this chapter we provide an alternative viewpoint to the scientific/experimental approach. Not all psychologists agree with the assumptions that are made in "scientific" psychology. This chapter introduces some of the main arguments for approaching psychology in a different way and looks at some of the issues surrounding doing psychology qualitatively.

Chapter 11: Qualitative data collection

Chapter 10 covered some of the arguments for conducting qualitative research in psychology. Chapter 11 looks at some of the ways that qualitative data can be collected. Semi-structured interviews, focus groups, diary studies, using Web-based data and obtaining data from media sources will all be outlined in this chapter.

Chapter 12: Observational methods

"If you want to find out about people, observe them." It is not quite as simple as that, but observational methods are a useful tool for psychologists. But how do we make observations? What do we observe? How do we record our observations? Chapter 12 will cover the various features of conducting observational research.

Chapter 13: Survey methods

"If you want to find out about people, ask them." Again, it is not that simple, but psychologists do ask people about themselves. What should you ask? How should you ask it? How should you collect people's answers? What things might influence the answers that people give you? This chapter will look at the issues involved in using surveys as a way to collect psychological information.

Section 3: Data analysis

Chapter 14: Introduction to statistics and describing data

This is where the stats start! This chapter will introduce you to statistics and why they are used. We will try to place the use of statistics in a context that emphasizes them as a tool for making sense of data. We will then (gently) introduce you to some basic descriptive statistics and will also introduce you to SPSS – the most common statistics computer package used by psychologists.

Chapter 15: Introduction to inferential statistics

In this chapter, we will introduce you to the logic behind inferential statistics. We use statistics to help us make inferences and to test our ideas, so this chapter is important preparation for the rest of the statistics chapters.

Chapter 16: Comparing differences between two samples or conditions

We sometimes measure people on some psychological construct under two different conditions. Alternatively, we often get two different groups of people to do the same thing and see if they differ on some measurement we take. This chapter will tell you how to statistically analyse whether there is any real difference between the two groups or between the two conditions. This chapter links back to Chapter 6.

Chapter 17: Comparing differences between more than two conditions: Part 1 – One-way designs

In this chapter we will cover the statistical tests used when you have more than two groups or more than two conditions. We will build on what was covered in the previous couple of chapters and introduce some new concepts, like the Analysis of Variance (ANOVA) test.

Chapter 18: Comparing differences between more than two conditions: Part 2 – Factorial designs

Chapter 18 will extend the analysis techniques that were introduced to in the previous chapter, to include designs that are a bit more complicated. Again, we will look at how to analyse designs that have more than two groups or conditions using ANOVA, but we will also add more variables into the mix and discuss the impact that these might have on your analysis and the interpretation of your results.

Chapter 19: Testing for relationships and making predictions

As well as looking for differences between groups or between conditions, we also sometimes look for relationships between things. This chapter will cover the statistical techniques for determining when a relationship between two things is meaningful and how to make predictions about the values of one thing based on the values of another.

Chapter 20: Analysing nominal data

Not all things can be measured in the same way (as we outline in Chapter 4) and sometimes our data will consist of things that exist in categories (males/females, redheads/brunettes etc.). This is a different type of data to other things that can be measured on a scale and we need different statistics to deal with data like this. This chapter covers how to analyse this type of data.

Chapter 21: Advanced statistical methods

This chapter will go into some of the more advanced techniques such as multivariate analyses, factor analysis, analysis of covariance, meta-analysis, loglinear analysis, discriminant analysis, logistic regression, path analysis and structural equation modelling. These techniques are becoming more prevalent and so we have included them in this book as an introduction to more complex forms of analyses.

Chapter 22: Analysing qualitative data

So far, all of the analysis techniques we have included have been quantitative in nature, but not all psychological research involves number-crunching. In this chapter we will introduce you to the main forms of qualitative analysis, including grounded theory, interpretative phenomenological analysis, discourse analysis and protocol analysis.

Section 4: The research process in context

Chapter 23: Planning research

This chapter will give you some handy hints on getting a research project off the ground. How do you get ideas for research? How do you know if your idea is a good one? How do you turn these ideas into questions that you can actually test? What do you need to do before starting research? How do you find out what other research has been done on this question? How do you obtain articles that are relevant to your research? How do you read these articles critically? What things should you think about before data collecting? What might you be able to do to make the data-collecting process run smoothly? What do you do after you have collected your data? As you can see from these questions, this chapter is all about the practical things that are involved in undertaking a research project from beginning to end.

Chapter 24: Ethics in psychological research

The penultimate chapter deals with ethics. Being near the end of the book should not be considered a reflection on the importance of this topic, as ethical considerations should feature in every aspect of your work as a psychologist, whether student or professional. This chapter will introduce you to the main ethical issues that psychologists must consider. We will cover studies from psychology's history that raised ethical questions and we will look at some ethical questions that relate specifically to Internet research and to research with animals. We will also look at integrity in research, and consider issues such as research fraud and plagiarism. Being involved in psychology carries with it a great responsibility, and this chapter should help guide your thinking about proper conduct.

Chapter 25: Communicating and reporting research – reports, presentations and posters

So, you have come up with an idea, designed a study to test it, conducted the study and analysed the data. What do you do next? You have to tell the world about it. This chapter will look at some ways psychologists disseminate their findings, both to other psychologists and to the world at large. Research reports are probably the most common way to do this, so this chapter will give you detailed guidance on how to write such a report according to the standard format that most psychology journals adhere to. We will also give you guidance on orally presenting your research to groups of peers, and on how to create a poster that illustrates your findings in a concise and visually appealing way.

A final word . . .

We know what it is like to embark on a research methods and data analysis course. It can be quite a daunting experience. We know this from our years of teaching this subject, but we also know it from our experience as students. For many students (and this certainly applied to me, SW, when I was a student) the relevance of this part of the degree does not become apparent until there is a requirement to conduct a research study. Inevitably, this involves designing a study to answer a question and then analysing the data. You would be amazed at how many students suddenly realize at this point that the research methods and data analysis classes that they were made to sit through in previous years actually were useful. Some students thank their lucky stars that they paid attention in these classes while others end up in a state of acute panic when faced with a research study to design, conduct, analyse and report. The reason for the panic is that they failed to devote the time required to build up a working knowledge of this part of their course and this has now come back to haunt them. This is a phenomenon that is never going to go away, but if we can make you aware of it now then we might succeed in preventing at least some people from falling into the same trap.

Much of this is not easy. We know. But it is important. If you realize this early and then dedicate yourself to learning it, you will be saving yourself a lot of trouble further down the line (trust us on this). In this book we hope to make the journey as painless as it can possibly be. We also hope that there will be some subject matter in the following pages that captures your imagination and that might even be enjoyable.[3] Let's get started . . .

---

3   If this is the case then we would love to hear from you . . . in fact, all feedback (good or bad) is appreciated.

SECTION 1

Conceptual Issues – Getting Started in Research

Science and Knowledge

Take a deep breath, as this is a long chapter. It is also a very important one. Our aim here is to introduce you to how we establish knowledge about the world. We hope to convince you that science is a very effective tool for building our knowledge about the natural world, whether that is physical, chemical, biological or psychological knowledge. Everyone has heard of science, but this chapter will tell you what it actually is and will dispel some widely held myths about it. When reading this chapter, always ask yourself "how do we come to know *anything*?" The amazing thing about science is that, once you have an understanding of the basic principles, you can apply them to find out just about anything you want to know about the natural world, including behaviour and psychological processes. That is why it is so powerful, that is why it is so important and that is why this chapter is so long! We hope you find it interesting.

After studying this chapter and working through the exercises, you should be able to:

● State the various ways in which our "knowledge" about the world comes about and, where appropriate, critique these techniques

● Define *science* and give an account of the characteristics of scientific practices

● Outline the main features of the scientific method

● Determine the difference between basic and applied research, and recognize the overlaps between the two

- Define what "theories" are in scientific terms, and describe what they are for and what constitutes a scientific theory

- State what Popper and Kuhn had to say about science from their philosophical perspectives

- Distinguish between science, non-science and pseudoscience, stating what criteria can be used to make this distinction

Knowledge and where it comes from

How do you know what you know? It's a strange question, but think about it. Where does your knowledge come from? You probably learned much of what you know at school or college, but how do you know what you learned is "true"? How do you know what is true and what is not? This is a big question and there is a whole area of philosophy dedicated to questions like this. It's called **epistemology** and it looks at what knowledge actually is (the nature of knowledge), where it comes from (the origins of knowledge) and whether there are boundaries to what we can possibly know (the limits of knowledge).

Epistemology
A branch of philosophy that deals with the nature and origins of knowledge.

There are a few ways in which we can develop explanations and fix our beliefs about the way the world is. Sometimes these explanations and beliefs will be correct (that is, they will match the way the world actually is) and sometimes they will be wrong. Below are some possible methods we can adopt in attempting to understand the world around us. All of them differ in how reliable they are in reflecting the way things actually are.

The method of tenacity and belief-based explanations

It is the way it is because I SAY SO.

This is not so much a way of obtaining knowledge rather than a way of sticking rigidly to your own views about how the world is. If you think the world is a particular way and you have a commitment to that idea for whatever reason, then you might be reluctant to change your mind regardless of what anyone else might tell you, and regardless of any other data that you might be presented with. So, if you are committed to the idea that the stars in the night sky are painted on a massive blanket that angels pull over the earth at night-time, then you would be utilizing the method of tenacity if you absolutely refused to budge on that belief, no matter what other information you were given about why the night sky looks the way it does.

Belief-based explanations/ method of tenacity
An explanation for behaviour that is accepted without evidence because it comes from a trusted source or fits within a larger framework of belief.

Belief-based explanations arise from individuals or groups who (through upbringing, personal need or indoctrination) have accepted the truth of their beliefs by faith alone. The thing about these explanations is that no evidence is required. If evidence suggests that the explanation is incorrect, then the evidence is discarded or reinterpreted to make it appear consistent with the belief. For example, certain religions hold that Earth was created only a few thousand years ago. The discovery of fossilized remains of dinosaurs and other creatures (apparently millions of years old) challenged this belief. To explain the existence of these remains, people defending the belief stick rigidly to their favoured explanation, and suggested that fossils are actually natural rock formations that resemble bones or that the fossils are the remains of the victims of a great flood. Thus, rather than calling the belief itself into question, any apparently contrary evidence is interpreted to appear consistent with the belief. This is not a good strategy for finding out about the world around you. Adopting an approach based on prior held beliefs that you rigidly stick to may actually prevent you from discovering valid features of the world, if these features contradict your own viewpoint. See the "In the Know" box below for more on this.

In the Know

Nowhere is the contrast between the belief-based approach and the scientific approach more striking than in the current debate between evolutionary biologists and the so-called creation scientists, whose explanation for fossils is described above. To take one example, consider the recent discoveries based on gene sequencing, which reveal the degree of genetic similarity among various species. These observations and some simple assumptions about the rate of mutation in the genetic material allowed biologists to develop "family trees" indicating how long ago the various species separated from one another. The trees drawn up from the gene-sequencing data agree amazingly well with, and to a large degree were predicted by, the family trees assembled from the fossil record. In contrast, many creationists deny evolution and assume that all animals alive today have always had their current form and that fossils represent the remains of animals killed in the Great Flood. This view could not have predicted relationships found in the genetic material, so instead, they must invent another *post hoc* explanation to make these new findings appear consistent with their beliefs.

In addition to the differences described thus far, scientific and belief-based explanations also differ in tentativeness. Whereas explanations based on belief are simply assumed to be true, scientific explanations are accepted because they are consistent with existing objective evidence and have survived rigorous testing against plausible alternatives. Scientists accept the possibility that better explanations may turn up or that new tests may show that the current explanation is inadequate.

Using authority

It is the way it is because HE SAYS SO.

On many occasions, when we want to find something out, we ask someone who we think will know the answer. This might be an expert, a parent, a teacher or anyone else we think has the knowledge that we are looking for. When you use expert sources (whether books or people), you are using the **method of authority** (although it is not really a "method"). Although useful in the early stages of acquiring knowledge, the method of authority does not always provide valid answers, for at least two reasons. First, the source that you consult may not be truly authoritative. Some people are more than willing to give you their "expert" opinions on any topic regardless of how little they

Method of authority
Relying on authoritative sources (e.g. books, journals, scholars) for information.

actually know about it (writers are no exception). Second, sources are often biased by a particular point of view. A sociologist may offer a very different explanation for something compared with the explanation offered by a behaviourally orientated psychologist. For these reasons, the method of authority by itself is not adequate for producing reliable explanations. In general, it is never a good idea to completely rely on authority for your knowledge.

Although appealing to authority is not the final word in the search for explanations of behaviour, the method does play an important role in the acquisition of scientific knowledge. Information that you obtain from authorities on a topic can familiarize you with the problem, the available evidence, and the proposed explanations. With this information, you could generate new ideas about causes of behaviour. However, these ideas must then be subjected to rigorous scientific scrutiny rather than being accepted at face value.

Using rationality

It is the way it is because it logically must be that way.

René Descartes proposed in the seventeenth century that valid conclusions about the universe could be drawn through the use of pure reason, a doctrine called *rationalism*. This proposal was quite revolutionary at the time because most scholars of the day relied heavily on the method of authority to answer questions. Descartes' method began with scepticism, a willingness to doubt the truth of every belief he held. Descartes noted, as an example, that it was even possible to doubt the existence of the universe. What you perceive, he reasoned, could be an illusion, or even a dream. Could you prove otherwise?

After establishing doubt, Descartes moved to the next stage of his method: the search for "self-evident truths", statements that must be true because to assume otherwise would contradict logic. Descartes reasoned that if the universe around him did not really exist, then perhaps he himself also did not exist. It was immediately obvious to Descartes that this idea contradicted logic – it was self-evidently true that if he did not exist, he certainly couldn't be thinking about the question of his own existence. And it was just as self-evidently true that he was thinking. Most of us would agree with the idea that if we are thinking, then we must exist.

These two self-evident truths can be used as assumptions from which deductive logic will yield a firm conclusion:

Assumption 1: Something that thinks must exist.
Assumption 2: I am thinking.
Conclusion: I exist.

Using only his powers of reasoning, Descartes had identified two statements whose truth logically cannot be doubted, and from them he was able to deduce a conclusion that is equally bullet-proof. It is bullet-proof because, if the assumptions are true and you make no logical errors, deduction guarantees the truth of the conclusion. This particular example of the use of his method was immortalized by Descartes in his famous declaration "Cogito, ergo sum" (Latin for "I think, therefore I am").

Descartes' method came to be called the **rational method** because it depends on logical reasoning rather than on authority or the evidence of one's senses. Although the method satisfied Descartes, we must approach "knowledge" acquired in this way with caution. The power of the rational method lies in logically deduced conclusions from self-evident truths. Unfortunately, there are not many self-evident truths. If one (or both) of the assumptions used in the deduction process is incorrect, the logically deduced conclusion will not be valid.

Rational method
Developing explanations through a process of deductive reasoning.

Consider the following:

Assumption 1: All men like football.

Assumption 2: John is a man.

Conclusion: John likes football.

Now, obviously, the first assumption is not correct, which means that the conclusion is not a valid one (it's entirely possible that John *hates* football). So for this method to work, the assumptions must be true beyond doubt, and things that are true beyond doubt are very difficult to find.

Deductive reasoning

The example above is a form of **deductive reasoning**. Deductive reasoning *starts* with general statements about the world (e.g. all men like football) and then attempts to say something about particular observations (e.g. one particular man – John). Here is another example:

Deductive reasoning
Reasoning that goes from the general to the specific (i.e. from general statements to specific observations); forms the foundation of the rational method of enquiry.

1 All research methods books are boring (general statement)
2 This is a research methods book

Therefore,

3 This research methods book is boring.

Now, apart from the fact that we hope you are not bored already, think about the following. Deductive reasoning attempts to move from general statements to specific observations. In other words, the general statements come *before* the observations. But how can we come up with any general statements before we have made any observations? Surely the observations have to come first (e.g. we would have had to look at various research methods books before forming a general statement about them being boring). Maybe we can use observations as a basis for constructing general principles about the world. This is called "inductive reasoning".

Inductive reasoning

When you use **inductive reasoning**, you try to use observations that you already have to form general principles. This will allow you to say something about what to expect in the future. For example, if you were to use observations about what has happened every time you dropped a ball (it fell to the floor) then, if you were using inductive reasoning, you would go on to say that there is a general principle at work

Inductive reasoning
Reasoning that uses observations as a basis for forming general principles.

that means you will see the same result at every point in the future when you drop a ball. This seems reasonable, but the Scottish philosopher David Hume pointed out a problem with induction. The problem is that your observations are never complete. What this means can be illustrated using swans. If you live in the northern hemisphere, it is likely that all of the swans you have ever seen have been white. If you want to use these observations to say something about "the colour of swans", then you would conclude that "all swans are white". However, if you were to then go to Australia or New Zealand, it is likely that you would see black swans. This means that your original conclusion (based on inductive reasoning) was false. That is what we mean when we say that your observations are never complete – you just do not know if the *next* observation is going to be the one that refutes the claim that you have made on the basis of your past observations.

Although it has shortcomings, the rational method still plays an important role in science. The tentative ideas that we form about the relationships between things are often deduced from earlier assumptions. For example, having learned that fleeing from a fire or trying to get into a crowded arena causes people to behave irrationally, we might deduce that "perceived availability of reinforcers" (with the reinforcers being either "escaping death" or "getting a front-row seat") is responsible for such behaviour. However, scientists do not just blindly accept that such a deduction is correct. What must then happen is that the deduction is tested in some way that will determine whether or not it is valid.

Using scientific methods

Although explanations for behaviour and general laws cannot adequately be formulated by relying solely on authoritative sources and using inductive or deductive reasoning, these methods (when combined with other features) form the basis for the most powerful approach to knowledge that we have: the **scientific method**. This is what we are going to look at next. To get us started, have a look at Figure 2.1. It is a summary of how the scientific method is used to find out things about our world. The terms and the process will be the subject of much of the rest of this chapter.

Figure 2.1 is a rough outline of the steps in the scientific method. We start with some observations that are of interest. Once we have got enough of these, we develop a theory (see below) to organize and explain our existing data, and to make predictions about new data that has not been collected yet. These predictions are formulated into hypotheses, which are then put to the test through research. The observations and measurements that we get from the research are then used to assess the theory from which the hypotheses derived. Basically, this is the way science works. But what is science in the first place?

Science

Think of a question. Any question. It does not matter what it is, as long as it is a question. Now think about how you might find the answer to that question. Was your question easy to answer or difficult? What was it about your question that made it easy or difficult to answer? Exactly what was it that you decided you would have to do if you wanted to answer your question?

Scientific method
Approach to knowledge that emphasizes empirical rather than intuitive processes, testable hypotheses, systematic and controlled observation of operationally defined phenomena, data collection using accurate and precise instrumentation, valid and reliable measures, and objective reporting of results; scientists tend to be critical and, most importantly, sceptical.

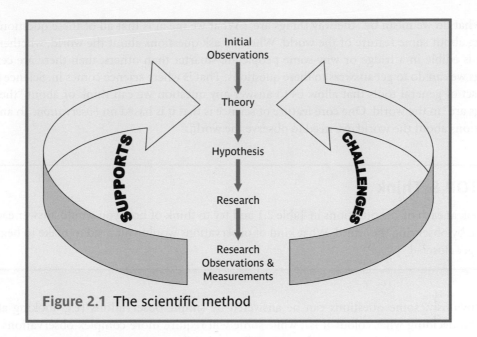

Figure 2.1 The scientific method

This gets us started on the issue of science's contribution to our knowledge about the world. Science is many things (see below), but it is basically about asking questions. Scientists ask questions of "nature", and then see how nature answers those questions. Nature never lies, so the real trick is asking "good" questions and understanding the answers that you get. That is what this chapter is about. It is a starter course on becoming a scientist and asking scientific questions.

Think back to your question. How easy your question was to answer, and exactly what was required to answer it, was probably dependent on the type of question that you asked. Some questions are easy to answer while others are difficult (Table 2.1)

Table 2.1 Easy and difficult questions

Easy-to-answer questions	Difficult-to-answer questions
What colour is the sky?	Why is the sky blue?
What is edible in my fridge?	Why do we need to eat?
Who is the smartest person in my class?	Why are some people smarter than others?

Although these questions differ in terms of their difficulty, they are all questions that are answerable.

Q. What do the questions in Table 2.1 have in common?

A. They are all questions about "the way things are".

What do we mean by "the way things are"? What we mean is that all of these questions are asking about some feature of the world. When we ask questions about the world, whether it is what is edible in a fridge or why some people are smarter than others, then there are certain things we can do to get answers to these questions. That is where science comes in. Science gives us a set of general tools that allow us to answer any question we can think of about "the way things are" in the world. One core feature of science is that it is based on *observation*. To answer questions about the world, we need to observe the world.

STOP & Think

Look at each of the questions in Table 2.1 and try to think of how you would answer each one by observing the world. What kind of observations would you need to make to begin to get close?

Obviously, some questions can be answered by simple observations (e.g. looking at the sky and deciding what colour it is), while some will require more complex observations (e.g. observing brain function in people with different intelligence quotients (IQs) and deciding whether the brain works differently for each group). Despite the obvious differences, the important point is that observations can answer questions. That is the real beauty of science. That is what gets us so excited about science. If you have got any sort of curiosity about the way the world works, then an understanding of science can help you answer just about any question that you care to ask – any question at all about the natural world and everything in it. Is that not great? If you are already on a psychology course or a science course, then you must have already asked yourself some of these questions, maybe about aspects of the mind or behaviour. With knowledge of the process of science, you can start to answer those questions. The left-hand column of Table 2.2 shows you some questions that might seem "crazy" to some people but are actually answerable if we were to make careful observations.

Not all questions are straightforward, however. Some questions may look like ones about the way the world works, but are actually questions that cannot be answered by observations (and may not be answerable at all). Many of these questions are philosophical in nature, and the right-hand column of Table 2.2 has some questions of this type. Take a minute to look at each type of question and understand why they are different.

Table 2.2 Scientific and non-scientific questions

Scientific questions	Non-scientific questions
Does eating fish increase our IQ?	What makes a good song?
Is our handwriting linked to our personality?	What is "justice"?
Can homoeopathic remedies cure some illnesses?	Is capital punishment right or wrong?

The "non-scientific" questions do not really refer to an aspect of the world that we can find a definitive answer for that is (in principle) the same for everyone and everywhere. Your idea of what makes a "good" song might be different to my idea, and there is no absolute and conclusive answer to "what makes a good song".[1] Similarly, your opinion on capital punishment may be different to mine, and there is no way of deciding once and for all who is right or wrong. The question of what "justice" consists of might be answered differently now than it might have been in the Middle Ages when many people were subjected to horrific (by our standards) acts in the name of justice. However, even though we might disagree with some of the methods of our ancestors, there is no way of deciding that one sense of justice is the "right" one, because the concept is so abstract and does not have an independent existence. If, however, we look at conceptions of nature in the past, we can see that many ideas were just plain wrong. For example, for many hundreds of years, the general opinion was that the Earth was the centre of the universe, and everything else moved around it. Modern science has since shown this idea to be wrong. This is because, unlike the question about "justice", the question about where the Earth is in relation to the other planets and to the Sun has only one correct answer, and we eventually reached that answer through a careful process of observation and theorizing.

Questions in the left-hand column of Table 2.2 refer to aspects of the world that can be revealed through careful observations, and do not depend on your or my opinions. We can use careful observations to decide whether homoeopathic remedies really do work or not, and the results of these observations will not depend on your opinion or on my opinion and they also will not depend on whether you make the observations in Madrid or in Papua New Guinea. However, even though these questions are scientific, it does not automatically mean that the things they ask about are valid. The point of science is to separate out the ideas that really do reflect a real aspect of the world from the questions that do not. We could study the effects of homoeopathic remedies again and again, as could other people in different places, and if we kept finding that they did not cure certain illnesses then we would be forced to conclude that nature had answered our question with a resounding "no". Even if you set out to show that homoeopathic remedies worked because you strongly believed that they did, if enough well-conducted observations suggest otherwise then that is the conclusion that you have to accept. It does not matter if you *really* believed in homoeopathy and you were absolutely convinced it was going to work. Careful observation will always be a more reliable indicator of the way the world works than your gut feeling or your prior beliefs. These ideas are expanded upon later.

Science and scientists

We often hear people say that they do not trust science. This seems like a strange thing to say as science is just a tool for finding out about the world. Perhaps what people mean when they speak of their distrust of science really refers to a suspicion they have about scientists. This seems a little bit unfair. They are certainly no more devious than any other group. What people probably mean when they make this statement is that they do not really understand most

---

1   Although it may be possible to scientifically study what makes a "catchy" song. But not everyone thinks catchy songs are good. It is the "goodness" judgement that's not scientific in this example.

scientific discoveries, but they are aware that the findings of science often force us to question some deeply held (and often cherished) beliefs about the way the world is. Additionally, scientific progress sometimes raises some profound ethical issues that can be extremely challenging for us as members of society. To realize this, you need only think about how Einstein's famous e = mc^2 equation eventually led to the development of nuclear weapons. Einstein certainly did not intend that his findings would lead to such a destructive weapon. By all accounts, Einstein was a kind and gentle person whose intentions were purely to gain a better understanding of nature. But his insights did eventually lead to the development of nuclear weapons, so you can see how sometimes an innocent piece of scientific curiosity can have massive political and ethical consequences. So, a combination of poor understanding, challenges to worldviews and a fear of how scientific knowledge might be applied (and perhaps abused) is most likely what lies behind people's alleged distrust of science. Although some of these fears are justified, merely expressing them as an overall distrust of science is unfair.

Scientist
A person who adopts the methods of science in his or her quest for knowledge.

The terms science and **scientist** probably conjure up a variety of images in your mind. A common image is a person in a white laboratory coat surrounded by bubbling flasks and test tubes. Alternatively, our laboratory-coated scientist might be involved in some nefarious endeavour that will threaten the existence of humankind. Books, movies and television have provided these images. Just think about the classic horror films of the 1940s and 1950s (e.g. *Frankenstein*), and it is not hard to see where some of these images come from. It is also not hard to see why they annoy scientists so much, except, perhaps, the ones who genuinely do wear white coats and are surrounded by bubbling flasks all day long.

Just as psychologists do not actually spend their lives analysing every person they meet, these images of scientists do not really accurately capture what science really is and what real scientists do. As we said above, science is a set of methods used to collect information about phenomena in a particular area of interest and build a reliable base of knowledge about it. This knowledge is acquired via research, which involves a scientist identifying a phenomenon to study, developing hypotheses, conducting a study to collect data, analysing the data and disseminating the results. This process is described below and is known as the *scientific method*. Science also involves developing theories to help better describe, explain and organize scientific information that is collected. At the heart of any science (psychology included – see the following chapter) is that information is obtained through **observation and measurement** of phenomena. So, if we want to find out some psychological "fact", we must go out and make the relevant observations that are going to help us find out about the psychological phenomena that we are interested in. Science also requires that any explanations for phenomena can be modified and corrected if new information becomes available. Nothing in science is taken as an absolute truth. Scientists should always be willing to revise their ideas if new observations suggest that their old ideas were wrong. This is important. Students often say "science has proved that . . .". This is not strictly the case, because "ultimate" proof is difficult (maybe even impossible) to establish. All scientific observations, conclusions and theories are *always* open to modification and perhaps even abandonment as new evidence is discovered, although it is also important to remember that some scientific ideas are so well established that they are considered to be "laws" and it's unlikely that we will ever have to change what we think about them (that helium is lighter than

ch. 3
pp.48–54

air, for example; this is unlikely to ever be disputed, to the relief of balloon manufacturers everywhere – see "Theory versus law" later in this chapter).

A scientist is someone who does science (obviously). More specifically, a scientist is a person who adopts the methods of science in his or her quest for knowledge. Despite the stereotyped image of the scientist, scientists engage in a wide range of activities designed to acquire knowledge in their fields. These activities take place in lots of different settings and for a variety of reasons. For example, you have scientists who work for pharmaceutical companies trying to discover new medications for diseases. You have scientists who brave the bitter cold of the Arctic to take ice samples that they can use to track the course of global climate change. You have scientists who sit in observatories with their telescopes looking at the sky, searching for and classifying celestial bodies. You have scientists who work at universities and do science purely to acquire knowledge in their chosen fields (e.g. psychology, biology or physics).

In short, science is a diverse activity involving a diverse group of people doing a wide range of things. Despite these differences, all scientists share a common goal: *to acquire knowledge through the application of scientific methods and techniques.*

Characteristics of science

Like most complex ideas, science is not easily defined. There are four characteristics of science that we are going to look at, but even these are not the full story. These are *empiricism, the public nature of science, the replication of scientific results* and *theory*. These four characteristics are included in nearly all definitions of **science**.

Empiricism

An empirical answer is one that is based on observation. We mentioned the importance of observation above, and empiricism is just the fancy name for it. Think of **empiricism** as experiencing things for yourself or as collecting data to answer your questions. The essence of empiricism is that observers attempt to discover facts in a completely unbiased manner. As we highlighted above when talking about testing homoeopathy, an important feature of science is that scientific answers come from unbiased observations, not opinions. To use another example, think about the moon.

> **Science**
> A method of inquiry that uses unbiased empirical observation, public methods, reproducible results and theory to reveal universal truths about the universe.

> **Empiricism**
> Philosophical and scientific approach to knowledge that uses unbiased observation to discover truths about the world.

There was a time when people speculated that the moon was made of green cheese. Questions about what the moon is made of are legitimate questions about "the way things are" (in this case, the moon). So we should be able to make observations and see whether or not the moon is, in fact, made of green cheese. After the invention of the telescope, astronomers made better observations and saw that the moon's surface was not smooth and did not really look cheese-like. Later, new technology (the mass spectrometer) revealed much more about what the moon's surface was made of (again, non-cheese-like material). During the first *Apollo* mission in 1969, actual moon rocks were collected and returned to Earth. Not surprisingly (except to the "green-cheese" theorists – of whom there were probably very few by this point), they were not made of cheese. Today, the physical nature of the moon is no longer a matter of speculation. Anyone who still thinks the moon is made of green cheese is wrong, no matter how convinced they might seem. Using telescopes, spectrometers and lunar samples, scientists possess a fairly complete picture of the moon's distinctly un-cheesy surface. The answer to the question of the moon's composition, although not completely known, has been revealed by empirical observations made from Earth and from actual lunar samples.

In a general sense, all science and all psychology depends on observations that are carefully planned and conducted. Much of what you will learn in this book relates to becoming a skilled and unbiased observer. Making such observations is one of the first steps towards becoming a scientist. Planning our everyday decisions is probably a good idea. In research, however, planning to collect data is a requirement, not an option.

Public nature

Publish
Recording of scientific results, methods, and theories to create a permanent knowledge base of science.

Replication
Repeating an experiment with the same procedures or with planned changes in the procedures to confirm the original results.

A second characteristic of science is its public nature. Typically, scientists **publish** their findings in scientific journals. These journals are where we can find most scientific results, methods and theories. Some of that publication is now in online journals, making access much easier for you (and other scientists). Regardless of the medium used, published data are a defining characteristic of science. Why? Openly publishing ideas and findings allows as many people as possible to have access to them. Publication means that once a scientist discovers an answer empirically, others need not repeat the research – they can just look up the answer. Alternatively, if a scientist (or anyone else) wants to scrutinize the research, then it is all out in the public domain. This is designed to make the whole process open and honest. If someone publishes something and you think there is something wrong with their conclusions, then you can read their findings and see if there are any obvious mistakes. The information that is published will also allow you to conduct a similar study to see for yourself whether the answers are valid or not – this is **replication**.

Replication

Replication is an important part of science because it creates confidence in scientific conclusions. Scientists are sceptical by training and they want to admit only correct conclusions into the collection of scientific "knowledge". They know that data must be collected properly so when they publish their conclusions, they also publish the methods they used to reach those conclusions. In this way, other scientists who wish to replicate (or verify) the original results can use the same methods. When other scientists obtain results similar to those originally published, the original conclusions are confirmed. However, when other scientists fail to replicate, the original conclusions are called into question and additional replications are attempted. If those fail, too, the original results and conclusions may be discarded altogether. By doing this, scientists are ensuring that their findings are of the highest standard, and reflect as much as possible the way the world really is.

Basic and applied research

As noted above, scientists work in a variety of areas to identify phenomena and develop valid explanations for them. The goals established by scientists working within the field may vary according to the nature of the research problem. For example, the goal of some scientists is to discover general laws that explain particular classes of behaviours. In the course of developing those laws, psychologists study behaviour in specific situations and attempt to isolate the things that affect it.

Other scientists within the field are more interested in tackling practical problems than in finding general laws. For example, they might be interested in determining which of several therapy techniques is best for treating severe phobias. These are two subtly different approaches. An important distinction has been made between basic research and applied research along the lines just presented.

Basic research

Basic research is conducted to investigate issues relevant to the confirmation or disconfirmation of theoretical or empirical positions. The major goal of basic research is to acquire *general* information about a phenomenon, with little emphasis placed on applications to real-world examples of the phenomenon. For example, research on the memory process may be conducted to test how much irrelevant information (known as "interference") influences the way we forget things. The researcher would be interested in discovering something about the forgetting process while testing the validity of a theoretical position. Of less immediate interest would be the application of results to forgetting in a real-world situation.

> **Basic research**
> Research carried out primarily to test a theory or empirical issues.

Applied research

The focus of **applied research** is somewhat different. Applied researchers are more interested in investigating problems based in the real world. Although you may still work from a theory when formulating your hypotheses, your primary goal is to generate information that can be applied directly to a real-world problem. A study by James Ogloff and Neil Vidmar (1994) on pre-trial publicity would be best classified as applied research. It informs us about a very real problem facing the court system. The results of studies such as Ogloff and Vidmar's can help trial and appeals court judges make decisions concerning limitations placed on jury exposure to pre-trial publicity. Further examples of applied research can be found in the areas of clinical, environmental and industrial psychology (among others).

> **Applied research**
> Research carried out to investigate a real-world problem.

Overlaps between basic and applied research

Basic and applied research are not always completely separate. Some research areas have both an applied and a basic flavour. Elizabeth Loftus is a psychologist who has done a lot of work on the psychology of the eyewitness. Loftus (1979) has extensively studied the factors that affect the ability of an eyewitness to accurately perceive, remember and recall a criminal event. Her research certainly fits the mould of applied research. But her results also have some implications for theories of memory, so they also fit the mould of basic research. In fact, many of Loftus's findings can be organized within existing theories of memory.

Test yourself

Identify basic and applied research questions by placing a check mark in the appropriate column. (Answers are provided at the bottom of the page.[2])

Examples of research questions	Basic	Applied
1 What are the predictors of teenage sexual behaviour?		
2 In what way can video games increase aggression among children?		
3 How do neurons generate neurotransmitters?		
4 Does memory process visual images and sound simultaneously?		
5 How can peer groups influence romantic behaviours?		
6 Which coping strategies are best for tsunami survivors?		

Both basic and applied research are important, and neither can be considered superior to the other. In fact, progress in science is dependent on a synergy between basic and applied research. Much applied research is guided by the theories and findings of basic research investigations. For example, applied research on expert testimony in jury trials is guided by basic research in perception and cognition. In turn, the findings obtained in applied settings often require modification of existing theories and spur more basic research. Thus, the study of actual eyewitness testimony leads to richer and more accurate knowledge of basic perceptual and cognitive processes.

Theories about theories

What is a theory?

Theories are extremely important in science. People use the word "theory" in all sorts of different ways. You might say "I have a theory that Jack is going to propose to his girlfriend on their trip to Paris." In this case, "theory" really means "hunch" or "intuition". In a murder-mystery novel, a detective is said to develop a "theory" of who the killer might be. In this context, the word theory is used as another word for "hypothesis". That is, the detective has an idea about who is guilty that he or she will then test. The word also has been used to describe ideas that are developed about unverifiable events. For example, many ideas exist about how the miracles recounted in the Bible actually occurred. In this context, a "theory" is used to provide the final explanation for a phenomenon that has long passed and cannot be studied directly. Sometimes people say something is "just a theory", and this is often meant in a derogatory way. When used in this way, it is usually based on a misunderstanding of what a scientific theory actually is. A scientific theory is grounded in actual data: observations that have been made and hypotheses

---

2   Answers: basic = 1, 3, 4; applied = 2, 5, 6.

that can be tested through research. When we use it in science, the term theory means something more than it does in our everyday lives. A scientific theory is more than a simple hypothesis.

Theories are "ideas" about how nature works. Psychologists propose theories about the nature of behaviour and mental processes, as well as about the reasons people and animals behave and think the way they do. A psychological theory can be developed on different levels; for example, the theory can either be developed on a physiological or on a symbolic level. Take schizophrenia – psychologists want to come up with a theory of schizophrenia; what causes it, why some people develop it and some don't, and so on. A physiologically based theory of schizophrenia would propose biological causes that might be genetic. A theory developed on a symbolic level would be more likely to propose psychological causes such as patterns of emotional conflict or stress in a person's life. It would also be possible for a theory of schizophrenia to include both biological and psychological causes.

Theories often differ in their scope – the range of phenomena they seek to explain. Some theories attempt to explain very specific phenomena. For example, Brown and Kulik's (1977) theory attempted to explain the phenomenon of "flashbulb memory". A flashbulb memory is when we remember very specific personal circumstances surrounding particularly surprising and emotional events in our lives, such as the horrific events of 11 September 2001. Other theories have much broader scope as they try to describe and explain more complex phenomena such as love (Sternberg, 1986) or human cognition (Anderson, 1990; 1993; Anderson and Milson, 1989).

In general, the greater the scope of a **theory**, the more complex it is likely to be. Most theories in contemporary psychology tend to be relatively modest in scope, attempting to account only for a limited range of phenomena.

But what are theories for?

Theories serve important functions in increasing our understanding of the area that we are interested in. First, theories *organize and explain* a variety of specific facts or descriptions in the chosen field. Having a whole load of "facts" based on observations is all very well, but sooner or later you are going to have to organize them and make sense of them. That is where theories come in. Such facts and descriptions are not very meaningful by themselves, and so we need theories so we can impose a framework on them. This framework makes the world more comprehensible by providing a few abstract concepts around which we can organize and explain a variety of different observations.

As an example, consider how Charles Darwin's (1859) theory of evolution organized and explained a variety of facts concerning the characteristics of animal species. Up until then, all scientists had was a collection of observations about these characteristics. The theory of evolution was a framework within which these observations could be organized and understood. Similarly, in psychology one theory of memory asserts that there are separate systems of short-term memory and long-term memory. This theory accounts for many specific observations about learning and memory, including such phenomena as the different types of memory deficits that result from a severe blow to the head versus damage to the hippocampus area of the brain, and the rate at which a person forgets material he or she has just read.

Second, theories *generate new knowledge* by focusing our thinking so that we notice new aspects of nature – theories guide our observations of the world. The theory generates hypotheses

Theory
A logically organized set of propositions (claims, statements, assertions) that serves to define events (concepts), describe relationships among these events, and explain the occurrence of these events.

Theories
Organize and explain facts; generate new knowledge; can be tested (and falsified); can be modified if needed.

about the world, and the researcher conducts studies to see whether these hypotheses are correct. If the studies confirm the hypotheses, the theory is supported. As more and more evidence accumulates that is consistent with the theory, we become more confident that the theory is correct.

Such testable hypotheses are falsifiable (see below) – the data can either support or refute the hypotheses. A scientific theory that is supported by a large body of research is no longer just an idea; it enables us to explain a great deal of observable facts. Research may reveal weaknesses in a theory when a hypothesis that is generated by the theory is not supported. Researchers can then modify the theory to account for the new data. Sometimes a new theory will emerge that accounts for both new data and the existing body of knowledge.

In the Know

Evolutionary theory is still helping psychologists generate hypotheses (Buss, 2009; Gaulin & McBurney, 2000). For example, evolutionary theory asserts that males and females have evolved different strategies for reproduction. All individuals have an evolutionary interest in passing their genes on to future generations. However, females have relatively few opportunities to reproduce, have a limited age range during which to reproduce, and must exert a tremendous amount of time and energy during pregnancy and then, after giving birth, caring for their children. Males, in contrast, can reproduce at any time and have a reproductive advantage by being able to produce as many offspring as possible. Because of these differences, the theory predicts that females and males will use different criteria when selecting mates. Females will be more interested in males who can provide support for child-rearing – in other words, females should prefer males that are higher in status, have more economic resources and are more dominant. Males will choose females who are younger, healthier and more physically attractive. Research supports these predictions across a variety of cultures (Buss, 1989). Although research supports evolutionary theory, alternative theories can be developed that may better explain the same findings, because theories are living and dynamic. Eagly and Wood (1999) interpreted the Buss research in terms of social structure. They argue that gender differences arise from the fact that there are male–female differences in the division of labour – males are responsible for the economic welfare of the family and females are responsible for care of children – and these differences account for gender differences in mate selection preferences. Research on this topic continues.

Theories are usually modified as new research defines the scope of the theory. This is an important part of science. They are not static. The necessity of modifying theories is illustrated by the theory of short-term versus long-term memory. Originally, memory theorists thought that the long-term memory system described long-term memory as a warehouse where we kept our permanent fixed memories. However, research by cognitive psychologists, including Loftus (1979), has shown that memories are easily reconstructed and reinterpreted. In one study, participants watched a film of an automobile accident and later were asked to tell what they saw in the film. Loftus found that participants' memories were influenced by the way they were questioned. For example, participants who were asked whether they saw "the" broken headlight were more likely to answer yes than were participants who were asked whether they saw "a" broken headlight. Results such as these have required a more complex theory of how long-term memory operates because it is now clear that it is anything but a warehouse for things we have encountered in the past. Modification of theories based on new evidence is an important feature of science.

As we have noted, everyday use of the term "theory" leads to confusion over what a theory really is. Confusion also can be found within the scientific community over the term. Let's spend a little bit of time looking at how theories are different from hypotheses and laws.

Theory versus hypothesis

Students often confuse theory with *hypothesis*, and even professional scientists make this error. Basically, theories are more complex than hypotheses. *A theory* is a collection of general principles that outline how a particular phenomenon works. These general principles can be used to explain observations that have already been made, and they can also be used to make predictions about new observations. The predictions about what new observations relating to the phenomena might be like are *hypotheses*. It is important not to mix up these two terms. For example, you might observe that more crime occurs during the period of a full moon than during other times of the month. This might lead you to think that the observed relationship is caused by the illumination that the moon provides for night-time burglary. But this is not a theory. It is a hypothesis. You could test this hypothesis by comparing crime rates during periods of full moon that were clear with crime rates during periods of full moon that were cloudy.

Even if you find that crime rates were higher during the full moon, you still have not got a theory. All you have done is made a fairly simple set of observations. In other words, you have developed a hypothesis and you have attempted to test it through observation. All highly commendable, but you are not theorizing yet. A theory would account for exactly *why* crime rates during periods of the full moon were higher. A good theory would specify the action and interaction of a system of variables (environmental conditions, the minds of criminals, opportunities for crime, time of year, economic conditions, etc.). Because of the complexity of the system involved, no single observation could substantiate the theory in its entirety. It would take many observations (i.e. many hypotheses being tested systematically) before we could start to evaluate the overall theory.

Theory versus law

A theory that has been substantially verified is sometimes called a law. However, most laws do not derive from theories in this way. Laws are usually empirically verified, quantitative relationships between two or more variables and thus are not normally subject to the disconfirmation that theories are. For example, E.L. Thorndike's (1932) law of effect states that any behaviour in a given situation that is followed by a satisfying state of affairs will become more likely to occur within that situation. This law derives from Thorndike's research using kittens in a puzzle box (sorry, animal-lovers). A kitten was placed in the puzzle box and if it made the necessary response, the box opened and the kitten received a small piece of fish. Thorndike noticed that on successive trials, the kitten's behaviour became more efficient. At first, the kitten's random explorations of the puzzle box produced the desired response by accident. Eventually, the kitten learned to make the response as soon as it was placed in the puzzle box. The law of effect was not derived from a theory but from Thorndike's empirical observations.

Empirical laws like this are not theories grown solid through verification. They are relationships that must be explained by theory. For example, a theory relating to Thorndike's law of effect would specify the exact psychological and perhaps the physiological mechanisms underlying *how* the kittens came to learn in the way that they did. Such a theory would explain why the relationship described by the law of effect occurs.

Mechanistic explanations versus functional explanations

Mechanistic explanations
Mechanistic explanations explain *how things work.*

Functional explanations
Functional explanations explain *what things do.*

Theories provide explanations for observed phenomena, but not all explanations are alike. When evaluating a theory, you should think about whether the explanations provided are *mechanistic* or *functional*. What do we mean by this? A **mechanistic explanation** describes the mechanism (the physical components) and the chain of cause and effect through which conditions act on the mechanism to produce its behaviour; it basically describes *how* something works. In contrast, a **functional explanation** describes an attribute of something (such as physical attractiveness) in terms of its function – that is, what it *does* (i.e. its *function* – hence the name). For example, in women, beauty signals reproductive health, according to evolutionary psychologists. This would be a functional explanation of beauty as it describes *why* the attribute or system exists.

Mechanistic explanations tell you how a system works without necessarily telling you why it does what it does; functional explanations refer to the purpose or goal of a given attribute or system without describing how those purposes or goals are achieved. A full understanding requires both types of explanation.

Although you can usually determine a mechanism's function once you know how it works, the converse is not true. Knowing what a system does gives only hints as to the underlying mechanism through which its functions are carried out. Think about the buttons on your television's remote control.

You can quickly determine their functions by trying them out – this one turns on the power; that one changes the volume; the next one changes the channel. From these observations, you could develop a functional understanding of the remote control. However, without some knowledge of electronics, you may have no idea whatever how this or that button accomplishes its function, and even with that knowledge, there may be dozens of different circuits (mechanisms) that can do the job. So, even though you have a functional understanding, you might still lack a mechanistic understanding. Knowing what a button does in no way tells you how it does it.

Given the choice between a mechanistic explanation and a functional one, you should usually prefer the mechanistic one. Unfortunately, arriving at the correct mechanism underlying a given bit of human or animal behaviour often may not be possible given our current understanding of the brain. We still don't have a full understanding of how that lump of meat we call our brain actually does what it does, and this makes mechanistic explanations for behaviour very difficult. For example, we currently have no firm idea how memories are stored in the brain and subsequently accessed (although there has been plenty of speculation). Yet we do have a fair understanding of many functional properties of the brain mechanisms involved. Given what we do know, it is possible to construct a theory of memory that attributes it with certain properties without getting into the specific details about the physical mechanism that might underlie how a particular memory is accessed and retrieved and so on.

Characteristics of a good theory

In the history of psychology, many theories have been advanced to explain behavioural phenomena. Some of these theories have stood the test of time, whereas others have fallen by the wayside. Whether or not a theory endures depends on several factors, including the following:

1 *Ability to account for data.* To be of any value, a theory must account for most of the existing data within its domain. Note that the amount of data is "most" rather than "all" because at

least some of the data may be unreliable. Observers aren't perfect and sometimes our observations can be wrong for a variety of different reasons. A theory can be excused for failing to account for erroneous data. However, a theory that fails to account for well-established facts within its domain is in serious trouble. The phrase "within its domain" is crucial here. If the theory is designed to explain the habituation of responses, it can hardly be criticized for its failure to account for schizophrenia. Such an account clearly would be beyond the scope of the theory.

2 *Explanatory relevance.* A theory must also have explanatory relevance. That is, the explanation for a phenomenon provided by a theory must offer good grounds for believing that the phenomenon would occur under the specified conditions. If a theory meets this criterion, you should find yourself saying, "Ah, of course! That was to be expected under these conditions!" If someone were to suggest to you that the rough sleep you had last night was caused by the colour of your socks, you would probably reject this on the grounds that it lacks explanatory relevance – the explanation (sock colour) is irrelevant as an explanation for the phenomenon (sleeplessness). There is simply no good reason to believe that wearing a particular colour of socks would affect your sleep. To be adequate, the theory proposed by your friend to explain the relationship between your socks and your sleeplessness must define some logical link between socks and sleep, which in this case is unlikely.

3 *Testability (or falsifiability).* Another condition that a good theory must meet is testability (see also the section on Karl Popper below). A theory is testable if it is capable of failing some empirical test. That is, the theory specifies outcomes under particular conditions, and if these outcomes do not occur, then the theory is rejected. The criterion of testability is a major problem for many aspects of Freud's psychodynamic theory of personality. Freud's theory provides explanations for a number of personality traits and disorders, but it is too complex and loosely specified to make specific, testable predictions. For example, if a person is observed to be stingy and obstinate, Freudian theory points to unsuccessful resolution of the anal stage of psychosexual development. Yet diametrically opposite traits also can be accounted for with the same explanation. There is no mechanism within the theory to specify which will develop in any particular case. When a theory can provide a seemingly reasonable explanation no matter what the outcome of an observation, you are probably dealing with an un-testable theory.

4 *Prediction of novel events.* A good theory should predict new phenomena. Within its domain, a good theory should predict phenomena beyond those for which the theory was originally designed. Strictly speaking, these predicted phenomena do not have to be new in the sense of not yet observed. Rather, they must be new in the sense that they were not taken into account in the formulation of the theory. As an example, consider Einstein's theory of relativity. This theory accounted for the same data and produced the same predictions for a wide range of phenomena as did Newtonian mechanics. However, Einstein's theory went beyond Newton's to predict new phenomena not expected to occur from Newton's point of view. One implication of Einstein's view was that if two totally accurate clocks were set to the same time and one of the clocks was shot into orbit while the other remained on Earth, then the clock in orbit would appear to lose time relative to the one on Earth. This experiment was actually conducted using super-accurate atomic clocks, and the predicted loss of time was in fact detected.

5 *Parsimony.* **Occam's Razor** (sometimes spelled Ockham's Razor) is a name that you should never forget if you keep doing science. The medieval English philosopher William of Occam popularized an important principle previously stated by

Occam's Razor
The principle which states that a problem should be stated as simply as possible, with the fewest propositions possible.

Aristotle. Aristotle's principle states: "Entities must not be multiplied beyond what is necessary." Occam's refinement of this principle is now called Occam's Razor and states that a problem should be stated in the simplest possible terms and explained with the fewest propositions possible. Today we know this as the law of parsimony.

What does this mean? Well, it's basically a principle that states that, whenever you have two (or more) competing explanations for the same phenomenon, and they all account for the data, then the simplest one is the one you should favour, as it is most likely to be true. In other words, you should always try to minimize the number of assumptions or entities that a given explanation posits. So, imagine you wake up one morning to find your house is flooded. Staying in the house is your 5-year-old nephew, who tells you that evil pixies came in the night and turned on all the taps before disappearing again. That would certainly account for the flooding. But it is probably more likely that your nephew turned all the taps on then made up the story about the pixies once he realized he was going to be in trouble. This is the simplest explanation, because it does not involve positing an unnecessary amount of entities ("evil pixies" being the entities in this particular case) in order to explain what has happened. As the alternative explanation makes fewer assumptions, we prefer it. In the above example, you can imagine Occam's Razor slicing away the un-needed evil pixies to produce a more **parsimonious explanation**.

> **Parsimonious explanation**
> An explanation or theory that explains a relationship using relatively few assumptions.

In teaching, we often have to teach students to prefer the simplest explanations, even if the simplest explanations are not the most exciting ones. I once asked a student how we might account for the experience of a person who had recently emerged from a coma, and reported strange experiences and distant lights. The student suggested that this might be evidence of a spiritual dimension that the coma victim had experienced. However, a simpler explanation would hold that the brain of the individual was "firing" (to use a simplistic term) in such a way so as to produce these strange experiences. Even though the person was in a coma, his brain was still working, and given that the brain is the seat of all our experiences, the more likely explanation is that the brain gave rise to these experiences as well. There is no need to suggest further entities such as spiritual dimensions as the explanation concerning the way the brain "fires" in such a state is simpler and has as much explanatory power.

Playing with Occam's Razor

Occam's Razor is the only razor you can safely play with, and you can use it in many situations. We'd recommend getting into the habit of assessing explanations with Occam in mind. Think about how you might apply Occam's Razor to the following things:

(a) A serial killer tells the police that he is not responsible for his actions, as he was only following orders from God.

(b) A medium tells you that your dead aunt wants you to know that she approves of your new boyfriend/girlfriend.

(c) A magician makes a coin disappear right in front of your eyes.

Strategies for testing theories

A major theme developed in the preceding sections is that a good scientific theory must be testable with empirical methods. In fact, the final step in the business of theory construction is to subject the propositions of your theory to rigorous empirical scrutiny:

1 *Following a confirmational strategy*. A theory is usually tested by identifying implications of the theory for a specific situation that has never previously been examined and then setting up the situation to see whether the predicted effects actually happen. If the predicted effects do occur, the theory is said to be supported by the results, and your confidence in the theory increases. If the predicted effects do not occur, then the theory is not supported, and your confidence in it weakens.

When you test the implications of a theory in this way, you are following what is called a **confirmational strategy** (i.e. a strategy of looking for confirmation of the theory's predictions). A positive outcome supports the theory.

Looking for confirmation is an important part of theory testing, but it does have an important limitation. Although the theory must find confirmation if it is to survive (too many failures would kill it), you can find confirmation until doomsday and the theory may still be wrong.

Confirmational strategy
A strategy for testing a theory that involves finding evidence that confirms what is already believed.

2 *Following a disconfirmational strategy*. Even when a theory's predictions are relatively precise, many alternative theories could potentially be constructed that would make the same predictions. Because of this fact, following a confirmational strategy is not enough. To test a theory requires more than simply finding out if its predictions are confirmed. You also must determine whether outcomes not expected, according to the theory, do or do not occur.

This strategy follows this form:

If the theory is correct, then X won't happen.

Thus

If X happens, then the theory is not correct.

Because a positive result (X happens) will disconfirm the prediction (rather than confirm it), this way of testing a theory is called a **disconfirmational strategy**.

Disconfirmational strategy
A method of testing a theory that involves conducting research to provide evidence that disconfirms the predictions made by the theory.

3 *Using confirmational and disconfirmational strategies together*. Adequately testing a theory requires using both confirmational and disconfirmational strategies. Usually, you will pursue a confirmational strategy when a theory is fresh and relatively untested. The object during this phase of testing is to determine whether the theory can predict or explain the phenomena within its domain with reasonable precision.

If the theory survives these tests, you will eventually want to pursue a disconfirmational strategy. The objective during this phase of testing is to determine whether outcomes that are unexpected from the point of view of the theory nevertheless happen. If unexpected outcomes do occur, it means that the theory is, at best, incomplete. It will have to be developed further so that it can account for the previously unexpected outcome, or it will have to be replaced by a better theory.

Philosophy of science

The nature and conduct of science has been a topic of interest for philosophers, who have had much to say about many of the ideas outlined in the previous sections. In this quick detour, we are going to examine two important twentieth-century philosophers of science: Karl Popper and Thomas Kuhn. In the early 1900s, as science became a prominent part of the intellectual world, philosophers began to study it from their own perspective. Karl Popper (1902–94) proposed a method to determine the worth of scientific theories. Thomas Kuhn (1922–96) discovered that the traditional way of thinking about science's progress had been largely unrecognized.

Karl Popper and falsifiability

Karl Popper (Figure 2.2) believed that some of science's theories were not really scientific. He believed that Einstein's general relativity theory was scientific but that Freud's psychoanalytic theory was not. General relativity hinged upon gravity bending light, a suggestion that violated existing theories in physics. Arthur Eddington was a scientist who, in 1919, managed to test a prediction that Einstein had made about how light might bend during an eclipse. Nobody had ever tested Einstein's prediction before, so the outcome of this test was crucial in deciding whether his theory was a good one. Eddington's observations confirmed Einstein's prediction (Coles, 1999) and this inspired Popper. Using Einstein's theory as a model, Popper proposed that all scientific theories be judged as to how falsifiable they were. Falsifiable theories made predictions that could be shown to be false. On the other hand, non-falsifiable theories made ambiguous predictions that were difficult or impossible to test. For Popper, authors of scientific

Figure 2.2 Karl Popper

theories should state their predictions in a way that data could destroy the entire theory. Such theories were falsifiable and, thus, were good scientific theories. **Falsifiability** became Popper's method for determining the worth of a scientific theory. Unlike the majority of scientists, Popper reversed their usual order of observation, experiment, theory. Instead, Popper argued that theory should be the first step in science. A falsifiable theory points the scientist to the observations and experiments necessary to falsify the theory. The more the theory resists scientists' attempts at falsification, the better it is. Thus, according to Popper, *all* tests of a theory are actually attempts to falsify it.

> **Falsifiability**
> Karl Popper's criterion for deciding the worth of a scientific theory. Falsifiable theories allow their predictions to be tested.

Thomas Kuhn and scientific revolutions

The inspiration for Thomas Kuhn's description of the growth and death of scientific theories came after he read old science textbooks. Kuhn (Figure 2.3) wondered how someone as smart as Aristotle could have had such wrongheaded ideas about motion. Aristotle believed that moving objects travelled in straight lines only. For Aristotle, the path of an arrow shot into the air was an upside-down *V*. Galileo's observations, however, showed that the arrow's path was a parabola. As van Gelder (1996, p. B7) noted, Kuhn eventually realized that Aristotle's views were not "bad Newton"; they were just different. From then on, Kuhn looked for historical evidence of intellectual conflict; he found it. Science, he claimed, was normally a peaceful enterprise whose practitioners agreed about the problems to be addressed and the methods to use. Those scientists, he said, shared a

Figure 2.3 Thomas Kuhn

Paradigm
A global viewpoint that determines which scientific questions are asked and the methods used to answer them.

paradigm, a shared viewpoint that determines what questions are asked and what methods are used. Every now and then, however, a discipline might go through a period of doubt and strife when a new theory challenged an existing paradigm. Kuhn called those periods of intellectual conflict *scientific revolutions*. For Kuhn, revolutions occurred when an old paradigm no longer worked and was replaced by a new paradigm. Over time, the theorists supporting the new paradigm became more numerous, whereas those supporting the old paradigm either converted or retired. Eventually the scientific revolution was complete. Very soon after the publication of Kuhn's book, *The Structure of Scientific Revolutions* (1962), other philosophers began to address (and criticize) Kuhn's views of science and its progress.

Kuhn's ideas about scientific progress have sparked debate about how they apply to psychology. Some psychologists believe that, as a young science, psychology has yet to develop any paradigms at all. Psychology is pre-paradigmatic, to use Kuhn's terminology. Other psychologists, however, believe that Kuhn's idea of scientific revolutions is not applicable to psychology. Instead, psychology's wide variety of topics reflect a tradition of independent research and theorizing, none of which is amenable to the kind of synthesis suggested by Kuhn. Recently, Sternberg and Grigorenko (2001) argued for a unified conception of psychology based on phenomena and not on methods of inquiry. Furthermore, they see "unified psychology" as a multi-paradigmatic, multidisciplinary and integrated approach in which researchers should attempt to break free of smaller and restrictive mindsets.

Science and pseudoscience

Finally in this chapter, we are going to look at what distinguishes a true science from non-science and pseudoscience. Some things can masquerade as science when, on closer inspection, they are anything but scientific. This is unfortunate as the general public often do not know how to tell good science from bad science, and can get duped by people peddling false science as if it were valid. The difference lies in the methods used to collect information and draw conclusions from it. A true science (like psychology, physics, chemistry and biology) relies on established scientific methods to acquire information, and adheres to certain rules when assessing the validity of information obtained. A non-science can be a legitimate academic discipline (like history or philosophy) that applies systematic techniques to the acquisition of knowledge (for example, providing explanations for the First World War or describing the nature of the soul).

Pseudoscience
Claims that are made on the basis of evidence that is designed to appear scientific; however, such evidence is not based on the principles of the scientific method.

Pseudoscience is another animal all together. The term pseudoscience literally means "false science". According to Robert Carroll (2006), "pseudoscience is [a] set of ideas based on theories put forth as scientific when they are not scientific" (http://skepdic.com/pseudosc.html). Some notorious examples of pseudoscience include phrenology (determining your personality by reading the bumps on your head) and astrology (using the position of the stars and planets to explain behaviour and personality, and to predict the future).

Scott Lillenfeld (2005) lists several qualities that define a pseudoscience:

- Using ad hoc hypotheses to explain away falsification of a pseudoscientific idea or claim
- No mechanisms for self-correction and consequent stagnation of ideas or claims

- Reliance on a confirmational strategy rather than a disconfirmational one to test ideas or claims
- Shifting the burden of proof to sceptics and critics away from the proponent of an idea or a claim
- Over-reliance on anecdotal evidence and testimonials to support an idea or claim
- Avoidance of the peer review[3] process that would scientifically scrutinize ideas and claims
- A failure to build on an existing base of scientific knowledge
- Excessive use of impressive-sounding jargon that lends false credibility to ideas and claims
- Failure to specify conditions under which ideas or claims would not hold true.

Lillenfeld points out that no one of the above is sufficient to identify an idea or claim as pseudoscientific. However, the greater the number of the above qualities an idea or claim has, the more confident you can be that the idea or claim is based on pseudoscience and not legitimate science.

Rory Coker (2007) provides a nice contrast between a true science and a pseudoscience. He identifies several crucial differences between science and pseudoscience that can help you assess whether an idea or claim is truly scientific or based on pseudoscientific beliefs. This contrast is shown in Table 2.3. Coker also suggests several additional characteristics of pseudoscience. First,

Table 2.3 Distinguishing science from pseudoscience

Science	Pseudoscience
Findings published in peer-reviewed[3] publications using standards for honesty and accuracy aimed at scientists	Findings disseminated to general public via sources that are not peer reviewed. No pre-publication review for precision or accuracy
Experiments must be precisely described and be reproducible. Reliable results are demanded	Studies, if any, are vaguely defined and cannot be reproduced easily. Results cannot be reproduced
Scientific failures are carefully scrutinized and studied for reasons for failure	Failures are ignored, minimized, explained away, rationalized or hidden
Over time and continued research, more and more is learned about scientific phenomena	No underlying mechanisms are identified and no new research is done. No progress is made and nothing concrete is learned
Idiosyncratic findings and blunders "average out" and do not affect the actual phenomenon under study	Idiosyncratic findings and blunders provide the only identifiable phenomena
Scientists convince others based on evidence and research findings, making the best case permitted by existing data. Old ideas are discarded in the light of new evidence	Attempts to convince based on belief and faith rather than facts. Belief encouraged in spite of facts, not because of them. Ideas never discarded, regardless of the evidence
Scientist has no personal stake in a specific outcome of a study	Serious conflicts of interest. Pseudoscientist makes his or her living off of pseudoscientific products or services

Source: Based on information obtained from Coker (2007).

---

3 "Peer review" is the process where scientific work is checked by experts. Before anything can be published in a scientific journal, it has to be reviewed by other experts (peers) in the area, to ensure that the quality of the work is good enough. It is science's in-built quality control mechanism.

pseudoscience often is unconcerned with facts, and "spouts" dubious facts when necessary. Second, what research is conducted on an idea or claim is usually sloppy and never includes independent investigations to check its sources. Third, pseudoscience inevitably defaults to absurd explanations when pressed for an explanation of an idea or claim. Fourth, by leaving out critical facts pseudoscience creates mysteries that are difficult to solve. The full list of these and other characteristics of pseudoscience can be found at https://webspace.utexas.edu/cokerwr/www/index.html/distinguish.htm.

> **Scientific explanation**
> A tentative explanation for a phenomenon, based on objective observation and logic, and subject to empirical test.

Contrast pseudoscience with how a true science operates. A true science attempts to develop scientific explanations to explain phenomena within its domain. Simply put, a **scientific explanation** is an explanation based on the application of accepted scientific methods. Scientific explanations differ in several important ways from non-scientific and pseudoscientific explanations that rely more on common sense or faith.

Scientism: a final note for sceptics . . .

We have presented a very positive view of science in this chapter. Some people might be sceptical about this, and might ask whether we have been too sycophantic towards science. This is a valid criticism, and should be briefly addressed. Unquestioning reverence of science is sometimes known as "scientism". Some people might call it "science worship". Science is not perfect, and so we should be keenly aware of its limitations. It is a human endeavour and its weaknesses emerge from this fact. Humans are not perfect and so science is not perfect. Humans make mistakes, have biases, have personal and political agendas, and so on. Some of these things will have an influence on the scientific process, and so we must acknowledge this and avoid unquestioning worship of science. It is certainly not something that is above criticism. Some people have noticed these things and have adopted the opposite stance – becoming extremely negative towards science and sceptical of scientific knowledge. This is not really helpful, because it fails to acknowledge the things that science gets right. Although not perfect, the scientific process is a very powerful tool (maybe the most powerful we have) for making sense of the world around us. It has its problems, but that does not mean we should discard it completely. A pragmatic approach is probably the most useful, acknowledging that science, as practised by humans, cannot be absolutely perfect, but also recognizing that it is useful and can tell us a lot about the world around us. Questions about science are interesting and they continue to fascinate philosophers and stimulate debates, many of which have implications for psychology. We will look at some of these issues and some **criticisms of science** in Chapter 10. For the moment, however, we appreciate that we have been very positive towards science in the current chapter, but would hope that we are not so deferential that it results in accusations of scientism.[4]

> ch. 10

---

4   For further reading on these issues, see Haack (2007).

Summary

We can find out about the world in various ways. The method of tenacity involves sticking to what you believe, no matter what, while the method of authority involves looking to an expert to inform our beliefs. Rational methods are based on logic and reason, while the scientific method is based on a combination of reasoning and actual observations. Scientists work in a wide variety of areas, but have a common goal: *to acquire knowledge through the application of scientific methods and techniques*. Science is empirical (based on observation and measurement), it is public and it usually involves replicability. Scientific research can be basic (involved with conceptual issues) or applied (concerned with applying scientific knowledge to real-world problems), although there are overlaps between these. Theories, laws and hypotheses are all important features of science, and certain criteria exist for determining what makes a "good" theory. Linked to this is the important distinction between science and pseudoscience. Philosophers of science, such as Popper and Kuhn, have commented on the nature of the scientific process and the way scientists go about knowledge gathering.

 Questions

1 What is science and what do scientists do?

2 How do basic and applied research differ, and how are they similar?

3 What is pseudoscience and how does it differ from science?

4 How do belief-based and scientific explanations differ?

5 What are the defining characteristics and weaknesses of the method of authority and the rational method?

6 What is the scientific method, and why is it preferred in science?

7 What is the definition of a scientific theory?

8 How does a theory differ from a hypothesis or a law?

9 How do mechanistic and functional theories differ? Which type is better, and why?

10 What roles do theories play in science? (Describe each role in detail.)

11 What are the defining characteristics of a "good" theory?

12 What is meant by confirmation and disconfirmation of a theory?

13 What is the difference between a confirmational and a disconfirmational strategy? How are they used to test a theory?

14 How are theories tested?

15 Explain why rigorous tests of a theory that seek to falsify a theory's propositions can be more informative than tests that seek to confirm a theory's propositions.

Activities

1 Read several editorials in your daily newspaper and identify the sources used to support the assertions and conclusions. Did the writer use intuition, appeals to authority, scientific evidence, or a combination of these? Give specific examples. Identify two reasons you would give another person as to why they should critically evaluate the results of the research reported in the news media (e.g. television, magazines).

2 Identify ways that you might have allowed yourself to accept beliefs or engage in practices that might have been rejected if you had engaged in scientific thinking. For example, I continually have to remind some of my friends that a claim made in an email may be a hoax or a rumour. Provide specific details of the experience(s). How might you go about investigating whether the claim is valid?

3 Think of at least five "common-sense" sayings about behaviour (e.g. "Like father, like son"; "Absence makes the heart grow fonder"). For each, develop a hypothesis that is suggested by the saying and a prediction that follows from the hypothesis.

4 Theories serve two purposes: (1) to organize and explain observable events, and (2) to generate new knowledge by guiding our way of looking at these events. Identify a consistent behaviour pattern in yourself or somebody close to you (e.g. you consistently get into an argument with your sister on Friday nights). Generate two possible explanations for this occurrence (e.g. because you work long hours on Friday, you're usually stressed and exhausted when you get home; because your sister has a chemistry test every Friday afternoon and she's not doing well in the course, she is very irritable on Fridays). How would you gather evidence to determine which explanation might be correct? How might each explanation lead to different approaches to changing the behaviour pattern, either to decrease or increase its occurrence?

5 Identify which one of the four characteristics of science each statement relates to.[5]

(a) I like science because there are no secrets and everything is above board.

(b) The thing I like about science is that undiscovered things are predicted by principles.

(c) I'm going to take a scientific approach and look for myself.

(d) It is easy to find scientific stuff because so much is online.

(e) The neat thing about science is that the facts are explained by an overarching idea.

(f) The facts that get put into textbooks have been observed several times at least.

5 Answers: (a) public nature; (b) theory; (c) empiricism; (d) public nature; (e) theory; (f) replication.

Psychology as a Science

OVERVIEW

To reward your endurance in getting through Chapter 2, we have made this chapter a short one. In Chapter 2 we introduced you to science and scientific thinking. Some of the examples we used were psychological in nature and others were not. In this chapter, we are going to focus on psychology. Psychology occupies a rather strange position in that it is usually considered to be quite different from other sciences such as physics and chemistry, but it also stands apart from disciplines such as sociology and anthropology. By the end of this chapter, you should understand the particular challenges psychologists face when investigating mind and behaviour in a scientific way. You should also be able to give an account of the ways in which psychologists have faced these challenges in the past and produce an argument defending psychology's status as a science.

OBJECTIVES

After studying this chapter and working through the exercises, you should be able to:

- State the main differences between psychology and "hard sciences" in terms of the way they approach their phenomena of interest
- Demonstrate an understanding of the main challenges involved in studying psychology scientifically
- Outline the ways in which psychologists have approached their discipline throughout psychology's short history and, where appropriate, critique these approaches
- Give an account of the main issues surrounding both the definition and the measurement of constructs within psychology
- State what an "operational definition" is and why it is important

Psychology and science

What is psychology? If you are on a psychology course, this is a question that you will probably already have thought about. Most definitions would probably include something about "the study of mental processes and behaviour", and this is a fairly good account of what psychology is. Sometimes you might find psychology described as the "scientific" study of mental processes or behaviour. Although there are psychologists who would argue with that description (and we will meet some of them in **Chapter 10**) the majority of psychologists do consider their discipline to be a scientific one. If you think back to **Chapter 2** then you will remember that science is concerned with "observation" and "measurement". This means that the way we employ scientific methods is going to be closely related to what it is we are studying. Different areas of science look at different things and this is going to have implications for the way scientists in each area make their observations and measurements. Not everything can be observed and measured in the same way.

> ## STOP & Think
>
> What do we mean by "not everything can be observed and measured in the same way"? Think about the differences between how we might measure something like "distance to the moon" compared to how we might measure something like "facial attractiveness".

Fuzzy science

Psychology has often been called a "fuzzy" science, or a "soft" science.

Sometimes this is used as a put-down intended to denigrate psychology's scientific status. If you have friends studying physics, chemistry or biology, you might have heard them say that psychology is not a "proper" science. What does this mean? Well, it does not mean that psychologists have a poorer understanding of scientific methods than scientists in other disciplines, nor does it mean that psychologists are any worse at employing scientific methods than other scientists. When people say this, they are actually referring to the phenomena under study. Think about the things that physicists, chemists and biologists study. Physicists are interested in physical properties of the world such as matter and particles. They look to develop laws indicating the way in which these physical properties interact and they look to uncover the forces that act upon matter. Chemists study physical matter as well, but they are interested in its composition and structure and how it changes during chemical reactions. Biologists are concerned with living organisms and, among other things, how these organisms are structured, how they function and how they evolve.[1]

The thing that all of these disciplines have in common is that, on the whole, the things of interest are all relatively easy to define and measure.[2] What do we mean by this? To use a simple

---

1   We are aware that these definitions of physics, chemistry and biology are embarrassingly simplistic, and we apologize to students of any of them for this. We are just trying to make a simple point.

2   Again, this may be an oversimplification. Our point is merely that psychology faces unique challenges when practised as a science that other disciplines do not.

example, imagine you're interested in the acceleration of an object due to gravity in a vacuum. This is a physics question and it is answerable by creating a situation that allows you to make the measurements that will answer your question. If you have set up the experiment in the correct way and you know how to operate the measuring equipment adequately, then you will get a fairly accurate measurement that informs you about the phenomena you are interested in. Likewise, in chemistry, if you are interested in how two chemicals interact at a certain temperature then it should not be difficult to find out as long as you are careful in your preparation and measurement. Furthermore, both of these investigations can be replicated again and again, by you and others, and the results are likely to be the same (as long as you conducted the measurement adequately in the first place and as long as the replications are conducted to the same standard). It doesn't matter if you have had an argument with your neighbour just before the test; it doesn't matter if your new shoes are hurting you – the thing you are measuring is not likely to depend on these things. Because the scientific question relates to objective, measurable things "out there" in the world, then the answer you get from a well-conducted investigation will always be the same.

Challenges for psychology

Psychology is slightly different to mainstream "hard" sciences. Psychology deals with people (forgetting, for the moment, animal and comparative psychology) and people are complex. A person is far more complex than a chemical in a test tube or an object falling in a vacuum. Being psychologists, we are interested in psychological complexity rather than our biological or chemical complexity, and humans are psychologically complex for a number of reasons. First, we have astonishingly complex brains.

The human brain has 100–150 billion neurons, with each single neuron connecting with approximately 10 000 other ones. It has been described as the most complex thing in the known universe. As you know, this amazing thing inside each of our heads is responsible for everything we are interested in as psychologists. Not only do we have physically complex brains, but there are an enormous amount of things that can influence our behaviour and our thinking.

This complexity makes it very hard to study psychological phenomena in the same way we might study phenomena in other areas of science. Take something like memory, a very common thing to study in psychology. Memories are part of an individual's psychological make-up. This means that they are very difficult to study objectively (see below for more on this). There are all sorts of things that might influence an individual's memory capabilities. In any laboratory study on human memory it is conceivable that whether or not a person had been involved in an argument with his neighbour prior to the study would affect his concentration, which would in turn impact upon how he performs on whatever memory task he is given. There are lots of other things that could influence his performance in your experiment and there is no way you can account for them all.

The point is that the complexity of factors that are interacting and influencing our psychological make-up and behaviour is vast. In psychology, we are usually unable to isolate the particular psychological phenomenon in which we are interested in the same way as we can isolate phenomena in other sciences. There is an enormous number of factors that can potentially influence the thing we want to measure, and this means that psychology is rarely a precise science in the same way other "hard" sciences are. This is one reason why students of other science subjects sometimes accuse psychology of being a "soft" science.

This is not the only problem. Psychologists also have trouble defining things in a way that most "hard" sciences do not. Take something like "intelligence". It is clear that some people are more intelligent than others, but what exactly *is* intelligence?

Does it make sense to have one measure of overall intelligence that applies to everyone everywhere? Some researchers say that it does, while others would say that this does not accurately reflect the broad spectrum of what counts as "intelligence". Obviously, how you define it is going to influence how you then measure it. And, even if you can agree a way of measuring it, how can you be sure that your measurement is actually measuring "intelligence" and not something else? This suggests that some things we study in psychology are far from having definitions that everyone agrees on. This is not common in most other areas of science.

Where does this leave psychology? Given the multitude of things that can influence people and the problems in defining some of the things we are interested in, can we ever hope to isolate measurable phenomena in the same way that other sciences can? The short answer to this is "no". But do not let this put you off or fool you into thinking that psychologists cannot make progress. Those interested in the mind can still use scientific principles in their investigations. Let's explore these issues in more detail.

Addressing the challenges

Psychologists have recognized the difficulties they face in studying mind and behaviour for a long time. As well as the problem of complexity and a large, open sphere of influence (both described above) we have the further problem of what we should be measuring. We use terms like "attitudes" and "personality" and "depression", but what do these really mean? If we are trying to be scientific and stick to objective observation and measurement, then we are going to have to think long and hard about how to observe and measure things like this. There does not seem to be an easy way to define "attitude". Even if we could define it, how could we observe it? We will return to these questions shortly, but first, let's look at how psychologists have faced up to these challenges in the past.

The idea of applying scientific thinking and methods to phenomena of mind, behaviour and cognition emerged during the nineteenth century. Much of the early work was in psychophysics, which sought to demonstrate mathematical relationships (laws) between a physical stimulus from the environment and a psychological perception within a person. Also in the mid-nineteenth century, Paul Broca (1861) discovered a relationship between the brain and a specific behaviour by performing an autopsy on a man who had lost the ability to speak. The autopsy showed a lesion in his left temporal lobe, a part of the brain now named Broca's area.

Although there had been a move in the nineteenth century to apply scientific thinking and methods to phenomena of mind, behaviour and cognition, it was a physiologist turned psychologist named Wilhelm Wundt (1832–1920) who first intentionally established scientific psychology (Figure 3.1).

In 1879, Wundt established the first research laboratory devoted to the scientific study of psychology, and his research was directed primarily towards consciousness. Wundt and his

Figure 3.1 Wilhelm Wundt

students studied the mind by examining their thoughts while they engaged in controlled, experimental situations. This method is called **introspection**.

Psychologists eventually abandoned introspection because of its methodological flaws. It quickly became clear that it was not a method that had scientific validity. Scientists try to be as objective as possible in their methods and it was clear that introspection was problematic given that it is inherently subjective. For example, two people could introspect when taking part in the same task and both give different (perhaps even conflicting) accounts of what their thought processes were. Given that all we have to work with are subjective accounts, there is no way of determining who (if anyone) is "correct". Clearly, this is a problem if we are trying to obtain scientific (and thus objective) data on the mind.

John B. Watson (1878–1958) introduced a new methodology, **behaviourism** (Watson, 1913), which replaced introspection and its emphasis on the mind.

Behaviourists defined psychology and psychological research in terms of changes in behaviour in response to changes in the environment. They rejected introspection as a method due to its flaws, and partly due to a keen ambition to establish psychology as a science, and stated that only externally observable behaviours could be considered as valid data. Obviously this position ruled out any internal psychological phenomena from being studied. Eventually these internal processes were reintroduced into psychology by people who realized that it did not make sense to exclude them given their obvious role in our mental lives. Thus, cognitive psychology emerged after the Second World War using a new metaphor, *computation*. Cognitive psychologists study cognitive processes (perception, memory, learning and others) scientifically by studying many factors relating to internal cognitive processes. Among other measures, cognitive psychologists look at response times (linked to how long

Introspection
A method by which the researcher pays attention to his or her own psychological processes while engaged in a task.

Behaviourism
A school of thought in psychology which holds that the only valid unit of measurement in psychology is observable behaviours.

the process takes) and accuracy measures (linked to knowledge that must be accessed). In using these things, the internal processes that had been ignored by behaviourists could be studied in an objective way that did not face the same criticisms as the introspective methods did.

Defining psychological things

As we have seen, one of the main challenges to psychology concerns how we define the things that we want to investigate. It is extremely important to have a clear definition of what you are studying as early as you possibly can, because a clear definition will help you in your quest to observe and measure.

Concepts

Concept
An abstract idea or unit of knowledge that refers to something in the external world and can be conveyed to others in a meaningful way.

Concepts are everywhere. They are like the glue that binds the social world together. We can use the term "concepts" to refer to things (both living and inanimate), to events (things in action), and to relationships among things or events. "Dog" is a concept, as is "barking", and so is "obedience". Concepts are the symbols that allow us to communicate. Clear, unambiguous communication of ideas requires that we use concepts that are clearly defined. If we all used ambiguous concepts, then nobody would know what anyone else was talking about.

STOP & Think

What is the difference between "dog" as a concept and "justice" as a concept? Do you think this difference matters? Why?

In everyday conversation we often get by without having to worry too much about how we define a concept. Many words are commonly used and apparently understood even though neither party in the conversation knows exactly what the words mean. That is, people frequently communicate with one another without being fully aware of what they are talking about! This may sound ridiculous but, to illustrate our point, try the following. Ask a few people whether they believe that intelligence is mostly inherited or mostly learned. You might try arguing a point of view opposite to theirs just for fun. After discussing the roots of intelligence, ask them what they mean by "intelligence". You will probably find that most people have a difficult time defining this concept, even after debating its origins. Despite this difficulty in finding an adequate definition, people are frequently willing to debate an important point regarding intelligence, and even take a definite stand on the issue, without being able to say exactly what "intelligence" is. When someone does provide a definition, it is unlikely to be exactly the same as that given by another person. Clearly, in order to attempt to answer the question of whether intelligence is mainly inherited or mainly learned, we need to have an exact definition that everyone involved can accept.

Constructs and operational definitions

The study of "concepts" is so important in psychological science that researchers refer to concepts by a special name: constructs.

A **construct** is a concept or idea; examples of psychological constructs include intelligence, depression, aggression and memory. One way in which a scientist gives meaning to a construct is by defining it operationally. What does this mean? Scientists are masters of measuring. They measure distances as large as the diameter of the Milky Way (100 000 light years) and as small as the diameter of an atom (one ten-billionth of a metre). Obviously those distances are measured with different methods. Scientists measure time as long as the age of the universe (13.7 billion years) and as brief as the duration of a computer's command (one-billionth of a second). Like distances, long and short times are measured with different methods. In psychology, scientists measure the memory of animals as simple as molluscs and as complex as humans. Again, the way in which you measure memory in each of these cases is different. To completely understand a concept such as distance, time or memory, you must understand how the measurements are made.

> **Construct**
> A concept or idea used in psychological theories to explain behaviour or mental processes; examples include aggression, depression, intelligence, memory and personality.
>
> **Operational definition**
> Procedures or operations used to measure a variable or establish a condition.

An explanation of how to make a measurement is called an **operational definition**. An operational definition is a description of the procedures used by the researcher to measure a variable or create levels of a variable. These procedures are connected in a logical way to the concept or condition that is being operationally defined.

To illustrate operational definitions of psychological concepts, contrast them with their dictionary definitions. Table 3.1 lists five psychological variables, their dictionary definitions, and one or more operational definitions. You already know that dictionary definitions almost always help us understand a concept better. An operational definition adds to that understanding by telling us how the concept is measured. Notice in Table 3.1 that several variables have two or more operational definitions. Some things in psychology can be measured in different ways by different researchers and that is why it is important to give an account of your measurement technique when referring to a psychological construct.

For "frustration", we listed two operational definitions. The first gives the procedures that have been used to create frustration in children: "Abruptly remove toys that a child is playing with." The second operational definition has been used with rats: "Withhold reinforcement for performing a previously reinforced behaviour." The procedures to follow to create frustration are fairly clear and there is a logical connection between the procedures and concept. A good operational definition is one that leaves you saying "I understand what you mean", or "I can measure it the same way" or "I can create the same conditions."

Operational definitions tell you exactly what to do to replicate a measurement, but they do not always produce feelings of assurance. For example, hunger seems to be more than merely "hours without food". Happiness seems to be more than a score on a test. However, operational definitions communicate clearly, which is an important element of mutual understanding, and especially important in a scientific research context. If you cannot communicate clearly how you are defining and measuring a construct, then other researchers will not be able to follow up your work.

Table 3.1 Dictionary and operational definitions of psychological terms		
Psychological variable	**Dictionary definition**[a]	**Operational definition (to measure or create)**
Frustration	State of insecurity and dissatisfaction arising from unresolved problems or unfulfilled needs	1 Abruptly remove toys that a child is playing with 2 Withhold reinforcement for performing a previously reinforced behaviour
Hunger	Craving or urgent need for food	1 Hours of food deprivation 2 Percentage of *ad libitum* weight
Depression	State of feeling sad	Beck Depression Inventory score[b]
Happiness	State of well-being and contentment	Subjective Happiness Scale score[c]
Memory	Power or process of reproducing or recalling what has been learned and retained	1 Trials to relearn 2 Custom-made multiple-choice test 3 fMRI activity

Notes:
a. *Merriam Webster's Collegiate Dictionary*, 11th edn (2004).
b. Beck et al. (1988).
c. Lyubomirsky (1999).

Operational definitions are very important to think about. One of the most common mistakes that undergraduates make when embarking on their first research project is failing to think about their operational definitions. It is all too easy to get carried away with your great ideas, but at every step along the way, you need to stop and think "OK – how am I actually going to measure this?" If you get into the habit of thinking about operational definitions, then it will be of benefit to you in further research that you might conduct.

Problems with operational definitions

Although we strongly advise that operational definitions are crucial in any psychological research project, there are some issues to keep in mind. One problem is that, if we do not like one operational definition of intelligence, there is nothing to prevent us from giving intelligence another operational definition. Does this mean that there are as many kinds of intelligence as there are operational definitions? Each time a new set of questions is added to a paper-and-pencil test of intelligence, do we have a new definition of intelligence? The answer, unfortunately, is that we do not really know. To determine whether a different procedure yields a new definition of intelligence, we would have to seek additional evidence. For example, do people who score high on one test also score high on the second test? If they do, the new test may be measuring the same construct as the old one.

Illustration 3.1 If balancing a ball on your nose is an operational definition of intelligence, would seals be considered more intelligent than humans?

Another criticism of using operational definitions is that the definitions are not always meaningful. For example, defining intelligence in terms of how long one can balance a ball on one's nose is an operational definition that most people would not find very meaningful (Illustration 3.1). How do we decide whether a construct has been meaningfully defined? Once again, the solution is to appeal to other forms of evidence. How does performance on a balancing task compare to performance on other tasks that are commonly accepted as measures of intelligence? We must also apply common sense to the situation. Do people usually consider balancing a ball evidence of intelligence? Probably not. Scientists are generally aware of the limitations of operational definitions; however, a major strength of using operational definitions is that they help to clarify communication among scientists about their constructs. This strength is assumed to outweigh the limitations.

Measuring psychological things

As we have already said in this chapter, we cannot touch a mood, an attitude, a memory or a thought. We cannot put these things down in front of us and measure them in the same way we would measure other physical things. But just because we cannot directly measure them does not make them any less real. This is one of the interesting things about psychology. No one would argue that our thoughts are not real. That would seem ridiculous. They are as real as anything else. Descartes, whom we met in Chapter 2, argued that our thoughts are the most real thing we can experience because we can doubt the existence of just about anything else but our own thoughts.

So, given that these things are real, we need to find ways to measure them. That is not easy. How do you measure a thought?

These days we have fantastic machines that can measure the blood flow in your brain, or the electrical signals that happen when you think. These are the most advanced machines we have in psychology. But they are still not measuring thoughts. All they are measuring is things that are *associated* with thoughts. If you have a thought, there is an associated electrical signal. We can measure the electrical signal, but that electrical signal is not the same thing as the thought. If we gave an expert the isolated electrical signal to analyse, he would find it absolutely impossible to figure out what the thought was that caused it, which would suggest that these electrical signals must not be the same as the thoughts that give rise to them. It's a tricky situation. It would be wrong to say that thoughts do not exist just because we cannot directly see them. Of course they exist. Just because something cannot be seen does not mean that we cannot hypothesize about it. Physics is probably the "hardest" of all the sciences, yet physicists have never seen sub-atomic particles, or even a black hole. That does not stop them from studying these

Dynamic processes
Memory, mood, judgement, etc.

Stable characteristics
Intelligence, personality, certain beliefs, etc.

things. They just have to study them in indirect ways, and that is what psychologists have to do. Psychologists do their best to measure things that are closely associated with thoughts, attitudes, feelings and so on.

To get an idea about the ways in which we should approach measurement, it is sometimes useful to think of psychological phenomena as belonging to two very broad categories: **dynamic processes** and **stable characteristics**.

Having split up the psychological world into these two broad categories, psychologists investigate these phenomena in slightly different ways.

Dynamic processes

ch. 6

ch. 7
pp.114–123

When we measure dynamic processes like memory, we are interested in on-the-spot measurements. What this means is that we set up a **well-controlled situation** in which we can measure the phenomenon of interest. We might then look at these on-the-spot measurements and **compare them with other groups** of people, or see how the measurements might differ in different situations. The fact that these things are dynamic means that they're likely to change from time to time, so you have to make sure that you "capture" them in exactly the right way that makes most sense to answer the question that you are asking. As an example, think about mood. Your mood is going to be different if you have just sat and watched a sad film about death for two hours than it would be if you had just won the lottery. So, mood is dynamic. It changes. It is not stable. It would not make any sense for me to give you a "mood test" and then say "the type of mood you have is . . . sad". We would need to say "under these conditions, your mood is sad . . . under *these* conditions, your mood is . . .". It is the same for memory. Because your memory might work differently under different conditions, we have to take this into consideration when we study it. We have to be very careful that we know exactly what aspect of memory we are testing, and we also have to know exactly what type of conditions we are testing under. For example, your memory capabilities will probably be different depending on the type of thing you are trying to remember. If I were to give you 15 random letters to remember or 15 words related to food, then your memory for each of these types of things is probably going to be different.

Stable characteristics

Stable psychological characteristics are things like personality and intelligence. Certain types of attitudes are also thought to be stable over time. Unlike dynamic processes, we can expect these things to be relatively constant. Your core personality, who you are, is not going to change much depending on the situation. Neither is your intelligence or your core attitudes. If you are an intelligent person, your intelligence is not going to fluctuate depending on whether you have just watched a sad film or not. This has implications for our measurement techniques. Many stable psychological characteristics can be measured using paper-and-pencil tests or questionnaires. We will come back to **survey methods** in Chapter 13.

These categories are fairly arbitrary, and are rarely (if ever) explicitly commented upon by professional researchers. That said, it is useful to keep them in mind when you are thinking about psychological phenomena and how to proceed with measuring them.

STOP & Think

Think of some other psychological phenomena and decide whether they are dynamic processes or stable characteristics. Is it easier to categorize some things compared to others? What does this tell you about these phenomena?

Using scientific principles in psychology

Although there are clearly challenges when approaching psychological topics from a scientific viewpoint, we hope that you can see that a scientific approach is possible. All of the things that we stated in Chapter 2 about the nature of science apply to psychology. We can measure and observe psychological phenomena as long as we take great care in defining what we are studying and are clear in the steps we are taking to measure the psychological construct that is of interest. Despite being challenges, these issues are part of what makes psychology such a fascinating science. The debates of constructs and measurement are extremely interesting and really get to the heart of what it is that we are interested in. Arguments among psychologists about the nature of intelligence, personality, attitudes, emotions, beliefs, attitudes, conscious experience and so on force us to think carefully about what these things are and how to study them. The complexity of these constructs and the complexity of people in general should not be considered a barrier to understanding. Instead, we should view the complexity as a springboard allowing us to further our knowledge about these interesting and elusive things.

The way we make our observations and measurements must also be carefully thought through, and this forces us to think about the relationship between the construct itself and the way we are measuring it. For some things this will be less of an issue. For example, using response time as a measure can unambiguously tell us that there is a meaningful relationship between the time taken to respond and the way things are organized in our minds. For example, one finding from cognitive psychology is that we recognize a word quicker if that word has just been preceded by another word that is semantically related to it (e.g. cat–dog; a phenomenon known as semantic priming). Now, in this case, the measurement we have made relates to response time. We have good reason to believe that, in studies such as this, response time acts as an indirect measure relating to the organization of concepts in our minds. However, despite the fact that the measurement itself is not really controversial, the way the finding is interpreted opens up another area of debate among psychologists, who often interpret the same findings in different ways. Again, this is entirely in line with scientific thinking, as the way to resolve the debate is to posit a **theoretical framework** that explains the finding and makes predictions about future studies, which are then developed into hypotheses and empirically tested. In this way we can slowly paint a picture that reveals the nature of the mind, and which theory is correct and which is not. For other things, such as intelligence, the debate will focus on many things, including the nature and definition of the construct itself and the ways in which it is measured.

There's a further implication for psychology and it relates to the complexity of people that we mentioned previously. As we stated, there are lots of things that can influence you in any task that you do. As well as this, everyone is different. Everyone will come to a task with different experiences, a different personality, etc. What this means is that everyone will perform slightly differently for lots of reasons. Why is this important? We stated above that psychology is not a precise science. What this means is that we cannot take measurements from just one person and assume that they are going to be representative of everyone else. That would be too simplistic given the complexity of people and all the things that can potentially have an influence on the measurement that you are taking. What we have to do is test many people. All of these people are going to be different in lots of different ways, so we need to think about how we are going to organize all the measurements we take, what the measurements actually mean and what we can conclude from them. This is one of the reasons that psychology employs statistics in its quest to find out about the mind. The complexity of the subject matter demands that we must make many observations and the variation between these observations require that we use statistical analyses to make sense of them. **We will introduce you to these ideas in the second part of the book,** but we hope that this very brief justification helps you understand the common question we are asked by undergraduates: "why do we need to do statistics in a psychology degree?"

Alternatives to scientific psychology

This chapter has focussed mainly on how psychology can be seen as a science. However, not all psychologists are keen to take such a scientific approach. These psychologists argue against the notion that our observations are an accurate reflection of reality. Instead, they argue that reality is something that we actively construct, and this construction is a result of historical, cultural and linguistic influences. As such, many psychologists would say that there is no such thing as independent "knowledge" but rather there are multiple "knowledges" that reflect the particular way that the knowledge has been subjectively developed. This is at odds with a scientific view, which holds that it is possible to obtain knowledge in a fairly objective manner. The alternative approach is also highly critical of the way scientific psychologists use constructs and operational definitions. The argument is that, although psychologists appear to acknowledge the limitations of the definitions and measurements that they employ, they still proceed as if they are measuring "things" (e.g. emotion) when it might be the case that these "things" are a construct of the psychologists rather than having an independent existence. We will return to this issue more fully in **Chapter 10.**

Summary

This chapter has introduced you to the concept of approaching psychology as a science, which is probably the most common approach. Psychology, however, is different to "hard" sciences like physics, chemistry and biology because of the things that it measures: behaviour and mental processes. This leads to psychology facing challenges relating to the definition and measurement of the things that it studies, which can be broadly split into two categories: "dynamic processes" and "stable characteristics". Which category a phenomenon belongs to determines the way in which it is measured. The issues raised in this chapter are at the core of modern psychology because, to know about anything, we must be able to first define it, and then to find out its properties, both of which are hard to do for psychological and behavioural phenomena.

Questions

1 What is the major advantage of using operational definitions in psychology? In what two ways has the use of operational definitions been criticized?

2 In what ways might psychology be distinguished from "hard" sciences such as physics, chemistry and biology?

3 What are the main challenges facing those who want to study the mind from a scientific perspective?

4 What is an operational definition and how does it differ from a definition you might find in a dictionary?

5 Why did psychology abandon introspection as a method of finding out about mental processes?

6 What's the difference between "dynamic processes" and "stable characteristics" in reference to psychological phenomena?

Activities

1 List three psychological phenomena that you think are "stable characteristics" and three that you consider to be "dynamic processes".

2 For each of the psychological phenomena that you listed in (1), provide a brief operational definition for it.

3 Ask two friends (who do not study psychology) what they understand by the term "intelligence".

    (a) In what ways do their definitions differ from each other?

    (b) Do their definitions differ from one you might expect from a psychology student? In what way? What does this tell you?

    (c) Do either of your friends' definitions suggest a meaningful way of measuring "intelligence"?

SECTION 2

Methods and Issues in Research

Chapter 4

The Language of Research

OVERVIEW

Although this is an "introductory" chapter, it has some important material. We will cover some of the language and concepts used when discussing methods and research in psychology. Although this part covers quite a lot of terms, there are other terms that we have decided to cover in other chapters, so it is not quite a complete account of all the terms you'll encounter in this book.

OBJECTIVES

After studying this chapter and working through the exercises, you should be able to:

- Define the following terms:
  - Variables
    - Independent variable
    - Dependent variable
  - Operational definition
  - Levels of measurement
    - Nominal
    - Ordinal
    - Interval
    - Ratio

o Hypotheses

  ■ Experimental/alternative hypothesis

  ■ Null hypothesis

  ■ Two-tailed/one-tailed hypotheses

o Reliability

o Validity

● Identify what level of measurement is being used for various types of measure

● Give an account of the ways in which the reliability and validity of a measure can be assessed

"This is like learning a foreign language"

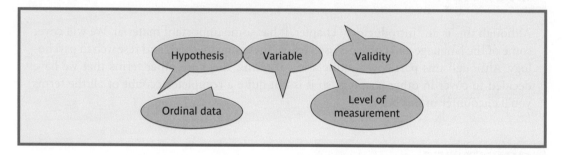

If you have already been to some research methods classes, you may be a bit confused by all of the new terms you have to learn. Learning about research is one of those things that can sometimes feel like learning another language. Although there are lots of new words to get to grips with, the ideas they convey are usually remarkably straightforward, despite what you might think. In this section, we will run through the main bits of jargon that you will hear again and again both in this book and in any research methods classes you might attend. It is important that you become familiar with these terms and what they mean, because most of what follows will only make sense if you are. We should probably warn you that the same concept can sometimes have two or more different terms associated with it, while other single terms can be used to mean slightly different things. This can be frustrating when you are learning about research methods, but it is just something that we all have to live with. We will be as consistent as we can in our use of terms, and will make it clear what term we'll be adopting where more than one exists.

Variables

height height **height height** height

Figure 4.1 Height can vary – it's a "variable"

Variables are things that vary. Obviously. Variables are central to most quantitative methods, so an understanding of them is crucial (Figure 4.1). More specifically for psychological research, a variable is any event, situation, behaviour or individual characteristic that varies. Examples of variables a psychologist might study include performance on a cognitive task, word length, intelligence, gender, reaction time, rate of forgetting, aggression, speaker credibility, attitude change, anger, stress, age and self-esteem. Each of these can vary. Some can vary more than others. A variable must have two or more levels or values. For some variables, the values will have true numeric (quantitative) properties. Suppose that you were to give people a cognitive-performance test on which you measured their score over 50 questions. The values can range from a low of 0 correct to a high of 50 correct; these values have numeric properties. In other words, the score on the test that reflects cognitive performance is "countable" (or "quantitative"). Sometimes we look at variables that do not have numeric values, but instead simply identify different categories. An example is gender; the values for gender are male and female. These are different, but they do not differ in amount or quantity. Gender is a variable, but it can only vary in two ways – male or female.

> **Variable**
> Any characteristic that varies in some way. A variable will have two or more values.

Independent and dependent variables

In many types of research, the variables that are being studied are usually conceptualized as having a cause-and-effect connection. That is, one variable is considered to be the "cause" and the other variable the "effect". Researchers using both experimental and non-experimental methods view variables in this fashion, although there is less ambiguity about the direction of cause and effect when the experimental method is used. Researchers use the terms **independent variable** and **dependent variable** when referring to the variables being studied. The variable that is considered to be the "cause" is the independent variable, and the variable that is the "effect" is the dependent variable.

Independent and dependent variables are key components of experiments. In an experiment, the researcher manipulates one variable and then measures the effect of that manipulation. The manipulated variable is the independent variable, and the second variable that is measured is the dependent variable (i.e. it "depends" on the independent variable). This will be covered in the following two chapters.

> **Independent variable**
> Variable whose values are manipulated by the researcher; it is expected to have an effect on the dependent variable.
>
> **Dependent variable**
> The outcome variable measured in a study; it is expected to change as a result of changes in the independent variable.

ch. 5
p.91

Operationally defining variables

While we are on the subject of variables, it is worth reminding yourself about a concept that we introduced in the previous chapter. Once you have decided which variables you should be looking at in a study, you need to immediately ask yourself, "How am I going to measure these?" It is a very important question, as some things are easy to measure and some things are not. If you choose something that is hard to define (and thus hard to measure) then you could be making life very difficult for yourself, especially when you come to analyse the data that you collect. If you cannot remember what an **operational definition** is, then have a quick look back at the section in the last chapter. Briefly, an operational definition is the set of procedures you go through to measure a variable or construct that you are interested in. You really do need to give this issue some thought as early as possible in the research process. In fact, you should get into the habit of *always* asking yourself "How is this measured?" when confronted with a variable or potential variable.

ch. 3
pp.49 – 51

Levels of measurement

Another issue that is related to variables and their measurement concerns what we call the "level of measurement". What do we mean by this? We've established that variables are things that vary. But the way you measure the variable is not always the same. The way height varies is measured differently to the way gender varies. Perhaps the best way to explain this concept is by example. Think of a 100 m athletics final. There are various ways we can measure the results of this race, using a variety of different things that vary (i.e. variables). If we wanted to, we could place each athlete into categories. We would need to choose which category was important, but we might want to split them up into those who were fast and those who were slow. However, this does not really tell us much. We certainly would not be able to tell who actually won, as each competitor would exist only in one of two categories, "fast" or "slow" (Table 4.1).

Table 4.1 Alphabetical list of 100 m competitors and whether they completed the race in a "fast" or a "slow" time[1]

Competitor's name	Fast or slow	Competitor's name	Fast or slow
C. Bjoness	Slow	M. McGuigan	Fast
D. Brooks	Fast	D. McNeil	Slow
D. Bryceland	Slow	T. McShane	Slow
A. Dale	Fast	A. Millar	Slow
R. Henry	Fast	K. Montgomery	Fast
K. Houston	Slow	S. Munro	Slow
C. Hutchison	Slow	G. Richardson	Fast
R. Kerr	Slow	A. Sommerville	Fast
K. Locke	Slow	C. Thirlwall	Slow
S. McGrath	Fast	S. Wilson	Fast

Table 4.1 does not tell us much. It does not even tell us who won the race. Another way of measuring the performance of the competitors would be to order each one according to their position in the race. The winner would obviously have come first, and we could then give each other competitor a position (2nd, 3rd and so on).

1st	S. Wilson	11th	K. Houston
2nd	R. Henry	12th	D. Bryceland
3rd	M. McGuigan	13th	S. Munro
4th	A. Dale	14th	C. Bjoness
5th	A. Sommerville	15th	A. Millar
6th	D. Brooks	16th	D. McNeil
7th	K. Montgomery	17th	C. Thirlwall
8th	S. McGrath	18th	K. Locke
9th	G. Richardson	19th	C. Hutchison
10th	R. Kerr	20th	T. McShane

This is more informative as it tells us who won, who came second and so on, but it does not tell us everything. We do not know whether the winner won by a large margin or whether he stole the race by a thousandth of a second. To know this, we would need to have the actual time that it took each athlete to complete the 100 m sprint. If we measured the outcome of the race in terms of how long it took each athlete to finish, then we would not only know who took less than 10 seconds and who took more than 10 seconds and also who finished in what position, but we would also know how much the winner won by and what margin there was between all the other competitors.

1st	S. Wilson (9.71)	11th	K. Houston (10.03)
2nd	R. Henry (9.72)	12th	D. Bryceland (10.11)
3rd	M. McGuigan (9.74)	13th	S. Munro (10.41)
4th	A. Dale (9.77)	14th	C. Bjoness (10.44)
5th	A. Sommerville (9.80)	15th	A. Millar (10.49)
6th	D. Brooks (9.81)	16th	D. McNeil (10.56)
7th	K. Montgomery (9.86)	17th	C. Thirlwall (11.00)
8th	S. McGrath (9.88)	18th	K. Locke (11.01)
9th	G. Richardson (9.92)	19th	C. Hutchison (15.19)
10th	R. Kerr (10.01)	20th	T. McShane (15.20)

If you understand this, then you basically understand the concept of levels of measurement, which is something that students sometimes struggle with in their initial research methods classes. Let us explore the concept in a bit more detail.

---

1 Apologies to any old school friends whose name I (SW) have left off the above list of competitors in this mythical race. If any of the "competitors" are unhappy with their position, then I can upgrade you in future editions of this book for a small fee.

Table 4.2 Levels of measurement

Level	Description	Example	Distinction
Nominal/ categorical	Categories with no numeric scales	Males/females; Introverts/extroverts	Impossible to define any quantitative values and/or differences between/across categories
Ordinal	Rank ordering Numeric values limited	2-, 3- and 4-star restaurants; Ranking television programmes by popularity	Intervals between items not known
Interval	Numeric properties are literal Assume equal interval between values	Intelligence; Aptitude test score; Temperature	No true zero
Ratio	Zero indicates absence of variable measured	Reaction time; Weight; Age; Frequencies of behaviours	Can form ratios (someone weighs twice as much as another person)

ch. 14
p.284

There are four different "**levels of measurement**" (Table 4.2). Some variables can be measured on all four levels, some on only one. Knowing which level of measurement that you are using when you measure a variable is important because which one you use has huge implications for what you can then do with the data and how you can analyse them. Students who do not think about this at the start are often left with data that they either cannot analyse, or can analyse only in a limited way that is uninformative and does not answer the question that they posed. We are aware that we seem to keep emphasizing that things are important, but they are, and we just want you to avoid the pitfalls that have befallen many students and researchers before you. You should learn the characteristics of each scale and be able to identify the type of scale a given variable represents.

Nominal scales (or "categorical scales")

Nominal scale
Measurement scale in which numbers or names serve as labels and do not indicate a numerical relationship. Sometimes called "categorical" scale as we put things into categories when using it.

To measure something on a **nominal** (or categorical) **scale**, you simply divide it up into categories (hence "categorical") and the categories are given names (hence "nominal"). Some things can only be measured in this way. For example, sex may be male or female. You cannot measure it numerically. To say that male is "higher" or "lower" than female does not make sense. They exist as distinct categories. Variables whose values differ in quality and not quantity are said to fall along a nominal scale. In the example above, splitting up athletes into those who completed the race in a "fast" time and those who completed the race in a "slow" time would be an example of a nominal scale – each competitor will be assigned to one of the two categories.

Sometimes the categories of a nominal variable are identified by numbers. For example, each athlete in the 100 m race will have been assigned a number that they wear on their vest. So, D. Brooks might be known as 007. This is often the case in research. We often assign numbers so that participants remain anonymous, and to make it easier to enter each participant's details into statistical software (it is easier to enter numbers than actual names). When this is the case, you need to remember that the numbers are meaningless. They are arbitrary numbers that are usually assigned to make it easier to enter this information into statistical programmes such as SPSS (you would need to remember to "tell" SPSS that these numbers represent categories rather than any actual numerical measurements). This is important to remember because sometimes we have a tendency to start doing calculations whenever we see numbers in front of us. Any calculations done on numbers that have been used to represent categories will be meaningless, because the numbers are completely arbitrary (D. Brooks is not number 007 for any particular reason, so using that number in any calculations will result in meaningless data).

Although it makes no sense to apply mathematical operations to nominal values (even when these values are represented by numbers), in some cases you can *count* the number of cases (observations) falling into each nominal category and apply mathematical operations to those counts. So, you could count the *number* of athletes who completed the race in under 10 seconds and the number who completed it in over 10 seconds. We could then do some statistical analysis on these counts. **Chapter 20** discusses how to do this.

Ordinal scales

At the next level of measurement are variables measured along an **ordinal scale**. When you use an ordinal scale, you put things in order. Usually, the order you put them in reflects some kind of property. You might line everyone up in your class from left to right starting with the tallest and working your way down to the shortest, assigning them values (1st, 2nd etc.) as you go along. This would be an example of using an ordinal scale, as would the example above of placing the athletes in the order they finished the race.

> **Ordinal scale**
> Measurement scale in which numbers indicate rank order, but equal differences between numbers do not indicate equal differences between the thing measured.

The drawback of an ordinal scale is that you do not know the difference between the points on the scale. If you gave your data to someone who was not in your class, they would know that Kenny was taller than David, but they would not know by how much. Likewise, if you only assign positions to the athletes then you do not know by how much the winner won the race – you only know the positions. Because you do not know the actual amount of difference between ordinal values, mathematical operations such as addition, subtraction, multiplication and division, which assume that the quantitative distance between values is known, are likely to produce misleading results. For example, if three athletes are ranked first, second and third, the difference in *ranking* between first and second and between second and third are both 1.0. This implies that the competitors are equally spaced in terms of performance. However, it may be the case that the winner romped home in world-record time a full 2 seconds ahead of his nearest rival, while the difference between the 2nd placed sprinter and the 3rd placed was a mere thousandth of a second. Measuring on an ordinal scale does not give you this information as the distance between the points on the scale is not equal.

Interval and ratio scales

Interval scale
Scale in which equal differences between measurements indicate equal differences in the thing measured. Does not have a "true" zero point.

Ratio scale
Scale of measurement in which the distance between the points on the scale is known and equal, and which has a "true zero" point (meaning that a score of zero indicates that none of the measured property is present).

If the spacing between values along the scale is known and is equal, then the scale is either an **interval scale** or a **ratio scale**. In either case, you know that one unit is larger or smaller than another, as well as by how much.

A ratio scale has a true zero point that literally indicates the absence of the quantity being measured. An interval scale has a zero point that does *not* indicate the absence of the quantity. With interval scales, the position of the zero point is established on the basis of convenience, but its position is purely arbitrary.

The difference between interval and ratio scales is something that can be tricky to grasp. What do we mean by "true zero point"?

Think about temperature. There are various ways of measuring temperature (Fahrenheit and Celsius being the ones we generally use) and they all have different zero points. The Celsius scale for temperature is an interval scale. Its zero point does not really indicate the absence of all temperature. Zero on the Celsius scale is the temperature at which ice melts – a convenient, easy-to-determine value. Although this temperature may seem cold to you, things can get much colder. In contrast, the Kelvin scale for temperature is a ratio scale. Its zero point is the temperature at which all heat is absent. You simply cannot get any colder.

In deciding whether a scale is interval or ratio, you need to think about two things: are the distances between the points on the scales equal and does it make sense to say that 0 means that none of the measured property is present? Examples of ratio scales (ones that measure from 0 upwards) are height, weight, distance and so on.

In psychological research, when you measure the number of items correctly answered in a test of cognitive performance, you are using a ratio scale. Zero responses means literally that there are no correct responses. Other examples of psychological research data measured on a ratio scale are the number of items recalled in a memory experiment, the number of errors made in a signal-detection experiment, and the time required to respond in a reaction-time experiment. Again, zero on these scales indicates an absence of the quantity measured. In contrast, if you have participants rate how much they like something on a scale from 0 to 10, you are using an interval scale. In this case, a rating of zero does not necessarily mean the total absence of liking. It is not a "true" zero.

For practical purposes, an important difference between interval and ratio scales concerns the kinds of mathematical operations that you can legitimately apply to the data. Both scales allow you to determine by how much the various data points differ. For example, if someone makes 30 correct responses on a test and someone else makes 15, you can confidently state that there is a 15-response difference between these people. If the data are measured on a ratio scale (as in this example), you can also correctly state that one participant made half as many correct responses as the other (i.e. you can divide one quantity by the other to form a ratio). Making ratio comparisons makes little sense when data are scaled on an interval scale. Consider the IQ scale of intelligence, which is an interval scale. If one person has an IQ of 70 and another an IQ of 140, saying that the person with the 140 IQ is twice as intelligent as the person with the 70 IQ is nonsense. The reason is that even a person scoring zero on the test may have some degree of intelligence. Having said that, interval and ratio data are treated very similarly when it comes to statistics, so they often tend to be considered together.

Variables and levels of measurement

The four basic scales of measurement help clarify the level of information conveyed by the numbers that result from measuring some variable. However, not all measures fall precisely into one or the other scale category. Many psychological measures do not seem to fall along a scale of precisely equal intervals, which would be needed for the measure to be interval level. However, the distances between values along the scale are known with greater precision than would be implied by merely ranking them in order (which would make the data ordinal level). To use one example, many psychologists interested in attitudes ask people to rate their attitudes on a scale such as the following:

Smoking should be banned in all public places:

1	2	3	4	5	6	7
Strongly disagree	Disagree	Slightly disagree	Neutral	Slightly agree	Agree	Strongly agree

One problem with this is that it is not clear whether data collected on a scale like this should be considered interval or ordinal or even nominal. If it is to be treated as interval level, then the distance between each point would have to be equal. But is this reasonable? Does it make sense to say that the distance between point 3 "Slightly disagree" and 4 "Neutral" is the same as the distance between point 6 "Agree" and point 7 "Strongly agree"? In fact, does it even make sense to measure attitudes on scales like this at all? Despite these reservations, researchers usually treat such measures as if they had full interval-scale properties.

Choosing a level of measurement

There are two main considerations when choosing a level of measurement, and those are the information that the scale gives you about the variable and the statistical measures that you would like to apply to the data.

One way to think about the four scales of measurement described is in terms of the amount of information that each provides. The nominal scale provides the least amount of information; all you know is that the values differ in some non-numerical way. The ordinal scale adds crude information about quantity (you can rank the order of the values). The interval scale refines the measurement of quantity by indicating how much the values differ. Finally, the ratio scale indicates precisely how much of the quantity exists. When possible, you should adopt the scale that provides the most information.

In the second part of this book we will introduce you to the statistical tests that we can do once we have collected data from a research project. When designing a study, it is a good idea to think about what kind of statistics you might want to do on the data in order to answer the research questions that you have posed. Which level of measurement you have employed will have implications for the kinds of statistics you can then do on the data. Typically, the statistics that are used for nominal and ordinal data are less powerful (i.e. less sensitive to relationships among variables) than are the statistics used for interval or ratio data. On a practical level, this means that you are less likely to detect a significant relationship among variables when using a nominal or an ordinal scale of measurement.

ch. 15
pp.338–340

ch. 15
p.334

Test yourself

Identify the level of measurement associated with each of the following psychological measures.[2]

Examples of measurements	Nominal/ categorical	Ordinal	Interval	Ratio
1 Shoe size?				
2 Hair colour?				
3 Time taken to respond to a red-dot displayed on a screen?				
4 Score on a "sociability scale" measured by a questionnaire?				
5 Ranking of horror films from "most scary" to "least scary"?				
6 Overall number of correct responses on a grammar test?				

Summary for part 1

Many of the things that psychologists study can be considered variables (things that vary). But things can vary in different ways, which will affect how we measure them. Nominal/ categorical variables are variables that are not measured numerically. Instead, "categories" are assigned (such as "brown hair/blonde hair/red hair"). It is possible to count the number of occurrences within each category, but note that it is impossible to assign a numerical figure that measures "hair colour". Variables measured on the ordinal scale are placed in a meaningful order (e.g. 1st, 2nd, 3rd). This does not tell us about the distances between the items, however. Variables measured on the interval and ratio scales are given numerical values on a scale. The distance between consecutive values is equal, and known. Ratio level data has a true zero point, whereas the interval scale does not.

Measurement

We have been speaking in this chapter about variables, about operational definitions and about levels of measurement. In Chapter 2, we emphasized how important observation and measurement are for gaining an understanding of the world around us that is scientific. Think about what this means. "The world around us" suggests something external to us. If we were studying something external to us, then we would expect that measurement would not be too difficult. Measuring physical properties of the world can be challenging, but we usually have good ways of making these measurements and observations. We know how to measure height, speed, weight, mass and so on. Biological and chemical properties are sometimes more difficult, but once again we have fairly good ways of making measurements in these areas. As psychologists,

2 Answers: 1 = interval; 2 = nominal/categorical; 3 = ratio; 4 = interval; 5 = ordinal; 6 = ratio.

we are interested in things that we might consider to be more difficult to measure. Many of the things psychologists are interested in are going on inside people's heads.

Psychology differs from the traditional sciences in the sense that many of the things that psychologists measure are not directly observable. Think back to the section in Chapter 3 entitled "Measuring psychological things". We cannot touch a mood, an attitude, a memory or a thought. We cannot put these things down in front of us and measure them in the same way we would measure certain other physical things. Instead, we need to devise other ways of measuring them. Nobody is suggesting (any more) that psychological processes are less real than anything else. They most certainly are. The behaviourist approach to the problem was to focus on actual externally observable behaviours rather than the internal, private (and "hard to study") processes that were going on inside a person's head. But this was not satisfactory. The processes that go on inside your head *are* important, and we should not just ignore them. The behaviourists were correct when they noted that these processes were hard to measure. How do you measure a thought? But that should not prevent us developing techniques that allow us to study the psychological world in a scientific manner. That is why we need to pay close attention to things like operational definitions and we need to be clear what we mean by the constructs that we talk about in psychology.

ch. 3
p.51

Given the central role of measurement in science, and given how difficult it is to measure psychological "things", it is important that we are aware of issues concerning measurement. This brings us on to the important concepts of "reliability" and "validity".

Reliability of measurements

Reliability refers to how consistent or how stable your measure is. Your everyday definition of reliability is probably quite close to the scientific definition. For example, you might say that Dr Richards is "reliable" because she always starts her lecture at exactly at 10 a.m. each day; in contrast, Professor Taylor might be called "unreliable" because, while he sometimes begins class exactly on the hour, on any given day he may appear anytime between 10 a.m. and 10.20 a.m.

Reliability
The consistency or dependability of a measure.

Similarly, a reliable measure of a psychological variable such as intelligence will give you the same result each time you administer the intelligence test to the same person. Imagine you gave someone an intelligence test on Monday and found them to have an above average IQ. You then give them the same test a week later and their score now indicates they are considerably below average. You test them a final time and find that the test is now indicating that they are of average intelligence. It is unlikely that the person's intelligence is fluctuating over such a short space of time, so there must be something about the test itself that is unreliable. Put simply, a reliable measure does not fluctuate from one reading to the next. If the measure fluctuates a lot, there is too much error in the measurement device.

A more formal way of understanding reliability is to use the concepts of true score and measurement error. Any time you measure something, the measurement you get can be thought of as having two components: (1) a *true score*, which is the real score on the variable, and (2) **measurement error**.

Obviously you would hope that any measurement you make is going to have as little error as possible and be a true reflection of the thing that you are measuring. But errors do occur and they occur for a variety of reasons, as we will see in later

Measurement error
The degree to which a measurement device deviates from the true score value.

chapters. An unreliable measure of intelligence contains a lot of error and does not provide an accurate indication of an individual's true intelligence. In contrast, a reliable measure of intelligence – one that contains little measurement error – will yield an identical (or nearly identical) intelligence score each time the same individual is measured.

When conducting research, you usually can measure each person only once; you cannot give the measure 50 or 100 times to discover a true score. Because of this, it is very important that you use a reliable measure. Your single administration of the measure should closely reflect the person's true score. The importance of reliability is obvious. An unreliable measure of length would be useless in building a table; an unreliable measure of a variable such as intelligence is equally useless in studying that variable. Researchers cannot use unreliable measures to study variables or the relationships among variables. Hopefully, you can see that this is just common sense. Trying to study behaviour using unreliable measures is a waste of time because the results will be unstable and will be impossible to repeat. To put it another way, you would not drive a car that had an unreliable speedometer. An unreliable speedometer would give you different measures every time you drove (even if you always drove at the same speed). You would have no idea what speed you were actually going at. Likewise, unreliable measures in psychology are equally as useless.

Reliability is most likely to be achieved when researchers use careful measurement procedures. In some research areas, this might involve carefully training observers to record behaviour; in other areas, it might mean paying close attention to the way questions are phrased or the way recording electrodes are placed on the body to measure physiological reactions.

Let's look at some ways in which researchers assess reliability. We will look at test–retest reliability, internal consistency reliability and interrater reliability.

Test–retest reliability

Test–retest reliability
Determining reliability by administering a test a second time and comparing the two scores.

Test–retest reliability is assessed by measuring the same people at two different points in time. So, test–retest reliability looks at consistency over time – if someone took a test on one day, are they likely to have the same result if they take that test again the following week? As we mentioned above, the reliability of a test of intelligence could be assessed by giving the measure to a group of people on one day and giving it to them again a week later. We would then have two scores for each person, and we could assess the relationship between the first test score and the second retest score. If people's scores at time 1 are sufficiently similar to their score at time 2, then this suggests that we have got a reliable test, and the measure reflects true scores rather than measurement error.

Given that test–retest reliability involves administering the same test twice, there is the possibility that people remember the test from the first time they did it. This could influence their performance and might artificially inflate the scores on the second test in a way that reflects their previous experience of the test rather than an underlying psychological construct being reliably measured. *Alternate forms reliability* is sometimes used to avoid this problem; this involves administering two *different* versions (or "forms") of the same test to the same individuals at two points in time. If the test is different, then the people taking it for the second time should not be influenced by their memory of the first test.

ch. 3
p.53

Intelligence is a variable that can be expected to stay relatively constant over time (i.e. it is a relatively **stable characteristic**); thus, we expect the test–retest reliability for intelligence to be very high. However, some variables may be expected to change from one test period to the next

ch. 3
p.52

(i.e. they are dynamic). For example, a mood scale designed to measure a person's current mood state is a measure that might easily change from one test period to another and so test–retest reliability might not be appropriate. On a more practical level, obtaining two measures from the same people at two points in time may sometimes be difficult. To address these issues, researchers have devised other ways to assess reliability that don't rely on two separate assessments.

STOP & Think

Apart from intelligence, can you think of any other psychological measures that would be appropriate to apply test–retest reliability?

Internal consistency reliability

It is possible to assess reliability by measuring individuals at only one point in time. We can do this because most psychological measures are made up of a number of different questions, called "items" (each time you do a psychological questionnaire, every question is called an "item"). An intelligence test might have 100 items, a measure of extroversion might have 15 items, or a multiple-choice examination in a class might have 50 items. A person's test score would be based on the total of his or her responses on all of the items. In the class, an examination consists of a number of questions about the material, and the total score is the number of correct answers. A measure of extroversion might ask people to agree or disagree with items such as "I enjoy the stimulation of a lively party." An individual's extraversion score is obtained by finding the total number of such items that they say applies to them.

Internal consistency reliability is the assessment of reliability using responses at only one point in time. Because all items measure the same variable, they should yield similar or consistent results (if you genuinely are an extrovert, then your scores on different extrovert questions should be similar). One indicator of internal consistency is **split-half reliability**. In its simplest form, split-half reliability is the **correlation** of an individual's total score on one half of the test with the total score on the other half. The two halves are created by randomly dividing the items into two parts. So, to use extroversion as an example, you would take all the questions measuring extroversion, randomly split them into two halves and then see how closely related scores were on each half. If the measure of extroversion is reliable, then there should be a close association as the questions are all measuring the same underlying thing.

Split-half reliability is relatively straightforward and easy to calculate, even without a computer. One drawback is that it does not take into account the contribution of each individual item in assessing how reliable the measure is. It would be useful to know whether some items were "better" than others at measuring the thing you are interested in.

Another internal consistency indicator of reliability, called **Cronbach's alpha**, is based on the individual items themselves. Here the researcher calculates the degree of association between each item and every other item. The value of *alpha* is the average

---

Internal consistency reliability
Reliability assessed with data collected at one point in time with multiple individual measures of a psychological construct (e.g. multiple questions on a questionnaire). A measure is reliable when the multiple measures provide similar results.

Split-half reliability
Determining reliability by dividing a test in half and correlating the two part scores.

ch. 19
pp.463–480

Cronbach's alpha
An indicator of internal consistency reliability assessed by examining the average correlation of each item (question) in a measure with every other item.

ch. 19

of all the measured correlations. It is also possible to examine the correlation of each individual item score with the total score based on all items. Such **item–total correlations** and Cronbach's alpha are useful because they provide information about each individual item. Any items that do not seem to be associated with the other items can be eliminated from the measure to increase reliability, due to the fact that the item does not seem to be doing as good a job at measuring the construct as the other items are. See Chapter 19 for statistical details on how to calculate correlations.

Item–total correlation
The correlation between the score on one item of a measurement device and the overall total score.

Interrater reliability
Method of detecting inconsistent measuring by comparing observations of two independent observers.

Interrater reliability

In some research, raters observe behaviours and make ratings or judgements. To do this, a rater uses instructions for making judgements about the behaviours – for example, by rating whether the behaviour of a child at a playground is aggressive and how aggressive the behaviour is. One way of doing this is to have one rater make judgements about aggression. However, if you have only one person rating the behaviours, then you do not know whether their observations are completely reliable. We do not know whether the person we have got rating the behaviour might have a different view of what counts as "aggression" to someone else. The solution to this problem is to use at least two raters who observe the same behaviour. **Interrater reliability** is the extent to which raters agree in their observations. If two raters are judging whether behaviours are aggressive and they tend to agree on what is aggressive and what is not, then we say we have high interrater reliability. We cover this issue in more detail when discussing observational methods in Chapter 12. A summary of the different types of reliability is shown in Figure 4.2.

ch. 12

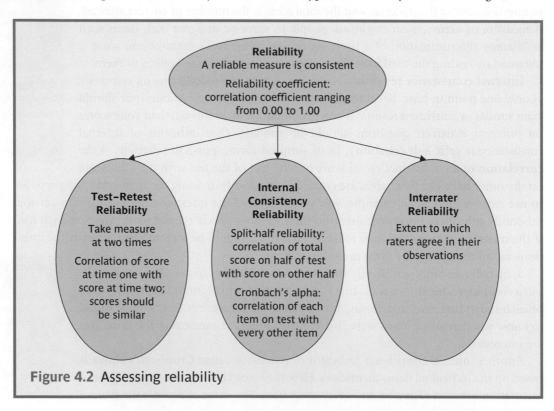

Figure 4.2 Assessing reliability

Reliability and accuracy of measures

Reliability is clearly important when researchers develop measures of behaviour. However, reliability is not the only thing that researchers worry about. Reliability tells us about measurement error but it does not tell us about whether we have a good measure of the variable of interest in the first place. To use a silly example, suppose we want to measure intelligence. The measure we develop looks remarkably like the device that is used to measure shoe size at the local shoe store. We ask you to place your foot in the device and we use the gauge to measure your intelligence. There are numbers that provide a scale of intelligence so we can immediately assess a person's intelligence level. Will these numbers result in a reliable measure of intelligence? The answer is that they will! It is a reliable measure. Consider what a test–retest reliability coefficient would be. If we administer the "foot intelligence scale" on Monday, it will be almost the same the following Monday; the test–retest reliability is high. But is this an accurate measure of intelligence? Obviously, the scores have nothing to do with intelligence; just because we labelled that device as an intelligence test does not mean that it is a good measure of intelligence. So even though the measure is reliable, that does not always mean that it is measuring what you want it to measure. What we also need to consider is whether our measure is *valid*.

Validity of measurements

If something has **validity**, it is "true" in the sense that it is supported by available evidence. The speedometer on a car should be a valid measure of speed and the measure should not be related to anything else (like oil temperature). Likewise, a measure of a personality characteristic such as shyness should be an accurate indicator of that trait and an individual's score on that measure should be a good indication of how shy they actually are. As we have stated a few times, it is crucial that you think about the construct that you want to measure in your study. You need to have an **operational definition** and this operational definition is basically the set of procedures that you will go through to measure the construct. Obviously, you would hope that the measure you take is a good one. You hope that the operational definition you have come up with is going to give you a measurement that is a true reflection of the construct itself. In other words, we would hope that the measure we take actually measures what we intend it to measure. If our measure of shyness was poorly operationally defined, we might find that it does not actually reflect shyness at all, but something else. This would be problematic as we have not measured the thing we thought we were measuring.

> **Validity**
> The extent to which your measure is measuring what it is supposed to.

ch. 3
p.49

The extent to which our measure is "tapping into" the construct it is supposed to, is known as **construct validity**. This refers to the adequacy of the operational definition that we have employed for the variable that we are looking to measure. To what extent does the operational definition of a variable actually reflect the true theoretical meaning of the variable? This is very important as it would be a waste of time to spend hours collecting data that you think is measuring one thing, only to find out that it was actually measuring something completely different.

> **Construct validity**
> The degree to which a measurement device accurately measures the theoretical construct it is designed to measure.

Indicators of construct validity

How do we know that a measure is valid? Ways that we can assess validity are summarized in Table 4.3. Construct validity information is gathered through a variety of methods. The simplest

Table 4.3 Indicators of construct validity of a measure	
Face validity:	
The content of the measure appears to reflect the construct being measured.	
Criterion-oriented validity:	
Scores on the measure are related to a criterion (an indicator of the construct).	
Types of criterion-oriented validity:	
• **Predictive validity**	Scores on the measure predict behaviour on a criterion measured at a time in the future.
• **Concurrent validity**	Scores on the measure are related to a criterion measured at the same time (concurrently).
• **Convergent validity**	Scores on the measure are related to other measures of the same construct.
• **Discriminant validity**	Scores on the measure are *not* related to other measures that are theoretically different.

Face validity
The degree to which a measurement device appears to accurately measure a variable.

way to argue that a measure is valid is to suggest that it appears to accurately assess the intended variable. This is called **face validity** – the evidence for validity is that the measure appears "on the face of it" to measure what it is supposed to measure. Face validity is not very sophisticated as it involves a subjective judgement of whether, given the theoretical definition of the variable, the content of the measure appears to actually measure the variable. That is, do the procedures used to measure the variable appear to be an accurate operational definition of the theoretical variable? Thus, a measure of a variable such as shyness will usually appear to measure that variable and might include items such as "I often feel insecure in social situations" rather than items such as "I learned to ride a bicycle at an early age", which doesn't seem to have anything to do with shyness (and so would lack "face validity").

Face validity is not really sufficient to conclude that a measure is valid. Appearance is not a very good indicator of accuracy. Some very poor measures may have face validity. For example, most personality measures that appear in popular magazines usually have several questions that look reasonable but often do not tell you anything meaningful. The interpretations of the scores may make fun reading, but there is no empirical evidence to support the conclusions that are drawn in the article. In addition, many good measures of variables do not have obvious face validity. For example, is it obvious that rapid eye movement during sleep is a measure of dream occurrence? Instead of relying on face validity, researchers assess validity by conducting research with the measure itself.

Construct validity research examines the relationship between scores on the measure and some criterion (outcome) – termed **criterion-oriented validity**. A researcher looks at the theory underlying the construct being measured and then makes a prediction about how scores on the measure will relate to *another* variable – called a criterion. This sounds confusing, but it should become clear as we go along. There are four types of criterion-related research approaches that differ in the type of criterion that is employed: *predictive validity*, *concurrent validity*, *convergent validity* and *discriminant validity*. Let us look at each of these in turn.

Criterion-oriented validity
Determined by the degree to which the test correlates with another (criterion) variable.

Predictive validity

Research that uses a measure to predict some future behaviour is using the **predictive validity** approach. So, with predictive validity, the "criterion" is some future behaviour. Predictive validity is clearly important when studying measures that are designed to improve our ability to make predictions. If you are given a test at school that is designed to be an indicator of your future success at university, then your future performance at university would be the "criterion". If it is found that the school test is a good indicator of how well you go on to do in your academic studies, then that test would have high predictive validity. If people tend to perform well in the school test but this did not relate to how well they did at university, then the school test would have low predictive validity.

> **Predictive validity** Determined by assessing the relationship between the measure and some future behaviour associated with the measure.

Concurrent validity

Concurrent validity is demonstrated by research that examines the relationship between the measure and a criterion behaviour at the same time (concurrently). This can be done in many ways, but one way of doing it is to study whether two or more groups of people differ on the measure in expected ways. Suppose you have a measure of shyness. Your theory of shyness might lead you to expect that salespeople whose job requires making "cold calls" to potential customers would score lower on the shyness measure than salespeople in positions in which potential customers must make the effort to contact the company themselves. If you do find this, then you could say that the measure is likely to be measuring shyness, although you must be cautious in drawing these conclusions as it is possible that these two groups differ in *other* ways as well, and it might be one of these that the measure is picking up.

> **Concurrent validity** Determined by assessing the relationship between the measure and a concurrent criterion behaviour.

Another approach to concurrent validity is to study how people who score either low or high on the measure behave in different situations. For example, you could ask people who score high versus low on the shyness scale to describe themselves to a stranger while you measure their level of anxiety. Here you would expect that the people who score high on the shyness scale would exhibit higher amounts of concurrent anxiety when asked to do this.

Convergent validity

For some constructs there might be more than one operational definition. In psychology, there is often more than one way of measuring the same construct (just look at the number of different intelligence tests there are). Any given measure is a particular operational definition of the variable being measured. There will sometimes be other operational definitions – other measures – of the same or similar constructs. **Convergent validity** is the extent to which scores on the measure in question are related to scores on other measures of the same construct or similar constructs. Measures of similar constructs should "converge" – for example, one measure of shyness should correlate highly with another shyness measure or a measure of a similar construct such as social anxiety. Intelligence measures can be validated in similar ways. If various measures of intelligence are all giving similar results (converging) then this gives them some degree of validity as they must all be measuring the same thing.

> **Convergent validity** A measure is assessed by how closely it is associated with other measures of the same construct.

Discriminant validity

Discriminant validity
Determined by the degree to which the measure is distinct from other measures, thus demonstrating that the initial measure is tapping into something distinct.

Sometimes we explicitly expect our measure to be distinct from other variables. When the measure is *not* related to variables with which it should not be related we call this **discriminant validity**. The measure should discriminate between the construct being measured and other constructs that we expect to be unrelated. In research on the discriminant validity of their shyness measure, Bortnik et al. (2002) found no relationship between scores on the shyness questionnaire that they developed (the "Shy Q") and several conceptually unrelated interpersonal values such as valuing forcefulness with others. This shows that their measure was measuring something unique compared with the scales measuring other constructs. Thus, it was possible to discriminate the "shyness" measure from the other things.

In the Know

The Sensation Seeking Scale (Zuckerman, 1979) is an excellent illustration of construct validity research in which multiple studies support predictions made by a theory. Zuckerman's research was stimulated by a psychological theory of optimal levels of physiological arousal. The theory states that people have a need to maintain an optimal level of arousal. When arousal is too low, people will be motivated to do things to increase arousal; when arousal is too high, individuals will attempt to reduce arousal. The theory helps to explain many behaviours, such as the hallucinations and other disturbances that people experience when they are placed in sensory deprivation environments. Zuckerman decided to study this theory by focusing on individual differences; he asked why some people consistently seem to seek out novel or arousing sensations (e.g. parachuting, listening to loud music, driving in car races) while other people avoid arousing sensations.

The Sensation Seeking Scale was developed to study such individual differences in personality. The scale itself includes items intended to measure thrill seeking, susceptibility to boredom, and other aspects of sensation seeking. The reliability of the scale was assessed, of course. After determining that the scale was reliable, construct validity research could begin. Over a period of many years, research by Zuckerman and others demonstrated that people who score high on the scale do in fact behave differently from people who score low. High sensation seekers engage in more dangerous activities, drive faster and prefer less intellectual activities, for example. Other research with the Sensation Seeking Scale examined how the measure is related to other similar and different personality constructs. Work on the Sensation Seeking Scale has ultimately led to research on the biological basis for sensation seeking, such as identifying what brain mechanisms are responsible for arousal needs and whether the trait has a genetic basis. Zuckerman's research illustrates a systematic programme of research on the validity of a measure of a psychological construct.

The fact that an entire body of research exists on the Sensation Seeking Scale illustrates an important point about validity and the entire process of scientific inquiry. A single study is only one indicator of the validity of a measure. Our confidence in the validity of a measure is built up over time as numerous studies investigate the theory of the particular construct being measured. Further, measures of variables usually have a limited life span. As research findings accumulate, researchers refine the measure and sometimes develop new measures that do a better job of helping us understand the underlying variable being studied.

STOP & Think

What is the difference between "validity" and "reliability"?

Hypotheses

"Hypothesis" and its plural "hypotheses" are words that you will already have encountered in this book, and you will see them with increasing regularity. There are a few different meanings associated with the term "hypothesis", so it is worth outlining what we might mean when we use it, as it has an "everyday" meaning as well as what we mean when we use it in relation to science and research.

In general, a **hypothesis** is a tentative explanation for something. Hypotheses frequently attempt to answer the questions "How?" and "Why?" At one level, a hypothesis may simply suggest how particular things might be related. For example, in our popular culture we frequently associate white or brightness with "good" and black or darkness with "bad" (Meier et al., 2004). For example, in the film *Star Wars*, Luke Skywalker and Princess Leia were dressed in white and Darth Vader was completely in black. Across many religions (e.g. Buddhism, Christianity, Hinduism, Islam, Zoroastrianism) there is an association between light and goodness (e.g. "God") and between darkness and evil (e.g. "Satan"). Whether something is considered good or bad is referred to as an *affective judgement*. On the other hand, our experience of brightness (and darkness) is a sensory perception. In their research, Meier and his colleagues hypothesized that the association between affective judgements and sensory perceptions of brightness is automatic – that is, people automatically judge brighter objects as "good" and darker objects as "bad".

> **Hypothesis**
> 1. A tentative explanation for something. 2. A statement about what might be observed in a study.

To test their hypothesis, researchers asked participants to judge whether 100 words presented on a computer screen were negative or positive. Fifty of the words were previously rated as reflecting positive affect (e.g. chocolate, love, pretty, sleep), and 50 of the words represented negative affect (e.g. bitter, cancer, devil, rude). The researchers manipulated whether the words were presented in a bright font or a dark font. Their results indicated that when the affect and the brightness of the word conflicted (e.g. love presented in a dark font), participants took longer and made more errors when judging whether the word was positive or negative, compared to when the words "matched" the associated brightness (e.g. love presented in a bright font).

Hypotheses should usually be derived from a theory. Although this is not always the case, and they sometimes come from "hunches" or the intuitions of the researcher, it is normally the case that a hypothesis is related to a theory as a way of testing the **theory**.

ch. 2
pp.28–36

If you think back to Chapter 2, you might remember that a good theory will make predictions about what should happen in novel situations (that is, research that has not been done yet) if that theory is correct. In other words, a theory makes *predictions* about what should be observed if the theory is an accurate one. These predictions can be formulated into hypotheses that are then tested by conducting a research study.

Meier and his colleagues (2004) looked at theories suggesting that the human brain has developed in a way that makes conceptual thinking, such as affective judgements, automatically tied to physical perception. Based on these theories, the researchers suggested that people cannot judge the affect of a word (or any other object) without first automatically considering its physical features, such as brightness. In their study, when the brightness conflicted with the correct affective judgement, additional processing (i.e. time, thought) was required for people to override their automatic association and to make the correct judgement about whether the word was negative or positive.

Nearly everyone has proposed hypotheses to explain some human behaviour at one time or another. For example:

- Why do people commit apparently senseless acts of violence?
- What causes people to start smoking cigarettes?
- Why are some students academically more successful than others?

One characteristic that distinguishes casual, everyday hypotheses from scientific hypotheses is testability. If a hypothesis cannot be tested, it is not useful to science. Three types of hypotheses fail to pass the "testability test". A hypothesis is not testable when its constructs are not adequately defined, when the hypothesis is circular, and when the hypothesis appeals to ideas not recognized as part of the natural world.

Hypotheses are not testable if the concepts to which they refer are not adequately defined

ch. 2
p.33

Consider a hypothesis saying that a would-be assassin shot a US president or other prominent figure because he was mentally disturbed. This hypothesis would not be **testable** unless a very clear definition of "mentally disturbed" can be agreed upon. The reason that this might be difficult is that one researcher might say that the individual was mentally disturbed while another might disagree and say that the man was acting without any psychological problems. "Mentally disturbed" is itself a vague term that can be interpreted in many different ways. Unfortunately, psychologists and psychiatrists cannot always agree on what terms such as "mentally disturbed" mean because the concept does not have just one definition that everyone agrees with.

Hypotheses are also not testable if they are circular

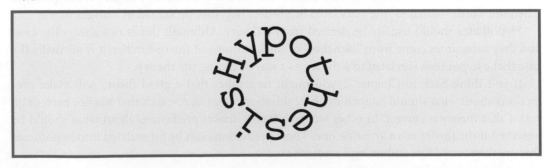

A circular hypothesis occurs when an event itself is used as the explanation of the event. As an illustration, consider the statement that an "8-year-old boy is distractible in school and having trouble reading because he has an attention deficit disorder". How is attention deficit disorder defined? It's defined by the inability to pay attention. So the statement simply says that the boy does not pay attention because he does not pay attention – that is a circular hypothesis.

Hypotheses are not testable if they refer to "supernatural" concepts

A hypothesis also may be untestable if it appeals to ideas or forces that are outside the natural world. Science deals with everything in nature. These are things that are observable (in some way – even if not directly but at least through instruments), demonstrable and empirical. To suggest that people who commit horrendous acts of violence are under orders from the Devil is not testable because it invokes a principle (the Devil) that is "supernatural" and thus not observable or demonstrable by any scientific technique. Such hypotheses might be of interest to philosophers or theologians but not to the scientist. A question you must ask when considering a hypothesis for testing is "Is this measurable in principle?"

Research hypotheses

We have covered the concept of what a "hypothesis" is above, but now we will move on to how we use the word in a more specific way relating to research.

Research hypotheses are particularly important in quantitative studies. As we will see in the coming chapters, quantitative research involves looking for relationships between variables. At the beginning of any research project, you will need to have a clear statement of what you think the relationship between the variables is going to be. You need to make a statement about what might happen in your study. This is your research hypothesis. There are two main types of research hypothesis, and they are the logical opposites of each other.

Alternative hypothesis

Alternative hypotheses are sometimes known as the "experimental hypotheses" as well as "research hypotheses". They are sometimes abbreviated to H_{alt}, H_{exp} or H_1. These all refer to the same thing. It is called the "alternative" hypothesis because it is the alternative to the null hypothesis, which we explain below. The alternative hypothesis is a statement about what the relationship between the variables in your study might be. As stated above, you usually create this hypothesis on the basis of what you expect to happen given one particular theoretical position, although you might be working on a "hunch" and doing some explorations as to whether your hunch is justified. Usually, however, you will have an idea about what the relationship between the variables will be if the theory is correct. To use a crude example, you might have a theory about the way caffeine influences the central nervous system. You might then develop a hypothesis about how people who drink coffee prior to a motor-skills test perform compared to a group who drink a decaffeinated drink. Your alternative hypothesis in this case might be "performance on a motor-skills test will be different for a group of coffee drinkers' compared to a group who do not drink coffee".

Null hypothesis (or H_{null} or H_0)

The null hypothesis (or H_{null} or H_0) is the logical opposite of the alternative hypothesis. In other words, this is a statement about what you would expect if there were *no* relationship between the variables in your study. It essentially says "this is what we will find if there's nothing going on". You may think it is a bit odd to state the null hypothesis. In a research report you would usually state either the null hypothesis or the experimental hypothesis and not both, as it is easy to work out the null hypothesis by looking at the experimental hypothesis, and vice versa. In the example above, the null hypothesis would be "there will be no difference in motor performance between a group of coffee drinkers and a group who do not drink coffee". One reason that you need to know about the null hypothesis is that the statistical tests that you will use to assess the relationship between the variables actually test against the null hypothesis. What this means (and we will come to this in **Chapter 15**) is that it is the null hypothesis that you test and your results will tell you how likely it is that your null hypothesis is actually true.

ch. 15

One-tailed hypothesis/two-tailed hypothesis (also known as directional hypothesis/non-directional hypothesis)

One-tailed (directional) hypothesis
Alternative hypothesis in which the direction of a difference is specified.

Two-tailed (non-directional) hypothesis
Alternative hypothesis in which no direction of difference is specified – both directions are covered by the hypothesis.

A further way to look at research hypotheses concerns whether they are "**one-tailed**" or "**two-tailed**". The difference between these involves whether or not you are making a specific prediction about the direction of the relationship between the variables. This sounds more complicated than it is. If, in the above example, you expect drinking coffee to enhance performance in the motor-skills task, then you would use a one-tailed hypothesis. This would be "the group of coffee drinkers will show enhanced performance on the motor-skills task than the group who do not drink coffee". What this means is that the "direction" of the relationship is specified: the coffee drinkers will be *better* than the non-coffee drinkers. A hypothesis can also be two-tailed (or non-directional) in which you state that you think there will be *something* going on, but you are not stating which direction it will be in. So a two-tailed hypothesis might state that "there will be a difference between the two groups in their motor-skills performance". Note that this hypothesis merely states that there will be a difference, but does not say which group will show enhanced performance. A two-tailed hypothesis is careful not to make any distinct predictions about the direction of the effect.

Deciding on whether to adopt a one-tailed or two-tailed hypothesis will depend on your knowledge of the previous research and the theory. If you are doing exploratory work then you might decide to adopt a two-tailed hypothesis because you probably will not be entirely sure what the relationship between the variables might be. There are also statistical implications resulting from whether you decide upon a one-tailed or a two-tailed hypothesis.

Summary for part 2

How reliable and valid our measures are is important. Reliability refers to the extent to which our measure is consistent and dependable. Types of reliability include test–retest reliability (looking at the consistency of a measure over time); internal consistency reliability (looking at how consistent a measure is within the items that make it up) and interrater reliability (which looks at how consistent different raters are in their ratings of a variable). Validity refers to the extent to which a measure is measuring what it is supposed to. Again, there are various types of validity. Face validity is the extent to which the measure *appears* to be measuring what it is supposed to. Criterion-oriented measures of validity test against a criterion, which is an indicator of how good the construct is. Criterion-oriented validity can be predictive (when scores of the measure are used to predict behaviour on a criterion measured at another time), concurrent (when scores on the measure are related to a criterion measured at the same time), convergent (when scores on the measure are related to scores on another measure that is designed to measure the same construct) and discriminant (when scores on a measure are tested against another measure that is theoretically distinct and should be independent). A hypothesis is a tentative explanation for something, and also a statement of what you might expect to find in a research study. The alternative hypothesis states what the relationship between the variables will be if there is a genuine effect, while the null hypothesis states what will be found if there is no effect.

Questions

1. What is meant by the reliability of a measure? Distinguish between true score and measurement error.

2. Describe the methods of determining the reliability of a measure.

3. What is the validity of a measure?

4. What are the ways you can assess the validity of a measure?

5. What is construct validity? Distinguish between convergent and discriminant validity.

6. What is meant by criterion-oriented validity?

7. Why is face validity not sufficient to establish the validity of a measure?

8. Distinguish between nominal, ordinal, interval and ratio scales.

Activities

1 Here are a number of references to variables. For each, identify whether a nominal, ordinal, interval or ratio scale is being used:

   (a) The temperatures in cities throughout the country that are listed in most newspapers.

   (b) The birth weights of babies who were born at Wilshire General Hospital last week.

   (c) The number of hours you spent studying each day during the past week.

   (d) The amount of the tip left after each meal at a restaurant during a three-hour period.

   (e) The number of votes received by the Labour and Conservative candidates in the last local election in your constituency.

   (f) The position of a brand in a consumer magazine's ranking of DVD players.

   (g) Your friend's score on an intelligence test.

   (h) Yellow walls in your office and white walls in your boss's office.

   (i) Ethnic group categories of people in a neighbourhood.

2 Think of an important characteristic that you would look for in a potential romantic partner, such as humorous, intelligent, attractive, hardworking, religious and so on. How might you measure that characteristic? Describe two methods that you might use to assess construct validity.

Chapter 5

Introduction to Methods

OVERVIEW

In this chapter we will discuss methods, which are techniques for doing research. We give a brief description of the main methods that are covered in the book. Some of the material in this chapter is quite difficult. Do not get disheartened if you do not fully understand the methods the first time you read about them. It is not uncommon to have to look over these things a few times before they sink in.

OBJECTIVES

After studying this chapter and working through the exercises, you should be able to:

- Define what a "method" is
- Identify the general differences between qualitative and quantitative methods
- Understand and give a basic description of:
  - Experimental methods
  - Correlational methods
  - Observational methods
  - Survey methods
- Give an account of "internal validity" and how it relates to research
- Define various factors that are considered threats to internal validity
- Give an account of "external validity" and how it relates to research
- Define various factors that are considered threats to external validity
- Demonstrate a basic understanding of the relationship between external and internal validity and how this affects research decisions

Before you do *anything*

If you have found a topic that you are interested in, you might think that it is now just a matter of getting stuck into researching it. Unfortunately, it is not that simple. Once you have identified a general area that you want to explore, you have to become familiar with the relevant research in that area that has already been published. It is unlikely that you will be the first person who has ever been interested in this topic, so if you are going to contribute something worthwhile then you need to know what people have done in this research area in the past. You will also have to have a good understanding of what the current thinking is in the area, whether there are any outstanding questions in the field, what the competing theories are that can explain the phenomena, whether or not there are any controversies or debates among researchers and so on. **There are lots of things you have to do before you can embark on your research**, and most of them involve searching the literature and then reading (and understanding) the relevant articles and the key issues contained within them.

ch. 23

We should point out that this whole process is often lengthy and sometimes frustrating. First, you will spend hours in front of computers putting words into search engines, looking for articles that have been published that might be relevant to your chosen topic. You will then trawl through the output of dozens of searches, looking for anything that seems as if it might be important for you to read. Once you have done this (and it sometimes takes days) you then have to actually *get* the articles (many articles can be downloaded, but you might have to go hunting in libraries or somehow arrange for the article to be sent to you, either through the kindness of the author or by paying for it directly from the publisher).

ch. 4 p.77

All the library research and critical reading that you have done has now put you on the threshold of the next major step in the research process: developing your idea into a testable **hypothesis**. This hypothesis will usually be a tentative statement relating two (or more) variables that you are interested in studying, although as we will see when we talk about qualitative research, this is not always the case.

Your research hypothesis should flow logically from the sources of information that you read before developing your research question. What we mean by this is that, given what you already know from previous research (either your own or what you read in the literature), you should be able to make a tentative statement about what you think might happen in the study that you are about to do.

Hypothesis development is an important step in the research process because it will influence your later decisions concerning how you actually set up and conduct your study (i.e. the method you employ and the design of your study). These things will be the focus of this chapter and the following one. If you do not take time in thinking about your hypothesis and what you hope to find, then you may end up with a poorly conceptualized study and any findings that you end up with might not be valid, making the whole thing a waste of your (and your participants') time.

What is a method?

Method
A particular approach to answering a research question.

The term "method" is one that we use again and again throughout this book, but what is a method? To put it simply, a **method** is a way of doing something. If the "thing" that you are doing is research, then the method is the way you do your research. In essence, it is nothing more complicated than that. A method is the overall approach that you will take. Once you have identified a particular area that you are interested in studying, you need to decide how you are going to study it – and this will include the way in which you will proceed in conducting the research that you intend to do. In psychology, there are a few different ways that we can answer the questions that we ask. We outline some of the general approaches below.

What are the different types of methods you could use?

There are multiple methods that can be employed in psychological research. In this section we will give a brief summary of some of the major subdivisions, noting that we will return to look at each one in more detail in future chapters.

Quantitative and qualitative methods

One of the most important decisions you will make is whether to adopt a quantitative or qualitative approach. At a fundamental level, these approaches are quite different to each other, and some would say that they are completely incompatible. That said, there are researchers who use both quantitative and **qualitative methods**, although it is usually the case that any one study can only be either qualitative or quantitative.

Qualitative method
Research characterized by richness of experience and narrative results.

Quantitative method
Research characterized by measurement and numerical results.

Quantitative research is concerned with measurement. The previous two chapters have emphasized a particular position concerning science and psychology's role as a science. Treating psychology in this way naturally leads to adopting quantitative techniques. If we are going to view psychology as a science, then we must adopt the techniques of other sciences and at the heart of these will be measurement and quantification of the phenomena that we are studying. Thus, all **quantitative methods** will necessarily involve measurement of some kind.

Although this is arguably the predominant position in psychology, there are psychologists who argue that this is *not* the correct way to study psychological phenomena. The main arguments for **the qualitative approach will be introduced in Chapter 10**. At this point it will be enough to say that most qualitative researchers reject the notion that we can treat psychological phenomena as something that we can objectively measure and quantify. They point out that quantitative research tends to ignore several important factors in human experience. For example, one critique of a quantitative approach is that it ignores the meanings that people attribute to events and experiences. So, rather than looking at relationships between "variables", qualitative research is more concerned with the richness (or the "quality" – hence the name) of the experience under study. Qualitative researchers would argue that we lose a lot of important information about the texture of experiences by reducing them to cold numeric measurements.

ch. 10

We will explore these debates in future chapters, but for now it is worth pointing out that the method you adopt should be appropriate to the psychological phenomena you are studying. Some things will be better studied in a quantitative way (cognitive processes, for example) while other things might be more amenable to qualitative research (many social psychological phenomena, for example).

For the purposes of this chapter, we will now outline various different methods that psychologists use. Correlational methods and experimental methods are exclusively quantitative, although the other methods described below can be either quantitative or qualitative (or have elements of both), depending upon how you decide to proceed.

Correlational methods

Sometimes it is informative for us to understand how variables are related to each other rather than how one influences another. In correlational research, your main interest is to determine whether two (or more) things covary and, if so, to establish the nature of the relationship between them. Or, to put it another way, it looks to see the extent to which things are co-related (the clue is in the name). If one variable changes in value, is this related to a change in the other variable?

Correlational method
A method that looks for relationships between variables.

In **correlational** research, you make no attempt to manipulate variables but observe them "as is". For example, imagine that you wished to determine the nature of the relationship, if any, between how anxious students are before an examination and how well they perform. You have got a hunch that the students who are less anxious are the ones who get better scores on their psychology examinations. On examination day, you have each student rate his or her own level of pre-test anxiety and, after the examinations have been marked, you determine the examination performances of those same students. Your data consist of two scores for each student: self-rated anxiety level and examination score. You then analyse your data to determine **the relationship (if any) between these variables.**

ch. 19

The most important thing to remember with correlations is that just because two things are correlated with each other, it does not mean that one is causing the other (an old mantra, "correlation is not causation", is worth remembering). Whether the linkage between two variables is causal remains an open question.

✺ In the Know

In 2002 Andrea Wilson sued the maker of the popular video game *Mortal Kombat* after Wilson's son, Noah, was killed by his friend Yancy. It was alleged that, when he committed the murder, Yancy was acting out a violent scene that he had encountered previously in the game. This allegation presupposes a direct relationship between playing graphically violent fantasy games and displaying aggressive behaviour in real life. This hypothesis was tested in a correlational study by Craig Anderson and Karen Dill (2000).

Anderson and Dill (2000) recruited 227 introductory psychology students for the study and had them fill out a set of self-report questionnaires. The questionnaires assessed a variety of factors including personality factors (irritability and trait aggression), delinquency (aggressive behaviour and non-aggressive delinquency), severity of exposure to video game violence, time spent playing video games, perceived likelihood of being a victim of certain crimes, and feelings of safety. The resulting data were analysed to determine what relationships existed among these variables.

Among other results, Anderson and Dill (2000) found that low exposure to video game violence was associated with relatively low levels of aggressive behaviour and non-aggressive delinquency, regardless of the level of aggressive personality. In contrast, high exposure to video game violence was associated with relatively high levels of non-aggressive delinquency, but only for those scoring high in aggressive personality.

Anderson and Dill's (2000) results suggest a relationship between playing violent video games and delinquent behaviours, both aggressive and non-aggressive. Furthermore, they noted that the positive association found between exposure to violent video games and aggressive personality was consistent with a developmental model in which exposure to violence in video games and other media contributes to the development of an aggressive personality.

What qualifies Anderson and Dill's (2000) study as a correlational study? In their study, aspects of the participants' personalities, their exposure to video games and to violent content in those video games, and self-reported levels of aggressive behaviour and non-aggressive delinquency were all simply recorded as found. No attempt was made to manipulate variables in order to observe any potential effects of those variables.

Causation and the correlational approach

Given Anderson and Dill's (2000) results (see the "In the Know" box), you might be tempted to conclude that exposure to violent video games causes aggressive behaviour and non-aggressive delinquency. However, this conclusion that a causal relationship exists is inappropriate even though the relationship appears real. Two obstacles stand in the way of drawing clear causal inferences from correlational data: the third-variable problem and the directionality problem.

The third-variable problem

To establish a causal relationship between two variables, you must be able to demonstrate that variation in one of the observed variables could *only* be due to the influence of the other observed variable. In the example, you want to show that variation in the level of exposure to violent video games causes variation in the levels of aggressive behaviour and non-aggressive delinquency. However, because the students (and not the researchers) chose how much exposure they received to violent video games, it is possible that the observed relationship between video game violence and aggressive or delinquent behaviours may actually be due to the influence of something else – a third variable. A strong suspect in this case is the level of aggressive personality. Perhaps those who have more aggressive personalities are both more likely to enjoy playing violent video games and more likely to display aggressive behaviour and non-aggressive delinquency. It might be the case that it is degree of aggressive personality and not the amount of exposure to violent video games that is the real cause of differences in aggressive behaviour and non-aggressive delinquency.

The possibility that correlational relationships may result from the action of an unobserved "third variable" is called the **third-variable problem**. This unobserved variable may influence both of the observed variables (e.g. exposure to video game violence and aggressive behaviour), causing them to vary together even though no direct relationship exists between them. The two observed variables may be strongly correlated even though neither variable causes changes in the other.

To resolve the third-variable problem, you must examine the effects of each potential third variable to determine whether it does, in fact, account for the observed relationship.

Third-variable problem
A problem that interferes with drawing causal inferences from correlational results. A third, unmeasured variable affects both measured variables, making it appear as though the measured variables are correlated even though they do not influence each other.

The directionality problem

> ## STOP & Think
>
> Before reading on, think about whether the *direction* of causality implied in the "In the Know" box above (that playing violent video games causes violent behaviour) is the only way to think about the link.

A second reason why it is hazardous to draw causal inferences from correlational data is that, even when a direct causal relationship exists, the direction of causality is sometimes difficult to determine. This difficulty is known as the directionality problem.

The directionality problem lurks in Anderson and Dill's (2000) finding of a positive relationship between level of aggression (as self-reported by the students in their questionnaires) and the amount of exposure to violent video games. You might be tempted to conclude that students become more aggressive from playing violent video games, but it seems just as reasonable to turn the causal arrow around. Perhaps finding gratification in aggressive behaviour leads to a preference for playing violent video games. It is difficult, and sometimes impossible, to determine the direction of what is influencing what.

Why use correlational research?

Given the problems of interpreting the results of correlational research, you may wonder why you would want to use this approach. However, correlational research has a variety of applications, and there are many reasons to consider using it. In this section, we discuss three situations in which a correlational approach makes good sense.

Gathering data in the early stages of research

During the initial, exploratory stage of a research project, the correlational approach's ability to identify potential causal relationships can provide a rich source of hypotheses that later may be tested experimentally.

Inability to manipulate variables

In an experimental design, variables are manipulated to determine their effects on other variables. A second reason for choosing a correlational design over an experimental one is that manipulating the variables of interest may be impossible or **unethical**. For example, imagine that you were interested in determining whether psychopathic personality develops when a child is raised by cold, uncaring parents. To establish a clear causal connection between the parents' behaviour towards the child and psychopathic personality, you would have to conduct an experiment in which the parents' behaviour was manipulated by assigning infants at random to be raised by either normal parents or cold, uncaring ones. However, this experiment would be impossible to carry out (who would allow their child to participate in such an experiment?) and, because of its

ch. 24

potential for inflicting serious harm on the child, unethical as well. In such cases, a correlational design may be the only practical and ethical option.

Relating naturally occurring variables

A third situation in which a correlational research design may be chosen over an experimental design is one in which you want to see how naturally occurring variables relate in the real world. Such information can be used to make useful predictions even if the reasons for the discovered relationships are not clear. Certain theoretical views also may lead to predictions about which real-world variables should be correlated with which. These predictions can be tested by using a correlational design.

We will cover analyses of correlational designs in Chapter 19.

ch. 19

Regression

Regression is a technique that is related to correlational methods. However, when we do a regression, we aim to make predictions about what values we might get on one variable, based on the values that we have got for another variable. Obviously, if we are going to be able to make accurate predictions, then the relationship between the variables must be strong. As an example, imagine we are in charge of a factory. Workers in the factory are assembling toys, to be ready for the Christmas rush. A good worker can put together 20 toys every hour. If we are hiring new workers, how will we be able to tell if they are a good worker or not? Luckily, we have a new idea about how to find this out. We think that giving people some simple tests and measuring how well they do on them will be a good indicator of how many toys that person will be able to assemble in an hour. This is ideal for regression. We would give the test to a sample of people and measure how many toys they were assembling per hour. We could then look to see whether or not we could predict job performance (the "criterion" or "target" variable) based on the values from the test scores (the "predictor" variable). If our prediction was accurate, then we would be justified in using the tests when choosing who to employ, because the tests will be a good indication of how that person will do when assembling toys. We cover regression techniques in more detail in Chapter 19.

> **Regression**
> Statistical technique used to make predictions about scores on one variable based on scores of other variable(s).

Some research does not look for correlation or causation, but instead aims to provide a thorough and useful description of the behaviour under study. This can be done in a number of ways, some of which are described below. One thing to remember about the techniques we are about to summarize is that they do not *necessarily* always have to lead to purely descriptive information. This may sound a bit confusing, but what we mean by this is that we can sometimes use these techniques for solely descriptive accounts and at other times, in certain circumstances, we might choose to actually make some quantitative measurements which can then be used to look for (say) correlations.

Observational methods

Observing behaviour is something we all do every day. Every time we meet another person or are involved in a social situation we are observing behaviour. It is probably no surprise, therefore, that psychologists also use **observational methods** to learn about behaviour. However, the observational methods that psychologists

> **Observational methods**
> A series of methods that focuses on systematically observing individuals or groups either in their natural environment or in other situations. Data from observational methods can be quantitative or qualitative.

use are different from the way you might make observations in your day-to-day life. Psychologists have to make their observations as precisely as they can, often in well-defined conditions and usually in a systematic and objective manner with careful record-keeping.

Although it might seem straightforward, there are actually many different ways in which psychologists employ observational techniques. First, observation can be done either with intervention or without intervention. What this means is that the observer might simply stand back from the situation or behaviour they are observing and let it unfold in front of them. This is sometimes called **naturalistic observation** as the observer actively tries to keep as much of a distance between themselves and what they are studying as possible. They let it all happen in a natural manner and keep a record of what they think is important. This is in contrast to observation with intervention in which the researcher is actively involved in the thing that they are observing either to a greater or lesser extent. Observation with intervention can range from setting up a situation in a laboratory and watching the subsequent behaviour through a one-way mirror (a technique often used when studying infants) to a researcher actually joining a particular social group and taking part in their activities in order to gain an insight into the behaviours and the psychological factors that underpin them (a technique known as **participant observation**).

A further consideration is the way in which the observations are recorded. Again, there are a number of ways in which psychologists can record their findings. Sometimes the method of recording is highly structured and might involve ticking off behaviours that have previously been agreed to be important (e.g. the number of times an infant looks at his or her caregiver in a particular situation). In other observational studies, the method of recording will be more open and might involve written descriptions of the behaviour such as a diary account. How the observations are recorded will depend largely upon what the researchers are aiming to find out from the observation. These techniques and the issues surrounding **observational methods** will be covered more fully in Chapter 12.

> **Naturalistic observation**
> An observational method that involves the researcher studying behaviour as it occurs "naturally", without any attempt to intervene.

> **Participant observation**
> An observational method that involves the researcher actually becoming an active member of the group that he or she is studying.

ch. 12

Survey methods

Observational research allows you to infer what people must have been thinking or feeling to have behaved in a certain way, but your inferences might not always be correct. A more direct way to deal with the nature of people's thoughts, opinions and feelings is to ask them. Survey research does just this although just as observational methods are more sophisticated than our everyday methods of observing, **survey methods** are also more than simply asking people questions. Psychologists have developed a number of ways that can be used to ask people about various psychologically interesting phenomena, such as attitudes and beliefs. Again, like observational methods, there are various different versions that surveys can take. Sometimes survey research will be mainly questionnaire based and respondents will be asked a series of questions relating to the phenomena under study. Designing these questionnaires is not straightforward and there are many complicated issues concerning exactly what to ask in the questionnaire and exactly what "construct" you are "tapping into". Developing a questionnaire that reliably measures the thing you're interested in is a long and complex process.

> **Survey methods**
> A series of methods that ask individuals to respond to questions relating to the phenomena under study. Can be quantitative or qualitative, and can be conducted in a number of mediums.

In addition to questionnaires, there are other survey methods available to researchers. Sometimes the main method of data collecting will be through mail surveys, personal interviews, telephone interviews or Internet surveys. Survey research can be both qualitative and quantitative, but in both cases care must be taken in constructing the survey. Only a well-constructed survey will give you the best data possible relating to the phenomena of interest. Another feature of survey research is choosing the most appropriate group of people to test. Surveys and the issues surrounding them are covered in **Chapter 13**.

What makes a good method and what method should you choose?

It is a bit unfair to talk of methods being "good" or "bad". Methods are probably best described as being "appropriate" or "inappropriate" ways of answering research questions. Sometimes it will be clear that an experiment is the best way to answer your question, while at other times your research will be obviously correlational. Usually, it is fairly clear what type of method you should use. As long as you have a good understanding of your research question, the method that is most appropriate will be a straightforward decision. One mistake that students often make is that they do not have a thorough understanding of what they are trying to achieve with their projects, and this then leads to unnecessary head-scratching when it comes to choosing a method (and analysing the data). If you are embarking on a research project for the first time, then it really is important that you have a firm grasp of the aims of your project and the questions you are asking. Once you have chosen a general method to use, you then have to start designing the research that you will conduct. Choosing a method is the first step. Once you have decided upon a method, you are then faced with the task of actually designing the study that you will do.

Experimental methods

Experimental methods have dominated mainstream psychology in recent times. One of the primary reasons that psychologists conduct experiments is to make empirical tests of hypotheses they derive from psychological theories. An experiment allows the researcher to test a hypothesis in a controlled way.

> **Experimental method**
> A well-controlled form of research that looks for cause–effect relationships.

Imagine you are interested in the idea that exercising for 30 minutes influences mood. One way you could study this would be to do an experiment. You might get two groups of people and have one of these groups exercise for 30 minutes and then measure their current mood. For the other group, you get them to do some non-strenuous activity for 30 minutes (preferably something that was not likely to influence their mood) and then measure this group's current mood. You might hypothesize that "participants who have exercised for 30 minutes will have a more positive current mood than participants who have not taken part in 30 minutes of exercise". If the people in the first group tend to be different to those in the second in their reported mood, then you might conclude that it is the 30 minutes of exercise that has caused this difference, and thus your hypothesis has been supported. This is a very simple example of an experiment. Experimental methods are usually laboratory based and are extremely popular in many areas of psychology. The reason that they are so popular is because they offer a powerful tool in understanding certain psychological processes. Not everything can be studied in the laboratory, so in psychology we usually find that laboratory-based experimental methods are used mainly for studying physiological, cognitive or sensory phenomena, although these are not the only areas of psychology to use experimental methods.

An experiment allows you to identify a causal relationship between two (or more) variables. To put it as simply as we can, an experiment is when you put a person (usually one person, although occasionally more) into a situation and you measure some psychological factor that relates to the phenomenon you are interested in (in the example above, this would be "current mood"). In addition to this, you want to know what factors might influence the psychological factor that you are looking at. Usually in an experiment we manipulate some feature of the situation and then see how this manipulation influences the psychological phenomena that we are studying. In the example above, the manipulation involves either getting people to exercise for 30 minutes or getting them to do something non-strenuous for 30 minutes before measuring their current mood. So, to use the terms we introduced in Chapter 4, the study we have just described has an **independent variable and a dependent variable**. The independent variable is under the control of the researcher and in this case involves whether or not a participant exercises for 30 minutes. The dependent variable is the thing we are measuring to see if the manipulation influences it. So the dependent variable in this study would be "current mood". We are interested in discovering whether the dependent variable (mood) *depends* (hence the name) on the independent variable (exercise).

ch. 4
p.61

STOP & Think

How would you test the idea that exercise improves mood? Think of some ways that you might do this, and see if your ideas match the ways we will describe below and in the following two chapters.

In an experiment you test a number of people and see how they perform under different conditions. If there is a definite pattern in the results, then you can say with a certain degree of confidence that the conditions that you manipulated were having a causal influence on the behaviour that you were measuring. To be able to do this, it is extremely important that you conduct your experiment in a controlled environment. You would not do an experiment on the effects of mixing two chemicals if the test tube you were mixing them in was contaminated with lots of other chemicals. It is the same for psychology. If you want to find out if A (exercise) causes B (increased positive mood) then you need to be sure that there is nothing else that could contaminate your experiment by influencing mood without you knowing about it. For example, you would have to make sure that people in the no-exercise group were not all friends who were

Extraneous variable
Any variable that is not systematically manipulated in an experiment but that still may affect the behaviour being observed.

suffering from a hangover after a long night drinking in the student union. This would obviously impact upon the mood that they were in, so any differences between them and the group who you get to exercise for 30 minutes might actually be due to their sore heads rather than anything to do with the independent variable (exercise or no exercise) itself. This would be an example of an **extraneous variable**. A large part of doing experiments is making sure that there aren't any other factors that could be influencing the causal relationship that you are looking for. The section on **experimental control** in Chapter 6 deals with this in more detail.

ch. 6
p.106

In the Know

Music tempo and productivity
Jeffery Miller and his adviser, Blaine Peden, had participants listen to music while working on arithmetic problems (Miller & Peden, 2003). Their hypothesis was that changes in the tempo of music would have an effect on the number of arithmetic problems completed and the number of errors made. We describe the part of their experiment in which 33 undergraduates mentally added three 3-digit numbers and wrote answers, working for 2 minutes. The arithmetic problems were simple; they required no "carrying" to the next column. While performing the mental arithmetic, all of the participants heard Bach's Brandenburg Concerto No. 3 in G Major. For one-third of them, the tempo was 96 beats per minute (bpm) and there was no increase in tempo while the concerto was playing (0 per cent increase). For another third of the participants, the tempo increased from 96 bpm to 120 bpm during the 2 minutes (a 25 per cent increase). For the final third, the tempo increased 50 per cent (from 96 to 144 bpm). Special software changed the tempo of the music without changing the pitch. Each participant's answer sheet was scored two ways. One score was the number of problems worked (which ranged from 11 to 42), and the other score was the number of errors made (which ranged from 0 to 5).

As the music tempo increased, the number of problems worked decreased. At the 0 per cent increase, 25.0 problems were completed, on average. For the 25 per cent increase in tempo, the mean was 20.7 problems and for the 50 per cent increase, the participants worked 16.2 problems, on average. This reduction in the number of problems worked was **statistically significant**. As for the number of errors, the change in tempo did not produce any significant differences. In fact, few errors were made at any tempo. Thus, an increase in music tempo produced a decrease in the number of problems worked but had no effect on the number of errors.

ch. 15
p.332

Experimental methods are hugely important in modern-day psychology and we will be looking at them in more detail in Chapter 6.

ch. 6

Test yourself

Identify the method employed in each of the studies described.[1]

Study	Observational	Survey	Correlational	Experimental
1 A researcher is interested in how people behave when they see a lost wallet on a bench. She finds a quiet park and leaves a wallet where passers-by are likely to see it. She then retreats to a room overlooking the bench, and notes down whether the passers-by who notice the wallet pick it up or ignore it. She also notes down what they do with the wallet if they do pick it up.				

1 Answers: 1 = observational; 2 = correlational; 3 = experimental; 4 = survey.

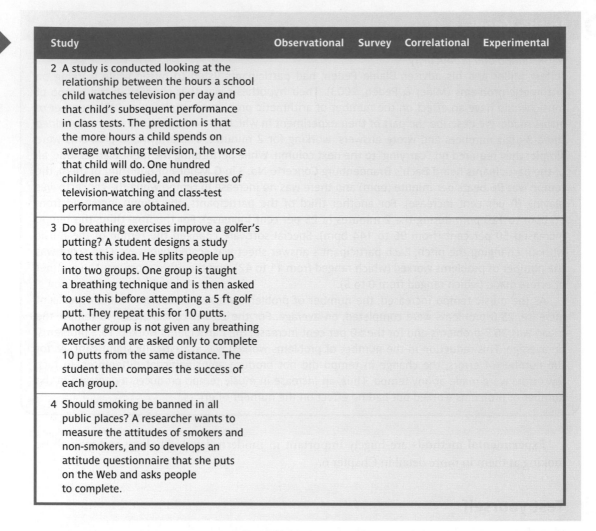

Study	Observational	Survey	Correlational	Experimental
2 A study is conducted looking at the relationship between the hours a school child watches television per day and that child's subsequent performance in class tests. The prediction is that the more hours a child spends on average watching television, the worse that child will do. One hundred children are studied, and measures of television-watching and class-test performance are obtained.				
3 Do breathing exercises improve a golfer's putting? A student designs a study to test this idea. He splits people up into two groups. One group is taught a breathing technique and is then asked to use this before attempting a 5 ft golf putt. They repeat this for 10 putts. Another group is not given any breathing exercises and are asked only to complete 10 putts from the same distance. The student then compares the success of each group.				
4 Should smoking be banned in all public places? A researcher wants to measure the attitudes of smokers and non-smokers, and so develops an attitude questionnaire that she puts on the Web and asks people to complete.				

Internal and external validity

ch. 4
p.73

Whatever the design of your study, you need to consider carefully two important but often conflicting attributes of any design: internal and external validity. We have already covered (in quite a bit of detail) issues relating to the **validity of measures** but researchers also need to consider issues relating to the validity of their *study* as a whole. In this section, we define these concepts and briefly discuss the factors that you should consider relating to internal and external validity when choosing a research design.

Internal validity

Much of your research will be aimed at testing the hypotheses that you developed long before you collected any data. The ability of your research design to adequately test your hypotheses is known as its **internal validity**. Essentially, internal validity is the ability of your research method to test the hypothesis that it was designed to test.

In an experiment, this means showing that variation in the independent variable (and *only* the independent variable) caused the observed variation in the dependent variable. In a correlational study, it means showing that changes in the value of your **criterion variable** relate solely to changes in the value of your predictor variable and not to changes in other, extraneous variables that may have varied along with your predictor variable.

Internal validity is threatened whenever extraneous (confounding) variables can provide alternative explanations for the findings of a study, or as Huck and Sandler (1979) call them, rival hypotheses. As an example, imagine that a teacher wants to know whether a new teaching method works better than the traditional method used with students in an introductory psychology course. She decides to answer this question by using the new method to teach her morning section of introductory psychology and using the traditional method to teach her afternoon section. Both sections will use the same text, cover the same material and receive the same tests. The effectiveness of the two methods will be assessed by comparing the average scores achieved on the test by the two sections. Now, imagine that the teacher conducts the study and finds that the section receiving the new method receives a substantially higher average grade than the section receiving the traditional method. She concludes that the new method is definitely better for teaching introductory psychology. Is she justified in drawing this conclusion?

> **internal validity**
> The ability of your method to adequately test the hypothesis it was designed to test.
>
> **Criterion variable**
> An outcome variable that provides an indicator of a psychological construct, against which scores on other measures can be validated.

The answer, as you probably suspected, is no. Several rival hypotheses cannot be eliminated by the study, explanations that are at least as credible as the teacher's view that the new method was responsible for the observed improvement in average grade.

Consider the following rival hypotheses:

1 The morning students did better because they were "fresher" than the afternoon students.

2 The morning students did better because their teacher was "fresher" in the morning than in the afternoon.

3 The teacher expected the new method to work better and thus was more enthusiastic when using the new method than when using the old one.

4 Students who registered for the morning class were more motivated to do well in the course than those who registered for the afternoon class.

These rival hypotheses do not exhaust the possibilities; perhaps you can think of others. Because the study was not designed to rule out these alternatives, there is no way to know whether the observed difference between the two sections in student performance was due to the difference in teaching methods, teacher enthusiasm, alertness of the students or other factors. Whenever two or more variables combine in such a way that their effects cannot be separated, a confounding of those variables has occurred. In the teaching study, teaching method is confounded by all those variables just listed and more. Such a study lacks internal validity.

Confounding effects such as this are minimized by implementing controls. We cover various control techniques in the next chapter.

Threats to internal validity

History
A threat to internal validity in which the occurrence of an event other than the treatment produces changes in the research participants' behaviour.

Maturation
A threat to internal validity in which naturally occurring change within the individual (associated with the passage of time) may be responsible for the results.

Statistical regression
A threat to internal validity in which participants who have been selected based on extreme scores move closer to the population mean on retesting (also called regression to the mean).

Biased selection
A threat to internal validity in which groups of participants are not equivalent prior to treatment.

Testing effects
A threat to internal validity in which taking a pre-test changes behaviour without any effect on the independent variable.

Confounding variables occur in both experimental and correlational designs, but they are far more likely to be a problem in the latter in which tight control over extraneous variables is usually lacking. Campbell and Stanley (1966) identify seven general sources of confounding that may affect internal validity: **history**, **maturation**, **testing effects**, instrumentation, **statistical regression, biased selection** of participants, and experimental mortality (Table 5.1).

History may confound studies that rely on making multiple observations that are taken over time. Specific events may occur between observations that affect the results. For example, a study of the effectiveness of an advertising campaign against drunk driving might measure the number of arrests for drunk driving immediately before and after the campaign. If the police institute a crackdown on drunk driving at the same time that the advertisements air, this event will destroy the internal validity of your study.

Maturation refers to the effect of age or fatigue. You might, for example, assess performance on a proofreading task before and after some experimental manipulation. Decreased performance on the second proofreading assessment may be due to fatigue rather than to any effect of your manipulation.

Testing effects occur when a pre-test sensitizes participants to what you are investigating in your study. As a consequence, they may respond differently on a subsequent (post-intervention) measure than if no pre-test were given. For example, if you measure participants' racial attitudes and then manipulate race in an

Table 5.1 Factors affecting internal validity

Factor	Description
History	Specific events other than the treatment occur between observations
Maturation	Performance changes due to age or fatigue confound the effect of the treatment
Testing	Testing prior to the treatment changes how participants respond in post-treatment testing
Instrumentation	Unobserved changes in observer criteria or instrument calibration confound the effect of the treatment
Statistical regression	Participants selected for treatment on the basis of their extreme scores tend to move closer to the mean on retesting
Biased selection of participants	Groups of participants exposed to different treatments are not equivalent prior to treatment
Experimental mortality	Differential loss of participants from the groups of a study results in non-equivalent groups

experiment on person perception, participants may respond to the treatment differently than if no such pre-test of racial attitudes was given.

In *instrumentation*, confounding may be introduced by unobserved changes in criteria used by observers or in instrument calibration. If observers change what counts as "verbal aggression" when scoring behaviour under two experimental conditions, any apparent difference between those conditions in verbal aggression could be due as much to the changed criterion as to any effect of the independent variable. Similarly, if an instrument used to record activity of rats in a cage becomes more (or less) sensitive over time, it becomes impossible to tell whether activity is really changing or just the ability of the instrument to detect activity.

Statistical regression threatens internal validity when participants have been selected based on extreme scores on some measure. When measured again, scores will tend to be closer to the average in the population. Thus, if students are targeted for a special reading programme based on their unusually low reading test scores, they will tend to do better, on average, on retesting even if the reading programme has no effect.

Biased selection of participants threatens internal validity because participants may differ initially in ways that affect their scores on the dependent measure. Any influence of the independent variable on scores cannot be separated from the effect of the pre-existing bias. This problem typically arises when researchers use pre-existing groups in their studies rather than assigning participants to groups at random. For example, the effect of a programme designed to improve worker job satisfaction might be evaluated by administering the programme to workers at one factory (experimental group) and then comparing the level of job satisfaction of those workers to that of workers at another factory where the programme was not given (control group). If workers given the job satisfaction programme indicate more satisfaction with their jobs, is it due to the programme or to pre-existing differences between the two groups? There is no way to tell.

Finally, experimental mortality refers to the differential loss of participants from groups in a study. For example, imagine that some people drop out of a study because of frustration with the task. A group exposed to difficult conditions is more likely to lose its frustration-intolerant participants than one exposed to less difficult conditions. Any differences between the groups in performance may be due as much to the resulting difference in participants as to any difference in conditions.

Enhancing internal validity

The time to be concerned with internal validity is during the design phase of your study. During this phase, you should carefully plan which variables will be manipulated or observed and recorded, identify any plausible rival hypotheses not eliminated in your initial design, and redesign so as to eliminate those that seriously threaten internal validity. Discovering problems with internal validity after you have run your study is too late. A poorly designed study cannot be fixed later on.

External validity

A study has **external validity** to the degree that its results can be extended (generalized) beyond the limited research setting and sample in which they were obtained. A

External validity
The extent to which the results of a research study can be generalized beyond the limits of the study sample, to different populations, settings and conditions.

common complaint about research conducted in the artificial conditions of the laboratory, using white rats or students, is that it may tell us very little about how white rats and college undergraduates (let alone animals or people in general) behave under the conditions imposed on them in the "real world".

The idea seems to be that all studies should be conducted in such a way that the findings can be generalized immediately to real-world situations and to larger populations. However, as Mook (1983) notes, it is a fallacy to assume "that the purpose of collecting data in the laboratory is to predict real-life behaviour in the real world" (p. 381). Mook points out that much of the research conducted in the laboratory is designed to determine one of the following:

1 whether something can happen, rather than whether it typically does happen

2 whether something we specify ought to happen (according to some hypothesis) under specific conditions in the lab does happen there under those conditions

3 what happens under conditions not encountered in the real world

In each of these cases, the objective is to gain insight into the underlying mechanisms of behaviour rather than to discover relationships that apply under normal conditions in the real world. It is this understanding that generalizes to everyday life, not the specific findings themselves.

Threats to external validity

In Chapter 2, we distinguished between **basic research**, which is aimed at developing a better understanding of the underlying mechanisms of behaviour, and **applied research**, which is aimed at developing information that can be directly applied to solve real-world problems. The question of external validity may be less relevant in basic research settings that seek theoretical reasons to determine what will happen under conditions not usually found in natural settings or that examine fundamental processes expected to operate under a wide variety of conditions. The degree of external validity of a study becomes more relevant when the findings are expected to be applied directly to real-world settings. In such studies, external validity is affected by several factors. Conducting your study in a highly controlled laboratory setting (as opposed to a naturalistic setting) is one such factor. Data obtained from a tightly controlled laboratory may not generalize to more naturalistic situations in which behaviour occurs. Other factors that affect external validity, as discussed by Campbell and Stanley (1966), are listed and briefly described in Table 5.2. Many of these threats to external validity are discussed in later chapters, along with the appropriate research design.

Internal versus external validity

Although you should strive to achieve a high degree of both internal and external validity in your research, in practice you will find that the steps you take to increase one type of validity tend to decrease the other. For example, a tightly controlled laboratory experiment affords you a relatively high degree of internal validity. Your findings, however, may not generalize to other samples and situations, leading to a reduction in external validity. Often the best that you can do is reach a compromise on the relative amounts of internal and external validity in your research.

Table 5.2 Factors affecting external validity

Factor	Description
Reactive testing	Occurs when a pre-test affects participants' reaction to an experimental variable, making those participants' responses unrepresentative of the general population
Interactions between participant selection biases and the independent variable	Effects observed may apply only to the participants included in the study, especially if they are a unique group (such as university undergraduates rather than a cross-section of adults)
Reactive effects of experimental arrangements	Refers to the effects of highly artificial experimental situations used in some research and the participant's knowledge that he or she is a research participant
Multiple treatment interference	Occurs when participants are exposed to multiple experimental treatments in which exposure to early treatments affects responses to later treatments

Whether internal or external validity is more important depends on your reasons for conducting the research. If you are most interested in testing a theoretical position (as is often the case in basic research), you might be more concerned with internal than external validity and hence conduct a tightly controlled laboratory experiment. However, if you are more concerned with applying your results to a real-world problem (as in applied research), you might take steps to increase the external validity while attempting to maintain a reasonable degree of internal validity. These issues need to be considered at the time when you design your study.

As just mentioned, the setting in which you conduct your research strongly influences the internal and external validity of your results. The kinds of setting available and the issues that you should consider when choosing a research setting are the topics that we take up next.

Summary

Methods are ways of approaching research questions and can be quantitative (involving measurement) or qualitative (focusing more on experiences). Correlational methods look at how closely related two variables are. Regression is linked to correlation, but attempts to make predictions about one variable based on the values of another. Observational methods are systematic attempts at observing and recording behaviour in a variety of conditions. Observation can be naturalistic (in which the behaviour is observed in a natural setting) or can involve the researcher becoming involved to various degrees. Survey methods involve investigating psychological phenomena by asking questions. Experimental methods involve cause–effect relationships between an independent variable and a dependent variable under well-controlled conditions. Internal validity refers to how well a particular method answers the research questions that it was designed to answer. External validity is the degree to which the outcome of a study can be generalized beyond the research setting and sample.

Questions

1   What is the difference between qualitative and quantitative methods?
2   How would you define an "experimental method"?
3   What is the difference between "experimental" methods and "correlational" methods?
4   Identify and describe two problems with correlational research.
5   In what circumstances might a researcher use a correlational design instead of an experiment?
6   What is internal validity, and why is it important?
7   What factors threaten internal validity?
8   What is external validity, and when is it important to have high levels of external validity?
9   How do internal and external validity relate to one another?

 Activities

1   Have a look at the study we describe on mood and exercise. Can you think of a way that we might investigate the link between mood and exercise using a correlational design rather than an experimental one? What would be the benefits and drawbacks of doing the study like this?

2   Again, imagine we are interested in testing the relationship between exercising and mood. What issues relating to validity and reliability might we have to consider if we were doing this study (a) as an experiment and (b) as a correlational study?

3   Imagine you are interested in whether meditation makes people happy. How might you do this as (a) a correlational study and (b) an experimental study? Think carefully about the potential confounding factors in both studies.

6

Introduction to Experimental Methods

OVERVIEW

In Chapter 5 we introduced you to some methods that we can employ when investigating psychological phenomena, and one way of doing this is through the use of experiments. This chapter will introduce you to the fundamental building blocks of experimental methods. Experimental methods have their own language, and so one purpose of this chapter is to introduce you to new terms and ideas that relate to experiments. Some of these will be familiar from previous chapters, and some will be new. We will be covering the role of independent and dependent variables in experiments, applying a hypothesis to an experiment, and the dangers of error and how to control for it. This is a fairly short chapter, but it does contain information that you will need to know before we move on to experimental designs in the following two chapters.

OBJECTIVES

After studying this chapter and working through the exercises, you should be able to:

- Recognize the basic components of experimental designs
- Demonstrate knowledge of the role that independent and dependent variables play in experimental methods
- Understand what "hypotheses" are and how they are used by experimenters
- Recognize experimental "error" and display an understanding of how to deal with it

Why experiment?

We briefly introduced the idea of experiments in the previous chapter, and we emphasized their importance in psychology. Why are they so important? They are important because they give us a chance to study phenomena in an objective way. Experiments give us an opportunity to understand the way in which things work (psychological things if psychology is your area of study). To find out how something works, it is usually informative to isolate it and then investigate its various properties. Often, we will be interested in how it interacts with other factors and what conditions tend to influence it. For example, if we discover through experimentation that our mood is influenced by exercise, then this tells us something valuable about the nature of "mood" and how it can be influenced and interact with other physiological functions. So, experiments isolate things and allow us to study them in ways that have the potential to reveal their underlying nature. Experiments in psychology are based on the same principles as experiments in any other area. The unique thing about psychology is the nature of the "things" that we are trying to isolate and study. **Psychological phenomena are difficult to study**, but that does not mean we cannot do experiments. We can; and, believe it or not, they do not all involve putting electrodes on people's heads.

ch. 3
p.51 – 53

Experiments are powerful tools for researchers. They allow us to test our hypotheses in a systematic and controlled way and can reveal important causal relationships between variables. This is the way in which experiments contribute towards our knowledge of psychological phenomena.

ch. 4
p.61

Psychology experiments involve putting people into a certain situation and either asking them to perform a task or merely observing how they behave; the measure that we get from the task or behaviour is the **dependent variable**. Usually, we will measure their response or behaviour under two or more conditions. These conditions are levels of the **independent variable**. So, the researcher is mainly interested in how the different conditions influence the performance of the task or the behaviour.

> ## STOP & Think
>
> What's the difference between an independent variable and a dependent variable?

It is at this point that we will start to make heavy use of the terms that we have introduced in previous chapters. If you find yourself reading the next few sections and wondering what it all means, then have a look back at Chapters 3 and 4, where most of the basic terms are introduced. The first thing to do is look at the basic features of experiments.

Fundamentals of experiments

The following are some fundamental concepts associated with experiments:

- Researchers manipulate an independent variable (sometimes called a *factor*) in an experiment to observe the effect that this has on the dependent variable. In psychology, the dependent variable is usually a measure of behaviour or a measure of a psychological process.

- Experimental control is an essential ingredient of experiments. A well-controlled experiment will rule out any unwanted influences (confounds) that might affect the dependent variable.

- If **confounding** does occur, then a plausible alternative explanation for the observed relationship exists, and the experiment lacks internal validity. Plausible alternative explanations are ruled out by holding conditions constant and balancing.

> **Confounding**
> Occurs when the independent variable of interest systematically covaries with a second, unintended independent variable.

Experiments allow us to exercise a relatively high degree of control in a situation. Researchers hope that studying a psychological phenomenon in a well-controlled environment will allow them to say with a certain degree of confidence that it was the manipulation of the independent variable that actually caused the observed changes. Why are we interested in observing changes in a dependent variable? Because this is how we get to understand psychological processes. Knowing how something is influenced, whether it is by different scenarios or by different types of input, will inform us about what that thing is and how it works. If we are interested in memory and we discover that our memory for events is influenced by what "remembering strategies" we use, then this reveals something about the nature of memory. This is why we do experiments – they allow us to discover features of psychological processes or behaviours by telling us how these things operate in a variety of scenarios.

So, an experiment is ultimately a carefully controlled situation in which a researcher manipulates an independent variable and measures the effect that this has on the dependent variable. As much as it is possible, the researcher takes great care in making sure that there is nothing else that could influence the dependent variable other than the manipulation that is made to the independent variable. In reality, there may be other things having an effect, so the researcher has to identify them and deal with them in some way. This is the problem of error and how to control for it. We cover this later in the chapter.

What all experiments must have

Before we describe the different types of experimental design, let us briefly cover some things that are common to all experiments.

Independent and dependent variables

The whole point of an experiment is to establish the relationship between the independent and the dependent variables. These are terms that are central to understanding experiments, so please refer back to Chapter 4 for definitions if you are unsure.

ch. 4 p.61

What does "manipulate the independent variable" actually mean?

One thing that we have mentioned a few times is the experimenter "manipulating the independent variable", so let us explain what this really means and how it relates to experiments. It sounds quite complicated and perhaps a little technical. It's not. In most experiments, the independent variable is *categorical*. What this means is that it can be split into two or more categories. In experiments these are called either "levels" or "conditions". Most experiments look for differences in the measurement of the dependent variable (which is the behaviour or psychological phenomena that the researcher is interested in measuring) between these categories. To manipulate the independent variable, you decide upon at least two different values (or "levels") and you then measure the dependent variable in each level.

You will also sometimes hear it said that the independent variable is "under the control" of the researcher. Sometimes people interpret this as meaning the researcher is actively involved in manipulating something during each experimental session. This is not (normally) the case. The researcher's control of the independent variable relates to the design of the study and all of the "control" is done well before the participant arrives to take part. The researcher designs the study and decides what the levels of the independent variable will be. That is the sense in which the independent variable is under the researcher's control. These ideas may seem a bit abstract, but have a look at the example that we are about to describe, which should make this concept clearer.

An example

ch. 5
p.91

Think back to the **example we used in Chapter 5**: whether exercising for 30 minutes resulted in enhanced mood. In this experiment, we had two groups of people. One of these groups exercised for 30 minutes. The other group did not. We then measured the "current mood" of everyone in both groups. We were looking for a difference in the average mood of the group that exercised as compared to the group that did not exercise. If we found a difference, then we might be able to say that it was the 30-minute exercise that had caused the difference in mood between the two groups. We might then be able to make a statement about the effect that exercise has on mood. Let us break down that simple experiment into its component parts (Table 6.1).

In this experiment, the "manipulation of the independent variable" is simply having two different activities that people can do prior to having their mood measured. They can either take part in 30 minutes' exercise, or they can do some other non-strenuous activity. It is nothing more complicated than that. The only "manipulation" that happens in the study is having two different categories of "things" that people will do before you measure their mood. Most independent variables in experiments are like this.

Table 6.1 Components of an experiment on exercise and mood

Type of variable/name of variable	Level of measurement	Operational definition
Independent (activity undertaken)	Nominal (two-conditions/levels) 1. Exercises for 30 minutes 2. Does not exercise for 30 minutes	Whether or not participants take part in 30-minute exercise before having mood measured
Dependent ("current mood")	Interval/ratio	Score measured on validated "current mood" scale

Hypotheses

ch. 4
pp.79–80

ch. 15
pp.330–332

All experiments are designed in order to test a **hypothesis**. For reasons that will be covered in Chapter 15, it is actually the **null hypothesis that an experiment tests**, but before you begin designing *any* experiment, it is vital that the experimenter has a clear idea of what the experimental and the null hypotheses are. To put it simply, they are statements about what pattern of results you might expect to find. The experimental hypothesis, remember, is a statement about what you will find if there is a causal relationship between the variables, while the null hypothesis is a statement about what you would find if there is *no* causal relationship between the variables. Having a clear hypothesis will make designing the experiment easier as it will usually state what the *conditions* (or the "levels" of the independent variable) are and what pattern of results you might expect to see when the conditions are compared. Table 6.2 gives examples of some hypotheses.

Table 6.2 Hypotheses

Alternative hypothesis	Null hypothesis
Exercising for 30 minutes will result in an increase in "current mood" (one-tailed)	There will be no difference between "exercise" and "no exercise" groups when current mood is assessed.
Ingesting caffeine will lead to a difference in reaction times compared to ingesting a placebo[1] (two-tailed)	There will be no difference in reaction time performance between those who ingest caffeine and those who ingest a placebo.
Heterosexual males will spend, on average, more time giving directions when asked by an attractive female compared to when asked by another male (one-tailed)	There will be no difference in how long heterosexual males spend giving directions to attractive females or other males.
One-month-old babies will spend more time looking at pictures of their mother's face than they will looking at pictures of a stranger's face (one-tailed)	There will be no difference in how long one-month-old babies spend looking at pictures of their mother's face compared to pictures of a stranger's face.

People

All psychology experiments need participants! And, most of the time, our participants are people. We would not be able to investigate psychological processes or behaviour if we did not have people to test. Who we test is a big issue to psychologists. We need to give careful consideration to the people that we recruit to take part in our experiment. This decision will be linked to what the hypothesis of the study is and the type of psychological phenomena we are interested in. There is also the issue about how we are going to get these people. There has to be a process we go through which results in people turning up in our laboratories and happily putting themselves forward for study. What is this process and what are the implications for our study? Are some people more appropriate than others for a particular study? What effect will our choice of participants have on the outcomes of our research? There are specific issues that relate to the

---

1 "Placebos" are explained on page 110.

ch. 9

people who take part in experiments, how we recruit them and what we do with them. These issues are addressed in Chapter 9.

Experimental control

In the perfect experiment, the only thing that could possibly influence the dependent variable would be the independent variable. That is, if the independent variable has two "conditions", then any difference we see in our measurement of the dependent variable must be a result of us measuring it in these two different conditions, with nothing else having any effect on our measurement. In the example that we have been using, the perfect experiment on exercise and mood would be one in which there is nothing else whatsoever that could influence the measure of mood that you are using as your dependent variable except whether or not people took part in 30 minutes of exercise prior to having their mood measured. If this was the case, and there was absolutely nothing else that could influence mood, then any observed differences would *have* to be due to exercise (or lack of it). Unfortunately there is no such thing as the perfect experiment. There are always going to be other things that can influence your dependent variable. But that does not mean we cannot do experiments. What it means is that we have to attempt to minimize the effects of these other influences, and the way we do that is by controlling our experiment as much as we can. A tightly controlled experiment is one in which these other influences are understood and can either be measured or can be prevented from having a significant and consistent effect that might obscure the influence of the independent variable on the dependent variable.

Internal validity

ch. 5
p.94

If we have a poorly controlled experiment, then there is a real threat to that experiment's **internal validity**. An experiment lacking in internal validity is almost useless as it means we cannot be sure whether or not our independent variable is the true cause of the observed measures of the dependent variable.

Imagine that you are doing an experiment. You have two conditions (levels of the independent variable) and a dependent variable. You conduct the experiment and find that the measure of the dependent variable is different when measured in these two conditions. You then conclude that you have found an interesting effect. However, your experiment is poorly controlled, and *unknown to you* there are other things that are influencing your measure of the dependent variable. If you do not know about them, then your conclusion is false. This means that your experiment lacks internal validity. That is why **control** is so important. The more control we have the more valid our experiment becomes.

Different types of experiments need to employ different measures of control, and we will cover each of these in turn when discussing the designs.

Control
The act of reducing unwanted effects in an experiment by incorporating techniques that reduce them as much as possible.

Error
Anything that might influence your dependent variable that is beyond the control of the investigator. Also known as "extraneous" or "confounding" variables.

Explaining error

The point of controlling our experiments is to reduce what is known as "**error**", and the key to any good experiment is to ensure there is as little "error" as possible. What do we mean by this? Error is what we call the influence of variables *other* than your independent variable. As we mentioned above, we do not want anything influencing our measure of the dependent variable that has nothing to do with our manipulation of the independent variable. If there is some other influence that is beyond our control, then this is error. We do not like it, as it causes confusion about the extent to which our manipulation has actually had a real influence. Other influences that are outside of our control serve only to muddy the waters, and make it difficult to draw conclusions. These other things that might be having an influence are "error" and are sometimes called "*extraneous*" variables or "*confounding*" variables.

Sources of error

In the real world, it is rarely possible to hold constant all the potential extraneous variables that could affect the value of your dependent variable. For example, participants in your experiment are not robots, and they will differ from each other in many different ways. Some of these differences might influence the way they perform in your study and this will affect your measure of the dependent variable. Given that most experiments consist of the same procedure being repeated over and over again with different people, it is impossible to expect that the environmental conditions will be absolutely constant each time you test a new participant. Even the same person will not be exactly the same from moment to moment. These variations might affect your dependent variable, causing fluctuations in scores that have nothing to do with your independent variable.

An example may help clarify this concept.[2] In an experiment on the effects of THC (the active ingredient in marijuana and cannabis) on a simulated air-traffic-control task, one group is exposed to a dose of THC (the experimental group) and one is not (the control group). Within each group, all participants would have been exposed to the same level of the independent variable, which means that, in the experimental group, each participant will have been given exactly the same dose of THC. However, it is unlikely that all participants in a group would perform exactly the same, producing exactly the same scores on the dependent measure (which is the number of errors on the simulated air-traffic-control task). Participants differ from one another in many ways that affect their performance. Some may be more resistant to THC, have better attention skills or have greater perceptual abilities than others, for example. The variation in scores produced by these other things is the error that we are discussing.

STOP & Think

What other things might influence people's performance in this study that are not related to how much THC they have been given?

---

2   We are changing the example here just for a bit of variety. If you prefer the exercise/mood example, then do not worry as it will be used again soon.

Table 6.3 Scores from hypothetical THC experiment		
	Control group	Experimental group
	25	13
	24	19
	18	22
	29	18
	19	23
Average score	23	19

Table 6.3 shows the scores achieved by participants in this hypothetical experiment. The scores for each group have been averaged, and the averages are presented at the bottom of the table. Judging from the averages, it appears that THC reduced the participants' scores on the dependent variable. This might make you think that THC has a detrimental effect on people's ability to perform tasks relating to air traffic control. However, look again at the averages for each group and you'll notice that 19 is not much lower than 23. Note that the lowest score in *both* groups is 18 and the scores across the two conditions look quite similar. It is possible that, given the variability in scores evident within each group, the difference in the means may reflect nothing more than pre-existing participant differences that did not quite balance out across the two conditions of the experiment. The problem is that you cannot tell which explanation is correct simply by looking at the means. The problem of error is therefore serious. It limits your ability to determine the effectiveness of your independent variable.

Handling error

Fortunately, there are ways you can cope with the problem of error in your experiments. You can take steps to reduce error, you can take steps to increase the effect of your independent variable, you can randomize error across groups and you can statistically control for it. Let's look at each of these strategies in more detail.

Reducing error

The main way that we might reduce error is to hold all potential extraneous variables constant by treating participants within a group as similarly as possible. For example, you could test participants in an isolated room to eliminate any distractions from outside. You could make sure that you read instructions to all participants within a group in exactly the same way. You should also follow the same procedures for all participants within a group. Error can also be reduced by using participants matched on characteristics that you believe contribute to error. For example, you could use people who are of the same age or educational level. A similar tactic is to match participants across groups on some characteristic relating to the dependent variable in a matched-groups design or use the same participants for all levels of your independent variable in a within-subjects design. (We discuss matching and using within-subjects designs in Chapter 7.)

ch. 7

Increasing the effectiveness of the independent variable

Another way to deal with error is to make sure you select the correct levels of your independent variable for your experiment. A weak manipulation (e.g. too low a dose of THC in the example above) may not influence your dependent variable at all, leaving the effect of your independent variable buried in whatever other error is having an influence. Of course, it is difficult to know beforehand just how to manipulate your independent variable, but you can get some idea about the levels to include from previous research and by conducting a pilot study before you run your actual experiment.

Randomization

Regardless of the steps that you take to minimize error, you can never eliminate it completely. One way to deal with error is to randomize as much as possible in your experiment. What this consists of is making sure that any potential error is balanced out over all conditions. What you definitely do not want is for all of the error to be having an effect in one condition only. If you can balance the error over all conditions, then it should have a cancelling effect and any difference between conditions that remains should (hopefully) be the result of your independent variable. We go into more specific details about randomization when discussing measures of control in each of the designs we discuss below. It is important to note that randomization is not mere coin-tossing. Many computer packages offer a "random-number" function, and some researchers still make use of "random-number" tables in order to achieve a desirable level of randomization.

Statistical analysis

Although random assignment tends to equalize error across groups, there is no absolute guarantee that it will completely get rid of all the error. Despite your best efforts to eliminate error, some will remain. How, then, can you determine whether an effect observed in your data was caused by your manipulation and not by error? Although you can never be sure, you can estimate the probability with which error alone would produce differences between groups at least as large as those actually observed. These statistical techniques will be covered in Chapters 16 to 19.

chs 16–19

Placebo control and double-blind experiments

A special case of control relates to the potential effects of expectations held by both participants and experimenters. "Demand characteristics" are one possible source of bias due to the expectations

Expectancy effects
When a researcher's preconceived ideas about how participants should behave are subtly communicated to participants and, in turn, affect the participants' behaviour.

Experimenter effects
When the behaviour of the researcher influences the results of a study (e.g. through expectancy effects or uneven treatment of participants across conditions).

that participants have when they come to take part in your study (**expectancy effects**). Demand characteristics refer to the cues and other information that participants use to guide their behaviour in a psychological study. Participants do not take part in a psychology study with complete naivety. They often have expectations and sometimes look for information that they think might be helpful for them. For example, research participants who know they have been given alcohol may have expectations about what they will experience, such as relaxation or giddiness. What might then happen is that these participants behave according to these expectations rather than in response to the effects of the alcohol per se.

Potential biases can also arise in experiments due to the expectations of the experimenters. The general term used to describe these biases is **experimenter effects**. Experimenter effects may pose a problem if the experimenters treat participants differently in the different groups of the experiment. If an experimenter treats groups differently, other than in ways that are required to implement the independent variable, then this would be a potential source of error. Experimenters sometimes have certain expectations about how participants should perform in each particular condition of the experiment. These expectations might lead the experimenter to treat the participants in such a way that influences them towards performing in a way that matches their expectation. This is not always a conscious act by the experimenter, but it is obviously undesirable, because, again, the only thing that we want to influence performance is the manipulation of the independent variable itself. If performance is influenced by the way the experimenter treats the participants, then this is a confounding variable. In an experiment involving alcohol, for instance, experimenter effects could occur if the experimenters read the instructions more slowly to participants who had been given alcohol than to those who had not. If this happens then we might not know if any observed effects are due to alcohol or due to "the speed at which the experimenter reads the instructions". Another way that experimenter effects can occur is if experimenters make biased observations when they know which treatment the participant has received. For example, biased observations due to experimenter effects might arise in the alcohol study if the experimenters were more likely to notice unusual motor movements or slurred speech among the "drinkers" (because they "expect" drinkers to behave this way).

Researchers can never eliminate the problems of demand characteristics and experimenter effects, but there are special research designs that control these problems. Researchers use a

Placebo control
A technique for reducing "expectancy effects" in which participants do not know whether they are given a "genuine" treatment or not.

placebo control group as one way to control demand characteristics. A placebo (from the Latin word meaning "I shall please") is a substance that looks like a drug or other active substance but is actually a completely inert, or inactive, substance. Some research even indicates that there can be therapeutic effects from the placebo itself. Pishkin and Shurley (1983) used a placebo control group to control for demand characteristics in an experiment testing the effectiveness of two drugs (doxepin and hydroxyzine). The drugs were tested to determine if they reduce arousal levels of psychiatric patients in response to stress. The placebo participants were given capsules identical to the two drugs, but the placebo capsules contained only lactose, a sugar found in milk. None of the participants in the placebo control group realized their pill contained no medicine so all groups had the same "awareness" of taking a drug, meaning that everybody in the study had similar expectations. In other words, the demand characteristics were similar for the groups – participants in both groups expected to experience the effects of a drug. Any differences between the experimental groups and the placebo control group could legitimately be attributed to the actual effect of the drug taken by the experimental participants, and not to what participants might expect from taking the drug.

The use of placebo control groups in combination with a double-blind procedure can control for both demand characteristics and experimenter effects. In a **double-blind procedure** both the participant and the observer are blind to (completely unaware of) what treatment is being administered. In an experiment such as the Pishkin and Shurley (1983) study, two researchers would be needed to accomplish the double-blind procedure. The first researcher would prepare the drug capsules, and code each capsule in some way; the second researcher would distribute the drugs to the participants, recording the code for each drug as it was given to an individual. This procedure ensures there is a record of which drug each person received, but neither the participant nor the experimenter who actually administers the drugs (and observes their effects) knows which treatment the participant received. This means that any expectations that the experimenter may have about the effects of the treatment are controlled because the researcher who makes the observations is unaware of who received the treatment and who received the placebo. Similarly, demand characteristics are controlled because participants remain unaware of whether they received the drug or placebo.

> **Double-blind procedure**
> A way of controlling for expectancy effects in both participants and observers in which all parties directly involved in the administration of treatments are unaware of who is receiving the placebo treatment and who is not.

Summary

This has been a short chapter that serves as a "gateway" for the next two chapters. In this chapter we introduced you to the basics of experimental methods, which are popular and powerful tools in psychological research. All experiments have some features in common. They have an independent variable that is manipulated by the experimenter, and a dependent variable which is measured. Experiments are conducted to test hypotheses. For an experiment to be valid, it must be well controlled. Only an experiment that has minimized error as much as possible can be considered informative. Reducing error can be done in a number of ways, including proper randomization techniques, placebo and double-blind controls, and maximizing the effectiveness of the independent variable. In the following two chapters, we will describe various types of experimental design that experimental researchers can adopt.

- Be able to recognize when a complex design is appropriate for a given research question
- Understand how "control" is achieved in all types of experimental design in order to reduce the effects of confounding variables
- State the main threats to validity in all designs discussed

Between-subjects designs

The first type of design we want to discuss is known by a few names. This is a bit annoying, as you may read about the same design with a different name in another textbook or hear it called something else in research methods classes. We will call it the "between-subjects" design, but just for reference here are some other names for it:

- between-groups design
- between-samples design
- independent samples
- independent groups design
- independent subjects design

Between-subjects design
An experimental design in which independent groups of participants take part in each condition.

A between-subjects[1] design is when you have an independent variable (sometimes known as a "factor") with two or more conditions (or "levels") and you test a *different* group of people (drawn from the same underlying population) in each of these conditions. So, in a study like this, you will have a sample of people who will take part in your experiment and you then assign each one of these people to one and *only* one of the conditions. In a **between-subjects design**, nobody can take part in any more than one condition. In other words, the samples that you test in each condition are independent of each other (hence the final three names for this design on the list above).

The imaginary (and increasingly tedious) study on whether exercise influences people's mood that we have mentioned more than a few times is an example of a between-subjects design. Let's see why.

As you can see in this study (Figure 7.1), each person takes part in only one condition. The two groups are independent of each other because of this. We get mood measures from everyone in each condition and then we see if there is a difference in mood between the participants in the groups (hence the name and why this design is sometimes called a "between-groups" design).

Between-subjects designs are as simple as that. Sometimes you will find that **the design has more than two conditions**, but the basic rule that any one participant can take part in only one

p.136

---

1   It's generally considered conventional to refer to humans taking part in psychology studies as "participants" while animals are referred to as "subjects". These conventions were adopted by the American Psychological Association (APA, 2001) but some psychologists have resisted them (see, e.g. Roediger, 2004). The British Psychological Society also recommends using the more respectful term "participants", but this usage hasn't yet become common when talking about research designs, where "between- or within-subjects" is still commonly used. We will use "subjects" when referring to designs (e.g. within-subjects) because that terminology is still widely employed. When we speak about people, we will adopt the term "participants". It's just another one of those things we have to get used to, but if you can, try to remember that whenever you see the word "subjects" used to describe a design, it really means "participants".

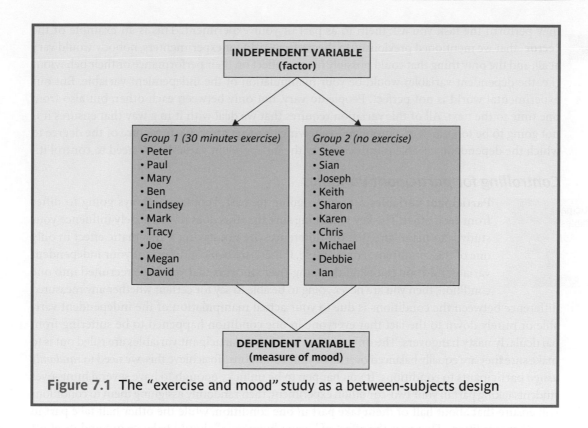

Figure 7.1 The "exercise and mood" study as a between-subjects design

condition during the course of the study holds true. There are some issues that we need to consider if we are to ensure that any conclusions about cause–effect relationships between the independent and dependent variables are as valid as possible.

Control in between-subjects designs

Like all experiments, between-subjects designs must be carefully controlled. There are two main issues when considering **control** in a between-subjects design. The first relates to participants.

> **Control**
> The act of reducing unwanted effects in an experiment by incorporating techniques that reduce them as much as possible.

Participant variables

In a between-subjects design, each participant gets assigned to one condition only. As we mentioned previously, all participants are different. Some will be shy and introverted; some will be outgoing and extroverted. Your participants will have had different experiences in their lives, and they will have had different experiences in the hours leading up to your experiment. Some might be coming to your study in a bad mood because of an argument they have had with their boyfriend, some might be coming to take part after having just been offered a new job. Some might be hung over from a wild night in the student union; some might be wide awake after several strong coffees. In short, there are many different things that make the people who you get to take part in your study different. All of these things could potentially influence the way

ch. 6
p.106

they perform the task you ask them to as part of your experiment. This is an example of the "**error**" that we mentioned previously. In the perfect world for experimenters, nobody would vary at all, and the only thing that could possibly have an effect on their performance or their behaviour (i.e. the dependent variable) would be your manipulation of the independent variable. But our experimental world is not perfect. People do vary, not only between each other, but also from one time to the next. All of this variation requires that we deal with it in a way that ensures it is not going to be too much of a problem in allowing us to get an accurate picture of the degree to which the dependent variable is influenced by the independent variable. We need to control it.

Controlling for participant variables

Participant variables
The natural ways in which participants in experiments differ from each other.

Participant variables are always going to exist. People are always going to differ from each other. The key to making sure that this does not adversely influence your study is to make sure that the differences are not having a systematic effect in only one of the conditions. For example, if there are two conditions of your independent variable and you put all of the hung-over students that you have recruited into one condition, then you are never going to be able to say for certain whether any measured difference between the conditions is due to your actual manipulation of the independent variable or purely down to the fact that everyone in one condition happened to be suffering from particularly nasty hangovers. The only way to ensure that participant variables are ruled out is to make sure they are equally balanced over all of your conditions. To achieve this, we need to *randomly assign* participants to conditions. If you happen to be unlucky enough to have several hung-over students taking part in your two-condition experiment, then randomly assigning them to conditions will ensure that about half of them take part in one condition, while the other half take part in the other condition. That way, the effect of "being hung over" should balance out and its effect will be cancelled out over the two conditions, meaning that any remaining difference between the two groups should be purely a consequence of your manipulation of the independent variable.

Random assignment will prevent any systematic biases, which are the enemy of the experimenter. If you randomly assign participants to conditions, then the groups will be equivalent in terms of participant variables such as income, intelligence, age or political attitudes. In this way, participant variables cannot be an explanation for the results.

Holding conditions constant

If you have two conditions in your study, with independent groups taking part in each condition, then it is essential that the *only* factor that differs between the two conditions is the independent variable. Apart from this, there should be nothing else that differs in the experience of the people in each group. By ensuring that conditions are constant in every way except the ways relating to the independent variable, then you are increasing your ability to state that the cause of any observed effect is due to your manipulation of that independent variable. That may sound complicated, but the logic behind it is straightforward. If there are other things that differ between the two conditions, then how would you know whether your measure of the dependent variable is due to your manipulation of the independent variable or whether it is due to one of these "other things"? By making sure that as little as possible varies except what you actually want to vary, then you can rule out any potential "confounds". This is sometimes more difficult than it might seem, as we will see below.

An imaginary study on the effects of exercise on mood

For any readers who have not yet encountered this **example**, this is a study that is designed to investigate whether taking part in exercise can influence current mood. Imagine that you are conducting this study as part of your psychology course and see how this experiment might be conducted. We will consider some issues relating to it below.

ch. 6
p.104

Box 7.1 Exercise and mood – doing the study using a between-subjects design

Experimental (alternative) hypothesis: Participants taking part in 30 minutes of exercise will show an improvement in mood compared to participants who take part in 30 minutes of non-strenuous activity.

In this experiment, there are two conditions of the independent variable (exercise versus no exercise) and you need to get two independent groups to take part in each condition. That is, each person who takes part in your study will be assigned to one and only one of the conditions. They will either do exercise for 30 minutes or they will not. All participants' mood will be measured after a 30-minute period of either exercising or not exercising.

Obviously, as the researcher, you are going to have to make a decision about which participants get allocated to which group. It is sometimes tempting to allocate people on the basis of what is convenient. For example, say you have a friend who works in a leisure centre and she tells you that you can have access to the gym for an hour before it opens the following Sunday. This gives you an opportunity to collect all of the data for the "exercise" group in one day. You decide that you are going to get 20 people to take part in this condition. How do you find these 20 people? You decide that you should put posters up around the gym advertising your study and asking for anyone who is willing to participate to sign up at the reception desk and to come along at 9 a.m. the following Sunday. When Sunday comes, you are thrilled to discover that there are 20 people waiting for you who are all keen to participate. You lead them into the gym and give each participant 10 minutes on an exercise bike, 10 minutes on a treadmill and 10 minutes on a rowing machine. After the 30 minutes of exercise are complete, you then administer the scale of "current mood". You collect the questionnaires and thank your participants for taking part. Job done! You now have data for the "30 minutes exercise" condition.

Now all you need to find so you can complete your data collection is a group to take part in the "no exercise" condition. You no longer need the gym, so you decide to book a tutorial room in your university for a couple of hours. You find that Friday morning is the only time available, so you book the room. Friday morning arrives and you realize that you have not got any participants yet, so you decide to see if you can find anyone in the student union bar. Luckily, you manage to get 20 people to agree to give up half an hour of their time. You take them to the classroom you have booked and give them three tasks to do. For 10 minutes they do a word-search puzzle. For another 10 minutes they read a magazine article about wildlife. For the final 10 minutes they play a simple computer game. You then give them the same "current mood" questionnaire as you gave the participants in the "exercise" condition, before thanking them for their time and sending them on their way. You now have data for both conditions.

Participant variables in the exercise/mood experiment

> ## STOP & Think
>
> Before continuing, try to figure out what "participant variables" may be a source of error in the study described above. Think about the ways in which these participant variables might have influenced the outcome of the experiment.

So, what might be wrong with the way the above study was conducted? Well, the main consideration is that participants were *not* randomly allocated to conditions. Participants were recruited for the "exercise" condition by putting up posters in the leisure centre, while participants for the "no exercise" condition were recruited in the student union bar. Think about all the ways in which these two groups of people might differ. On the whole, the people recruited from the leisure centre are likely to belong to a different demographic profile than the group of students. They might differ in age and income. There might be more people with families in the leisure-centre group. The lifestyles of the two groups are also likely to differ. Perhaps the group recruited from the leisure centre are generally more health-conscious than the students. Additionally, people who actively respond to a poster by signing up to take part and then turning up on a Sunday morning might be different in terms of motivation (and in many other ways) to students who agreed to take part after being asked spontaneously by the researcher.

Does all of this matter? Yes, it does. If you did find that the "30 minutes exercise" group had generally higher scores of "current mood", then you need to consider whether this is a result of the exercise itself or something else. Given that the two groups are likely to differ in many ways, it is entirely possible that the differences between them might be the cause of any observed differences in "current mood" that you find. It might not be the exercise that you ask one group to do that makes this group appear to have a more positive mood. They might just be more positive as a group anyway. Likewise, by allocating all the students to the "no exercise" group, you might find the "current mood" levels of students who are in the student union bar on a Friday morning to be somewhat lower than those of the group that volunteered to do exercise for 30 minutes on a Sunday. These participant variables that are influencing your dependent variable have got nothing to do with your independent variable (i.e. exercise/no exercise). As such, any observed differences cannot be said to be due to your manipulation, which would mean that your study is not valid. If you had randomly assigned participants to the conditions, then you would have got an evenly balanced mix of people taking part in each condition. By doing this, any participant variables would not be having an effect in only one condition.

A short note on sampling

We cover sampling later in Chapter 9, but at this point we should point out that the way the participants were recruited in the study above would only have added to the bias. If you sample in this way, then you should expect that the people whom you recruit will have participant variables related to the non-random way in which they were selected. A **random sample** that does not consist of one or two distinct "types" is the best way to select participants.

ch. 9
p.163

Controlling conditions in the mood/exercise experiment

What else might be a source of error in this study? Consider the conditions. We have an experimental condition in which participants are asked to take part in 30 minutes of exercise, and we have a control condition in which they are not. Our aim is to see whether exercise can influence "current mood". Think, for a moment, about the control condition. What do you get the people in this condition to do? The perfect version of this experiment would get them to do something for 30 minutes that was not going to influence their mood in any way at all. If we could do that, then we could compare the "uninfluenced" control group with the "influenced" (through exercise) experimental group. But is this realistic? We have to give them *something* to do during the 30-minute period. If we had them sitting in a room doing absolutely nothing, then it's likely that they would become bored, which in itself would influence their mood. In the example above, they are given three tasks to do for 10 minutes each. Is it possible to find a task that is definitely not going to influence mood in some way? Probably not. Word searches might frustrate participants who were not good at them, or excite ones who particularly enjoyed word games. Reading a magazine article on wildlife might have an emotional effect that could influence mood. Playing a simple computer game might not be fun for everyone. All of these things might influence the measure of mood that you take at the end of the 30-minute period. This is unfortunate, as you ideally would prefer it if the mood of this group were completely uninfluenced by anything, allowing you to get as "pure" a measure as possible of the effect of exercise in the experimental group.

So what can we do? In general, we need to think in advance about what the two conditions consist of and we need to try to make them as similar as possible, with the sole exception of the manipulation that you are interested in. In the mood/exercise study, this is very difficult as we have to give the no exercise group something to do. The only way around this is to choose the tasks you give this group very carefully. Do not have the "no exercise" group do anything that is likely to influence everyone's mood in the same way. It would be a bad idea, for example, to show them a harrowing film about death. Likewise, it would be bad to play them uplifting music. These are things that are likely to affect all of the participants' mood in similar ways. If you choose neutral tasks that are likely to affect people in different ways, then you are minimizing the bias as much as is possible.

In the Know

The logic of the experimental method and the application of control techniques that produce internal validity can be illustrated in an experiment investigating eyewitness behaviour, which was conducted by Loftus and Burns (1982). Participants in their experiment viewed a film that contained a violent scene. Loftus and Burns were investigating the effect of witnessing a mentally shocking event on the participants' memory for information that was presented in the film seconds before the violent scene. The experiment was done at the University of Washington. The 226 students who volunteered to participate were tested in small groups, and each small group was randomly assigned to view one of two films. Approximately half of the students (115) were assigned to view a violent version of a film. Near the end of the film, these students saw a robber, while running to a getaway car, turn and fire a shot towards two men who were pursuing him. The shot hit a boy in the face, and the boy fell bleeding to the ground. The other half of the students viewed a non-violent version of the film that was identical to the violent version until just before the shooting. At this point in the film, the camera switched back to inside the bank, where the students saw the bank manager telling the customers and employees what happened and asking them to remain calm. The violent and non-violent versions of the film represent the two levels of the independent variable that was manipulated in the experiment.

After viewing the film, students in both groups answered 25 questions about events in the film. One question was critical: it asked for the number on the football top worn by a boy playing in the parking lot outside the bank. The boy wearing the football top (see Figure 7.2) was visible for 2 seconds during the film – the 2 seconds before the shooting (violent version) or the 2 seconds before the scenes back in the bank (non-violent version). The dependent variable was the students' response to the question about the number on the back of the top. The version of the film participants saw did affect their recall. Just over 4 per cent of the students correctly recalled the number in the violent condition, whereas nearly 28 per cent did so in the non-violent condition. Thus, Loftus and Burns concluded that a mentally shocking event can impair memory for details immediately preceding the event.

Figure 7.2 Black and white representation of scene viewed by students, showing boy with the number 17 on his football top
Source: Loftus and Burns (1982).

Control in action: eyewitness memory

Have a look at the "In the Know" box above. How did Loftus and Burns (1982) incorporate elements of control in their study? In their experiment, several factors that could have affected the participants' memory were kept the same across the two conditions. The students viewed exactly the *same* film except for the critical incident, they were given the *same* experimental instructions at the beginning of the experiment and received the exact *same* questionnaire at the end.

This is a good example of how researchers hold conditions constant to make sure that the independent variable is the only thing that differs systematically across the groups. If the two groups had differed on a factor other than the film manipulation, then it would have been impossible to interpret the results. For example, if the participants in the violent version had viewed a film depicting a boy in the background wearing a *different* top than that seen in the non-violent version, then we would not know whether the difference in recall was due to viewing the violent version of the film or due to the fact that the top was different (e.g. one of the tops might have been generally less distinct, with a smaller or less noticeable number). By holding constant the boy playing in the background and the football top (among other things) in the two versions of the film, Loftus and Burns avoided any potential confounds resulting from differences between the two conditions. If we hold a factor constant in all conditions of our study, then there is no way that this can then be said to be the cause of our observed effect. Loftus and Burns knew that the difference in memory that they found for the number on the back of the football top was not anything to do with the top itself, because that was constant in both conditions.

It is important to recognize, however, that we choose to control only those factors we think might influence the behaviour we are studying – what we consider plausible alternative causes. For instance, Loftus and Burns held the setting constant by testing all their participants in the same room, but it is unlikely they specifically controlled the room temperature to be constant between groups because room temperature probably would not affect memory (at least when varying only a few degrees). They also tested students in "small groups," but there was no apparent attempt to hold constant the size of the group. Again, it doesn't seem plausible that small variations in the size of groups watching the film would have a substantial effect on recall. The point is that we control only those factors we believe are potentially relevant – that is, those additional factors that might affect the behaviour of interest. Nevertheless, we should constantly remain alert to the possibility that there may be **confounding** factors in our experiments whose influence we had not anticipated or considered.

> **Confounding**
> Occurs when the independent variable of interest systematically covaries with a second, unintended independent variable.

Matched-groups designs

In some cases, you know or suspect that there are certain subject characteristics that are likely to be sources of error. You might know in advance that certain factors are linked to your measurement of the dependent variable. For example, participants often differ considerably in their reaction times to simple stimuli. Some people have naturally fast reaction times, and some people have naturally slow reaction times. If you are studying the effect of stimulus complexity on reaction time, this large inherent variation in reaction time that is already present in your participants could pose a problem by creating large amounts of error, which could swamp any effect of stimulus complexity. You could randomize the way in which you allocate people to conditions, as suggested previously, but another way to deal with this issue is to use a matched-groups design.

A **matched-groups design** is one in which you match sets of participants on some feature that you think is important. Once matched, they are then distributed at random, *one per group*, into the groups of the experiment. Figure 7.3 illustrates this process. You begin by obtaining a sample of participants (group at the top of

> **Matched-groups design**
> A between-groups design in which participants in each group are matched on a variable that is thought to correlate with the dependent variable.

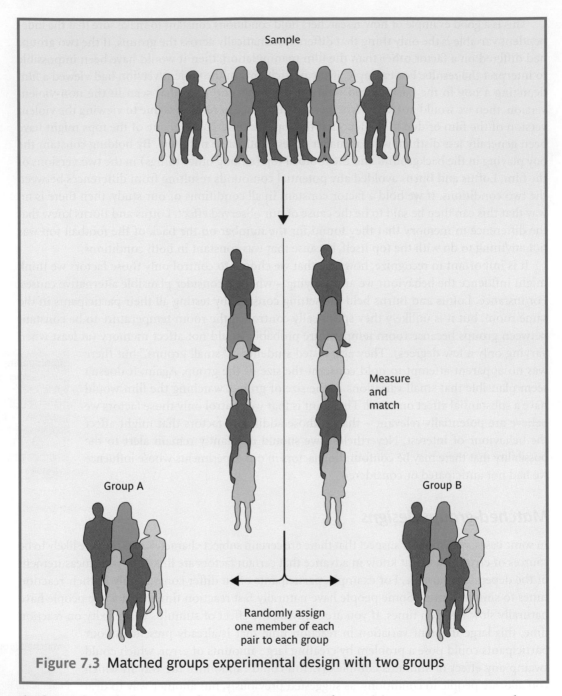

Figure 7.3 Matched groups experimental design with two groups

the figure) from the larger population. Next, you assess the participants on one or more characteristics that you believe exert an influence on the dependent measure and then group the ones whose characteristics match. In a reaction-time experiment, for example, participants could be pre-tested for their simple reaction times and then grouped into pairs whose reaction times were similar. These pairs of participants are shown in the middle portion of Figure 7.3.

Once you have matched your pairs, you then distribute them randomly across the experimental groups. In the reaction-time experiment, for example, one participant of each pair is randomly assigned to one of the treatments (perhaps to a high-stimulus-complexity condition); the other participant then automatically goes into the other treatment (in this case, a low-stimulus-complexity condition). This assignment to treatments is shown at the bottom of Figure 7.3. Doing this ensures that you have equal numbers of naturally fast (on reaction time measures) and naturally slow people in each of the conditions.

From here on, you conduct the experiment as in any other randomized between-subjects design. You expose your participants to their respective levels of the independent variable and record the resulting data. Then you compare the data from the different groups to determine the effect of the independent variable.

Logic of the matched-groups design

Because each of the matched participants goes into a different group, the effect of the characteristic on which the participants were matched gets distributed evenly across the treatments. As a result, this characteristic contributes little to the differences between the groups. The error contributed by this characteristic has, therefore, been minimized. This makes it more likely that any effect of the independent variable will be detected.

Advantages and disadvantages of the matched-groups design

The advantage of matching over random assignment is that it allows you to control subject variables that may otherwise obscure the effect of the independent variable under investigation. Randomization should balance these features out, but there is a chance that there will be an imbalance between the experimental conditions. If you already know that a particular participant variable is likely to have an influence, then matching ensures the balance between groups rather than leaving it to the randomization process. Where such variables exist, matching can increase the experiment's sensitivity to the effect of the independent variable (if such an effect is present). This is a big advantage. You may be able to discover effects that you would otherwise miss. Additionally, you may be able to demonstrate a given effect with fewer participants, thus saving time and money. However, using a matched design is not without risks and disadvantages.

One risk involved in using a matched design concerns what happens if the matched characteristic does *not* have the effect on the dependent variable that you initially thought it might. Matched designs require you to use somewhat modified versions of the statistics you would use in an unmatched, completely randomized design. These statistics for matched groups are somewhat less powerful than their unmatched equivalents. This means that they are less able to discriminate any effect of the independent variable from the effect of uncontrolled, extraneous variables.

If the matched characteristic has a large effect on the dependent variable, eliminating this effect from group differences will more than compensate for the reduced sensitivity of the statistic, resulting in a more sensitive experiment. However (and this is an important "however"), if the matched characteristic has little or no effect on the dependent variable, then matching will do no good. Worse, the loss of statistical power will result in a reduced ability to detect the effect of the independent variable, meaning that you might conclude that the independent variable has no effect at all *when it actually does*. For this reason, you should use matching only when you have good reason to believe that the matched variable has a relatively strong effect on the dependent measure. When using a matched design, you also must be sure that the instrument used to determine the match is valid and reliable. If you want to match on IQ, for example, be sure that the test you use to measure IQ is valid and reliable. Of course, for some characteristics, such as race, age or sex, this is usually not a problem.

Analysis of between-subjects experiments

One question that you may have asked yourself while reading about between-subjects designs is "how do we know whether or not our manipulation of the independent variable has been successful?" Unfortunately it is not enough to merely look at the scores obtained by each group and decide on the basis of this. We must employ a statistical analysis that will allow us to say with a certain degree of confidence whether any differences between the groups were significant (and thus probably due to a real causal effect of our manipulation) or non-significant (and thus probably due to random fluctuation that does not suggest the independent variable has had an influence). We cover statistical analysis for between-subjects designs like the ones we have just described in **Chapter 16**.

ch. 16

Summary of between-subjects designs

1 Each participant takes part in *only one* condition.
2 Randomization of participants to conditions can reduce error due to participant variables.
3 Holding conditions constant means that the experience is as similar as possible in each condition apart from the manipulation of the independent variable. This also reduces error.
4 If you know which participant variables might have an influence, you can eliminate their effect by using a "matched-pairs" design.

Test yourself

Fill in the blanks in the following statements, choosing from the words below each.[2]

1 A between-subjects design is one in which the _____ variable has two or more _____. The _____ variable is measured in each condition, using _____ groups. A defining feature of a between-subjects design is that each participant takes part in _____ of the conditions.

conditions; independent; different; one; dependent

2 Participant variables are a source of _____. They could potentially be a _____ factor, having an influence on your _____ variable that has nothing to do with your _____ variable. One way of dealing with participant variables is to make sure that participants are _____ assigned to _____.

conditions; confounding; dependent; independent; error; randomly

Within-subjects designs

The second major design that we want to cover is known as a *within-subjects* design. Again, it is known by several names, including:

- within-subjects design
- within-groups design
- related design
- related samples design
- repeated measures design
- paired samples design

In the between-subjects design that we introduced in the previous section, we randomly assign participants to the conditions of the independent variable. Each person can be exposed to only one of the conditions. We then measure the dependent variable and see whether participants in each group differ from each other. In a **within-subjects design**, each participant takes part in *all* conditions (see Figure 7.4). If your independent variable has two levels, then every person in your study will be measured in each of them. It's called "within-subjects" because it involves looking at the changes in performance *within* each participant across the conditions of the independent variable. It is also widely known as a "repeated measures" design because you are repeating your measurement(s) of the dependent variable in multiple conditions using the same participants.

> **Within-subjects design**
> An experimental design in which each participant takes part in *all* conditions of the independent variable.

Two ways to conduct a within-subjects design

1 The first way is to test people on different occasions. Conducting the experiment in this way involves getting each person to take part in one of the conditions (during which you measure their behaviour or some other psychological phenomenon) and then you send them away. Then, after a period of time (which can vary from hours to weeks, and sometimes months), you invite them back to take part in another condition, during which you measure the dependent variable again. How many times you get them to come back will obviously depend upon how many conditions there are in your study.

2 The other way of conducting a within-subjects design is to have each participant take part in a number of "trials" in one session. A "trial" is usually something simple, like getting the participant to rate a face for attractiveness. However, not all of these trials will be of the same type. Each individual trial will belong to one of the conditions of the independent variable. So, you might be testing the hypothesis that "famous" faces are seen to be more attractive than "non-famous" faces. Participants might rate 50 faces for attractiveness in the space of one 30-minute session. However, half of those faces will be famous and half will not. Thus, the participant has taken part in *both* conditions of the independent variable (i.e. she has rated both famous *and* non-famous faces for attractiveness) but has done so in one experimental session. This is a way of conducting a within-subjects design that does not require participants to come back on separate occasions, although not every within-subjects design can be conducted in this way.

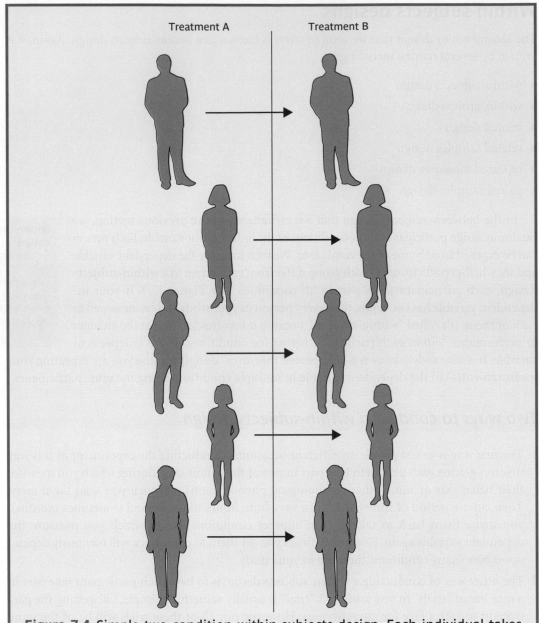

Figure 7.4 Simple two-condition within-subjects design. Each individual takes part in both conditions

Advantages of the within-subjects design

p.115 **Earlier in this chapter,** we noted that scores within a group can differ for reasons which have nothing to do with your independent variable. These differences arise from the effects of other things, which might include the naturally occurring differences between the participants (such as their personality, intelligence, socio-economic status etc.) as well as momentary fluctuations that change each subject's performance from moment to moment (e.g. hangovers or their experiences in the immediate period leading up to them taking part in your experiment). We called this "error". Such error can be a serious problem because it may mask any effects of your independent variable. One of the strategies that we suggested for dealing with error was "matching". We suggested that matching can help reduce this important source of error. If we know the characteristics that are likely to be important, then we can carefully make sure that there are equal numbers of participants with those characteristics in each of the conditions of the independent variable. In other words, we "match" the participants in each of the groups.

The within-subjects design pushes the logic of matching to the limit. If you think about it, the best "match" for someone is themselves. A within-subjects design means that you do not need to worry about the differences between the people in condition A and the people in condition B, because it is the *same* participants who will take part in each condition. What this means is that all participant-related factors (such as age, weight, IQ, personality, religion and gender) are literally identical across treatments (because it is the same person who is taking part in the conditions). Any differences that we end up finding between the conditions of the independent variable cannot be due to error arising from such differences, as might have been the case in the between-subjects design. Because of this reduction in error, the within-subjects design is more powerful, which means that it is more sensitive in detecting the causal effect of your manipulation of the independent variable. As a within-subjects design reduces error then this is a big benefit of using them.

A second benefit of this increased power is that you can use fewer participants in your experiment. For example, a between-subjects design that had two conditions and required 20 participants per treatment would require 40 people. The equivalent within-subjects experiment would require only 20 participants, taking part in *each* condition, representing significant savings in time, materials and money.

Confounds in within-subjects designs

Within-subjects designs are not perfect, however. Although the within-subjects design has its advantages, it also has some important disadvantages, which may prevent its use in certain situations. One disadvantage is that a within-subjects design is more demanding on participants because each participant must be exposed to every level of the independent variable. A complex design involving, for example, nine conditions would require a great deal of time to complete. It may be difficult to find people willing to take part in such an experiment. Those who do take part may become bored or fatigued after being in an experiment that might be several hours long. You can get around the problem of fatigue and boredom by administering only one or two treatments per session, spreading sessions out over some period of time. However, if you take this approach, you may lose some participants from the experiment because they fail to show up for one or more sessions.

Practice effects

A second and potentially more serious problem with the within-subjects design is its ability to produce "**practice effects**" (sometimes called "order effects" or "carryover effects"). Practice effects occur when a previous condition that a participant has taken

Practice effect
The influence taking part in one condition has on subsequent performance in other conditions.

part in alters their behaviour in a subsequent condition. Taking part in the first condition can some-times change the participant, and those changes carry over into the other conditions, influencing behaviour. This upsets the "perfect match" of participant characteristics that the within-subjects design is supposed to provide, because by the time the participant comes to take part in subsequent conditions, they already have experience of the previous ones. As such, they are not going into the later conditions with exactly the same mindset as they started out with.

In what ways might practice effects influence participants? If you have an experiment in which participants are required to attend and participate on two occasions, then once they have taken part in the first condition of your study, they may draw on their experience of this first testing session when they return to take part in the later one(s). Here is an example: imagine volunteering to take part in a psychology study and turning up to be tested. How would you feel? You might be a little nervous. You might feel apprehensive. You might not know what to expect and this could cause you to be anxious. You might wonder what happens in a psychology experiment? Are you going to be psychoanalysed? Will they put electrodes on your head? All of these things could potentially influence how you behave and how you perform on any tasks that the researcher asks you to do. However, if it is a within-subjects experiment in which you are asked back for a second time, then it is likely that you would be a little bit more at ease when you arrive to take part in the second condition. You might have a clearer idea about what to expect. You realize that nothing bad will happen to you. After all, you have already done it once before. Being comfortable with the situation could again influence your performance. In addition to that, you have already done the task once. You know what to do. You have had practice. Practising a task inevitably changes how you do that task in the future, so when you turn up to take part in the second condition, you might benefit from the effects of having done the task previously.

If you have a within-subjects experiment in which participants experience all conditions in one session, practice effects can also have an influence if you present all of the items or trials from one condition, followed by all of the items or trials from a second condition – for example, if you have a very simple reaction-time study, and you are looking at whether people react faster to red or blue dots on a screen (yes, this is another imaginary study, but it is quick and easy to under-stand). So you set up your study as a within-subjects design, meaning that every participant will be asked to respond to both red dots and blue dots (i.e. they will take part in both conditions of the independent variable). You then sit the participant down in front of a computer monitor and present 20 red dots, asking the participant to respond as quickly as they can when one appears. After the 20 red dots you present 20 blue dots. When you look at your results you find that people seemed to be responding more quickly to the blue dots. Does this mean anything significant? Probably not. By the time the blue dots were presented, the participant had got to know the task, had become comfortable and was probably more confident. Thus, it is likely that the faster reaction times are not due to the colour of the dots, but to the effects of practice. The participant would probably have got faster reaction times during the later trials if the dots were all the same colour, purely because he was getting better at the task through practice alone.

The mood/exercise experiment as a within-subjects design

It is possible to conduct our exercise/mood study as a within-subjects design. When we de-scribed it in the previous section, we employed a between-subjects design in which two *different* groups of people took part in each condition (either exercise or no exercise). To do this study using a within-groups design, we would find one group of people and test them all in each condition. That is, we would test people's moods in one condition and then ask them to return a second time to take part in the second condition, at which point we would test their moods again.

Box 7.2 Exercise and mood – doing the study using a within-subjects design

Experimental hypothesis: Taking part in 30 minutes of exercise will improve participants' current mood compared to taking part in 30 minutes of non-strenuous activity.

In this experiment, there are two conditions of the independent variable (exercise versus no exercise). To conduct the study using a within-subjects design, you need to recruit participants and test them in *both* conditions (Figure 7.5).

You manage to recruit 10 willing volunteers who agree to be tested on two separate occasions. You have a friend who works in a leisure centre and she tells you that you can have access to the gym for an hour before it opens the following Friday. This gives you an opportunity to collect all the data for the "exercise" condition in one day.

Rather than wait until then, you think it would be a worthwhile use of your time to collect the "no exercise" data as soon as possible, so you book a room in your university and ask your 10 volunteers to take part in that condition first. You take them to the classroom you have booked and give them three tasks to do. For 10 minutes they do a word-search puzzle. For another 10 minutes they read a magazine article about wildlife. For the final 10 minutes they play a simple computer game. You then give them a "current mood" questionnaire before thanking them for their time and sending them on their way, reminding them that it would be very helpful if they could turn up at the leisure centre the following week to take part in the second part of the study.

When Friday comes, you are thrilled to discover that all 10 participants have remembered, and are keen to participate. You lead them into the gym and give each participant 10 minutes on an exercise bike, 10 minutes on a treadmill and 10 minutes on a rowing machine. After the 30 minutes of exercise are complete, you then administer the scale of "current mood". You collect the questionnaires and thank your participants for taking part. Job done! You now have data for the "30 minutes exercise" condition as well as the "no exercise" data you collected the previous week.

STOP & Think

Before continuing, try to figure out what "extraneous variables" might be a source of error in the above study. Think about the way that the experiment has been conducted and whether there are any factors that might have been better controlled.

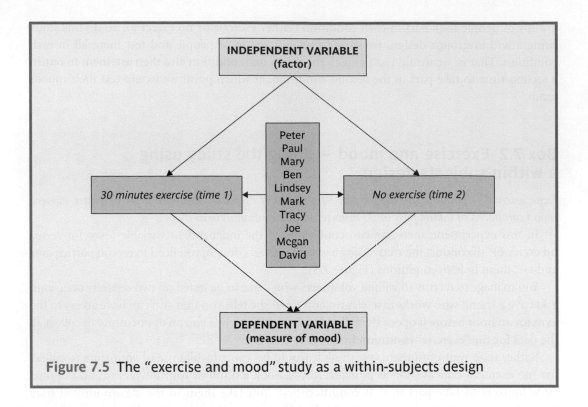

Figure 7.5 The "exercise and mood" study as a within-subjects design

Confounds in the exercise/mood experiment

It is important to note that the idea of "practice" effects does not always equate to the everyday meaning of the word "practice". Sometimes it refers to the general effect that doing something more than once has. If we are to conduct our exercise/mood study as a within-subjects design, then there are potential practice effects due to the fact that we are testing the same participants on the same dependent variable on two different occasions. In this study, we have to be very careful to look out for things that might influence "mood". As we mentioned above, taking part in a psychology study might be stressful, especially if you do not know what to expect. This might influence mood.

In the exercise/mood study described above, all participants were tested in the "no exercise" condition first, before being tested in the "exercise" condition a week later. It is possible that the participants were more at ease on the second occasion. Having already taken part in the first part of the experiment, they may have been less apprehensive and felt more comfortable with the task. This might have resulted in them being in a better mood on the second occasion. Likewise, turning up for the first time without fully knowing what to expect may have had a negative effect on their mood. If this was indeed the case, then any differences observed between the two conditions may not have been a direct result of the independent variable, but may instead have been due to the fact that they all took part in the conditions in the same order. In setting up the experiment in this way, it becomes difficult to establish whether or not it was the exercise compared to no exercise that was influencing mood. One way to think about this is as follows. Imagine you did not do anything different to the participants on each occasion you tested them. Imagine that they merely turned up, filled in a questionnaire and then went away again. Then, a week later, they did exactly the same thing. It is possible that their scores on the second occasion would be different, purely because they have the experience of having participated previously. That is a "practice effect" and is considered a confounding variable because it is something that can influence your dependent variable that is not your independent variable.

The problem of practice in within-subjects designs has received plenty of attention from researchers, who have developed strategies to deal with it. The next section identifies potential sources of practice. After that, we describe several design options that can help you deal with potential practice effects.

Sources of practice effects

Practice effects can arise from a number of sources, including the following:

1 *Learning*. If a subject learns how to perform a task in the first condition, performance is likely to be better if the same or similar tasks are used in subsequent conditions.

2 *Fatigue*. If performance in earlier conditions leads to fatigue, then performance in later conditions may deteriorate, regardless of any effect of the independent variable. For example, if measuring your dependent variable involves having participants squeeze against a strong spring device to determine their strength of grip, the participants are likely to tire if repeated testing takes place over a short period of time.

3 *Habituation*. Under some conditions, repeated exposure to a stimulus leads to reduced responsiveness to that stimulus because the stimulus is becoming more familiar or expected. This reduction is known as habituation. Your participants may jump the first time you surprise them with a sudden loud noise, but they may not do so after repeated presentations of the noise.

4 *Sensitization*. Sometimes exposure to one stimulus can cause people to respond more strongly to another stimulus. In a phenomenon called potentiated startle, for example, a rat will show an exaggerated startle response to a sudden noise if the rat has recently received a brief foot shock in the same situation.

5 *Contrast*. Because of contrast, exposure to one condition may alter the responses of participants in other conditions. If you pay your participants a relatively large amount for successful performance on one task and then pay them less (or make them work harder for the same amount) in a subsequent task, they may feel underpaid. Consequently, they may work less than they otherwise might have. This change occurs because participants can compare (contrast) the treatments.

6 *Adaptation*. If participants go through a period of adaptation (e.g. becoming adjusted to the dark), then earlier results may differ from later results because of the adaptive changes. Adaptive changes may increase responsiveness to a stimulus (e.g. sight gradually improves while you sit in a darkened theatre) or decrease responsiveness (e.g. you readjust to the light as you leave the theatre). Adaptation to a drug schedule is a common example. If adaptation to the drug causes a reduced response, the change is called tolerance.

Dealing with practice effects

It should be obvious that we want to minimize practice effects as much as possible. They are confounding variables and reduce our ability to draw conclusions from our experiments. One of the simplest and most effective ways to handle this potential confound is to make sure that the effects of practice are balanced out over all conditions. This will have a cancelling effect and there should be no consistent effect in only one condition.

p. 128

This can be achieved in a couple of ways. **In the simple reaction-time experiment described previously** (in which we present 20 red and 20 blue dots to participants) the simplest thing to do would be to randomize the order in which the dots are presented. By doing this, we can be sure that there will be an equal number of red and blue dots presented to the participant in the first half of the session (when reaction times might be slow) and in the second half (when reaction times start to get better). That is an improvement on our earlier design in which all the red dots were presented at the start and all the blue dots at the end. By randomizing the order that they are presented in, no one condition (red or blue) benefits more than the other from the effects of practice. The practice effect has been balanced in both conditions and thus cannot have a consistent influence in one condition only.

You can also deal with practice effects in three other ways. You can (1) use counterbalancing to even out practice effects across conditions, (2) take steps to minimize practice, and (3) separate practice effects from treatment effects by making the order of testing an independent variable in itself.

Counterbalancing
A technique that orders the levels of an extraneous variable so that their effects balance out over the different levels of the independent variable.

Counterbalancing. In **counterbalancing** you assign the various treatments of the experiment in a different order for different participants. This is the most straightforward way to deal with the problem of practice effects, especially for those conditions in which participants are returning on more than one occasion. Once again, the goal is to distribute any practice effect equally across conditions so that it does not produce differences in the average scores that could be mistaken for an effect of the independent variable. Two counterbalancing options are complete counterbalancing and partial counterbalancing.

1   Complete counterbalancing provides every possible ordering of treatments and assigns at least one participant to each ordering. If you have two conditions (A and B) then you need to make sure that half the participants take part in condition A followed by condition B and half the participants take part in condition B followed by condition A. This is known as an ABBA design (for obvious reasons). Any practice effect manifesting itself in condition B which is a result of taking part in condition A first is immediately balanced out by reversing the order of testing for the remaining participants, who take part in condition B followed by A. In doing so, half of the participants will show practice effects in condition B and half will show them in condition A, leading to a cancellation of the overall effect. Complete counterbalancing is practical for experiments with a small number of conditions, but it becomes a bit trickier as the number of conditions gets larger. For an experiment using only four conditions, there are 24 possible orders that the four conditions can be done in, which would require at least 24 participants to complete the counterbalancing.

2   Partial counterbalancing includes only some of the possible orders. The orders to be used in the experiment are chosen randomly from the total set with the restriction that each condition appears equally often in each position. Table 7.1 displays all 24 possible orders for a four-treatment experiment, followed by a subset of eight randomly selected orders that meet this criterion.

Table 7.1 Twenty-four possible treatment orders for a four-treatment within-subjects design and a randomly selected subset in which each treatment appears equally often in each position

Entire set of orders for four conditions	Randomly selected subset
1 ABCD	1 DABC
2 ABDC	2 ABCD
3 ACBD	3 CDAB
4 ACDB	4 BCDA
5 ADBC	5 DCBA
6 ADCB	6 ADCB
7 BACD	7 BADC
8 BADC	8 CBAD
9 BCAD	
10 BCDA	
11 BDAC	
12 BDCA	
13 CABD	
14 CADB	
15 CBAD	
16 CBDA	
17 CDAB	
18 CDBA	
19 DABC	
20 DACB	
21 DBAC	
22 DBCA	
23 DCAB	
24 DCBA	

When you use partial counterbalancing, you assume that randomly chosen orders will randomly distribute practice effects among the conditions.

A further way to achieve balancing is to use a technique known as a *Latin square*. In a Latin square, each condition appears at each ordinal position once. In Table 7.2, you can see that each condition is represented as the first condition on one occasion, the second condition on one occasion, the third condition on one occasion and the fourth condition on one occasion. Additionally, in a Latin square, each condition precedes and follows each other condition at least once. So, the order "BA" appears once, as does the order "AB". The order "AC" appears once, as does the order "CA", and so on for every combination of conditions.

Table 7.2 Latin square

Ordinal position			
1st	2nd	3rd	4th
B	A	C	D
A	D	B	C
D	C	A	B
C	B	D	A

PRACTICE

Taking steps to minimize practice. The second way to deal with practice effects is to try to minimize or eliminate them. Not all sources of practice can be minimized. For example, permanent changes produced by learning inevitably carry over into subsequent conditions and affect behaviour. There is no way of magically wiping your participants' prior experience and returning them to the state they were in prior to taking part in the first condition. However, if you are not interested in the effect of learning per se, you may be able to pre-train your participants before introducing your experimental treatments. This is something that is common in psychophysical experiments (testing such things as sensory thresholds), experiments on cognitive processes and experiments on human decision making. It involves making use of "practice sessions" in order to familiarize participants with the experimental tasks that they are being asked to do. The practice brings their performances up to desired levels, where they stabilize, and effectively eliminates any changes that might be caused by practice were the participants to be tested completely "cold" (i.e. without having had any experience at all of the task at hand). In essence, you are letting participants benefit from "practice" before you actually start measuring them.

Adaptation and habituation changes can be dealt with similarly. Before collecting data from the participants, allowing time for them to adapt or habituate to the experimental conditions can eliminate practice from these sources. Another way to deal with habituation (if habituation is short term), adaptation and fatigue is to allow breaks between the treatments. If the breaks are sufficiently long, they will allow participants to recover from any habituation, adaptation or fatigue induced by the previous treatment.

You can take steps to minimize practice effects in combination with either of the other two strategies. If you simply want to control practice, you could take these steps and then use counterbalancing to distribute whatever practice remains across treatments.

Making treatment order an independent variable. A third way to deal with the problem of practice is to make order of testing an independent variable in itself. Your experimental design will expose different groups of participants to different orderings of the conditions, just as in ordinary counterbalancing. However, you include a sufficient number of participants in each group to permit statistical analysis that should reveal the actual effect that the order of testing has on your dependent variable. For example, if you were going to conduct a one-factor experiment to compare the effect of two memorization strategies on recall, you could design the experiment to include the order of testing as a second independent variable. So not only are you looking at the strategies themselves and investigating the differences between them, you are also investigating the differences that might exist that are dependent upon the order that people take part in the two conditions. This is called a multi-factor design; it requires a special type of analysis to separately evaluate the effect of each and we introduce this design in the next section.

Analysis of within-subjects designs

As with between-subjects designs, it's not enough for us to simply look at the scores from each condition to be able to decide if there is a real causal effect. We must conduct statistical analyses to be able to make a decision like this. We cover these statistical techniques in **Chapter 16**.

ch. 16

Summary of within-subjects designs

1 Each participant takes part in *all* conditions.
2 Practice effects are a potential source of error in within-subjects designs, but can be minimized by:
   (a) Randomizing or counterbalancing of the order in which participants take part in the conditions
   (b) Randomization the order that stimuli are presented over the course of an experimental session
   (c) Minimizing the overall effects of practice by allowing participants "practice trials" that serve to get them performing at a desired level before testing takes place.

Test yourself

Identify the mistakes in the following statement. What should it say instead?[3]

1 Within-samples designs are ones in which participants take part in all levels of the dependent variable. Practice effects are a source of error in these designs and can be dealt with by randomizing the way participants are allocated to conditions.

Complex experimental designs

In this section we will consider more complex designs than we have covered so far. Up until this point we have focused on experimental designs that have two levels of the independent variable, such as the exercise/mood study (the levels being "exercise" and "no exercise"). These are the simplest experimental designs that can be used and they are useful in a variety of studies. However, sometimes researchers need a more complex design to be able to more fully understand the phenomena that they are studying.

---

3   "Within-subjects designs are ones in which participants take part in all levels of the independent variable. Practice effects are a source of error in these designs and can be dealt with by randomizing the order of testing."

Increasing the number of conditions: multi-level designs

Multi-level designs
Experimental designs in which the independent variable has more than two levels (or conditions).

In some studies, researchers want to test more than one level of the independent variable. It often makes sense to have three (or more) conditions in a single study. These are called **multi-level designs**. As with designs that have two levels, multi-level designs can be either within-subjects or between-subjects. All of the issues raised above concerning error and control apply to multi-level designs. So, for the mood/exercise study, we might decide that we wanted to compare whether "light" and "heavy" exercise, as well as no exercise at all, had any influence on mood. So what we have done is added another condition (or level) to the independent variable (giving us three in total: "light exercise", "heavy exercise" and "no exercise"). This is illustrated in Figure 7.6.

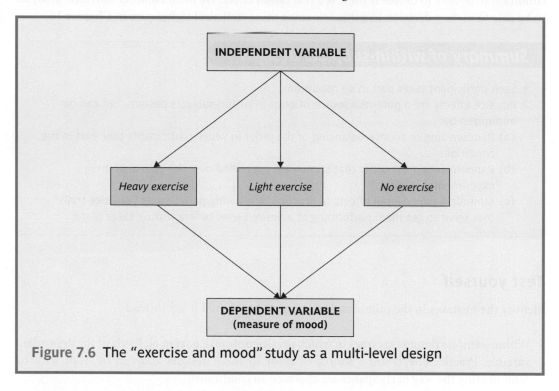

Figure 7.6 The "exercise and mood" study as a multi-level design

Again, it can be conducted as a within-subjects design or a between-subjects design. If it is conducted as a between-subjects design, then you will need to recruit a further group of participants to take part in the extra condition. If it is conducted as a within-subjects design, then you will have to ask your participants to come back on a third occasion to take part in the extra condition. Both of these scenarios present problems, as recruiting a large number of participants can be time consuming and difficult, while getting participants to return on more occasions increases the likelihood that some people will drop out before they have done all three conditions. A further consideration if the study is conducted as a within-subjects design is **counterbalancing**, which becomes more difficult as the number of conditions increases. That said, it is usually not a major problem as long as the number of conditions is manageable.

p.132

ch. 17   Analysis of **multi-level design** is covered in Chapter 17.

Increasing the number of independent variables: factorial designs

Sometimes, one independent variable is just not enough. Researchers often manipulate more than one independent variable in a single experiment. Typically, two or three independent variables are operating simultaneously. This type of experimental design is a closer approximation of real-world conditions, in which independent variables do not exist by themselves. Researchers recognize that in any given situation, a number of variables are operating to affect behaviour.

Factorial designs (sometimes known as "multi-factor" designs) are designs with more than one independent variable (or *factor*). In a factorial design, all levels of each independent variable are combined with all levels of the other independent variables. The simplest factorial design – known as a 2 × 2 (two by two) factorial design – has two independent variables, with each independent variable having two levels.

An experiment by Smith and Ellsworth (1987) illustrates a 2 × 2 factorial design. Smith and Ellsworth studied the effects of asking misleading questions on the accuracy of eyewitness testimony. Participants in the experiment first viewed a videotape of a robbery and were then asked questions about what they saw. One independent variable was the type of question – misleading or unbiased. The second independent variable was the questioner's knowledge of the crime: the

> **Factorial design**
> Research design that has more than one independent variable; every level of one independent variable is combined with every level of every other independent variable.

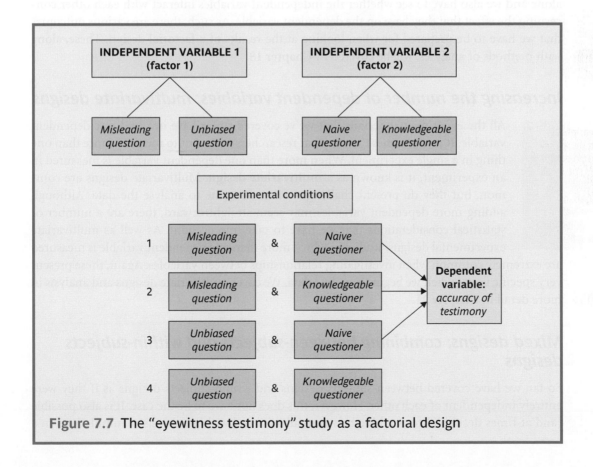

Figure 7.7 The "eyewitness testimony" study as a factorial design

person asking the questions had either viewed the tape only once (a "naive" questioner) or had seen the tape a number of times (a "knowledgeable" questioner).

This 2×2 design results in four experimental conditions: (1) knowledgeable questioner–misleading questions, (2) knowledgeable questioner–unbiased questions, (3) naive questioner–misleading questions, and (4) naive questioner–unbiased questions. This is shown in Figure 7.7.

A 2×2 design always has four groups. The general format for describing factorial designs is

Number of levels of first IV	$\times$	Number of levels of second IV	$\times$	Number of levels of third IV

and so on. A design with two independent variables, one having two levels and the other having three levels, is a 2×3 factorial design; there are six conditions in the experiment. A 3×3 design has nine conditions.

Analysis of factorial designs

When conducting factorial designs, there are a number of different challenges when interpreting the results. We now have more than one independent variable and each one of these might have several conditions attached to it. We have to look at the effect of each independent variable alone and we also have to see whether the independent variables interact with each other concerning the effect that they have on the dependent variable. As such, there are various outcomes that we have to be prepared for when looking at the results of a factorial design. These, along with methods of analyses, will be covered in **Chapter 18**.

ch. 18

Increasing the number of dependent variables: multivariate designs

Multivariate design
A research design in which multiple dependent measures are analysed with a single, multivariate statistical test.

All the experimental designs that we've covered so far have involved one dependent variable. It is sometimes the case that researchers will want to measure more than one thing in a single experiment. When more than one dependent variable is measured in an experiment, it is known as a **multivariate design**. Multivariate designs are common, but they do present challenges when we come to analyse the data. Although adding more dependent variables may seem straightforward, there are a number of statistical considerations that we have to take into account. As well as multivariate experimental designs, studies in which more than one dependent variable is measured are extremely common when investigating relationships between variables. Again, these present very specific issues when we begin to analyse data. We cover multivariate designs and analysis in more detail in **Chapter 21**.

ch. 21

Mixed designs: combining between-subjects and within-subjects designs

So far, we have covered between-subjects designs and within-subjects designs as if they were entirely independent of each other. However, this does not have to be the case. It is also possible (and at times desirable) to combine between-subjects and within-subjects manipulations in a single experiment. A **mixed design** (sometimes called a split-plot[4] design) is one that includes a between-subjects factor *and* a within-subjects factor. In using a design like this, we can investigate the effects of both between-subjects factors and within-subjects factors.

Imagine we are conducting our mood/exercise experiment as a within-subjects design. That is, we ask participants to take part in two conditions: one in which we measure their mood after 30 minutes of exercise and another in which we measure their mood after 30 minutes of non-strenuous activity. All participants take part in both conditions (and we are careful to counterbalance the order in which they participate, using an ABBA counterbalance). This is a typical within-subjects design. However, we might want to add a further between-subjects factor. We might have a hunch that exercise does not have the same effect at all times of the day. So we might add "time of test" as a further independent variable. This variable might have two levels: morning and evening. We now have a mixed design. We have a within-subjects factor that involves participants taking part in "exercise" and "no exercise" conditions, and we also have a between-subjects factor in which half of the participants take part in mornings and half take part in evenings. You may recognize this design as a 2×2 factorial design, and it is illustrated in Figure 7.8.

> **Mixed design**
> A design that includes both independent groups (between-subjects) and repeated measures (within-subjects).

Covariate designs

Sometimes, you know that some of the differences that exist between participants (such as IQ or reaction time) are likely to have an influence on the dependent variable that you are measuring. If you know for certain that this is the case, then you can build these differences into your experiment by measuring them and then controlling for their effects in the statistical analysis you conduct on the data. You do this by measuring the value of the variable for each participant together with the value of the dependent variable. This additional variable is called a *covariate*. The name derives from the fact that you expect the covariate to covary with the dependent variable.

By including a covariate in your experimental design, you can effectively "subtract out" its influence (or any variable correlated with it) on the dependent variable and thus reduce error and improve the sensitivity of your experiment to the effect of your independent variable. These designs are quite easy to implement. Simply by collecting additional data on potentially relevant correlational variables, you can convert a standard experimental design into one that examines the impact of those variables on the relationship between the independent and dependent variables.

> **Covariate designs**
> Designs in which a variable that is known to correlate with the dependent variable is measured and its effect "subtracted out".

An example of a **covariate design** would be one in which you think "age" might be an important factor that you wish to control for. So, if you are doing an experiment on whether a particular drug works to combat the symptoms of arthritis, you

---

4   The term "split plot" comes from agricultural research in which the design was first developed (it referred to a plot of land). In the split-plot design, a field was divided into several plots. Different plots received different levels of a given treatment (different pesticides). Each plot was then split into subplots, and each subplot received a different level of a second treatment (e.g. different fertilizers). Thus, each plot received all the levels of fertilizer, but only one level of pesticide. In psychological research, each "plot" is a group of participants who all receive the same level of the between-subjects variable. Within a given plot, the subplots represent the different levels of the within-subjects variable to which all members of that group are exposed.

would have an independent variable with two conditions ("drug-treatment" versus "placebo"). However, if you know that the symptoms worsen with age, you might want to add age as a covariate, which means you can subtract out the effects of age and get a result that is a purer measure of how effective the drug is compared to a placebo, regardless of the ages of the participants.

ch. 21
As this is primarily a statistical form of control, we will cover it in more detail in **Chapter 21**.

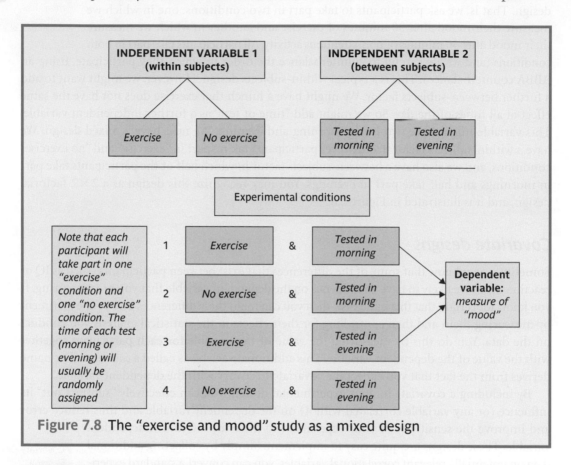

Figure 7.8 The "exercise and mood" study as a mixed design

Summary of complex experimental designs

1 When you increase the number of conditions of an independent variable above two, then your study is a "multi-level" design. Multi-level designs can be within subjects or between subjects.
2 When you increase the number of independent variables in your study, it is known as a "factorial" (or "multi-factor") design.
3 Any design that measures more than one dependent variable is called a "multivariate" design.
4 "Mixed designs" combine within-subjects and between-subjects factors.
5 "Covariate" designs are those in which a variable that is thought to covary with the dependent variable is measured so its effect can then be "subtracted" out.

Test yourself

Fill in the blanks.[5]

1 Factorial designs have more than one _____ variable.
2 A multi-level design is when we have _____ or more _____ of the _____ variable.
3 A _____ design is one that has more than one dependent variable.

Questions

1 What is a within-subjects design? What are the disadvantages of using a within-subjects design?

2 Why might some researchers prefer to use a within-subjects design rather than a between-subjects design if both are viable options?

3 What are some of the ways of dealing with the problems of a within-subjects design?

4 What other names are "between-subjects" designs sometimes given?

5 What are the main components of a "between-subjects" design?

6 In what situations would it be appropriate to randomly assign participants to conditions?

7 What kind of error gets minimized by randomizing the order of testing in a within-subjects design?

8 What do we call designs that have one independent variable, with more than two conditions?

9 What is a factorial design?

10 When would a researcher decide to use the matched-pairs design? What would be the advantage of this design?

11 You are a participant in a study that is investigating fatigue in computer users. Specifically, it wants to test to see whether a new specially designed ergonomic workstation can reduce fatigue in users who work consistently for more than 45 minutes. The study is a mixed design with both within-subjects and between-subjects factors. The within-subjects factor is "time of day" and has three levels – "morning", "afternoon" and "evening". The between-subjects factor is "workstation" and has two levels – "traditional" and "ergonomic". Fatigue is measured by asking participants to take part in a cognitive test of alertness. As a participant, how many times will your fatigue be measured?

12 Describe some of the ways in which practice effects might occur in within-subjects designs.

Activities

1 Professor Foley conducted a cola taste test. Each participant in the experiment first tasted 200 ml of Coca-Cola, then 200 ml of Pepsi-Cola and, finally, 200 ml of RC Cola. A rating of the cola's flavour was made after each taste. What are the potential problems with this experimental design and the procedures used? Revise the design and procedures to address these problems. You may wish to consider several alternatives and think about the advantages and disadvantages of each.

2 Your laboratory group has been assigned the task of designing an experiment to investigate the effect of time spent studying on a recall task. Thus far, your group has come up with the following plan: "Participants will be randomly assigned to two groups. Individuals in one group will study a list of five words for 5 minutes, and those in the other group will study the same list for 7 minutes. Immediately after studying, the participants will read a list of ten words and circle those that appeared on the original study list." Refine this experiment, giving specific reasons for any changes.

3 Read each of the following research scenarios and then fill in the correct answer in each column of the table (answers below).

Scenario	Number of independent variables	Number of experimental conditions
(a) Participants were randomly assigned to read a short story printed in either 12-point or 14-point font in one of three font style conditions: Courier, Times Roman or Arial. Afterwards they answered several questions designed to measure memory recall.		
(b) Researchers conducted an experiment to examine gender and physical attractiveness biases in juror behaviour. Participants were randomly assigned to read a scenario describing a crime committed by either an attractive or unattractive woman or an attractive or unattractive man who was described as overweight or average weight.		

Answers:

(a) 2 IVs (font size and font style); 6 conditions

(b) 3 IVs (gender, attractiveness, weight level); 8 conditions

Chapter 8

Quasi-experimental and Developmental Designs

OVERVIEW

The previous chapter introduced experimental designs in which the experimenter has full control over the independent variable. This is not always possible, however. In this chapter, we start by looking at "quasi experiments", which share many features with other experimental designs, except the control that the experimenter has over the independent variable. In the second part of this chapter, we look at developmental designs, which are used when we need to look at how something changes (or develops) over a period of time.

OBJECTIVES

After studying this chapter and working through the exercises, you should be able to:

• Distinguish quasi-experiments from "true" experiments

• Describe the advantages and disadvantages of using quasi-experimental designs

• Describe various types of quasi-experimental design, including time series designs, non-equivalent group designs, pre-test/post-test designs, and state under what circumstances each design is appropriate

• Demonstrate an understanding of developmental designs and their advantages and disadvantages

Quasi-experiments

The experiments that we described in the previous chapter are examples of what we call "true experiments". In true experiments, the researcher has complete control over the independent variable and can manipulate it in any way that is appropriate to test the hypothesis. The experimenter can also control extraneous variables by employing a range of techniques described previously. However, sometimes it is not possible to conduct a study in this way. In some cases, we might not be able to have complete control over the independent variable. If we wanted to test for differences between naturally occurring groups then we would not have any control over what group a person belonged to (given that it was naturally occurring). This means that it is impossible to randomly assign to groups, which we said previously was an important feature of some experimental designs. For example, if we wanted to test for differences between males and females on a spatial reasoning task, then "gender of participant" would be our independent variable. Obviously, we do not have control over this variable. We cannot "assign" people to the male and female groups.[1] The groups already exist and we use this naturally occurring difference. In cases such as this, in which we do not have full control over the independent variable, it is known as a **quasi-independent variable**. A quasi-independent variable is a variable that resembles an independent variable in an experiment. It is created by assigning participants to groups according to some characteristic that they already possess (such as age, gender or IQ), rather than using random assignment.

Quasi-independent variable
A variable resembling an independent variable in an experiment, but whose levels are not assigned to participants at random (e.g. participant's age).

> ## STOP & Think
>
> We have already mentioned some naturally occurring variables that prevent random assignment to conditions but that might be useful as independent variables. Can you think of some more?

Causal inferences in quasi-experiments

Quasi-experiment
An experiment in which the researcher is not in full control of the independent variable (e.g. when a naturally occurring variable such as gender is used as the independent variable).

Because participants enter the **quasi-experiment** already assigned to their treatment levels, it is always possible that any relationship discovered may be due to the action of some third, unmeasured variable that happens to correlate well with the quasi-independent variable. This means that the results of studies employing quasi-independent variables may be misinterpreted. For example, if we used gender as a quasi-independent variable and found that there was indeed a difference between males and females on a spatial reasoning task, we might be tempted to conclude that it was gender per se that was the "cause" of the difference. We are less entitled to draw this conclusion in a study in which the independent variable is not completely

---

1   We have seen more than one student report in which this fact has been overlooked, including the immortal line "gender was manipulated in this study".

under our control as we do not know whether there is something else that correlates with "gender" that is the underlying cause of our observed effect. Even so, the knowledge that a relationship exists may be important. This is especially true when quasi-experimental variables are added to an experimental design. Such combinations of both experimental and quasi-experimental variables often resemble the factorial designs described in the previous chapter.

Quasi-experimental designs

Pure **quasi-experimental designs** (sometimes known as non-experiments or *ex post facto* designs when the independent variable consists of a naturally occurring variable) are those that resemble experimental designs but use quasi-independent rather than true independent variables. Quasi-experimental research has some advantages and some disadvantages.

> **Quasi-experimental design**
> A design that resembles characteristics of a true experiment (e.g. some type of intervention or treatment is used and comparison is provided), but lacks the degree of control that is found in true experiments.

Advantages and disadvantages of quasi-experiments

One advantage of quasi-experimental designs is that they allow you to evaluate the impact of a quasi-independent variable under naturally occurring conditions. In those cases in which you manipulate the independent variable or even simply take advantage of a naturally occurring event, you may be able to establish clear causal relationships among variables. However, quasi-experimental research does have drawbacks that affect the internal and external validity of your research. The major problems with the quasi experiment are related to issues of internal validity. Because the researcher does not completely control the quasi-independent variable and other related variables, confounding variables may cloud any causal inferences drawn from the data collected. A partial solution to these problems is to include appropriate *control groups* in your quasi-experiment.

In the following sections, we examine several types of quasi-experimental design.

Time series designs

In the **time series design**, you make several observations (O) of behaviour over time prior to (O_1 to O_4) and immediately after (O_5 to O_8) introducing your intervention. For example, you might measure children's school performance on a weekly basis for several weeks and then introduce a new teaching technique (the intervention). Following the introduction of the new teaching technique, you again measure school performance on a weekly basis. A contrast is then made between pre-intervention and post-intervention performance. The basic time series design is shown in Figure 8.1.

> **Time series designs**
> Designs in which observations are made both before and after an intervention or event.

Intervention

O_1 O_2 O_3 O_4 O_5 O_6 O_7 O_8

Figure 8.1 Basic time series design

Interrupted time series design

Interrupted time series design
A variation of the time series design in which changes in behaviour are charted as a function of time before and after some naturally occurring event.

A variation on the basic time series design is the **interrupted time series design** in which you chart changes in behaviour as a function of some naturally occurring event (such as a natural disaster or the introduction of a new law) rather than manipulate an independent variable. In this design, the naturally occurring event is a quasi-independent variable (it is outside your control – after all, you cannot decide when a natural disaster will happen). As with the other time series designs, you make comparisons of behaviour prior to and after your participants were exposed to the treatment.

For such studies, you may have to use archival data. If you want to find out how a natural disaster has affected a particular behaviour, it is unlikely that you will have collected data concerning that behaviour prior to the natural disaster occurring. It is not usually the case that researchers collect data and then wait for a disaster to happen, after which they collect more data and see how the behaviour has been affected. Instead, it is more likely that you will have to rely on data that already exist from prior to the event occurring. As an example, if you were interested in conducting a prospective study of the impact of Hurricane Katrina on the nearby residents, you probably would have had a problem conducting your research. You would have had to predict when a powerful storm would develop and the exact track it would take. Unless you were extremely lucky (or knew more about hurricanes than the experts), you probably would not have been prepared to study the impact of such a natural disaster on human behaviour with a quasi-experiment. A more practical design here would make use of available archival data.

In other instances, you might be aware that an event is going to happen (e.g. the introduction of a new law such as a public smoking ban) which will allow you to collect data before and after the critical event takes place.

Non-equivalent group designs

Non-equivalent group designs
Designs in which one group is tested before and after an intervention, while another group serves as a "control" group for whom no intervention is employed.

In the **non-equivalent control group design**, you include a time series component (i.e. O_1 O_2 O_3 Intervention O_4 O_5 O_6) along with a "control group" that is *not* exposed to the intervention (i.e. O_1 O_2 O_3 No intervention O_4 O_5 O_6). The essence of the nonequivalent control group design is that a comparable group of participants is chosen and observed for the same period as the group for which the treatment is introduced. The control group is non-equivalent because it comes from a different underlying population (or community).

In the Know

A study reported by YunHee Shin (1999) illustrates a multiple time series design with a non-equivalent control group. Shin investigated the impact of an outdoor walking exercise programme on the physical health and emotional well-being of elderly Korean women. A sample of women was recruited from an apartment complex for the elderly and enlisted in the walking programme. The walking programme consisted of a 5-minute warm-up period followed by 30–40 minutes of walking, 10 minutes of stretching, and a 5-minute cool-down period. The women in this group constituted the experimental group. A second sample of women recruited from another apartment complex for the elderly made up the control group and was not enlisted in an exercise programme (participants in the control group were matched to the participants in the experimental group for age and activity level). Shin found no significant differences between the experimental and control groups on three of the measures obtained before the exercise programme was begun. However, there were significant differences between the groups *after* the exercise programme. In all cases, participants in the experimental group showed better physiological indicators than participants in the control group.

Drawbacks of non-equivalent group designs

Although the non-equivalent control group design allows you to make comparisons that you ordinarily might not be able to make, it does have some drawbacks. First, the validity of the design will be compromised if your two groups differ on some important variable before the study begins. For example, in the example above, living conditions in the apartment complex of participants in Shin's (1999) control group were worse than those in the complex of the experimental participants, and this could account for differences found. To minimize this problem, your groups must be matched as closely as possible prior to your study. Second, if either group is selected on the basis of extreme scores on the pre-test, then any shift of scores from pre-test to post-test towards the less extreme values may be due to their scores naturally "correcting" themselves rather than to the effect of your treatment. For example, if the members of the experimental group in Shin's study were selected because they were in very poor health to start with, any improvement might be due to a tendency for extreme scores to drift towards the average, and not due to the exercise programme.

Pre-test/post-test designs

As the name suggests, a **pre-test/post-test design** includes a pre-test of participants on a dependent measure before an intervention, followed by a post-test after the intervention. The pre-test/post-test design differs from the previously discussed quasi-experimental strategies in that the pre-test/post-test design is a true experimental design that resembles a standard within-subjects design. However, it lacks certain important controls for rival hypotheses.

Pre-test/post-test designs are used to evaluate the effects of some change in the environment (including interventions such as drug treatment or psychotherapy) on subsequent performance. You might employ a pre-test/post-test design to assess the effect of changes in an educational environment (e.g. introduction of a new teaching method). The design can also be used to test the effects of an experimental manipulation on behaviour. By using a pre-test/post-test design, you can compare levels of performance before the introduction of your change to levels of performance after the introduction of the change.

> **Pre-test/post-test design**
> An experimental design in which the dependent variable is measured both before (pre-test) and after (post-test) manipulation of the independent variable.

In the Know

Daniel Bernstein, Cara Laney, Erin Morris and Elizabeth Loftus (2005) conducted an experiment using a pre-test/post-test design to see if implanting a false memory could affect food aversions. Now, it is well established that false memories of events can be implanted and can be as vivid as real memories, but can implanting a false memory generate an aversion to foods? This is what Bernstein et al. wanted to find out.

In their experiment, participants completed a food history inventory (FHI) that asked them about their experiences with various foods when they were younger. Participants rated the likelihood that a food-related experience happened to them before age 10 (1 = definitely did not happen, 8 = definitely did happen). Embedded in the FHI were two items concerning getting sick after eating a hard-boiled egg or a dill pickle spear. A week later, participants returned to the laboratory and were given false feedback. They were told that, based on their answers to the FHI, they had got sick after eating a particular food. Half of the participants were told that they had got sick after eating a hard-boiled egg and the other half after eating a dill pickle. After receiving the false feedback, participants again completed the FHI and a measure of the kinds of foods they were likely to eat or not eat.

When Bernstein et al. (2005) compared participants' responses on the first FHI with those on the second, they found that telling a participant that he or she had got sick on a food increased the belief that the event actually happened. That is, participants who were told that they got sick after eating hard-boiled eggs were more confident that this actually occurred than they were before getting the false feedback. The same effect was found for participants who were told that they had got sick after eating dill pickle spears. Neither group showed any change to the opposite food item (e.g. those told that they had got sick on eggs did not increase their belief that they had got sick on pickles). Bernstein et al. also found that the false feedback affected the likelihood that participants would eat the food on which they had supposedly got sick. Those who were told they got sick on eggs were less likely to eat hard-boiled eggs, and those who were told they got sick on dill pickles were less likely to eat dill pickles.

Problems with the pre-test/post-test design

Evaluating changes in performance after some change would seem simple: just measure a behaviour, introduce the change, and then measure the behaviour again. This looks like a simple within-subjects experiment with two levels: pre-treatment and post-treatment. As with any within-subjects design, practice effects may play a part and could confound the effect of the manipulation. Giving your participants the pre-test may change the way they perform after you introduce your manipulation – for example, by drawing their attention to the behaviours you are assessing, providing practice on the test, introducing fatigue, and so on. Normally, you would control such practice effects through counterbalancing. Unfortunately, you cannot counterbalance the pre-test and post-test administrations (think about it!). Thus, a simple pre-test/post-test design leads to problems with internal validity. To ensure internal validity, you must include control groups. Figure 8.2 illustrates the simplest control measure possible for a design such as this.

As you can see in Figure 8.2, the design includes two independent groups of participants. Group 1 (the experimental group) receives your intervention (e.g. false feedback about getting sick after eating a food) between the pre-test and post-test. Group 2 (the control group) also receives the pre-test and post-test but does not receive the intervention (no false feedback). The

Group 1:	Pre-test	Treatment	Post-test
Group 2:	Pre-test		Post-test

Figure 8.2 The simplest practical pre-test/post-test design: a mixed design with pre-test/post-test as the within-subjects factor and with treatment versus no treatment as the between-subjects factor

pre-test and post-test are given to the participants in the experimental and control groups at the same time intervals. Take a look back at the Bernstein et al. (2005) study described in the "In the Know" box. You will find that there was no true control group in their design. All participants received some form of feedback manipulation. If you have been paying attention, you may have recognized this design from earlier in this chapter: it is simply a mixed design with pre-test/post-test as the within-subjects factor and with treatment versus no treatment as the between-subjects factor.

For this design to qualify as a true experiment, participants must be randomly assigned to your groups. You could use naturally formed groups in a pre-test/post-test format, but then the between-subjects component would involve a quasi-independent variable and your conclusions regarding the effect of this variable would be weaker. It is also important to note that although the two-group pre-test/post-test design ensures a degree of internal validity, it does not preclude potential problems with external validity. Your results may not generalize beyond the immediate research setting. Although this problem can affect any experiment, a particular problem of this design is that participants may be sensitized by the pre-test. Having had the pre-test, participants may now perform differently than they would have without the pre-test (this is essentially the old **practice effect** problem rearing its head again). For example, the experimental group may do better than the control group when both groups receive a pre-test but not when the pre-tests are omitted. Campbell and Stanley (1966) suggest two remedies to the problem.

ch. 7
p.149

Solomon four-group design

The first remedy is to use a design called the **Solomon four-group design**. This design is illustrated in Figure 8.3. Note that there are four groups in this design. Groups 1 and 2 are identical to those in the two-group design. The additional groups allow you to test for any possible sensitization effects of the pre-test. Groups 3 (treatment and then post-test) and 4 (post-test only) allow you to evaluate the impact of your treatment in the absence of a pre-test. By comparing this effect with the impact of your treatment when a pre-test is included, you can determine whether inclusion of the pre-test actually does alter the effect of your treatment.

Campbell and Stanley's (1966) second remedy is to entirely eliminate the pre-test. Minus the pre-test, this design is a simple two-group experiment. The decision to eliminate the pre-test depends on the question being asked. Situations may exist in which the pre-test is needed to completely answer a research question. For example, you may want to know how much students learn in a given course. However, because some students may come into a course already having some background in the subject, good performance on the final examination would not necessarily mean that the students had learned anything new. To eliminate this problem,

Solomon four-group design An expansion of the pre-test–post-test design that includes control groups to evaluate the effects of administering a pre-test on your experimental treatment.

Group 1:	Pre-test	Treatment	Post-test
Group 2:	Pre-test		Post-test
Group 3:		Treatment	Post-test
Group 4:			Post-test only

Figure 8.3 The Solomon four-group design

you might administer a pre-test on the first day of class over the same material to be assessed in the final examination. The results of this pre-test would provide a baseline against which you could measure any change attributable to the course.

Developmental designs

Developmental design
Research design in which participant age is used as a quasi-independent variable.

Sometimes we are interested in looking at how behaviour changes in relation to age, or over a long period of time. These studies use one of the specialized **developmental designs** discussed in this section: the cross-sectional design, the longitudinal design and the cohort-sequential design.

These designs represent a special case of quasi-experimental designs in which a characteristic of the participant (age) serves as a quasi-independent variable. Because age cannot be assigned to participants randomly, it must be used as a quasi-independent variable. Consequently, interpretations that you make from your data should not focus solely on causal relationships between age and behaviour change. We also should note that although we are presenting these designs as developmental designs, they often have applications outside of developmental psychology.

The cross-sectional design

Cross-sectional design
A developmental design in which the researcher recruits a "cross-section" (often related to age) of the population available at the time of the research.

Suppose you were interested in evaluating the changes in intelligence with age. One way to approach the problem is to use a **cross-sectional design**. In the cross-sectional design, you select several participants from each of a number of age groups. Figure 8.4 illustrates the general strategy of the cross-sectional design.

What you are doing is creating groups based on the chronological ages of your participants at the time of the study. So you might recruit a group of 5–8-year-olds, a group of 9–14-year-olds and so on. To answer the question "Does intelligence change with age?" you would test various age groups and then look for any differences between them. Assume that you are interested in investigating the developmental changes in intelligence across the life span (birth to death). Your hypothesis is that intelligence increases steadily during childhood and adolescence, levels off during early and middle adulthood, and declines in late adulthood. To evaluate this hypothesis with a cross-sectional design, you would obtain participants representing the different age groups elaborated in your hypothesis. You would then administer a standardized intelligence test (e.g. the Stanford–Binet) to each group and compare results across age groups.

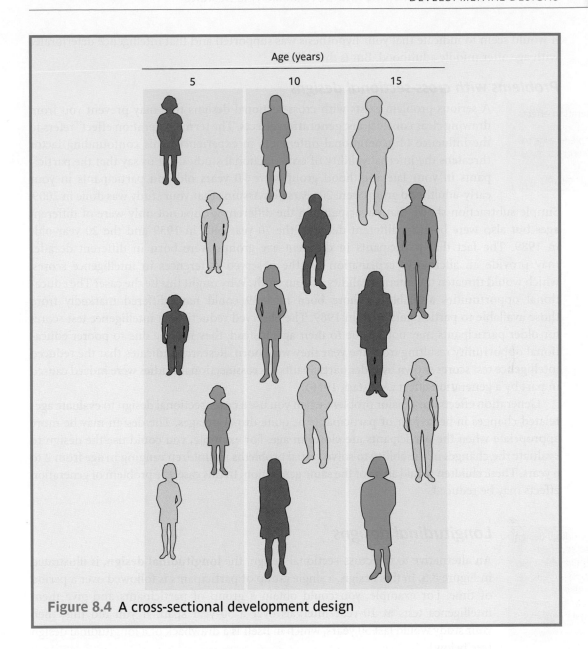

Figure 8.4 A cross-sectional development design

Advantages of cross-sectional designs

An advantage of the cross-sectional design is that it does not take long. You do not have to follow the same participant for 10 years in order to assess how their intelligence is changing as they get older. Instead, you pick a "cross-section" of the population, with groups consisting of participants of different ages from the population. If you found data consistent with your hypothesis, for example, what would you conclude? The purpose of the study was to draw conclusions about changes in intelligence across the life span. If you did indeed find that this pattern existed (with intelligence increasing until adolescence, levelling off and then declining in late adulthood) then it would seem to indicate that your hypothesis was supported and that intelligence deteriorates with age after middle adulthood. But is this valid?

Problems with cross-sectional designs

Generation effects
A confounding variable relating to differences that exist due to the generation of participants.

A serious problem exists with cross-sectional designs that may prevent you from drawing clear conclusions: **generation effects**. The term "generation effect" refers to the influence of generational differences in experience. This confounding factor threatens the internal validity of cross-sectional studies. Let us say that the participants in your late-adulthood group were 70 years old and participants in your early-adulthood group were 20 years old. Assume that your study was done in 2009. Simple subtraction shows that participants in the different groups not only were of different ages but also were born in different decades: the 70-year-olds in 1939 and the 20-year-olds in 1989. The fact that participants in different age groups were born in different decades may provide an alternative explanation for the observed differences in intelligence scores, which would threaten the internal validity of your study. Why might this be the case? The educational opportunities available to those born in 1939 could have differed markedly from those available to participants born in 1989. The observed reduction in intelligence test scores for older participants may not be due to their age. Instead, they may be due to poorer educational opportunity resulting from the year they were born. Research indicates that the reduced intelligence test scores shown by older participants in cross-sectional studies were indeed caused in part by a generation effect (Anastasi, 1976).

Generation effects are a major problem when you use a cross-sectional design to evaluate age-related changes in behaviour of participants of quite disparate ages. The design may be more appropriate when the participants are closer in age. For example, you could use the design to evaluate the changes in the ability to solve verbal problems in children ranging in age from 2 to 6 years. These children would all be of the same generation. In this case, the problem of generation effects may be reduced.

Longitudinal design
Developmental design in which the researcher measures or observes participants over a specified period of time.

Longitudinal designs

An alternative to the cross-sectional design, the **longitudinal design**, is illustrated in Figure 8.5. In this design, a single group of participants is followed over a period of time. For example, you could obtain a group of participants and give them intelligence tests at 10-year intervals over a 50-year span. If you did this, then your study would last 50 years, which in itself is a drawback of a longitudinal design (see below).

Advantages of the longitudinal design

Although it has some disadvantages (which we discuss in the next section), the longitudinal design has an attractive quality. It permits you to see developmental changes clearly. You can witness the development of a behaviour. This advantage may make the longitudinal design worth the rather large investment of time it takes to collect data.

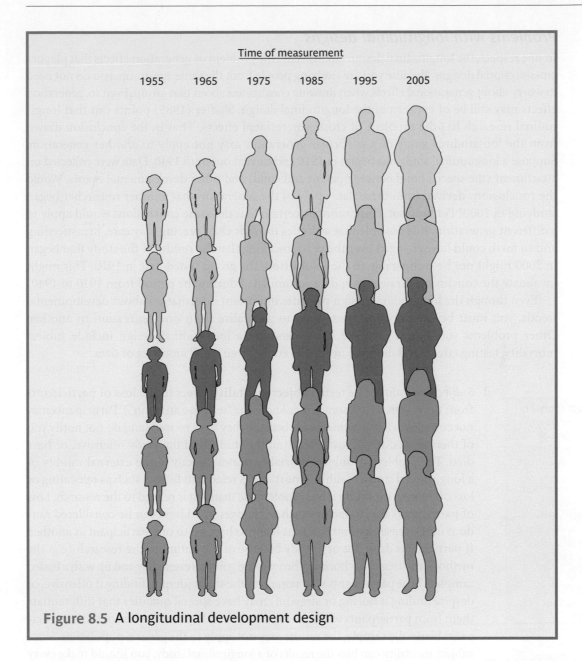

Figure 8.5 A longitudinal development design

Returning for the moment to the issue of changes in intelligence with age, longitudinal research indicates that intelligence for the most part changes very little with age.[2] A few areas of intelligence, such as measures requiring reaction time or perceptual skills, do seem to decline with age. However, the large declines seen with the cross-sectional design do not emerge in the longitudinal data.

---

2   Although a counter-argument could be made that this is due to the problems associated with the longitudinal design, mainly having only the healthiest, most motivated, most practised individuals left at the end of the study.

Problems with longitudinal designs

In one respect, the longitudinal design circumvents the problem of generation effects that plagues cross-sectional designs. Because you are studying people from the same age group, you do not need to worry about generational effects when drawing conclusions about that group. Even so, generation effects may still be of concern in the longitudinal design. Shaffer (1985) points out that longitudinal research has the problem of cross-generational effects. That is, the conclusion drawn from the longitudinal study of a particular generation may not apply to another generation. Suppose a longitudinal study was begun in 1910 and carried out until 1940. Data were collected on attachment (the special bond between parent and child) and other developmental events. Would the conclusions derived from these data apply to the generation that another researcher began studying in 2000? Perhaps not. You cannot be certain that the same conclusions would apply to a different generation. It is possible that attitudes towards child rearing, day care, breastfeeding and so forth could have changed over the years, meaning that the results of the study that began in 2000 might not be comparable to the results from the group tested first in 1910. This might invalidate the conclusions drawn from data accumulated during the period from 1910 to 1940.

Even though the longitudinal design provides important information about developmental trends, you must be careful when attempting to generalize from one generation to another. Other problems you should consider when choosing a longitudinal design include subject mortality, testing effects and the time needed to collect even small amounts of data.

Subject mortality
A reference to participants withdrawing from your study. Subject mortality is a particular problem in longitudinal research, in which researchers use the same participants over a long period of time.

Multiple observation effects
A threat to internal validity associated with longitudinal research, in which participants' scores may change for reasons related to repeated testing over time (e.g. practice effects, factors other than participant age).

1 *Subject mortality.* The term **subject mortality** refers to the loss of participants from the research (it is sometimes known as "selective attrition"). Participants may not complete a longitudinal study because they have moved (and do not notify you of their new address), lost interest in the study, find the study offensive, or have died. The problem of subject mortality relates directly to the external validity of a longitudinal study. If subject mortality is related to factors such as relocating or loss of interest, mortality is less problematic than if it is related to the research. Loss of participants due to factors such as changes in address can be considered random in the sense that moving is as likely to happen to one participant as another. If participants drop out of a study because of the nature of the research (e.g. the methods are stressful or boring), then you are going to eventually end up with a biased sample. Those participants who remain in the study (despite finding it offensive, or despite finding it boring or stressful) may have special qualities that differentiate them from participants who quit for this reason. Because the loss of those participants biases the sample, the results may not apply to the general population. Since subject mortality can bias the results of a longitudinal study, you should make every effort to evaluate why participants do not complete the study. Subject mortality may be more problematic with longitudinal research that spans a long period of time. The longer the time period, the more difficult it is to keep track of participants.

2 *Multiple-observation effects.* In a longitudinal design, you make multiple observations of the same participants across time. This very procedure raises problems that may threaten the internal validity of your longitudinal research. There are two **multiple observation effects** that threaten internal validity.

First, we have to consider practice effects. Improved performance on the tests over time may be related more to the participants' increasing experience with taking the tests than to changes related to age per se. For example, increases in intelligence scores with age may stem from the fact that participants develop a strategy for taking your test, not from any age-related changes in cognitive abilities. The solution to the problem of practice is relatively simple: (1) use multiple forms of a test to evaluate behaviour at different times, or (2) use different tests that measure the same behaviour at different times.

The second problem that results from observing the same participants over time is that other factors tend to arise and become confounded with age. For example, if evaluations of behaviour are made at five-year intervals, it is not possible to say conclusively whether the changes observed were due to increased age or to some other factor not related to age. An example may help to clarify this point. Suppose you were interested in evaluating the strength of attachment between a parent and child. You choose a longitudinal design and evaluate attachment behaviours at two-year intervals. You notice a change in attachment. Is the change caused by the fact that the child has grown older, or by other factors such as a shift in attitudes towards children or increased use of day care? It is difficult to know. The longitudinal design suffers from a problem in which the prevailing attitudes at the time of behaviour assessment may influence behaviour as much as the change in chronological age. This problem is not as easily handled as the problem of practice effects. You cannot account for whatever attitudes are prevailing at the time you are collecting data. You might try to deal with it by including a large enough sample so that any effects of attitudes could be statistically controlled while you are evaluating age-related changes in behaviour. However, such large samples of people who are willing to make a long-term commitment to a research project may be hard to find, and even if you do find willing participants, those people may themselves constitute a biased sample.

The cohort-sequential design

A disadvantage of the cross-sectional and longitudinal designs is their relative inability to determine whether factors other than age are influencing the observed changes in behaviour. The **cohort-sequential design** combines the two developmental designs and lets you evaluate the degree of contribution made by factors such as generation effects. However, the cohort-sequential design does not eliminate generation effects; it simply lets you detect them and consider them in interpreting your data.

Figure 8.6 illustrates a cohort-sequential design. Notice that the design embodies the features of both the cross-sectional and longitudinal designs. Along the vertical edge of Figure 8.6 is listed the year of birth. The participants making up one level of this variable (e.g. 1980) constitute a cohort group. A cohort group consists of participants born at a specified time. In our example, there are three cohort groups: participants born in 1980 (Cohort A), 1990 (Cohort B) or 2000 (Cohort C). These three cohort groups constitute the cross-sectional component when comparisons are made across cohort groups. Along the horizontal edge of the figure is listed the time of measurement. The different measurement times constitute the longitudinal component when we look at a single cohort group across different times of measurement.

Cohort-sequential design
Developmental design that combines features from cross-sectional and longitudinal designs in order to evaluate the contribution of "generation effects".

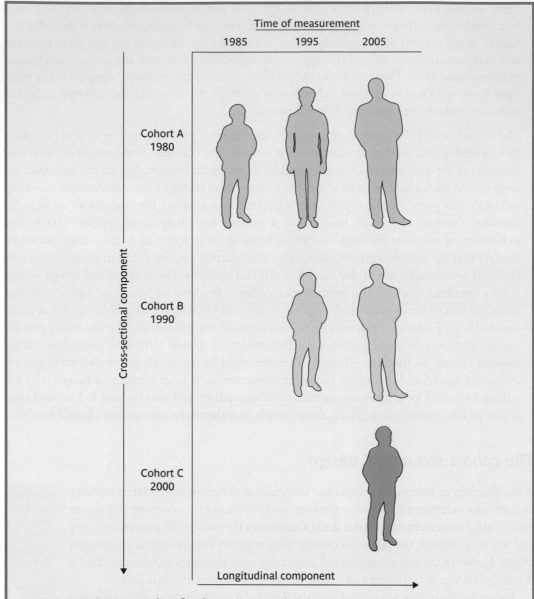

Figure 8.6 An example of cohort-sequential development design. Comparisons across time of measurement represent the longitudinal component, and comparisons across cohort groups represent the cross-sectional component of the design

By comparing participants from different cohort groups of the same age (e.g. comparing the data from 5-year-olds across cohort groups), we can identify potential generation or cohort group effects. This design is thus useful for evaluating developmental changes in behaviour while affording the capability to detect potentially important cohort effects.

Summary

In this chapter, we introduced a number of alternatives to "true" experimental designs. Quasi-experiments are those in which the independent variable is not under the full control of the experimenter. When this is the case, the independent variable is known as a quasi-independent variable. Examples of quasi-independent variables include those that occur naturally (gender, for example). Time series designs are those in which observations are made at various times before and after an intervention. A non-equivalent group design is one that uses a time series component, but also has a "control" group that is not exposed to the intervention. Pre-test/post-test designs measure participants on a dependent variable, using a design that is similar to a "true" within-subjects experimental design. However, pre-test/post-test designs cannot control for practice effects in the way a true experiment would. Control groups are usually employed in these designs, with the Solomon four-group design being a popular example. Developmental designs look at how a measure changes over time. Cross-sectional designs do this by measuring a "cross-section" of the population representing different age groups, while longitudinal designs are long-term studies that measure the same participants over a particular period of time. Cohort-sequential designs incorporate features from both cross-sectional and longitudinal designs, with the aim of evaluating the contribution of "generation effects".

 # Questions

1 Why might a researcher use a quasi-experimental design rather than a true experimental design?

2 What are the advantages and disadvantages of quasi-experimental designs?

3 Describe the non-equivalent control group pre-test/post-test design. Why is this a quasi-experimental design rather than a true experiment?

4 Describe the interrupted time series and the control series designs. What are the strengths of the control series design as compared to the interrupted time series design?

5 Distinguish between longitudinal, cross-sectional and sequential methods.

6 What is a cohort effect?

7 Explain how the addition of a non-equivalent control group to a simple interrupted time series design reduces the threat to the internal validity of the design.

8 Why might it not be possible to conclude that the treatment and control groups in a non-equivalent control group design are equivalent even when the pre-test scores are the same for both groups.

9 What are the defining characteristics of the pre-test/post-test design, and what are the design's strengths and weaknesses?

10 What is the Solomon four-group design, and why would you consider using it?

11 What are the defining qualities of the cross-sectional developmental design?

12 What are the advantages and disadvantages of the cross-sectional developmental design?

13 What are the defining qualities of the longitudinal developmental design?

14 What are the advantages and disadvantages of the longitudinal developmental design?

15 What is a cohort-sequential design, and when would you use one?

 ## Activities

1 The captain of each precinct of a metropolitan police department selected two officers to participate in a programme designed to reduce prejudice by increasing sensitivity to racial and ethnic group differences and community issues. The training programme took place every Friday morning for three months. At the first and last meetings, the officers completed a measure of prejudice. To assess the effectiveness of the programme, the average prejudice score at the first meeting was compared to the average score at the last meeting; it was found that the average score was in fact lower following the training programme. What type of design is this? What specific problems arise if you try to conclude that the training programme was responsible for the reduction in prejudice?

2 Many elementary schools have implemented a daily "sustained silent reading" period during which students, faculty and staff spend 15–20 minutes silently reading a book of their choice. Advocates of this policy claim that the activity encourages pleasure reading outside the required silent reading time. Design a non-equivalent control group pre-test/post-test quasi-experiment to test this claim. Include a well-reasoned dependent measure as well.

3 For the preceding situation, discuss the advantages and disadvantages of using a quasi-experimental design in contrast to conducting a true experiment.

4 Dr Cardenas studied political attitudes among different groups of 20-, 40- and 60-year-olds. Political attitudes were found to be most conservative in the age-60 group and least conservative in the age-20 group.

   (a) What type of method was used in this study?

   (b) Can you conclude that people become more politically conservative as they get older? Why, or why not?

   (c) Propose alternative ways of studying this topic.

5 A quasi-experiment was used to determine whether multimedia instruction is effective. Two sections of introductory psychology were taught by the same instructor, both in the early afternoon. In one section (the treatment group) the instructor used multimedia instruction. In the other section the instructor covered the same material but did not use multimedia instruction. Students did not know when they registered for the course whether multimedia instruction would be used, but the students were not randomly assigned to sections. Students' knowledge of the course material was assessed using two forms of a comprehensive introductory

psychology test. The comprehensive test can be considered a reliable and valid test that can be used to compare the effectiveness of the instruction in the two sections. The students in both sections were tested on the second day of class (the pre-test) and at the final (the post-test). Different forms of the test were used at the pre-test and at the post-test.

(a) What quasi-experimental design is used in this study?

(b) The instructor initially considered doing a true experiment rather than a quasi-experiment. Comment critically on the fairness of random assignment if you were arguing in favour of doing a true experiment to test the effectiveness of multimedia instruction.

(c) Explain why the quasi-experimental design used by the instructor is more effective than if the instructor had tested only students who had received multimedia instruction. Identify one threat to internal validity that was controlled in this study that would not have been controlled if only students who received multimedia instruction had been tested.

Chapter 9

Sampling

OVERVIEW

Throughout this text we have referred to "participants". Participants are sometimes called "subjects", a term that is still used when describing certain types of experimental design (e.g. within subjects and between subjects). Regardless of what the current name for them might be, these are the people who take part in your experiment; the people whom you measure or observe in some way. Who are they? Where do they come from? How do you get them to take part? Can you test anyone? These are important questions that may have important implications for your research. We will cover the main issues relating to choosing and recruiting participants in this chapter.

OBJECTIVES

After studying this chapter and working through the exercises, you should be able to:

- State the difference between a population and a sample
- Identify threats to "representativeness" and how this might affect validity
- Distinguish the difference between probability and non-probability sampling techniques
- Describe the basic procedures involved in obtaining a sample through the following methods of probability sampling: simple random sampling, stratified random sampling, cluster sampling
- Describe the basic procedures involved in obtaining a sample through the following methods of non-probability sampling: convenience sampling, purposive sampling, quota sampling
- Outline the main advantages and disadvantages of each type of sampling technique discussed in the chapter
- Demonstrate an understanding of the factors involved in acquiring volunteers to participate in research, including the main advantages and disadvantages

Populations and samples

Imagine that you are interested in investigating the effect of a new computer-based teaching technique on how well 13–14-year-olds learn mathematics. Would it be feasible to include every 13–14-year-old in the world in your experiment? Obviously not, but what is the alternative? You may have thought to yourself, "I will have to choose *some* 13–14-year-olds for the experiment." If this is what you thought, you are already considering an important distinction in research methodology: populations versus samples.

In the hypothetical experiment, you could not hope to include all 13–14-year-olds. "All 13–14-year-olds" constitutes the **population** under study. Because it is usually not possible to study an entire population, you must be content to study a sample of that population. A sample is a small subgroup chosen from the larger population.

> **Population**
> An entire group (or entire set of scores) that is of interest to you as a researcher.

Often researchers find it necessary to define a subpopulation for study. In your imaginary study, cost or other factors may limit you to studying a certain region of the country. Your subpopulation might consist of 13–14-year-olds from a particular city, town or district. Furthermore, you might limit yourself to studying certain school classes (especially if the district is too large to allow you to study every class). In this case, you are further dividing your subpopulation. In effect, rather than studying an entire population, you are studying only a small segment of that population. That small segment is known as a **sample**.

> **Sample**
> A smaller subgroup drawn from the larger population.

A population can be defined in many ways. For example, if you were interested in how prejudiced attitudes develop in young children, you could define the population as those children enrolled in nurseries and early primary school classes. If you were interested in visualization techniques in professional golfers, then you would define your population as all golfers who play in a professional capacity. In any case, you may need to limit the nature of the subject population and sample because of the special needs of the research.

It is important to emphasize at this point that samples are of little or no interest on their own. A new computer-based teaching technique is not going to be implemented only for the hundred or so 13–14-year-olds that you tested it on. Similarly, the social psychologist is not interested solely in the attitudes of the 50 people he surveyed. *Populations, not samples, are of primary interest.* The sample is a way of obtaining data about the population without testing every single member of that population. This is an important distinction. The "power" of samples to describe the larger population is based on the assumption that the measures that are taken from the sample are applicable to the population from which the sample was drawn.

The ability to apply findings from a sample to a larger population is known as generalization. In Chapter 5, we noted that studies whose findings can be applied across a variety of research settings and subject populations possess a high degree of external validity. Thus, the ability to generalize findings to a larger population contributes to the external validity of a study.

> **Representativeness**
> How closely your sample resembles the population from which it was selected.

The ability to generalize from a sample to the population depends critically on the **representativeness** of the sample.

ch. 5 p.97

Representativeness

Regardless of the technique that you use to acquire your sample (which we will cover shortly), your sample should be representative of the population of interest. A **representative sample** closely matches the characteristics of the population. Imagine that you have a bag containing 300 golf balls: 100 are white, 100 are orange and 100 are yellow. This is your population. You then select a sample of 30 golf balls. A representative sample would have 10 balls of each colour. A sample having 25 white and 5 orange would not be representative (because the ratio of colours does not approximately match that of the population) and would be considered a non-representative or **biased sample**.

Clearly, individuals in a population differ in many ways, and populations differ from each other. For example, one population might be 40 per cent male and 60 per cent female, whereas in another population the distribution might be 75 per cent female and 25 per cent male. A sample is representative of the population to the extent that it exhibits the same distribution of characteristics as the population.

> **Representative sample**
> A sample that closely matches the characteristics of the population.
>
> **Biased sample**
> A sample that is not representative of the population it is supposed to represent.

STOP & Think

Q. If a representative sample of 200 adults has 80 men and 120 women, which of the above-mentioned populations does it represent?
A. The population that is 40 per cent male and 60 per cent female.

For any researcher to be able to say something about the population as a whole, the sample that he or she tests must be representative of that population. What things might influence this?

Threats to representativeness

The major threat to representativeness is bias. A biased sample is one in which the distribution of characteristics in the sample is systematically different from the target population. A sample of 100 adults that included 80 women and 20 men would probably be biased if the population from which it came was 60 per cent female and 40 per cent male. In this case, women would be over-represented and men would be under-represented in the sample. There are two sources of bias: **selection bias** and **response bias**. Selection bias occurs when the procedures used to select the sample result in the over-representation of some segment of the population or, conversely, in the exclusion or under-representation of a significant segment. Response bias occurs when an unrepresentative section of your target population respond to your recruitment efforts or decide to participate.

> **Selection bias**
> Threat to the representativeness of a sample that occurs when the procedures used to select a sample result in the over- or under-representation of a significant segment of the population.
>
> **Response bias**
> A source of bias in your data caused by participants failing to return completed surveys.

If the results of a study are to generalize to the intended population, you must be very careful when you select your sample. The best way of choosing your sample is to identify the population that you are interested in, and then draw a **random sample** of individuals from that population. In a random sample, every person in the population must have an equal chance of being chosen for the study. But how do we do this? Is it even feasible to do this? Let's find out.

Sampling techniques

There are two basic techniques for **sampling** individuals from a population: **probability sampling** and **non-probability sampling**. In probability sampling, each member of the population has a specifiable probability of being chosen. Probability sampling is very important when you want to make precise statements about a specific population on the basis of the results of your survey. In non-probability sampling, we do not know the probability of any particular member of the population being chosen. Although this approach is not as sophisticated as probability sampling, non-probability sampling is quite common and useful in many circumstances.

Probability sampling

Simple random sampling

With **simple random sampling**, every member of the population has an equal probability of being selected for the sample. If the population has 1000 members, each member has one chance out of a thousand of being selected. Suppose you want to sample students who attend your school. A list of all students would be needed and, from that list, students would be chosen at random to form the sample.

When conducting telephone interviews, researchers commonly have a computer randomly generate a list of telephone numbers with the dialling prefixes used for residences in the city or area being studied. This will produce a random sample of the population because most residences have telephones (if many people do not have telephones, the sample would be biased). Some companies will even provide researchers with a list of telephone numbers for a survey in which the telephone numbers of businesses and numbers that telephone companies do not use have been removed. You might have noticed that this procedure results in a random sample of households rather than individuals. Survey researchers use other procedures when it is important to select one person at random from the household.

Random sampling is an effective way to obtain a sample that is representative of the larger population. However, the term "simple" random sample is a bit misleading. Obtaining a random sample like this is far from simple if the population is large. A truly random sample would require that *every* member of your population has an equal chance of being selected to become part of your sample. This might mean choosing a sample from a population of *millions*. This is not practical. If you are doing psychological research on a phenomenon that is generally thought to be universal in humans, then your population is the *entire population of the world*. A truly

Random sample
A sample drawn from the population such that every member of the population has an equal opportunity to be included in the sample.

Sampling
The process of choosing members of a population to be included in a sample.

Probability sampling
A way of sampling from a population that specifies the specific probability that each member has of being picked.

Non-probability sampling
Sampling techniques that do not specify how likely it is that any member of the population may be selected.

Simple random sampling
The purest form of probability sampling, in which every member of a population has an equal chance of being selected.

random sample would mean that every single person on the planet would have an equal chance of being selected. Obviously, this is an impossible task (even if you could achieve the selection process, would you really be able to fly people in from all over the world just to take part in your study?). So can we sample in a more practical way?

Stratified random sampling

Stratified random sampling
A probability sampling technique that identifies relevant "strata" and samples randomly within each of these strata.

In **stratified random sampling**, the population is divided into subgroups called strata (singular: stratum) and random sampling techniques are then used to select sample members from each stratum. It is up to the researcher to choose which "strata" are appropriate. Any number of dimensions could be used to divide the population, but the dimension (or dimensions) chosen should be relevant to the problem under study.

To clarify this type of sampling, imagine you are doing a study on religious beliefs. You want to sample from the population and you require your sample to be representative of the religious beliefs of the population as a whole. So you decide that the best way to do it is to use stratified random sampling. You choose the strata based on the following religious faiths: Christians, Muslims, Jews, Buddhists, Sikhs, Hindus. You would use information about how these religions are represented in the population as a whole and would then sample accordingly. So, if you know that 15 per cent of the population are Sikhs, then 15 per cent of your sample must also be Sikhs. You would then sample the appropriate number of Sikhs randomly from the Sikh population.

Stratified random sampling has the advantage of a built-in assurance that the sample will accurately reflect the numerical composition of the various subgroups. This kind of accuracy is particularly important when some subgroups represent very small percentages of the population. For instance, if you know that Buddhists make up 5 per cent of a city of 100 000, then a simple random sample of 100 people might not include any Buddhists; a stratified random sample would include five Buddhists chosen randomly from the population. In practice, when it is important to represent a small group within a population, researchers will "oversample" that group to ensure that a representative sample of the group is surveyed; a large enough sample must be obtained to be able to make inferences about the population. Thus, if your campus has a distribution of students similar to the city described here and you need to compare attitudes of Buddhists and Christians, you will need to sample a large percentage of the Buddhist students and only a small percentage of the Christians to obtain a reasonable number of respondents from each group.

Cluster sampling
A probability sampling technique that identifies clusters of individuals and then randomly samples an appropriate number of clusters. Every member of the selected cluster is entered into the sample.

Cluster sampling

It might have occurred to you that obtaining a list of all members of a population might be difficult. What if you cannot gain access to a list of all members of the population? What if you want to study a population that has no list of members, such as people who work in health care agencies? In such situations, a technique called **cluster sampling** can be used. Rather than randomly sample from a list of individuals, the researcher can identify "clusters" of individuals and then sample from these clusters. After the clusters are chosen, all individuals in each cluster are included in the sample. For example, if you are interested in sampling from a population of students, but you cannot get access to a complete list of registered students, you might choose to use cluster sampling. To sample in this way, you would start by identifying all classes being taught – the classes are the clusters of students. You could then randomly sample from this list of classes and have all members of the chosen classes complete your survey (making sure, of course, that no one completes the survey twice). So, if you know that there are 100 classes being taught in the month that you are collecting your data, you would randomly select 20 (say) of these classes and then have each student in each of these 20 classes complete your survey. That is cluster sampling.

Non-probability sampling

In contrast, non-probability sampling techniques are quite arbitrary. A population may be defined, but little effort is expended to ensure that the sample accurately represents the population. However, among other things, non-probability samples are cheap and convenient. Three types of non-probability sampling are convenience sampling, purposive sampling and quota sampling.

Convenience sampling

One form of non-probability sampling is **convenience sampling** or "haphazard" sampling. Convenience sampling could be called a "take-them-where-you-find-them" method of obtaining participants. Thus, you would select a sample of students from your university in any way that is convenient. You might stand in front of the student union at 9 a.m., ask people who sit around you in your classes to participate, or visit a couple of halls of residence and see who you can get to agree to participate. Unfortunately, such procedures are likely to introduce biases into the sample so that the sample may not be an accurate representation of the population of all students. Thus, if you selected your sample from students walking by the student union at 11 a.m., your sample excludes students who do not frequent this location (such as those who do not get out of bed until after this time), and it may also eliminate afternoon and evening students. Sample biases such as these limit your ability to use your sample data to estimate the actual population values. Your results may not generalize to your intended population but instead may describe only the biased sample that you obtained.

> **Convenience sampling**
> A method of sampling that involves recruiting participants at the researcher's convenience. Also known as "haphazard" sampling.

Although convenience sampling has its drawbacks, it is widely used by psychologists (and especially students embarking on research projects). There are a few reasons for this, but the main one is that most research does not, in reality, require that a sample must strictly match the population exactly. Unless there are obvious biases that are likely to limit the conclusions that you can draw, convenience samples arc often considered to be "good enough" especially if the construct under study is a general psychological process. However, do think carefully about any potential biases that a convenience sample may introduce and be sensitive to the potential effects of these biases on your measure.

> **Purposive sampling**
> A sampling technique in which individuals are selected due to them belonging to a pre-defined group. Selection of individuals is not random.

Purposive sampling

A second form of non-probability sampling is **purposive sampling**. The purpose is to obtain a sample of people who meet some predetermined criterion. Sometimes when visiting the cinema, researchers will ask customers to fill out a questionnaire about one or more movies. They are always doing purposive sampling. Instead of sampling anyone walking towards the theatre, they take a look at each person to make sure that they fit some criterion – under the age of 30 or an adult with one or more children, for example. This is a good way to limit your sample to a certain group of people. However, it is not a probability sample.

A type of purposive sampling that is often used in qualitative research is known as *snowball sampling*. This is when you use your initial participants to either recruit or suggest other participants who might be willing to take part in the study. Thus, the number of participants you have "snowballs" from a small initial few, to an increasingly larger sample.

Quota sampling

Quota sampling
A non-probability sampling technique involving the researcher having to fill a "quota" of participants that belong to pre-defined subgroups of the population. Similar to stratified sampling with the exception that the selection is not random within each subgroup.

A third form of non-probability sampling is **quota sampling**. A researcher who uses this technique chooses a sample that reflects the numerical composition of various subgroups in the population. Thus, quota sampling is similar to the stratified sampling procedure previously described; however, the sample that is obtained in each "strata" is not randomly selected.

To illustrate, suppose you want to ensure that your sample of religious people includes 19% Muslims, 23% Jews, 41% Christians, 12% Sikhs and 5% Buddhists because these are the percentages of the total population.

A quota sampling technique would make sure you have these percentages, but you would still choose your sample using haphazard techniques. You would not identify all members of each strata and randomly sample from this; nor would you identify clusters and sample a randomly selected cluster. Instead, you would go out and sample the required number of Christians, Muslims etc. in a convenient (but arbitrary) way – for example, you might just sample the first people you could find that fitted into the strata. Quota sampling is a bit more sophisticated than convenience sampling, but the problem remains that no restrictions are placed on how individuals in the various subgroups are chosen. The sample does reflect the numerical composition of the whole population of interest, but respondents within each subgroup are selected in a haphazard manner. Because of this, there is the potential for bias. If you are the researcher and you are left to decide whom to sample, then you may only ask people who look "friendly" and avoid anyone who looks like they might not be cooperative. By doing that, you have immediately introduced a bias into your sample by excluding certain people purely because of the way they looked to you.

ch. 6
p.104
ch. 7
p.117

STOP & Think

Flick back to Chapters 6 and 7 and **have a look at the experiment on how exercise influences mood** (both the between-subjects and within-subjects versions). Now that you know about sampling, can you identify what sampling method was used in these hypothetical studies and provide a critique of them, illustrating in what way they might violate "representativeness"? Can you recommend a better sampling technique that the researchers could have employed?

Test yourself

Identify the sampling technique used.[1]

	Simple random sampling	Quota sampling	Cluster sampling	Stratified random sampling
1 A researcher has been told to collect a sample of 100. In this sample, there must be ten 18–25-year-olds, twenty-five 26–35-year-olds, forty 36–45-year-olds and twenty-five 46–55-year-olds. To achieve this, she stands at the entrance of a shopping centre and asks people who she thinks will fit into the age groups she has been requested to sample.				
2 A market researcher wants to collect data on customer attitudes towards tipping in small restaurants. She identifies 30 small restaurants in her area, and then randomly selects five of them. She visits these five restaurants and samples all the diners who are eating there when she visits.				
3 A professor of education is employed by the government to run a study on student satisfaction in UK universities. She needs to sample 3000 students. To do this, the government provides her with a database containing the names of every student currently attending university. She employs a computer to randomly select her sample.				
4 A researcher into stress is interested in studying stress levels of various members of the armed forces. He identifies the appropriate proportion of junior and senior personnel in the army, navy and RAF. He then randomly selects within these categories.				

Sampling techniques are summarized in Table 9.1 on the next page.

Sampling in the real world

Unfortunately, having a completely random sample of individuals from the population is an ideal that is rarely met in psychological research. Instead, psychology researchers tend to sample in very specific ways. In this section, we'll look at some of the ways in which researchers sample, and look at the pros and cons of such approaches.

---

1 Answers: 1 = quota sampling; 2 = cluster sampling; 3 = simple random sampling; 4 = stratified random sampling.

Table 9.1 Advantages and disadvantages of sampling techniques

Sampling technique	Example	Advantages	Disadvantages
Simple random sampling	A computer program randomly chooses 100 students from a list of all 10 000 students at University X	Representative of population	May cost more. May be difficult to get full list of all members of any population of interest
Stratified random sampling	The names of all 10 000 University X students are sorted by subject and a computer program randomly chooses 50 students from each subject	Representative of population	May cost more. May be difficult to get full list of all members of any population of interest
Cluster sampling	Two hundred clusters of psychology subjects are identified at universities all over the UK. Out of these 200 clusters, 10 clusters are chosen randomly, and every psychology subject in each cluster is sampled	Researcher does not have to sample from lists of individuals in order to get a truly random sample	May cost more. May be difficult to get full list of all members of any randomly chosen cluster
Haphazard sampling	Ask students around you at lunch or in class to participate	Inexpensive, efficient, convenient	Likely to introduce bias into the sample; results may not generalize to intended population
Purposive sampling	In an otherwise haphazard sample, select individuals who meet a criterion, e.g. an age group	Sample includes only types of individuals you are interested in	Likely to introduce bias into the sample; results may not generalize to intended population
Quota sampling	Collect specific proportions of data representative of percentages of groups within population, then use haphazard techniques	Inexpensive, efficient, convenient, slightly more sophisticated than haphazard sampling	Likely to introduce bias into the sample; results may not generalize to intended population; no method for choosing individuals in subgroups

Students as participants

Non-random sample
A specialized sample of participants used in a study who are not randomly chosen from the population.

In practice, most psychological studies use a **non-random sample**, usually of individuals from a highly specialized subpopulation – students. The continued use of students as research participants (particularly those from the USA) has generated much controversy (see, e.g. McNemar, 1946) but this group continues to be the most common source of research participants used by psychologists.

Students are used so often because most psychological research is conducted in academic institutions, where students form a readily available pool of potential research participants. In fact, many psychology departments set up a participant pool, usually consisting of introductory psychology students, to provide participants for psychological studies. They are essentially a captive pool of individuals that can be tapped easily. Sampling from a relatively small subject pool is much easier than drawing a random sample from the general population, and greatly reduces the time and financial costs of doing research. However, using such a non-random sample has a downside. If you choose to use students in order to save time, effort and money, you may be sacrificing the generality of your results, and the study will have less **external validity**. Students differ from the non-student population in a number of ways (such as in age or socio-economic status). These differences may limit your ability to apply your results to the larger population. You may be limited to generalizing only to other students.

ch. 5
p.97

However, some researchers suggest that the issue of using college students in research may be overblown (Kardes, 1996). Kardes maintains that student populations are fine when you are studying basic psychological processes (e.g. memory), although problems may occur when you are interested in making specific applications of your findings (Kardes, 1996). Research on the issue of student versus non-student participants has produced mixed results. A few studies (such as Feild & Barnett, 1978) have found differences between student and non-student participants. In contrast, Tanford (1984) reports a jury simulation study in which student participants did not differ significantly from "real jurors" on most of the measures included in the study. Given these inconsistent findings, the true impact of using students as participants is difficult to assess. You should, however, recognize that your results *may* have limited generality should you use students.

Acquiring human participants for research

Whether your research is experimental or non-experimental, you must consider three factors when acquiring participants for your research: (1) the setting in which your research will take place, (2) any special needs of your particular research, and (3) any institutional, departmental and ethical policies and guidelines governing the use of participants in research.

The research setting

The way in which you recruit participants will depend of the setting of your research. In this chapter, we will focus mainly on recruiting participants for laboratory research and for experimental research in the "real world" (or "the field" as we sometimes call it) although do keep in mind that other methods require different methods of recruitment. We will cover other methods in the appropriate chapters.

Laboratory research

If you choose to conduct your research in a laboratory setting, there are two main ways of acquiring participants. First, you can seek volunteers from whatever participant population is available. For example, you could recruit participants from your university library. These participants would obviously participate on a voluntary basis (you cannot drag people into your laboratory against their will). As we indicate later, voluntary participation has both positive and negative consequences for your research. Second, you can use a participant pool if one exists. Individuals in the participant pool may be required to participate in a certain number of studies (with an alternative to the research option provided). If you adopt this strategy, you must make sure that your recruitment procedures do not put pressure on participants to participate or coerce them in any way. Even when using a participant pool, participation in a research study must be voluntary.

Field research

Field research requires you to select your participants while they are in their natural environment. How you acquire your participants for field research depends on the nature of your study. If you were running a field experiment, you could use one of two methods for acquiring participants, again depending on the nature and needs of your study. Some field experiments are actually carried out much like laboratory experiments except that you take your "show" (equipment, assistants, measuring devices etc.) on the road and set up in the participant's natural environment. In this type of field experiment, the researchers maintain about as much control over participant selection and assignment as they would if the experiment were conducted in the laboratory. However, the researchers are at the mercy of whoever happens to be available in the place you choose to set up your experiment on any given day. Thus, with field research, you have less control over participants than in the laboratory.

In another type of field experiment, you set up a situation and wait for participants to happen along. A field experiment reported by Michael Shohat and Jochen Musch (2003) conducted in Germany illustrates this strategy. Shohat and Musch were interested in studying ethnic discrimination. They set up auctions on eBay to sell DVDs, and manipulated the ethnicity of the seller. On one eBay listing, the seller had a Turkish username. On another, the seller had a German username. The researchers recorded the number of hits on each listing as well as the average price paid for the DVDs. In this kind of field experiment, you have less control over who participates in your research. Whoever happens to sign in to eBay at a particular time and search for DVDs would be potential participants.

The needs of your research

Special needs of your research may affect how you acquire participants. In some cases, you may have to screen potential participants for certain characteristics (such as gender, age or personality characteristics). For example, in a jury study, you might screen participants for their level of authoritarianism and include only authoritarians in your research. To do this, you must first pre-test participants using some measure of authoritarianism and then recruit only those who fall into the category you want. Bear in mind that doing this affects the external validity of your findings. The results you obtain with participants who score high in authoritarianism may not apply to those who show lower levels of authoritarianism.

As another example, you may need children of certain ages for a developmental study of intelligence. Acquiring a sample of children for your research is a bit more involved than acquiring a sample of adults. You must obtain permission from the child's parent or guardian, as well as from the child him or herself. You often have to obtain permission from the child's school (or local education authority). In practice, some parents may not want their children to participate and some local education authorities allow only a certain number of research projects to gain access to their schools. This again raises issues of external validity. Your sample of children of parents who agree to allow participation may differ from the general population of children.

Institutional policies and ethical guidelines

Any time you conduct research with humans or animals, you must make sure that your procedures follow ethical guidelines. We will cover these issues in **Chapter 24** but it is very important that you are aware that these guidelines exist and what the main ethical principals are. Most countries have guidelines prescribed by the professional body that regulates psychology (in the UK this is the British Psychological Society; in the USA it is the American Psychological Association). Academic institutions, educational authorities and health authorities often have their own ethics regulations. These procedures not only relate to how you treat participants and proceed with your study, but also how you recruit participants to take part. Make sure you are familiar with these guidelines before developing a research project.

ch 24

Voluntary participation and validity

A basic rule of research is that research participants cannot be forced, coerced or unduly induced into participating in your research. In other words, participants must voluntarily agree to be in your research. This raises an important question: are volunteer participants representative of the general population? There are undoubtedly differences between individuals who choose to participate in research and those who do not. Because a sample made up entirely of volunteers is biased, the external validity of your experiment may be affected. This is known as the volunteer bias.

There are two assumptions inherent in the previous discussion: (1) volunteers differ in meaningful ways from non-volunteers, and (2) the differences between volunteers and non-volunteers affect the external validity of your research.

Factors that affect the decision to volunteer

Two categories of factors affect a person's decision to volunteer. These are characteristics of the participant that either increase or decrease the likelihood that he or she will volunteer, and situational factors. We explore each of these next.

Participant-related characteristics

Rosenthal and Rosnow (1975) provide the most comprehensive study of the characteristics of the volunteer subject in their book *The Volunteer Subject*. Table 9.2 lists several characteristics that, according to Rosenthal and Rosnow, distinguish volunteers from non-volunteers. Associated with each characteristic is the degree of confidence Rosenthal and Rosnow believe that you can have in the validity of each attribute.

In some cases, no clear, simple effect of a variable is apparent on whether or not a person will volunteer for behavioural research. For example, Rosenthal and Rosnow (1975) point out that first-borns may respond more frequently than later-borns to an "intimate" recruitment style for an experiment dealing with group dynamics. Later-borns may respond more frequently than first-borns to a request for participants for an experiment involving stress. Similarly, a sociable person may be more likely to volunteer for an experiment that appears to be "sociable" in nature, and would be less likely to volunteer for an experiment in which there is little or no contact with others. Also, volunteers may show better adjustment than non-volunteers in experiments that require self-disclosure. Other research suggests that volunteers also may be more field dependent

Table 9.2 Characteristics of people who volunteer for research
Maximum confidence
1 Volunteers tend to be more highly educated than non-volunteers
2 Volunteers tend to come from a higher social class than non-volunteers
3 Volunteers are of higher intelligence in general, but not when volunteering for atypical research (such as hypnosis, sex research)
4 Volunteers have a higher need for approval than non-volunteers
5 Volunteers are more social than non-volunteers
Considerable confidence
1 Volunteers are more "arousal seeking" than non-volunteers (especially when the research involves stress)
2 People who volunteer for sex research are more unconventional than non-volunteers
3 Females are more likely to volunteer than males, except where the research involves physical or emotional stress
4 Volunteers are less authoritarian than non-volunteers
5 Jews are more likely to volunteer than Protestants; however, Protestants are more likely to volunteer than Catholics
6 Volunteers have a tendency to be less conforming than non-volunteers, except where the volunteers are female and the research is clinically oriented
Source: adapted from Rosenthal and Rosnow (1975).

(rely heavily on environmental cues) than are non-volunteers (Cooperman, 1980) and more willing to endure higher levels of stress in an experiment (Saunders, 1980). Thus, participant characteristics separate the person who volunteers from the person who does not.

Where does all of this leave us? It is clear that under some circumstances volunteers and non-volunteers differ. These differences may translate into lower external validity for findings based on volunteer participant samples. The best advice we can give is to be aware of the potential for volunteer bias and take it into account when interpreting your results.

Situational factors

In addition to participant characteristics, situational factors also may affect a person's decision to volunteer for behavioural research. According to Rosenthal and Rosnow (1975), you can have "maximum confidence" in the conclusion that people who are more interested in the topic being researched and who have expectations of being favourably evaluated will be more likely to volunteer for a particular research study. You can have "considerable confidence" that potential participants will be more likely to volunteer if they perceive the research as being important, if they feel guilty about not participating and if they are offered incentives to participate. Other factors that have less impact on the decision include personal characteristics of the person recruiting the participants, the amount of stress inherent in the experiment and the degree to which participants feel that volunteering is the "normative, expected, appropriate thing to do"

(Rosenthal and Rosnow, 1975, p. 119). Finally, you can have only "minimum confidence" that a personal acquaintance with the recruiter or public commitment to volunteering will affect the rate of volunteering (so do not count on your friends to volunteer).

As with the participant-related factors, the operation of the situational factors may be complex. For example, people are (perhaps not surprisingly) generally less likely to volunteer for experiments that involve stress or aversive situations.

The general conclusion from the research of Rosenthal and Rosnow (1975) is that there are several participant-related and situational characteristics that are likely to affect an individual's decision about volunteering for a particular research study. The decision to volunteer may be influenced by a variety of factors that interact with one another. In any case, it is apparent that volunteering is not a simple random process. Certain types of people are disposed to volunteer generally and for certain specific types of research. The next question is whether or not this volunteer bias affects the outcome of an experiment.

Volunteerism and internal validity

Ideally, you want to establish that it is your independent variable which causes observed variation in your dependent variable. However, variables related to voluntary participation may, quite subtly, influence your dependent variable. Thus, **volunteerism** may impact upon "inferred causality" (Rosenthal & Rosnow, 1975), which closely relates to internal validity.

> **Volunteerism**
> A threat to internal validity in which factors related to voluntary participation in a study may influence results.

Rosenthal and Rosnow conducted a series of experiments investigating the impact of volunteering on inferred causality within the context of an attitude change experiment in which they found that volunteers were more likely to be persuaded by a persuasive communication that they had heard (compared with non-volunteers who heard the communication without having previously indicated that they would be willing to volunteer for psychology studies). The authors suggest that this may have been due to the volunteers' "need for approval" and their desire to please the experimenter. Obviously, this has important implications for how we interpret causality in our studies because in cases such as this, it is a feature of "volunteers" that appears to be influencing the measure of the dependent variable rather than the independent variable itself. If this occurs, then the internal validity of the study is compromised.

Volunteerism and external validity

Ideally, we would like the results of any research that we conduct to generalize beyond our research sample. Volunteerism may affect our ability to do this. It may be the case that any results you find apply only to participants with the characteristics of the volunteers you used in your research. Thus, volunteerism may affect external validity as well as internal validity.

To see how volunteerism affects the external validity of a study, consider an experiment conducted by Irwin Horowitz (1969). This study investigated the relationship between the level of fear aroused by a persuasive communication and attitude change. Horowitz examined the impact of fear arousal along with a second variable: whether participants were volunteers or not. Participants in a "high-fear" group were exposed to a persuasive communication that pointed out the dangers of drug abuse (participants read a pamphlet and saw a film). The high-fear communication presented graphic descriptions of drug abuse. Participants in the low-fear group only read the pamphlet (they did not see the film), and the graphic references to dire consequences of drug abuse were eliminated. Attitudes were measured on a post-experimental questionnaire. What Horowitz found was that the high-fear communication affected volunteers and non-volunteers differently. The volunteers showed more attitude change in response to the high-fear communication than did the non-volunteers. However, little difference emerged between volunteers and non-volunteers in the low-fear condition. Thus, the relationship between fear arousal and attitude change was different for volunteer and non-volunteer participants. These results suggest that using volunteer participants in an attitude-change experiment may produce results that do not generalize to the general population.

Remedies for volunteerism

Are there any remedies for the "volunteerism" problem? Rosenthal and Rosnow (1975, pp. 198–9) list the following actions that you can take to reduce the bias inherent in the recruitment of volunteers:

1 Make the appeal for participants as interesting as possible, keeping in mind the nature of the target population.

2 Make the appeal as non-threatening as possible so that potential volunteers will not be "put off" by unwarranted fears of unfavourable evaluation.

3 Explicitly state the theoretical and practical importance of the research for which volunteering is requested.

4 Explicitly state in what way the target population is particularly relevant to the research being conducted and the responsibility of the potential volunteers to participate in research that has potential for benefiting others.

5 When possible, potential volunteers should be offered not only pay for participation but also small courtesy gifts simply for taking the time to consider whether they will want to participate.

6 Have the request for volunteering made by a person of status as high as possible and preferably by a woman.

7 When possible, avoid research tasks that may be psychologically or biologically stressful.

8 When possible, communicate the normative nature of the volunteering response.

9 After a target population has been defined, make an effort to have someone known to that population make an appeal for volunteers. The request for volunteers itself may be more successful if a personalized appeal is made.

10 For situations in which volunteering is regarded by the target population as normative, conditions of public commitment to volunteer may be more successful. If non-volunteering is regarded as normative, conditions of private commitment may be more successful.

Evaluating samples

Samples should be representative of the population from which they are drawn. A completely unbiased sample is one that is highly representative of the population. How do you create a completely unbiased sample? First, you would randomly sample from a population that contains *all* individuals in the population. Second, you would contact and obtain completed responses from *all* individuals selected to be in the sample. Such standards are rarely achieved. Even if random sampling is used, there can be bias from two sources: the sampling frame used and poor response rates. Moreover, even though non-probability samples have more potential sources of bias than probability samples, there are many reasons why they are used and should be evaluated positively.

Sampling frame

The **sampling frame** is the actual population of individuals (or clusters) from which a random sample will be drawn. Rarely will this coincide perfectly with the population of interest – some biases will be introduced. If you define your population as "residents of my city", the sampling frame may be a list of telephone numbers that you will use to contact residents between 5 p.m. and 9 p.m. This sampling frame excludes persons who do not have telephones or whose schedule prevents them from being at home when you are making calls. Also, if you are using the telephone directory to obtain numbers, you will exclude persons who have unlisted numbers. As another example, suppose you want to know what doctors think about the portrayal of the medical profession on television. A reasonable sampling frame would be all doctors listed in your telephone directory. Immediately you can see that you have limited your sample to a particular geographical area. More important, you have also limited the sample to doctors who have private practices – doctors who work only in clinics and hospitals have been excluded. When evaluating the results of the research, you need to consider how well the sampling frame matches the population of interest. Often the biases introduced are quite minor; however, they could have consequences.

> **Sampling frame**
> The actual population from which the sample will be drawn. Will match the "true" population to a greater or lesser degree depending on the sampling technique.

Summary

When obtaining a sample from a population it is important to rule out bias and maximize representativeness. Sampling techniques can be split up into two broad categories: probability sampling (which specifies the probability that a member of the population will be chosen) and non-probability sampling (which does not specify the likelihood that any given member of the population will be chosen). Types of probability sampling include: simple random sampling; stratified random sampling and cluster sampling. Non-probability sampling can be achieved by techniques known as convenience sampling, purposive sampling and quota sampling. All of these have advantages and disadvantages associated with them, and the sampling technique used should be both ethical and appropriate for the purposes of the research being conducted. When researchers sample, there are issues to be considered involving the use of students and, more generally, volunteers. Both groups have particular features that may lead to bias when tested on certain things. When evaluating the results of research, the degree of correspondence between the sampling frame and the population of interest should be considered.

Questions

1 Distinguish between probability and non-probability sampling techniques. What are the implications of each?

2 A population is the _____ group of cases that you are interested in, while a sample is a _____ of that population.

3 Distinguish between simple random, stratified random and convenience sampling.

4 What is the difference between quota sampling and stratified sampling?

5 Distinguish between cluster sampling and quota sampling.

6 What is "representativeness" and why is it important for validity?

7 What are the main advantages and disadvantages of using volunteers as participants?

8 What can be done to combat the problem of "volunteerism"?

 Activity

1 Suppose you want to know how many books in a bookshop have only male authors, only female authors, or both male and female authors (the "bookshop" in this case might be a large retail store, the textbook section of your university bookshop, or all the books in the stacks of your library). Because there are thousands of books in the store, you decide to study a sample of the books rather than examine every book there. Describe a possible sampling procedure using a non-probability sampling technique. Then describe how you might sample books using a probability sampling technique. Now speculate on the ways that the outcomes of your research might differ using the two techniques.

Chapter 10

Introduction to Qualitative Research

OVERVIEW

This chapter serves to introduce you to qualitative research. It is also a companion chapter to Chapter 2, in which we covered issues relating to the nature of knowledge and scientific approaches to knowledge. In the current chapter, we look at these ideas from a different perspective. And we do mean a different perspective. There is a genuine philosophical debate concerning the nature of knowledge and where it comes from, and this chapter will give you a general outline of another way of approaching these issues. This debate has direct consequences for researchers who, after all, make "obtaining knowledge" their job. We hope that you can read about the issues and appreciate the essence of the debate. We also use this chapter to introduce you to qualitative research and the features that are common to all qualitative methods.

OBJECTIVES

After studying this chapter and working through the questions, you should be able to:

- Give an account of the main critiques of the positivist position and its related assumptions
- Describe *relativism* and *social constructionism*, and the ways in which they approach knowledge
- State the main criticisms of quantitative methodologies in psychology
- Describe the main features of the qualitative paradigm

- Recognize when a qualitative approach to psychological questions might be most appropriate and why

- Outline some ways in which qualitative researchers can approach issues of reliability and validity, and account for why these are difficult topics for qualitative research

- Critique qualitative techniques and place the issues within a broader context

Introduction

Psychologists are interested in people, and their job is to understand them. You might say that psychologists aim to *know* about people. But how do they get this knowledge? Where does a psychologist's knowledge about people come from? In previous chapters, we have emphasized the way in which psychology has aligned itself with science. It uses scientific methods in its investigations into the mind and behaviour. However, the story is not as straightforward as this. There is an alternative position that questions the fundamental assumptions that science is based on. Additionally, there are psychologists who have critically examined the way in which scientific psychology is conducted and the knowledge that can be gained from such an approach. The result of these critical analyses of science and psychology has led many psychologists to adopt a qualitative approach to research. This chapter will introduce you to the basic concepts, first by covering the arguments against a strict scientific approach to knowledge acquisition and then describing an alternative position. After this, we will explore how this has influenced psychology and what a qualitative approach can offer. We finish by evaluating the material introduced in the chapter and offering a perspective on the issues.

One thing to note before reading this chapter is that we have deliberately polarized some of the positions we cover. The versions of the arguments we offer against science and against quantitative methods are, perhaps, at the extremes. We have made the issues deliberately black and white to begin with, because this is the easiest way to introduce the ideas. If we were to cover all the subtle nuances of the debate, then the bigger issues would be swamped by shades of grey. Towards the end of the chapter we acknowledge this and offer some concluding thoughts on how to approach research realistically, without committing oneself to an extreme position. To get further into the issues and for a fuller appreciation of the subtleties involved, see Willig and Stainton-Rogers (2008).

Revisiting knowledge

ch. 2
p.16

How do you know what you know? If you have already read Chapter 2 of this book, you might remember that we started that chapter with this question. The question is about "**knowledge**" and we mentioned previously that there is a whole branch of philosophy that is dedicated to questions related to what "knowledge" is and where it comes from: *epistemology*.

In Chapter 2, we described a few methods that you could employ to build an understanding of the world around you. One of these was the "scientific method", and we stated that, on balance, this was probably the best method you could use if you wanted to discover facts about the world

ch. 2
p.25

ch. 2
p.20

and how it works. We then went on to describe the **scientific method**, sketching out its characteristics and explaining its merits as a way of gaining knowledge. One of the characteristics that we discussed was *empiricism*. If you have not read Chapter 2 or have forgotten what **empiricism** was, then it might be worthwhile flicking back and reminding yourself. Empiricism is based on observation. If you want to find out about how the world is, you observe it. Making more and more observations allows us to build up an ever-increasing body of knowledge. The scientific method that we described in that chapter places emphasis on the manipulation of certain variables and the measurement of the effects such manipulations have on a dependent variable. This is done to test a hypothesis, and the outcome of an experiment is usually an appraisal of whether the manipulation of the independent variable(s) has had an influence on the dependent variable in relation to the hypothesis that was stated at the outset.

Positivism and realism

For empiricism to give you an accurate account of how the world is, we must first assume that there is a real world "out there" (let us call it "reality"). This position is broadly known as **realism**. Once we have made this assumption, we'll probably want to know things about this reality. To do this we can adopt **positivism**, which states that the best way to find out about reality is through empirical observations of it.

    For positivism to give us a reliable account of reality, we must assume that there is a straightforward relationship between the reality that we are trying to describe (and explain) and our observations of it. We assume that our observations reflect reality in an unproblematic way, and it is these objective observations that allow us to determine the truth about how it works. This is what science in its purest form is based upon. This approach holds that there is one "true" story to tell about the world out there and about any particular feature of it that you decide to study. The purpose of science is to make enough objective observations (using the scientific method) so that we can gradually build up a picture that gets closer and closer to the "true story". Obviously, for this approach to give us a true account our observations must be good. If our observations are "good" (in the sense of being impartial and objective) and they really do reflect reality, then there's nothing to stop us using these observations as a basis for creating an accurate representation of the world that we are trying to describe and explain. But is it really that simple?

> **Realism**
> The view that there is a real world "out there".
>
> **Positivism**
> The view that knowledge about reality can be reliably obtained through empirical observations.

Box 10.1 Fundamental assumptions of positivistic science

1 There is a reality.

2 This reality is knowable.

3 We can gain knowledge about reality through empirical observations.

4 The observations are an unproblematic reflection of the way reality is.

5 Our interpretations of the observations are objective and unbiased.

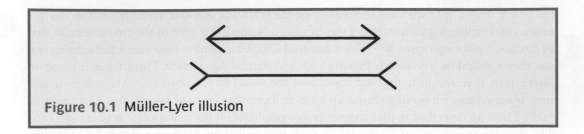

Figure 10.1 Müller-Lyer illusion

Problems with positivism

Positivism looks good in principle. It looks like it should work. However, in practice it has some problems. Most modern scientists agree that complete objectivity is difficult, if not impossible, to achieve. Let's see why.

Seeing is (not) believing – part 1

The first problems we encounter are with the empirical part of positivism. If our observations are going to help us describe and understand the world, they had better be good observations. When we talk about "observation" it is natural to think about it in terms of what we see through our eyes. Although not all observations are like this, we will use this as a way of showing you how observations are not always as perfect as we would like them to be. First, the way we see the world is not always directly and perfectly related to how the world actually is. For positivism to work, we would ideally like our observations to be true accounts of reality. It is easy to show that this sometimes is not the case. In the Müller-Lyer illusion (Figure 10.1), we usually see the bottom of the two lines as being longer than the top one. However, if you measure them, you will find that they are exactly the same length. This is just one example of how our observation does not match reality. Sometimes observations are not a reliable way to determine how "the world is".[1]

STOP & Think

Can you think of any other examples where our observations of the world are mistaken?

Seeing is (not) believing – part 2

Second, an objective appraisal of the facts would require most people to view the observations in exactly the same way. If the observations are a true reflection of the real world, then there should not be any room for disagreement. Again, we know that this does not always happen. To use another simple example, look at Figure 10.2. The "facts" are the same for two people looking

---

1 Of course, in this particular case, there is an alternative observation that we can make – measuring the lines with a measuring instrument such as a ruler. This will help in this case, but it will not always be clear whether or not you require a secondary observation and neither will it always be clear what a secondary observation should be. Moreover, how could you be sure that your second observation was better than the first?

Figure 10.2 Duck/rabbit

at it, in the sense that they are both looking at exactly the same thing. The problem, however, is that they may reach different conclusions about what the observation relates to. Some might see a duck, some might see a rabbit. Despite the facts (the ink-marks on the page and the image on the retina) being identical, two different observers might reach different conclusions about what they actually see. Objectivity is not guaranteed as people do not always view the same thing in the same way.

Do these things matter? That is the big question! Some people argue that, although these examples might appear trivial, they do illustrate that our observations about "reality" can sometimes be distorted. If they can be distorted, then we cannot claim that they are a perfect, unproblematic representation of the reality that we are trying to describe. If this is the case, and if it holds for observations in general, then positivism is in trouble because it is based on the idea that our observations are reliable indications of an underlying "real world". This would mean that all of these assumptions about how we can use observations to find out the truth about how reality works would have to be called into question.

More objections to objectivity

There is another way in which the positivist/empiricist position might be criticized. Again, taking science in its literal and purest form, we would expect scientists to be objective individuals who "let the data speak for themselves". In this picture, the scientist is the cold dispassionate observer who follows wherever his observations take him.[2] Again, this is unrealistic. Any time we look at something, we cannot help evaluate it in some way, and this evaluation is usually based on what we already know about it (or what we think we know about it). We will always have preconceived ideas or expectations when we make an observation. We cannot help it. This raises the possibility that *all* observations are "theory laden". This means that any observation we make comes with an evaluation attached, which is usually based on whatever "theory" or preconceived notion we have already formed about the thing we are observing. Again, this seems to rule out the pure objectivity that a strict interpretation of science would require.

If our observations are not 100 per cent trustworthy in the ways described above, where does that leave science? There are many positions on this. Scientists would admit that observations are not perfect, but they are reliable enough to be used in an informative way that allows us to

---

2   Or her. One critique of science has come from the feminist movement, with the argument being that science is male dominated both in terms of its practice and its focus. This is beyond the scope of the current text, but see Haraway (1988) or Harding (1991) for examples.

gain knowledge about the world. They would argue that enough observations from enough people showing the same outcome is a good way to get as *close* to objective knowledge as possible. Although it is true that our observations can never be perfect, science is getting ever closer to having a very accurate picture of reality. Others would disagree. They would say that the scientists' insistence that they can know about the nature of "reality" is naive and that there is always a barrier between the thing that they are trying to measure and the way they observe and measure it. After all, is it really possible that anyone can ever have direct access to "reality"?[3] Our observations are always going to be mediated by our sensory apparatus, by our existing knowledge and by our own particular way of interpreting things. We can never "climb outside of our heads" and observe reality in a way that does not require us to use our senses to look at things and use our minds to interpret what our observations mean. Pure objectivity would require us to look at the world in a way that was completely incapable of being biased in any way. It would also require us to look at the world in a way that wasn't linked to any of our previous ideas or notions that we have in our heads. Obviously we can't do either of these things.

The trouble with truth

A further criticism of the positivist approach is based on its approach to "truth". We have used the words "true" and "truth" frequently, both in the current chapter and in previous parts of this book, but what is truth? Truth is a slippery idea when you try to pin it down. In a scientific sense, it refers to the "way things really are" – the underlying nature of reality. Using the term "truth" in this way suggests that there is one (and only one) correct answer for every scientific question that you might want to ask, and positivism holds that it is possible to obtain this answer. But can you ever know when you have reached ultimate truth? Many people think that you cannot. You have nothing to measure it against. We do not have a "truth-ometer" that tells us how close or how far away we are from knowing the true nature of reality.

People in the past held beliefs (based on observations) that they were sure were true, but that turned out not to be. For example, casual observations do not suggest that the world is rotating. People once thought it was stationary until further observations suggested that their version of truth was mistaken. How can we be certain that *our* ideas about what is true are not also mistaken? Scientists would argue that more and more observations nudge us slowly and surely towards "truth". They would suggest that scientific observations increase our knowledge, but is it really possible for any one scientist, or group of scientists, to claim once and for all that they know the "truth" about reality? If this is not possible, then what is science progressing towards? Perhaps there is no such thing as ultimate truth that has an independent existence that we can discover. Even if there is an "ultimate truth", is it likely that humans will ever have direct access to it? Critics of science disagree with the claim that we are edging our way towards truth and would counter that by suggesting that it is entirely possible that our current ideas about what is "true" might be completely overhauled by some scientific revolution in the future of which we currently cannot conceive. Their point is: how would we ever be able to say "we now know the absolute truth"?

---

3   Some critics would say that there is no such thing as reality in the first place.

Alternative epistemologies

Given the criticisms of the positivist/empirical approach to knowledge that we have outlined above, what alternatives are there? One starting point is based on an idea introduced in the previous section. If you agree with the suggestions that there is no way of knowing when we have arrived at ultimate "truth" and that knowledge can never be entirely certain, then there must be an alternative way of looking at things. Perhaps knowledge is *constructed* in a subjective way rather than objectively "discovered". If all knowledge is a subjective construction built up by individuals (or groups of individuals), then there is no objective way that we can choose between different points of view. If we take the above objections seriously enough and suggest that observations and theories do not give us a reliable picture of reality, then that can lead us to conclude (if we are willing to follow the logic all the way) that there is no way of being able to decide whether *any* given observation or theory is better than any other. If you accept that there are no absolute truths, then you are adopting *relativism*.

Relativism

Relativism holds that truth is not something that can be objectively discovered and is not something universal that everyone can agree on. Instead, any claim about truth or about knowledge is relative to the context in which the claim is made. The context can be cultural (in which knowledge claims are relative to the culture in which they are made), historical (in which knowledge claims are relative to the historical period in which they are made), social (in which knowledge claims are relative to the social group that holds them) or linguistic (in which knowledge claims are relative to the language that is used to make them). The thing that all of these forms of relativism have in common is that they do not take any kind of knowledge as being absolute. What does this actually mean? To understand, think about the common phrase "beauty is in the eye of the beholder". This statement is based on a form of relativism. It means that there is no such thing as "objective beauty" that absolutely everyone will agree on. Some people will find some things (or people) beautiful, while others will disagree with them. If you tell someone that you think a film star is beautiful and they respond by saying "eeurgh, she's ugly", then this is relativism at work. Beauty is relative to the person who is making the judgement (i.e. the "beholder") and judgements about beauty do not depend on some objective measure of it.

> **Relativism**
> A position that suggests all knowledge is relative to the context in which it emerges.

Social constructionism

One approach that has developed from relativism is **social constructionism**. Social constructionists argue that all human experience is mediated by social factors and that our "reality" is constructed as a result of this. This probably sounds confusing, so we will try to break it down a little. Some things are undoubtedly socially constructed. Think about money. The paper that a £20 note is printed on is not worth £20. But you do not point this out to a shopkeeper when you use it to buy something that costs £20. Instead, the value of the £20 note has been agreed by society. Society has agreed that these particular pieces of paper have a specific value that is more than the paper is actually worth. The value of the £20 note is purely a social construction

> **Social constructionism**
> The view that all knowledge is constructed and is a direct result of the society in which it exists.

that in no way reflects the "reality" of the value of the paper itself. This is one social construction that most people can agree on, but some people take the idea further.

Think about "madness". What does "madness" actually mean? You probably have your own definition and it may or may not be the same as someone else's (in the same way that your idea of who is "beautiful" might not be the same as someone else's). However, our society *in general* has agreed upon a set of criteria by which people might be considered to be "mad". This is also a social construction and it is relative because our own society's agreement on what counts as "mad" may be different from that of another society, existing in another culture. Additionally, what we consider to be "mad" today is not what societies hundreds of years ago would have considered "mad", and vice versa, so our definition of it is relative to the historical time at which it was made as well as being culturally relative. Further to that, you may have noticed that we have used scare quotes every time we have mentioned the word "mad". Why was that? We used quotes around "mad" because it's not a word that is generally used any more in the society in which we are writing this book. It has been agreed by certain parts of society that "mad" is a term that is derogatory and should not be used. Instead, other terms have taken its place. In that sense, even the word "mad" is a social construction that is relative to the time in which it is used (and the culture – certain societies still do not have any problems with calling people "mad"). So, given that our society's version of "madness" is different to other societies', and given that our version of "madness" is different to what people thought it to be in the past, then we can say that knowledge about "madness" is relative. There are multiple versions of what counts as "madness" and it does not make sense to say that one is more right than another – they are all equally right within their own cultural or historical domain.

So, we can agree that some forms of knowledge (knowledge about the value of certain bits of paper and knowledge about who is "mad") are social constructions. Is there a line between things that are not social constructions and things that are? Strict social constructionists would say that *all* forms of knowledge are constructed socially. This viewpoint suggests that, whatever it is that you are considering, there is more than one type of "knowledge" that is relevant to it, and whatever type of knowledge that an individual subscribes to is a construction that is based on the context in which that individual exists. It is in this sense that social constructionists state that scientific knowledge itself has been socially constructed by scientists. Scientists form a particular type of group (a "society") and, according to this viewpoint, what is considered to be "true" within this group is just one version of reality that has been constructed by the members of the group. From this point of view, there is no such thing as a "right" or "wrong" theory or a "right" or "wrong" viewpoint, and it makes no sense to think of knowledge as being something that is "discovered". Instead, every theory and viewpoint is as valid as any other because a strict relativistic position suggests that there is no objective way of deciding between them.

Social constructionism in psychology

If all the discussion above has seemed a bit abstract and confusing, it is probably worth illustrating how social constructionists view certain psychological phenomena. Psychological research from a social constructionist perspective attempts to understand the various ways in which psychological "reality" is constructed within a particular historical and social context. For example, psychological constructs like "emotions" may not be objective and measurable, but may instead be viewed as concepts that have been socially constructed in such a way that the only context in which they are meaningful is the society in which they are used. Mesquita et al. (1997) describe a large degree of cultural diversity in the way various societies talk about emotions. The vocabulary used to describe emotions tends to vary considerably depending upon the cultural group that is under study. Additionally, there are also cultural variations in the ways in which emotional phenomena are described and communicated within everyday interactions. These findings may lend support to the idea that there are no universal emotions and what is called "emotion" is a direct result of shared cultural values in addition to the modes of interaction that are relevant in communicating ideas about the construct. As such, a social constructionist view of emotions (and any other psychological concept that you submit to this analysis) does not have an objective existence other than that which has been socially constructed.

Look at some of the words we used in the paragraph above: "talk", "vocabulary", "described" and "communicated". This should give you a hint as to what might play a key role in social construction. Language is central to the way we construct aspects of our world. It would be very hard to construct anything socially if we did not have the tools of language to do so. This is one reason why qualitative psychologists are so concerned with language. It is the key feature that allows us to have social relationships and build up a coherent narrative about our place in the world and our experience of it. We will talk more about language below. For a fuller discussion of social construction, see Burr (1995).

In the Know

The social construction of anorexia nervosa
Julie Hepworth published a book in 1999 entitled *The Social Construction of Anorexia Nervosa*. In it, Hepworth challenges the view that anorexia nervosa is best conceptualized as a psychopathology, and follows the various ways in which the medical community and society in general came to "construct" anorexia nervosa as a psychiatric condition. Hepworth traces the history of what became known as anorexia back to the fourteenth century, during which time "self-starvation" behaviours were often associated with saints and considered to be holy acts. After the witch-hunts of the Middle Ages, during which time many thousands of women were accused and executed for alleged witchcraft, the interpretation of women's mental health moved from the domain of religion to the domain of medicine, with the concept of "hysteria" being a ubiquitous explanation for many behaviours displayed by women (including self-starvation behaviour). In the eighteenth century, the concept of "insanity" became dominant, leading to the proliferation of the infamous Victorian-era insane-asylums. Individuals who starved themselves were increasingly considered to be insane and were confined to these asylums. In 1874, William Gull defined his observations of self-starvation and coined the term "anorexia nervosa", which was the moment that the condition entered into medical science. However, Gull did not "discover" anorexia nervosa. These behaviours had always existed and had been viewed in a variety of different ways throughout history. Hepworth offers an account of the various social practices that gave rise to Gull's "discovery" and the subsequent way in which the construct was developed throughout the decades to be seen eventually as being a psychopathological behaviour that primarily affects women. The point is that anorexia nervosa is undoubtedly a distressing condition, but the way that it is currently conceptualized is a product of a variety of social practices and that one's view of it is necessarily relative to the social and historical context in which it is made – if one lived in the fourteenth century, then one would have a very different view of the same condition to that one might have in the twenty-first century.

Quantitative versus qualitative psychology

Positivism in psychology

When psychologists talk about their discipline as being scientific in nature, they usually adopt a positivist position. Although scientific psychologists are aware that the phenomena they study are difficult to measure (and sometimes difficult to define) they still adopt positivism and employ the scientific method in order to study the mind. A large proportion of psychological research is still grounded in this position. This approach lends itself primarily to quantitative methods of investigation. These are methods in which mental phenomena are measured in some way that is usually numerical. When we talk about "variables" and measurement, we are talking about quantitative methods. Variables are, by definition, things that change (vary) and quantitative researchers measure these changes. The measurement can take various forms. For example, we might measure how many people exist in one category compared to another (say, how many people exercise at least once a week compared to how many never exercise) or we might measure the extent to which a variable changes (say, by asking people how many hours of exercise they do in an average week). Either way, we are getting numerical data. Psychology has traditionally aligned itself with other "natural" sciences that have adopted a positivist approach and emphasized the importance of quantitative measurements. But this is not the only way to do psychology.

ch. 4
p.61

The qualitative critique

Measuring experience

Psychology's subject matter is unique in many ways and is distinct from those of the natural sciences. Human experience and behaviour are rich in meaning. People are not passive "subjects" who are waiting to be measured. Psychological phenomena are complex and exist in a tapestry that includes the social, historical and cultural environment in which they take place. Measuring people is not the same as measuring other physical phenomena. The physical world of the natural sciences does not change over time and can be measured at the researcher's convenience without any consequence to the measurement. In contrast, many features of human psychology may be sensitive to all sorts of things. For example, the manner in which something psychological is measured, the time at which the measurement is made and the social context within which the measurement is made are all things that might have an important role to play in studying the phenomena in question. The complexity, richness and uniqueness of human experience have led some psychologists to question whether quantification is really the most appropriate way to study humans. Is it appropriate to attempt to isolate psychological phenomena and attach numerical measurements to them? Can we really expect that the complexities of psychological life can be neatly identified and divided up into variable-sized chunks that can then be studied in experiments? Our minds, our inner life and our experiences exist within a network of influencing factors that is large and does not lend itself to being easily packaged into discrete boxes. We attach meaning to our experiences, so how is it possible that our quantitative measures will be able to tell us anything about this meaning or the ways in which we interpret our experience? Reducing human experience to numbers may devalue it and might actually be self-defeating if it results in the loss of important and revealing information about the nature of people's experience. Most things can be measured numerically if you try hard enough, but that does not mean we should do so and it does not necessarily mean that our measurement will tell us everything that is useful. We can measure things like mood and emotion and attitudes on numerical scales, but will the numbers we end up with give us a full picture about moods, emotions and attitudes? Or is it likely that there will be features related to each of these things that are not captured by the quantitative way in which they are measured? Does a quantitative measure of "current mood" tell us anything about someone's mood as they are experiencing it? It seems unlikely. To get a complete picture, some researchers argue that psychologists should be interested in more than the numerical measure. They should also be interested in what a mood feels like to an individual, and how that experience interacts with the other aspects of that person's life. Studying mood in this way will tell us something different compared to knowing a person's score on a current mood questionnaire. Issues such as these have led some psychologists to adopt a qualitative approach to psychological questions.

Laboratory environments

Further critiques of quantitative methods derive from the way in which they are conducted. Laboratory-based experiments are generally viewed to be artificial environments which will not always be conducive to natural behaviours. This means that they are lacking in **ecological validity**.

Ecological validity
How much a particular method of research resembles "real life" in the context of the research.

ch. 5
p.97

Ecological validity is closely related to **external validity**, which we covered in Chapter 5, but it is not exactly the same. A study can be said to have ecological validity if the method employed closely resembles "real life". The more realistic a method of investigation is, the more ecological validity the study has.[4] Laboratory studies are highly controlled and usually follow a strict, regimented procedure. The situations into which participants are placed are unfamiliar, from sitting in front of a computer to lying in a brain-scanning machine.

Critics have been quick to point out the drawbacks of laboratory-based research, and it is no surprise that many of the criticisms tend to focus on the artificiality of the environment. If participants are placed into this environment, then how much confidence can we have that their behaviour will not be influenced by it? Not only that, but the tasks we ask people to do once they are in the laboratory rarely reflect anything that they would encounter in everyday life. Learning lists of words, solving abstract puzzles, viewing parts of faces; are these strange tasks really going to enlighten us about how memory, problem solving or perception work? In general, the laboratory is a place in which individual phenomena (memory, perception etc.) are studied in isolation, outside of any normal social context. Additionally, more often than not the participant is almost entirely unaware of *why* she is being asked to undertake these various tasks, which is another way in which the laboratory setting is unlike any naturally occurring environment. Laboratory-based quantitative research methods tend to lack ecological validity, and these concerns have led some researchers to endorse a more natural approach that places emphasis on people's actual experiences.

4   This is slightly different to external validity, which deals with how "generalizable" the findings from a study might be. It is entirely possible that a study's findings are generalizable (high external validity), but do not have high ecological validity.

Assumptions about people

A further criticism that might be levelled at the traditional quantitative paradigm is that it assumes certain things about its subject matter. For example, a large proportion of quantitative research makes the assumption that the psychological phenomena under investigation are, in some broad sense, universal in the population as a whole. Although this may be the case for some things, there are other things that might not be as universal as researchers would like to believe. For example, the way in which people interpret instructions given to them in an experiment, or the meaning they attach to questionnaire items, might be dependent upon their cultural background. If this is the case then this is obviously going to influence the way they perform the task or answer the questions. This would then suggest that the measurement instrument cannot be said to be entirely valid, as it may be measuring something different in different people. Some things, therefore, might be valid only if the participants and the researchers all share an understanding of the task and the meaning of any terms that are used. Qualitative researchers acknowledge this and make the context in which the research takes place a key component of their studies.

Box 10.2 Qualitative critique of quantitative psychology

1 "Objectively" measuring humans is impossible.
2 Reducing experience to quantitative values means losing its inherent richness.
3 Attempts to isolate psychological "phenomena" fail to reflect the context in which they truly operate.
4 Laboratory-based experiments are unnatural environments that constrain natural behaviours and reactions.
5 Social context of behaviour is ignored.
6 Tasks often fail to resemble anything people would usually do.
7 Cultural contexts are rarely taken into consideration.

Qualitative research in psychology

A qualitative approach to psychological questions is hard to define as there is more than one way of doing psychology qualitatively. Qualitative researchers range from those who adopt a strict social constructionist position to those who are sympathetic to empiricism, despite its potential problems. Broadly, however, qualitative research is based on *interpretation of experience* and the *meaning* that is attached to experience. Qualitative approaches serve a different function to quantitative techniques. They are not concerned with relationships between variables in the same way that quantitative research is. What this means is that a qualitative approach will be able to tell you about different aspects of a particular phenomena. Sometimes this will be instead of quantitative research (in cases where the phenomena cannot be studied quantitatively or where the researcher's epistemological position prohibits positivism), while sometimes it will be a companion to it (in cases where the phenomena can be studied using both approaches, and when the researcher's epistemological position permits a mixed-method approach). Approaching psychological phenomena qualitatively will often shed light on the things that quantitative measurement cannot address, such as accounts of first-person experience. Also, qualitative researchers acknowledge that the researcher plays a vital part in any study involving other people, and that all research in psychology necessarily involves a social interaction between people (even if it is only a participant and an experimenter). This particular feature of qualitative research is a direct response to the claim that pure objectivity is impossible, and is particularly difficult when studying behaviour. Instead, qualitative researchers argue that attempts to eliminate subjective interpretations are unnecessary, and the interpretative process itself should be a key feature of the study. In addition to the interpretation that the researcher makes, emphasis is also placed on the way the participant interprets his or her own experiences and the meaning that they take from these experiences.

What can be studied qualitatively?

Most features of the mind (with a few exceptions) come with experiences, and humans are in the habit of interpreting and attaching meaning to their experiences, either through language or through some other form of interpretative system. Any phenomena to which these things apply would be open to qualitative study. Although we might be able to measure, say, memory performance in brain-damaged individuals, the qualitative flip-side is to gain an account of these patients' lived experience with such an impairment. Note that these two approaches will answer very different questions about the phenomena under study. Additionally, people often use language in order to achieve something in the world. It might be to convey information; it might be to withhold information; it might be to persuade someone in some way. Whenever language is employed, qualitative techniques can be used. As always, careful consideration must always be given to the question that you are addressing.

Perhaps not surprisingly, it is in social psychology that qualitative research has thrived. Social psychology deals with interactions between individuals in a social context and focuses on the way in which people experience their social environment. This makes the phenomena of social psychology particularly suited to a qualitative approach (see McKinlay & McVittie, 2008, for an excellent account of a variety of social psychological phenomena from a qualitative perspective).

Health psychology is another area in which qualitative techniques are increasingly employed (see, e.g. Chamberlain & Murray, 2008). Health psychology is often concerned with how people experience their own health and illness. An appreciation of these issues can be invaluable, because it can inform how health practices are delivered and it can also inform health policy. Developmental psychology is another area in which qualitative techniques are increasingly being employed, by investigating children's knowledge and experience of the world (Burman, 2008). These are just some areas that can benefit from qualitative methodologies, but there are a lot more. For a comprehensive account, see Willig and Stainton-Rogers (2008).

Which method should I use?

We have presented the two extreme positions (positivism versus relativism) in this chapter. Although there are psychologists who fall squarely into one or the other of these camps, there are many who will be somewhere in the middle. When this is the case, then the decision about which method to use will depend on the phenomena under study and the research question that you are asking. The most important thing at the outset of any research project is to have a full and clear understanding of the question you want to address. A full understanding of the research aims will shed light on how best to proceed. Keep in mind that qualitative and quantitative approaches ask different kinds of questions and allow for different kinds of conclusions. If you are not interested in investigating relationships between variables, and if you find yourself asking questions about people's experiences and the way they attach meaning to these experiences, then a qualitative approach is best.

It is also important that you understand *why* you have decided to utilize one particular type of research over the other. Careful thought must be given at the design stage to what the most appropriate methodology is likely to be, and this will depend on many factors, including your own philosophical position concerning epistemology and whether or not quantification is going to answer your question more satisfactorily than a qualitative study. It will also depend on the way you view the phenomenon itself – is it likely to be something that is "measurable" in a way that is genuinely informative, or would it be better to get people's own accounts of it? As is the case for all methods, the old saying "horses for courses" applies to this question.[5] We return to some of these issues in the final sections of this chapter.

Sampling

ch. 9
We covered **sampling in** the previous chapter but it is worth mentioning again in relation to qualitative research. Obviously, how and who you sample will be determined by the research question you are addressing. As such, there are some sampling methods that might be appropriate for quantitative research, but would not be suitable for a qualitative study. For example, most quantitative researchers would advocate probability sampling as much as possible when conducting research. However, in many qualitative studies, random sampling would not be worthwhile because the resulting sample might have very little to contribute to the topic under investigation. Qualitative research, therefore, does not overly concern itself with sample sizes and ensuring representativeness. Instead, the sample is chosen according to how appropriate the cases are in

Theoretical sampling
A method of sampling used in some qualitative research in which additional sampling is undertaken according to how much new theoretical insight it might provide.

relation to the research question being asked. That is why many qualitative researchers use **purposive sampling** in which the participants (or cases) that are chosen meet some criteria that are linked to the research question. Another form of sampling that is often used in qualitative research is **theoretical sampling**. Theoretical sampling is commonly linked to **Grounded Theory**. It involves adding new cases to the sample in order to provide more insight into the theory that is being developed from the data analysis. What this means is that researchers will selectively add new cases in order to develop the theory further. The researcher must ask herself "what cases should I sample next?" during the data collection process, and must also decide when "theoretical saturation" (the point at which adding new cases will not provide substantially more insight than has already been achieved) has taken place.

 ch. 9
p.165

 ch. 22
pp.548–55

---

5 This is a phrase that I (SW) remember hearing in my undergraduate methods class, and at the time I did not realize what it meant. Without wishing to be patronizing, I will explain it just in case there is anybody who, like I was, is unfamiliar with this term. It basically means that, in a horse race, it is often not the "best" horse that wins, but the horse that is most suited to the ground on the day of the race. In the current context it means that the method you should choose is the one most suited to the purpose of the research.

STOP & Think

Quantitative and qualitative research place different emphases on sampling techniques. In what way might these different approaches to sampling influence the conclusions that can be drawn from both quantitative and qualitative research respectively?

The fundamentals of qualitative research

We will cover methods of qualitative data collection in the next chapter, but before that we would like to cover some features that we consider to be common to all qualitative methods. These are reflexivity, interpretation and meaning, and language.

Reflexivity

Qualitative research tends not to make any claims about objectivity in the way that much quantitative research does. Instead, qualitative researchers openly admit that there is a large subjective component to their work, but view this as a further source of information rather than a weakness. As such, qualitative research usually involves an element of **reflexivity**. This is the practice of reflecting upon the research process and providing an account of the researcher's role in it, from the choice of topic to the conduct of the investigation itself. Doing this allows researchers to account for the subjective factors that they themselves bring to the investigation and to speculate about the role that they have played and the impact that they have had. It also involves the researcher commenting on the context in which the investigation took place and how this may have impacted upon the attempt to understand the phenomenon in question. Both the researcher and the participant (if participants are involved) will bring their own meanings to the research, and reflexivity is an opportunity to explore this and the effects that may have resulted. In doing so, the qualitative researcher is being open and honest about the subjective nature of the research, and is allowing whoever is reading the research to form their own judgement on the relative impact of these subjective factors.

> **Reflexivity**
> The practice of reflecting upon a qualitative research process for the purpose of identifying subjective and contextual factors that may have influenced the outcome.

Interpretation and meaning

Most qualitative research in psychology will be concerned with **interpretation and meaning**. Quantitative methods based on a positivist approach to knowledge will try to avoid interpretation as much as possible in order to obtain a "pure" objective representation of the phenomenon under study. Qualitative researchers, on the other hand, do not do this. Psychology is the study of people by people. A qualitative psychologist will argue that an inevitable consequence of this is that we will be unable to completely screen out any interpretations that we might bring to a situation, and we should instead be looking to understand these interpretations in the context

> **Interpretation and meaning**
> The basis of the majority of qualitative research is an interpretation of experience (both the participants' and the researcher's) and the meaning that is attached to the experience.

in which they occur. As such, qualitative researchers will seek to actively include interpretations in their research, because they believe that interpretations are devices that allow us to bridge the gap between the thing that we are interested in (the object of our psychological investigation) and the way we represent it. The suggestion is that the phenomenon under study will always be mediated by the people involved in terms of their interpretation of it, and so we should look to the interpretation as a source of information rather than try to reduce it. Closely related to this is the issue of meaning. We all attach meaning to our experiences, but this meaning is ignored by quantitative research. Qualitative researchers recognize the importance of the meanings we impose upon our experiences of the world and the interactions we have within it. Interpretation and meaning are, therefore, core features of qualitative approaches to psychology.

Language

Language
The fundamental "unit of analysis" for qualitative research. Language is considered a vehicle to convey interpretation and meaning.

How do we attach meaning to things and how do we interpret our experience? **Language** is the medium by which these things usually operate.[6] Most qualitative techniques rely on close scrutiny of language. This can take many forms, including the language used by researchers engaged in observations to describe the events being observed, language used by participants to describe their experiences, language used in written text or language used between individuals engaged in a social exchange. The way language is treated will depend upon the particular methodology that is being used, but, as a vehicle for meaning and interpretation, language is central to qualitative techniques. In the **next chapter** we will describe the ways in which qualitative researchers collect their data (which is usually language based) and in Chapter 18 we will cover the analysis techniques that can be employed with this data.

 ch. 18

ch. 11

Reliability and validity

In previous chapters, we have spoken about validity and reliability as being indicators of how "good" the quantitative measures being used are. A good quantitative measure of anything psychological will be reliable in the sense that it will give you consistent results when a replication is attempted. Validity relates to measures of psychological constructs (i.e. an indication about the degree to which the measure is "tapping into" what it is supposed to) and to quantitative studies as a whole (i.e. the extent to which the relationship between the variables can be considered a "true" account). Validity can also be "external", which is a measure of the degree to which the findings can be generalized to a larger population or to environments outside the one that the research was conducted in. There are objections to this, and they stem from the objections to positivism that we described earlier in this chapter. For validity and reliability to make any sense, the researcher must make some assumptions about "objectivity". In other words, a quantitative researcher making a claim about a measure's validity must claim to know what a "good" (i.e. objective) measure of a phenomenon would look like. We have already seen that there are various objections to this claim.

---

6   Although it does not have to be. Sometimes we interpret our experiences in other ways. For example, through a painting or a photograph, which are not language based. These things can also be used in qualitative research. Although language is the most common medium, any representational system can be used.

That leaves us with two problems. First, if we rule out objectivity (which allows us to recognize "good" measures or "good" research when we see it), then does that not mean that we do not have any criteria by which to judge validity? If we do not have any standards of what a "good" measure is, how do we know if what we are doing is valid? This is one of the central issues in qualitative research. Second, the concepts of validity and reliability are much more difficult to apply in qualitative research, which does not make measurements in the way that quantitative research does. If a measure is reliable, it generally means it produces the same measurement from time A to time B. But would it make sense to apply that definition to a qualitative observation (for example)? If two people interpret a similar experience in different ways, this is not an indication that their accounts are "unreliable". Instead it might be telling us something that is potentially important about the way people experience things.

One way to deal with these issues is to adopt a relativist position (see, e.g. Smith & Hodkinson, 2005). As we outlined above, the relativist position states that there are no objective criteria that can be used to judge "good" and "bad" research. Instead, everything is judged in a relative manner, meaning that there is no way to decide between two pieces of research except in terms of how they have been relatively accepted or rejected by the community of researchers (or an even larger societal group). By this account, relativists would argue that there are no "fixed" criteria for judging research. Instead, research is assessed within the context in which it takes place (e.g. social, historical, geographical, political, cultural). Those who adopt this position argue that it is complex sociocultural factors that give any kind of research its perceived credibility, and these are transient according to the context. The result of this position is that research can never be said to be truly valid/invalid or reliable/unreliable (indeed, these terms are meaningless if a strict relativist position is adopted).

However, not every qualitative researcher is a relativist. Merrick (1999) addresses such issues, and recommends that "reliability" when applied to qualitative research should be understood in the more common everyday sense of the word. She recommends that we ask questions concerning how much we can depend upon the research process itself and the findings that emerge from it. This will include questions relating to the methods that were used, who was involved, how it was conducted and how the information gathered was analysed. Merrick calls this "trustworthiness" and it encompasses all aspects of "good practice" that other researchers should be able to recognize. A feature of this is the process of reflexivity, described previously, in which the researcher makes an honest assessment about the role that he or she has played in the process, and any potential biases or interpretations that may exist as a result of the interactions that occurred.

The issue of validity is a more difficult one. Merrick (1999) suggests that one way of addressing the validity problem is to rely on a consensus of judgement in which interpretive conclusions are assessed on the basis of how much agreement there is between researchers. This, however, becomes problematic when deciding how to deal with alternative views (they cannot be "wrong" or even "less valid" than other views, given the rejection of such statements by many qualitative epistemologies).

One way to approach the issue of validity is by using **triangulation**. This refers to the assessment of the outcome of a particular investigation by looking at it from a number of standpoints. The alternative standpoints can originate from a variety of different sources, and should emphasize that any one problem can be approached

Triangulation
The process of assessing the outcome of a piece of research by viewing it from a number of differing perspectives. If the perspectives converge on the same conclusion, "triangulation" can be said to have occurred.

in a number of ways. For example, we can utilize different methods to look at the same question. We can use different researchers, all bringing their own interpretations, frameworks, strengths and weaknesses. If the outcomes of our different approaches all produce similar results, then we can say that triangulation has occurred and this gives the findings more credibility than if there were not this convergence. In a loose sense, we could say that the findings were more valid given the triangulation.

However, the triangulation method would be dismissed by some researchers, which highlights the difficulties involved in addressing these issues. During the writing of this chapter, we received some feedback from qualitative researchers about what we had written. Most of them had something to say about the way we had handled the issues of reliability and validity. All of them said something different. Some suggested that we should place more emphasis on the political and social factors that influence judgements about the perceived "quality" of qualitative research. Some said we should pay more attention to the consequences of the research as a measure of how "good" the research is (e.g. who gains/who loses? Is there more of an advantage for anyone involved compared to anyone else?). Others wanted us to state the importance of the fit between data and theory, as well as the transparency that comes with reflexivity. The comments we received all made sense, but they were wide-ranging and, at times, disparate. This is a feature of the intellectual conversation that qualitative researchers continue to have with themselves about how they can best assess their research. This is a good thing, because it demonstrates the open debate that is still happening as to how notions of validity and reliability might apply to qualitative research, but it also highlights how difficult the issue is. The discussion over which criteria should be used to evaluate qualitative research is ongoing. For a readable and sober summary of some of the main issues, see Willig (2001).

Evaluation of qualitative methods and critiques

If the critiques of science and of quantitative psychology presented in this chapter are to be taken seriously, then why is not everyone doing qualitative psychology? The time has come to take a step back and take stock of some of the issues we have covered in this chapter.

Problems with qualitative methods

What many researchers see as being strengths of qualitative methods, others see as being weaknesses. Qualitative researchers emphasize the "richness" of the information that their methods provide. This richness is a direct result of the way in which qualitative data is collected and the natural environment in which this data collection occurs. This is thought to produce information that directly reflects an individual's experience of the social world and the meanings that they attach to it. However, a critic of qualitative methods would point to the large amount of data collected in qualitative studies, which then has to be organized and interpreted by the researcher. The possibility arises that this process itself allows the researcher to conduct this organization and interpretation in any way he or she sees fit. There is no way to ensure that the analysis is not biased by the researcher conducting it. After all, if the basis of qualitative methods is "interpretation" then what is to stop any number of people interpreting the same qualitative data in any number of ways? This would be truly relativistic, but just how informative would it

p.191

pp.193–194

be? In short, the standard accusation is that qualitative techniques are too subjective and tied to each investigator's particular viewpoint to be useful. Although this subjectivity is recognized and often directly addressed through the processes of reflexivity and triangulation, these techniques are not always fail-safe ways of ensuring that subjectivity does not bias conclusions in a way that cripples the research and prevents any real insight being gained from it. While qualitative researchers are to be applauded in their attempts to address the criticisms of quantitative psychology, the subjectivity that they promote is seen by many as being their ultimate weakness.

Making sense of the debate

Despite the critiques that we have described in the current chapter, science still has a monopoly on the knowledge business. Why is this? The first thing to note is that we have described the most extreme version of the positivist agenda, and we did so to illustrate the fundamental assumptions. Most scientists, if they were pushed on the matter, would admit that positivism in this pure form is untenable. However, this is not to say that they would agree with the critics of science. You need only look at medical advances and the applications of scientific principles in technology to realize that scientific knowledge is useful on some "real" level. Strip away the social and cultural baggage that goes along with Western medicine and you will find that it actually does a very good job of dealing with disease. Science seems to work. Despite the conceptual critiques aimed at it, science has had many undeniable successes and the critiques must be considered with that in mind. Scientists might also claim that the assertions of relativism are merely an intellectual exercise in scepticism that is useful only in a general conceptual analysis of epistemological positions. A favourite taunt that is often aimed at the social constructionists is to invite them to jump out of a high window and then ask them whether they consider gravity to be socially constructed.[7] This, however, may also be unfair because it, too, is based on an extreme version of social constructionism. Just as the majority of quantitative researchers would not defend an extreme positivist position, most qualitative researchers would acknowledge that staunch relativism is not particularly useful either. As interesting as the critiques are and as logical as the arguments may be, there are always going to be parts of psychology and the cognitive sciences that necessarily adopt the techniques of science, not because the practitioners are naive or out of touch or are stubbornly refusing to move away from old ideas, but because there is simply no better way to do things in their area. The enlightened researcher will be aware of the critiques and acknowledge them, but will also realize that they probably are not as problematic in certain areas as some people would suggest. It would be our advice to you to understand the arguments for and against positivism and the scientific method, and for and against relativism and qualitative methods, and then make your own judgement. You do not have to adopt one position and stick stubbornly to it, but an appreciation of the arguments can only be useful.

Mixed methods
Using both qualitative and quantitative methodologies to approach a particular research question.

Mixed methods

Increasingly, psychologists are adopting **mixed methods**, incorporating both quantitative and qualitative techniques. For many psychological topics, this makes sense,

---

7   We have not been able to track down the exact source of this comment, but it is believed to have been Alan Sokal, who has written about science and relativism, and who perpetrated one of the most famous hoaxes in recent scientific history to illustrate his position. For more, see Sokal and Bricmont (2003).

because adopting one or the other will potentially exclude a great deal of potentially illuminating data. For example, one of us (SW) has recently conducted a qualitative study on the way people express superstitious, paranormal and magical beliefs. Most of the work done previously on this topic was quantitative, and focused on the various correlations between quantifiable measures of (for example) reasoning skills and quantifiable measures of paranormal and superstitious beliefs (measured using questionnaires). However, it became clear that these techniques were missing a great deal of what people actually mean when they speak about these beliefs. For example, it is not uncommon for someone to profess scepticism about superstitions (and reflect this on a questionnaire) but still be reluctant to walk under a ladder or open an umbrella indoors. Quantitative research will usually miss these things, so by qualitatively studying people's conceptualizations of the phenomena in question, a whole new avenue of interesting data can be uncovered. On the other hand, a solely qualitative approach will find it difficult to discover whether reasoning skills are different in those who believe in such things and those who don't, which is why a mixed-method approach is to be recommended.

Confused?

At this point, it's natural to be a bit confused. Many textbooks on research methods will primarily adopt a quantitative or a qualitative approach and give only a brief cursory account of the alternative position. We didn't want to do this and so we have presented arguments for and against science.[8] Who is right and who is wrong?[9] Unfortunately, it is not as simple as that. Both arguments for and against positivism have strengths and weaknesses, as have arguments for and against a form of relativism. Stripped down to the fundamentals, the extremes of both positions are irreconcilable. Staunch scientists will continue to adopt a version of positivism and employ empirical methods, while hard-line relativists will always point out the problems with the scientists' basic assumptions and state that a relativist position can help avoid the pitfalls of strict positivism.[10] In practice, many researchers acknowledge that both approaches can be useful in different circumstances. Not everything can be studied qualitatively and not everything should be studied quantitatively. As well as introducing you to the qualitative critique of science, this chapter was also intended to make you think about the issues. Unfortunately, we do not have space to cover all the subtleties and nuances involved in the debate between scientists and their critics, just as we cannot cover all of the arguments for and against a qualitative approach to psychology. We hope that the reader consults works on the philosophy of science if these issues are of interest (see, e.g., Couvalis, 1999, for an introductory account).

When it comes to actually conducting research, we would strongly recommend that you think about the assumptions that underlie your methodology and be able to defend why you have chosen one method rather than another. Hopefully, your decision will be guided by some of the issues discussed in this book. It is also worth remembering that many researchers

---

8   We have not covered *all* of the arguments, however. For an excellent account of what science is, see Chalmers (2004) appropriately titled "What is this thing called science?"

9   A meaningless question in itself if you are a strict relativist.

10   Although we cannot help but mention an inherent paradox with the strict relativist position: the statement "everything is relative" must itself either be a relative statement or a statement of an absolute truth. If considered to be relative, then this statement itself does not rule out the possibility that absolute truths might exist. If the statement is absolute, on the other hand, then it would be an example of an absolute statement, suggesting that not all truths are relative, and discrediting the relative position.

employ both quantitative and qualitative methods when approaching an issue that can be studied by both. Now that we have given you the basics, the following chapter will look at how qualitative researchers actually collect their data.

STOP & Think

Think back to the mood/exercise study that we used in Chapter 7. So far, we have described various ways to do this study that have involved quantitative measurement and experimental designs. Based on what you've read in the current chapter, can you think of how you might approach this topic in a qualitative way? What benefits/drawbacks might go along with doing a qualitative study to look at the "exercise/happiness" link?

Summary

In Chapter 2 we presented a case for science, and suggested that it was the best way of finding out how the world works. In the current chapter, we attacked that viewpoint and outlined objections to it that suggest it is built on unstable foundations. In particular, the assumptions that positivism rests on, which include objectivity and empiricism, can be viewed as being mistaken. As an alternative, relativism and its close relations can be adopted as an epistemological stance, which in turn leads to the endorsement of qualitative methodologies. These involve a rejection of the main drawbacks of quantitative techniques (measurement, laboratory-based studies), and focus on interpretation and meaning.

Questions

1 What is positivism and what assumptions underlie it?
2 Why might positivism be problematic?
3 What alternative epistemology offers an alternative to positivism?
4 In what way do alternative epistemologies differ from positivism?
5 What criticisms have been made about quantitative approaches to psychology?
6 What are the mean features of qualitative research?
7 Should qualitative researchers be concerned with reliability and validity? Why/why not?
8 What can be done to establish validity in qualitative research?
9 What weaknesses might there be with qualitative approaches to psychology?
10 Is the qualitative paradigm likely, in your opinion, to replace quantitative methods as the main way of doing research in psychology? Why/why not?

Chapter 11

Qualitative Data Collection

OVERVIEW

Chapter 10 introduced you to qualitative research and some of the assumptions that underlie it. Another way in which qualitative methods are distinct from quantitative methods is in the way data are collected. Qualitative projects use a variety of techniques, all of which reflect the emphasis that qualitative researchers place on extracting meaning from their data. In this chapter, we will introduce you to some (but by no means all) of the ways that qualitative data can be collected. We will start with interviews, which are probably the most common means to collect data. We will then move on to focus groups, which are becoming more popular, before covering diary methods, Web-based techniques, and media and text sources.

OBJECTIVES

After studying this chapter and working through the questions, you should be able to:

- Identify the issues involved in choosing an appropriate research question for a qualitative study
- Give an account of the main features involved in using interviews as a way to collect qualitative data
- Describe what makes a "good" interview and what the characteristics are of a "good" interviewer
- Describe the advantages and disadvantages of "focus groups", and how they differ from one-to-one interviews
- Describe and evaluate other forms of qualitative data collection, including diary studies, Web-based data, and media and text sources

Introduction

One of the main strengths of qualitative research is in the richness of the data that it produces. Rather than reducing things to numbers, qualitative researchers like to focus on content and meaning and the actual things people say. Qualitative researchers undertaking a research project need to give careful consideration to the nature of the data that they will collect and the way in which they will collect it. "New" data can be obtained by engaging people in discussions about the issues that are of interest to the researcher. This type of data collection will usually be in the form of interviews or focus groups. Alternatively, researchers can use data that already exist. This might involve analysing Internet postings or text that has been drawn from the media. By their very nature, qualitative methods will not attach numbers to things in the way that quantitative methods might, but that is not to say there won't be any reduction of the data at all. One of the main challenges of qualitative research is to ensure that the data that are collected reflect the source as much as possible. This is sometimes not as easy at it sounds. For example, a written transcript of an **interview** will inevitably lose some of the richness that the actual interview will have had, purely because it cannot accurately convey all of the features of the original interaction. The tone of the interviewee's voice, her body language, how much eye-contact she makes with the interviewer, as well as other situational factors such as a raised eyebrow, an almost imperceptible smirk or a nervous twitch – all things that will be lost in a written account of the interview, even if that account replicates verbatim what was said. A videotape of the interview will reproduce many of these things, but even this will fail to capture all aspects of the situation. In many interviews and focus groups, the things mentioned above will not matter and will have very little impact on the meaning that is conveyed by the words used. In other cases, body language may be important. When pre-existing data are used, then the researcher must acknowledge that the data have already been through the interpretative filter of the individual (or individuals) from whom they originated. Generally, qualitative research attempts to minimize how much gets "lost in translation", but this will depend on the nature of the research itself. In this chapter, we will look at various methods of collecting qualitative data. First, however, let us look at some things to be considered before the data collection can begin.

> **Interview**
> A one-to-one discussion with a participant on a specified topic.

Choosing a research question

Quantitative methods employ hypotheses. A hypothesis is a statement about a potential relationship between the variables under study. Hypotheses are usually derived from a theory and then empirically tested. Qualitative research, however, does not involve variables and many qualitative researchers do not subscribe to strict empiricism, so hypotheses as formulated in this way are not appropriate for qualitative studies. Instead, a **research question** is established. The research question that you choose is going to have an impact upon the way in which you collect your data. For example, a research question that asks "How do Scottish adolescent males define excessive drinking behaviours?" is going to require a different approach to data collection than a research question that asks "How have Republican and Democrat American presidential candidates spoken about their religious beliefs during presidential campaigns?"

> **Research question**
> The question that a researcher addresses with a given piece of research.

Research questions do not appear out of nowhere. They are usually based upon literature that has already raised important issues, such as drinking practices among Scottish youths or the role that religion plays in American politics. Another feature of qualitative research questions is that they do not make specific predictions in the same way as quantitative hypotheses do. Instead, the question is framed in a way that allows the researcher to explore the question freely without an explicit statement about what outcomes are expected. You may also have noticed that both of the questions above begin with the word "how". This is common in qualitative research and we ask questions in this way because we want to know more than just "what" (for example) presidential candidates say about their religious beliefs. Asking "how" is asking about the process involved in constructing their discourse on the issue, which allows us to look at whether the candidates have tried to conceal their religious beliefs, whether they have tended to qualify them with an accompanying statement about the importance of the separation of church and state or whether they have actively promoted their beliefs as being a defining feature of their candidacy. Maybe they did all of these things depending on the audience that they were speaking to. Asking "how" questions will open up the research in a way that merely asking "what" would not.

Another feature of research questions in qualitative research is that they will sometimes be directly related to the method used. Sometimes the philosophy underlying a particular approach will determine the way in which the question is asked and the way in which the data are analysed. For example, a social constructionist approach will necessarily ask questions about how a particular phenomenon is constructed and how this construction is represented in language (e.g. "How do sport psychologists construct 'success' in their interactions with sportsmen and sportswomen?"). This approach limits the research question compared to other methodologies, which allow for a wider range of questions to be addressed. When using a qualitative method known as "**Grounded Theory**" a researcher will ask a general question (e.g. "How do people make decisions regarding recycling?") and gather data relating to the question. Then a process of analysis will begin in which theoretical categories are generated from the data in such a way that the theoretical categories are "grounded" in the data that the researcher has got (if you do not understand this, do not panic; we will explain it in Chapter 22). This technique is different in its underlying assumption to social constructionist approaches, and as a result of this difference, researchers using Grounded Theory can ask questions that social constructionists would not, such as questions relating to processes, decisions and experiences.

ch. 22
pp.554–556

As is always the case, the method that you choose should be appropriate to your research question and no method is generally better or worse than any other. Once your research question has been formulated, there are two decisions that have to be made:

1 How am I going to collect the data?
2 How am I going to analyse the data?

These two questions are not independent of each other and decisions regarding one question should be made with the other question in mind. A general piece of advice is that you should never begin data collection without knowing how those data will be analysed (this advice is just as true for quantitative research as it is for qualitative work). The philosophy that underpins your method of analysis will also underpin your method of data collection, so you should view these two components as being complementary to each other. We will cover analysis techniques in Chapter 22, so for the moment, let us focus on the various ways in which you can collect qualitative data.

Interviews

Interviews are perhaps the most common way of collecting qualitative data. Bingham and Moore (1959) described an interview as a conversation with a purpose. In qualitative research, the main purpose is to explore the interviewee's experiences and subjective views on a topic. There are many different ways to conduct interviews. In this chapter we will describe the main features of **semi-structured interviews**, and in Chapter 13 we will cover interviews that are considerably more structured in nature. Semi-structured interviews are interviews in which the researcher has a small number of questions relating to the themes that are to be explored, but allows the interview to progress in a flexible manner, often letting the natural interaction with the interviewee guide the direction that the interview takes. An important component of semi-structured interviews is the natural rapport that is established between the interviewer and the interviewee, as this can often determine the quality of the data produced.

ch. 13

> **Semi-structured interview**
> A one-to-one discussion between a researcher and a participant on a specific topic. The researcher has some prepared questions or topics for discussion, but will let the interview develop naturally.

STOP & Think

Imagine you were conducting an interview. What things would you have to think about and/or prepare before you started?

Before the interview

The worst thing that a researcher can do is undertake an interview without preparation. Although semi-structured interviews are "looser" than their more highly structured counterparts, this does not mean they require less preparation, and there are a number of things that the interviewer has to consider before sitting down with the first interviewee. The first thing, obviously, is the research question. An interview without a research question is nothing more than a semi-formal chat – and will produce little, if any, useful data.

Selecting participants

Once the research question has been set, the researcher needs to think about who is going to be interviewed. In many projects the participants will be directly linked to the research question that is being addressed (you are not going to recruit adolescent males if you are asking about experiences relating to being a single mother). Not all research questions will have an obvious target group and, so, careful consideration needs to be given to who is going to be interviewed. Once you have got an idea of whom to interview, you need to ask them. This might not be as straightforward as it seems, because the way in which you approach potential interviewees is likely to shape their perception of you, which could have implications for the development of a rapport between interviewer and interviewee. For example, they may view you as an authority figure, which immediately impacts upon the way they will interact with you during the interview itself. Additionally, being asked to be interviewed is quite a big deal for many people, which is something that is easy to forget if you are doing the interviewing. Potential interviewees might be nervous, or suspicious about your motives. Others might be keen to talk to you for a whole host of reasons that are unrelated to your research question. Again, these are issues that are mostly unavoidable, but awareness of them can help the researcher make good decisions about who to contact and how to contact them, and will be important to note during the reflexivity exercise that will usually take place after the interviews have been conducted and the data analysed.

ch. 24
pp.601 – 603

Once participants have been selected and approached, it is essential that they give their **consent** to be interviewed. This is an issue that we will get into in Chapter 24 but, for the moment, be aware that the interviewee should be informed as to the general aims of the research and the topics that will be discussed. They should be made aware of any potentially sensitive issues that may be a part of the interview and they should be informed of their right to stop the interview and withdraw from the research at any time they wish. They should also be informed that the data will be confidential and that they will not be identifiable in any records or subsequent research publications. The interviewee should give their explicit consent that they are happy with these arrangements and also happy to be recorded (if an audio or video recording is to be made of the interview). They should also be told that they are allowed to request to have the researcher exclude any material that they are not comfortable with from the record of the interview, and should also be offered the opportunity to view a copy of the final report.

The interview schedule

Interview schedule A list of pre-prepared questions or discussion topics for use by an interviewer.

Most interviewers will have a list of pre-prepared questions or topics for discussion. This is the "**interview schedule**" and the questions or topics will usually be limited in number. Regardless of how many questions there are in the interview schedule, it should be treated flexibly so that the interview can progress naturally. Semi-structured interviews allow the interviewer to break away from the prepared questions to follow up issues that have been raised by the interviewee and that may not have been anticipated at the outset. This makes the semi-structured interview a flexible research tool in a way that strict quantitative methods (including the structured interviews that we will discuss in **Chapter 13**) struggle to be. What is actually taken into the interview depends on the interviewer and their style of interviewing. Some researchers like to prepare one schedule and stick to it for all participants, while others prefer to tailor their schedule to each individual interviewee. Some like to have a list of specific questions to ask, while others prefer to have a list of general topics to cover. There are always drawbacks to whatever technique is chosen. For example, if you use specific questions, then it is likely that you will stick to them rigidly and the interview may take on a more "formal" or structured tone. If you decide to use topic headings, then there is a danger that the questions that emerge from your reading of the headings may not be as open as they might have been had they been written in advance. This is particularly likely with inexperienced interviewers, so if you fall into this category, we would advise you to prepare questions in advance. A well-prepared interviewer will be knowledgeable enough to know what type of thing is likely to come up during the course of the interview, but will be also be prepared to let the interview cover unexpected areas of discussion.

ch. 13

The questions themselves should usually be open-ended in nature. Open-ended questions allow interviewees freedom to express their answers in any way they choose. Questions that require a "yes" or "no" answer should be avoided. For instance, it would be better to ask a woman who had recently given birth a question like, "*Tell me about your experience of antenatal provisions in your area*" rather than "*Did you feel you had sufficient antenatal provisions in your area while you were pregnant?*" Like all good Scouts, the motto of a good interviewer is "be prepared".

Piloting the interview

Once you think that you have the material ready, it is worthwhile doing one or two practice (or "pilot") interviews. These can be with friends or family or someone who is similar to the people who you will interview in the main study. This will help you identify any problems with definitions or other terms that you are using and it will also give you an indication about what things are likely to come up. It is also an opportunity to become familiar with any recording equipment that you will be using and it will be useful for familiarizing yourself with the general experience of interviewing someone – it can be quite disconcerting when you do it for the first time!

During the interview

The interview process itself begins before the interview does. All interviews are social interactions and this interaction begins as soon as the interviewer meets the interviewee. This is when the initial rapport will be developed, so the researcher should look to develop a good relationship with the interviewee at this point. Interviewees might be apprehensive or nervous, so it is up to the interviewer to put them at their ease and make them feel comfortable. Given that the interview is a social interaction, there are certain factors that may contribute to it. The researcher may be seen as being an authority figure by the interviewee, and the interaction may also be influenced by the researcher's social status, gender, age or ethnicity. The effect of all of these factors should be considered by the researcher in the reflexivity exercise.

Conducting the interview

The first thing to do just before the interview begins is to start the recording device (if you are using one). You do not want to get halfway through the interview and realize that you forgot to press "record". Obviously, this will require that you are familiar with how the recording device works and where the best position to place it is to ensure a recording that is loud and clear enough. You should also have enough tapes/discs/batteries etc. to be able to quickly change them if required during the interview.

When the interview itself begins, it is good practice to begin with more general questions before moving on to specific or private issues. This will help get both the interviewee and the interviewer "loosened up" before getting into a more detailed discussion of the relevant issues. As well as the interview schedule, the interviewer should have certain "prompt" questions that can be used whenever the interviewee does not know how to respond or responds with an answer that requires elaboration or clarification. Prompt questions might include "How did that make you feel?", "Can you tell me more about your experience?" or "Can you give me a concrete example of that?" Willig (2001) advises that a good way of getting information from interviewees is to express ignorance. A naive interviewer assumes no prior knowledge and so the interviewee is sometimes required to "state the obvious", which can reveal interesting information about the way he or she views the subject under discussion.

The semi-structured interview is a dynamic process, and this requires that the interviewer be able to "think on her feet" and respond to what the interviewee is saying in a relevant and appropriate way. This will often involve going off on an unexpected tangent while keeping the discussion relevant to the research question. The interviewer may have to ask unprepared questions spontaneously as the interview progresses. For this, there is no substitute for experience and most people will learn this skill as they go along.

It is particularly important that the interviewer does not guide the interviewee towards particular viewpoints. Questions that use evaluative language should be avoided (e.g. "Why did you behave so immorally?") as should anything that gives too much away concerning the interviewer's opinion or position on an issue. The interviewer should endeavour to stay neutral on any sensitive issues, although this must be balanced with avoiding appearing too "cold", "distant" or "unsympathetic", all of which could have implications for the rapport between interviewer and interviewee.

After the interview

The very last question of the interview should ask the interviewee if there is anything they would like to add. Once the interview is over, the interviewer should read any notes that he or she has made to the interviewee to gain an agreement that they give a fair reflection of what was said. If no notes were taken, then this is not a problem because the interviewer should send a transcript of the interview to the interviewee for approval at the earliest possible time. This allows the interviewee to look at what was said and to request deletion of any material they are not comfortable with.

Transcribing the interview

Transcription
A detailed written account of the interaction between an interviewer and interviewee.

To most researchers, transcribing the interview is the most tedious part of the process. This is when the researcher listens back to the recording of what was said during the interview and painstakingly notes down every word, and in some cases, every sigh, grunt and laugh. The **transcription** is a detailed written account of the interaction between the interviewer and the interviewee. There are various ways that the transcription can be done, and which way you use will depend on the form of qualitative analysis. Some analyses will be primarily interested in what was said, whereas other forms of analysis will also require the *way* it was said to be taken into account, along with all the "umm"s and "errr"s, which are sometimes important features of the interaction. Transcribing is not merely noting down all the words that were used. A good transcription (regardless of analysis) will also note where the two speakers interrupt each other or overlap with each other. It will also indicate anything else that a reader needs to know about the nature of the interaction, which might include interruptions and unexpected events that both participants respond to (in one interview I conducted, the chair broke halfway through and so that had to be conveyed in the transcript).

The first thing you need to do in a transcription is indicate who is speaking. This is usually easily done by giving each person a codename and using this (or their initial) to indicate who is saying what. There are a number of other ways in which you can indicate the nature of the interaction:

- Shouting can be indicated by using capital letters (although we would hope there was not much shouting in most interviews).
- Words or parts of words that have been emphasized by the speaker can be underlined.

  Square brackets [] have a number of uses:

- They can be used to indicate something that happens in the room (e.g. [chair breaks]).
- They can be used when one of the speakers makes a gesture or does something that is not strictly verbal (e.g. [rolls eyes] or [laughs]).
- They can also be used to indicate when a word is not clear from the recording (e.g. . . . [unclear] . . . or [inaudible]).
- If one speaker interrupts the other, this can be indicated with marking the point at which the speaker was interrupted with a square bracket and then marking the start of the "interrupter's" comments by a square bracket directly below the preceding line (see the example below).
- Overlaps in speech can be indicated by placing an equals sign (=) at the end of the first person's speech (where the overlap begins) and another equals sign at the start of the second person's speech (where they take up the discussion and carry on).
- Pauses or hesitations can be indicated by round brackets around a space, i.e. ( ). If the pause is long then you should indicate how long within the round brackets, e.g. (3 seconds).

Here is an example transcript from an interview conducted by a student on people's paranormal and superstitious beliefs. The interviewer is "I" and the participant is "B".

Box 11.1 Example transcript

I: But ( ) do you think (3 seconds) it is possible to influence objects and events just by thinking about them?

B: (4 seconds) Logic, and the way that I normally reason the way that I think tells me "No". However, erm, I definitely have behaviours I do thoughts I have to have, ehm, in order to try and influence things that I know I don't have any real influence over. So for all I would say "No", I don't think it makes <u>any</u> difference whatsoever whether I stand on my head and do a cartwheel as to whether Germany is gonna score another goal ( ) when they're about to take a penalty, ehm, I have to touch that coffee table with my index and middle finger [

I:]Ehm, why do you think that <u>works</u>?

B: It doesn't work, but I feel compelled to do it and I want to do it and I feel better that I've done it, ehm, and I think why not do something that's simple, unobtrusive, ehm, doesn't do anybody any harm in any way shape or form, makes me feel ehm slightly more comfortable . . . ehm why not do it?

I: Would you think that something bad would happen if you wouldn't do it?

B: Ehm (4 seconds) rationally no, I know it wouldn't ( ) But I would rather do it so why not do it?

I: Well, that's true.

B: Ehm () and there's been there's times when I've <u>not</u> done these things because ehm (2 seconds) it would be odd because somebody's just turned round and asked me a question, so if I say: 'Well, if you hang on a minute cause I just need to go touch a few things in a certain sequence =

I: = [laughs]

B: and I'll get back to you ehm then I cannot do it and it's fine, I know it has no bearing, it has no consequence for me, and a few moments later it's I've forgotten about it [

I:]So, it doesn't make you feel worried or =

B: = no.

Reflexivity

Reflexivity
The practice of reflecting upon a qualitative research process for the purpose of identifying subjective and contextual factors that may have influenced the outcome.

As we outlined in the previous chapter, **reflexivity** is an exercise that many qualitative researchers conduct at the end of a piece of research in which important subjective or contextual factors are identified and their potential influence on the outcomes of the research discussed. In interviews, the nature of the relationship between the interviewer and the interviewee may be an important feature in determining the outcome of the interview. If you interview people you know and are friends with, then this is undoubtedly going to impact upon the interaction during the interview, so an honest reflective account must be given about the likely nature of this and how it may have contributed to the data obtained.

ch. 10
p.191

Other issues that should be considered concern the interpretation that is placed on the data. Is it likely that the researcher is bringing his or her own particular viewpoint to the analysis? Could the data collected from the interview be interpreted in other ways? Has the researcher been selective in choosing parts of the interview to focus on at the expense of other parts? Why might this have been the case? Was the selection based on the researcher's preconceived ideas about what might emerge from the interview?

The researcher should also reflect upon the interviewee's experience. Were they treated well? Was there an environment that encouraged an honest and open discussion? Did the interviewee seem nervous or uneasy? How serious was the power imbalance between interviewer and interviewee? How might these things have affected the discussion?

Reflexivity is an important part of all qualitative research, but particularly so in interviews, given their social nature and the degree of interpretation.

In the Know

The 10 commandments of interviews (Berg, 2007)
In his book *Qualitative Research Methods for the Social Sciences* (2007), Berg suggests 10 commandments of interviews. We think these are very useful rules to follow for anyone conducting qualitative interviews:

1 *Never begin an interview cold* – Berg doesn't mean you should wear a woolly hat. His suggestion is that you should spend a bit of time talking to your interviewee before the interview begins. Small talk can help put both interviewer and interviewee at ease and can help establish a rapport.

2 *Remember your purpose* – the interview should stay on track and the discussion should remain relevant to the research question.

3 *Present a natural front* – do not appear as if you are reading from a script. Ask your questions in a natural way and try to be relaxed and as supportive as possible.

4 *Demonstrate aware hearing* – this relates to non-verbal responses to what the interviewee is saying. These might include nodding your head to show that you are listening, smiling if they say something funny, consoling them if they get upset and so on. It is not conducive to good interviewing to appear uninterested or unaware.

5 *Think about appearance* – there are no rules concerning what you should wear, but you should give it some thought. In general, your appearance should be appropriate to the person you are interviewing.

6 *Interview in a comfortable place* – the location of the interview should be comfortable to both participants. If the interviewee is not comfortable or is worried about being overheard, then this will impact upon the responses.

7 *Do not be satisfied with monosyllabic answers* – yes-and-no answers are not informative at all and should always be followed by a probe question, such as "Can you tell me a little bit more about that?" Berg suggests that even an uncomfortable silence might yield additional information after a probe question.

8 *Be respectful* – this should be obvious, but you should make the interviewee feel like an integral part of the research process. You may have to reassure them that you are genuinely interested in their opinion and hearing about their experiences. If they say something that you do not agree with, then treat the comment with respect, even if your natural reaction is to chastise them. Chastising them will only put them on the defensive and prevent them from giving you further information that will be of use.

9 *Practise, practise and practise some more* – you cannot learn good interviewing technique from reading about it in books like this. The only way to become good at it is to do it.

10 *Be cordial and appreciative* – your interviewee has graciously given up their time to speak to you, often about personal issues, so you should thank them and offer them the opportunity to ask you questions about the research. Your general aim should be to send the interviewee away feeling that they have had a good experience.

Focus groups

A **focus group** is a type of interview that is conducted with a small group of people. The researcher (sometimes known as the "moderator") will lead the group in a discussion that focuses on an issue or a topic of interest to the researcher. Focus groups have previously been a popular way for companies to conduct market research, but they have increasingly been adopted by the social sciences, and are often used whenever a social issue is to be studied, such as those relating to health education and promotion (Basch, 1987). Although they have sometimes been described as "group interviews", this description is not entirely appropriate. Focus groups are more dynamic than semi-structured interviews, and the moderator's role is to facilitate the discussion rather than conduct an interview. Although they are different to interviews, many of the issues we discussed above will also apply to focus groups, including the need for thorough preparation and the post-interview

Focus group
A small group of participants interact with each other and an interviewer who poses questions.

activities. The focus group method is becoming more popular in psychology because it generates a lot of rich data and involves discussions and interactions that are often informative and illuminating.

Features of focus groups

The focus group is based around a series of questions (the focus group schedule) developed by the researcher. As is the case with interview schedules, this can consist of specific questions or a list of topics. The researcher's style can vary as well, but generally the researcher acts as a moderator and will encourage discussion between members of the group, pose questions, and keep the conversation flowing and on track. It is not normally the case that the moderator will ask questions to each member in turn.

This method is distinctive because it offers an opportunity to study the interaction between people as they discuss various ideas and express opinions. Often, ideas will be challenged by members of the group, which might then lead to those ideas being defended and justified by other members. This provides the researcher with insights into some of the techniques used by individuals to persuade others, defend a position or jointly construct meaning. The data produced are different to those that would be obtained from a one-to-one interview in which the interviewer cannot challenge or undermine the ideas expressed by the interviewee.

Who takes part?

Participants taking part in focus groups can share key features or can be different on certain features. Whether you choose participants with something in common or not will depend on the research question that you have set and the information that you wish to obtain from the group discussion. Sometimes it will be informative to have members of the group who have conflicting views, while other times this will not be appropriate. Members can belong to a pre-existing group (e.g. friends, work colleagues) or be strangers to each other. Again, this decision will depend upon the type of interaction you are hoping to see and on the research question that is being addressed.

Advantages of focus groups

One of the main advantages of the focus group as a method of qualitative data collection is how naturalistic it is. The discussions that take place between group members will closely resemble natural conversation and will have a dynamic quality that incorporates more ways of communicating than would usually be evident in a more formal interview setting. For example, group members might joke with each other, tell anecdotes, disagree, argue and so on.

A further advantage is in the method's flexibility. Focus groups can be used as the primary method of collecting qualitative data or can be employed in conjunction with other methods as part of a **triangulation** effort. Also, groups can be held in a variety of settings, from the psychology lab to anywhere in "the field". They can be one-off events or can be conducted on more than one occasion, either with the same group (usually discussing different topics or a variation on a theme), or with different groups.

ch. 10
pp.193–194

Disadvantages of focus groups

Although it might not always be viewed as a disadvantage, focus groups do produce a large amount of data. All of the discussion must be transcribed and then analysed, which are both time-consuming tasks. Organizing focus groups can also present a challenge: first, due to the difficulty in identifying the most appropriate group of people to take part and, second, in arranging for them all to be in the same place at the same time. Conducting the focus group is another challenging aspect. The researcher who acts as group moderator must be skilled in facilitating the discussion and mediating between members of the group. The moderator must be in charge of guiding the discussion while at the same time not dominating it. He or she must have "people management" skills and should ensure that all group members have an equal opportunity to voice an opinion, including members who are less keen to do so. These are skills that will (normally) require training and practice.

For a more detailed account of focus groups and the issues involved in conducting them, see Morgan (1997).

In the Know

Jackson and Cram (2003) conducted six focus group interviews with 16- to 18-year-old female students in New Zealand. The groups ranged in size from four to twelve, but most consisted of six to eight students. The interviews explored the sexual double standard, the idea that some behaviours are acceptable for males but not for females. Jackson conducted all of the interviews. Because she was only a few years older than the women interviewed and had a youthful appearance, the participants felt comfortable talking with her. Each focus group session lasted 2 hours. The researchers made transcripts of all the sessions and conducted a multistage qualitative analysis to find patterns related to the women's perceptions of their sexuality. The data that emerged centred around three themes: (1) challenging the language of the double standard, (2) articulating sexual desire, and (3) exploring the role of sex in adolescence that is created by peers, the media and other social sources. The women possessed a sophisticated understanding of their own sexuality, saw themselves as actors and had created ways of viewing themselves outside the double standard.

Diary studies

Some researchers are interested in the experiences that individuals have over a period of time and so may ask people to keep diaries, the contents of which will be analysed by the researcher at a later date. When a participant is asked to keep a diary, they are usually required to keep a record of their feelings, activities and experiences. This is usually in written form, but it can also be recorded via a tape recorder or other recording device.

The researcher must have clear research aims before asking people to complete diaries. A clear focus concerning what aspects of the participants' lives are to be recorded is essential, and this must be explained to the participants in a clear way. For example, if you are interested in eating behaviours, then you would have to make sure that you provided each participant with a set of instructions outlining exactly what you wish them to record in the diary. In this case it may be instances of every piece of food that is eaten, what it is and when it was consumed. You might also want them to indicate how satisfied the food made them feel as well as recording at which points in the day they felt hungry, while also indicating the extent of the feeling of hunger by rating it on a scale from 1 to 10. To help facilitate this, you might provide them with a diary that has spaces for "food consumed", "time consumed" and "satisfaction (1–10)" as well as spaces for "time hunger felt" and "degree of hunger felt (1–10)". Although it's tempting to think of **diary studies** as being very little work for a researcher, they often involve more than providing the participants with a blank notebook and asking them to fill it in. Consideration needs to be given about the types of experiences you are interested in and the form of information that you would like to get from each participant. Diary studies will be most successful when the participant is clear on what he or she is supposed to be recording and when.

> **Diary studies**
> A method of qualitative data collection in which individuals keep diaries related to experiences or events of interest over an extended period of time.

There are three main ways that diary studies can be implemented. The most straightforward version is when the participant fills in the diary with appropriate information at intervals predetermined by the researcher. So, for example, the participant might be asked to complete details about their current mood every two hours or may be asked to sum up their stress levels at the end of each day. A second way of conducting a diary study is to give each participant a signal indicating when to input the desired information. This signal may be in the form of a "beeper" or an alarm, but it will sound at various intervals over the course of the day. Third, participants can be instructed to enter information in their diary in response to certain events that happen to them. For example, the researcher might be interested in the factors involved in smoking and will ask participants to provide details about their psychological state and their activities whenever they decide to have a cigarette, while also providing information about how the cigarette made them feel at the time.

Advantages of diary studies

Diary studies do have certain advantages over other types of qualitative data collection. The data that diary studies provide are unique as they allow an insight into events and experiences "as they happen" and will also provide an insight into how these events progress over a period of time. In asking participants to complete diaries on a regular basis, there is less of an issue concerning the reliability of memory for events, which may sometimes be a problem when asking people to recall experiences from their past in interviews or focus groups. Additionally, diary studies can sometimes offer a more personal account of feelings that participants might be reluctant to talk about in interviews or focus groups.

Disadvantages of diary studies

If your aim is to obtain an account of people's routines and experiences, then there is the possibility that keeping a diary will itself alter these things. If this happens then the diary might not be a true reflection of the relevant aspects of the participant's life.

Another potential disadvantage is that there is no way of ensuring that the participant has completed the diary in the way the researcher requested by closely following the instructions that were given. It is common for participants to forget to complete the diary and then to fill in the blanks immediately prior to handing it back to the researcher.

Also, there may be differences between people in how they complete the diary. Some people will be more open than others and will happily provide detailed information. Others, however, may find keeping such a personal record uncomfortable and may omit important personal details. There might also be variation in what people consider to be "relevant" information, with some leaving out large chunks of information that they consider irrelevant that others would decide to include.

Dropout rates are also fairly high in diary studies, as the participants are often asked to keep to a strict regime. Participants sometimes find it difficult to find time to complete the diary entry or simply forget to do so. A successful diary study will be one in which the participants are motivated and interested in the study. If they start to find it boring or if they lose interest, then it is likely they will drop out.

For a brief introduction to diary methods, see O'Connor and Ferguson (2008).

Ethnographic studies

Ethnography is closely linked to "**participant observation**", which is a method that we describe in the next chapter. It is, however, widely used in the social sciences, and is worthy of a mention of its own. Ethnographic research is concerned with experiences "as they are lived". This means that the researcher gains an insight by immersing herself in the daily life of the social world under study. In doing so, the ethnographer aims to gain an acute understanding of the issue that is being researched. Ethnography is not actually a single method; it is a variety of methods that are all utilized during the period in which the researcher is participating in the activities of the group in which he or she has placed herself. As a result of this, the ethnographic researcher will employ many of the methods that we have described elsewhere in this book. For example, the researcher might use **observational techniques** in which information is gathered from within a social group. **Interviews** might also be used at some stage of the researcher's investigations, and he or she might also make use of archival or **Web-based data**. At some point in the study, a researcher might even choose to select a particularly interesting or illuminating case and conduct a **case study**. The ethnographic researcher aims to build up a coherent account of the key issues which will emerge from the variety of methods that are utilized. The use of multiple methods is particularly useful, because it allows for **triangulation**, which lends credibility to the conclusions that might be offered. A further feature of ethnographic work that is to be commended is the inherent realization that embedding a researcher within a particular social context will inevitably influence the phenomena under study. The result of this is recognition that the researcher will undoubtedly play an important role, and so must practise **reflexivity** in accounting for what this influence may be and what consequences it may have had. For example, members of the social group might be unwilling to reveal certain bits of information to the researcher, or might be motivated to distort information, either for impression-management purposes or for some other reason. As well as the way in which the phenomena are influenced by the researcher, there are a number of other issues to consider. First, there is the problem of access. An ethnographic researcher must gain access to the social group in which he or she will place him or herself and conduct the studies. There are obvious problems in gaining access to particular groups that might be suspicious of "outsiders" (e.g. extremist organizations), but even where access is possible, it must be obtained through some form of negotiation, and this itself might have

ch. 13
pp.201&269

ch. 12
p.239

ch. 12
p.225

ch. 12

p.212

ch. 10
pp.193–194

ch. 10
p.191

ch. 12
& ch. 24

implications for the subsequent investigation. Linked to this are ethical considerations relating to such "infiltration" of a social group. Each study will be different and will present its own **ethical problems,** and we cover some of these in the following chapter and in Chapter 24. A further practical issue to consider is the nature of the data collection and the way in which it is recorded. It often will not be possible to take copious amounts of notes while actively participating in a social group, nor will it always be possible or appropriate to record on video or audio the information that might be relevant. There are many ways in which information can be recorded, and the researcher must make an informed decision about how best to record the data that she deems important. Field notes are often used, although these are open to distortions of memory. How information is recorded and kept is something that deserves careful thought before the researcher enters the field, and there are no hard-and-fast rules about how best to do so. Given the variety of methods that can be employed, and the wide range of skills that are required, ethnographic research is usually the domain of experienced and well-trained researchers.

Using Web-based data

The Internet is a gold-mine of data for qualitative researchers and can be utilized in a number of ways. There are web pages for everything imaginable and, as the Internet grows, so do the possibilities for research. The most obvious way that the Internet can be used is by collecting first-person accounts that have been posted by individuals. Discussion boards, guestbooks, support groups, chat rooms and blogs are just some of the places in which researchers might find rich first-person accounts of a wide range of human experience. At this stage, we are only talking about accounts that have *already* been posted on the Internet. We briefly cover below using the Web to gather *new* data (e.g. by asking people to provide you with details relating to specific questions you ask) but you should be aware that this has its own set of ethical issues. In the two sections that follow, we are discussing using information that already exists on the Internet.

Advantages of Web-based data

Web-based data
First person accounts that have been posted on the Internet by an individual.

The **web-based data** that can be obtained from the Internet are often rich in detail and can be very specifically focused on a particular topic. The relative anonymity that the Internet offers allows people to speak openly and truthfully in a way that they might not in an interview or less anonymous environment. This makes the Internet a useful resource for studying experiences of a highly sensitive nature which participants are unlikely to disclose in a face-to-face setting. Given the size of the Web and its increasing accessibility, there will always be a vast amount of data for the qualitative researcher to use.

Disadvantages of Web-based data

Unfortunately, the same anonymity also allows people to lie with little chance of being found out, so this must also be taken into consideration. The wealth of potential data can also be seen as a drawback as it requires an individual researcher to spend considerable time searching for appropriate material to be used. Another potential drawback concerns the demographics of Internet users. Not everyone has access to the Web, and so not every potential viewpoint will be represented. In fact, it is possible that the viewpoints that are available on the Internet are those of an unrepresentative sample of "Internet users", who may be considerably different to people who have no access to the Internet and cannot put forward an alternative position. This will always be a problem, but it will become less of an issue as Internet access becomes available to more and more people worldwide.

Ethical considerations

Although we will cover ethics in **Chapter 20**, there are some specific ethical issues that are related to Web research. When collecting data in a traditional sense (i.e. in quantitative studies or by asking people questions) one of the main ethical principles of research is that participants must give informed consent. People must have enough information about the aims of the study to allow them to make a reasoned decision about whether to participate or not. Anonymity is also an important right of any participant. However, if you are collecting pre-existing data that has been posted on the Internet, then the individuals who have posted it will not have given their consent for it to be used. This does not always mean that it would be unethical to do so. There are certain factors that must be taken into account whenever a researcher is considering using Web-based data. First, is the material in the public domain? If the material already exists and is accessible to the general public, then it can be used (provided that the anonymity of the poster is maintained). By "already exists" we mean material that has been posted on the Internet for reasons other than the research that is being conducted by the qualitative researcher. For many sources, this will be easy to establish, but for others there will have to be further questions asked. For example, is there an assumption on the part of the individual who has posted the material that their account will be publicly available? If so, then informed consent does not need to be explicitly obtained. A useful analogy can be drawn with pinning a message on a public noticeboard (e.g. in a library or a local shop). Any individual who does this cannot reasonably expect that their message will not be seen (and possibly used) by other members of the public, many of whom will not be known to the original poster. In this sense, many internet messageboards are similar to public noticeboards, and any material on them should be considered to be in the public domain and thus OK to use. However, if there is any expectation of privacy on the part of the individual posting the message, then great care must be taken. For example, if the messageboard is open to members only or is password protected, then this is equivalent to a real-world messageboard that only certain people can view (e.g. in a private office). In cases such as this, the researcher must ensure that a person's privacy is not compromised. In these instances, it is up to the researcher to exercise a degree of common sense in making ethical judgements that take into account the rights of the individual who has posted the material. If there are any doubts, then it is sometimes possible to contact the individual via email and ask their permission. If this is not possible and the researcher is still in doubt as to the ethics of including material, then he or she should consult with a senior researcher or an ethics panel. If the researcher is *still* unsure, then it is best to err on the side of caution and exclude the material.

ch. 20

Other Web techniques

The Internet can also be used for more traditional data collecting. Questionnaires can be sent out via email lists or posted on websites or messageboards; interviews can be conducted using personal messaging software, over email or using webcams and so on. Again, the main advantage is in the amount of data that can be obtained. Although initial effort must be made in preparing questionnaires or interview schedules, there is no need to arrange face-to-face interviews or to travel anywhere to collect data. The usual disadvantages apply. How trustworthy the data will be is open to question, and Internet data gathering is notorious for its high dropout rates. A further issue concerns obtaining informed consent. Researchers usually require participants to give informed consent in the form of a record that can be kept (whether it's a "click" on a website or a recorded verbal agreement) and this is sometimes difficult to obtain over the Internet. Generally, however, "new" qualitative data are rarely obtained via the Internet.

Media and text sources

The final source of qualitative data that we wish to cover concerns the use of text that already exists. There are countless sources of textual data that a qualitative researcher can utilize, including (but by no means limited to) documents, stories and articles in newspapers and magazines, biographies and autobiographies, interviews, letters to the editor, government memos, reports, adverts, public information documents, documentaries, diaries, leaflets, advertisements, feature films, speeches, computer games and so on. Depending upon what your research question is, you may find that there are valuable data to be found out there if you know where to look. These sources are often referred to as "archival".

It is often the case that research of this type is mainly concerned with assessing the way a particular phenomenon or group has been portrayed by the media. For example, Guillaume and Bath (2008) looked at the way in which the media represented information about the MMR (measles, mumps and rubella) vaccination during the period in which it was linked with autism in children, while Gormly (2004) investigated the way in which Islam was represented on an American Christian evangelical television show in the aftermath of the 9/11 terrorist attacks in the USA. The media pervade our lives and present us with a rich source of data on an enormous number of topics.

Using this type of data is useful as the author will often be commenting on an issue from a particular perspective. For example, a right-leaning author in a right-leaning newspaper may be criticizing a left-leaning government's policy on crime. This allows a researcher an opportunity to investigate the way the arguments have been presented and the discursive techniques that have been employed. Any researcher who decides to analyse media data should have a keen understanding of the context in which the original material was created. No data exist in a vacuum but this is particularly true of anything that originates in the media. The sociocultural and historical context in which a piece of text was written will often shed light on its nature, and the researcher must be aware of these factors and take them into consideration when analysing the material.

Although we are including media and text sources in a chapter about data collecting, the real challenge of using data from these sources is in the analysis used. Most often, **discourse analysis** will be used.

ch. 22
pp.559–561

Advantages of media and text sources

One of the most obvious advantages in using material that has already been written and printed is that it reduces the need to collect new data and transcribe it. Although the researcher still has to find appropriate material to use, there is no need to recruit participants, set up interviews and transcribe what was said. There is also the advantage that there is no possibility that the researcher can influence the data that are collected, which is always a possibility when conducting interviews or focus groups. Data that are collected from the media is already "out there" and exist for another purpose, allowing the researcher to analyse them without influencing them. Additionally, print media (newspapers and magazines) are useful indicators of societal trends and opinions, which are often of interest to researchers who want to investigate the way in which the "mainstream" represents various issues. The wide range of **media sources** can often allow the researcher to compare and contrast the various ways in which the same issue has been dealt with by a variety of sources and the rhetorical devices that have been used by each one.

> **Media sources**
> Sources of data derived from various media (e.g. magazines, television, speeches).

Similar advantages apply to other sources, such as autobiographies. These can be a rich source of data as the author will be constructing a position or an argument that he or she will then support and defend in various ways. A skilled qualitative researcher can learn a lot about how this is achieved through analysis of the language used and the meaning conveyed.

Disadvantages of media and text sources

Despite the seemingly endless possibilities for analysing pre-existing text, researchers should exercise caution. Because of the vast amount of potential data that exist in printed (and other) media and the relative ease of access to this, there is a temptation to turn to them more often than is appropriate. Only very specific research questions (such as those involving the way a particular topic is portrayed by the media or the way in which an individual argues and defends a position) can be researched using these methods alone. More commonly, the use of archival data will be one of a number of methods (**triangulation**) being employed to address a research question. There is no doubt, however, that some studies will inevitably benefit from the rich data on a topic that already exists in the public domain.

ch. 10
pp.193–194

For more detailed accounts of collecting and analysing material obtained from the media or other texts, see Richardson (2006) or Mautner (2008).

Analysis of qualitative data

All data have to be analysed in some way, and qualitative data are no different. The analysis of the data you collect is intimately linked with the question that you have set, the data that you have chosen to collect, the way in which you have collected this, and even the way in which you have transcribed this. There is more than one way of analysing qualitative data and it is yet another important decision that must be made early in the research process. Because many techniques are incompatible with each other, you need to know prior to collecting the data what you will do with them in the analysis stage. If you do not, then you may end up with data that are inappropriate to be analysed in the way that is best suited to address the question that you have set. Some forms of analysis have a very specific philosophical underpinning and not all forms of qualitative analysis are interchangeable. For example, some analysis techniques will mainly identify themes and focus on the content that exists in the data. Other techniques will focus on the discursive techniques used by speakers. We cover **qualitative analyses** techniques in Chapter 22 and you should refer to this chapter before deciding upon which qualitative method of data collection is most appropriate.

ch. 22

Questions

1 What are the main differences between interviews and focus groups?

2 What factors may impact upon the "rapport" that an interviewer builds with an interviewee?

3 What qualities is a good interviewer likely to have?

4 What makes a good qualitative research question and why?

5 Under what circumstances would a researcher choose to conduct a focus group?

6 What are the advantages and disadvantages of using data from media and printed sources?

7 Highlight some of the main ethical issues involved in using Web-based data.

Activities

1 Compose a research question relating to "giving up smoking". Describe how you might gather data relating to this question through:

- interviews
- focus groups
- diary methods
- Web-based data
- media and text sources.

2 As there is no better way to learn than by "doing", create a research question and an interview schedule that will allow the interviewee to provide the information that you are looking for. If you can, conduct the interview according to the "10 commandments of interviews" and transcribe it according to the guidelines provided.

Chapter 12

Observational Methods

OVERVIEW

In Chapter 2 we stated that science is concerned with observations. This is true. You cannot understand anything without observing it. However, in social sciences, "observational methods" are a family of techniques that researchers use when attempting to understand behaviour. This family of techniques is quite varied and can take the form of both quantitative and qualitative methods. In this chapter we will cover various ways of observing behaviour and recording observations. You will see that there are many issues relating to this method that we must take into consideration, and that the observer is not always passively recording behaviour as it occurs. We will take a look at reasons why psychologists sometimes intervene to create special situations for their observations, and we will introduce you to methods for recording and for analysing observational data. Finally, we will describe important challenges that can make it difficult to interpret the results of studies using observation, before introducing you to some of the ethical issues involved in conducting observational techniques.

OBJECTIVES

After studying this chapter and working through the exercises, you should be able to:

- Recognize the ways in which psychologists use "observation" as a way to investigate behaviour
- Explain what both "observation with intervention" and "observation without intervention" are, and recognize the differences between them

- Describe what the different types of "observation with intervention" are and what drawbacks there are with each

- Describe what the different types of "observation without intervention" are and what drawbacks there are with each

- Recognize the ways in which observations can be coded and measured, both in quantitative and qualitative approaches

- Give an account of the limitations of observational methods and the potential ways of addressing these limitations

- Appreciate the ethical issues involved in using observational methods

Introduction

All of us observe behaviour every day. Observations are crucial for our day-to-day lives. Failing to be observant while walking or driving can be life threatening. When in another country, we usually have to observe how people behave if we want to avoid embarrassment. We can learn a lot by observing people's behaviour when they are in a queue at the supermarket, travelling on a bus or sitting in a classroom. Psychologists also rely on observations to learn about behaviour, but the observations that psychologists make differ in many ways from our everyday observations. When we observe casually we may not be aware of the various factors that bias our observations, and we rarely keep formal records of our observations. Instead, we rely on our memory of events even though our own experience (and the observations of psychologists) tells us that our memory is not perfect. The observations that psychologists make, on the other hand, are made in ways that allow them to get the most information possible from the situation being observed and are made in a systematic way with careful record keeping.

The primary goal of observational methods is to describe behaviour. Psychologists strive to describe behaviour as fully and accurately as possible. This is not an easy thing to achieve and researchers face serious challenges in reaching this goal. Clearly, it is impossible for researchers to observe *all* of a person's behaviour. There is far too much behaviour for it all to be observed. This is why anyone conducting an observational study must rely on observing samples of people's behaviour, and must decide whether their samples are good representations of the behaviour being studied.

Researchers also face a second challenge in trying to describe behaviour fully: behaviour frequently changes depending on the context in which it occurs. Consider your own behaviour. Do you behave the same at home as in school, or at a party compared to in a classroom? Does your observation of others lead you to conclude that context is important? Have you ever noticed that children sometimes change their behaviour when they are with their parents? Social psychologists have been aware for a long time that behaviour can be affected by the presence of another person. The effect may be one of social facilitation (i.e. improved performance) or social inhibition, as when performance is impaired by the presence of another. Complete descriptions of behaviour require that observations be made across many different situations and at different times.

Observation provides a rich source of hypotheses about behaviour and so observation can also be a first step in discovering why we behave the way we do. For example, Kagan et al. (1988)

observed the reactions of a group of 2- and 3-year-old children in the presence of an unfamiliar person or object. The researchers identified those children who were consistently shy, quiet and timid, and those who were consistently sociable, talkative and affectively spontaneous. When the same children were observed at 7 years of age, a majority of the children in each group exhibited similar behaviours. Based on these observations the researchers developed a hypothesis relating shyness in childhood to extreme social anxiety in adulthood, and argued that both were the result of temperamental differences present at birth.

Sampling behaviour

Before conducting an observational study, researchers must make some important decisions about when and where observations will be made. In most observational studies the investigator cannot observe *all* behaviour. It is clear that we can observe only certain behaviours, occurring at particular times, in specific settings and under particular conditions. In other words, behaviour must be *sampled*. This sample is used to represent the larger population of all possible behaviours. By choosing times, settings and conditions for their observations that are representative of a population, researchers can generalize their findings to that population. The sampling of times, situations and conditions will strongly influence the most important dimension of **sampling** – who the participants will be. Results can be generalized only to participants, times, settings and conditions similar to those in the study in which the observations were made. The key feature of representative samples is that they are "like" the larger population of participants, times, settings and conditions from which they are drawn. For example, observations made of classroom behaviour at the beginning of a school year are probably not going to give you results that are typical of the behaviours you might see at the end of the school year.

> **Sampling**
> The process of choosing members of a population to be included in a sample.

Time sampling

Researchers typically use a combination of **time sampling** and situation sampling to identify representative samples. In time sampling, researchers seek representative samples by choosing various time intervals for their observations. Intervals may be selected systematically (e.g. observing the first day of each week), randomly, or both.

> **Time sampling**
> A technique to sample behaviour that involves selecting observations to be made at various time intervals.

   Let us look at how time sampling could be used to observe children's classroom behaviour. Researchers might want to observe the children in a classroom for a total of two hours each day. If the researchers restricted their observations to certain times of the day (say, mornings only), they would not be able to generalize their findings to the rest of the school day (because it is possible that behaviour would be different later in the day). One approach to obtaining a representative sample is to schedule observation periods systematically throughout the school day. Observations might be made during four 30-minute periods beginning every two hours. The first observation period could begin at 9 a.m., the second at 11 a.m. and so on. Another possibility would be to schedule 10-minute observation periods every half hour during the school day. A random time-sampling technique could be used in the same situation by distributing four 30-minute periods (or a dozen 10-minute periods) randomly over the course of the day. A different random schedule would be determined each day on which observations are made. Times would vary from day to day but, over the long run, behaviour would be sampled equally from all times of the school day.

Systematic and random time-sampling procedures are often combined. Sometimes researchers systematically schedule intervals during which observations can be made systematically but observations within any given interval are made at random times. For example, having scheduled four 30-minute observation periods at the same time each day (e.g. 9 a.m., 11 a.m.), an observer might then decide to observe only during 20-second intervals that are randomly distributed within each 30-minute period. Whatever time-sampling procedure is used, the observer must carefully consider both the advantages and limitations of the schedule in terms of its potential to yield a representative sample of behaviour.

Time sampling is not an effective method of sampling behaviour when the event of interest occurs infrequently. Researchers who use time sampling for infrequent events may miss the event entirely. Alternatively, if the event lasts a long time, time sampling may lead the researcher to miss an important portion of the event, such as its beginning or end.

Event sampling

Event sampling
A technique to sample infrequent or formally scheduled behaviour. It involves selecting specific events to be observed which must meet predetermined criteria.

Event sampling is a more effective and efficient sampling method for infrequent events. In event sampling the observer records each event that meets a predetermined definition. For example, researchers interested in observing children's reactions to special events in school, such as a holiday play, would use event sampling. The special event defines when the observations are to be made. Researchers would certainly not want to use time sampling in this situation in the hope that a special event might occur during one of their randomly selected observation periods. Event sampling also is useful in situations other than for observing formally scheduled events like a school play. Researchers are often interested in events that occur unpredictably, such as natural or technical disasters. Whenever possible, observers try to be present at those times when an event of interest occurs or is likely to occur. For example, in a study of children's "rough-and-tumble" play, an observer positioned herself in the corner of a playground to observe members of a nursery school class (Smith & Lewis, 1985). Due to the relatively low frequency of this behaviour, event sampling was the method of choice in this study. The researcher made observations whenever an episode of rough play began, and continued to observe until it ended. Although event sampling is an efficient method for observing unpredictable events, the use of event sampling can easily introduce biases into the behavioural record. For instance, event sampling could lead an observer to sample at the times that are most "convenient" or only when an event is certain to occur. The resulting sample of behaviour at these times may not be representative of the same behaviour at other times. In most situations, an observer is likely to achieve a representative sample of behaviour only when some form of time sampling is used.

Situation sampling

Situation sampling
A technique to sample behaviour that involves observing the behaviour of interest in as many different locations and under as many different circumstances as possible.

Researchers can significantly increase the external validity of observational findings by using **situation sampling**. Situation sampling involves observing behaviour in as many different locations and under as many different circumstances and conditions as possible. By sampling different situations, researchers reduce the chance that their results will be peculiar to a certain set of circumstances or conditions. Animals do not behave the same way in zoos as they do in the wild. Children do not always behave the same way with one parent as they do with the other. By sampling different situations, a researcher can also increase the diversity of the subject sample and achieve greater generality than could be claimed if only specific types of individuals were observed. As part of a naturalistic observation of beer drinking among college students, investigators purposely sampled behaviour in various situations where beer was served, including five town bars and a student centre (see Geller et al. 1986).

In most situations researchers observe the behaviour of all the individuals who are present at the time and place they selected to sample. If, for example, researchers wished to observe how well students can concentrate while studying in the library in the morning and in the evening, they would observe all students in the library at the designated times. There are situations when there may be more going on than can be effectively observed. For example, if researchers observed students' food selections in the dining hall during peak hours, they would not be able to observe all of the students. In this case, and in others like it, the researcher would use individual sampling to determine which students to observe. Similar to the procedures for time sampling, the researcher could either select students systematically (e.g. every tenth student) or select students randomly.

Individual sampling

With *individual sampling*, you select a single participant for observation over a given time period (e.g. 10 minutes) and record his or her behaviour during that period. Over successive time periods, repeat your observations for the other individuals in the observed group. Individual sampling is most appropriate when you want to preserve the organization of an individual's behaviour over time rather than simply noting how often particular behaviours occur.

Test yourself

Identify the type of behaviour sampling.[1]

	Time sampling	Situation sampling	Individual sampling	Event sampling
1 Jenny is interested in studying male-bonding behaviour during sports events. She attends a rugby match, a football match and a televised cup-final event in her local pub. In all these locations, she makes careful notes on the way that the males around her interact with each other.				
2 An organizational psychologist "shadows" a senior manager for a week, making notes on the styles of interaction that she has with colleagues and customers.				

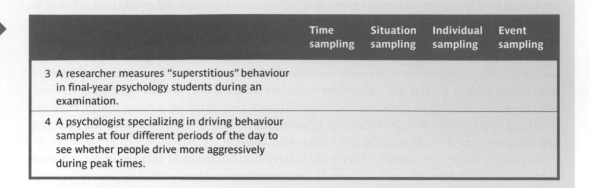

	Time sampling	Situation sampling	Individual sampling	Event sampling
3 A researcher measures "superstitious" behaviour in final-year psychology students during an examination.				
4 A psychologist specializing in driving behaviour samples at four different periods of the day to see whether people drive more aggressively during peak times.				

Classification of observational methods

Observational methods can be classified on two dimensions. The first important distinction is between *observation with intervention* and *observation without intervention*. The second dimension involves the methods of recording behaviour. Observation studies can be distinguished in terms of whether all (or nearly all) of the behaviour is recorded or whether only particular parts of behaviour are recorded. In some situations researchers seek a comprehensive description of behaviour and they achieve this by recording behaviour using film, tapes or lengthy verbal descriptions. More often, researchers record specific units of behaviour that are related to the goals of a particular study. For example, Chambers and Ascione (1987) observed children while they played either an aggressive video game or a video game with pro-social content. Children who played the aggressive game were later observed to put less money in a donation box and were less likely to help sharpen pencils than children who played the pro-social game. Thus, in this study, the researchers recorded specific responses related to the children's pro-social behaviour. We will discuss observational methods first in terms of the extent of observer intervention and then in terms of methods for recording behaviour.

Observation without intervention

> **Naturalistic observation**
> An observational method that involves the researcher studying behaviour as it occurs "naturally", without any attempt to intervene.

One way of approaching an observational study is to try to be as removed as possible from the thing that you are observing. This is known as observation without intervention. When employing this technique, the researcher is detached from the behaviours or the group under study and exists only as a "passive" observer. Naturalistic observation is one form of observation without intervention.

Naturalistic observation

Observation of behaviour in a natural setting, without any attempt by the observer to intervene in what is being observed, is frequently called **naturalistic observation**.

An observer using this method of observation acts as a passive recorder of what occurs, and the major goals are to discover behaviours that occur naturally in a particular environment and to investigate the relationship among variables that are present. Given that the researcher is interested in naturally occurring behaviours, the events that are being observed are not manipulated or controlled in any way by the observer. Observing people in a psychology laboratory would not, for instance, be considered naturalistic observation, as the laboratory situation has been created specifically to study behaviour. In that sense, the laboratory is an artificial rather than a natural setting. In fact, observation in natural settings serves, among other functions, as a way of establishing the external validity of laboratory findings – bringing the laboratory into the "real world". Observation of behaviour in Internet discussion groups and chat rooms is another way that researchers have sought to describe behaviour as it normally occurs, although this recent form of "naturalistic" observation raises serious **ethical issues**, which we will discuss in Chapter 24.

ch. 24

A researcher uses naturalistic observation when he or she wants to describe and understand how people in a social or cultural setting live, work and experience the setting. So, if you want to know about bars as a social setting, you need to visit one or more bars over an extended period of time, talk to people, observe interactions and become accepted as a "regular" (cf. Cavan, 1966). If you want to know how people persuade or influence others, you can get a job as a car salesperson (cf. Cialdini, 1988). If you want to understand the process of coping after detection of breast cancer, you could become involved in a breast cancer support group on the Internet or at a local hospital.

In the Know

Hartup (1974) chose naturalistic observation to investigate the frequency and types of aggression exhibited by pre-schoolers in a children's centre. He distinguished hostile aggression (person orientated) from instrumental aggression (aimed at the retrieval of an object, territory or privilege). Although he observed boys to be more aggressive overall than girls, his observations provided no evidence that the types of aggression differed between the sexes. As a result of his observations, Hartup was able to conclude that there was no evidence that boys and girls were "wired" differently when it came to "hostile aggression".

Hartup's study illustrates why a researcher may choose to use naturalistic observation rather than to manipulate experimental conditions related to behaviour. There are certain aspects of human behaviour that moral or ethical considerations prevent us from controlling. For example, researchers are interested in the relationship between early childhood isolation and later emotional and psychological development. However, we would all agree (hopefully) that taking children from their parents in order to raise them in isolation was an unacceptable thing to do. Alternative methods of data collection must be considered if this problem is to be investigated. For example, the effect of early isolation on later development has been studied through experimentation on animal subjects (Harlow & Harlow, 1966); descriptions of so-called feral children raised outside of human culture, presumably by animals (Candland, 1993); case studies of children subjected to unusual conditions of isolation by their parents (Curtiss, 1977); and systematic observation of

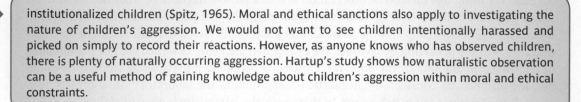

institutionalized children (Spitz, 1965). Moral and ethical sanctions also apply to investigating the nature of children's aggression. We would not want to see children intentionally harassed and picked on simply to record their reactions. However, as anyone knows who has observed children, there is plenty of naturally occurring aggression. Hartup's study shows how naturalistic observation can be a useful method of gaining knowledge about children's aggression within moral and ethical constraints.

Advantages and disadvantages of naturalistic observations

Naturalistic observation gives you insight into how behaviour occurs in the real world. The observations you make are not tainted by an artificial laboratory setting, and you can, therefore, be reasonably sure that they are representative of naturally occurring behaviour. In other words, properly conducted naturalistic observation has extremely high external validity. Because naturalistic observation allows you only to *describe* the observed behaviour, you cannot use this technique to investigate the underlying causes of those behaviours. Additionally, naturalistic observation can be time consuming and expensive. Unlike some types of observation in which participants record their own data, naturalistic observation requires the researcher to be there, engaged in observation, during the entire data-collecting period, which may last hours, days, or longer.

Naturalistic observation obviously cannot be used to study all issues or phenomena. The approach is most useful when investigating complex social settings, both to understand the settings and to develop theories based on the observations. It is less useful for studying well-defined hypotheses under precisely specified conditions. However, although naturalistic observation research is a difficult and challenging procedure, it yields invaluable knowledge when done well.

STOP & Think

Try to think of some phenomena that would be particularly suited to naturalistic observations. What do they have in common? Is there anything you can think of that definitely wouldn't be suitable to be studied in this way? Why not?

Observation with intervention

Let's face it. Scientists like to tamper with things. They like to intervene in order to observe the effects and perhaps to test a theory. Intervention rather than non-intervention characterizes most psychological research. Although the types of intervention employed by psychologists are too numerous and diverse to classify, their reasons for intervening are generally one or more of the following:

1 To precipitate or cause an event that occurs infrequently in nature or that normally occurs under conditions that make it difficult to observe.

2 To investigate the limits of an organism's response by varying systematically the nature and/or the qualities of a stimulus event.

3 To gain access to a situation or event that is generally not open to observation.

4 To arrange conditions so that important antecedent events are controlled and consequent behaviours can be readily observed.

5 To establish a comparison by manipulating one or more independent variables to determine their effect on behaviour.

There are three important methods of observation that researchers use when they choose to intervene in natural settings: participant observation, structured observation and the field experiment. How much intervention is involved and what the intervention actually consists of varies across these three methods. We will consider each method in turn.

Participant observation

In **participant observation**, observers play a dual role. They observe people's behaviour and they also participate actively in the situation they are observing. In *undisguised participant observation*, individuals who are being observed know that the observer is present for the purpose of collecting information about their behaviour. The researcher becomes a part of the group that is under study and the group know that this is the case. This method is used frequently by anthropologists who seek to understand the culture and behaviour of groups by living and working with members of the group.

> **Participant observation**
> Study of naturally occurring situations by researchers who are participants in the situation.

In *disguised participant observation*, those who are being observed do not know that they are being observed. As you might imagine, people do not always behave in the way they ordinarily would when they know their behaviour is being recorded. Politicians, for instance, often make different statements when speaking to the press, depending on whether their comments are "on" or "off" the record. Our own behaviour is likely to be affected by knowing that we are being watched. Because of this possibility, researchers may decide to disguise their role as observers if they believe that people being observed will not act as they ordinarily would if they know their activities are being recorded. Disguised participant observation raises ethical issues (e.g. privacy and informed consent) which must be addressed prior to implementing the study. We will cover some of these issues later in this chapter and in **Chapter 24**.

ch. 24

Disguised participant observation in action

Picture this. In the early 1970s a psychologist recruits you to participate in an experiment. You are to present yourself to a mental hospital, use a false name and state that you are hearing voices (a symptom typical of schizophrenia). If you are admitted to the hospital, you are to act completely normally and give the actual details of your life (other than your real name), and no longer report hearing voices. You agree to participate and, to your great surprise, when you go to the mental hospital you are admitted quickly. Your diagnosis is schizophrenia. Once in the hospital, you act normally. In addition, you go out of your way to be friendly and cooperative with the staff. You accept the medication they give you, but you secretly dispose of it afterwards (as do many of the other patients, you discover). The only strange thing you do is to take notes about your experiences. At first, you take notes covertly, but soon you realize that you may take them openly. No one on the staff is really watching you (or the other patients) closely. Some of the patients, however, ask you why you are there. They are convinced that you do not belong in a mental hospital. The staff, on the other hand, believe that you really do belong there. They see your note taking as a symptom of schizophrenia.

A psychologist called Rosenhan (1973) actually conducted the study, which was to become one of the most famous and controversial observational studies in psychology's history. He wanted to find out if the staff at mental hospitals could reliably distinguish between normal and abnormal behaviour and how long it would take for a "sane" person to be released. The hospitals ranged from large to small, rural to urban, research to private and old to new. He discovered that, regardless of type of hospital, the staff did not distinguish real patients from pseudo-patients (a pseudo-patient is a person playing the role of a patient. In reality, pseudo-patients were confederates of the experimenter; none had a prior history of psychopathology.) Pseudo-patients were admitted and hospitalized from 7 to 52 days, with an average hospitalization of 19 days. All were discharged, but not because they were cured. They were labelled schizophrenic in remission (not cured, but without any symptoms).

Rosenhan (1973) argued that labelling is a very powerful determinant of perception in a mental health setting. Time and time again, the pseudo-patients' normal behaviours were interpreted as symptoms of schizophrenia and not as indicators of normal behaviour. Once admitted, the pseudo-patients (and real patients, too, presumably) could do little to convince the hospital staff to change their diagnosis. Apparently, once the pseudo-patients were labelled schizophrenic, they were stuck with that label no matter how they behaved subsequently. There are, however, reasons to challenge this specific conclusion and other aspects of Rosenhan's (1973) study (see "In the Know" box). Another finding was that the pseudo-patients and staff had very little interaction with each other despite their close proximity. Rosenhan's experiment is an example of participant observation, and the effect of his research was profound. Today, procedures for admission to mental health hospitals are much more stringent and the definition of schizophrenia is more complex.

In the Know

Thinking critically about "On being sane in insane places"
In his article, "On being sane in insane places", Rosenhan (1973) questioned the nature of psychiatric diagnosis and hospitalization. How could normal people be labelled as schizophrenic, one of the most severe mental illnesses we know? Why did the hospital staff not recognize the pseudo-patients were faking their symptoms? After days or weeks of hospitalization, why didn't the staff recognize that the pseudo-patients were "sane", not insane?

These are important questions. After Rosenhan's research article was published in the journal *Science*, many psychologists and psychiatrists met and wrote articles in response to Rosenhan's questions (e.g. Spitzer, 1976; Weiner, 1975). Presented below are just a few of the criticisms of Rosenhan's research:

- We cannot criticize the staff for making a wrong diagnosis: a diagnosis based on faked symptoms will, of course, be wrong.

- The pseudo-patients had more than one symptom; they were anxious (about being "caught"), reported they were distressed and sought hospitalization. Is it "normal" to seek admission into a mental hospital?

- Did the pseudo-patients really behave normally once in the hospital? Perhaps normal behaviour would be to say something like, "Hey, I only pretended to be insane to see if I could be hospitalized, but really, I lied, and now I want to go home."

- Schizophrenics' behaviour is not always psychotic; "true" schizophrenics often behave "normally". Thus, it is not surprising that the staff took many days to determine that the pseudo-patients no longer experienced symptoms.

- A diagnosis of "in remission" was quite rare, and reflects staff members' recognition that a pseudo-patient was no longer experiencing symptoms. However, research on schizophrenia demonstrates that once a person shows signs of schizophrenia, he or she is more likely than others to experience these symptoms again. Therefore, the diagnosis of "in remission" guides mental health professionals as they try to understand a person's subsequent behaviour.

- "Sane" and "insane" are legal terms, not psychiatric. The legal decision of whether someone is insane requires a judgement about whether a person knows right from wrong, which is irrelevant to this study.

As you can see, Rosenhan's research was controversial. Most professionals now believe that this study does not help us to understand psychiatric diagnosis. However, several important long-term benefits of Rosenhan's research have emerged:

- Mental health professionals are more likely to postpone a diagnosis until more information is gathered about a patient's symptoms; this is called "diagnosis deferred".

- Mental health professionals are more aware of how their theoretical and personal biases may influence interpretations of patients' behaviours, and guard against biased judgements.

- Rosenhan's research illustrated the depersonalization and powerlessness experienced by many patients in mental health settings. His research influenced the mental health field to examine its practices and improve conditions for patients.

Participant observation allows an observer to gain access to a situation that is not usually open to research. The pseudo-patients in the Rosenhan study, for instance, felt what it was like to be labelled schizophrenic and not to know how long it would be before they could return to society. An important contribution of Rosenhan's study was its illustration of the dehumanization that occurs in institutional settings – something that may not have been so apparent had the study been conducted using a different methodology.

Issues in participant observation

The participant observation technique that Rosenhan used differs from naturalistic observation in that the observer is not only part of the observed environment but also a participant in the situation being studied. Participant observation has a greater potential for researcher bias, and that problem must be addressed in the design of the research. Typically, participant observation is used when naturalistic observation would be impractical or impossible. A participant observer's role in a situation can pose serious problems in carrying out a successful study. Observers may lose the objectivity required for valid observations if they identify too closely with the individuals under study. Changes in a participant observer are sometimes dramatic and are not easily anticipated. As a striking example of this, take the experiences of a criminologist who used undisguised participant observation to study police officers at work. Kirkham (1975) went through police academy training like any recruit and became a uniformed patrol officer assigned to a high-crime area in a city of about half a million. His immersion in the daily activities of an officer on the beat led to marked changes in his attitudes and personality. As Kirkham himself noted:

> As the weeks and months of my new career as a slum policeman went by, I slowly but inexorably began to become indistinguishable in attitudes and behaviour from the policemen with whom I worked . . . According to the accounts of my family, colleagues and friends, I began to increasingly display attitudinal and behavioural elements that were entirely foreign to my previous personality – punitiveness, pervasive cynicism and mistrust of others, chronic irritability and free-floating hostility, racism, a diffuse personal anxiety over the menace of crime and criminals that seemed at times to border on the obsessive. A former opponent of capital punishment, I became its vociferous advocate in cases involving felony murder, kidnapping and the homicide of police officers – even though as a criminologist I continued to recognise its ineffectiveness as a deterrent to crime. (1975, p. 19)

Participant observers must be aware of the threat to objective reporting that arises due to their involvement in the situation they are studying. This threat necessarily increases as degree of involvement increases.

Another potential problem with observer involvement is the effect the observer can have on the behaviour of those being studied. It is more than likely that the participant observer will have to interact with people, make decisions, initiate activities, assume responsibilities and otherwise act like everyone else in that situation. Whenever observers intervene in a natural setting, they must ask to what degree participants and events are affected by their intervention. Is what is being observed the same as it would have been if the observer had never appeared? It is difficult to generalize results to other situations if intervention produces behaviour that is specific to the conditions and events created by the observer.

The extent of a participant observer's influence on the behaviour under observation is not easily assessed. Several factors must be considered, such as whether participation is disguised or undisguised, the size of the group entered and the role of the observer in the group. The disguised participant observation in the Rosenhan study appears to have been successful. Rosenhan and his associates seem not to have significantly affected the natural environment of the hospital unit by assuming the role of patients. However, some of the patients – though none of the staff – apparently detected the sanity of the pseudo-patients, suggesting to the observers that they were there to check up on the hospital.

When the group under observation is small or the activities of the participant observer are prominent, the observer is more likely to have a significant effect on participants' behaviour. This problem confronted several social psychologists who infiltrated a group of people who claimed to be in contact with aliens from outer space (Festinger et al., 1956). A leader of the group said he had received a message from the aliens predicting a cataclysmic flood on a specific date. The flood was to stretch from the Arctic Circle to the Gulf of Mexico. Because of the attitudes of members of the group towards "non-believers", the researchers were forced to make up bizarre stories in order to join them. This tactic worked too well. One of the observers was even thought to be a spaceman bringing a message (honestly, we are not making this up!). The researchers had inadvertently reinforced the group's beliefs and influenced in an undetermined way the course of events that followed. By the way, the flood never occurred, but at least some of the group members came to use this disconfirmation as a means of strengthening their initial belief. They began to seek new members by arguing that it was the strength of their faith that had prevented the prophesied flood.

Thus, although participant observation may permit an observer to gain access to situations not usually open to investigation, the observer using this technique must seek ways to deal with the possible loss of objectivity and the potential effects that a participant observer may have on the behaviour under study.

Structured observation

There are a variety of observational methods using intervention that are not easily categorized. These procedures differ from naturalistic observation because researchers intervene to exert some control over the events they are observing. The degree of intervention and control over events is less, however, than that seen in field experiments (which we describe in the next section). We might call these techniques "**structured observation**", although you may find other terms in different texts (e.g. some people prefer the term "**systematic observations**"). Often the observer intervenes in order to cause an event to occur or to "set up" a situation so that events can be more easily recorded than they would be without intervention. In other cases the observer may create quite elaborate procedures to investigate a particular behaviour more fully. This approach is much less global than naturalistic observation research. The researcher is interested in only a few very specific behaviours, the observations are quantifiable and the researcher frequently has developed prior hypotheses about the behaviours.

Simons and Levin (1998) used structured observation to study a phenomenon called "change blindness". Change blindness occurs when people fail to notice things that have changed in their immediate environment. With so much going on around us, it is impossible for us to notice every little change. Simons and Levin demonstrated, however, that people often fail to notice changes even when they are paying attention, and sometimes fail to notice fairly big changes. In their study the researchers used confederates (that is, individuals who were "in" on the research and were working for the researcher) who were placed in the research situation and instructed to behave in a certain way in order to create a situation for observing behaviour. One confederate approached a pedestrian and asked for directions. About 15 seconds into the conversation two other confederates rudely passed between them carrying a door. As the door passed, the original confederate and one of the people carrying the door swapped places with each other.

Structured observation A type of observational method that looks at a specific quantifiable behaviour in a particular setting. It involves more intervention from the researcher than naturalistic observation, but does not involve as much manipulation as experimental studies.

Systematic observation Observations of one or more specific variables, usually made in a precisely defined setting.

Figure 12.1 Frames from a video of a subject from Simons and Levin's (1998) change-blindness study. Frames a–c show the sequence of the switch. Frame d shows the two experimenters side by side

This structured observation created a changed environment with the *new* confederate now continuing the conversation with the pedestrian (see Figure 12.1). The new confederate typically made eye contact with the pedestrian, but differed from the original confederate in height, voice and clothing. The amazing finding was that only about half of the pedestrians noticed the switch; half of the pedestrians were blind to the change and did not realize that the person they had been speaking to had changed into a different person after the people carrying the door had gone past!

Structured observations may occur in a natural setting, as in the Simons and Levin (1998) study, or in a laboratory setting. Animal researchers also frequently structure an observational situation to create events that would normally be difficult to observe in natural settings. An interesting example in this regard comes from a series of studies investigating differences in the cognitive capacity of apes and humans. One type of structured observation involves assessing the gaze-following behaviour of chimpanzees (see Povinelli & Bering, 2002). A human caretaker makes eye contact with the chimpanzee and then looks above the chimpanzee. Observations reveal that chimpanzees do indeed follow the caretaker's gaze (i.e. looking above); however, controversy exists as to what this behaviour really means. Do apes "understand" the mental state of the human caretaker (i.e. that the person has seen something)?

Developmental psychologists also frequently use structured observations. Jean Piaget (1896–1980) is perhaps most notable for his use of these methods. In many of Piaget's studies, a child is first given a problem to solve and then given several variations of the problem to test the limits of the child's understanding. The observer acquaints the child with the problem and then asks questions to probe the child's reasoning processes. These structured observations have provided a wealth of information regarding children's cognition and are the basis for Piaget's "stage theory" of intellectual development. Piaget-type tasks are also frequently used by animal researchers to investigate aspects of animal cognition. In one such study, orang-utans outperformed squirrel monkeys on a classic test of object permanence, the ability to represent cognitively the existence of a hidden object (de Blois, Novak & Bond, 1998.)

Structured observation represents a compromise between the passive non-intervention of naturalistic observation and the systematic manipulation of independent variables and precise control that characterize laboratory experiments. The advantage of such a compromise is that it permits observations to be made under conditions that are more natural than the artificial conditions imposed in a laboratory. However, as always, there is a price to pay. The failure to follow similar procedures each time an observation is made may make it difficult for other observers to obtain the same results when investigating the same problem. Uncontrolled, and perhaps unknown, variables may play an important part in producing the behaviour under observation. For example, observers who use structured observations like those used by Piaget do not always follow exactly the same procedure from one observation to another. This inconsistency in procedure across observations is a potential problem with these techniques.

Field experiments

ch. 4
p.61

Sometimes researchers want to conduct well-controlled experiments that don't take place within the confines of a laboratory. In situations such as this, an observer might wish to manipulate one or more independent **variables** in a natural setting in order to determine their effect on behaviour. This is called a **field experiment**. We mention field experiments in this chapter because they represent the most extreme form of intervention in observational methods. The essential difference between field experiments and other observational methods is that researchers exert more control in field experiments. In a field experiment, researchers will typically manipulate an independent variable to create two or more conditions and they measure the effect of the independent variable on behaviour. Field experiments are commonly used in social psychology. For example, confederates have posed as robbers when bystander reaction to a crime has been investigated (Latané & Darley, 1970) and as individuals pushing in to a queue in order to study the reactions of those already waiting in line (Milgram et al., 1986).

> **Field experiments**
> A method of observation that closely resembles experimental methods, with the exception that the studies are conducted in a more natural setting than the laboratory.

There are many reasons why researchers do experiments in natural settings. One reason for conducting field experiments is to test the **external validity** of a laboratory finding. It is sometimes important to find out if an effect observed in the laboratory works in a similar way in another setting. Other reasons for experimenting in natural settings are more practical. Doing experiments in natural settings allows researchers to achieve an important goal of the scientific method. That is, research in natural settings is likely to be associated with attempts to improve conditions under which people live and work. The government may experiment with a new tax

ch. 5
p.97

system or a new method of job training for the economically disadvantaged. Schools may experiment by changing lunch programmes, after-school care or curricula. A business may experiment with new product designs, methods of delivering employee benefits or flexible work hours. In these cases, as is true in the laboratory, it is important to determine whether the "treatment" caused a change. Did a change in the way patients are admitted to a hospital emergency room cause patients to be treated more quickly and efficiently? Did a college energy conservation programme cause a decrease in energy consumption? Knowing whether a treatment was effective permits us to make important decisions about continuing the treatment, about spending additional money, about investing more time and effort, or about changing the present situation on the basis of our knowledge of the results.

Recording observations

Observational methods differ in the degree of observer intervention. The passive non-intervention of naturalistic observation is at one end of the intervention dimension, and the active manipulation of independent variables that characterizes field experiments is at the other end. Observational methods also differ in the way in which behaviour is recorded. Whenever you observe something, you have to make a record of what you observed. It should be obvious that we cannot rely solely on our memory of the events and the behaviours that we observed. We have to use another way of recording the behaviours so that we can refer to them later and analyse them if appropriate. Sometimes researchers aim to provide a comprehensive description of behaviour and the situation in which it occurs. More often they focus on only certain behaviours or events. Whether it is all behaviour in a setting or only selected aspects that are observed will depend on the purpose of the study and the researchers' goals. Decisions about how behaviour is recorded will also depend on whether the investigator is doing qualitative or quantitative research.

Observational methods can be broadly classified as being primarily quantitative or qualitative. **Qualitative research** may be characterized in a number of ways that distinguish it from quantitative approaches. We covered qualitative research in the previous two chapters so we will not cover it in depth again here beyond what is necessary. Qualitative research focuses on people behaving in natural settings and describing their world in their own words; quantitative research tends to focus on specific behaviours that can be easily quantified (i.e. measured). Qualitative researchers emphasize collecting in-depth information on a relatively few individuals or within a very limited setting; quantitative investigations generally include larger samples. The conclusions of qualitative research are based on interpretations drawn by the investigator; conclusions in quantitative research are based upon statistical analysis of data.

As an example to help understand the distinction, imagine that you are interested in describing the ways in which the lives of teenagers are affected by working. You might take a quantitative approach by developing a questionnaire that you would ask a sample of teenagers to complete. You could ask about the number of hours they work, the type of work they do, their levels of stress, their school grades and their use of drugs. After assigning numerical values to the responses, you could subject the data to a quantitative, statistical analysis. A quantitative description of the results would focus on such things as the percentage of teenagers who work and the way this percentage varies by age (we cover **survey methods** such as this one in the following chapter).

Now suppose you decided to take a qualitative approach to describing behaviour. You might conduct a series of focus groups in which you gather together groups of 8 to 10 teenagers and engage them in a discussion about their perceptions and experiences with the world of work. You would ask the teenagers to tell you about the topic using their own words and cognitive frameworks. To record the focus group discussions, you might use a videotape or audiotape recorder and have a transcript prepared later, or you might have observers take detailed notes during the discussions. A qualitative description of the findings would focus on the themes that emerge from the discussions and the manner in which the teenagers conceptualized the issues. Such description is qualitative because it is expressed in non-numerical terms using language and images.

Other methods, both qualitative and quantitative, could also be used to study teenage employment. For example, a quantitative study could examine data collected from a government department that has relevant data; a qualitative researcher might work in a fast-food restaurant as a management trainee. Keep in mind the distinction between quantitative and qualitative approaches to describing behaviour as you read about other specific observational methods discussed in this chapter. Both approaches are valuable and provide us with different ways of understanding behaviour. The most important point to remember is that how you choose to record behaviour determines how the results of your study are eventually measured, summarized, analysed and reported.

Qualitative measures of behaviour

When researchers seek a comprehensive record of behaviour, they often use **narrative records**. Narrative records provide a more or less faithful reproduction of behaviour as it originally occurred. To create a narrative record, an observer can write descriptions of behaviour or use audiotape recordings, videotapes and films. Once narrative records are created, researchers can study, classify and organize the records. Particular hypotheses or expectations about the behaviours under observation can be tested by examining the records that have been obtained. Narrative records differ from other forms of recording and measuring behaviour because the classification of behaviours is done *after* the observations are made. Thus, researchers must make sure that the narrative records capture the information that will be needed to evaluate the hypotheses they are testing in the study.

> **Narrative records** Records intended to provide a more or less faithful reproduction of behaviour as it originally occurred.

Hartup (1974) obtained narrative records as part of his naturalistic study of children's aggression. He investigated a number of different aspects of children's aggression, including the relationship between particular kinds of events that preceded aggressive behaviour and the nature of the aggressive episodes that followed these precipitating events. Consider this sample narrative record from Hartup's study (1974, p. 339):

Marian [a 7-year-old] . . . is complaining to all that David [who is also present] had squirted her on the pants she has to wear tonight. She says, "I'm gonna do it to him to see how he likes it." She fills a can with water and David runs to the teacher and tells of her threat. The teacher takes the can from Marian. Marian attacks David and pulls his hair very hard. He cries and swings at Marian as the teacher tries to restrain him; then she takes him upstairs . . . Later,

Marian and Elaine go upstairs and into the room where David is seated with a teacher. He throws a book at Marian. The teacher asks Marian to leave. Marian kicks David, then leaves. David cries and screams, "Get out of here, they're just gonna tease me."

Hartup (1974) instructed his observers to use precise language in describing behaviour, and to avoid making inferences about the intentions, motives or feelings of the participants. Note that we are not told why David might want to throw a book at Marian or how Marian feels about being attacked. Hartup believed that certain antecedent behaviours were related to specific types of aggression. By strictly excluding any inferences or impressions of the observers, individuals coding the narrative would not be influenced by what the observer inferred was going on. Thus, the content of the narrative records could be classified and coded in a more objective manner.

Not all narrative records are as focused as those obtained by Hartup, and it is not always the case that narrative records always avoid inferences and impressions of the observer. Narrative records are also not always meant to be comprehensive descriptions of behaviour. For example, field notes include only the observer's running descriptions of the participants, events, settings and behaviours. Field notes are used by journalists, social workers, anthropologists, ethologists and others, and they do not always contain an exact record of everything that occurred. Events and behaviours that especially interest the observer are recorded and are likely to be interpreted in terms of the observer's specialized knowledge or expertise. For example, an ethologist (someone who studies animal behaviour) might record how the behaviour of one species appears to parallel that of another. Field notes tend to be highly personalized, but they are probably used more frequently than any other kind of narrative record. Their usefulness as scientific records is completely dependent on the accuracy and precision of their content. Accuracy and precision depend critically on how well the observer has been trained and the extent to which the observations that are recorded can be verified by independent observers and through other means of investigation.

Practical, as well as methodological, considerations dictate the way in which narrative records are made. As a general rule, records should be made during or as soon as possible after behaviour is observed. The passage of time blurs details and makes it harder to reproduce the original sequence of actions.

Decisions about what should be included in a narrative record must be made before the observational study begins. We have seen, for example, that verbal narratives may differ in terms of the degree of observer inference that is appropriate or the completeness of the behavioural record. Thus, these aspects of a narrative record, as well as others, must be decided upon prior to beginning a study. Once the content of narrative records is decided, observers must then be trained to record behaviour according to the criteria that have been set up. Practice observations may have to be conducted and records critiqued by more than one investigator before any "real" data are collected.

Quantitative measures of behaviour

Often researchers are only interested in certain behaviours or specific aspects of individuals and settings. They may have specific hypotheses about the behaviours they expect to see. If this is the case, they will need clear definitions of the behaviours they are investigating. For example, assume you want to do a naturalistic observation study investigating how members of the public act towards individuals with obvious physical disabilities. In order to conduct your study, it would be necessary to define what constitutes a "reaction" to a physically disabled individual. Are you interested, for example, in helping behaviours, approach/avoidance behaviours, eye contact, length of conversation, or in some other behavioural reaction? As well as considering what behaviours you will use to define people's "reactions", you will also have to decide how you are going to measure these behaviours. Assume, for example, that you have decided to measure people's reactions by observing eye contact between individuals who do not have obvious physical disabilities and those who do. You would still need to decide exactly how you should measure eye contact. Should you simply measure whether a passerby does or does not make eye contact, or do you want to measure the duration of any eye contact that is made? You will sometimes find it useful to use more than one measure, a research strategy that is recommended whenever it is possible. The decisions you make will depend on the particular hypotheses or goals of your study. In making your decisions, you should take advantage of information you can gain by examining previous published studies that have used the same or similar behavioural measures.

Coding systems

Numerous behaviours can be studied using systematic observation. The researcher must decide which behaviours he or she is interested in, choose a setting in which the behaviours can be observed, and most importantly, develop a **coding system** to measure the behaviours. What do we mean by coding system? Well, we need a way of recording the data. To record the data, we need to know which behaviours are important for our study and which are not. As well as this, we need to be able to distinguish one "type" of behaviour from another. A coding system is simply a way of "tagging" behaviours as belonging to some pre-defined category or having a quality that the researcher has deemed to be important. Sometimes the researcher develops the coding system to fit the needs of the particular study. Coding systems should be as simple as possible, allowing observers to easily categorize behaviours. The need for simplicity is especially important when observers are coding live behaviours rather than viewing videotapes that can be re-viewed or even coded on a frame-by-frame basis. An example of a simple coding system comes from a study by Barton et al. (1980) in which nursing home residents and staff were observed. Only five categories were used: (1) resident independent behaviour (e.g. doing something by oneself, such as grooming), (2) resident dependent behaviour (asking for help), (3) staff independence-supporting behaviour (praise or encouragement for independence), (4) staff dependency-supportive behaviour (giving assistance or encouraging taking assistance), and (5) other, unrelated behaviours of both residents and staff. Their results illustrate one of the problems of care facilities: staff perceive themselves to be "care providers" and so most frequently engage in dependency-supportive behaviours.

> **Coding system**
> A method for data reduction in which units of behaviour or particular events are identified and categorized according to specific criteria.

Levels of measurement

Quantitative measures of behaviour differ depending upon the level of measurement that you decide to use. Thus, it is important for you to be familiar with the types of measurement scales used in behavioural research. Behaviour can be quantified in different ways, and the different levels of measurement that can be used will influence how data are subsequently analysed. There are four measurement scales that apply to both physical and psychological measurement: nominal, ordinal, interval and ratio. If you're unfamiliar with these, then we recommend flicking back to **Chapter 4**. You will need to keep these four levels of measurement in mind as you select statistical procedures for analysing the results of the research you will be doing. In this section we will describe how the measurement scales can be used in observational research.

ch. 4
pp.62 – 66

1 *Nominal scales.* Observational researchers often use checklists to record nominal scale measures. The observer could record on a checklist, for example, whether individuals make eye contact with a physically disabled person, whether children in a classroom are talking or are quiet, whether people use seat belts or do not use seat belts, and so on. Characteristics of participants – such as age, race and sex – are also frequently recorded using a checklist, as are features of the setting – such as time of day, location and whether other people are present. Researchers are often interested in observing behaviour as a function of participant and context variables. Do males use seat belts more than females? Are people who drive inexpensive cars more likely to let another driver out at a junction than people who drive expensive cars? These questions can be answered by observing the presence or absence of certain behaviours (seat-belt use or "letting other drivers out at junctions") for different categories of participants and settings (male and female, expensive and inexpensive cars).

2 *Ordinal scales.* Tassinary and Hansen (1998) used an ordinal scale to measure male and female undergraduate students' reactions to line drawings of female figures. The figures varied on physical dimensions such as height, weight and hip size. The undergraduates rank-ordered sets of figures in terms of attractiveness and fecundity (i.e. capability of bearing children). According to evolutionary psychology theory, female attractiveness is defined on the basis of cues simultaneously signalling both physical attractiveness and reproductive potential. One specific prediction based on evolutionary psychology theory is that the waist-to-hip ratio should be an invariant perceptual cue for both attractiveness and fecundity. Contrary to this expectation, the results of this study showed that relative hip size and weight were positively related to the rankings of fecundity and negatively related to physical attractiveness.

3 *Interval scales.* In order to quantify behaviour in an observational study, observers sometimes make ratings of behaviours and events. Observers usually make ratings on the basis of their subjective judgements about the degree or quantity of some trait or condition. For example, Dickie (1987) asked observers to rate parent–infant interactions. The basis of this study was an attempt to assess how successful a parent-training programme had been. Her observers visited the home of each family and rated both the mother and the father while the parents interacted with their infant child. During most of the observation period, the observers sat in the room with the infant and asked the parents to "act as normal as possible – just as if we [the observers] weren't here". She also used structured observations involving assigned play with each parent. Parent–infant interactions were rated on 13 different dimensions, including degree of verbal, physical and emotional interaction. For each dimension a continuum was defined that represented different degrees of this variable rated on a 7-point scale. A rating of 1 represented the absence or very little of the characteristic and larger numbers represented increasingly more of the trait.

Table 12.1 Example of rating scale used to measure a parent's warmth and affection towards an infant child

Scale value	Description
1	There is an absence of warmth, affection and pleasure. Excessive hostility, coldness, distance and isolation from the child are predominant. Relationship is on an attacking level.
2	
3	There is occasional warmth and pleasure in interaction. Parent shows little evidence of pride in the child, or pride is shown in relation to deviant or bizarre behaviour by the child. Parent's manner of relating is contrived, intellectual, not genuine.
4	
5	There is moderate pleasure and warmth in the interaction. Parent shows pleasure in some areas but not in others.
6	
7	Warmth and pleasure are characteristic of the interaction with the child. There is evidence of pleasure and pride in the child. Pleasure response is appropriate to the child's behaviour.

Source: from materials provided by Jane Dickie.

Table 12.1 outlines one of the dimensions used by the observers in this study: warmth and affection directed towards the child. Note that precise verbal descriptions are given with the four odd-numbered scale values to help observers define different degrees of this trait. The even-numbered values (2, 4, 6) are used by observers to rate events that they judge fall between the more clearly defined values. The investigators found that parents who had taken part in a programme aimed at developing competency in dealing with an infant were rated higher than were untrained parents on many of the variables.

At first glance, a rating scale such as that used by Dickie would appear to represent an interval scale of measurement. There is no true zero, and the intervals seem to be equal. Many researchers treat such rating systems as if they represent interval scales of measurement. Closer examination, however, reveals that most of the rating scales used by observers to evaluate people or events on a psychological dimension really yield only ordinal information. For a rating system to be truly an interval level of measurement, a rating of 2, for instance, would have to be the same distance from a rating of 3 as a rating of 4 is from 5 or a rating of 6 is from 7. It is highly unlikely that human observers can make subjective judgements of traits such as warmth, pleasure, aggressiveness or anxiety in a way that yields precise interval distances between ratings. How can we be sure that one judgement concerning warmth and affection is "1 point better" than another judgement? It does not seem to make sense. However, most researchers assume an interval level of measurement when they use rating scales. Deciding what measurement scale applies for any given measure of behaviour is not always easy. If you are in doubt, you should seek advice from knowledgeable experts so that you can make appropriate decisions about the statistical description and analysis of your data.

4 *Ratio scales.* If you decided that you wanted to measure duration of eye contact between people, then this would represent a ratio level of measurement because units of time (e.g. seconds) have equal intervals and "zero" is a meaningful value (i.e. no eye contact).

Another important measure of behaviour is frequency of occurrence. Checklists can be used to measure the frequency of particular behaviours in the same individual or group of individuals by making repeated observations of the same individual or group over a period of time. The presence or absence of specific behaviours is noted at the time of each observation. In these situations, frequency of responding can be assumed to represent a ratio level of measurement. That is, if "units" of some behaviour (e.g. occasions when a child leaves a classroom seat) are being counted, then zero represents an absence of that specific behaviour. Ratios of scale values would be meaningful as long as, for instance, an individual with 20 units had twice as many units as someone with 10.

Electronic recording and tracking

Behaviour is sometimes measured by using electronic recording and tracking devices. For example, as part of a study investigating the relationship between cognitive coping strategies and blood pressure among college students, participants were outfitted with an ambulatory blood pressure monitor (Dolan et al., 1992). College students wore the electronic recording device during two "typical" school days, one of which included an examination. Participants also completed a questionnaire assessing coping strategies and kept detailed logs of their daily activities. The researchers compared blood pressure readings for different times of the day and as a function of coping style. Students classified as exhibiting "high self-focused coping" (that is, who showed tendencies "to keep to themselves and/or blame themselves in stressful situations", Dolan et al., 1992, p. 233), had higher blood pressure responses during and after an exam than did those who were classified as low in self-focused coping strategies. The use of electronic recording in research is likely to grow with technological advances such as personal digital assistants (PDAs).

1 *Experience sampling.* Researchers also have used an innovative procedure known as the experience sampling method (ESM), which involves giving people electronic pagers, usually for a week at a time. Participants are asked to report on their activities whenever the pager goes off. In one study of adolescents' interactions with their families, 220 middle- and working-class youth provided reports at two periods in their lives, grades 5 to 8 and grades 9 to 12 (Larson et al., 1996). When randomly "beeped", the adolescents used a checklist to indicate who they were currently with. They also used 7-point scales to indicate their current emotional state and perceptions of the people they were with. They also were required to answer some open-ended questions about their activities at that moment in time. As might be expected, the data revealed a sharp decline in the time adolescents spend with family members between the ages of 10 to 18.

2 *Internet diaries.* Park, Armeli and Tennen (2004) used an "Internet daily diary methodology" to obtain measures of stress and coping by university undergraduates. A total of 190 students participated by logging into a secure Internet website on each of 28 days. (Email reminders were sent each day.) Participants recorded information about the day's most stressful event. They then

rated the event for how controllable they thought it was, and answered questions about their mood and strategies of coping. Positive moods were linked more with problem-focused coping strategies than avoidance strategies, especially when stressors were viewed as controllable.

Both ESM and daily diary methods rely on participants' self-reports of mood and activities, and not on direct observation of their behaviour. As such, it is important that techniques be devised to detect biases in data collection (e.g. possible omission or misrepresentation of personal activities by participants – it is possible that the "beeper" goes off just as the individual is doing something that they would be too embarrassed to report). These problems can be weighed against the time and labour costs sometimes required to obtain a comprehensive description of behaviour through direct observation.

Other observational methods

We have covered some of the main types of observational methods, but there are a few more that are difficult to classify. In this section, we will briefly cover other methods that might be considered to be "observational".

Case studies

A **case study** provides a description of an individual. This individual is usually a person, but it may also be a setting such as a business, school or neighbourhood. A naturalistic observation study is sometimes called a case study, and in fact the naturalistic observation and case study approaches often overlap. We have included case studies as a separate category in this chapter because case studies do not necessarily involve naturalistic observation. Instead, the case study may be a description of a patient by a clinical psychologist or a historical account of an event such as a model school that failed. A "**psychobiography**" is a type of case study in which a researcher applies psychological theory to explain the life of an individual, usually an important historical figure (cf. Elms, 1994). Thus, case studies may sometimes use such techniques as library research and telephone interviews with persons familiar with the case, but no direct observation at all (cf. Yin, 1994).

> **Case study**
> A detailed description of one individual case (usually a person) that represents an instance that is rare or of particular interest to the researcher.
>
> **Psychobiography**
> A type of case study in which a researcher applies psychological theory to explain the life of an individual, usually an important historical figure.

Depending on the purpose of the investigation, the case study may present the individual's history, symptoms, characteristic behaviours, reactions to situations or responses to treatment. A case study is usually done when an individual possesses a particularly rare, unusual or noteworthy condition. One famous case study involved a man with an amazing ability to recall information (Luria, 1968). The man, known as "S", could remember long lists and passages of prose with ease, apparently using mental imagery for his memory abilities. Luria also described some of the drawbacks of S's ability. For example, he had difficulty concentrating because mental images would spontaneously appear in his mind and interfere with his thinking. Another case study example concerns language development; it was provided by "Genie", a child who was kept isolated in her room tied to a chair, and was never spoken to until she was discovered at the age of $13\frac{1}{2}$ (Curtiss, 1977). Genie, of course, lacked any language skills. Her case provided psychologists and linguists with the opportunity to attempt to teach her language skills and discover which skills could be learned. Apparently, Genie was able to acquire some rudimentary language skills, such as forming childlike sentences, but she never developed full language abilities.

In the Know

This example illustrates the way that individuals with particular types of brain damage can allow researchers to test hypotheses (Stone et al., 2002). The individual in question, RM, had extensive limbic system damage. The researchers were interested in studying the ability to detect cheaters in social exchange relationships. Social exchange is at the core of our relationships; one person provides goods or services for another person in exchange for some other resource. Stone et al. were seeking evidence that social exchange can evolve in a species only when there is a biological mechanism for detecting cheaters; that is, those who do not reciprocate by fulfilling their end of the bargain. RM completed two types of reasoning problems. One type involved detecting violations of social exchange rules (e.g. you must fulfil a requirement if you receive a particular benefit); the other type focused on non-social precautionary action rules (e.g. you must take this precaution if you engage in a particular hazardous behaviour). Individuals with no brain injury do equally well on both types of measures. However, RM performed very poorly on the social exchange problems but did well on the precautionary problems, as well as other general measures of cognitive ability. This finding supports the hypothesis that our ability to engage in social exchange relationships is grounded in the development of a biological mechanism that differs from general cognitive ability.

Case studies are valuable in informing us of conditions that are rare or unusual and thus providing unique data about some psychological phenomenon, such as memory, language or social exchange. Insights gained through a case study may also lead to the development of hypotheses that can be tested using other methods.

Archival research

Archival research
Analysis of existing records or documents that were obtained from archives (e.g. statistical records, survey archives, written records).

Archival research involves using previously compiled information to answer research questions. The researcher does not actually collect the original data. Instead, he or she analyses existing data such as statistics that are part of public records (e.g. number of divorce petitions filed), reports of anthropologists, the content of letters to the editor or information contained in computer databases. Judd et al. (1991) distinguish among three types of archival research data: statistical records, survey archives and written records.

Statistical records

Statistical records are collected by many public and private organizations. The Office of National Statistics maintains the most extensive set of statistical records available to researchers for analysis, including census data. There are also numerous less obvious sources, including public health statistics and test score records kept by testing educational organizations.

Gilovich and his colleagues (1985) were interested in the so-called "hot-hand" in basketball. This is the belief that some basketball players go on successful streaks during a game, causing them to "get into a groove" and repeatedly score shot after shot. It is a feeling common among players, many of whom state that they sometimes feel that they just cannot miss when they are "on fire". In contrast, it is often commented that some players go on "cold" streaks during which they just cannot seem to make a single shot no matter what they do. Gilovich et al. decided to test this to see if it really was the case that basketball players went on these runs of success or failure. They formulated a hypothesis based on the assumption that, if the "hot-hand" (or "cold-hand") really happened, then a player would be more likely to score after scoring his previous shot (or several previous shots) than he would if he had missed his previous shot. Gilovich et al. obtained records from a professional basketball team that happened to keep data relating to its players' shots (both hits and misses) and analysed the data to see if there were any obvious patterns. Contrary to what many basketball fans would have expected, they did not find any evidence that that the "hot" (or "cold") hand existed, with players being no more likely to score a shot after having scored their previous shot. Interestingly, they also interviewed several of the players from the team whose shots they analysed, and the players themselves indicated a belief that they shoot in "streaks" despite what Gilovich et al. found when they looked at their patterns of successful shooting.

Public records can also be used as sources of archival data. In a study looking at the link between temperature and aggression, Anderson and Anderson (1984) demonstrated a relationship between temperature and violent crime statistics in two US cities. Data on both variables are readily available from agencies that keep these statistics.

Survey archives

Survey archives consist of data from surveys that are stored on computers and available to researchers who wish to analyse them. Major polling organizations make many of their surveys available and it is usually possible to find survey data from political and social research organizations online. Survey archives are now becoming increasingly available via the Internet at sites that enable researchers to analyse the data online. These archives are extremely important because most researchers do not have the financial resources to conduct large surveys of randomly selected national samples; the archives allow them to access such samples to test their ideas.

Written and mass communication records

Written records are documents such as diaries and letters that have been preserved by historical societies, ethnographies of other cultures written by anthropologists, and public documents as diverse as speeches by politicians or discussion board messages left by Internet users. Mass communication records include books, magazine articles, films, television programmes and newspapers.

As an example of archival research using such records, Schoeneman and Rubanowitz (1985) studied prominent "problem pages" in newspapers, in which readers wrote in with personal problems and appeals for advice. The researchers were interested in the causes people gave for problems they wrote about in their letters. Letters were coded according to whether the writers were discussing themselves or other people, and whether the causes discussed in the letters were internal (caused by the person's own actions or personality) or external (caused by some situation external to the person). When people discussed themselves, the causes of the problems were primarily external, but when other people were described, more of the problems were seen as internally caused (also see Fischer et al., 1987).

Archival data may also be used in cross-cultural research to examine aspects of social structure that differ from society to society. A variable such as the presence versus absence of monogamous marital relationships cannot be studied in a single society. In North America, for example, monogamy is the norm and bigamy is illegal. By looking at a number of cultures, some monogamous and some not, we can increase our understanding of the reasons that one system or the other comes to be preferred. This method was adopted in a study by Rosenblatt and Cozby (1972) on the role of freedom of choice in mate selection. Some societies have considerable restrictions on whom one can marry; other societies give great freedom of choice to young people in deciding on a spouse. In the study, anthropologists' descriptions (called *ethnographies*) of a number of societies were used to rate the societies as being either low or high in terms of freedom of choice of spouse. The ethnographies also provided information on a number of other variables. The results indicated that, when there is freedom of choice of spouse, romantic love and sexual attraction are important bases for mate selection. However, it was also found that freedom of choice of spouse was linked with greater antagonism in the interactions among young males and females. The Rosenblatt and Cozby study used the Human Relations Area Files (HRAF), a resource available in many university libraries, to obtain information from the ethnographies. The HRAF consists of anthropologists' descriptions of many cultures, which have been organized according to categories such as courtship and marriage customs, and child-rearing practices. Thus, it is relatively easy to find specific information from many societies by using the HRAF.

 Test yourself

Identify the method used.[2]

Scenario	Case study	Naturalistic observation	Structured observation	Archival research
1 Researchers conducted an in-depth study with certain 9/11 victims to understand the psychological impact of the attack on the World Trade Center in 2001.				
2 Researchers recorded the time it took drivers in college parking lots to back out of a parking space and compared the time when another car was waiting to the time when another car was not waiting for the space.				
3 Contents of mate-wanted personal advertisements in three major cities were coded to determine whether men and women differ in terms of their self-descriptions.				

2   Answers: 1 = case study; 2 = structured observation; 3 = archival research; 4 = case study; 5 = archival research; 6 = naturalistic observation.

> 4 The researcher spent over a year meeting with and interviewing Aileen Wuornos, the infamous female serial killer who was the subject of the film *Monster*, to construct a psychobiography.
>
> 5 Researchers examined unemployment rates and the incidence of domestic violence police calls in six cities.
>
> 6 A group of researchers studied recycling behaviour at three local parks over a six-month period. They concealed their presence and kept detailed field notes.

Issues in observational research

As with any methodology, there are a number of issues that we have to be aware of when considering adopting it. No methodology is perfect, and so we must acknowledge the potential weaknesses and think critically about each one as a technique for answering questions about behaviour. In the sections below we look at some issues with observational research, focusing mainly on some important things to consider about the nature of "observation" and the people who do it. We also consider briefly some of the ethical factors relating to this type of research.

Observer reliability

An important aspect of analysing observational data is assessing the reliability of the observations. Unless the observations are reliable, they are unlikely to tell us anything meaningful about behaviour. One way researchers assess the reliability of an observer is to ask, "Would another observer viewing the same events obtain the same results?"

Interrater reliability

ch. 4
p.72

We mentioned reliability in Chapter 4. In that chapter, we introduced the problem of "**interrater reliability**", in which reliability is measured by the degree to which two "raters" looking at the same behaviour agree with each other. In this section, we cover this in a bit more detail (although we'll call it "**inter-observer reliability**" given that this is a chapter on observational methods; do not worry, it's the same thing). When observers disagree we become uncertain about what is being measured and what behaviours and events actually occurred. Low inter-observer reliability is likely to result when the event or behaviour to be recorded has not been clearly defined. Imagine Hartup (1974) asking his observers to record aggressive episodes among children without giving them an exact definition of aggression. What exactly is aggression? Some observers might decide to define aggression as one child's physical attack on another; other observers might include verbal assaults in their definition of aggression. What is a playful push and what is an angry shove? Without a clear definition of behaviour or of the events to be recorded, observers do not always agree – and hence show low inter-observer reliability. In addition to providing precise verbal definitions, giving concrete examples of a phenomenon generally helps increase reliability

> **Inter-observer reliability**
> The extent to which two or more observers assessing the same behaviour or event agree about the relevant details.

among observers. Showing observers photographs or videotapes of aggressive and non-aggressive episodes would be a good way to improve their ability to classify aggressive behaviours reliably. Observer reliability is also generally increased by training observers and giving them practice doing the observations. It is especially helpful during the training and practice to give the observers specific feedback regarding any discrepancies between their observations and those of other observers.

The observations of a highly reliable observer are not necessarily accurate observations. Consider two observers who reliably agree about what they saw but who are both "in error" to the same degree. Neither observer is providing an accurate record of behaviour. For example, both might be influenced in a similar way by what they expect the outcome of the observational study to be. Instances are occasionally reported in the media of several observers claiming to see the same thing (for instance, an unidentified flying object, or UFO), only to have the event or object turn out to be something other than what observers claimed it to be (for instance, a weather balloon). Nevertheless, when two independent observers agree, we are generally more inclined to believe that their observations are accurate and valid than when data are based on the observations of a single observer. In order for observers to be independent, each must be unaware of what the other has recorded. The chance of both observers being influenced to the same degree by outcome expectancies, fatigue or boredom is generally so small that we can be confident that what was reported actually occurred. Of course, the more independent observers agree, the more confident we become.

Measures of reliability

The way in which inter-observer reliability is assessed depends on how behaviour is measured. When events are classified according to mutually exclusive categories (nominal scale), observer reliability is generally assessed using a percentage agreement measure. A formula for calculating percentage agreement between observers is:

$$\frac{\text{Number of times two observers agree}}{\text{Number of opportunities to agree}} \times 100$$

Hartup (1974) reported measures of reliability using percentage agreement that ranged from 83 per cent to 94 per cent for judges who coded narrative records according to type of aggression and nature of antecedent events. Although there is no hard-and-fast percentage of agreement that defines low inter-observer reliability, researchers generally report estimates of reliability that exceed 85 per cent in the published literature, suggesting that agreement that is lower than that is unacceptable. In many observational studies data are collected by several observers who observe at different times. Under these circumstances, researchers use only a sample of the observations to measure reliability. For example, two observers might be asked to record behaviour according to a time-sampling procedure such that there is only a subset of times during which both observers are present. Amount of agreement for the times when both observers were present can be used to indicate the degree of reliability for the study as a whole.

When observational data represent at least an interval scale, such as when time is the variable being measured, observer reliability can be assessed using a Pearson product-moment correlation coefficient *r*. This is a statistic that will be introduced in **Chapter 19**.

ch. 19

Thinking critically about observational research
Influence of the observer

Conducting a good observational study involves choosing how to sample behaviour and events to observe, choosing the appropriate observational method, and choosing how to record and analyse observational data. Now that you know the basics of observational methods, you also need to know about potential problems that can occur. The first problem occurs because people often change their behaviour when they know they are being observed. A second problem occurs when observers' biases influence what behaviour they chose to record. We will consider each of these problems in turn.

1 *Reactivity*. The presence of an observer can lead people to change their behaviour because they know they are being observed. When the observer influences the behaviour being observed, we call this the problem of **reactivity**. When individuals "react" to the presence of an observer, their behaviour may not be representative of behaviour when an observer is not present. Underwood and Shaughnessy (1975) relate how a student, as part of a class assignment, set out to observe whether drivers came to a complete stop at an intersection with a stop sign. The observer located himself on the street corner with clipboard in hand. He soon noticed that all the cars were stopping at the stop sign. He then realized that his presence was influencing the drivers' behaviour. When he concealed himself near the intersection, he found that drivers' behaviour changed and he was able to gather data to test his hypothesis.

> **Reactivity**
> When an observed participant changes his or her behaviour as a result of the observer's presence.

Research participants can respond in very subtle ways when they are aware that their behaviour is being observed. Participants are sometimes apprehensive and more than a little anxious about participating in psychological research. Measures of arousal, such as heart rate and galvanic skin response (GSR), may show changes that are purely due to the presence of an observer. Wearing an electronic beeper that signals when to record behavioural activities and mood also can be expected to affect participants' behaviour.

STOP & Think

Can you think of any other scenarios in which being observed might have an influence on the measurement being made?

> **Demand characteristics**
> Cues and other information used by participants to guide their behaviour in a psychological study, often leading participants to do what they believe the observer (experimenter) expects them to do.

Research participants often react to the presence of an observer by trying to behave in ways they think the researcher wants them to behave. When they know they are part of a research study, people usually want to cooperate and be "good" participants. Research participants often try to guess what behaviours are expected, and they may use cues and other information to guide their behaviour (Orne, 1962). These cues in the research situation are called **demand characteristics**.

Orne suggests that individuals generally ask themselves the question, "What am I supposed to be doing here?" To answer this question, participants pay attention to cues present in the setting, the research procedure itself and implicit cues given by the researcher. As participants try to guess what is expected, they may change their behaviours accordingly. Participants' responses to the demand characteristics of a research situation pose a threat to the external validity of psychological research. Our ability to generalize the research findings (**external validity**) is threatened when research participants behave in a manner that is not representative of their behaviour outside the psychological research setting. Interpretation of the study's findings is potentially threatened because participants may unintentionally make a research variable look more effective than it actually is or even nullify the effects of an otherwise significant variable.

ch. 5
p.97

The problem of demand characteristics can be reduced by limiting participants' knowledge about their role in a study or about the hypothesis being tested in the study. The researcher's goal in keeping participants unaware of important details regarding the study is to obtain more representative behaviour. This methodological "solution" to the problem of demand characteristics does raise ethical concerns about important issues such as informed consent (see later in this chapter and **Chapter 24**).

ch. 24

2 *Controlling reactivity.* There are several approaches that researchers use to control the problem of reactivity. One obvious way in which researchers can eliminate reactivity is by making sure that research participants do not detect the presence of the observer. Measures of behaviour when participants do not know they are being observed are referred to as unobtrusive (non-reactive) measures. Obtaining unobtrusive measures may involve concealing the observer or hiding mechanical recording devices such as tape recorders and videotape cameras. LaFrance and Mayo (1976) observed people in conversation without their knowledge. Observations were made in a variety of natural settings, such as restaurants and waiting rooms, so we can imagine that observers had to keep their stopwatches and data sheets hidden behind menus and potted plants in order to obtain unobtrusive measures of behaviour.

Yet another approach is for researchers to use disguised participant observation and to adopt a role in the situation other than that of observer. You may remember this procedure was used by social psychologists studying the behaviour of individuals who claimed to be in contact with aliens from outer space (Festinger et al., 1956). When researchers use unobtrusive measures, they assume that participants act as they ordinarily would because the participants do not know that an observer is present.

Another way to deal with reactivity is to adapt participants to the presence of an observer. Researchers make a reasonable assumption that as participants get used to an observer being present, they will come to behave normally in that person's presence. The speed at which contestants in reality shows like *Big Brother* forget they are being watched and behave as if they were not is one example of this. Adaptation can be accomplished through either habituation or desensitization. In a habituation procedure, observers simply introduce themselves into a situation on many different occasions until the participants cease to react to their presence.

In order to film a documentary entitled *An American Family*, which was shown in the US in the early 1970s, observers (with their cameras) moved into a California home and recorded the activities of a family over a seven-month period. Although it is impossible to tell how much of their behaviour was influenced by the observers' presence, the events that unfolded and remarks made by family members gave evidence of a habituation process having taken place. During filming, the family broke up, the mother asking the father to move out of the house. When interviewed later about having the divorce announced to millions of television viewers, the father admitted that they could have asked the camera crew to get out but that, by this time, "we had gotten used to it" (*Newsweek*, 1973, p. 49).

Desensitization as a means of dealing with reactivity is similar to the desensitization used in the behavioural treatment of phobias. In a therapy situation, an individual with a specific fear (say, an irrational fear of spiders) is first exposed to the feared stimulus at a very low intensity. The patient may be asked to think of things that are related to spiders, such as dusty rooms and cobwebs. At the same time the therapist helps the patient practise relaxation. Gradually the intensity of the stimulus is increased until the patient can tolerate the actual stimulus itself. Desensitization is often used by ethologists to adapt animal subjects to the presence of an observer. Prior to a violent death in the land of her beloved subjects, Fossey (1981; 1983) conducted fascinating observational studies of the mountain gorilla in Africa. Over a period of time she moved closer and closer to the gorillas so that they would get used to her presence. She found that by imitating their movements – for instance, by munching the foliage they ate and by scratching herself – she could put the gorillas at ease. Eventually she was able to sit among the gorillas and observe them as they touched her and explored the research equipment she was using.

Finally, non-reactive measures of behaviour can be obtained by observing behaviour indirectly. This may involve examining physical traces left behind or examining archival information, which are records kept by society about individuals and events. One researcher investigated the drinking behaviour of people living in a town that was officially "dry" (i.e. in which alcohol was prohibited) by counting empty alcohol bottles in their bins. Another researcher used the records kept by a library to assess the effect on a community of the introduction of television. Withdrawals of fiction titles dropped, but the demand for non-fiction was not affected (see Webb et al., 1981). Physical traces and archival data are important unobtrusive measures that can be valuable sources of information about behaviour.

3 *Ethical issues.* Whenever researchers try to control for reactivity by observing individuals without their knowledge, important ethical issues arise. For instance, observing people without their consent can represent a serious invasion of privacy. Deciding what constitutes an invasion of privacy is not always easy, and must include a consideration of the sensitivity of the information, the setting where observation takes place, and the method of dissemination of the information obtained.

Recent behavioural studies using the Internet introduce new ethical dilemmas. When researchers entered Internet chat rooms as disguised participant observers to find out what makes racists advocate racial violence (Glaser et al., 2002), the information they obtained could be seen as gathering incriminating evidence without the respondents' knowledge, not unlike a "sting" operation. The dilemma, of course, is that if informed consent were obtained it is very unlikely that respondents would cooperate. In this case, the relevant research ethics committee approved the research by agreeing with the researchers that the chat room constituted a "public forum", that these topics were common to that forum, and that the researchers had instituted sufficient safeguards to protect the respondents' identities (e.g. by carefully separating names, typically the pseudonyms commonly used by individuals in this chat room, from the responses). On the other hand, there are instances in which people have felt that their privacy was violated when they learned that researchers observed their online discussions without their knowledge (see Skitka and Sargis, 2005).

When individuals are involved in situations that are deliberately arranged by an investigator, as might happen in a structured observation or in a field experiment, ethical problems associated with placing participants at risk may arise. Consider, for instance, a study designed to investigate how college students' attitudes towards racial harassment are affected by hearing other students either condone or condemn racism (Blanchard et al., 1994). More than 200 white undergraduate women attending various universities were "naive participants". The women were approached by a white interviewer as they walked across campus, and were invited to answer a short series of questions about "how their college should respond to acts of racism" (Blanchard et al., 1994, p. 994). A female confederate, posing as a student, approached the interviewer so that she arrived at the same time as the naive participant. The interviewers asked both "students" the same five questions; however, the interviewer always questioned the confederate student first. At this point, the confederate responded by either condemning or condoning racists' acts. Of interest was the effect of these statements on the naive participants' responses to the same questions. The results were clear; hearing another student condemn racism produced more condemning responses relative to a no-influence control group, and hearing another student condone racism produced more condoning reactions to racism than hearing no one else express an opinion. Thus, as the authors suggest, the findings "imply that a few outspoken people can influence the normative climate of interracial social settings in either direction" (Blanchard et al., 1994, p. 997). Were the naive participants "at risk?" If you think the participants were at risk, what degree of risk was present? Did the goals of the study, and the knowledge potentially obtained, outweigh the risks involved in the study? Although participants were "debriefed immediately" in this study, is that sufficient to address any concerns that the naive students might have about how they behaved when confronted with racist opinions, or even to restore confidence in a science that seeks knowledge through deception? Attempting to provide answers to these kinds of questions highlights the difficulty of ethical decision making. (In responding to these ethical questions it may be helpful to look at **Chapter 24**, on ethics.)

ch. 24

Observer bias

Earlier in this chapter we described a study in which Rosenhan (1973) and his colleagues observed the interaction between staff members and patients in mental hospitals, and they found a serious bias on the part of the staff. Once patients were labelled schizophrenic, their behaviour was interpreted solely in light of this label. Staff members interpreted behaviours that might have been considered normal when performed by sane individuals as evidence of the patients' insanity. For example, the researchers later learned that note taking by the participant observers, which was done openly, had been cited by members of the staff as an example of the pseudo-patients' pathological state. Thus, the staff tended to interpret patients' behaviour in terms of the label that had been given them. This example clearly illustrates the potential danger of **observer bias**, the systematic errors in observation that result from an observer's expectations.

Observer bias
Systematic errors in observation often resulting from the observer's expectancies regarding the outcome of a study (i.e. expectancy effects).

1 *Expectancy effects.* In many scientific studies the observer has some expectations about what behaviour should be like in a particular situation or following a specific psychological treatment. This expectancy may be created by knowledge of the results of past investigations or perhaps by the observer's own hypothesis about behaviour in this situation. Expectancies can be a source of observer bias – expectancy effects – if they lead to systematic errors in observation (Rosenthal, 1966; 1976). Cordaro and Ison (1963) designed a study to document expectancy effects. The study required student observers to record the number of head turns and body contractions made by two groups of flatworms. Each student observer was allocated to one of two groups. One group was led to expect that the worms would display frequent turning and contracting, while the other group was led to expect that the worms would not turn and contract very much. The worms in the groups were, however, essentially identical. What differed was what the observers expected to see. Results showed that the observers reported twice as many head turns and three times as many body contractions when a high rate of movement was expected than when a low rate was expected. Apparently, the students interpreted the actions of the worms differently depending on what they expected to observe.

2 *Other biases.* An observer's expectancies regarding the outcome of a study may not be the only source of observer bias. You might think that using automated equipment such as film cameras would eliminate observer bias. Although automation reduces the opportunity for observer bias, it does not necessarily eliminate it. Consider the fact that, in order to record behaviour on film, the observer must determine the angle, location and time of filming. To the extent that these aspects of the study are influenced by personal biases of the observer, such decisions can introduce systematic errors into the results. Altmann (1974) describes an observational study of animal behaviour in which the observers biased the results by taking a midday break whenever the animals were inactive. Observations of the animals during this period of inactivity were conspicuously absent from the observational records. Furthermore, using automated equipment generally only postpones the process of classification and interpretation, and it is perfectly possible for the effects of observer bias to be introduced when narrative records are coded and analysed.

3 *Controlling observer bias.* Observer bias cannot be eliminated, but it can be reduced in several ways. As we mentioned, the use of automatic recording equipment can help, although the potential for bias is still present. Probably the most important factor in dealing with observer bias is the awareness that it might be present. That is, an observer who knows about this bias will be more likely to take steps to reduce its effect.

Observer bias also can be reduced by limiting the information provided to observers. When Hartup (1974) analysed the results of his observational study of children's aggression, the individuals who performed the analysis were not permitted to see all of the narrative records. When the nature of the aggressive act was classified, the antecedent events were blacked out; and when antecedent events were coded, the nature of the aggressive act was blacked out. Therefore, in making their classifications, the coders could not be influenced by information related to the event that they were coding. In a manner of speaking, the coders were "blind" to certain aspects of the study. Observers are blind when they do not know why the observations are being made or the goals of a study. Using blind observers greatly reduces the possibility of introducing systematic errors due to observer expectancies.

Summary

In this chapter, we have described some of the observational methods that are used by psychologists to describe behaviour as systematically and accurately as possible. There is more to observation than you may have first thought. For example, the thing you are observing must be sampled in some way (for example, by using time sampling, event sampling, situation sampling or individual sampling) and then observed using the most appropriate technique. There are many different ways to actually do the observing. Observations can be with or without intervention, which broadly relates to how much or how little interaction the researcher has with the participants under observation. Observation with intervention includes participant observation (which can be disguised or undisguised), structured observations and field experiments. Rosenhan's study in which he sent volunteers into psychiatric institutions is an example of disguised participant observation, and also highlights some of the ethical issues raised by such an approach. Naturalistic observation is an example of observation without intervention. It is when researchers observe behaviour "from a distance" without actually intervening in any way. Observational data can be qualitative or quantitative in nature, and must be recorded appropriately. When conducting observational research, it is important to think about the ethical issues involved and also about the potential influence (and bias) of the observers. In the next chapter, we will look at survey research.

Questions

1 What is archival research? What are the major sources of archival data?

2 Distinguish between participant and non-participant observation; between concealed and non-concealed observation.

3 What is a coding system? What are some important considerations when developing a coding system?

4 What is a case study? When are case studies used?

5 What is naturalistic observation? How does a researcher collect data when conducting naturalistic observation research?

6 Explain why researchers use sampling in observational studies, and describe what the proper use of sampling is intended to accomplish.

7 Explain whether high or low inter-observer reliability ensures that the observations are accurate and valid, and why this is the case.

8 Explain why participants' reactions to demand characteristics can be a threat to the external validity of psychological research and to the interpretation of a study's findings.

9 Identify three factors in participant observation that researchers need to consider to determine the extent of the observer's influence on the behaviour being observed.

10 Structured observation represents a compromise between naturalistic observation and laboratory experiments. What are the primary advantage and potential cost of this compromise?

Activity

1 Some questions are more readily answered using quantitative techniques, and others are best
   addressed through qualitative techniques or a combination of both approaches. Suppose you
   are interested in how a parent's alcoholism affects the life of an adolescent. Develop a research
   question best answered using quantitative techniques and another research question better
   suited to qualitative techniques. A quantitative question is, "Are adolescents with alcoholic
   parents more likely to have criminal records?" and a qualitative question is, "What issues do
   alcoholic parents introduce in their adolescent's peer relationships?"

Chapter 13

Survey Methods

OVERVIEW

The simplest way to find out what people's attitudes and beliefs are is to ask them. Although this may seem obvious, there are specific techniques that psychologists have developed that increase our chances of getting valid and reliable data from surveys. If you are doing a psychology degree, you have probably already filled out a questionnaire for a research student or staff member. This chapter will look at the various ways that we can collect survey data as well as looking at the procedures involved in developing questionnaires. We will also look at the ways in which we can assess whether our questionnaires are any good or not.

OBJECTIVES

After studying this chapter and working through the exercises, you should be able to:

- Identify the steps involved in preparing a questionnaire
- State the ways in which questions should and should not be worded in questionnaires and surveys, and what different types of questions there are
- Describe the different ways in which respondents might provide answers to questions
- Give an account of the different ways in which surveys can be administered, paying attention to the benefits and drawbacks of each approach
- Describe issues that relate to the reliability and validity of surveys, and ways in which these things can be assessed
- Think critically about survey research

Introduction

What are your favourite foods? How much sleep do you get? What type of car do you drive? Do you use the library on campus? Are you satisfied with your life at this point? Psychologists are often asked why they need to do complex experiments. Sometimes people wonder "what's so difficult about psychology? After all, if you want to know what people are doing, observe them; if you want to know how people think, ask them!" While this does not work for all areas of psychology (you would not ask someone "how good is your short-term memory?" as you would get a more reliable answer by actually testing their short-term memory), asking people about themselves can be a valuable source of information.

We discussed in Chapter 12 how psychologists use observational methods to study behaviour. However, one drawback of that technique is that it is sometimes difficult to infer what people were thinking as they behaved in the way that you observed. Any statements about their thought processes are usually the result of inferences made by the researcher, and these inferences do not always reflect the true thoughts and reflections of the people being observed. **Survey research** is designed to deal more directly with the nature of people's thoughts, opinions and feelings. Observational techniques are most useful when we hope to infer general principles of behaviour, but for this to be a valid and useful way of studying behaviour our observations must be more sophisticated than our everyday, casual ones. Likewise, survey research requires more than simply asking people questions.

> **Survey research**
> Research method in which participants are questioned directly about behaviour, and underlying attitudes, beliefs and intentions.

Social scientists, such as political scientists, psychologists and sociologists, use surveys in their research for a variety of reasons, both theoretical and applied. Surveys also are used to meet the more pragmatic needs of the media, political candidates, public health officials, professional organizations, and advertising and marketing directors. In other words, the scope and purpose of surveys can be limited and specific (such as finding out which candidate in an election tends to be favoured by the public), or they can be more global (such as when psychologists measure a person's "sense of well-being and satisfaction with life").

Surveys provide us with a methodology for asking people to tell us about themselves. They have become extremely important as society demands data about issues rather than relying on intuition and anecdotes. Lecturers gather data from students to help determine changes that should be made to their classes. Car companies want data from buyers to assess and improve product quality and customer satisfaction. Without collecting such data, we are totally dependent upon stories we might hear or letters that a graduate or customer might write. Other surveys can be important for making public policy decisions by lawmakers and public agencies. In **basic research**, many important variables are most easily studied using questionnaires or interviews, including attitudes, current emotional states and self-reports of behaviours.

ch. 2
p.26

What questions should you ask?

Surveys are all about asking questions. But asking questions is not as simple as it might seem. A great deal of thought must be given to writing questions for questionnaires and interviews. This section describes some of the most important factors to consider when constructing questions.

Steps in preparing a questionnaire

Constructing a questionnaire that will yield reliable and valid measurements is a challenging task. In this section we suggest guidelines that can help you meet this challenge, especially if you are constructing a questionnaire for the first time as part of a research project you are doing.

> ## STOP & Think
>
> Imagine you are preparing a questionnaire on young people's attitudes towards recreational drugs. What things do you think you will need to consider when deciding on the questions to be used?

The following six steps can serve as a guide as you prepare your questionnaire:

1 Decide what information should be sought.
2 Decide what type of questionnaire should be used.
3 Write a first draft of the questionnaire.
4 Re-examine and revise the questionnaire.
5 Pre-test the questionnaire.
6 Edit the questionnaire and specify the procedures for its use.

Step 1

The first step in questionnaire construction – deciding what information you are aiming to get – should actually be the first step in planning the survey as a whole. This decision, of course, determines the nature of the questions to be included in the questionnaire. It is important to predict the likely results of the proposed questionnaire and then to decide whether these "findings" will answer the questions of the study. Remember that that a poorly conceived questionnaire takes just as much time and effort to administer and analyse as a well-conceived questionnaire does. The difference is that a well-constructed questionnaire leads to interpretable results. The best that can be said for a poorly designed one is that it is a good way to learn how not to do it.

Step 2

Once the information to be sought from respondents[1] has been clearly specified, the next step is to decide on the type of questionnaire to be used. For example, will it be self-administered, or will trained interviewers be using it? This decision is determined primarily by the survey method that has been selected. For instance, if a telephone survey is to be done, trained interviewers will be needed. In designing the questionnaire, the researcher should also consider using items[2] that have been prepared by other researchers. For example, there is no reason to develop your own

---

1   "Respondents" is a term that we'll use in this chapter to refer to those "responding" to your questions. It is synonymous with "participants".
2   "Items" is a term that is used to refer to individual questions in a questionnaire, with each question being an "item".

instrument[3] to assess an attitude if a reliable and valid one is already available. Besides, if you use items from a questionnaire that has already been used, you can compare your results directly with those of earlier studies and you can benefit from any work that has already been conducted on establishing the validity and reliability of the measure.

Step 3

If you decide that no available instrument suits your needs, you will have to take the third step and write a first draft of your own questionnaire. Guidelines concerning the wording and ordering of questions are presented later in this section.

Step 4

The fourth step in questionnaire construction – re-examining and rewriting – is an essential one. It's tempting to think that once you've thought of a few questions you can go out and start getting people to answer them. It is not as simple as that. Questions that appear objective and unambiguous to you may strike others as slanted and ambiguous. It is helpful to have your questionnaire reviewed by experts, both those who have knowledge of survey research methods and those with expertise in the area on which your study is focused. For example, if you are doing a survey of students' attitudes towards the campus food service, it would be advisable to have your questionnaire reviewed by the campus food service manager. When you are dealing with a controversial topic, it is especially important to have representatives of both sides of the issue screen your questions for possible bias.

Step 5

By far the most critical step in the development of an effective questionnaire is doing a pre-test. A pre-test involves actually administering the questionnaire to a small sample of respondents under conditions as much as possible like those to be used in the final administration of the survey. Pre-test respondents must also be typical of those to be included in the final sample; it makes little sense to pre-test a survey of nursing home residents by administering the first draft of the questionnaire to university students. There is one way, however, in which a pre-test does differ from the final administration of the survey. Respondents should be interviewed at length regarding their reactions to individual questions and to the questionnaire as a whole. This provides information about potentially ambiguous or offensive items.

The pre-test should also serve as a "dress rehearsal" for interviewers, who should be closely supervised during this stage to ensure that they understand and adhere to the proper procedures for administering the questionnaire. If major changes have to be made as a result of problems arising during the pre-test, a second pre-test may be needed to determine whether these changes solved the problems originally encountered.

Step 6

After pre-testing is completed, the final step is to edit the questionnaire and specify the procedures to be followed in its final administration. To reach this final step successfully, it is important to consider guidelines for the effective wording of questions and for the ordering of questions.

---

3   "Instrument" is a term commonly used to refer to questionnaires. They are seen as "measurement instruments" where the thing being measured is some psychological property such as an attitude.

Defining the research objectives

The first step in designing a questionnaire is to clearly define the topic of your study. A clear, concise definition of what you are studying and what your research objectives are will yield results that can be interpreted unambiguously. Always ask yourself the question: "What is it that I want to know?" (this is a good thing to ask yourself at the planning stage of *any* study, regardless of what method you intend to use). Results from surveys that do not clearly define the topic area may be confusing. It is also important to have clear, precise **operational definitions** for the attitudes or behaviours being studied. Behaviours and attitudes that are not defined precisely also may yield results that are confusing and difficult to interpret. Clearly defining your topic at the start can help avoid serious problems further on in the research process.

ch. 3
p.49

Having a clearly defined topic has another important advantage: it keeps your questionnaire focused on the behaviour or attitude chosen for study. You should avoid the temptation to do too much in a single survey. Tackling too much in a single survey leads to a long questionnaire that may confuse, overburden or just bore your participants. It also may make it more difficult for you to summarize and analyse your data. Your questionnaire should include a broad enough range of questions so that you can thoroughly assess behaviour, but not so broad as to lose focus and become confusing. Your questionnaire should elicit the responses you are most interested in without much extraneous information. In general, there are three types of survey questions: questions that look at attitudes and beliefs; questions about facts and demographics; and questions about behaviours.

Attitudes and beliefs

Questions about attitudes and beliefs focus on the ways that people evaluate and think about issues. Should more money be spent on mental health services? Are you satisfied with the way that the police responded to your call? How do you evaluate this teacher?

Facts and demographics

Factual questions ask people to indicate things they know about themselves and their situation. In most studies, asking for some demographic information is necessary to adequately describe your sample. Age and gender are typically asked. Depending on the topic of the study, questions on such information as ethnicity, income, marital status, employment status and number of children might be included. Obviously, if you are interested in making comparisons among groups, such as males and females, you must ask the relevant information about group membership. It is unwise to ask such questions if you have no real reason to use the information, however.

Behaviours

Other survey questions can focus on past behaviours or intended future behaviours. How many times last week did you exercise for 20 minutes or longer? How many children do you plan to have? Have you ever been so depressed that you called in sick to work?

The questions to which your participants will respond are the heart of your questionnaire. Take great care to develop questions that are clear, to the point, and relevant to the aims of your research. The time spent in this early phase of your research will pay dividends later. Well-constructed items are easier to summarize, analyse and interpret than poorly constructed ones.

Writing questionnaire items

Writing effective questionnaire items that elicit the information that you want requires care and skill. You cannot simply sit down, write several questions and use those first-draft questions in your final questionnaire. Writing questionnaire items involves writing and rewriting items until they are clear and succinct, and then pre-testing them to ensure clarity, reliability and validity.

Cognitive psychologists have identified a number of potential problems with the way questions are worded (see Graesser et al., 1999). Many of the problems stem from a difficulty with understanding the question, including: (a) unfamiliar technical terms, (b) vague or imprecise terms, (c) ungrammatical sentence structure, (d) phrasing that overloads working memory, and (e) embedding the question with misleading information. Here is a question that illustrates some of the problems identified by Graesser et al.: "Did your mother, father, full-blooded sisters, full-blooded brothers, daughters or sons ever have a heart attack or myocardial infarction?" There is memory overload because of the length of the question and the need to keep track of all those relatives while reading it. The respondent must also worry about two different diagnoses with regard to each relative. Further, the term myocardial infarction may be unfamiliar to most people. How do you write questions to avoid such problems? The following things are important to consider when you are writing questions.

Simplicity

The questions asked in a survey should be relatively simple. People should be able to easily understand and respond to the questions. Avoid jargon and technical terms that people will not understand. Sometimes, however, you have to make the question a bit more complex to make it easier to understand. Usually this occurs when you need to define a term or describe an issue prior to asking the question. Thus, before asking whether someone approves of new anti-terrorist legislation, you will probably want to provide a brief description of what the content of this legislation is.

Double-barrelled questions

Avoid "double-barrelled" questions that ask two things at once. A question such as "Should senior citizens be given more money for recreation centres and food assistance programmes?" is difficult to answer because it taps two potentially very different attitudes. If you are interested in both issues, ask two questions.

Loaded questions

A loaded question is written to lead people to respond in one way. For example, the questions "Do you favour eliminating the wasteful excesses in the public school budget?" and "Do you favour reducing the public school budget?" are likely to elicit different answers. Questions that include emotionally charged words such as rape, waste, immoral, ungodly or dangerous may influence the way that people respond and thus lead to biased conclusions.

Negative wording

Avoid phrasing questions with negatives. This question is phrased negatively: "Do you feel that the city should not approve the proposed women's shelter?" Agreement with this question means disagreement with the proposal. This phrasing can confuse people and result in inaccurate answers. A better format would be: "Do you feel that the city should approve the proposed women's shelter?"

"Yea-saying" and "nay-saying"

Response set
A pattern of individual responses to questions on a self-report measure that is not related to the content of the questions.

When you ask several questions about a topic, there is a possibility that a respondent will employ a **response set** to agree or disagree with all the questions. Such a tendency is referred to as *"yea-saying"* or *"nay-saying"*. The problem here is that the respondent may in fact be expressing true agreement, but alternatively may simply be agreeing with anything you say. One way to detect this is to word the questions so that consistent agreement is unlikely. If you include a question and then ask a similar question with the meaning reversed, you would not expect many people to respond in the same way to each. For example, a study of family communication patterns might ask people how much they agree with the following statements: "The members of my family spend a lot of time together" and "I spend most of my weekends with friends." Similarly, a measure of loneliness (e.g., Russell et al., 1980) will phrase some questions so that agreement means the respondent is lonely ("I feel isolated from others") and others with the meaning reversed so that disagreement indicates loneliness (e.g. "I feel part of a group of friends"). Although it is possible that someone could legitimately agree with both items, consistently agreeing or disagreeing with a set of related questions phrased in both standard and reversed formats is an indicator that the individual is "yea-saying" or "nay-saying".

 ## Test yourself

Question wording – what is the problem?[4]

Read each of the following questions and identify the problems for each	Negative wording	Simplicity	Double-barrelled	Loaded
Professors should NOT be required to take daily attendance. 1 (Strongly disagree) and 5 (Strongly agree)				
Do you study or spend time with your friends in the afternoon?				
Do you still speed on the motorway?				
Would you like to be beautiful and a scholar?				
Do you believe the relationship between mobile phone behaviour and consumption of fast food is orthogonal?				
It would not be correct to follow that procedure, would it?				
Are you in favour of the boss's whim to cut lunchtime to 30 minutes?				

---

4 Answers: negative wording, double-barrelled, loaded, double-barrelled, simplicity, negative wording, loaded.

Responses to questions

Another important decision that a researcher must make concerns the way in which participants will be asked to respond to the questions asked. Is it enough just to ask participants about a topic and let them respond in any way they wish, or should we restrict their responses by asking them to choose between a limited number of possible responses? There are several types of responses and we cover the main ones below.

Open-ended versus closed-ended questions

Questions may be either closed- or open-ended. With closed-ended questions, a limited number of response alternatives are given; with open-ended questions, respondents are free to answer in any way they like. Thus, you could ask a person, "What is the most important thing children should learn to prepare them for life?", followed by a list of answers from which to choose (a closed-ended question), or you could leave this question open-ended for the person to provide the answer. Using closed-ended questions is a more structured approach; they are easier to code and the response alternatives are the same for everyone.

Open-ended questions

Open-ended questions are when you ask the respondent a question and let him or her provide any answer that they wish. Although they are primarily used in **qualitative research**, they can also feature as part of more structured interviews. Using open-ended questions requires time to categorize and code the responses, which usually makes the process more costly. Sometimes a respondent's response cannot be categorized at all because the response does not make sense, does not actually answer the question asked or the person could not think of an answer. Still, an open-ended question can yield valuable insights into what people are thinking. Open-ended questions are most useful when the researcher needs to know what people are thinking and how they naturally view their world; closed-ended questions are more likely to be used when the dimensions of the variables are well defined. Schwarz (1999) points out that the two approaches can sometimes lead to different conclusions. He cites the results of a survey question asking people about what things are important in preparing children for life. When "To think for themselves" was an option in a closed-ended list, 62% of respondents chose it; however, only 5% gave this answer when the open-ended format was used. This finding points to the need to have a good understanding of the topic when asking closed-ended questions.

> **Open-ended questions** Questions in a survey that allow the respondent to answer freely, either verbally or in writing.

ch. 11

The following example might appear in a survey like the Pew Global Attitudes Project (2006) on the attitudes of non-Westerners toward Westerners and Western culture: "How would you characterize Westerners as a group?" The participant writes an answer to the question in the space provided immediately below. Such information may be more complete and accurate than the information obtained with a closed-ended question (discussed next). A drawback to the open-ended item is that participants may not understand exactly what you are looking for or may inadvertently miss some answers. Thus, participants may fail to provide the needed information. Essentially, you must perform a **content analysis** on open-ended answers.

ch. 22
pp.548–551

Partially open-ended questions

Partially open-ended questions resemble restricted items but provide an additional, "other" category and an opportunity to give an answer not listed among the specific alternatives, as shown in this example adapted from the Pew survey:

What is most responsible for declining standards in written English?
__ The government
__ Teachers
__ Local education authorities
__ Tabloid newspapers
__ Other (specify) _____

Dillman (2000) offers several suggestions for formatting restricted and partially open-ended items. First, use a boldface font for the stem of a question and a normal font for response category labels (as we have done in the previous example). This helps respondents separate the question from the response categories that follow. Second, make any special instructions intended to clarify a question a part of the question itself. Third, put check boxes, blank spaces or numbers in a consistent position throughout your questionnaire (e.g. to the left of the response alternatives). Fourth, place all alternatives in a single column.

Closed-ended questions

With **closed-ended questions** (also called "restricted items"), there are a fixed number of response alternatives. In public opinion surveys, a simple "yes or no" or "agree or disagree" dichotomy is often sufficient. In more basic research, it is often preferable to have a sufficient number of alternatives to allow people to express themselves – for example, a 5- or 7-point scale ranging from "strongly agree" to "strongly disagree" or "very positive" to "very negative". Such a scale might appear as follows:

Strongly agree ____ ____ ____ ____ ____ ____ ____ Strongly disagree

This is an example of a rating scale. Rating scales are an integral feature of closed-ended questionnaires so we cover them in detail below.

Rating scales

Rating scales such as the one just shown are very common in many areas of research. Rating scales ask people to provide "how much" judgements on any number of dimensions – amount of agreement, liking or confidence, for example. Rating scales can have many different formats. The format that is used depends on factors such as the topic being investigated. Perhaps the best way to gain an understanding of the variety of formats is simply to look at a few examples.

Graphic rating scale

A **graphic rating scale** requires a mark along a continuous 100-millimetre line that is anchored with descriptions at each end.

How would you rate the movie you just saw?
Not very enjoyable _____ Very enjoyable

A ruler is then placed on the line to obtain the score on a scale that ranges from 0 to 100.

Semantic differential scale

The **semantic differential scale** is a measure of the meaning of concepts that was developed by Osgood and his associates (Osgood et al., 1957). Respondents rate any concept – persons, objects, behaviours, ideas – on a series of bipolar adjectives using 7-point scales.

> **Semantic differential scale**
> A rating scale which measures responses to words or concepts using scales labelled with two contrasting adjectives.

Smoking cigarettes is
Good ____: ____: ____: ____: ____: ____: ____ Bad
Strong ____: ____: ____: ____: ____: ____: ____ Weak
Active ____: ____: ____: ____: ____: ____: ____ Passive

Research on the semantic differential shows that virtually anything can be measured using this technique. Ratings of specific things (marijuana), places (the student union), people (the prime minister, accountants), ideas (abortion, tax reduction) and behaviours (attending church, using public transport) can be obtained. A large body of research shows that the concepts are rated along three basic dimensions: the first and most important is *evaluation* (e.g. adjectives such as good–bad, wise–foolish, kind–cruel); the second is *activity* (active–passive, slow–fast, excitable–calm); and the third is *potency* (weak–strong, hard–soft, large–small).

Non-verbal scale for children

Young children may not understand the types of scales we have just described, but they are able to give ratings. For example, you could ask children to "Point to the face that shows how you feel about the toy."

The examples thus far have labelled only the end points on the rating scale. Respondents decide the meaning of the other response alternatives. This is a reasonable approach, and people are usually able to use such scales without difficulty. Sometimes researchers need to provide labels to more clearly define the meaning of each alternative.

Likert scales

Here is a fairly standard alternative to the agree–disagree scale shown previously:

The government are doing all they can to combat violent crime
1. Strongly agree   2. Agree   3. Undecided   4. Disagree   5. Strongly disagree

_____   _____   _____   _____   _____

Surveys and questionnaires that use a series of items like the one above to measure an attitude (or construct) are known as Likert scales. Likert scales are named after Rensis Likert who wrote a paper on using scales to measure attitudes (Likert, 1932). A Likert scale provides a series of statements to which participants can indicate degrees of agreement or disagreement using the response scale illustrated above. The statements used in a Likert scale have all undergone extensive item – analysis in order that the researcher can be confident that they are reliable measures of the construct being studied.

In the first example above, the attitude statement is followed by five blank spaces labelled from "Strongly agree" to "Strongly disagree". The participant simply checks the space that best reflects the degree of agreement or disagreement with each statement. The second example, below, provides consecutive numbers rather than blank spaces and includes descriptions only at the ends. Participants are instructed to circle the number that best reflects how much they agree or disagree with each statement.

The government are doing all they can to combat violent crime

1	2	3	4	5
Strongly agree				Strongly disagree

The two scales above have five response options, although 7- and 10-point versions have also been used. In some cases, researchers have found it necessary to omit the "undecided" or "neutral" options for questionnaires in which they would prefer the participants to respond in one direction or the other and for questionnaires that appear to elicit "neutral/undecided" responses in a large number of participants. Once you've decided on the format of your Likert scale, you should stick to it for the whole questionnaire.

ch. 4
p.62

Scores on these scales are generally considered to be **interval data** as it is assumed that the distance between each point on the scale is equal and there is no true zero point. It is important to note that the data from such scales can only be considered in this way after it has been summated across all questions relating to the construct under study; in other words, the Likert scale requires that responses to all the relevant questions be taken into account before it can be considered as interval-level data. Some researchers would dispute this, however, and argue that scales such as these should be considered ordinal data because researchers have no justification in assuming that the distances between the points on the scale represent discrete measurable distances. Although this is a serious objection, most researchers using data obtained from these scales treat it as interval level.

Other alternatives for responses

Sometimes, a perfectly balanced scale may not be possible or desirable. Consider a scale asking a university professor to rate a student for a job or graduate programme. This particular scale asks for comparative ratings of students:

In comparison with other graduates, how would you rate this student's potential for success?

Lower 50%	Upper 50%	Upper 25%	Upper 10%	Upper 5%

Notice that most of the alternatives are asking people to make a rating in terms of the top 25 per cent of students. This is done because students who apply for such programmes tend to be very bright and motivated, and so professors rate them favourably. The wording of the alternatives attempts to force the raters to make finer distinctions among generally very good students.

Labelling alternatives is particularly interesting when asking about the frequency of a behaviour. For example, you might ask, "How often do you exercise for at least 20 minutes?" What kind of scale should you use to let people answer this question? You could list (1) never, (2) rarely, (3) sometimes and (4) frequently. These terms convey your meaning but they are too vague – how often would "sometimes" be? Would two people who say they exercise "sometimes" actually exercise for the same amount of time each week? Here is another set of alternatives, similar to ones described by Schwarz (1999):

_____ less than twice a week
_____ about twice a week
_____ about four times a week
_____ about six times a week
_____ at least once each day

A different scale might be:

_____ less than once per month
_____ about once a month
_____ about once every two weeks
_____ about once a week
_____ more than once per week

The first scale is a **high-frequency scale** because most alternatives indicate a high frequency of exercise. The other scale is referred to as low frequency. These labels should be chosen carefully because people may interpret the meaning of the scale differently, depending on the labels used. If you were actually asking the exercise question, you might decide on alternatives different from the ones described here. Also, your choice should be influenced by factors such as the **population** you are studying. If you are studying people who generally exercise a lot, you will be more likely to use a higher frequency scale than you would if you were studying people who generally do not do much exercise.

By offering only specific response alternatives, restricted items control the participant's range of responses. The responses made to restricted items are therefore easier to summarize and analyse than the responses made to open-ended items. However, the information that you obtain from a restricted item is not as rich as the information from an open-ended item. Participants cannot explain their responses or elaborate further on them. Also, you may fail to include an alternative that correctly describes the participant's opinion, thus forcing the participant to choose an alternative that is not really appropriate for that person.

High-frequency scale
A rating scale in which the response options for frequency of behaviour represent high frequencies.

Population
An entire group (or entire set of scores) that is of interest to you as a researcher.

Finalizing the questionnaire

Formatting the questionnaire

If it is to be effective, the printed questionnaire should appear attractive, coherent and professional. It should be neatly typed and free of spelling errors. Respondents should find it easy to identify the questions and the response alternatives to the questions. Leave enough space between questions so people do not become confused when reading the questionnaire. If you have a particular scale format, such as a 5-point rating scale, use it consistently. Do not change from 5- to 4- to 7-point scales, for example.

Ordering of questions

1 *The first few questions*

The order in which questions are included on a questionnaire has been shown to affect the responses of participants. The first few questions set the tone for the rest of the questionnaire, and determine how willingly and conscientiously respondents will work on subsequent questions. For self-administered questionnaires (i.e. those the participant will complete without interaction with the researcher), it is best to begin with the most interesting set of questions in order to capture the respondent's attention. Demographic data should be obtained at the end of a self-administered questionnaire. If you ask for these details first, it is likely that the participants will believe that the questionnaire is boring. For personal or **telephone interviews**, on the other hand, demographic questions are frequently asked at the beginning because they are easy for the respondent to answer and thus bolster the respondent's confidence. They also allow time for the interviewer to establish rapport before asking questions about more sensitive matters.

> **Telephone interview**
> Method of conducting a survey that involves calling participants on the telephone and asking them questions.

2 *The influence of order of questions on responses*

The order in which particular questions are asked can have dramatic effects, as illustrated in a study by Schuman et al. (1981). They found that people responded differently depending on the order of two questions concerning abortion: one general and one specific. The general question was: "Do you think it should be possible for a pregnant woman to obtain a legal abortion if she is married and does not want any more children?" The more specific question was: "Do you think it should be possible for a pregnant woman to obtain a legal abortion if there is a strong chance of a serious defect in the baby?" When the general question was asked first, 60.7 per cent of respondents said "yes", but when the general question followed the specific question, only 48.1 per cent of respondents said "yes". The corresponding values for the specific question were 84 per cent and 83 per cent agreement in the first and second positions, respectively. The generally accepted method for dealing with this problem is to use funnel questions, which means starting with the most general question and moving to more specific questions on a given topic.

3 *Filter questions*

Researchers also make use of filter questions – which are general questions asked of respondents to find out whether they need to be asked more specific questions. For example, the question,

"Do you own a car?" might precede a series of questions about the costs of maintaining a car. In this instance, the respondents would answer the specific questions only if their response to the general question was "yes". If that answer was "no", the interviewer would not ask the specific questions (in a self-administered questionnaire, the respondent would be instructed to skip that section). When the filter questions involve objective information (e.g. "Are you over 65?"), their use is relatively straightforward. Researchers must be careful, however, in using behavioural or attitudinal questions as filter questions. Smith (1981) first asked respondents whether they approved of hitting another person in "any situation you can imagine". Logically, a negative response to this most general question should imply a negative response to any more specific questions. Nonetheless, over 80 per cent of the people who responded "no" to the general question then reported that they approved of hitting another person in specific situations, such as in self-defence. Although findings such as this suggest that filter questions should be used cautiously, the need to demand as little of the respondent's time as possible makes filter questions an essential tool in the design of effective questionnaires.

4 *Sensitive questions*

The placement of items asking for sensitive information (such as sexual preferences or illegal behaviour) is an important factor. Dillman (2000) suggests placing objectionable questions after less objectionable ones, perhaps even at the end of the questionnaire. Once your participants are committed to answering your questions, they may be more willing to answer some sensitive questions. Additionally, a question may not seem as objectionable after the respondent has answered previous items than if the objectionable item is placed earlier in the questionnaire.

Refining questions

Before actually administering the survey, it is a good idea to give the questions to a small group of people as a pre-test and have them "think aloud" while answering them. The participants might be chosen from the population being studied, or they could be friends or colleagues who can give reasonable responses to the questions. For the "think aloud" procedure, you will need to ask the individuals to tell you how they interpret each question and how they respond to the response alternatives. This procedure can provide valuable information that you can use to improve the questions. It will also allow you to assess how easy it is for participants to "navigate" their way through the questionnaire, if it is a written version that you're using. There should be a logical "navigational path" (Dillman, 2000) that your respondent can follow. This path should lead the respondent through the questionnaire as if he or she were reading a book. One way to accomplish this is to use appropriate graphics (e.g. arrows and other symbols) to guide respondents through the questionnaire. In fact, Dillman talks about two "languages" of a questionnaire. One language is verbal and relates to how your questions are worded. The other language is graphical and relates to the symbols and graphics used to guide respondents through the items on your questionnaire.

Symbols and graphics can be used to separate groups of items, direct respondents where to go in the event of a certain answer (e.g. "If you answered 'No' to item 5, skip to item 7" could be accompanied by an arrow pointing to item 7), or direct respondents to certain pages on the questionnaire. Dillman suggests the following three steps for integrating the verbal and graphical languages into an effective questionnaire:

1 Design a navigational path directing respondents to read all the information on a page.

2 Create effective visual navigational guides to help respondents stay on the navigational path.

3 Develop alternate navigational guides to help with situations where the normal navigational guide will be interrupted (e.g. skipping items or sections).

However you decide to guide your participants through the questionnaire, it is always useful to pre-test first to assess whether or not your techniques are effective. If not, then you can refine them before collecting any "real" data.

Administering surveys

Face-to-face interview
Method of administering a questionnaire that involves face-to-face interaction with the participant.

After you develop your survey, you must decide how to administer it. You could mail your questionnaire to your participants, deliver your questionnaire via email or post it on the Internet, telephone participants to ask the questions directly, administer your questionnaire to a large group at once, or conduct **face-to-face interviews**. Each method has advantages and disadvantages and makes its own special demands. In the next few sections, we look at each method of administering surveys.

Mail surveys

Mail survey
Method of administering a survey that involves mailing questionnaires to participants.

Response bias
A source of bias in your data caused by participants failing to return completed surveys.

Non-response bias
A problem associated with survey research, caused by some participants not returning the questionnaire, resulting in a biased sample.

Response rate
The percentage of people selected for a sample who actually completed a survey.

In a **mail survey**, you mail your questionnaire directly to your participants and they complete and return it at their leisure. This is a convenient method. All you need to do is put your questionnaires into addressed envelopes and mail them off. Unfortunately, there are disadvantages to mail surveys. Some of these disadvantages are less serious than others. For instance, because respondents will not be able to ask any questions, the questionnaire used in the survey must be completely self-explanatory and easy to follow. A second less serious disadvantage is that the researcher has little control over the order in which the respondent answers the questions. As we noted previously, the order of questions may affect how respondents answer certain questions.

The main disadvantage of mail surveys, however, is when some participants do not complete and return your questionnaire. This is known as **response bias**. If the participants who fail to return the questionnaire differ in significant ways from those who do return it, your survey may give you answers that do not represent the opinions of the intended population.

Combating non-response bias

To reduce **non-response bias**, you should develop strategies to increase the likelihood that people will return your questionnaires. Dillman (2000) notes that the single most effective strategy for increasing **response rate** is to contact the respondents on more than one occasion. Dillman suggests making four contacts via mail. The first consists of a pre-notice letter sent to the respondent a few days before the questionnaire is sent. The pre-notice letter should inform the respondent that an important questionnaire will be coming in the mail in a few days. It also should inform the respondent what the survey is about and why it will be useful. The second mailing would deliver the questionnaire itself, accompanied by a cover letter. The cover letter should include the following elements in the order listed (Dillman, 2000): the specific request to complete the questionnaire, why the respondent was selected to receive the survey, the usefulness of the survey, a statement of confidentiality of the respondent's answers, an offer of a token of appreciation (if such an offer is to be made), an offer to answer questions and a real signature. The third mailing would take the form of a thank you postcard sent a few days or a week after the questionnaire was mailed. The postcard should thank the respondent for completing the questionnaire and remind the respondent to complete the questionnaire if they have not already done so. The fourth contact provides a replacement questionnaire, sent two to four weeks after the original questionnaire and accompanied by a letter indicating that the original questionnaire had not been received. The letter also should urge the respondent to complete the replacement questionnaire and return it.

You may be able to increase your return rate somewhat by including a small token of your appreciation, such as a pen or pencil that the participant can keep. Some researchers include a small amount of money as an incentive to complete the questionnaire. As a rule, it is better to send the token along with the questionnaire rather than make the token contingent upon returning the questionnaire. One study in the USA found that 57 per cent of respondents returned a survey questionnaire when promised $50 for its return whereas 64 per cent returned the questionnaire when $1 was included with it (James & Bolstein, 1990). Ironically, smaller rewards seem to produce better results than larger ones (Kanuk & Berenson, 1975; Warner et al., 1983).

Internet surveys

An increasingly popular method of administering questionnaires is to post them on the Internet. **Internet surveys** can be distributed via email, sent out via mailing lists or posted on a website. Which method you use depends on the nature and purpose of your survey. Email surveys are easy to distribute but do not permit complex navigational designs (Dillman, 2000). Consequently, email surveys are best for relatively short, simple questionnaires. Web-based surveys allow you to create and present more complex questionnaires.

Internet survey
A survey in which the questionnaire is administered electronically via the Internet.

There are numerous advantages of using the Internet for survey research. At the top of the list are efficiency and cost. Thousands, if not millions, of participants who vary in age, ethnicity and even nationality can be contacted through a few keystrokes on a computer. Time and labour are dramatically reduced compared to mail or telephone surveys, let alone personal interviews. Online questionnaires are paperless, thus saving natural resources and copying costs. Participants may respond when it is convenient and do so without leaving the comfort of their home, office, student halls or other Internet site.

In addition to reaching large and potentially diverse samples, Skitka and Sargis (2005) suggest that the Internet also has the potential for accessing groups that are typically under-represented in psychological research. The prevalence on the Web of chat rooms, special interest groups and support groups provides an "in" for a researcher seeking specific samples of participants, whether it be pet owners, members of hate groups, cancer survivors, victims of various crimes, or any of a multitude of respondent types that may not be as easily reached by more traditional survey methods. Because the Internet is truly a worldwide source of participants, it also opens up new possibilities for cross-cultural research (e.g. Gosling et al., 2004).

There are disadvantages to Internet surveys as well. A sample of respondents from the Internet may not be representative of the general population. How representative your sample is will depend on how many people in your target population have access to the Internet. In the past, computers were more likely to be owned by people with higher levels of education and income, and by certain other members of society. While this may still be the case, it may not be as big an issue as it once was as more and more people have access. Despite this, however, there is still a potential issue in getting your questionnaire to people who do have access, as not everyone uses the Internet in the same way. Another disadvantage is that one must have the resources available to post a survey on the Internet. This requires computer space on a server and the ability to create the necessary web pages or the resources to pay someone to create your net survey for you.

ch. 24
p.602

Lack of control over the research environment is also a major disadvantage of Internet surveys. As you will discover in Chapter 24, this lack of control raises serious **ethical issues** related to informed consent and protecting individuals from harm as a consequence of their participation (e.g. emotional distress over survey questions). Because the researcher is not present there is no easy way to determine if respondents understand clearly the instructions, are answering conscientiously and not frivolously or even maliciously, or creating multiple submissions. Respondents may participate alone or in groups, under distracting conditions, without the knowledge of the researcher (Skitka & Sargis, 2005).

Telephone surveys

In a telephone survey, you contact participants by telephone rather than by mail or via the Internet. You can ask some questions more easily over the telephone than you can in written form. Telephone surveys can be done by having an interviewer ask respondents a series of questions or by interactive voice response (IVR). Telephone surveys using live interviewers have lost popularity as new technologies have become available. Interactive voice response surveys involve respondents using a touch-tone telephone to respond to a series of pre-recorded questions. Modern IVR technologies also allow respondents to provide verbal answers in addition to numeric responses.

Selection bias
Threat to the representativeness of a sample that occurs when the procedures used to select a sample result in the over- or under-representation of a significant segment of the population.

Interviewer bias
Intentional or unintentional influence exerted by an interviewer in such a way that the actual or interpreted behaviour of respondents is consistent with the interviewer's expectations.

Generally, telephone surveys may not be the best way to administer a questionnaire. The plethora of "junk calls" to which the population is exposed has given rise to a backlash against telephone intrusions and various countries now have laws to protect people from unwanted calls. These laws, combined with caller ID and answering machines (which allow residents to screen their calls), make the telephone a less attractive medium for surveys now than in the past.

The telephone survey also has other drawbacks. A possible **selection bias** exists when respondents are limited to those who have telephones and the problem of **interviewer bias** remains. There is a limit to how long respondents are willing to stay on the phone, and individuals may respond differently when talking to a "faceless voice". The proliferation of mobile phones also adds an unknown effect, given that mobile phone users are frequently "on the go" or in business settings when they answer their phone. This cultural change may result in lower response rates from telephone surveys. Hippler and Schwarz (1987) suggest that people take less time to form judgements during phone interviews and they may have difficulty remembering the response options offered by the interviewer.

Group administered surveys

Sometimes you may have at your disposal a large group of individuals to whom you can administer your questionnaire. In such a case, you design your questionnaire as you would for a mail survey but administer it to the assembled group. For example, you might distribute a questionnaire to a first-year university class. Using such a captive audience permits you to collect large amounts of data in a relatively short time. You do not have to worry about participants misplacing or forgetting about your questionnaire. You also may be able to reduce any volunteer bias, especially if you administer your questionnaire during a class period. People may participate because very little effort is required.

As usual, this method has some drawbacks. Participants may not treat the questionnaire as seriously when they complete it as a group as when they complete it alone. Also, you may not be able to ensure anonymity in the large group if you are asking for sensitive information. Participants may feel that other participants are looking at their answers. (You may be able to overcome this problem by giving adjacently seated participants alternate forms of the questionnaire.) Also, a few partici-pants may express hostility about the questionnaire by purposely providing false information.

A final drawback to **group administered surveys** concerns the participant's **right to decline** participation. A participant may feel pressure to participate in your survey. This pressure arises from the participant's observation that just about everyone else is participating. In essence, a conformity effect occurs because completing your survey becomes the norm defined by the behaviour of your other participants. Make special efforts to reinforce the understanding that participants should not feel compelled to participate.

ch. 24
p.602

> **Group administered surveys**
> Administering a questionnaire to a group of participants at the same time.

Structured interviews

Yet another method for obtaining survey data is the face-to-face interview. We have already covered **interviews** as a method for qualitative data collection and many of the same issues apply.

ch. 11
p.201

Interviews involve the researcher talking to each participant directly. This can be done in the participant's home or place of employment, in your office, or in any other suitable place. If you decide to use a face-to-face interview, you need to keep several things in mind. First, you must decide how much structure you require in the interview. In a structured interview, you ask prepared questions. This is similar to the telephone survey in that you prepare a questionnaire in advance and simply read the ordered questions to your participants. In the unstructured[5] (usually referred to as semi-structured) interview you have a general idea about the issues to discuss but you do not have a predetermined sequence of questions. In this section, we will primarily focus on interviews in which the researcher asks a series of structured questions, but first we would like to clear up some of the differences between the two forms of interviews and the related methods of analysis.

Structured versus semi-structured/quantitative versus qualitative

As we mentioned in Chapter 11, qualitative interviews tend to encourage interviewees to talk openly about their views and their experiences. In most research of this type, semi-structured

---

5   Burman (1994) suggests that the term "unstructured" should not be used, as it falsely indicates that the researcher has no prior expectations or agenda.

interviews are used. Although it is usually the case that structured interviews are generally used for quantitative research and semi-structured interviews for qualitative research, this does not always have to be the case. The key factor is not how much structure there is in the interview process, but what you actually end up doing with the data that you obtain from the interview. The responses that you get from an interview can be coded numerically and analysed quantitatively regardless of whether the interview itself was highly structured or highly unstructured. That said, the type of data that you will usually get from less structured interviews will allow the interviewee to give a full and detailed account that is not constrained by the researcher's predetermined list of questions. Data collected in this way will usually be difficult to quantify and will best be dealt with using a qualitative method of analysis. After all, if you have an abundance of rich detailed data, much of this would be lost if you were to reduce it to numbers. Likewise, although it is possible to apply qualitative analyses to data from highly structured interviews, the structure will limit the responses that the interviewee can give and so this type of data is usually best coded and submitted to a quantitative analysis.

Advantages and disadvantages of structured interviews

An advantage of the structured interview is that all participants are asked the same questions in the same order. This eliminates fluctuations in the data that result from differences in when and how questions are asked. Responses from a structured interview are therefore easier to summarize and analyse. However, the structured interview tends to be inflexible. You may miss some important information by having a highly structured interview. The semi-structured interview is superior in this respect. You can gain some advantages of each type of interview by incorporating elements of each in one interview. For example, you can begin the interview with a structured format by asking prepared questions and then switch to an unstructured format later in the interview.

Using the face-to-face interview strategy leads to a problem that is not present in mail or Internet surveys but is present to some extent in telephone surveys: the appearance and demeanour of the interviewer may influence the responses of the participants. This is known as "interviewer bias" and it is also linked to the problem of demand characteristics that we briefly mentioned in the previous chapter. Subtle changes in the way in which an interviewer asks a question may elicit different answers. Also, your interviewer may not respond similarly to all participants (e.g. an interviewer may react differently to an attractive participant and an unattractive one). This can also bias the results.

ch. 12
p.245

The best way to combat this problem is to use interviewers who have received extensive training in interview techniques. Interviewers must be trained to ask questions in the same way for each participant. They also must be trained not to emphasize any particular words in a question or in the response list. The questions should be read in a neutral manner. Also, try to anticipate any questions that participants may have and provide your interviewers with standardized responses. This can be accomplished by running a small pilot version of your survey before running the actual survey. During this pilot study, try out the interview procedure on a small sample of participants. This can be done with just about anyone, such as friends, colleagues or students, and it will allow you to correct any problems that arise.

Another potential problem with the interview method is that the social context in which the interview takes place may affect a participant's responses. For example, in a survey of sexual attitudes, known as the "Sex in America" survey (Michael et al., 1994), some questions were asked during a face-to-face interview. Some participants were interviewed alone, whereas others were interviewed with a spouse or other sex partner present. Having the sex partner present changed the responses to some questions. For example, when asked a question about the number of sex partners one had over the past year, 17 per cent of the participants interviewed alone reported two or more. When interviewed with their sex partner present, only 5 per cent said they had two or more sex partners. It would be better to conduct the interviews in a standardized fashion with only the participant present.

Summary

Although each of the techniques discussed has advantages, the mail survey has been the most popular. The mail survey can reach large numbers of participants at a lower cost than either the telephone survey or face-to-face interview, and produces data that are less affected by social desirability effects (answering in a way that seems socially desirable). For these reasons, consider mail surveys first.

After designing your questionnaire and choosing a method of administration, the next step is to assess the reliability and validity of your questionnaire. This is typically done by administering your questionnaire to a small but representative sample of participants. Based on the results, you may have to rework your questionnaire to meet acceptable levels of reliability and validity. In the next sections, we introduce you to the processes of evaluating the reliability and validity of your questionnaire.

Assessing the reliability of your questionnaire

Constructing a questionnaire is typically not a one-shot deal. That is, you do not just sit down and write some questions and magically produce a high-quality questionnaire. Developing a quality questionnaire usually involves designing the questionnaire, administering it, and then evaluating it to see if it does the job it's supposed to.

One dimension you must pay attention to is the reliability of your questionnaire. In Chapter 4, we defined *reliability* as the ability of a measure to produce the same or highly similar results on repeated administrations. This definition extends to a questionnaire. If, on testing and retesting, your questionnaire produces highly similar results, you have a reliable instrument. In contrast, if the responses vary widely, your questionnaire is not reliable.

ch. 4 p.69

In Chapter 4, we described two ways to assess the reliability of a measure: the test–retest method and the split-half method. In the next sections, we discuss the application of these two methods when assessing the reliability of a questionnaire.

Assessing reliability by repeated administration

Evaluating test–retest reliability is the oldest and conceptually simplest way of establishing the reliability of your questionnaire. You simply administer your questionnaire, allow some time to elapse, and then administer the questionnaire (or a parallel form of it) again to the same group of people. How closely responses on the later administration resemble the ones from the initial administration of the questionnaire is an indicator of how reliable it is. Although this method is relatively simple to execute, you need to consider some issues before using it.

First, you must consider how long to wait between administrations of your questionnaire. An inter-test interval that is too short may result in participants remembering your questions and the answers they gave. This could lead to an artificially high level of test–retest reliability. If, however, you wait too long, test–retest reliability may be artificially low. According to Tim Rogers (1995), the inter-test interval should depend on the nature of the variables being measured, with an interval of a few weeks being sufficient for most applications. Rogers suggests that test–retest methods may be particularly problematic when applied to the following:

1 *Measuring ideas that fluctuate with time.* For example, an instrument to measure attitudes towards universal health care should not be evaluated with the test–retest method because attitudes on this topic seem to shift quickly.

2 *Issues for which individuals are likely to remember their answers on the first testing.*

3 *Questionnaires that are very long and boring.* The problem here is that participants may not be highly motivated to accurately complete an overly long questionnaire and therefore may give answers that reduce reliability.

Some of the problems inherent in using the *same* measure on multiple occasions can be avoided by using alternate or parallel forms of your questionnaire for multiple testing sessions. This is known as the *parallel-forms* method.

For the parallel-forms method to work, the two (or more) forms of your questionnaire must be equivalent so that direct comparison between them is meaningful. According to Rogers (1995), parallel forms should have the same number of items and the same response format, cover the same issues with different items, be equally difficult, use the same instructions and have the same time limits. In short, the parallel versions of a test must be as equivalent as possible.

Although the parallel-forms method improves on the test–retest method, it does not solve all the problems associated with multiple testing. Using parallel forms does not eliminate the possibility that rapidly changing attitudes will result in low reliability. As with the test–retest method, such changes make the questionnaire appear less reliable than it actually is. In addition, practice effects may occur even when alternate forms are used. Even though you use different questions on the parallel form, participants may respond similarly on the second test because they are familiar with your question format.

Assessing reliability with a single administration

Because of the problems associated with repeated testing, you might consider assessing reliability by means of a single administration of your questionnaire. As noted in **Chapter 4**, this approach involves splitting the questionnaire into equivalent halves and deriving a score for each half; the correlation between scores from the two halves is known as split-half reliability. This technique works best when your survey is limited to a single specific area (e.g. sexual behaviour) as opposed to multiple areas (sexual behaviour and sexual attitudes).

ch. 4
p.71

Although the split-half method circumvents the problems associated with repeated testing, it introduces others. First, when you split a questionnaire, each score is based on a reduced (by half) number of items. Reducing the number of items that you use to measure reliability can lead to the measure of reliability itself being reduced. Consequently, the split-half method may underestimate reliability. Second, it is not clear how splitting should be done. If you simply do a first-half/second-half split, artificially low reliability may occur if the two halves of the form are not equivalent or if participants are less motivated to answer questions accurately on the second half of your questionnaire and therefore give inconsistent answers to your questions. One remedy for this is to use an odd–even split. In this case, you derive a score for the odd items and a score for the even items.

Perhaps the most desirable way to assess the split-half reliability of your questionnaire is to apply the Kuder–Richardson formula. This formula yields the average of all the split-half reliabilities that could be derived from splitting your questionnaire into two halves in every possible way. The resulting number (designated KR20) will lie between 0 and 1; the higher the number, the greater is the reliability of your questionnaire. A KR20 of .75 indicates a "moderate" level of reliability (Rogers, 1995).

In cases in which your questionnaire uses a Likert format, a variation on the Kuder–Richardson formula known as *coefficient alpha* is used. Like KR20, coefficient alpha is a score between 0 and 1, with higher numbers indicating greater reliability. Computation of this formula can be complex. For details, see a text on psychological testing (e.g. Cohen and Swerdlik, 2005; Rogers, 1995).

Increasing reliability

Regardless of the method that you use to assess the reliability, there are steps you can take to increase the reliability of your questionnaire (Rogers, 1995):

1 Increase the number of items on your questionnaire. Generally, higher reliability is associated with increasing numbers of items. Of course, if your instrument becomes too long, participants may become angry, tired or bored. You must weigh the benefits of increasing questionnaire length against possible liabilities.

2 Standardize administration procedures. Reliability will be enhanced if you treat all participants alike when administering your questionnaire. Make sure that timing procedures, lighting, ventilation, instructions to participants and instructions to administrators are kept constant.

3 Score your questionnaire carefully. Scoring errors can reduce reliability.

4 Make sure that the items on your questionnaire are clear, well written and appropriate for your sample (see our previous discussion on writing items).

Assessing the validity of your questionnaire

In Chapter 4, we discussed the validity of a measure and described several forms of validity that differ in their method of assessment: content validity, criterion-related validity, construct validity and face validity As with other measures, a questionnaire must have validity if it is to be useful. In other words, it must measure what it is intended to measure. For example, if you are designing a questionnaire to assess political attitudes, the questions on your test should tap into political attitudes and not, say, religious attitudes.

ch. 4 pp.73–74

Here we review content validity, **construct validity** and criterion-oriented validity as applied to a questionnaire. For more detailed definitions of these forms of validity, flick back to Chapter 4.

In a questionnaire, *content validity* assesses whether the questions cover the range of behaviours normally considered to be part of the dimension that you are assessing. To have content validity, your questionnaire on political attitudes should include items relevant to all the major issues relating to such attitudes (e.g. crime and justice, health care, the economy and defence). The *construct validity* of a questionnaire can be established by showing that the questionnaire's results agree with predictions based on theory.

Establishing the *criterion-oriented validity* of a questionnaire involves correlating the questionnaire's results with those from another, established measure. There are two ways to do this. First, you can establish *concurrent validity* by correlating your questionnaire's results with those of another measure of the *same* dimension administered at the same time. In the case of your questionnaire on political attitudes, you would correlate its results with those of another, established measure of political attitudes. Second, you can establish *predictive validity* by correlating the questionnaire's results with some behaviour that would be expected to occur, given the results. For example, your questionnaire on political attitudes would be shown to have predictive validity if the questionnaire's results correctly predicted election outcomes.

The validity of a questionnaire may be affected by a variety of factors. For example, as noted earlier, how you define the behaviour or attitude that you are measuring can affect validity. Validity also can be affected by the methods used to gather your data. In the "Sex in America" survey, some respondents were interviewed alone and others with someone else present. One cannot be sure that the responses given with another person present represent an accurate reflection of one's sexual behaviour (Stevenson, 1995). Generally, methodological flaws, poor conceptualization and unclear questions can all contribute to lowered levels of validity.

Response rate

Random sample A sample drawn from the population such that every member of the population has an equal opportunity to be included in the sample.

The response rate in a survey is simply the percentage of people in the sample who actually completed the survey. Thus, if you mail 1000 questionnaires to a **random sample** of adults in your community and 500 are completed and returned to you, the response rate is 50 per cent. Response rate is important because it indicates how much bias there might be in the final sample of respondents. Non-respondents may differ from respondents in any number of ways, including age, income, marital status and education. The lower the response rate, the greater the likelihood that such biases may distort the findings and in turn limit the ability to generalize the findings to the population of interest.

In general, mail surveys have lower response rates than telephone surveys. With both methods, however, steps can be taken to maximize response rates. With mail surveys, an explanatory postcard or letter can be sent a week or so prior to mailing the survey. Follow-up reminders and even second mailings of the questionnaire are often effective in increasing response rates. It often helps to have a personally stamped return envelope rather than a business reply envelope. Even the look of the cover page of the questionnaire can be important (Dillman, 2000). With telephone surveys, respondents who are not home can be called again and people who cannot be interviewed today can be scheduled for a call at a more convenient time. Sometimes an incentive may be necessary to increase response rates. Finally, researchers should attempt to convince people that the survey's purposes are important and their participation will be a valuable contribution.

Thinking critically about survey research

Correspondence between reported and actual behaviour

Regardless of how carefully survey data are collected and analysed, how valuable they are depends on the truthfulness of the respondents' answers to the survey questions. Should we believe that their responses on surveys reflect people's true thoughts, opinions, feelings and behaviour? The question of the truthfulness of verbal reports has been debated extensively, and no clear-cut conclusion has emerged. In everyday life, however, we regularly accept the verbal reports of others as valid. If a friend tells you she enjoyed reading a certain novel, you may ask why, but you do not usually question whether the statement accurately reflects your friend's feelings. There are some situations in everyday life, however, when we do have reason to suspect the truthfulness of someone's statements. When looking for a used car, for instance, we might not always want to trust the "sales pitch" we receive. Generally, however, we accept people's remarks at their face value unless we have reason to suspect otherwise. We apply the same standards to the information we obtain from survey respondents.

By its very nature, survey research involves reactive measurement. Respondents not only know their responses are being recorded, but they may also suspect their responses may prompt some social, political or commercial action. Hence, pressures are strong for people to respond as they think they "should" believe and not as they actually believe. The term often used to describe these pressures is social desirability (the term "politically correct" refers to similar pressures). For example, if respondents are asked whether they favour giving help to the needy, they may say "yes" because they believe this is the most socially acceptable attitude to have. In survey research, as was true with observational research, the best protection against reactive measurement is to be aware of its existence. The "In the Know" box covers a couple of instances where researchers checked the truthfulness of participants' responses.

You now have a great deal of information about methods for asking people about themselves. If you engage in this type of research, you will often need to design your own questions by following the guidelines described in this chapter and consulting sources such as Judd et al. (1991) and Converse and Presser (1986). However, you can also adapt questions and entire questionnaires that have been used in previous research. For example, Greenfield (1999) studied the new phenomenon of Internet addiction by adapting questions from a large body of existing research on addiction to gambling. Consider using previously developed questions, particularly if they have proven useful in other studies (make sure you do not violate any copyrights, however). A variety of measures of social, political and occupational attitudes developed by others have been compiled by Robinson and his colleagues (Robinson et al., 1968, 1969, 1991).

In the Know

Sometimes researchers can examine the accuracy of verbal reports directly. For example, Judd et al. (1991) describe research by Parry and Crossley (1950) wherein responses obtained by experienced interviewers were subsequently compared with archival records for the same respondents kept by various agencies. Their comparisons revealed that 40% of respondents gave inaccurate reports to a question concerning contributions to United Fund (a charitable organization), 25% reported they had registered and voted in a recent election (but they did not) and 17% lied about their age. A pessimist might find these figures disturbingly high, but an optimist would note that a majority of respondents' reports were accurate even when social desirability pressures were high, as in the question pertaining to charitable contributions.

Another way researchers can assess the accuracy of verbal reports is by directly observing respondents' behaviour. An experiment concluded by Latané and Darley (1970) illustrates this approach. They found that bystanders are more likely to help a victim when the bystander is alone than when other witnesses are present. Subsequently, a second group of participants was asked whether the presence of others would influence the likelihood they would help a victim. They uniformly said that it would not. Thus, individuals' verbal reports may not correspond well to behaviour. Research findings such as these should make us extremely cautious of reaching conclusions about people's behaviour solely on the basis of verbal reports. Of course, we should be equally cautious of reaching conclusions about what people think solely on the basis of direct observation of their behaviour. The potential discrepancy between observed behaviour and verbal reports illustrates again the wisdom of a multi-method approach in helping us identify and address potential problems in understanding behaviour and mental processes (Figure 13.1).

Figure 13.1 How people say they would respond to this type of situation does not always match what they actually do

Summary

This has been another long chapter. Hopefully, between this chapter and the previous one, you can see that there is more to observations and asking questions than you might originally have thought. Both methods are varied in the ways that they can be employed and there are benefits and drawbacks of adopting each technique and the specific variations that are attached to it. By now you should have a fairly good grasp of the basics of how we do research in psychology. One thing we have not covered is what to do with all the data that you collect. The data that you collect need to be analysed in order for you to answer the research question that you have set. The next section of the book deals with how to approach these analyses. As you go through it, always try to link the analysis with the method that you used to collect the data that you are analysing. Linking the method to the analysis can sometimes make the process clearer as it reminds you of why you are doing the analysis in the first place.

Questions

1. Explain why there is likely to be a serious threat to the interpretability of the results of a survey when a convenience sample is used.

2. What are the advantages and disadvantages of using questionnaires versus interviews in a survey?

3. Explain why you would choose to use a mail survey, personal interviews, telephone interviews or an Internet survey for your survey research project.

4. What are some factors to take into consideration when constructing questions for surveys (including both questions and response alternatives)?

5. What are the steps involved in designing a questionnaire?

6. How do open-ended and closed-ended questions differ, and what are the advantages and disadvantages of each?

7. Why is the first question on a questionnaire so important?

8. What are some of the factors that you should pay attention to when constructing questionnaire items?

9. What can you do to combat non-response bias?

10. What techniques are used to assess the reliability of a questionnaire?

11. How can the reliability of a questionnaire be increased?

12. What techniques are used to assess the validity of a questionnaire?

13. Why is it important to have a representative sample for a survey?

14. Distinguish between probability and non-probability sampling techniques. What are the implications of each?

15 Distinguish between simple random, stratified random and convenience sampling.

16 Distinguish between cluster sampling and quota sampling.

17 Explain the "parallel forms" method of assessing reliability.

Activity

1 Select a topic for a survey. Write at least five closed-ended questions that you might include in the survey. For each question, write one "good" version and one "poor" version. For each poor question, state what elements make it poor and why the good version is an improvement.

SECTION 3

Data Analysis

Introduction to Statistics and Describing Data

OVERVIEW

In this chapter, you will be introduced to the wonderful world of statistics. We will describe how and why statistics are useful, and why there is no need to be afraid of them. One major use of statistics is to simplify, summarize or condense large amounts of data in order that people can make sense of them, and this will be the focus of this chapter.

OBJECTIVES

After studying this chapter and working through the exercises, you should be able to:

- Distinguish between descriptive and inferential statistics
- Explain how and why level of measurement can affect choice of statistics
- Calculate (by hand or computer) and explain the mean, median and mode
- Calculate (by hand or computer) and explain the range, interquartile range, variance and standard deviation
- Select the most appropriate measures of central tendency and spread for a given set of data
- Construct and explain frequency distributions, frequency polygons, histograms, stem-and-leaf plots and boxplots
- Construct and explain bar graphs, line graphs, scatterplots and pie charts

Some words of advice before we begin

The simple word statistics has the power to strike fear into the hearts of students (and academics) everywhere, conjuring up pictures of incomprehensible mathematical formulae and endless calculations. So, if you have started to read this chapter with a feeling of trepidation and slight apprehension, then you are not alone. However, please stick with us and read on – it will be worth it in the end.

"Doing" statistics is not about learning endless formulae and you definitely do not need a degree in mathematics to be able to do it. It is similar to using a computer – most of us use computers without fully understanding how they work. We may know what we want the computer to do, but we do not necessarily know how it does it. For many social scientists and psychologists, the same is true for statistics. We can use statistics to do a specific function, but we usually do not need to understand the precise mathematical calculations. Statistical computer programs can do the calculations for us, leaving us to focus more on interpreting and understanding the results.

One of the most commonly used statistical computing programs is SPSS (Statistical Package for the Social Sciences*); we will be referring to it throughout this book, focusing on how to make sense of the SPSS output and what this means in terms of your research question. We will end this chapter with an introduction to SPSS, but due to lack of space and the fact that not everyone uses the package, you will not find detailed instructions for the SPSS statistical procedures here. Instead, go to our website (www.mcgraw-hill.co.uk/textbooks/wilsonandmaclean) or consult one of the many excellent SPSS textbooks (e.g. Kinnear and Gray, 2010; Pallant, 2010; see also Field, 2009).

As wonderful as statistical programs such as SPSS are, it is still really helpful to have a go at doing a statistical test by hand. This will aid your understanding immeasurably and help to demystify the whole process, as well as producing a feeling of satisfaction and pride at getting through it all unscathed. For these reasons, we have included statistical formulae throughout the statistics chapters and will take you through the procedures step by step.

Whether you plan on doing statistics mainly by hand or computer, or a mixture of both, it is important that you at least understand the general principles behind the statistical methods covered here – why certain tests are used and what the results mean. Please do not think that you can get away with knowing nothing about statistics or that the computer will do everything for you. Unfortunately, this is not the case. The real trick is knowing just enough to allow you to do what you need to do.

As you go through the statistical chapters, you may find that you will not understand all of the concepts straight away. This is normal, but if you put in a little effort and try the exercises, you will be surprised by how easily it all fits into place. One of the nice things about this sort of topic is that once you understand a concept, it is very difficult to "un-understand" it.

What is statistics and why am I studying it?

Many students question why they have to study statistics as part of their degree; they see it as irrelevant, boring and pointless. This could not be further from the truth. In fact, you come

---

*   The current name for the product is IBM SPSS Statistics, but it has previously been called PASW statistics and simply just SPSS. We will refer to the program as SPSS as it's the most common and widely used (and saves space!).

across statistics every day even though you are probably not aware of it. Examples include: today's average temperature, crime rates, examination grades, chances of contracting flu, etc.

Put simply, statistics help us to understand data more easily. For instance, if a weather forecaster wanted to see if temperatures are increasing year on year, she could examine the maximum and minimum temperatures for each day of the year for a period of 25 years. Not only would she have mountains of data to trawl through (two temperatures for 365 days a year for 25 years = 18 250 values), but it would be extremely difficult for her to spot any patterns or trends in the masses of data. It would be much easier, quicker and altogether better if she just calculated the average temperature for each year and looked to see if there was an increase. This is statistics. Calculating the average is a statistical method and a neat way of summarizing the data to make it easier to understand and comprehend. Other statistical methods do a similar job.

So, whenever you do any kind of study that involves collecting quantitative (numerical) data, you need to know what you are going to do with it. Statistical methods can be used to summarize, simplify or condense data, but they can also be used to help us draw conclusions based on the data that you have collected. For example, if you do some research and collect some numerical data from a sample of individuals, statistics can tell us whether the results can be generalized to a wider population. We can determine if the pattern of results is just a fluke or if it reflects a real pattern in the population. This is extremely useful information and has informed much of what we know in psychology and related subjects – without this knowledge, it would be difficult to test theories or interpret the measurements that we make in our studies.

As a student of psychology and/or the social sciences, it is vital for you to be able to summarize and make sense of data using statistics. On one hand, you will probably be conducting research of your own sometime, so you will need to be able to condense and understand your data, and see if your findings are meaningful. On the other hand, you will read many examples of research in your studies and without an understanding of statistics you will not be able to understand this research. So, statistics clearly is relevant and extremely useful and it is worthwhile putting in effort while studying the topic.

Descriptive versus inferential statistics

Generally, there are two main ways in which we use statistics and statistical techniques and these different uses are called **descriptive statistics** and **inferential statistics**. A descriptive statistic is a number, a collection of numbers or a graph that conveys a characteristic of a *sample*. If you remember, **a sample is a subset of a larger population**. (In contrast, a *parameter* is the name given to a characteristic of an entire *population*. Anything involving statistics, therefore, suggests that you are dealing with samples.) Descriptive statistics are useful because they can summarize or condense data. However, as they are dealing with samples, there is always a degree of uncertainty about them. You can never know with absolute certainty whether the information (data) that you have about the sample is an absolutely true reflection of the population as a whole. Inferential statistics are techniques that use sample data and concepts of probability to arrive at conclusions about populations. You could say that inferential statistics allow us to ask "Given the data from this sample, what is the likelihood that it represents the general population?" Inferential statistics help generate conclusions, and they also provide a measure of the uncertainty

Descriptive statistics
Numbers or graphs that summarize a set of sample data.

Inferential statistics
Set of methods used to reach conclusions about populations based on samples and probability.

ch. 9

that goes with the conclusion. No conclusion based on a sample will ever be 100% representative of the population. Given this, it is useful to know just how much uncertainty you are dealing with. This will allow you to judge how "good" (i.e. representative) the data from your sample is.

In this chapter, we will focus on descriptive statistics; the subsequent chapters are devoted to inferential statistics.

Levels of measurement

ch. 4
pp.62–68

Before we move on, it is time for a little revision. Recall that in Chapter 4 you were introduced to the concept of **levels of measurement** and that data can be measured on four different levels: nominal, ordinal, interval and ratio. The type of data you have will dictate what type of statistical method you can use, so it is vital that you understand the characteristics of the measurement scales before we discuss descriptive statistics. Note that in statistics, we tend not to worry about the difference between interval and ratio data – they are usually considered together. Table 14.1 summarizes the main characteristics of the different levels of measurement.

If you are still unclear about the differences between the levels, focus on what is being measured and not the numbers themselves. Here is another example that will hopefully hammer the point home. Look at Table 14.2, which shows three different measurements for two teams participating in a cross-country adventure race. Look at the first line, an 8 and a 16, which are the identification numbers of the two teams. What can you say about the two teams based on these two numbers? The two numbers tell you only that they are two different teams and nothing more. This is an example of a nominal scale – the numbers here are pretty arbitrary and could easily have been replaced with names or any other number. The numbers are only being used as labels or names.

Now look at the next pair of scores which are also 8 and 16. These two numbers indicate the order of crossing the finish line. Of course, the two different orders also tell us that there were

Table 14.1 Levels of measurement

Scale	Description	Example	Distinction
Nominal	Categories with no numeric scales	Males/females Introverts/extroverts Marital status	Impossible to define any quantitative values and/or differences between/across categories
Ordinal	Rank ordering Numeric values limited	2-, 3- and 4-star restaurants Ranking television programmes by popularity Finishing position in race	Intervals between items not known
Interval	Numeric properties are literal Assume equal interval between values	Intelligence Aptitude test score Temperature (°C/°F)	No true zero
Ratio	Zero indicates absence of variable measured	Reaction time Weight Age Frequencies of behaviours	Can form ratios (someone weighs twice as much as another person)

Table 14.2 Measurements of two teams on three variables in an adventure race		
Thing measured	Team A	Team B
Identification number	8	16
Finishing order	8	16
Hours required	8	16

two different teams. Team A finished before team B, but these two numbers tell nothing about the time between the two crossings. This is an example of an ordinal scale.

Finally, the bottom row again shows an 8 and a 16, which are the number of hours required to finish the race. The interpretation of these two numbers is that team A was twice as fast as team B (and also that it was faster and different). This is therefore an example of a ratio scale.

The point we are making here is that although the numbers look the same, what they represent is quite different and this all depends on the scale of measurement being used.

But what has this to do with statistics? Well, the scale of measurement used will dictate the amount of information provided, which in turn will influence what statistical methods you can use. The nominal scale provides the least amount of information; all you know is that the values differ in some quality. The ordinal scale adds crude information about quantity (you can rank the order of the values). The interval scale refines the measurement of quantity by indicating how much the values differ. Finally, the ratio scale indicates precisely how much of the quantity exists.

STOP & Think

Imagine you were designing a questionnaire and wanted to measure age. You have the option of asking people to select an age category (e.g. 18–24, 25–30) or reporting their actual age (e.g. 23 years). What levels of measurement are represented by these two options, and which would you choose and why?

Because the nominal and ordinal levels do not give you much information, statistical methods using these types of data are typically less powerful (i.e. less sensitive to relationships among variables) than statistics used for interval or ratio data. There are also many more statistical tests that can deal with interval or ratio data than with nominal or ordinal data, again because of the level of detail provided. Students who do not think about statistics until after they have collected data often find that they have got data which cannot be analysed properly. If you are designing a measure and have the option of using different levels of measurement, remember that you can always simplify if you have lots of detail (i.e. you can convert interval/ratio data into ordinal or nominal data), but you cannot get more detail if you have simple data to begin with (i.e. you cannot convert nominal data into ordinal or interval/ratio data).

With all of this information on levels of measurement in mind, it is now time to turn to the really exciting stuff, so strap yourselves in.

Descriptive statistics: measures of central tendency and spread

When summarizing data, there are two main things that need to be considered in order to gain a good understanding of a data-set: central tendency and spread.

Central tendency

Central tendency
Descriptive statistics that indicate a typical or representative score. Examples are mean, median and mode.

A measure of **central tendency** (a central tendency statistic) does what its name implies: it tells us about the score that the data tend to centre around. In other words, a measure of central tendency describes how an entire group scores as a whole, or on average. It is one value whose purpose is to tell us about what our data set is typically like. It summarizes the middle of the data for us. The most common measures of central tendency are the mean, median and mode. Each has its own strengths and weaknesses, and there are some situations in which a given measure of central tendency cannot be used.

The Mean

Mean
The arithmetic average; the sum of the scores divided by the number of scores.

When most people talk about an "average" score, they're usually referring to the arithmetic average, which is also known as the **mean**. So, the chances are that you are already familiar with the concept of the mean without even knowing it! The mean is calculated by adding together all of the scores and then dividing by the number of scores (the formula is shown in Figure 14.1, should you need it).

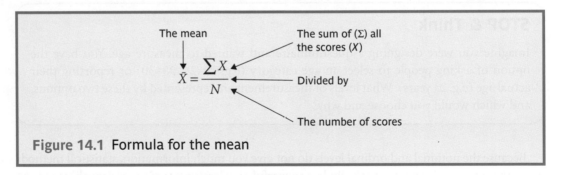

Figure 14.1 Formula for the mean

So, if you had the data-set 6, 7, 4, 8, 5, 8, the mean would be 6.33:

$$\text{Mean} = \frac{\text{Sum of all scores}}{\text{Number of scores}} = \frac{(6 + 7 + 4 + 8 + 5 + 8)}{6} = \frac{38}{6} = 6.33$$

The mean is suitable only for interval or ratio data.

The mean of a sample is abbreviated to M when reported in text – for example, in the results section of a report. You may also come across the symbol μ (Greek letter mu), which denotes the mean of an entire population (Greek letters are used to represent population values). However, as we very rarely know a population mean (it is usually impossible to test or measure absolutely everyone in a population), you will be much more likely to use M than μ in your own work. The symbol $\bar{X}$ (read "X bar") is another way of symbolizing the mean, but this is usually used only in statistical formulae and calculations.

The median

The **median** is the score that divides the set of scores in half (with 50% lying below and 50 per cent lying above the median). In scientific reports, the median is abbreviated as *Mdn*. To calculate the median, you order the scores from lowest to highest and then simply find the middle score. For example, if there are nine scores, the fifth score is the median, because there are four lower and four higher scores. What is the median of the following data-set: 7, 5, 2, 9, 4, 8, 1? The correct answer is 5 (put the scores in order: 1, 2, 4, 5, 7, 8, 9, and 5 is the middle score; see Figure 14.2).

> **Median**
> The point that divides a set of scores into equal halves; half the scores are above the median and half are below it.

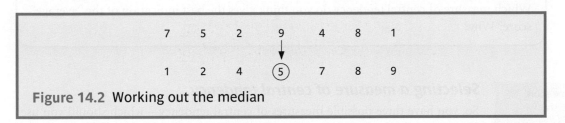

Figure 14.2 Working out the median

But what if you have an even number of scores? There will not be an actual middle score. In this case, the median is the midpoint between the two middle scores, so just add these two middle scores together and divide by 2 (i.e. the mean of the two middle scores). For the data-set 6, 7, 4, 8, 5, 8, the median would be 6.5 as 6 and 7 are the two middle scores when the scores are ordered (4, 5, 6, 7, 8, 8), and the mean of 6 and 7 is 6.5 (Figure 14.3).

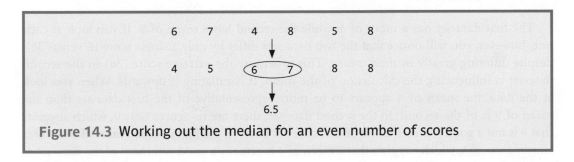

Figure 14.3 Working out the median for an even number of scores

The median can be used with ordinal, interval or ratio data, but it is most likely to be used with ordinal data. This is because calculation of the median considers only the rank ordering of scores and not the actual size of the scores.

The mode

The **mode** is the third measure of central tendency and is simply the most frequently occurring score. So, for the data-set 3, 4, 7, 4, 8, 2, 4, the mode would be 4 as that is the most frequent score – no calculation required! No mode exists for a data-set in

> **Mode**
> The score that occurs most frequently.

which every score is different; a set with two modes (i.e. with two most frequently occurring scores) is said to be *bimodal*.

The mode can be used with any of the four levels of measurement, but it is the only measure of central tendency which can be used with nominal data. For instance, if you are measuring gender and find there are 100 females and 50 males, the mode is "female" because this is the most frequently occurring category on the nominal scale. (It's tempting to think that the mode is 100, because we like attaching numbers to things. But it is not. The mode in this case is the most frequently occurring category, which is "female".)

STOP & Think

For the following data-set, calculate the mean, median and mode: 1, 2, 2, 2, 3, 5, 6, 6, 8, 10. Which measure of central tendency do you think gives the best indication of the "average" score? Why?

Extreme score
A score that lies towards the extremes of a distribution; sometimes defined as lying more than 3 × interquartile range from the other scores.

Selecting a measure of central tendency

So, you have three possible measures of central tendency – which should you use? The mean is by far the most commonly used, as it has the major advantage of being the most sensitive measure because its value is directly affected by the magnitude of each score. However, this sensitivity can sometimes be a problem if you have **extreme scores** or outliers.[1] Consider the following data-sets:

4, 3, 4, 5, 2, 6
4, 3, 4, 5, 2, 36

The first data-set has a mean of 4, while the second has a mean of 9. If you look at each one, however, you will notice that the two data-sets differ by only a single score (6 versus 36), despite differing greatly in their means. This is because the extreme score (36) in the second data-set is influencing the calculation of the mean. It is inflating it upwards. When you look at the data, the mean of 4 appears to be more representative of the first data-set than the mean of 9 is of the second. In the second data-set, there are no scores near 9, which suggests that 9 is not a good representation of that data-set at all. In the first data-set, most of the scores cluster around 4, which suggests that a mean of 4 is actually a good summary of the data-set as a whole.

If you have extreme scores it may be a better idea to use the median, which is not affected by the actual size of scores. In our example, it does not matter if the largest score is 6, 36 or even 106 – the median would still be 4. However, the price you pay for using the median is a loss in sensitivity (because you are not taking the values of the data points into consideration, instead you are using their position in an ordered set).

---

1   An outlier is a score that is far away in value from the rest of the data-set.

The mode is the crudest of all measures of central tendency, because the values of the score outside the most frequent score are not represented. Consider the following two sets of data:

2, 2, 6, 3, 7, 2, 2, 5, 3, 1
2, 2, 21, 43, 78, 22, 33, 72, 12, 8

In both of these sets the mode is 2 even though the second data set is very different to the first. In this case, the mode is probably not a good measure of central tendency for the second data-set, because it does not really tell us much about the nature of the data that we are looking at.

Another factor to think about when selecting a measure of central tendency is the level of measurement. If your data were measured on a nominal (categorical) scale, you can only use the mode – it would make no sense to calculate a median or mean gender, for example. Note that in statistical programs such as SPSS, nominal data are usually coded as numbers (e.g. 1 = males, 2 = females) and if you ask the computer to calculate a median or mean on these data, it will do it for you, even though it is completely meaningless. This is a common mistake and something you need to get your head around. Always ask yourself: "What is this number measuring?" With nominal variables, like gender, the number is not actually measuring anything – it is just there to stand in for "male" or "female". In cases like this, when the number is not measuring anything, making any calculations based on that number is meaningless. On the other hand, if your data were measured on an ordinal scale (ranked), you can use the median or the mode. If, however, you tried to calculate the mean of ordinal data, you would be making the incorrect assumption that the distance between each score is equal, when in fact we do not know anything about the distance between the scores on an ordinal scale. Finally, if your data were measured on an interval or ratio scale, then you can use the mean, median or mode – your choice will depend on whether or not there are outliers or extreme scores and which measure you think best describes your particular data-set.

Table 14.3 summarizes the key information on different measures of central tendency. Remember to think carefully about the type of data you have and look at the different scores in your data-set.

 ## Test yourself

For the following two data-sets, calculate the mean, median and mode:

1. 1   3   6   10   10   10   13   18   19
2. 8   9   9   10   10   10   11   11   12

What do you notice about the measures of central tendency for the two data sets? What characteristic of the data is not clear from looking at the measures of central tendency?

Table 14.3 Summary of measures of central tendency

	Mean	Median	Mode
Definition	*Arithmetic average*	*Middle score*	*Most frequently occurring score*
Use with:			
Interval/ratio data	✓	✓	✓
Ordinal data	✗	✓	✓
Nominal data	✗	✗	✓
Advantages	Sensitive Most commonly used	Not affected by outliers	Not affected by outliers Easy to calculate Can be used for all types of data
Disadvantages	Can be affected by outliers or extreme scores	Loss of sensitivity – based on ranks	Does not tell us anything about other scores

Spread

Knowing about a measure of central tendency is helpful, but it does not provide the whole picture about a data-set – it does not tell us if the scores in the set are close to or far away from the average. Consider the following two data-sets:

4, 5, 6, 6, 7, 8
1, 2, 3, 9, 10, 11

Spread
The degree of dispersion or variability of scores in a data-set. Examples of measures of spread include the range, interquartile range, variance and standard deviation.

Although they have the same mean (6), the two data-sets are quite different: the scores in the first set are all quite close to the mean, whereas the scores in the second set are a bit further from the mean. We can say that these data-sets differ in the **spread** (sometimes called dispersion or variability) of their scores. So, to give a good summary of a data-set, it is not enough to just give a measure of central tendency, you should also provide a measure of the spread. If we look only at the mean, we might conclude that the above data-sets are the same, when they definitely are not.

Range

Range
The highest score minus the lowest score.

The **range** is the simplest and least informative measure of spread. To calculate the range, you simply subtract the lowest score from the highest score. For the two data-sets considered in the previous paragraph, the range therefore would be 4 (8 − 4) for the first set and 10 (11 − 1) for the second (Figure 14.4).

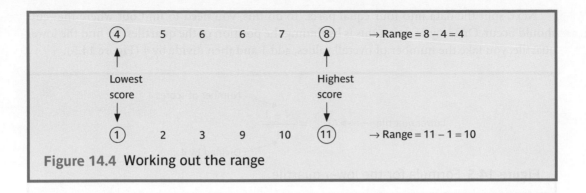

Figure 14.4 Working out the range

However, there are a couple of problems with the range, which can limit its usefulness. First, the range is based on only two scores from the data-set and consequently does not take into account all of the information that is available in the entire set of scores. Second, the range is very sensitive to outliers (i.e. unusually high or low scores). Compare the following two distributions of scores:

1, 2, 3, 4, 5, 6
1, 2, 3, 4, 5, 31

The range for the first distribution is 5, and the range for the second is 30. The two ranges are very different from each other, despite the fact that the two distributions are nearly identical (with the exception of one score). For these reasons, the range is rarely used as a measure of spread.

Interquartile range

The **interquartile range** is another measure of spread, but it is less sensitive to the effects of extreme scores and takes into account more information than the range. Imagine putting all the scores in a set in order, dividing it into quarters and then chopping off the extreme upper and lower quarters. The middle 50% of scores which are left (i.e. the two quarters you have not chopped off) represents the interquartile range; it represents the distance between the 25th percentile score and the 75th percentile score, also known as the lower and upper quartiles. Because the interquartile range does not include the lowest and highest scores in a set (they will have been chopped off with the highest 25% of scores and the lowest 25% of scores), it is not affected so much by outliers.

> **Interquartile range**
> A range of scores that captures the 50 per cent of a distribution that is between the 25th and 75th percentiles.

There are different ways of calculating the interquartile range because there is no single agreed definition of a quartile, so the easiest thing to do is to use a statistical computing package (such as SPSS) to do it for you and to use that method consistently. However, if you want to try it by hand, here is the most straightforward way of working it out.

Begin by organizing your data from the lowest value to the highest:

3, 4, 4, 5, 5, 6, 7, 7, 10, 12, 13, 15, 16, 16, 18

Next, split the data into four equal parts. To do this, you need to find out where the "cut" should occur. One way of doing this is by finding the position of the quartiles. To find the lower quartile, you take the number of overall values, add 1 and then divide by 4 (Figure 14.5).

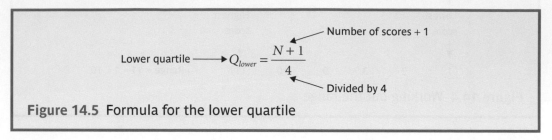

Figure 14.5 Formula for the lower quartile

So, for the data above, there are 15 values. Add 1 is 16. Divide 16 by 4 = 4. This means that the cut happens in the 4th position. If you count from the left, the value that is in the fourth position is "5". That's the lower quartile.

To work out the upper quartile, you do something similar, except you multiply $N + 1$ by 3 (Figure 14.6).

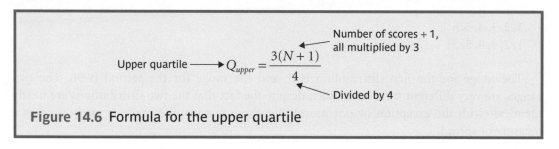

Figure 14.6 Formula for the upper quartile

So, for our data-set, 16 (i.e. 15 + 1) multiplied by 3 gives 48, and dividing by 4 gives 12. This means that the upper quartile is in the 12th position. The value that is in the 12th position in the data above is 15 (counting 12 along from the left-hand side).

If you add in the median (i.e. the value in the middle of your set of scores), you will see that the data are split into four sections: values below the lower quartile, values between the lower quartile and the median, values between the median and the upper quartile, and values that are above the upper quartile (Figure 14.7).

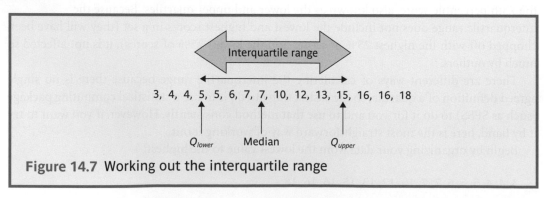

Figure 14.7 Working out the interquartile range

The interquartile range is the difference between the upper quartile and the lower quartile, so in our example the interquartile range is 10 (15 − 5).

In fact, the interquartile range is used in the most popular definition of what actually counts as an outlier in the first place (Hogan & Evalenko, 2006). Upper and lower **outliers** are defined as:

> **Outlier**
> A score separated from others and 1.5 (IQR) beyond the 25th or 75th percentile.

Upper outlier = 75th percentile + 1.5 IQR
Lower outlier = 25th percentile − 1.5 IQR

Variance

One measure of spread which uses information from all of the scores in a set is the **variance** (s^2). When you think about it, most of the scores in a data-set will vary around the mean. Some will be higher, some will be lower. The variance tells us the degree to which scores vary about the mean. Consider the following data-set: 2, 4, 5, 5, 7, 8, 9, 9, 10, 11. The mean is 7. To work out how far away each score is from the mean, we just calculate the difference, or deviation, between each score and the mean:

> **Variance**
> The average squared deviation from the mean.

Score:	2	4	5	5	7	8	9	9	10	11
Difference from the mean:	−5	−3	−2	−2	0	+1	+2	+2	+3	+4

To get an indication of how much the scores as a whole vary about the mean, you might think that you could just add up all the deviations, but there is a problem – because you have negative and positive values, they cancel each other out and you end up with a value of 0 (try it and see!). To get round this, we square the deviations (i.e. multiply them by themselves), remembering that when we square a negative value, it becomes positive.

Score:	2	4	5	5	7	8	9	9	10	11
Difference from the mean:	−5	−3	−2	−2	0	+1	+2	+2	+3	+4
Squared deviation:	25	9	4	4	0	1	4	4	9	16

You then add together all of the squared deviations, and find the average squared deviation by dividing the total squared deviations by $N − 1$ (N = number of scores). (See "In the Know" for further discussion of why we use $N − 1$.)

$$\text{Total squared deviation} = 25 + 9 + 4 + 4 + 0 + 1 + 4 + 4 + 9 + 16 = 76$$

$$
\begin{aligned}
\text{Variance} &= 76 \div (N − 1) \\
&= 76 \div (10 − 1) \\
&= 76 \div 9 \\
&= 8.44
\end{aligned}
$$

The equation to express these calculations is shown in Figure 14.8 (along with an alternative, which has things shifted around a bit to make it easier to calculate – it will still give you the same answer).

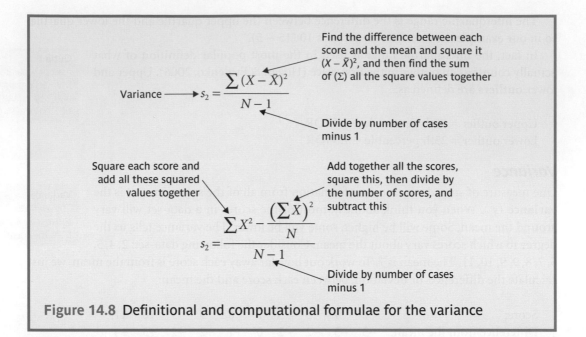

Figure 14.8 Definitional and computational formulae for the variance

In the Know

Why do we divide by N – 1?
Many textbooks answer this question by saying "for technical reasons" or "it just works". We are going to offer a rudimentary explanation that does not go into the mathematics. It is related to the concept of **degrees of freedom**, which we explain in Chapter 16. Do not worry if you do not understand it. It is very rare that you will ever need to understand it.

First, remember that we are trying to estimate the variance of the population. We have not measured the entire population – instead, we have measured a sample from it. We want our sample to be a good one. However (and get ready to ask "but why?"), if we divide by N, then our estimate will be wrong. It will be biased towards underestimating the variance in the population from which our sample is drawn. Dividing by $N – 1$ corrects for this bias. But why does the bias occur? It occurs because the mean $\bar{X}$ was calculated using the same data as were used to calculate S^2. When you do this, you introduce a bias, and the way to counterbalance the bias is to divide by $N – 1$. Confused? Don't worry, it is unlikely you will need to know much more than this.

Standard deviation

You may have noticed a problem with the variance: we squared the deviations but did not "undo" the squaring, meaning that the variance does not describe the amount of variability in the same units as the original scale. The **standard deviation** (symbolized as *s* in calculations; *SD* when reported in text) gets round this problem and is calculated by finding the square root of the variance. So, for our example, the standard deviation would be: $\sqrt{8.44} = 2.91$. Therefore, the average deviation of scores from the mean is 2.91. The formula is shown in Figure 14.9.

Standard deviation
A measure of spread of scores about the mean, the average deviation from the mean.

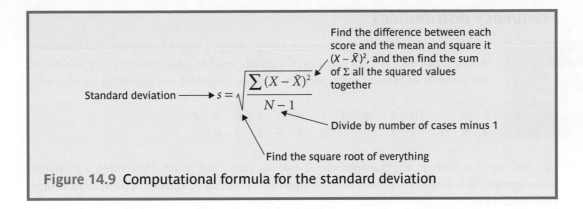

Figure 14.9 Computational formula for the standard deviation

The standard deviation is the most popular measure of spread. Large *SDs* tell us that the scores are widely spread from the mean; small *SDs* indicate that the scores are grouped together closely.

 ## Test yourself

For the following two data-sets, calculate the range, variance and standard deviation:

1. 1   3   6   10   10   10   13   18   19
2. 8   9   9   10   10   10   11   11   12

What can you say about the spread of scores in the data-sets?

Choosing a measure of spread

The choice of a measure of central tendency is affected by whether you have extreme scores or outliers, and the same is true for the choice of a measure of spread. Like the mean, the range, variance and standard deviation are all sensitive to outliers (meaning that just one extreme value could give you a measure of spread that is inaccurate). Remember, too, that the mean is used to calculate the standard deviation, so if you are not going to use the mean for a data-set, you probably should not use the standard deviation either. In cases where you have one or more outliers, the interquartile range may be the best measure of spread.

Descriptive statistics: summarizing data in tables and graphs

As well as calculating statistics such as measures of average and spread, we can also summarize and condense data in the form of graphs (figures) and tables. Often these are the best ways of getting a real feel for data.

Frequency distributions

Frequency distribution
Arrangement of scores or categories with the frequency of each score or category shown.

One of the simplest ways of summarizing data is to create **frequency distributions**. A frequency distribution consists of a set of possible categories or score values and the number of cases of each category or score. Consider the following set of scores:

```
5   7   2   10   5    6   4   1   8   0   5   6   8   4   5
9   8   3    3   4   10   7   6   4   5   5   9   6   7   8
```

You will see that there is, for example, one 0, two 3s, six 5s and so on. How often a particular score appears in a data-set is known as its "frequency". This can be summarized in tabular form (see Table 14.4).

By examining Table 14.4, you can see that the distribution is roughly symmetrical with a greater number of scores in the middle (lots of 6s and 5s) and fewer on both ends (not many 10s or 0s).

You may sometimes see frequency tables with ranges of scores rather than individual scores. For example, if you were conducting a study looking at intelligence quotients (IQ) and had IQ scores ranging from 65 to 134, a table with each individual IQ score would be extremely big. Instead, you can identify ranges of scores and how many cases are in that range. An example of data from a hypothetical IQ study is shown in Table 14.5.

Although a table provides a compact summary of the distribution, it is not particularly easy to extract useful information from it about centre, spread and shape. Graphical or semi-graphical displays are much better for this purpose.

Table 14.4 Frequency distribution table

Score	Frequency
10	2
9	2
8	4
7	3
6	4
5	6
4	4
3	2
2	1
1	1
0	1
Total	30

Table 14.5 Frequency distribution table of hypothetical IQ data

IQ	Frequency
125–134	5
115–124	12
105–114	22
95–104	25
85–94	26
75–84	7
65–74	3
Total	100

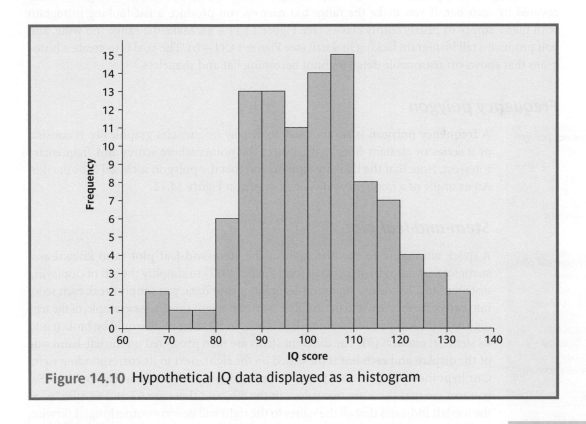

Figure 14.10 Hypothetical IQ data displayed as a histogram

Histograms

Figure 14.10 displays our IQ frequency data as a **histogram**. A histogram uses bars to display a frequency distribution for a quantitative variable (i.e. you cannot use a histogram to summarize frequencies for a nominal variable). Note that the bars in a histogram touch, indicating that the values are continuous and that there are no

Histogram
A graph of frequencies of a continuous variable constructed with contiguous (touching) vertical bars.

gaps in the range of scores. The x-axis (horizontal) represents the variable being measured and the y-axis (vertical) represents the frequency of the scores. Thus, the length of a bar indicates the frequency of scores falling within its range. It is important not to make the mistake of thinking that the x-axis represents individual scores (i.e. scores from each one of your participants). The x-axis represents the value, and the y-axis represents how often the value occurs in the entire data-set. In the histogram in Figure 14.10, you can see that there is only one instance of an IQ score between 70 and 75, because the bar only reaches "1" on the frequency (y) axis (75 is not actually shown on the x-axis, but we know that it is there because there are two bars between 70 and 80). Likewise, there is only one instance of an IQ between 75 and 80. However, if you look at the frequency of IQs between 100 and 105 (again, 105 is not actually on the graph, but we know it is the first bar between 100 and 110), we can see that it is 14. So, in this data-set, there were 14 cases of IQs between 100 and 105. At the other end, we can see that there were only two cases of an IQ between 130 and 135 and no instances of an IQ over 140.

A histogram's appearance changes depending on how wide you make the range of scores covered by each bar. If you make the range too narrow, you produce a flat-looking histogram with many empty or nearly empty classes (see Figure 14.11 – a). Make the range too wide, and you produce a tall histogram lacking in detail (see Figure 14.11 – b). The goal is to create a histogram that shows off reasonable detail without becoming flat and shapeless.

Frequency polygon

Frequency polygon
A frequency distribution graph of a continuous variable with frequency points connected by lines.

A **frequency polygon** is another way to display frequencies graphically. It consists of a series of straight lines that connect the points where scores and frequencies intersect. Note that the lines are straight and that the polygon is closed at both ends. An example of a frequency polygon is shown in Figure 14.12.

Stem-and-leaf plot

Stem-and-leaf plot
A frequency distribution in which scores are split into "stems" and "leaves", simultaneously showing the shape of the distribution and the individual scores.

A quick alternative to the histogram is the **stem-and-leaf plot** (also known as a stemplot), invented by statistician John Tukey (1977) to simplify the job of displaying distributions. To create a stem-and-leaf plot of your data, you simply break each score into two parts: the stem and the leaf. The stem part might consist, for example, of the tens digit, and the leaf part of the units digit. Thus, an IQ score of 98 would be broken into its stem (9) and leaf (8). The different stems are then presented on the left-hand side of the display, and each leaf is presented on the right, next to its corresponding stem. Our hypothetical IQ data are presented in stem-and-leaf format in Figure 14.13. So, you can see that there are two values in the 60s, and these are 67 and 68 (the "6" at the top left indicates that all the scores to the right will be sixty-something). Likewise, we can see that there are five IQ scores of exactly 90 (the 9 on the "stem" tells us that the "leaf" to the right shows all the scores in the nineties and there are five 0s indicating five scores of 90). You may notice that the stem-and-leaf plot looks like a histogram turned on its side.

Stem-and-leaf plots are easy to construct and display, and have the advantage over histograms and tables of preserving all the actual values in the data. For example, you can see in Figure 14.13 that four people had IQ scores of 85 and five had IQs of 90. However, stem-and-leaf plots can become

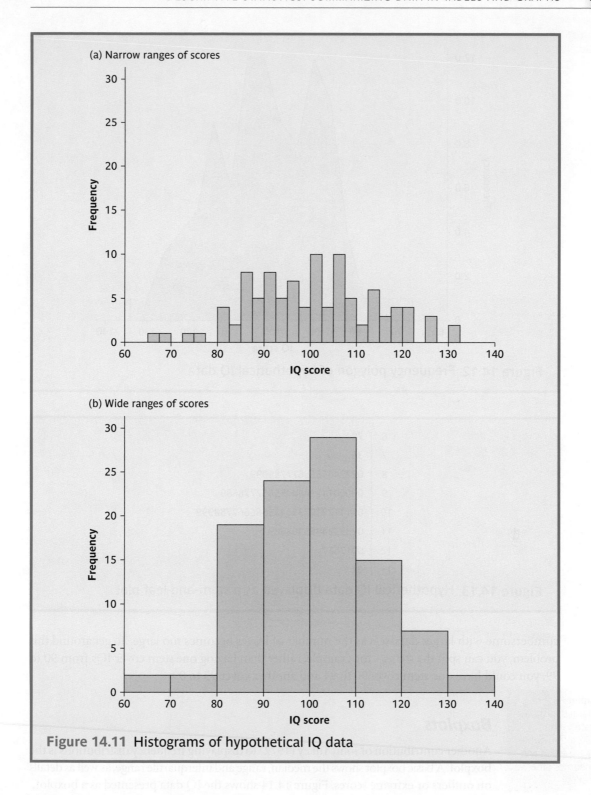

Figure 14.11 Histograms of hypothetical IQ data

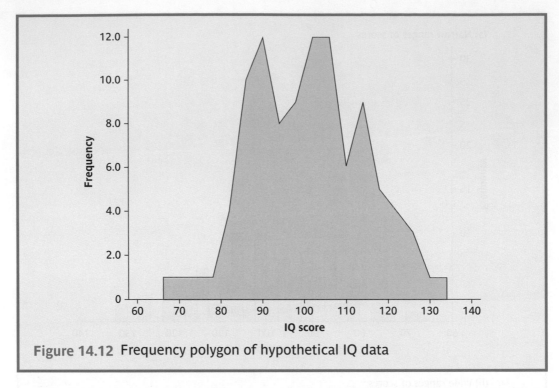

Figure 14.12 Frequency polygon of hypothetical IQ data

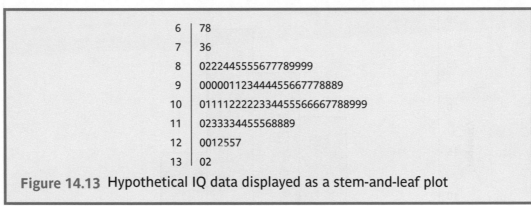

6	78
7	36
8	0222445555677789999
9	000001123444455667778889
10	0111122222334455566667788999
11	0233334455568889
12	0012557
13	02

Figure 14.13 Hypothetical IQ data displayed as a stem-and-leaf plot

cumbersome with larger data-sets as the number of leaves becomes too large. To get around this problem, you can split the stems – for example, rather than having one stem cover IQs from 90 to 99, you could have one stem cover 90 to 94 and another cover 95 to 99.

Boxplot
A graph that shows a distribution's range, interquartile range, median and sometimes other statistics.

Boxplots

Another contribution of John Tukey (1972) to displaying frequency distributions is the **boxplot**. A basic boxplot shows the median, range and interquartile range, as well as details on outliers or extreme scores. Figure 14.14 shows the IQ data presented as a boxplot.

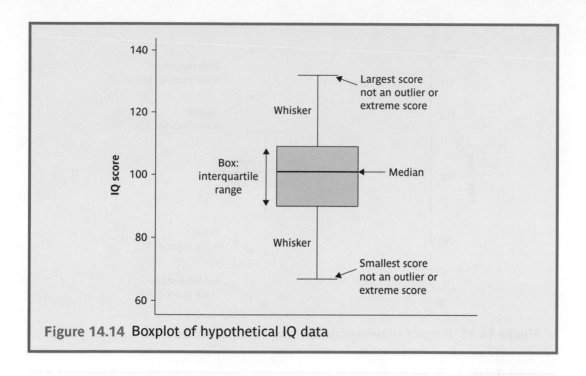

Figure 14.14 Boxplot of hypothetical IQ data

Figure 14.15 shows a boxplot with outliers and extreme scores. In SPSS, an outlier is defined as a score more than 1.5 box lengths away from the box, and an extreme score is more than 3 box lengths away (the box length is the interquartile range).

Examining your distributions

Frequency distributions such as histograms, stem-and-leaf plots and boxplots are used extensively as part of what is called **exploratory data analysis**. This is just a fancy name for inspecting the data thoroughly before proceeding with proper statistical analysis. If you have made any mistakes in entering data into your statistical package, or if there are anomalies in your data, exploratory data analysis should highlight these. It should also give you a general feel for the data and help you in making predictions about what you are likely to find in your later analysis.

You should inspect your frequency distributions for several important features. The first is the centre of the distribution – where do the scores tend to cluster? Next, look at the spread of scores – are the scores bunched up or spread about? Looking at the size of the box and the whiskers on a boxplot can give you an indication of the level of spread in the data (i.e. how spread out it is around the centre). A boxplot will also make clear any outliers or extreme scores. These may be genuine scores or may just be mistakes in data entry, so it is always worth checking. If it is just an error in data entry, correct it. However, if it's a valid but highly unusual score, you may want to consider removing it altogether. As we discussed earlier, statistics such as the mean and standard deviation can be affected by outliers or extreme scores, so treat them with caution – if included, these values can seriously affect the validity of your analysis.

> **Exploratory data analysis**
> Approach to analysing data that includes examining boxplots, stem-and-leaf plots and histograms, to gain an insight into the data prior to statistical analysis.

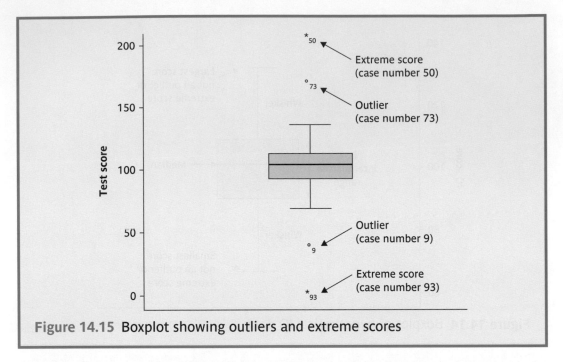

Figure 14.15 Boxplot showing outliers and extreme scores

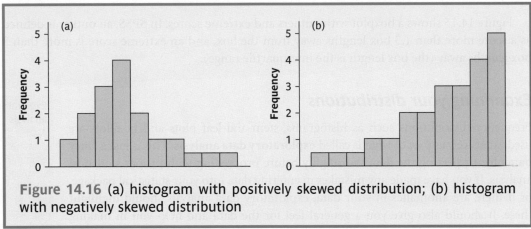

Figure 14.16 (a) histogram with positively skewed distribution; (b) histogram with negatively skewed distribution

Another important thing to look out for in frequency distributions is the shape of the distribution. Is there one peak or two? Is it symmetrical? Some distributions may be skewed, with a non-symmetrical distribution. This can be clearly seen in histograms which have a long "tail" trailing off in one direction and a short tail extending in the other. A distribution is positively skewed if the long tail goes off to the right, to the upper values (see Figure 14.16 – a), or negatively skewed if the long tail goes off to the left, to the lower values (see Figure 14.16 – b).

Many variables encountered in psychology tend to produce what is known as the "normal" distribution, which is symmetrical and hill-shaped – the well-known bell curve (Figure 14.17). This type of distribution has an important role to play in inferential statistics and we will return to it in the next chapter.

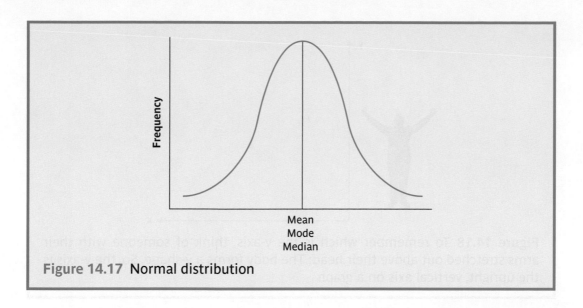

Figure 14.17 Normal distribution

Test yourself

Construct a stem-and-leaf plot and histogram for the following data-set:

6	7	12	15	21	24	26	32	32	33	35
36	37	41	44	45	48	50	56	57	61	63
67	70	70	71	72	74	76	82	84	85	91

What do you notice about the shape of the distribution?

Graphing your data

Frequency distributions are useful for preliminary exploration of data, but are rarely presented in reports and research articles. Instead, other types of graphical representations are often used to summarize data in these kinds of publications. It is a well-known saying that "a picture is worth a thousand words" and this is particularly true of graphs, which can make relationships between variables much clearer than would have been seen in a table of the same data, consisting of lots and lots of numbers. However, it must be remembered that at the same time, if you use a graph, you lose some of the numerical precision that you find in tables of data.

Elements of a graph

A basic graph represents data in a two-dimensional space. The two dimensions are defined by two lines intersecting at right angles, called the axes of the graph. The horizontal axis is called the abscissa or x-axis of the graph, and the vertical axis is called the ordinate or the y-axis of

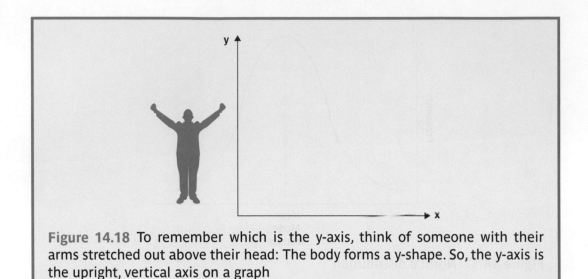

Figure 14.18 To remember which is the y-axis, think of someone with their arms stretched out above their head: The body forms a y-shape. So, the y-axis is the upright, vertical axis on a graph

the graph. If you have difficulty remembering which is the x- and y-axis, imagine someone standing upright with their arms stretched out above their head: their body is forming a y-shape (Figure 14.18). So, the y-axis is the upright, vertical axis on a graph.

Students also often have difficulty deciding which variable should go on the x-axis and which should go on the y-axis. You should think carefully about what you are trying to show in your graph. When graphing data from an experiment though, you normally represent the independent variable along the x-axis and the values of the dependent variable along the y-axis.

When presenting any graph, the golden rule is that the graph should be able to stand by itself. This means that all the information required to understand what the graph is showing should be with the graph and not hidden away in text. Therefore, graphs must have a meaningful title and all axes must be properly labelled.

Also, do not get carried away by applying three-dimensional effects and wacky colour schemes – the best graphs are simple and clear.

Bar graphs

Bar graph
A graph of the frequency, percentage or means of different categories.

You will probably be most familiar with the **bar graph** (or bar chart, Figure 14.19). This type of graph presents data for different categories as bars, with the length of the bar reflecting the value for that category. These values may be frequencies, percentages or means. Note that bar graphs have spaces between the bars, indicating that the bars are discrete and independent of each other. Indeed, the ordering of the bars along the x-axis is usually fairly arbitrary – the decision is based on convenience and simply what looks best. Similarly, the width of the bars has no real meaning and is chosen purely to provide a pleasing appearance.

Although they look similar, histograms are not the same thing as bar graphs. Remember that in histograms the bars touch, indicating that the variable is continuous (usually numerical) and not discrete (or categorical, like "male" and "female"). Also, the width of the bars in histograms covers a specific range of scores.

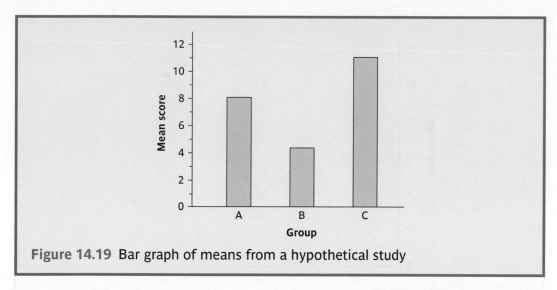

Figure 14.19 Bar graph of means from a hypothetical study

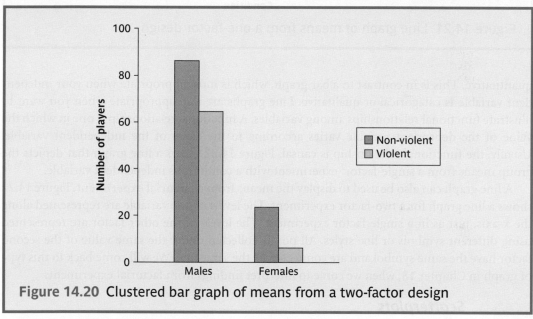

Figure 14.20 Clustered bar graph of means from a two-factor design

You can use a clustered bar graph to present data from a complex multifactorial design (Figure 14.20). Here, for each level of one independent variable there is a cluster of bars along the x-axis; the other variable is represented in the graph itself, with bars corresponding to the different levels of the variables being distinguished by a different colour or shading.

Line graphs

A **line graph** represents data as a series of points connected by a line. It is most appropriate when your independent variable, on the x-axis, is continuous and

> **Line graph**
> A graph that shows the relationship between two variables with points connected by a line.

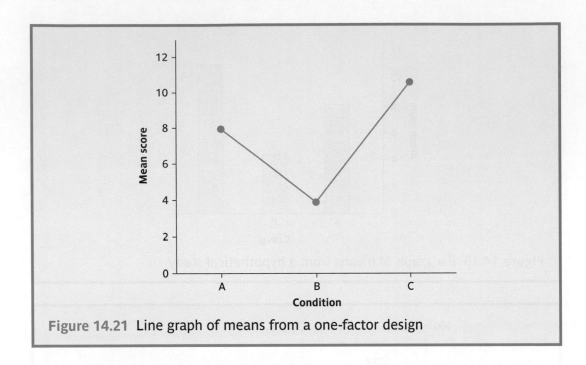

Figure 14.21 Line graph of means from a one-factor design

quantitative. This is in contrast to a bar graph, which is most appropriate when your independent variable is categorical or qualitative. Line graphs are also appropriate when you want to illustrate functional relationships among variables. A functional relationship is one in which the value of the dependent variable varies according to the value of the independent variable. Usually, the functional relationship is causal. Figure 14.21 shows a line graph that depicts the group means from a single-factor[2] experiment with a continuous independent variable.

A line graph can also be used to display the means from a factorial experiment. Figure 14.22 shows a line graph for a two-factor experiment. The levels of one variable are represented along the x-axis, just as in a single-factor experiment. The levels of the other factor are represented using different symbols or line styles. All points collected under the same value of the second factor have the same symbol and are connected by the same line. We will come back to this type of graph in **Chapter 18**, when we come to interpret findings from factorial experiments.

Scatterplots

Scatterplot
Graph in which pairs of scores on two variables are represented by separate points.

In correlational research, the data from the two dependent variables are often plotted as a scatterplot. On a **scatterplot**, each pair of scores is represented as a point on the graph (see Table 14.6 and Figure 14.23). To make a scatterplot, you plot the values of variable A along the x-axis and the values of variable B along the y-axis (or vice versa, it really does not matter). Then each pair of values is represented by a point within the graph.

We will return to scatterplots in **Chapter 19**, where you will see that they are extremely useful for inspecting relationships between variables.

---

2   Single-factor means that the experiment has only one independent variable.

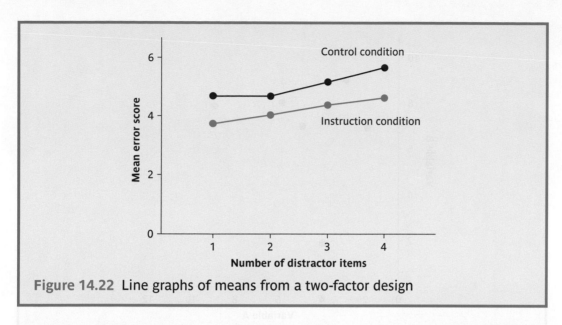

Figure 14.22 Line graphs of means from a two-factor design

Table 14.6 Bivariate data for a scatterplot

Participant number	Variable A	Variable B
1	5	7
2	4	2
3	9	8
4	2	7
5	6	8
6	3	9

Pie charts

If your data are in the form of proportions or percentages, then you might find a **pie chart** a good way to represent the value of each category. A pie chart represents the data as slices of a circular pie (see Figure 14.24). Although they may look nice, you very rarely see pie charts in results sections of reports or articles and so are best advised to leave them alone. Instead, they are more usually found in newspapers, magazines and some applied research reports.

> **Pie chart**
> Circular chart which has been divided into sectors according to the proportion or percentage for different categories.

Introduction to SPSS

In this section of the chapter, you will be introduced to the most popular statistical package, SPSS. We have a website accompanying this book that will take you through the basics of how to perform tests using this package (www.mcgraw-hill.co.uk/textbooks/wilsonandmaclean).

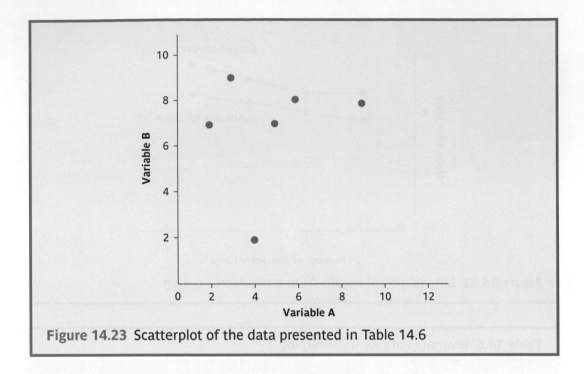

Figure 14.23 Scatterplot of the data presented in Table 14.6

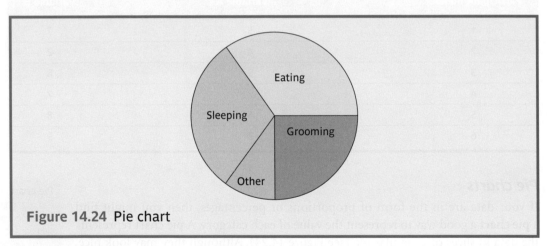

Figure 14.24 Pie chart

We decided that it was best to put most of the stuff related to SPSS on a website, because including it in the book was just too unwieldy, and we thought that you would get more benefit from actually sitting down at a computer and following instructions in that way rather than constantly referring to a text next to you. That said, this brief section does introduce you to the very basics, so you should be able to get started.

If you do not use this package, please just skip to the end of the chapter, but if you do use it, a word of caution – SPSS will do whatever you tell it to do. This means that you need to think carefully about what statistics you want from it and have an idea of what to expect. Just because

SPSS has produced a table of values does not mean that they are automatically correct! Use your judgement – if a graph or table looks strange, then something has probably gone wrong somewhere. Just because something has been produced by a computer does not make it correct.

Opening up SPSS

When you open up SPSS, you are greeted by a window asking you what you would like to do (see Figure 14.25).

You will normally choose one of two options here: (1) type in new data, to create a new data file, or (2) open an existing data source, to work with a previously saved data file (you may need to click on More Files . . . to find the file you want). Click OK once you have made your selection. If you want a bit of practice with SPSS, feel free to select Run the tutorial and take one of the tutorials.

When you open or create a data file, the SPSS Data Editor will open up. This consists of two views: Data View, which is a spreadsheet for your data, and Variable View, in which the variables to appear in the Data View are specified. The Data View and the Variable View are separate windows. One tells SPSS about the variables that you will be using, the other tells it the values of the data in each variable. You can switch between these two views using the tabs at the bottom left of the screen (see Figure 14.26).

Entering data

Before you can enter any data, you need to set up the Variable View with details of the variables. If you are not already in Variable View, click on the Variable View tab (near the bottom of the screen). In Variable View, each row represents one variable. When you switch to the Data View window, each variable that you enter will correspond to one column. To create a variable, click on the

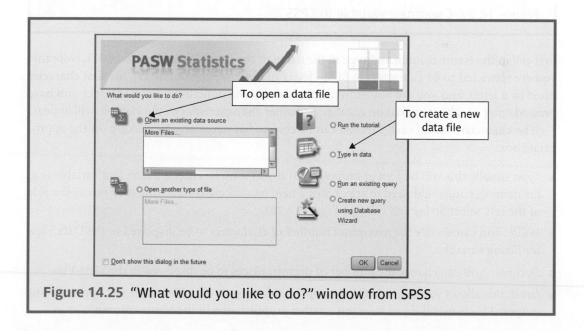

Figure 14.25 "What would you like to do?" window from SPSS

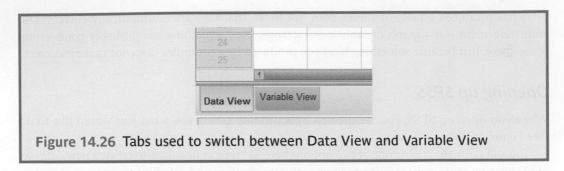

Figure 14.26 Tabs used to switch between Data View and Variable View

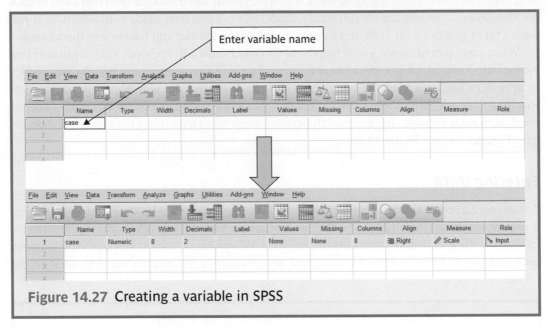

Figure 14.27 Creating a variable in SPSS

first cell in the Name column and type in the name of the variable (see Figure 14.27). Note that you are restricted to 64 characters in SPSS (fewer in older versions of SPSS), the first character must be a letter, and you are not allowed spaces and some punctuation marks. Once you have pressed enter or tab, or clicked on another cell, other characteristics of the variable will appear.

The characteristics of each variable can be changed as necessary, by clicking on the appropriate box:

- *Type*: usually this will be kept at numeric, but if you want to enter a letters in a variable (e.g. for names), you would need to select *String* here by clicking on the little grey box at the side of the cell, select *String* and *OK* (see Figure 14.28).

- *Width*: you can specify the maximum number of characters to be displayed in the Data View for String variables.

- *Decimals*: you can change the number of decimal places to be displayed in the Data View.

- *Label*: this allows you to give a full descriptive title to your variable which will appear in any output. This is useful if you have put a rather cryptic name in the Name column.

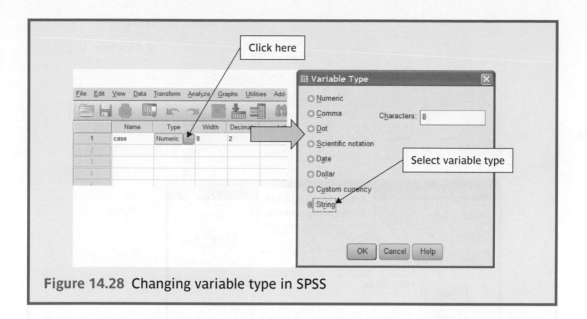

Figure 14.28 Changing variable type in SPSS

- *Values*: this is used when you have categories. Rather than making a String variable and typing in each category name, it is much easier and quicker to use a coding scheme where each category is assigned a specific value. For example, you may want a variable to specify participant gender – the code could be 1 = Male, 2 = Female. You need to tell SPSS what the coding scheme is and this is done by clicking the appropriate cell in the Values column and then on the little grey box to the right of the cell (see Figure 14.29). In the Value Labels box, enter the Value (i.e. number) and Label (i.e. category name) for the first category, click *Add*, and then repeat for all of the other categories. When finished, click *OK*.

- *Missing*: if you have missing data (e.g. someone did not give a response to a question in a questionnaire), you can simply not enter a value in your data file and SPSS will deal with that as missing data. However, a blank cell in your spreadsheet could just be an error in data entry rather than an actual missing data point. You may also want to distinguish between different types of missing data (e.g. ambiguous response, no response). To avoid this problem, you can assign code values to missing data; you tell SPSS about the code under the Missing column (see Figure 14.30).

- *Columns*: you can alter the width of the columns that appear in Data View here.

- *Align*: you can change whether data are left, right or centre aligned in Data View.

- *Measure*: you should specify whether you have Scale data (i.e. interval/ratio), Ordinal data or Nominal data by using the drop-down menu (see Figure 14.31). It's important that you get right as it can affect what options are available to you later if you are producing graphs.

- *Role*: in newer versions of SPSS you can change the role of variables. For example, you can specify whether the variable is input (e.g. independent variable), output (e.g. dependent variable or an outcome), both, none, or if it is being used to split or partition the data. You can do this using the drop-down menu (see Figure 14.32).

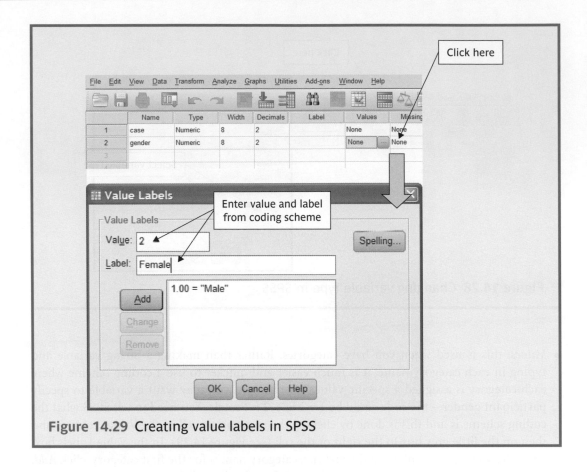

Figure 14.29 Creating value labels in SPSS

Figure 14.30 Specifying missing data in SPSS

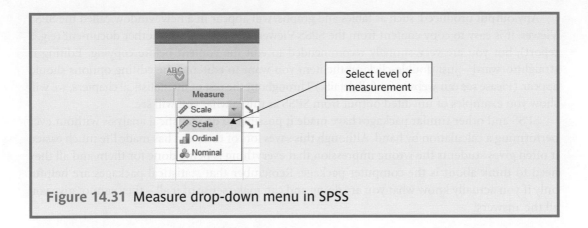

Figure 14.31 Measure drop-down menu in SPSS

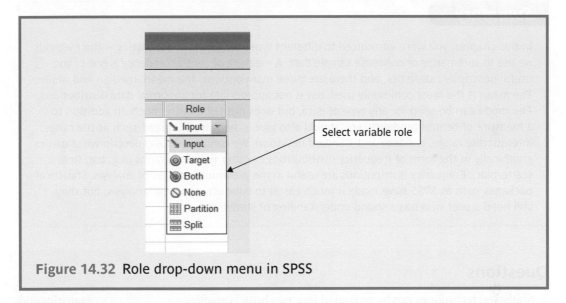

Figure 14.32 Role drop-down menu in SPSS

When you are satisfied that you have set up your variables, you are ready to enter data in Data View. Click on the Data View tab. You should see that you have a column in the Data View that corresponds to each variable created in Variable View. In the Data View, each row represents one case, and each column represents a variable.

To enter data, just click on the first cell in the first column of the Data View window, and get started. For any variables with value labels, you can use the drop-down menu or enter the value. You can switch between seeing the values and the value labels by clicking on the Value Labels button on the toolbar (also available in the View menu).

Once data are entered, you can start to use it, employing functions in the menus at the top of the screen. For example, if you got to the Analyze menu → Descriptive Statistics → Explore . . . , you can produce histograms, boxplots, stem-and-leaf plots and descriptive statistics. For details of the different procedures here, please have a look at our website (www.mcgraw-hill.co.uk/ textbooks/wilsonandmaclean).

Any output produced, such as tables and graphs, will appear in a new window called the SPSS Viewer. It is easy to copy content from the SPSS Viewer for pasting into another document (e.g. a report), but you are very strongly recommended to edit the content before copying. Editing is straightforward – just double-click on the item you want to edit and the editing options should appear. (Please see our website for full details.) Throughout the rest of the statistical chapters, we will show you examples of unedited output from SPSS as this is what you will see.

SPSS and other similar packages have made it possible to do statistical analysis without ever performing a calculation by hand. Although this saves lots of time and has made life much easier, it often gives students the wrong impression that everything is being done for them and all they need to think about is the computer package. Remember that statistical packages are helpful only if you actually know what you are doing and can make sense of it all – they cannot give you all the answers!

Summary

In this chapter, you were introduced to different types of descriptive statistics – the methods we use to summarize or condense sample data. A measure of central tendency is one of the useful descriptive statistics, and there are three main options: the mean, median and mode. The mean is the most commonly used, but is not appropriate for abnormal data distributions. The mode can be used for any type of data, but does not tell us very much. In addition to a measure of central tendency, you should also give a measure of spread such as the range, interquartile range, variance and standard deviation. We can also display descriptive statistics graphically in the form of frequency distributions or other types of graphs (e.g. bar, line, scatterplot). Frequency distributions are useful in the preliminary stages of analysis. Statistical packages such as SPSS have made it much easier to conduct statistical analysis, but they still need a user who has a sound understanding of statistics.

Questions

1 Statistical techniques can be separated into two broad categories: _____ statistics and _____ statistics.

2 How do the mode, median and mean differ, and under what conditions would you use each?

3 What measures of spread are available, and when would you use each?

4 Why is it useful to have both a measure of central tendency and a measure of spread for a data-set?

5 What should you look for when inspecting graphs of frequency distributions? Why?

6 Why is it important that you know what scale of measurement is being used when deciding on descriptive statistics?

7 Distinguish between a bar chart and a histogram. In what circumstances should you use each?

8 What are the important features of a graph that must be present?

Activities

1 Construct a stem-and-leaf display for the following set of numbers; then report what you have learned by examining the data in this way. 36, 42, 25, 26, 26, 21, 22, 43, 40, 69, 21, 21, 23, 31, 32, 32, 34, 37, 37, 38, 43, 20, 21, 24, 23, 42, 24, 21, 27, 29, 34, 30, 41, 25, 28.

2 Calculate the mean, median and mode (by hand or by computer) for the following data-set: 7, 7, 2, 4, 2, 4, 5, 6, 4, 5. Which measure do you think is the most appropriate?

3 Calculate the standard deviation (by hand or by computer) for the data in the previous activity. What does this tell you about the spread of data?

4 Describe the advantages and disadvantages of the three measures of central tendency: mean, median, mode.

5 Comment on descriptive statistics that are useful for ranked data.

Chapter 15

Introduction to Inferential Statistics

OVERVIEW

In the previous chapter we examined descriptive statistics and the ways in which we can summarize and condense data. But we can also use statistical methods for another purpose – to make inferences and draw conclusions. This is what we call inferential statistics. If we get a particular result in a study, inferential statistical methods can tell us about the likelihood of obtaining that result merely by chance alone. It is important that you understand the content of this chapter as the chapters which follow cover different inferential statistical methods and you will need to have the grounding provided in this chapter before moving on.

OBJECTIVES

After studying this chapter and working through the exercises, you should be able to:

- Distinguish between samples and populations
- Identify how the normal distribution curve can be used to identify probabilities of scores
- Explain the sampling distribution and standard error
- Calculate and explain z-scores
- Calculate and interpret a confidence interval
- Explain the logic of null hypothesis significance testing

- Distinguish between significant and non-significant results based on probabilities
- Distinguish between Type I and Type II errors
- Define the power of a statistical test and what factors can affect that power
- Define effect size and explain why it is useful

Samples and populations

Before discussing inferential statistics any further, it is important that you remind yourself of the differences between **populations and samples**. A **population** is the set of all cases of interest, whereas a **sample** is a subset of the population. Students often confuse the use of the word population in a research context with its use to describe everyone in a specific country or geographical area. Yes, sometimes your population of interest may be every single person in the UK (or another country or area, or even the world), but usually you will be focusing on a more specific group. For example, if you wanted to learn more about the attitudes of students at your university to the computing facilities, the population would be all of the students at your university, not all university students or the entire population of your country.

The goal of research is to tell a story about the population. However, measuring a large population is often practically impossible. This means that we have to conduct research on samples and generalize the results from the sample to the population from which it was drawn. However, there is a problem – how do we know that the results from the sample can actually be generalized to the population? Could the sample result merely be due to random error? How confident can we be that our sample is a good reflection of the population from which it came? This is where inferential statistics can help.

Inferential statistics is the name for a number of techniques that allow you to draw conclusions about populations based on data that you have obtained from a sample. Using what we know about probabilities, these techniques can also tell us about the degree of uncertainty that comes with the conclusion. If there is little uncertainty, researchers can generalize their findings to the population with some confidence (although they still acknowledge that there is a small chance that it is wrong – we can never be 100 per cent certain in statistics). If there is a great deal of uncertainty, researchers avoid drawing a conclusion from the sample.

Probability

Probability plays an important part in inferential statistics. Probability can be defined as the likelihood of the occurrence of some event or outcome. We all use probabilities in everyday life. For example, if you say that there is a high probability that you will pass this course, you mean that this outcome is likely to occur. You will

Population
An entire group (or entire set of scores) that is of interest to you as a researcher.

Sample
A smaller subgroup drawn from the larger population.

Inferential statistics
Set of methods used to reach conclusions about populations based on samples and probability.

Probability
Likelihood of the occurrence of an event or outcome.

have based this statement on specific information, such as your marks on coursework and examinations, and how much of this book you've understood. A weather forecaster may say that there is a 10% chance of rain; this means that the likelihood of rain is very low. A gambler gauges the probability that a particular horse will win a race on the basis of how that horse has performed in the past.

We can express probabilities in different ways. Imagine being asked to pick a card out of a full pack of cards. What is the probability of you picking a red card? There are 52 cards in the pack and 26 of them are red, so the probability of you choosing a red card is 26 out of 52. We can express this probability as a fraction (26/52 or 1/2), a percentage (50%) or in decimals (0.50). In statistics, we tend to express probabilities in decimals and usually do not bother with the 0 before the decimal point (e.g. .50 rather than 0.50), the reason being that all probabilities in statistics have a 0 before the decimal point, so putting it there is pretty pointless – if there were a 1 before the decimal point, that would indicate a 100% certainty and we can never be 100% certain in statistics.

STOP & Think

How would you express the probability of picking the following from a pack of cards? (1) Any hearts card; (2) any ace; (3) the Queen of Diamonds. Have a go at presenting the probabilities as fractions, percentages and decimals.

In research, we need to know whether the pattern of results that we have obtained from our sample accurately reflects the population that we sampled from or if it is due to random error in measurement. What do we mean by "random error in measurement"? Well, when we measure a sample, the data that we get are never going to be a perfect reflection of the population. There will always be some "error" (i.e. some fluctuation between our sample data and the data we would get if we measured the entire population on the thing that we are interested in). Good samples will give you information that is very close to the population. Bad samples will not – they will be very far away (i.e. they will be mostly "error"). The key question we ask in inferential statistics, therefore, is *what is the probability of our sample result being entirely due to error in measurement?* If this probability is very low, we can reject the possibility that what we have found is purely the result of random or chance error. If the probability is high, we have to accept that error or chance has produced the result. Inferential statistical methods can tell us what this probability is, and much of this is based around something called the normal curve.

STOP & Think

Much of what you will read in the following chapter about statistical tests is based on the sentence in italics above. Make sure you fully understand what this means.

The normal distribution curve

In the previous chapter, you were introduced to the concept of **frequency distributions**, which have an important role in inferential statistics and probability. Many variables such as IQ, shoe size and examination marks demonstrate what we call a normal distribution of scores, with most scores centred around the mean and few scores at the extreme ends of the distribution.

ch. 14
pp.296–303

The bell-shaped curve shown in Figure 15.1 is called the normal curve and is a mathematically defined, theoretical distribution of scores. In a **normal curve**, the peak of the distribution corresponds to the mean. Of course, the peak of the curve also indicates the most frequently occurring score (given that this is a frequency distribution), so the mode is the same score as the mean in a normal curve. You'll also notice

Normal curve
A mathematically defined, theoretical distribution with a particular bell shape. An empirical distribution of similar shape.

that the normal curve is symmetrical, with half of the distribution to the right of the mean and half to the left. The median (the middle score) is therefore the same as the mean and the mode.

In the Know

The term "normal" was adopted in the nineteenth century as the name for a curve that was proving important as mathematical statistics developed. Among some statisticians, the curve was thought of as an ideal; that is, it was the way the data should be distributed if there were no errors in measurement. This idea was quite mistaken, but it provides a clue to the selection of the term normal. The Latin adjective *normalis* means built with a carpenter's square or built exactly right. Thus, the ideal or proper curve should be called the normal curve according to those who adopted the name.

The normal curve has a special place in the history of statistics and statisticians have spent a lot of time studying it. One extremely useful thing that statisticians have learned about the normal curve is the probabilities of the scores in the distribution. If you look along the x (i.e. horizontal)

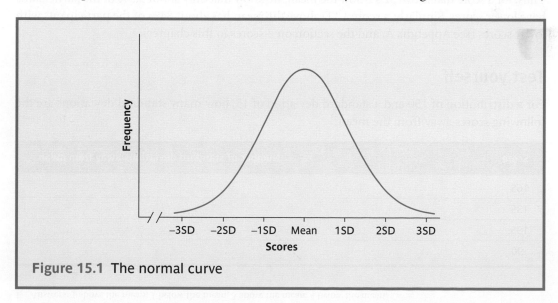

Figure 15.1 The normal curve

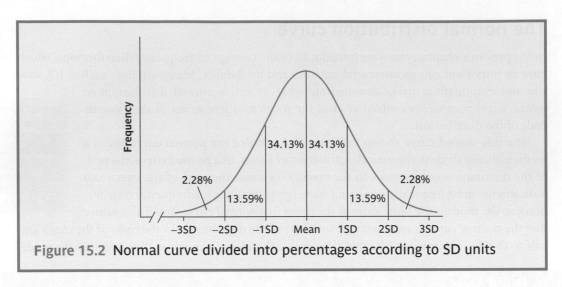

Figure 15.2 **Normal curve divided into percentages according to SD units**

ch. 14
pp.294–295

axis in Figure 15.1, you will see that the scores are expressed in terms of standard deviations rather than raw scores. We introduced the **standard deviation** in the previous chapter. The standard deviation is a measure of how "spread out" our data are around the central point. It's the average amount of deviation (from the mean) that exists in a distribution. Imagine a distribution of scores that has a mean of 100 and a standard deviation of 10. Now imagine an individual score of 110. The score of 110 is one standard deviation above the mean (because the standard deviation is 10 and the mean is 100). Likewise, a score of 90 is one standard deviation below the mean. A score of 120 is two standard deviations away from the mean . . . and so on. So, +1 *SD* means that a particular score is 1 *SD* above the mean, −2 *SD* means the score is 2 *SD*s below the mean (see the "Test yourself" box). It is useful to think of data in this way, because we know a lot about the proportions of the curve between the *SD* units. Those proportions are shown in Figure 15.2. Thus, for a score that is two *SD*s below the mean, we know that only about 2.3% of the participants have lower scores. Similarly, a score 1 *SD* above the mean has about 84% of the participants with lower scores (see Appendix A, and the section on *z*-scores in this chapter).

 ## Test yourself

For a distribution of 150 and a standard deviation of 15, how many standard deviations are the following scores away from the mean?[1]

Score	Number of standard deviations away from mean
165	
135	
195	
90	

There are some percentages that relate to normal curve that you will encounter frequently, so it is worth pointing them out now. One is that about 68% of scores in the normal curve lie between −1 SD and +1 SD (68.55% to be precise) and another is that about 95% (95.44%) of scores lie between −2 SD and +2 SD. But, because statisticians like to be as accurate as possible, it is important that you know that *exactly* 95% of scores lie between −1.96 and +1.96 SDs. What this means is that 2.5% of the curve is above +1.96 SD and 2.5% is below −1.96 SD.

STOP & Think

If exactly 95% of scores are between −1.96 and +1.96 standard deviations away from the mean, then why have we stated that 2.5% of the curve is above +1.96 SD and 2.5% is below −1.96 SD? You might find that it helps to sketch a diagram indicating a normal curve with the rough percentages that we're talking about.

But how does this relate to probability? Remember that we are discussing the percentage of scores in the distribution, and we can express probability as percentages, fractions or decimals. Thus, if we know that 95% of scores lie between 1.96 SDs above and below the mean, we can say that there is a 95% probability (.95 when expressed as a decimal) of any particular score coming from this region of the distribution. This means that there is only a 5% (.05) probability of a score being in the extreme range of the distribution, that is, above +1.96 SD and below −1.96 SD. (See Figure 15.3.) So, if you were to put all of the scores in a bucket and pull one out at random

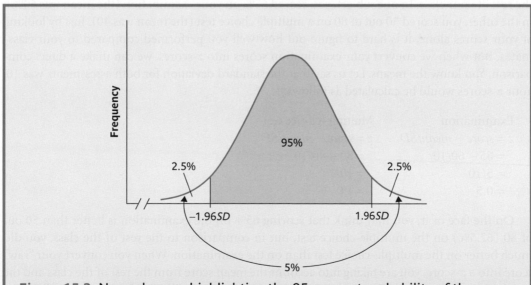

Figure 15.3 Normal curve, highlighting the 95 per cent probability of the scores between ±1.96 SD, and 5 per cent of the extreme scores

(blindfolded, obviously), then there is a 95% chance that the score you pick out will be from the region that lies between 1.96 standard deviations above the mean, and 1.96 standard deviations below the mean. There is only a 5% chance that you will get a score that is not in this region of the curve. You will see later that this 5% probability has an important role to play in inferential statistics.

Z-scores

Z-score
Standardized score in which raw score is described by how many standard deviations it is from the mean.

We can express how many *SD* units a point in the normal curve is from the mean using something called z-scores. A **z-score** is simply the number of standard deviations any particular score is away from the mean. For example, if a score is 1 *SD* above the mean, it would have a z-score of +1; a score that is 2.5 *SD*s below the mean would have a z-score of −2.5; and so on. To calculate a z-score, you subtract the mean from your raw score and then divide by the *SD*. To calculate a raw score when you know the z-score, you multiply the z-score by the *SD* and add the mean (if you completed the "Test yourself" box, you have already worked out z-scores because your answers *were* z-scores). You can see the equation for working out z-scores below. The other equation (on the right) is the equation for working out individual scores when you already know the z-score, mean and *SD* (it is just the z-score equation reorganized).

$$z = \frac{score - mean}{SD} \qquad score = zSD + mean$$

Converting raw scores into z-scores allows direct comparisons, even if scores are measured on different scales, and thus, for comparison of probabilities. For example, imagine you were studying two subjects as part of your course and you wanted to compare your performance to the rest of your class. In one subject, you scored 65% on your examination (the mean was 60%); in the other, you scored 50 out of 80 on a multiple choice test (the mean was 40). Just by looking at your scores alone, it is hard to figure out how well you performed compared to your classmates. But when we convert your examination scores into z-scores, we can make a direct comparison. You know the means. Let us say that the standard deviation for both assessments was 10. Your z-scores would be calculated as follows:

Examination   Multiple-choice test
z = score − mean/SD   z = score − mean/SD
  = 65 − 60/10   = 50 − 40/10
  = 5/10   = 10/10
  = 0.5   = 1.0

On the face of it, you may think that scoring 65% on the examination is better than 50 out of 80 (62.5%) on the multiple-choice test, but in comparison to the rest of the class, you did much better on the multiple-choice test than on the examination. When you convert your "raw" score into a z-score, you are taking into account the mean score from the rest of the class and the standard deviation. This allows you to work out where in this distribution your score lies. The z-score tells you this. Because we also know the properties of the normal curve, we can then work out how "probable" your score was (i.e. was it a "rare" score that lies far away from the mean, or was it a "common" score that lies close to the mean?). So, given that you worked out a z-score of 1.0 for the multiple-choice test, this means that this score was further away from the mean performance (and therefore less probable) than your examination score, meaning that you cannot always judge performance on the score that you got – you have to look at how you compared to the rest of the class (i.e. the average). You can work out exactly how "probable" your score was in relation to the rest of the distribution by consulting the table in Appendix A. To do this, look down the first column until you see the z-score you're checking (in this case let us use the z-score of 1.00). You will see two things. First, the area of the curve that is *between the mean and that z-score*. For this example, this is .3413. This means that there are 34.13% of scores that are between the mean and your score. The next figure is the area of the curve that lies *above your score*. In this case, this is .1587, which means that there are 15.87% of scores that are above yours.

Z-scores are referred to as standard scores because measurement scales (which can be in all sorts of different units – feet, centimetres, miles, camel-steps, hand-widths) are converted into a standardized format, with a mean of 0 and a standard deviation of 1. When z-scores are applied to a normal curve, the curve is called the standard normal curve. Thus, if we know a z-score from a normal curve, we can work out its probability (using Appendix A).

STOP & Think

Can you think of any circumstances in which researchers would want to standardize scores on different variables?

Test yourself [2]

Using Appendix A, work out the following;

a. The area of the curve between the mean and 1.5 standard deviations away from the mean (i.e. a z-score of 1.5)

b. The area of the curve that lies *above* a z-score of 1.65

c. The area of the curve that lies between the mean and a z-score of 1.9

d. The area of the curve that lies *below* a z-score of 1.30 (do not forget that there are 50% of the scores that lie *below* the mean)

---

2   Answers: a = .4332, or 43.32%; b = .0495, or 4.95%; c = .4713, or 47.13%; d = .9032, or 90.32% – we worked out the area between the mean and z = 1.3, which is 40.32%. However, this is only to the right of the mean (i.e. the scores between the mean and that z-score). To get *all* the scores *below* this z-score, we must think of the score *below* the mean. As 50 per cent of the scores lie below the mean, then 50% + 40.32% = 90.32%.

Sampling distribution of the means and standard error

Until now we have been considering the frequency distributions of scores from a sample. But there is another type of frequency distribution that we must consider. We can also create a frequency distribution by repeatedly taking samples of a given size (e.g. five scores) from a population (see Figure 15.4). Imagine that we took a sample of five scores and calculated the mean. We then took another five scores and calculated the mean of these scores. We did this again and again until we have lots of means. Not all of these means will be the same. Some will be high, some will be low. We could then use the means of these samples to form a distribution. This distribution is not of individual scores, but is of the means of the samples that we have taken again and again. We call this the **sampling distribution** of the mean. If you could take every possible sample of your chosen size (e.g. every possible sample of five scores), and make a histogram of the means from these samples, you would have a distribution of sample means (see Figure 15.5).

Sampling distribution
Frequency distribution showing means from all possible samples of a given size taken from a population.

Notice that the means of the various samples differ – some are higher than the population mean, some are lower and some are exactly the same as the population mean. If you look at the distribution of sample means (Figure 15.5), you may see something familiar.

STOP & Think

Where have you seen this type of distribution before? What do we know about this distribution?

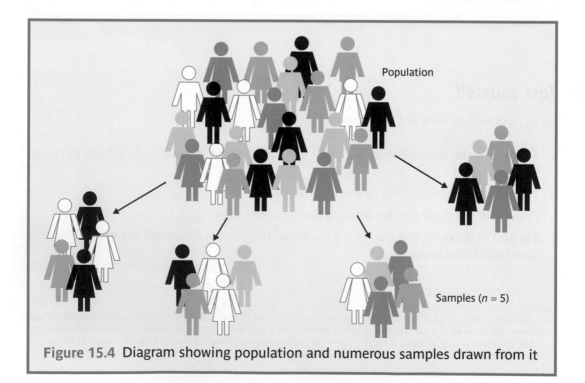

Figure 15.4 Diagram showing population and numerous samples drawn from it

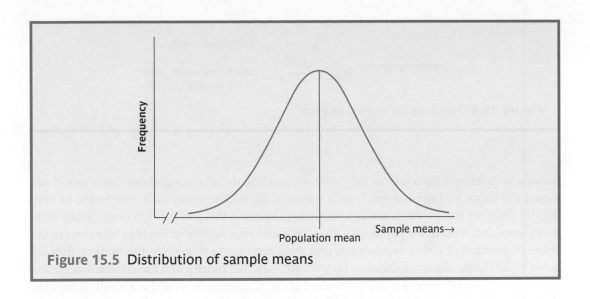

Figure 15.5 Distribution of sample means

Something called "central limit theorem" tells us that this sampling distribution of means will tend to closely approximate the normal distribution, even when the population of scores from which the samples were drawn is far from normal in shape. What this means is that, if you keep finding the mean of a sample of (say) five again and again, and then plot the means, you will find that they fall into a nice normal curve. A consequence of this is that the mean of *all* the *sample* means (i.e. add together all of the sample means and divide by the number of samples; it's a bit like a "supermean" – the mean of all the means in your distribution) will be equal to the population mean.

However, we do not usually sample again and again and again. Usually we sample from the population only once. When you measure one sample mean, how do you know it's a good estimate of the population mean? Just as the standard deviation tells us about the variability of scores in a sample, we can calculate a standard deviation to tell us about the variability in the sample means that were all drawn from the same population. This particular standard deviation is so important that it has a special name, the **standard error of the mean** (*SE*), or standard error for short. (You may also see it denoted as s_x or *SEM*.) Small standard errors suggest that you have a good estimate of the population mean; large standard errors indicate a greater degree of uncertainty about how good the sample mean is at estimating the population mean. The *SE* is calculated (Figure 15.6) by finding the standard deviation and dividing it by $\sqrt{N}$ (the square root of the sample size).[3]

> **Standard error of the mean**
> Standard deviation of the sampling distribution of means.

Notice that the sample size (*N*) is part of the calculation for the *SE*. As the sample size increases, the *SE* will decrease, and the uncertainty about the mean decreases. This makes sense. Imagine you have a population (say, 1000) and you take a very large sample (say 998). You keep sampling 998 people again and again, and then plot the means on a frequency distribution.

---

3   To be precise, what you are calculating here is an *estimated* standard error of the mean. If you were to calculate the standard error for the sampling distribution of the mean, you would need the population standard deviation, but we usually do not know this. Instead, we use the sample standard deviation as an estimate of the population standard deviation.

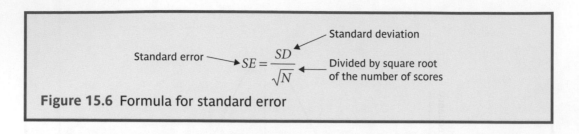

Figure 15.6 Formula for standard error

Because your sample each time is very close to sampling the whole population, you would not expect the mean to differ too much each time you did it. The mean each time might be very slightly different, but probably not by much. Also, the mean that you get each time is likely to be a very good indicator of the population mean (because your sample of 998 is so very close to the entire population of 1000). So when you plot these means on a frequency distribution, they are going to be tightly clustered (because they do not vary that much), and the standard deviation (in this case, given its special name of standard error) is going to be small (as a result of the tight clustering of scores). So, in this case, the larger the sample, the less error there is likely to be in your estimate of the population mean. In contrast, imagine you took only a small sample each time (say 10 cases). Because the sample is so small, each time you sample there is more chance that the means you get will be different to each other. You will get a wide variety of means (because your sample is considerably smaller and is not representative of the larger population). Each sample that you take might have considerably different means, and so when you plot these means on a distribution, there will be a large degree of variability. This means that the standard error will be high, and you can be less certain about how closely any given sample mean is to the overall mean of the population. Thus, with very large samples, you can be quite sure that the sample mean is very close to the population mean, so always try to have as large a sample as possible when conducting research.

In the chapters that follow, you will be introduced to other statistics, which, like the mean, can be repeatedly sampled to produce a sampling distribution. Some of these sampling distributions look similar to normal distributions, others are very different. Regardless of the shape of the sampling distribution, we can ask the same question – is our sample statistic representative of the value in the population?

Confidence intervals

Confidence interval
Range of scores that is expected with a specified degree of confidence to capture a parameter (population value).

So, the standard error gives us an indication of how close our sample mean is likely to be to the population mean. We can also use something called a **confidence interval** to tell us about the degree of precision and confidence in our sample measurement.

Sometimes, if you are watching the news during an election campaign, you will see the results of polls. The polls are supposed to give an indication of how people are likely to vote on election day. Obviously, this is an example of "sampling". Not everyone that will vote on election day will have been asked to take part in the poll, so the people who are asked are a "sample" from that larger population of voters. When the results of the polls are presented, you will often hear the newsreader say that they are accurate to within "plus or minus 5 percentage points", or something similar. Likewise, when you are reading the results of academic survey research you may see statements such as: "The results from the survey are accurate within 3 percentage points, using a 95% level of confidence." What do these statements mean?

Suppose you asked students in the academic survey to tell you whether they prefer to study at home or at university, and the survey results indicate that 61% prefer to study at home. You might realize that, although you do not know what the result would be if you tested the entire population of students, it is likely that the actual population value is somewhere between 58% and 64% (i.e. 61% ± 3%). This range of values with an upper limit and a lower limit is called a confidence interval, and is calculated for a specified amount of confidence (usually 95%). So, in our example, we can have 95% confidence that the range between the upper and lower limits (i.e. between 58% and 64%) includes the true population mean. The sample value lies in the middle of the confidence interval and is the best estimate of the population value. However, because you have only a sample and not the entire population, your result may be in error. The confidence interval gives you information about the likely amount of the error. The formal term for this error is **sampling error**, although you are probably more familiar with the term margin of error.

> **Sampling error**
> The deviation between the characteristics of a sample and a population.

The surveys you often read about in newspapers and the previous examples deal with percentages, but you apply the same logic to other types of data. For example, if you also ask students to report how many hours and minutes they studied during the previous day, you might find that the average amount of time was 76 minutes. A confidence interval could then be calculated based on the size of the sample; for example, the 95% confidence interval is 76 minutes plus or minus 10 minutes. It is highly likely that the true population value lies somewhere between 66 and 86 minutes.

Note that the size of the confidence interval is related to both the size of the sample and the level of confidence. As the sample size increases, the confidence interval narrows. This is because sample means obtained with larger sample sizes are more likely to reflect the population mean. Second, higher confidence is associated with a larger interval. If you want to be almost certain that the interval contains the true population mean (e.g. a 99% confidence interval rather than 95%), you will need to include a larger range of scores (you can be more confident that the population mean lies between 15 and 100 than you can that it lies between 50 and 70).

So how do you calculate a confidence interval? Think back to the normal curve. We know that 95% of scores lie between ±1.96 SDs (i.e. ±1.96 z-scores) from the mean. As the distribution of sample means (when we take the means of lots and lots of samples and plot them on a frequency distribution) also approximates a normal distribution, we can use the same logic to work out that 95% of sample means will lie between ±1.96 SE from the mean of this distribution (remember that the standard error, SE, is the standard deviation, SD, of the sampling distribution). So, if you know the sample mean and the SE, you can work out the confidence interval: multiply the SE by 1.96 and add this value to the sample mean to calculate the upper limit, and subtract it from the sample mean to calculate the lower limit.

Box 15.1 Example of confidence interval calculation

Sample mean = 15

Standard error = 5

Work out the 95% confidence intervals

1   95% of scores lie in the area between 1.96 standard errors below the mean and 1.96 standard errors above the mean

2   1.96 standard errors below the mean:

   $1.96 \times 5 = 9.8$

   $15 - 9.8 = 5.2$

3   1.96 standard errors above the mean:

   $1.96 \times 5 = 9.8$

   $15 + 9.8 = 24.8$

Therefore, the confidence intervals are 9.8 and 24.8, so we know with 95 per cent confidence that the interval between these two values contains the population mean.

However, there is a slight problem with this. The *SE* that we have been using is only an *estimate* based on sample data – to calculate the real *SE* we would need to know the *population* standard deviation and we normally do not know this because we do not have data from the whole population. Unless the sample size is large (and consequently the estimated *SE* is more likely to accurately reflect the real *SE*), using an estimate will mean that the distribution we are working with will not be exactly normal and this means that we cannot say for certain that 95% of the means lie between ±1.96 *SE* from the sample mean.

Instead, we have to use a different distribution (sorry). We call it the *t*-distribution, and we use it to work out confidence intervals. The shape of the distribution is related to the sample size and approaches normality when the sample is large. (We will be discussing the *t*-distribution in more depth in the next chapter.)

ch. 16
pp.345–346

So, when you have a particular sample size, there will be a corresponding *t*-distribution that you can use to calculate confidence intervals. There is a different *t*-distribution for every possible sample size, and statisticians have spent a lot of time working out probabilities for values under the various *t*-distributions and have published tables of these values (see Appendix C). For example, for a sample of five cases, it is known that 95% of values lie between ±2.78 on the *t*-distribution. If the mean was 10 and the *SE* was 2, we would multiply the *SE* by 2.78 (*not* 1.96) to give us 5.56; the upper limit would therefore be 15.56 (10 + 5.56) and the lower limit would be 4.44 (10 − 5.56). As the sample size increases, the critical values (i.e. the cut-off values in the distribution) become closer to the normal distribution values: for a sample of 10, 95% of values lie between ±2.26 on the *t*-distribution, for a sample of 25 it is ±2.06, for 120 is it 1.98, and so on.

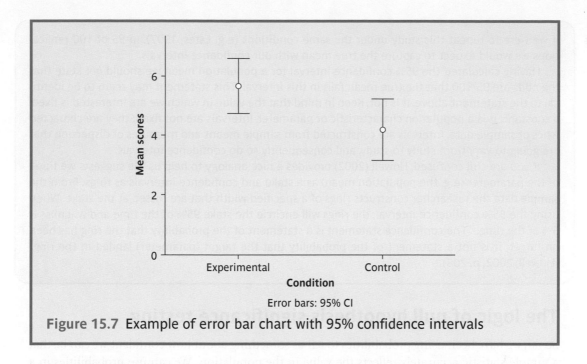

Figure 15.7 Example of error bar chart with 95% confidence intervals

> ## STOP & Think
>
> For a study with a sample of 10, $M = 50$ and $SE = 2.5$, what would be the 95 per cent confidence interval?

If this all seems a bit confusing, do not worry as SPSS (or another statistical package) can calculate confidence intervals for you as well as produce error bar charts which neatly show confidence intervals in graphical form (see Figure 15.7). The key thing to take away from this section is that you can recognize the usefulness of confidence intervals and have an understanding behind the basic concept of how they are calculated. It is becoming more common now to report confidence intervals in results so you need to be familiar with them.

In the Know

Interpreting confidence intervals for a single mean: rings and stakes
Having calculated the 95% confidence interval for a population mean we can state that the odds are 95/100 that the obtained confidence interval contains the true population mean.

The confidence interval either does or does not contain the true mean. A 95% probability associated with the confidence interval for a mean refers to the probability of capturing the true population mean if we were to construct many confidence intervals based on different random samples of the same size. That is, confidence intervals around the sample mean tell us what happens

▶ if we were to repeat this study under the same conditions (e.g. Estes, 1997). In 95 of 100 replications we would expect to capture the true mean with our confidence intervals.

Having calculated the 95% confidence interval for a population mean we should *not* state that the odds are 95/100 that the true mean falls in this interval. This statement may seem to be identical to the statement above. It is not. Keep in mind that the value in which we are interested is fixed, a constant; it is a population characteristic or parameter. Intervals are not fixed; they are characteristics of sample data. Intervals are constructed from sample means and measures of dispersion that are going to vary from study to study, and consequently so do confidence intervals.

If you are still confused, Howell (2002) provides a nice analogy to help us. He suggests we think of the parameter (e.g. the population mean) as a stake and confidence intervals as rings. From the sample data the researcher constructs rings of a specified width that are tossed at the stake. When using the 95% confidence interval, the rings will encircle the stake 95% of the time and will miss it 5% of the time. "The confidence statement is a statement of the probability that the ring has been on target; it is not a statement of the probability that the target (parameter) landed in the ring" (Howell, 2002, p. 208).

The logic of null hypothesis significance testing

So far, we have been using probabilities to tell us something about how confident we can be that a sample statistic accurately reflects the value in the population. We can use probabilities in a similar way to find out if a particular sample result (e.g. a difference between the means of two samples) accurately reflects the corresponding result that you would get it you happened to test the entire population. To do this, we use something called **null hypothesis significance testing** (NHST).

Recall from **Chapter 4** that we can state hypotheses,[4] or informed predictions, when conducting research. When we use NHST, we construct two hypotheses about the population: one is the **null hypothesis** (symbolized as H_0) and the other is the alternative (or experimental or research) hypothesis (symbolized as H_1). The null hypothesis is always a statement about independence or equality in populations (e.g. there will be *no difference* between two means), whereas the **alternative hypothesis** states that there will be an association or differences (e.g. there *will* be a difference between two means).

We can think of NHST as a battle between the null and alternative hypotheses: if the null hypothesis is incorrect, then we can infer that the alternative hypothesis is correct; if the null hypothesis is correct, then we cannot accept the alternative hypothesis as correct. In order to determine which of the two hypotheses is correct, we test the null hypothesis by asking the following question: *assuming that the null hypothesis is correct, what is the probability of obtaining our pattern of results?* In other words, what we are asking is "if there is absolutely no real effect, how likely is it that we would have got the results that we have?"

Using what we know already about probabilities and what we will learn about different statistics in the following chapters, we can work out this probability (which we

ch. 4
pp.77–80

Null hypothesis significance testing
An inferential statistics technique that produces accurate probabilities about samples when the null hypothesis is true.

Null hypothesis
The hypothesis that there is no effect in the population (e.g. no difference between means, no relationship between variables).

Alternative hypothesis
The hypothesis that there is an effect in the population (e.g. difference between means, relationship between variables); the opposite of the null hypothesis.

---

4 Note the difference between hypothesis (singular) and hypotheses (plural). This can sometimes be confusing.

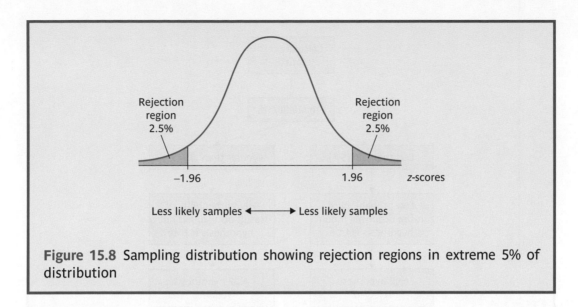

Figure 15.8 Sampling distribution showing rejection regions in extreme 5% of distribution

imaginatively call p). If p is high, this means that the pattern of results that we have got in our study is very likely (or highly probable) if the null hypothesis is actually correct. We would therefore have to accept that the null hypothesis is indeed correct and reject the alternative hypothesis.[5] In contrast, if p is low, then our pattern of results is highly *unlikely* to have occurred if the null hypothesis is correct. In this case, we would decide to reject the null hypothesis and accept the alternative hypothesis as correct.

You may be wondering why we are testing the null hypothesis in the first place. The reason is that the null hypothesis is a very precise statement (e.g. there will be no difference between two means) and gives us something to compare our results with. The alternative hypothesis, in contrast, is not so precise. For example, if the alternative hypothesis is that there will be a difference between two means, it does not tell us how big the difference should be. Because of this lack of precision, the only way we can say that the alternative hypothesis is correct is by rejecting the null hypothesis. In other words, you are *inferring* the alternative hypothesis is correct without actually testing it. (This is where the term inferential statistics comes from – inferences are being made about a population based on sample data.)

So, when we use NHST, we are making decisions about whether the null hypothesis or the alternative hypothesis is likely to be correct based on a probability. But how do we decide what level of probability represents a likely or unlikely result if the null hypothesis was true? Thankfully, there is a generally agreed cut-off point and it is one that we have already covered. Recall that 95% of scores in a normal distribution lie between ±1.96 z-scores from the mean, leaving us with 5% of the scores in the extreme tail-ends of the distribution (2.5% in each tail). These scores have a low probability (5%; see Figure 15.8).

This 5 per cent probability is the most commonly used "cut-off point" in NHST. If the calculated probability (p) is *greater* than 5% (sometimes written as $p > .05$), the result is considered to be

---

5   Technically speaking, we do not really "accept" the null hypothesis – we "fail to reject" it. This is because we may obtain a high probability for reasons other than the null hypothesis being true (e.g. small sample size, poor methodology), so we cannot accept that the null hypothesis is actually true. However, for our discussion we will use "accept" simply because it's easier to understand and less confusing. Please see Shaughnessy, Zechmeister and Zechmeister (2006) for a fuller discussion of this topic.

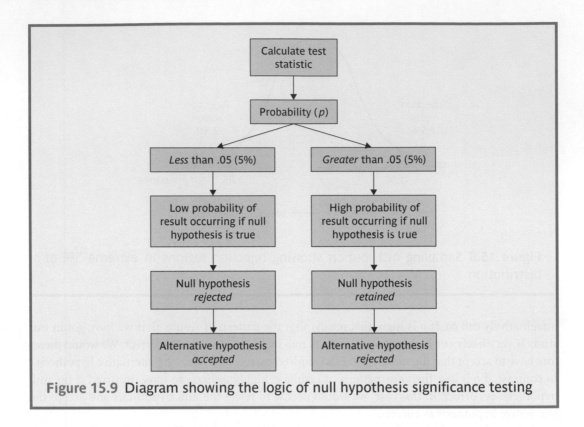

Figure 15.9 Diagram showing the logic of null hypothesis significance testing

likely if the null hypothesis was correct (i.e. null hypothesis accepted, alternative hypothesis rejected). If the probability (p) is *less* than 5% ($p < .05$), the result is considered to be unlikely if the null hypothesis was correct (i.e. null hypothesis rejected, alternative hypothesis accepted). If you obtain a probability of less than .05 (5%), then this is said to be **statistically significant**, and you would reject the null hypothesis and accept the alternative hypothesis. Note that in statistics "significant" has a specific meaning, so don't talk about something being "significant" if you just mean "important".

> **Statistically significant**
> Sample data with a probability less than .05 (5 per cent).

Another way to think about it is to consider that the probability tells us about the likelihood of the result occurring by chance alone (assuming the null hypothesis was true). A small probability (less than 5 per cent) tells us that there is a small likelihood that the result is due to random error or pure chance; a large probability tells us that there is a high likelihood that the result is due to random error or pure chance.

This section may seem confusing and counter-intuitive and it will probably take a while for you to digest it all, but persevere! Figure 15.9 presents a diagram to help clarify the process we have discussed.

Significance levels

We have seen that 5% or .05 is the probability value most commonly used to determine whether a result is statistically significant or not. There is nothing magical about this value – it

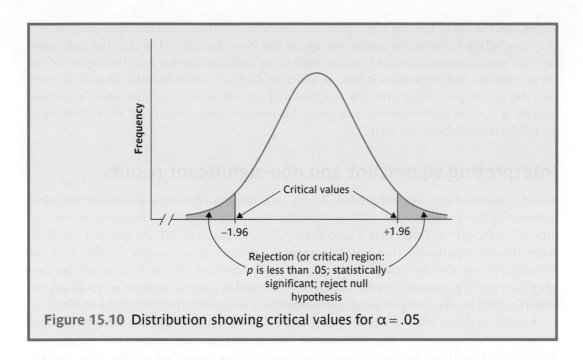

Figure 15.10 Distribution showing critical values for α = .05

was selected through consensus among statisticians and other scientists over the years and is fairly arbitrary. However, you may sometimes see people using a different level of probability as a cut-off point (e.g. 1% or .01). The probability that we decide to use to indicate whether an outcome is statistically significant is called the **level of significance**. The level of significance is indicated by the Greek letter **alpha** (α). So, we can speak about the .05 level of significance, the .10 level or the .01 level, which we report as α = .05, α = .10, α = .01, respectively.

Before you conduct any null hypothesis significance testing, you should decide on your significance level (alpha) and stick to it. (You most definitely should not adjust your alpha level after conducting statistical tests to give you your desired outcome; this is very dishonest and unethical.) If you conduct a statistical test and you find that the calculated probability (p) is less than your alpha level, then you have a statistically significant result. We can display this graphically (see Figure 15.10). The points associated with an alpha level, separating the significant tail-ends from the rest of the distribution, are called critical values. Thus, if α = .05, the critical values for the normal curve are ±1.96 (because, as we said earlier in this chapter, the most extreme 5% of the scores in a normal distribution lie in the regions that are above 1.96 standard deviations above the mean and the corresponding region that is below 1.96 standard deviations below the mean).

As indicated in Figure 15.10, the region of a sampling distribution that includes samples that are less likely than the chosen α level is called the **rejection region**. The distributions that we have considered so far can have rejection regions in the two extremes of the curve, but for others that we will discover later, the rejection region is in just one tail of the curve. Nevertheless, the principle is the same: regardless of the shape of the distribution the rejection region(s) will contain the most unlikely

Level of significance (alpha) The probability value that is the criterion for rejecting the null hypothesis; usually .05.

Rejection region The portion of a sampling distribution which includes samples with probabilities less than alpha.

values, and the size of the rejection region will depend on the chosen level of alpha (usually .05). If a value falls in the rejection region, we can say that its probability is less than the alpha level. In other words, we can say that it is very unlikely to find a result that is in this region of the curve when the null hypothesis is true, so when we do find a result like this, we will conclude that the null hypothesis is probably not true and we will accept the alternative hypothesis instead. It is quite important that you grasp this concept, because many of the statistics that we will be talking about rely on it.

Interpreting significant and non-significant results

This may sound all very well and good (or maybe not), but we need to exercise some caution when interpreting the results of NHST. The probabilities that NHST produces are conditional: a conditional probability is correct only if specified conditions hold. In NHST, the specified condition is that the null hypothesis is true. So if you obtain a significant result, this tells you that *if the null hypothesis is true*, the obtained result has a probability less than .05. You may sometimes hear people say that a *p*-value tells us the likelihood of the null hypothesis being true, but this is not strictly correct as when we are testing a null hypothesis we assume it's true in the first place.

Another problem with interpreting a significant result is that it does not demonstrate that the alternative hypothesis is definitely correct. We can only "provide support for" or "give evidence for" a hypothesis, but a significant result alone cannot prove that an alternative hypothesis is correct.[6] Why? We never test the alternative hypothesis directly. If we have a significant result, this tells us that our result is highly unlikely to occur by chance if the null hypothesis was true. We can therefore reason that the null hypothesis is probably not true and we then turn to our other hypothesis – the alternative hypothesis – and conclude that it is a better explanation for the data that we have than the null hypothesis. In other words, the alternative hypothesis is used only because the null hypothesis has already been eliminated. So although your results may support the alternative hypothesis, they most definitely cannot prove it!

Interpreting non-significant results can be equally problematic. If you obtain a non-significant *p*-value, this leaves the null hypothesis in contention but does not provide a strong statement of support. There may be a number of alternative explanations for a non-significant result other than the null hypothesis being true in the population, including poor research design and small sample size. However, Frick (1995) pointed out that if the study is well designed, has a reasonably large sample size and if several other studies have found similar results, you could be justified in concluding that the null hypothesis is in fact true.

Effect size

Another problem with interpreting significant results is that they do not tell us anything about the importance of a result. In the non-statistical world, we often use the word "significant" to mean important, but in the statistical world it means only one thing: the null hypothesis was rejected. It is entirely possible to have a highly significant result that is not important or has little practical significance. For example, if an expensive new psychiatric treatment technique

---

6   This is partly why you should never talk about "proving" something in psychology.

significantly reduces the average hospital stay from 60 days to 59 days, it might not be practical to use the technique despite the evidence for its effectiveness. The additional day of hospitalization costs less than the treatment.

So how can we find out about the importance of a result? This is where the concept of **effect size** comes in. Effect size measures tell us the magnitude of a treatment effect or of the strength of a relationship between two variables. In experimental research, an effect size measure indicates the degree of the effect that the independent variable has on the dependent variable. In the previous example we could say that the psychiatric treatment had little effect and so we would expect a small effect size. In correlational research effect size measures can tell you about the strength of the relationship between two variables.

What makes effect size measures so important and useful is that they are standardized and they do not depend on sample size. This allows for direct comparison of effect sizes across studies and indicates the relative importance of the result. Probabilities, in contrast, are directly related to sample size – the larger the sample size, the greater the likelihood of finding a significant result. This is because larger sample sizes give more accurate estimates of the actual population than smaller sample sizes. You cannot compare probabilities across different studies and conclude that because one result is more significant than another, that result is more important than another.

You are therefore recommended to report effect size when you are reporting probabilities as this will give the reader a fuller picture of what is going on. We will discuss effect size measures again in the following chapters, but for now you should appreciate that effect size provides a useful piece of information that you do not get from just looking at the *p*-values.

> **Effect size**
> A measure of the size of a treatment effect or strength of association; unaffected by sample size.

Type I and Type II errors

The decision to reject the null hypothesis is based on probabilities rather than certainties, and because of this degree of uncertainty we can sometimes make errors. For example, if you use an alpha level of .05, you can only have 95% confidence that you have made the correct decision – but there is still a 5% chance that you are wrong.

There are two possible outcomes of a null-hypothesis significance test: (1) reject the null hypothesis, or (2) accept the null hypothesis. There are also two possible truths about the population: (1) the null hypothesis is true, or (2) the null hypothesis is false. Combining these, we can have four possible situations: two kinds of correct decisions and two kinds of errors (see Figure 15.11).

As you can see from the decision matrix in Figure 15.11, you can make a correct decision if you reject the null hypothesis when it is actually false (i.e. the alternative hypothesis is true in the population), or if you accept the null hypothesis when it is actually true in the population. This is good. But more worrying are the errors that you can make.

Type I errors

A **Type I error** is made when we *reject* the null hypothesis when it is actually *true* (i.e. we conclude "there's nothing going on here" when in fact there is). In a situation

> **Type I error**
> Rejecting the null hypothesis when it is actually true; the probability of which is equal to alpha.

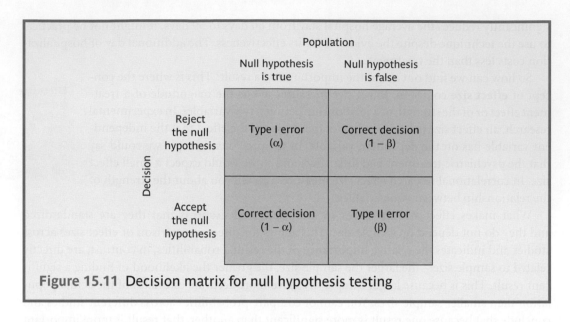

Figure 15.11 Decision matrix for null hypothesis testing

like this, we accept the alternative hypothesis when we should really be accepting the null hypothesis. For example, we might conclude from our study on exercise and mood discussed in Chapter 6 that the results we obtained were suggestive that exercise improves mood, when in actual fact there is no real discernible effect of exercise on mood. The probability of making this sort of error is determined by your choice of significance level (alpha). Therefore, if your chosen alpha level is .05 and you decide to reject the null hypothesis because a statistic has a probability of less than .05, there is a 5 per cent chance (or five chances out of 100) that your decision is wrong. The probability of making this type of error can be changed by increasing or decreasing the significance level. If we use a lower significance level of .01, for example, there is less chance of making a Type I error. However, as we will see, lowering the significance level does not solve all our problems.

Type II errors

A Type II error occurs when the null hypothesis is retained although in the population the alternative hypothesis is actually true. For example, we might conclude that there was no effect of exercise on mood when in actual fact mood does indeed improve mood. The probability of making this type of error is called beta, or β. Several factors control the value of β, including the significance (alpha) level. If we set a very low significance level to decrease the chances of a Type I error, the flip-side is that we make it very difficult to reject the null hypothesis.

> **Type II error**
> Retaining the null hypothesis when it is actually false; the probability of which is called beta.

Consequently, this makes it more likely that we will accept the null hypothesis, even if it was false – a **Type II error**. In other words, we can protect ourselves against making a Type 1 error, but in doing so we increase the chances of us making a Type II error. The two types of error are always in tension with each other. We will discuss the topic of β in more depth in the next section in relation to something called power.

STOP & Think

Can you think of a scenario in which making a Type I error (rejecting the null hypothesis when it is true) would have real consequences? Do the same for a Type II error (accepting the null hypothesis when it is false).

In the Know

The everyday context of Type I and Type II errors
The decisions and errors made in NHST can be applied to the kinds of decisions people frequently make in everyday life. For example, consider the decision made by a juror in a criminal trial. As is the case with statistics, a decision must be made on the basis of evidence: is the defendant innocent or guilty? However, the decision rests with individual jurors and does not necessarily reflect the true state of affairs: that the person really is innocent or guilty.

A juror's decision matrix is illustrated in Figure 15.12. To continue the parallel to the statistical decision, assume as the null hypothesis that the defendant is innocent (i.e. people are treated as innocent until proven guilty). Thus, rejection of the null hypothesis means deciding that the defendant is guilty, and acceptance of the null hypothesis means deciding that the defendant is innocent. The decision matrix also shows that the null hypothesis may actually be true or false.

		True state	
		Null is true (Innocent)	Null is false (Guilty)
Decision	Reject null (Find guilty)	Type I error	Correct decision
	Accept null (Find innocent)	Correct decision	Type II error

Figure 15.12 Decision matrix for a juror

There are two kinds of correct decisions and two kinds of errors like those described in statistical decisions. A Type I error is finding the defendant guilty when the person really is innocent; a Type II error is finding the defendant innocent when the person actually is guilty. In our society, Type I errors by jurors generally are considered to be more serious than Type II errors. Thus, before finding someone guilty, the juror is asked to make sure that the person is guilty "beyond reasonable doubt" or to consider that "it is better to have a hundred guilty persons go free than to find one innocent person guilty".

The decision that a doctor makes to operate or not operate on a patient provides another illustration of how a decision matrix works. The matrix is shown in Figure 15.13. Here, the null hypothesis is that no operation is necessary. The decision is whether to reject the null hypothesis and perform the operation or to accept the null hypothesis and not perform surgery. In reality, the surgeon is faced with two possibilities: either the surgery is unnecessary (the null hypothesis is true) or the patient will die without the operation (a dramatic case of the null hypothesis being false). Which error is more serious in this case? Most doctors would believe that not operating on a patient who really needs the operation – making a Type II error – is more serious than making the Type I error of performing surgery on someone who does not really need it.

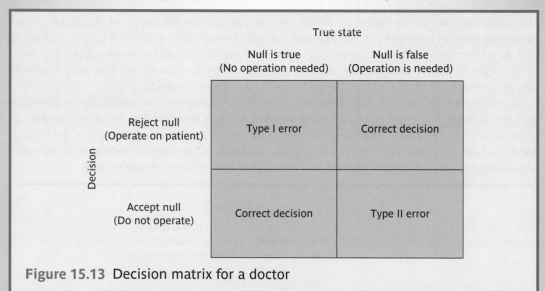

Figure 15.13 Decision matrix for a doctor

One final illustration of the use of a decision matrix involves the important decision to marry someone. If the null hypothesis is that the person is "wrong" for you, and the true state is that the person is either "wrong" or "right", you must decide whether to go ahead and marry the person. You might try to construct a decision matrix for this particular problem. Which error is more costly: a Type I error or a Type II error?

Power

Power
The probability of correctly rejecting a false null hypothesis.

Statistical **power** refers to a statistical method's ability to correctly reject the null hypothesis. A powerful statistical test is one that will find genuine effects when they are there to be found (i.e. when they truly exist in the population). If the null hypothesis is false in the population, the sample data may lead the researcher to reject the null hypothesis (correct decision) or to retain the null hypothesis (a Type II error, the probability of which is β). Therefore, the probability of arriving at a correct decision in this situation is $1 - \beta$. Mathematically, power is defined as $1 - \beta$. This means that the greater the power of a test, the higher the probability that it will detect that the null hypothesis is false. If that sounds confusing, think about it like this. Power is measured on a scale between 0 and 1. The closer to 1, the more powerful the test. Beta (β) is the probability of making a Type II error. We do not like making errors, so we want this to be as small as possible (probability, remember, is also measured on a scale between 0 and 1). Therefore, what we ideally want is the calculation of power to be as close to 1 as possible (i.e. as powerful as possible), meaning that we want β to be very very small (because 1 minus "something very very small" is going to be very close to 1).

Unlike α, which is set by the researcher, power is the result of a combination of factors. Unfortunately, researchers can control only some of these factors. Factors that influence the power of NHST are:

1 *Effect size.* If the effect size is large, a Type II error is unlikely. A large effect is like finding an enormous needle in a small haystack with plenty of helpers – i.e. it is not hard to detect. However, a small effect size may not be statistically significant with a small sample. That would be like looking for a small needle in a large haystack on your own – i.e. it is going to be very difficult to detect.

2 *Alpha level.* As you reduce your significance (alpha) level, you reduce the probability of making a Type I error (rejecting the null when it is actually true). In other words, you are making it more difficult to reject the null hypothesis (think about it like this – if you reduce your significance level, this means that you are making the "extreme" section of the curve where a significant score must be smaller and smaller). However, in doing so you are also reducing the probability of rejecting the null hypothesis when it is actually false (i.e. making a correct decision). So, by reducing your alpha level, you also reduce power, because power is the probability of correctly rejecting the null hypothesis.

3 *Sample size.* The larger the sample, the greater the power of the test. This is because larger samples provide more accurate estimates of population values.

It is becoming increasingly common for researchers to report power when presenting results. For example, the American Psychological Association's *Publication Manual* (2010) recommends that you discuss power when giving non-significant results. If your study has a high level of power and still cannot detect a significant result, this suggests that there is no effect or the effect is so small as to be of no importance. On the other hand, if your study has low power, a non-significant result raises the possibility that you have missed an effect that is actually real, i.e. committed a Type II error and accepted the null hypothesis when it is false.

But how much power should a statistical test have and how can you determine this? Unfortunately, there is no single agreed-upon desired level of power (Keppel, 1982), although a power between .70 and .90 is generally seen as acceptable (which means, roughly, that a test with power of .70 has a 70% chance of correctly rejecting the null hypothesis). If you set your alpha (significance) level and have an estimate of the effect size (usually based on previous research or theory), you can work backwards from a desired amount of power to estimate the sample size required to detect a significant result. These recommended sample sizes have been determined by statisticians and can be found in published tables or by using different computer programs. In this way, if you know your alpha level, the effect size and you have the recommended sample size, you can say that your study has the desired level power. (See Gravetter and Wallnau, 2007, or Keppel, 1982, for a discussion on how to estimate the required sample size.)

Obviously, power is an important concept – you want to be fairly confident that your statistical method can correctly reject the null hypothesis. However, too much power can be as bad as too little. If you ran enough participants, you could conceivably find statistical significance in even the most minute and trivial of effects. Your sample should be large enough to be sensitive to any effects but not so large as to produce significant but trivial results.

Selecting a statistical test

We have covered a lot in this chapter, so do not worry if you do not understand everything on first reading. We will come back to these concepts again and again over the next few chapters, in which you will be introduced to the different statistical tests. The same underlying principle applies though – each test calculates a particular statistic whose probability is then determined. If the probability is lower than your chosen significance level (usually .05), then the result is significant and the null hypothesis is rejected; if the probability is greater than your significance level, the null hypothesis is retained.

However, before getting to this stage you need to select the most appropriate statistical test. We will obviously be going through this in more detail in the following chapters, but there are a few general questions that you need to consider when identifying which test to use:

1 *What is your research question?* Your analysis should have a particular aim, so there is no point testing for relationships when you really want to test for differences. Often, your research question will refer to one of the following: testing for differences, testing for relationships or associations, or predicting scores or categories, or identifying underlying variables.

2 *What type of research design do you have?* Your research design should be directly related to the research question, so that may give you another clue about which test to select. For example, if you want to analyse data from an experiment it is likely that you will be comparing differences between different experimental conditions. Depending on your research design, you may need to answer some additional questions, e.g.:

   (a) *Between or within subjects design?* If comparing differences, you will need to identify if you are using a between-subjects (independent samples) or a within-subjects (repeated measures, paired samples) design, as this will dictate which test you can use.

   (b) *How many conditions?* If comparing differences, you will need to identify how many different conditions or groups you have.

   (c) *How many independent variables?* In some experimental designs, you can simultaneously manipulate two or more independent variables.

3 *What type of data do you have?* The scale of measurement (i.e. nominal, ordinal, interval/ratio) will dictate which statistical methods are available to you. As interval/ratio data provide the greatest level of detail, there are many more tests that can deal with this type of data than ordinal or nominal data.

4 *Parametric or non-parametric?* Some inferential statistical tests make specific assumptions about your data. Tests which make such assumptions are called parametric tests; tests which don't make these assumptions are called non-parametric tests. One of the most basic assumptions of parametric tests is that you have interval/ratio data. Parametric tests are therefore not suitable if you have nominal or ordinal data, and you should use a non-parametric

test instead. Another important assumption of parametric tests is that the sample was drawn from a normally distributed population. So if your data distribution is clearly skewed or your have outliers, this may indicate that this assumption has been violated. However, you can overcome this by transforming the data or removing outliers. Additionally, if comparing different groups, parametric tests assume that the variances of the different groups are highly similar (called homogeneity of variance). Despite their assumptions, parametric tests are usually preferred as they are more powerful than non-parametric tests (i.e. more likely to find a significant result) and also tend to be more flexible.

Figure 15.14 provides an overview of the statistical methods to be covered in the next five chapters. This will not make a lot of sense to you at the moment, but feel free to refer back to it as you go through the chapters.

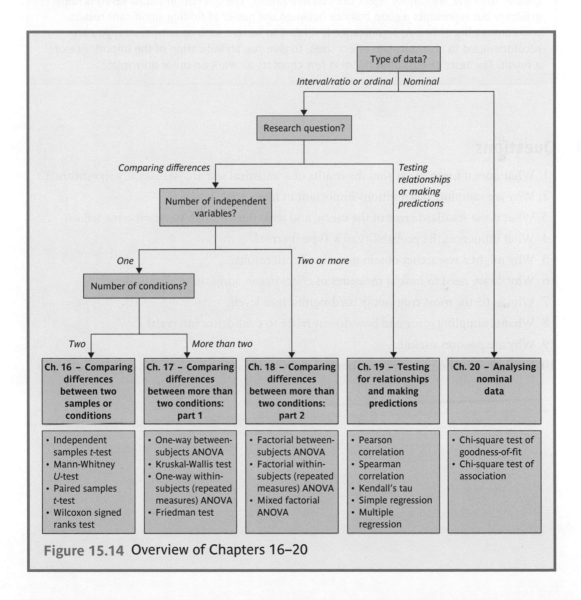

Figure 15.14 Overview of Chapters 16–20

Summary

In this chapter you have been bombarded with quite difficult – but fundamental – concepts, so it is worth taking your time and making sure that you have understood everything before moving on further with this text. Inferential statistics are the techniques we use to help us make inferences about populations based on sample data. We begin by stating hypotheses about the results and then use a statistical test to help us to determine if the null hypothesis (i.e. that there is no difference or relationship) is supported. A statistic, or characteristic of a sample, is calculated for a given set of data and its probability obtained. If the probability of a statistic is less than 5% (.05), we can say that it is highly unlikely to occur if the null hypothesis was true, and so we reject the null hypothesis and accept the alternative hypothesis as the best available explanation. If the statistic has a probability greater than 5%, we cannot reject the null hypothesis. The 5% cut-off (alpha level) is fairly arbitrary but represents a good balance between the power of finding significant results and committing errors. As significance is related to factors such as sample size, you are recommended to also calculate effect sizes, to give you an indication of the importance of a result. The tests discussed in the next few chapters all work on these principles.

Questions

1 What does it mean to say that the results of a statistical test are "statistically significant"?

2 Why are sampling distributions important in inferential statistics?

3 What is the standard error of the mean, and what does a small standard error tell us?

4 What influences the probability of a Type II error?

5 Why might a researcher obtain non-significant results?

6 Why do we need to look at measures of effect size in addition to significance?

7 Why is .05 the most commonly used significance level?

8 What is sampling error and how does it relate to confidence intervals?

9 Why are z-scores useful?

10 What proportion of scores on a normal distribution is above +1.96 SD?

Activities

1 Identify the factors that influence power and explain how power changes as each factor changes. If you were designing an experiment, what could you do to maximize power?

2 Assuming an alpha level of .05, for the following results, determine whether the following results are statistically significant or not, and identify whether the null hypothesis would be retained or not:

(a) $p = .49$

(b) $p = .0001$

(c) $p = .032$

(d) $p = .87$

(e) $p = .005$

3 In an experiment conducted by Prof. Lechiguero, one group of research participants is given 10 pages of material to proofread for errors. Another group proofreads the same material on a computer screen. The dependent variable is the number of errors detected in a 5-minute period. A .05 significance (alpha) level is used to evaluate the results.

(a) What is the null hypothesis? The alternative hypothesis?

(b) What is the Type I error? The Type II error?

(c) What is the probability of making a Type I error?

(d) What could you conclude if the results had a probability of .043?

4 Suppose that you work for the child social services agency in your county. Your job is to investigate instances of possible child neglect or abuse. After collecting your evidence, which may come from a variety of sources, you must decide whether to leave the child in the home or place the child in protective custody. Specify the null and research hypotheses in this situation. What constitutes a Type I and a Type II error? Is a Type I or Type II error the more serious error in this situation? Why?

5 Imagine that your friend wants to know about null hypothesis significance testing (yes, really!). Write a short summary of the logic behind null hypothesis significance testing that would help your friend.

Comparing Differences between Two Samples or Conditions

OVERVIEW

Before reading this chapter, you should be familiar with the concepts discussed in Chapter 15, particularly the logic of null hypothesis significance testing and interpreting probabilities. The tests discussed in this chapter are all used to compare differences between two averages. As you will see, the crucial distinction between the tests is whether the averages come from the same group of participants or different participants, and whether the parametric assumptions are met. If you want to find out how to compare differences between two samples when the outcome measure is a nominal variable (i.e. categories), you should go to Chapter 20.

OBJECTIVES

After studying this chapter and working through the exercises, you should be able to:

- Define degrees of freedom and describe how they can affect the *t*-distribution
- Describe how *t*-tests can be used to test hypotheses

- Distinguish between a one-tailed and two-tailed hypothesis in relation to *t*-tests

- Distinguish between the independent-samples *t*-test, paired-samples *t*-test, Mann-Whitney *U*-test and Wilcoxon Signed Ranks test

- Conduct analysis, interpret output and write up results for the independent-samples *t*-test, paired-samples *t*-test, Mann-Whitney *U*-test and Wilcoxon Signed Ranks test

Introduction

Many of the most widely used research designs involve looking for differences between two groups (if the design is between-subjects) or between two conditions (if the design is within-subjects). We covered designs like this in **Chapter 7**, so please have a look back if you think you need to refresh your memory or remind yourself of the different names that we use for these designs. When you use a design such as this, you are left with data from each of the groups (or conditions) and the challenge then becomes one of deciding whether or not there was a real difference between the two. You can summarize each group or condition using the descriptive statistics that we introduced in **Chapter 14**, leaving you with two means and two standard deviations. But how can we tell if the difference between the two groups or conditions is meaningful? How do we know whether our data are telling us anything interesting? This is where we use inferential statistics, and we will cover these methods of analysis in this chapter. First, however, it is time for some *t*.

ch. 7

ch. 14

The *t*-distribution

ch. 15
p.328

You may remember us mentioning something called the **t-distribution** in Chapter 15 (we were discussing calculating confidence intervals at the time, in case you have forgotten). The *t*-distribution is the sampling distribution of all possible values of a statistic called *t*. This statistic is very useful when we want to compare two means. When we want to compare two means, we can calculate a *t*-value and work out its probability based on where that value is in the *t*-distribution. Some *t*-values are very common (i.e. have a high probability of occurrence) and some are very uncommon (i.e. have a low probability). Using the probability associated with the *t*-value that we have calculated from our data, we can then make a decision about whether to retain or reject the null hypothesis.

The *t*-distribution is not just one distribution. It is actually a whole family of curves that vary according to their **degrees of freedom**. What are degrees of freedom? Degrees of freedom (*df*) can sometimes be a difficult concept to understand, but it can be defined as the number of observations that are free to vary to produce a known outcome. For example, if the mean of a group is 6.0 (the known outcome) and you know that there are five people in the group, this means that there are

> **t-distribution**
> Sampling distribution used to determine probabilities for *t*-tests.

> **Degrees of freedom**
> The number of observations free to vary; related to sample size.

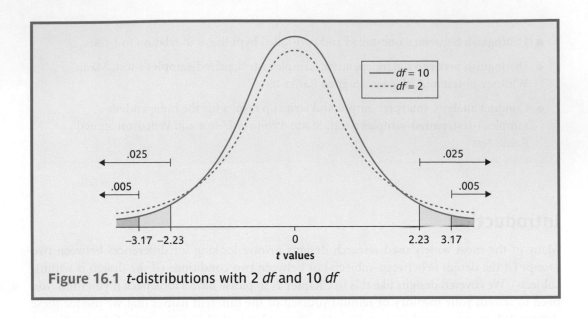

Figure 16.1 *t*-distributions with 2 *df* and 10 *df*

4 degrees of freedom. The reason for this is that, once you have any four scores (e.g. 2, 6, 8, 9), the fifth score is fixed because the mean must remain 6.0 (in this case the "unknown" score must be 5 to produce a mean of 6.0; it cannot vary given the other scores – hence the data set has 4 degrees of freedom). The larger your sample, the higher your degrees of freedom will be.

ch. 15
pp.319–326

Figure 16.1 shows two *t*-distributions, one with 10 *df* and one with 2 *df*. You may think that the curves look like **normal distributions**, but they actually have slightly fatter tails and narrower peaks than the normal curve. However, as the degrees of freedom increase, the *t*-distribution becomes more like the normal distribution, and when *df* = ∞ (infinity), the *t*-distribution and the normal distribution are identical. Like the standard normal curve, the *t*-distribution (regardless of *df*) has a mean of 0 and a standard deviation of 1.

Notice that for both of the *t*-distributions shown above, the larger the absolute value of *t*, the smaller the probability associated with that value. Larger absolute values of *t* are rare and do not appear very often (an absolute value ignores whether the number is positive or negative and just focuses on the value itself). In other words, *t*-values that are close to 0 (at the centre of the curve) will tend to have high probabilities (i.e. are very common), and more extreme *t*-values will tend to have lower probabilities (i.e. they are "rarer"). Also notice that as the degrees of freedom increase, the shape of the distribution changes and, consequently, so does the "cut-off" point for a significant value. This means that the point beyond which a value can be said to be in the most extreme 5 per cent of the distribution changes depending on the degrees of freedom (which is linked to sample size). What this all means is that when dealing with *t*-values, you must know the degrees of freedom or you will not be able to work out the probability of the *t*-value, and it is the probability of the *t*-value that tells us whether our means are significantly different from each other. Let us see how.

Test yourself

Assuming the same number of *df*, which of these *t*-values has the lowest probability?[1]

−2.5

−0.67

 0.00

 1.2

 2.3

The *t*-value

As we have already mentioned, *t*-values are often used to compare two means. For example, imagine you have conducted a study with two samples – one has a mean score of 5 and the other has a mean score of 7. Is this a statistically significant difference? It is impossible to say just by just looking at the two means. Having an indication of the spread of scores, though, would help us to determine if the difference was in fact highly unlikely or merely the result of random error or sheer chance.

This is where the *t* statistic comes in. Put simply, a *t*-value is a ratio of two aspects of the data – the difference between the means and the variability about those means:

$$t = \frac{\text{difference between means}}{\text{variability about the means}}$$

As the difference between means increases, the *t*-value will also increase. This is because the value on the top of the ratio will be large. On the other hand, *t*-values will tend to decrease as the variability about the means increases. This is because the value on the bottom of the ratio will be large. To illustrate this, have a look at the three sets of data in Table 16.1, each consisting of two groups.

In the first data-set in Table 16.1, there is relatively little variability about the mean – the scores in both groups are all very close to the mean of that group, and it looks as though there is a consistent difference in scores between the samples (with group 2 getting consistently higher scores than group 1). Thus, the *t*-value would be fairly high as the variability part of the *t*-ratio would be low. In the second set of data the means remain the same, but there is more variability in the scores in each group. The variability part of the *t*-ratio would be larger than before, and the *t*-value would become smaller as a result. The third data-set has the most variability of all and so would produce the smallest *t*-value. There appears to be a high degree of overlap between the groups, with people in group 1 scoring similarly to people in group 2; the difference

---

1   The correct answer is −2.50 as this is the most extreme value. The + or − sign does not matter.

Table 16.1 Three sample data-sets for two groups

	Low variability	Medium variability	High variability
Group 1 (Mean = 5)	5	2	1
	5	8	5
	5	7	3
	5	5	12
	4	5	2
	6	3	7
	SD = 0.4	SD = 2.28	SD = 4.05
Group 2 (Mean = 7)	7	4	1
	7	10	9
	7	5	5
	9	8	15
	6	7	4
	6	8	8
	SD = 1.10	SD = 2.19	SD = 4.86

between the means would be more likely to be due to random error than because of a consistent difference in the populations.

Testing hypotheses using *t*-tests

The name for the inferential statistical technique that uses *t*-values to test hypotheses is called, not surprisingly, a *t*-test (statisticians are not the most creative when naming their tests, as you will continue to see). There are a number of different tests, each appropriate for a different type of research design. However, the same logic applies: once you have calculated a *t*-value, you can obtain its probability based on the appropriate *t*-distribution. You can then make a decision about whether this *t*-value has a probability lower than your chosen significance level (usually .05). If the *t*-value is significant (i.e. its probability is *less* than your chosen significance level), then you can conclude that you have a statistically significant difference between the two means that you are comparing. If the *t*-value is not significant, you would have to conclude that there is no significant difference.

ch. 15
pp.330–332

As with all **NHST techniques**, we are testing the null hypothesis. (Remember that the probabilities that you obtain are referring to the probability of obtaining your statistic while *assuming the null hypothesis was true*.) In the case of *t*-tests, the null hypothesis is that there will be no difference between the means; the alternative hypothesis is that there will be a difference

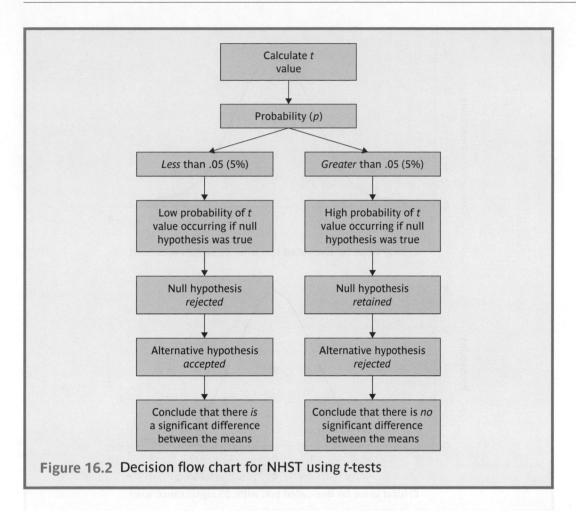

Figure 16.2 Decision flow chart for NHST using *t*-tests

between the means. So, if a *t*-value is in the extreme 5% of the distribution, this tells us that the result is highly unlikely if the null hypothesis were true. We would therefore reject the null hypothesis (assume that it is not true) and accept the alternative hypothesis (i.e. that there is a difference) as the best available explanation. If the *t*-value has a high probability, we cannot reject the null hypothesis and so have to conclude that there is no difference between the means. A simple decision flow chart is shown in Figure 16.2.

    In some cases, you may see people making a **directional** or **one-tailed hypothesis**, where they specify the direction of the difference in the alternative hypothesis. This can be contrasted with a non-directional or two-tailed test, where the alternative hypothesis makes no reference to the direction of the difference – it just states that there will be a difference. Choosing a one-tailed hypothesis over a **two-tailed hypothesis** has important implications for the significance cut-off points on *t*-distributions.

    Figure 16.3 shows the sampling distribution of *t*-values for 18 degrees of freedom. The first distribution shows the logic of a non-directional or two-tailed hypothesis. For a *t*-value to be significant, it should have a probability *(p)* of less than .05 (5 per

ch. 4
p.80

One-tailed (directional) hypothesis Alternative hypothesis in which the direction of a difference is specified.

Two-tailed (non-directional) hypothesis Alternative hypothesis in which no direction of difference is specified – both directions are covered by the hypothesis.

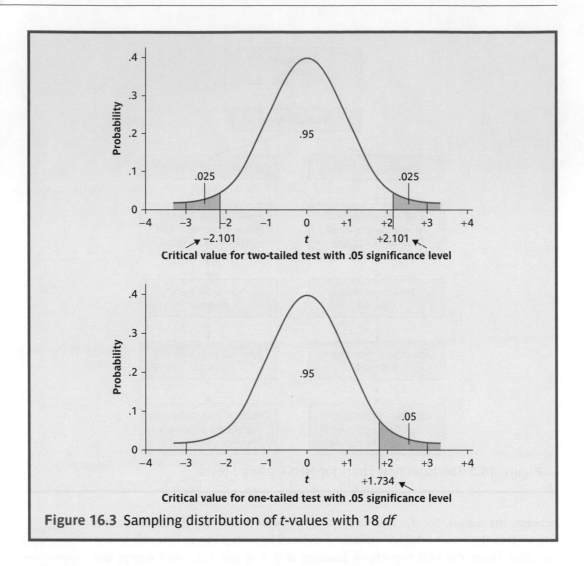

Figure 16.3 Sampling distribution of *t*-values with 18 *df*

cent). What this means is that the two means that you are comparing are significantly different from each other, and the difference is *not* just a result of chance fluctuation.

As a two-tailed hypothesis does not specify the direction of the difference, we need to look at *both* positive and negative *t*-values and so use both tails (i.e. the extreme end to the left and the extreme end to the right) of our distribution (hence "two-tailed"). In other words, for a *t*-value to be significant (in the most extreme 5%) in this situation, it needs to be either in the extreme 2.5% of the positive values or the extreme 2.5% of the negative values (2.55% + 2.5% = 5%).

The second distribution illustrates a one-tailed hypothesis, in which the direction has been specified. There is therefore no need to consult both tails of the distribution; we look at the extreme 5% in just one tail.

One thing you should notice is that the critical cut-off value of *t* changes depending on which hypothesis is being used. For the two-tailed test, the critical value of *t* is 2.101, but for the one-tailed test, it is 1.734. Suppose that you had obtained a *t*-value of 1.900. If you had initially stated a two-tailed hypothesis, this *t*-value would not be in the extreme tails of the distribution (remember, we look at the most extreme 5% of scores in both directions, above and below the mean, so our *t*-value would have to be in either the most extreme 2.5% of *t*-values below the mean or the most extreme 2.5% of *t*-values above the mean) and so would not be significant. In contrast, this particular *t*-value *would* be significant if you had used a one-tailed hypothesis (because for a one-tailed hypothesis we look only at the most extreme 5 per cent of scores in one direction, either above or below the mean).

Great, you may think – I can just use a one-tailed hypothesis and increase the likelihood of obtaining a significant result! Wrong. You are best advised to use a two-tailed hypothesis and stay away from one-tailed hypotheses unless you have very good reasons for using them. For example, imagine that you were conducting a study comparing males and females on some measure. The null hypothesis would be a statement of equality: that the males and females would not differ. A one-tailed alternative hypothesis would state the direction of a difference: for example, that males will have a higher mean than females. But what would you do if your data produced the opposite pattern – that males actually had a lower mean than females? By focusing on one tail of the distribution, you are discounting this possibility altogether and so cannot reject the null hypothesis and conclude that males score significantly lower than females (or females score significantly higher than males). However, if you had used a two-tailed, non-directional hypothesis, this would leave both options open. You should make a specific directional prediction only if you have a good reason to do so.

You should always specify your null and alternative hypotheses before conducting research, so you most definitely should not check your data first before making your hypothesis, or run a one-tailed *t*-test and a two-tailed *t*-test and then select the one which produces the most favourable result. Again, this is bad practice and would be considered dishonest. You must state your hypothesis first and stick with it. There are a few circumstances where you can justify the use of a one-tailed hypothesis, though. For example, when comparing a new product or procedure to an old one, a researcher may only want to know whether the new is better than the old. Equally, previous knowledge or research may suggest a consistent direction of difference, or you may want to test a particular theory which makes a specific prediction about the direction of difference.

If you are confused about whether to use a one-tailed or two-tailed hypothesis, it is best just to stick with two-tailed. If a *t*-value is significant using a two-tailed test, it will also be significant for a one-tailed test; the reverse, however, is not true. Additionally, if you use a two-tailed hypothesis to begin with, it will reduce the temptation to find an excuse to select a one-tailed test if you obtain a non-significant result with the two-tailed version.

Independent-samples *t*-test

Having discussed the logic behind *t*-tests, we're now ready to move on to the real thing at last! The first of the *t*-tests we will discuss is called the **independent-samples *t*-test** (you may also see it called the unrelated, unpaired, uncorrelated, between-subjects, between-groups or randomized *t*-test). We know that *t*-tests are used to compare means, so, as the name suggests, the independent-samples *t*-test is used

> **Independent-samples *t*-test** Parametric statistical test used to compare means from two separate samples.

Parametric test
A statistical test that makes assumptions about the nature of the underlying population (e.g. that scores are normally distributed).

Homogeneity of variance
The parametric assumption that variances of two samples are similar.

ch. 7
pp.114–119

to compare means from **two separate and distinct samples**. In other words, we use it to test for differences between two groups.

At the end of the previous chapter we briefly mentioned **parametric tests**, which are statistical tests that make certain assumptions about data. The independent-samples *t*-test is an example of a parametric test and it assumes that you have interval/ratio data and they are normally distributed. (You can check distributions by examining histograms.) Additionally, the independent-samples *t*-test assumes something called **homogeneity of variance**. This just means that the variance (the spread of scores around the mean) across the different conditions are equal – if one group has a very high variance and the other group has a low variance, this can cause problems for the calculation of *t*. If you use SPSS, there is a test – Levene's test for equality of variances – which can check that the data have met this assumption.[2] SPSS can also provide an alternative *t*-value if this assumption has not been met, so all is not lost. If you do not have access to a statistical computing package and are feeling brave, you can calculate Levene's test by hand (see Howell, 2007, for further details). You could also do an eyeball comparison of the variances of the two groups. If the variance of one group is much greater than the variance of the other – say by about twice as much if you are dealing with large samples or four times as much for smaller samples – this may indicate that this assumption has not been met (Coolican, 2001). If the assumptions of the *t*-test are met, you can proceed with the calculation of the *t*-value and its probability.

Example of independent-samples t-test

ch. 5
pp.91–92,
ch.7
pp.114–115,
117–119,
128–131

To illustrate an independent-samples *t*-test, let us think back to the **experiment** we introduced in Chapter 5 on whether taking part in exercise for 30 minutes might have an influence on mood. In this version of the study (which might also be called a between-subjects design) we had two groups of people. One group took part in physical activity for 30 minutes, while the other group did not. Participants were randomly allocated to one of the two groups. After 30 minutes, each participant was given a measure of their current mood, and what we are interested in is seeing if there is a significant difference between the ratings of current mood between people in the exercise condition and people in the no-exercise condition.

 Test yourself

What is the null hypothesis for this study? What is the alternative hypothesis? Is it one-tailed or two-tailed? Why?[3]

Data for the study are shown in Table 16.2.

---

2   It is easy to get confused about what Levene's test is actually doing. Remember that it is *not* testing the difference between your means. Instead, it is checking to see if the variances of the two groups are significantly different. We do not want them to be different, because then we cannot use parametric tests, so a non-significant outcome in a Levene's test is a good thing.

3   The null hypothesis is that there will be no difference between the means. The alternative hypothesis is that there will be a difference between the means. If no direction of difference is specified in the alternative hypothesis, it is a two-tailed hypothesis.

Table 16.2 Data for exercise and mood experiment

Group	Scores														
Exercise	10	10	9	9	8	8	8	8	7	7	7	6	6	6	6
	5	5	5	5	5	5	4	4	4	4	3	3	2	1	0
No exercise	10	9	8	8	8	8	6	6	5	5	5	5	5	4	4
	4	4	3	3	3	3	2	2	2	1	1	1	1	0	0

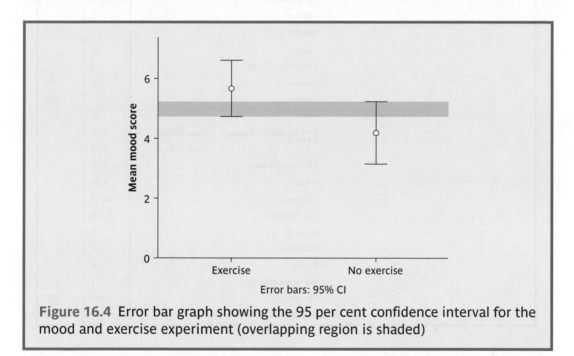

Error bars: 95% CI

Figure 16.4 Error bar graph showing the 95 per cent confidence interval for the mood and exercise experiment (overlapping region is shaded)

Before conducting any analysis, however, you should always explore the data thoroughly. The first thing to do is to obtain descriptive statistics such as the means and standard deviations. If you use SPSS you may obtain a table that looks something like this (Table 16.3; see our website for details of relevant procedures). Alternatively, you could calculate the means and standard deviations by hand.

As can be seen, the mean for the exercise group (5.67) appears to be higher than that for the no-exercise group (4.20). Is this difference significant? Remember that our sample means are only estimates of the population means, so it is useful to look at the 95 per cent confidence intervals for the means to get a better idea about the populations and if there really is a difference between them. The 95 per cent confidence interval for the exercise group is between 4.73 and 6.60, and for the no exercise group, it is between 3.17 and 5.23. Note that there is a small region of overlap between these two intervals as they both include means between 4.73 and 5.23. This can be shown graphically using an error bar graph (see Figure 16.4; the overlapping area is shaded). If there is no

Table 16.3 SPSS descriptives table for mood and exercise experiment

Descriptives

Group				Statistic	Std. Error
Mood score	Exercise	Mean		5.67	.458
		95% Confidence Interval for Mean	Lower Bound	4.73	
			Upper Bound	6.60	
		5% Trimmed Mean		5.72	
		Median		5.50	
		Variance		6.299	
		Std. Deviation		2.510	
		Minimum		0	
		Maximum		10	
		Range		10	
		Interquartile Range		4	
		Skewness		-.225	.427
		Kurtosis		-.237	.833
	No exercise	Mean		4.20	.504
		95% Confidence Interval for Mean	Lower Bound	3.17	
			Upper Bound	5.23	
		5% Trimmed Mean		4.13	
		Median		4.00	
		Variance		7.614	
		Std. Deviation		2.759	
		Minimum		0	
		Maximum		10	
		Range		10	
		Interquartile Range		4	
		Skewness		.389	.427
		Kurtosis		-.674	.833

overlap, this usually indicates that there is a significant difference between the groups. A degree of overlap, however, does not automatically mean that there is no significant difference.

The next thing to do it to check that the data meet the assumptions of the independent-samples *t*-test. First, we can conclude that we are dealing with interval/ratio data (i.e. can assume equal distances between values). A boxplot and histograms for the two samples can tell us about the data distributions (see Figures 16.5 and 16.6) and do not suggest anything odd – there is no evidence of outliers and the scores are fairly normally distributed. It looks as though the parametric assumptions have been met and we can proceed with our *t*-test.

Independent-samples t-test using SPSS

To run an independent-samples *t*-test in SPSS, please go to our website and use the online tutorial to guide you through the process. Once it has been run, you should end up with output that looks something like Table 16.4 (a and b).

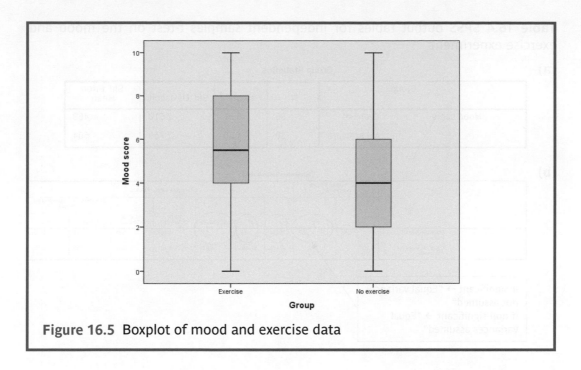

Figure 16.5 Boxplot of mood and exercise data

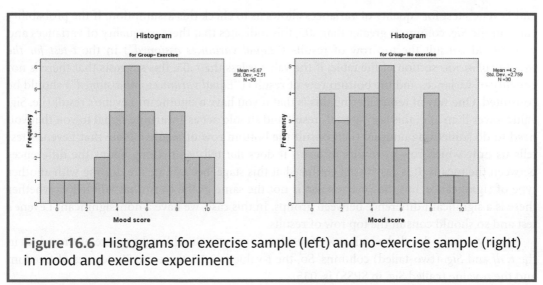

Figure 16.6 Histograms for exercise sample (left) and no-exercise sample (right) in mood and exercise experiment

You should initially check the group statistics table (Table 16.4 – a): the *N* column gives the number of cases (in this example, number of cases is simply the number of people) in each group (double-check that this is correct); the mean, standard deviation and standard error columns should be the same as in the descriptives table (Table 16.3) obtained during your preliminary analysis.

Next, we come to the independent-samples test table (Table 16.4 – b) – this is the important one! Remember that one of the assumptions of parametric tests is homogeneity of variance,

Table 16.4 SPSS output tables for independent samples *t*-test on the mood and exercise experiment

(a)

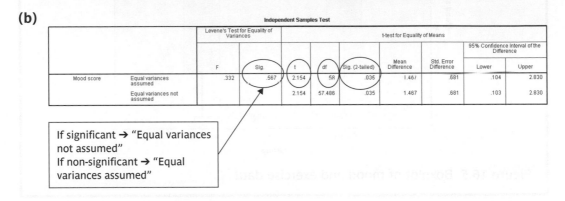

Group		N	Mean	Std. Deviation	Std. Error Mean
Mood score	Exercise	30	5.67	2.510	.458
	No exercise	30	4.20	2.759	.504

(b)

Independent Samples Test

		Levene's Test for Equality of Variances		t-test for Equality of Means						95% Confidence Interval of the Difference	
		F	Sig.	t	df	Sig. (2-tailed)	Mean Difference	Std. Error Difference	Lower	Upper
Mood score	Equal variances assumed	.332	.567	2.154	58	.036	1.467	.681	.104	2.830
	Equal variances not assumed			2.154	57.486	.035	1.467	.681	.103	2.830

If significant → "Equal variances not assumed"
If non-significant → "Equal variances assumed"

and Levene's test for equality of variances allows us to check this assumption. If the probability value in the *Sig.* column is greater than .05, this indicates that there is equality of variances and you should consult the top row of results ("*Equal variances assumed*") in the *t-test for the equality of means* section of the table; if the value is less than .05, this suggests that there is not equality of variances and the bottom row of results ("*Equal variances not assumed*") should be consulted. One way of remembering this is that if you have a significant Levene's result (i.e. Sig. value lower than .05), this is a "special" result and should act as a warning signal to you that you need to do something unusual (i.e. consult the bottom row of results). Note that Levene's test tells us only which row of results to use – it does *not* tell us anything about the differences between the means. It is easy to get confused at this stage, because we are dealing with another type of significance, but the Levene's test is not the same as the *t*-test that will tell us whether there is a significant difference between groups. In this case, we have a non-significant Levene's test and so should consult the top row of results.

Once you have decided which row of results to use, you should make a note of the values in the *t*, *df* and *Sig.* (two-tailed) columns. So, the *t*-value is 2.15, there are 58 degrees of freedom and the *p*-value (called Sig. in SPSS) is .035.

STOP & Think

Does this *p*-value indicate a significant difference?

As the *p*-value is less than .05, we can conclude that the obtained *t*-value is unlikely to have occurred if the null hypothesis was true – it suggests that there is a real difference between the two groups. In other words, there is a significant difference, with the exercise group scoring significantly higher on the measure of current mood compared to the no-exercise group.

The column headed **95% confidence interval of the difference** confirms this. This column gives us the upper and lower bounds for the 95% CI for the difference between the means, which are 0.10 and 2.83. Note that this confidence interval does not include the null hypothesis value of a difference of 0. In other words, we can be pretty confident that the mean difference between the populations is not 0, and conclude that there is a difference in the population means.

Effect size measure for independent-samples t-test

We do not just stop here, though. Recall that NHST tells us only about probability and nothing about the size of the effect being studied; we also need to use an **effect size**. For the independent samples *t*-test, the most appropriate effect size measure is **Cohen's *d***. Cohen's *d* expresses effect size in terms of standard deviation units. A *d*-value of 1.0 tells you that the means are 1 *SD* apart; a *d*-value of 0.2 tells you that the means are 0.2 *SD* apart, and so on.

> **Cohen's *d***
> An effect size measure suitable for *t*-tests.

Unfortunately, SPSS does not calculate Cohen's *d* for you so this is one thing you will need to do by hand, but it is very straightforward and can be done quickly. Cohen's *d* can be calculated most simply using the formula in Figure 16.7 with values from the *t*-test (see Rosenthal and Rosnow, 1991):

$$d = \frac{2t}{\sqrt{df}}$$

t value multiplied by 2

Divided by the square root of the degrees of freedom

Figure 16.7 Formula for Cohen's *d* for independent-samples *t*-test

So, for our current study, the effect size would be:

$$d = \frac{2t}{\sqrt{df}} = \frac{2(2.154)}{\sqrt{58}} = \frac{4.308}{7.616} = 0.566$$

Cohen (1988) categorized *d*-values between 0.2 and 0.5 as indicating a small effect size, values between 0.5 and 0.8 were medium effects, and *d*-values greater than 0.8 represented large effect sizes. So, the effect size for our study represents a medium effect.

Independent-samples t-test by hand

If you want to do the independent-samples *t*-test by hand, the formula is essentially the difference between the means divided by the variability about those means. If you have equal sample sizes, the formula in Figure 16.8 is appropriate:

ch. 15
pp.334 – 335

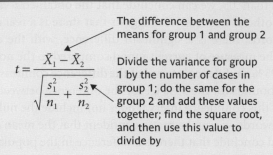

The difference between the means for group 1 and group 2

$$t = \frac{\bar{X}_1 - \bar{X}_2}{\sqrt{\dfrac{s_1^2}{n_1} + \dfrac{s_2^2}{n_2}}}$$

Divide the variance for group 1 by the number of cases in group 1; do the same for the group 2 and add these values together; find the square root, and then use this value to divide by

Figure 16.8 Formula for the independent samples *t*-test, with equal sample sizes

If you do not remember how to calculate the mean and variance, please look back at Chapter 14. For our mood and exercise study, the means and variance for group 1 are 5.67 and 6.30, respectively, and for group 2 are 4.20 and 7.61, respectively. Both groups had 30 cases. Substituting these values into the equation, you would have:

ch. 14
pp.286–28
293–294

$$t = \frac{5.67 - 4.20}{\sqrt{\dfrac{6.30}{30} + \dfrac{7.61}{30}}} = \frac{1.47}{\sqrt{0.21 + 0.25}} = \frac{1.47}{\sqrt{0.46}} = \frac{1.47}{0.68} = 2.16$$

Next, work out your degrees of freedom (*df*), which is just the total number of cases minus 2 (i.e. 60 − 2 = 58). Then go to a table of critical *t* values (Appendix C) and find the critical value for your *df* and significance level. If your actual *df* is not listed, use the next lowest *df* value instead, or try to find a more detailed table. For example, for a significance level of .05 and *df* = 55, the critical value is 2.004. Our *t*-value is more extreme than this critical value and so is significant (i.e. in the extreme 5 per cent of the distribution).

If you have unequal sample sizes, however, you need to use a slightly different formula to the one shown above. So, instead of using the individual group variances, you use something called the pooled variance, which is an average of the two variances and takes into account the different sample sizes. See Figure 16.9 for the formula for the pooled variance.

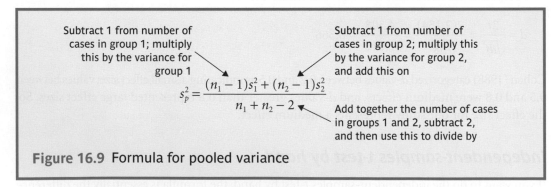

Subtract 1 from number of cases in group 1; multiply this by the variance for group 1

Subtract 1 from number of cases in group 2; multiply this by the variance for group 2, and add this on

$$s_p^2 = \frac{(n_1 - 1)s_1^2 + (n_2 - 1)s_2^2}{n_1 + n_2 - 2}$$

Add together the number of cases in groups 1 and 2, subtract 2, and then use this to divide by

Figure 16.9 Formula for pooled variance

Once you have calculated the pooled variance, you can substitute this in the *t*-test equation (see Figure 16.10).

The difference between the means for group 1 and group 2

$$t = \frac{\bar{X}_1 - \bar{X}_2}{\sqrt{\frac{s_p^2}{n_1} + \frac{s_p^2}{n_2}}}$$

Divide the pooled variance by the number of cases in group 1; do the same for group 2 and add these values together; find the square root, and then use this value to divide by

Figure 16.10 Formula for the independent samples *t*-test, with unequal sample sizes

So, for our mood and exercise data, the pooled variance would be:

$$s_p^2 = \frac{(n_1 - 1)s_1^2 + (n_2 - 1)s_2^2}{n_1 + n_2 - 2} = \frac{(30 - 1)6.30 + (30 - 1)7.61}{30 + 30 - 2}$$

$$= \frac{(29)6.30 + (29)7.61}{58} = \frac{182.70 + 220.69}{58} = \frac{403.39}{58} = 6.96$$

Using this value in the equation you have:

$$t = \frac{5.67 - 4.20}{\sqrt{\frac{6.96}{30} + \frac{6.96}{30}}} = \frac{1.47}{\sqrt{0.23 + 0.23}} = \frac{1.47}{\sqrt{0.46}} = \frac{1.47}{0.68} = 2.16$$

the same as before.

Calculating *t* by hand is not really that difficult – there are just a lot of steps – but you can see why many people prefer to use a statistical package.

Reporting results from independent-samples t-test

All that remains is to present your results in the most appropriate manner. There is a standard format for reporting *t*-test results, which includes the *t*-, *df* and *p*-values (see Figure 16.11).

Put *df*-value here, in the brackets

Put *t*-value here

$$t\,(df) = \underline{\hspace{2cm}}, \quad p = \underline{\hspace{2cm}}$$

Put *p*-value (Sig.) here

Figure 16.11 General format for reporting *t*-test results

With the values for the current study, this would give you:

$$t\,(58) = 2.51, \quad p = .035$$

If you calculated *t* by hand, you would need to write $p < .05$ (*p* is less than .05) or $p > .05$ (*p* is greater than .05), as you will not know the exact *p*-value. You are also strongly recommended to give the effect size and also to discuss the 95% CI for the difference. Thus, the results for the current study may be written up as:

> The mean mood rating for the no-exercise group ($M = 4.20$, $SD = 2.76$) was significantly lower than the mean mood rating for the exercise group ($M = 5.67$, $SD = 2.51$), $t(58) = 2.51$, $p = .035$. The 95% confidence interval for the difference between the population means was between 0.10 and 2.83. Cohen's $d = 0.57$, indicating a medium effect size.

In the Know

An example from the literature: contrasting two groups

Spinal cord injuries (SCIs) represent a major source of physical disabilities (Hess, Marwitz & Kreutzer, 2003). These injuries are often the result of car accidents or falls that involve rapid deceleration of the body and may result in mild traumatic brain injury (MTBI). Hess et al. note that when a patient with an SCI is taken into hospital, the possibility that MTBI exists is often overlooked because of the seriousness of SCIs. Often, patients with SCI show cognitive impairments normally associated with MTBI, such as memory loss, attention deficits and problems with processing information (Hess et al., 2003). The problem is that it is sometimes difficult to determine whether cognitive impairments are the result of MTBI or the emotional trauma associated with SCI.

David Hess, Jennifer Marwitz and Jeffrey Kreutzer (2003) conducted a study to differentiate between patients with MTBI (without SCI) and patients with SCI. Participants were patients with SCI or MTBI who had been treated at a medical centre. Participants' neuropsychological functioning was measured using a battery of tests assessing attention (two tests), motor speed, verbal learning, verbal memory (two tests), visuospatial skills and word fluency. Mean scores were computed on each measure for patients with SCI and MTBI. Hess et al. used a series of *t*-tests to determine if the SCI and MTBI patients differed significantly on any of the neuropsychological tests. They found significant differences between the two groups on 5 of the 10 tests. The results (shown in Table 16.5) showed that, as a rule, patients with SCI performed better than patients with MTBI. They also found that a high percentage of SCI patients showed significant impairment on several of the cognitive measures (even though they scored better than the MTBI patients). Hess et al. suggest that SCI patients might benefit from a comprehensive rehabilitation programme that targets cognitive functioning as well as emotional well-being.

Table 16.5 Means and *t*-values from the five significant differences found by Hess et al. (2003)

Test	SCI	MTBI	*t* (*df*)
Written attention test	41.6	30.4	2.40 (18)
Motor speed	91.4	126.1	−2.20 (31)
Verbal learning	47.1	37.9	2.40 (34)
Verbal memory (immediate recall)	25.9	18.7	3.16 (49)
Verbal memory (delayed recall)	21.4	10.7	4.73 (44)

Paired-samples *t*-test

ch. 7
p.125 – 135

A **paired-samples *t*-test** (sometimes called a repeated measures *t*-test or a within-subjects *t*-test) is used when you are comparing two means from samples which are not independent, but are related in some way. Most often, this just means that the same people have taken part under both conditions and so you are comparing the scores of one group of people under one condition with their scores under another condition. This is what is also called a repeated-measures or within-subjects design. Samples may also be related if participants have been matched for some reason such as being in the same family, the same income group, or because they had similar scores on a pre-test. It is for these reasons that you may sometimes see a paired-samples *t*-test called a correlated, related, dependent, within-subject or split plot *t*-test.

> **Paired-samples
> *t*-test**
> Parametric statistical
> test used to compare
> two means from
> the same sample or
> from paired or
> matched samples.

Just like the independent-samples *t*-test, the paired-samples *t*-test involves the calculation of a *t*-value and its probability. If the *t*-value has a probability less than .05, we can say that there the result is unlikely if the null hypothesis was true and we can conclude that we have a significant difference between the means.

However, the method used to calculate the *t*-value is different for the paired-samples *t*-test because it takes into account the fact that like is being compared with like. What this means is that all the random fluctuations that might exist when you have different people in each group are eliminated, because the same people are being used in two conditions. So, for example, participant A is being compared to herself, the only difference is that she is being measured in a different condition. Consequently, the paired-samples *t*-test tends to produce larger *t*-values than the independent-samples *t*-test when applied to the same data, thus making the paired-samples *t*-test more sensitive to any effect of the independent variable.

Example of paired-samples t-test

We can illustrate a paired-samples *t*-test using our mood and exercise study (again). Instead of one group taking part in exercise and a completely different group doing no exercise, imagine that we had one group of 15 participants who each took part in both conditions. In other words, each individual rated their mood twice: once after taking part in exercise and once after no exercise. The data are shown in Tables 16.6 and 16.7 and Figure 16.12.

As always, the first part of your analysis should be to explore the data (e.g. using the Explore procedure in SPSS – see our website for details). Examples of output are shown below.

Table 16.6 Data for exercise and mood experiment															
Condition							Scores								
Participant	1	2	3	4	5	6	7	8	9	10	11	12	13	14	15
Exercise	10	7	9	3	6	9	2	7	7	4	8	8	5	6	9
No exercise	9	7	8	4	6	7	4	4	6	2	5	6	4	3	9

Table 16.7 Descriptive statistics for mood and exercise study (within subjects)

Descriptives

			Statistic	Std. Error
Mood score after exercise	Mean		6.67	.607
	95% Confidence Interval for Mean	Lower Bound	5.37	
		Upper Bound	7.97	
	5% Trimmed Mean		6.74	
	Median		7.00	
	Variance		5.524	
	Std. Deviation		2.350	
	Minimum		2	
	Maximum		10	
	Range		8	
	Interquartile Range		4	
	Skewness		-.604	.580
	Kurtosis		-.411	1.121
Mood score after no exercise	Mean		5.60	.550
	95% Confidence Interval for Mean	Lower Bound	4.42	
		Upper Bound	6.78	
	5% Trimmed Mean		5.61	
	Median		6.00	
	Variance		4.543	
	Std. Deviation		2.131	
	Minimum		2	
	Maximum		9	
	Range		7	
	Interquartile Range		3	
	Skewness		.147	.580
	Kurtosis		-.850	1.121

STOP & Think

Based on the descriptive statistics, can you draw any preliminary conclusions about differences between the exercise and no-exercise conditions in this study?

 Once you are sure that the assumptions of the test have been met, you can move on to run the paired-samples *t*-test.

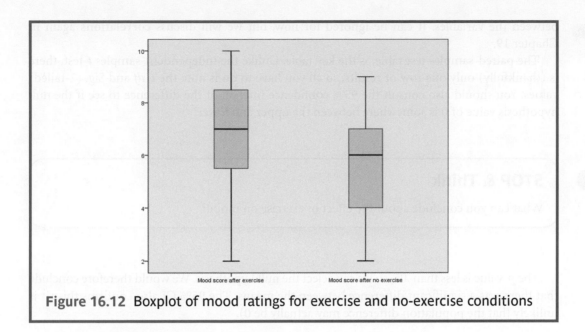

Figure 16.12 Boxplot of mood ratings for exercise and no-exercise conditions

SPSS output for paired-samples t-test

The SPSS output should look something like Table 16.8.

The paired-samples statistics table, gives the descriptive statistics – does it match the previous descriptives? The paired-samples correlations table, gives details on the relationship

Table 16.8 SPSS output tables for paired-samples *t*-test

Paired Samples Statistics

		Mean	N	Std. Deviation	Std. Error Mean
Pair 1	Mood score after exercise	6.67	15	2.350	.607
	Mood score after no exercise	5.60	15	2.131	.550

Paired Samples Correlations

		N	Correlation	Sig.
Pair 1	Mood score after exercise & Mood score after no exercise	15	.784	.001

Paired Samples Test

		Paired Differences					t	df	Sig. (2-tailed)
		Mean	Std. Deviation	Std. Error Mean	95% Confidence Interval of the Difference Lower	Upper			
Pair 1	Mood score after exercise - Mood score after no exercise	1.067	1.486	.384	.243	1.890	2.779	14	.015

between the variables. It can be ignored for now, but we will discuss **correlations** again in Chapter 19.

The paired-samples test table, is the key table. Unlike the independent-samples t-test, there is (thankfully) only one row of results, so all you have to do is note the t, df and Sig. (2-tailed) values. You should also consult the 95% confidence interval of the difference to see if the null hypothesis value of 0 is somewhere between the upper and lower.

STOP & Think

What can you conclude about the effect of exercise on mood?

The p-value is less than .05, so we can reject the null hypothesis. We would therefore conclude that there was a significant difference between the means. The 95% CI also confirms this (it is unlikely that the population difference may actually be 0).

Effect size measure for paired-samples t-test

You should also think about calculating an effect size. The formula for calculating Cohen's d for a paired-samples t-test is different to that for an independent-samples t-test, but still uses information provided in the output tables (Figure 16.13).

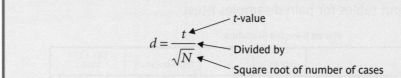

Figure 16.13 Formula for Cohen's d for a paired-samples t-test

Thus, for the within-subjects mood and exercise experiment, the effect size would be:

$$d = \frac{t}{\sqrt{N}} = \frac{2.78}{\sqrt{15}} = \frac{2.78}{3.87} = 0.72$$

This represents a large effect size – the independent variable had a strong effect.

Paired-samples t-test by hand

If you plan on doing the paired-samples t-test by hand, you will need to calculate difference, or D, scores (i.e. the difference between a participant's scores in both conditions). For our mood and exercise example, the differences are shown, using data in Table 16.9, below.

Table 16.9 Data for exercise and mood experiment, with difference scores

Condition	Scores														
Participant	1	2	3	4	5	6	7	8	9	10	11	12	13	14	15
Exercise	10	7	9	3	6	9	2	7	7	4	8	8	5	6	9
No exercise	9	7	8	4	6	7	4	4	6	2	5	6	4	3	9
D	1	0	1	−1	0	2	−2	3	1	2	3	2	1	3	0

The next stage is calculating the mean and standard deviation of these *D*-scores – just treat them as you would with any ordinary score. Remember, to find the mean, you add all the scores together and divide by the number of scores, giving you a mean *D* of 1.067 for our data. To find the standard deviation, you use the following formula (shown in Chapter 14).

$$Standard\ deviation = \sqrt{\frac{\sum (X - \bar{X})^2}{N - 1}}$$

The first thing you do is find the difference between each score and the mean; in this case, this would be the difference between each *D*-score and the mean *D*. You then square each difference and add them all together; divide by the number of scores minus 1, and then find the square root. Using our data, this should give you 1.49.

Getting the mean and standard deviation of the *D*-scores is the difficult bit. You are now ready to move on to the *t*-test formula at last (Figure 16.14).

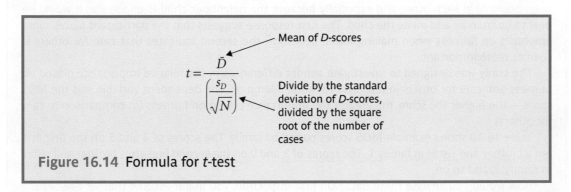

Figure 16.14 Formula for *t*-test

So, with our example data, we would have:

$$t = \frac{\bar{D}}{\left(\frac{s_D}{\sqrt{N}}\right)} = \frac{1.067}{\left(\frac{1.49}{\sqrt{15}}\right)} = \frac{1.067}{\left(\frac{1.49}{3.87}\right)} = \frac{1.067}{0.38} = 2.77$$

To calculate *df* for a paired-samples *t*-test substract 1 from the number of participants. Therefore, for our study *df* = 14 (i.e. 15-1). The critical value of *t* for 14 degrees of freedom and a .05 significance level is 2.131(from the table of critical *t*-values – Appendix C); our *t*-value is more extreme than this and is therefore significant.

Reporting the results of a paired-samples t-test

You write up the paired-samples *t*-test result in exactly the same way as for an independent-samples *t*-test. The results of the paired-samples *t*-test could be written up like this:

> The mean mood rating for the exercise condition (*M* = 6.67, *SD* = 2.35) was significantly higher than the mean mood rating for the no-exercise condition (*M* = 5.60, *SD* = 2.13), *t* (14) = 2.78, *p* = .015. The 95% confidence interval for the difference was between 0.24 and 1.89. Cohen's *d* = 0.72, indicating a large effect size.

In the Know

Paired-samples t-test versus independent-samples t-test

Jaffee and Hyde (2000) conducted a study looking at gender differences on a test that measures the importance of fairness in resolving moral dilemmas. Participants were assessed using the Moral Orientation Scale (MOS; Yacker & Weinberg, 1990), which consists of 12 scenarios about children's activities and the response that a parent or caregiver might make. Each scenario sets up a moral dilemma and participants select the choice they consider the best. For example, one scenario describes plans for a birthday party. The birthday child wants to invite most of his or her classmates, but not a nearby neighbour child who is also in the class. One response is that the neighbour child should be invited because it is not fair to exclude just one child. Another response is that neighbours help each other, and especially because the neighbour child is unpopular, it would be best to be friendly and invite the child. The first response suggests that the participant places more emphasis on fairness when making moral decisions; the second indicates that care for others is seen as more important.

The study was designed to investigate gender differences in the relative importance placed on fairness and care for others in response to moral dilemmas. The dependent variable was the MOS score – the higher the score, the greater the importance placed on fairness (in comparison to care for others).

Table 16.10 shows example MOS scores paired by family. The scores of 4 and 3 on the first line are a brother and sister in family 1. The scores of 3 and 0 on the second line are a brother and sister in family 2, and so on.

How would you analyse these data? On first inspection, you might assume that we are dealing with two separate groups (male and female) and so should use the independent-samples *t*-test. However, we are actually dealing with paired samples here – we are not comparing just any group of males with any group of females, but brothers with their own sisters. You may find it helpful to think of each brother–sister pair as an individual case, much like one participant being tested under two different conditions. Instead of one participant generating two scores, we have one family generating two scores.

Table 16.10 Moral Orientation Scale scores for males and females

Family	Males	Females
1	4	3
2	3	0
3	4	4
4	11	6
5	7	10
6	1	4
7	9	7
8	0	3
9	5	6
10	2	1
11	7	5
12	10	8

Note: Higher scores indicate greater importance of fairness compared to care for others.

Non-parametric equivalents of *t*-tests

As mentioned earlier, the *t*-tests make assumptions about the data. But what do you do if your data are not normally distributed or are not even interval/ratio in the first place? All is not lost – there are non-parametric equivalents of the independent- and paired-samples *t*-tests. However, when using non-parametric tests you sacrifice some power and are generally less likely to find a significant difference if there really is one.

STOP & Think

What type of error are you making if you fail to find an effect when it really exists?

Mann-Whitney U-*test*

The non-parametric equivalent of the independent-samples *t*-test is the **Mann-Whitney U-test**. So, if you are comparing two groups and either have ordinal data or interval/ratio data that do not meet the parametric assumptions, the Mann-Whitney *U*-test is the best option for you. Note, however, that the Mann-Whitney *U*-test works best when there are few, if any, tied scores. Tied scores occur when people have the same scores – this is likely to occur if you have a limited range of available scores.

Mann-Whitney U-test
Non-parametric test used to compare averages from two independent samples; the non-parametric equivalent of the independent-samples *t*-test.

The logic behind this test is fairly simple. All the scores from both groups are combined and ranked in order from lowest to highest. If there is a consistent difference between the groups, then the ranks for the scores in one group should be consistently above the ranks from the other groups, rather than being randomly distributed (in other words, we're looking to see if one group has consistently lower ranked scores than the other). A U-value is then calculated for each group by adding together the ranks for each group, and the probability of the smallest U-value is obtained. If this p-value is less than .05, we have a significant difference.

Example of Mann-Whitney U-test

The Mann-Whitney U-test can be demonstrated using the following example. Imagine that an experiment was designed to examine the influence of perceived reward on problem solving. Fourteen participants were randomly assigned to one of two groups. Everyone received the same difficult problem to solve, but one group were told that they would receive a monetary reward if they solved the problem; the other group (the control) were not told anything about a reward. The times taken to solve the problem (in minutes) are shown in Table 16.11.

On inspection of a boxplot of the data (Figure 16.15), it is clear that the data are not normally distributed – there are outliers – and a non-parametric test should be used.[4]

Calculating Mann-Whitney U by hand

The first step is to combine all of the scores and put them in rank order (from lowest to highest; Table 16.12). For each participant, give a score indicating the number of people in the other group who have a higher rank. For example, the participant in the No reward group who is ranked first has 7 people in the Reward group who have a higher ranking and so receives a score of 7. The next participant receives a score of 7, the next 6, and so on.

You then just add up the points for one group (e.g. No reward = 7 + 6 + 5 + 4 + 4 + 3 + 1 = 30). This is what we call a U-value. The process is then repeated for the other group (e.g. Reward = 6 + 5 + 4 + 2 + 1 + 1 + 0 = 19). Whichever of the U-values is the smallest is the test value (i.e. in this case it would be 19).

While this may seem simple enough, calculating U can be quite time-consuming if you have a large sample size. Consequently, there is also a formula that you can use to calculate U for each sample (see Figure 16.16).

Table 16.11 Time taken to solve problem

Condition	Time taken to solve problem (minutes)						
Reward	13.21	3.25	9.02	21.37	10.45	7.66	5.54
No reward	15.55	8.54	1.32	3.56	7.55	10.18	8.05

---

4 Alternatively, you could try to transform the data to give a normal distribution, or remove the outliers altogether. However, using a non-parametric test keeps all of the available data in their original form.

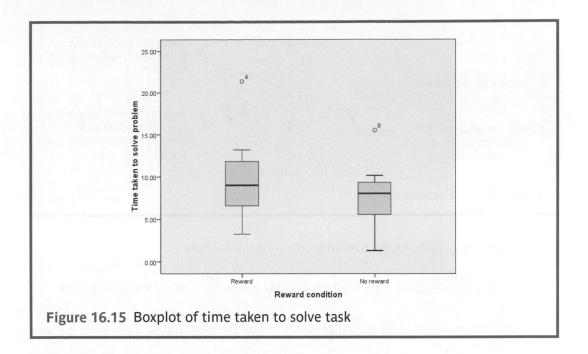

Figure 16.15 Boxplot of time taken to solve task

Table 16.12 Ranks, times and points for "Reward" and "No reward" groups

Rank position	Time	Group	Points
1	1.32	No reward	7
2	3.25	Reward	6
3	3.56	No reward	6
4	5.54	Reward	5
5	7.55	No reward	5
6	7.66	Reward	4
7	8.05	No reward	4
8	8.54	No reward	4
9	9.02	Reward	2
10	10.18	No reward	3
11	10.45	Reward	1
12	13.21	Reward	1
13	15.55	No reward	1
14	21.37	Reward	0

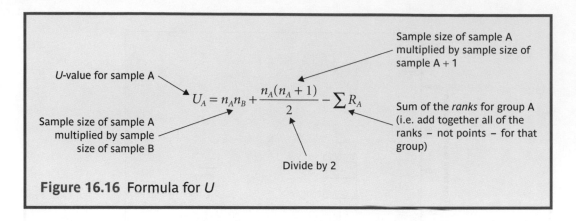

Figure 16.16 Formula for U

Therefore, the U-value for the Reward group using this formula is:

$$U_A = 7(7) + \frac{7(8)}{2} - (2 + 4 + 6 + 9 + 11 + 12 + 14) = 49 + \frac{56}{2} - 58 = 49 + 28 - 58 = 19$$

To calculate the U-value for the other group (group B), the formula is the same but uses group B values:

$$U_B = n_A n_B + \frac{n_B(n_B + 1)}{2} - \sum R_B$$

So, the U-value for the No reward group would be calculated as:

$$U_B = 7(7) + \frac{7(8)}{2} - (1 + 3 + 5 + 7 + 8 + 10 + 13) = 49 + \frac{56}{2} - 47 = 49 + 28 - 47 = 30$$

You should select the lower of your two U-values (i.e. 19), consult a table of U-values (Appendix F), and determine whether your U-value is more or less than the critical value in the table. If your U-value is greater than the critical value, you have a significant result. For a significance level of .05 and with 7 cases in each group, the critical value of U is 8, so we have a significant result.

SPSS output for Mann-Whitney U-test

To run the Mann-Whitney U-test in SPSS, please use the online tutorial. In newer versions of SPSS, output consists of a table which gives you the p-value and helpfully tells you if your null hypothesis should be retained or rejected (Table 16.13a). If you double-click on the table in your output, you can get more detailed information on the test (Table 16.13b). Take a note of the number of cases (N), the mean rank (i.e. the sum of the ranks divided by N), the value of Mann-Whitney U and its probability.

Reporting results from a Mann-Whitney U-test

There are no strict rules about how to report the result of a Mann-Whitney U-test apart from that you should include the U-value and its probability. It is also a good idea to include additional

Table 16.13 SPSS output for Mann-Whitney *U*-test

(a)

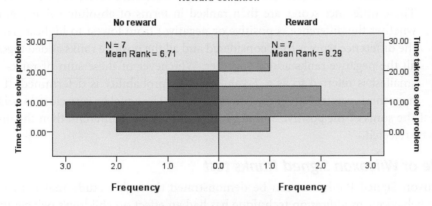

Hypothesis Test Summary

	Null Hypothesis	Test	Sig.	Decision
1	The distribution of Time taken to solve problem is the same across categories of Reward condition.	Independent-Samples Mann-Whitney U Test	.482	Retain the null hypothesis.

Asymptotic significances are displayed. The significance level is .05.

(b)   **Independent-Samples Mann-Whitney U Test**

Reward condition

	Total N	14
	Mann-Whitney U	19.000
	Wilcoxon W	47.000
	Test Statistic	19.000
	Standard Error	7.826
	Standardized Test Statistic	-.703
	Asymptotic Sig. (2-sided test)	.482
	Exact Sig. (2-sided test)	.535

information such as the sample sizes and sum of ranks. The results for the example could therefore have been written up as:

> The times taken to solve the problem for the Reward group ($n = 7$, mean rank $= 8.29$) and the No reward group ($n = 7$, mean rank $= 6.71$) were compared using a Mann-Whitney U-test. No significant difference was found, $U = 19$, $p = .482$.

Wilcoxon Signed Ranks test

Wilcoxon Signed Ranks test
Non-parametric test used to compare two averages from the same sample, or paired or matched samples; the non-parametric equivalent of the paired-samples t-test.

The **Wilcoxon Signed Ranks test** is the most appropriate non-parametric equivalent of the paired-samples t-test. Therefore, if you are analysing data from a study with two paired samples and the parametric assumptions have not been met, you should consider using the Wilcoxon Signed Ranks test.

In this test, for each pair of scores, the difference between them is calculated. These difference scores are then ranked in terms of absolute value (i.e. ignoring whether the difference is positive or negative) from lowest to highest. The sign of the difference score is then considered and all the positive ranks added together and all the negative ranks added together. Whichever of these sum of ranks values is smallest is referred to as a T-value, and its probability is determined. If the null hypothesis was true, then the two sums should be equal or very close to being equal. However, if the sums of the positive and negative ranks are very different, then the null hypothesis can be rejected.

Example of Wilcoxon Signed Ranks test

The Wilcoxon Signed Ranks test can be demonstrated through a study that is investigating whether a behaviour modification technique has had an effect on children's behaviour. Twelve sets of parents were asked to rate their children's behaviour on a scale of 1 to 20 (1 indicating that the child's behaviour is much worse than that of their peers, 20 indicating that the child's behaviour is much better than that of their peers). The parents were then given training on how to use a time-out technique to deal with bad behaviour – if their child misbehaved, they would be removed from the situation for a specified amount of time. After six weeks of implementing the time-out technique, the parents were once again asked to rate their child's behaviour to see if the time out had had any effect. The data for the 12 cases are shown in Table 16.14.

In this study, the researcher considered the ratings to be measured on an **ordinal scale** (i.e. we cannot assume equal distances between values and so cannot say, for example, that the distance between ratings of 1 and 6 are the same as the distance between ratings of 8 and 13). Consequently, the researcher opted for a non-parametric test. (Ratings scales are quite a grey area when it comes to deciding what type of data is being measured and which type of test to use. Some people think that rating scales should always be treated as ordinal and so should be analysed using non-parametric tests, whereas others think that it is acceptable to treat them as interval/ratio and use a parametric test. Unfortunately there is no easy answer, but if you are using a well-established, standardized measure, then you would be justified in considering the data to be interval/ratio. Also think about whether the distances between values are meaningful – for an interval/ratio scale they should be.)

ch. 4
pp.62–68

Table 16.14 Parent ratings of child's behaviour before and after using the time-out technique

Before using time-out technique	After using time-out technique
3	8
11	15
6	15
8	6
6	6
13	12
4	11
7	8
9	17
10	7
5	7
4	10

Calculating the Wilcoxon Signed Ranks test by hand

The first thing to do is to calculate the difference for each pair of scores. In the example below, the "before" score has been subtracted from the "after" score because this follows the expected direction of change. You should then rank the difference scores, ignoring the + or − signs and leaving out any 0 differences. Note that if you have any differences that are the same, identify the ranks that these values cover and choose the midpoint. For example, there are two difference scores with absolute values of 1 (absolute values are values that don't take the + or − signs into consideration). These two scores would cover the ranks of 1 and 2, so they would both receive the midpoint of these ranks, 1.5. You would then rank the next highest score as 3 (because 1 and 2 have already been used). As you can see, the next highest absolute value is 2, and there are two cases with a difference score of 2. These two cases would be given a rank of 3.5 (halfway between 3 and 4). We would then start ranking again from 5, and so on. This is shown in Table 16.15.

Once you have ranked the differences, you should then add together the ranks for all the positive difference scores and repeat for the negative difference scores. Whichever of these sum of ranks values is *smaller* is the *T*-value, whose probability will be determined.

In the example, the sum of ranks of positive differences would be: 7 + 6 + 11 + 9 + 1.5 + 10 + 3.5 + 8 = 56, and for negative differences it would be: 3.5 + 1.5 + 5 = 10. *T* is therefore 10 (the smaller of the two sum of ranks).

You can then inspect a table of critical values to determine if the *T*-value is statistically significant or not. For your specific number of cases (remember not to include any cases with a 0 difference) and alpha level, identify the critical value. If your *T*-value is less than this critical value, then you have a significant result. In our case, the critical value of *T* for 11 cases is 10; we have a significant result (only just!).

Table 16.15 Difference scores between "before" and "after" the time-out intervention, and the ranks of the difference scores

Case	Before	After	Difference	Rank
1	3	8	+5	7
2	11	15	+4	6
3	6	15	+9	11
4	8	6	−2	3.5
5	6	6	0	
6	13	12	−1	1.5
7	4	11	+7	9
8	7	8	+1	1.5
9	9	17	+8	10
10	10	7	−3	5
11	5	7	+2	3.5
12	4	10	+6	8

SPSS output for Wilcoxon Signed Ranks test

The SPSS procedure for the Wilcoxon Signed Ranks test can be found on our website. The output for the Wilcoxon Signed Ranks test is shown in Table 16.16. The first table tells you whether you should retain or reject the null hypothesis, and the rest of the output provides more detail on the test (remember to note the *p*-value).

> **STOP & Think**
>
> What is the *p*-value? Do we have a significant difference?

Reporting results from a Wilcoxon Signed Ranks test

As with the Mann-Whitney *U*-test, there are no hard-and-fast rules about how you should report the results of a Wilcoxon Signed Ranks test. However, you should provide the value of *T* (i.e. smallest sum of ranks) and the *p*-value. Sample size and sum of ranks could also be included. For example:

> One case showed no change in rating before and after the introduction of the time-out technique and was not included in the analysis. Ratings for the remaining 11 cases were analysed using a Wilcoxon Signed Ranks test, which revealed that behaviour ratings were significantly higher after using the time-out technique, $T = 10$, $p = .041$. The sum of ranks for increases in behaviour ratings was 56, and 10 for decreases in behaviour ratings.

Table 16.16 SPSS output for Wilcoxon Signed Ranks test

Hypothesis Test Summary

	Null Hypothesis	Test	Sig.	Decision
1	The median of differences between Behaviour rating before using time-out technique and Behaviour rating after using time-out technique equals 0.	Related-Samples Wilcoxon Signed Rank Test	.041	Reject the null hypothesis.

Asymptotic significances are displayed. The significance level is .05.

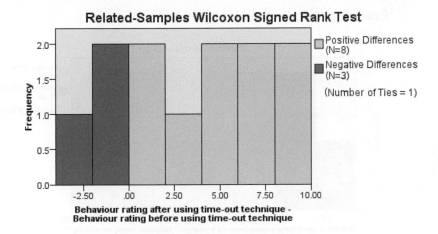

Related-Samples Wilcoxon Signed Rank Test

Positive Differences (N=8)
Negative Differences (N=3)
(Number of Ties = 1)

Behaviour rating after using time-out technique -
Behaviour rating before using time-out technique

Total N	12
Test Statistic	56.000
Standard Error	11.236
Standardized Test Statistic	2.047
Asymptotic Sig. (2-sided test)	.041

The Sign test

The Sign test is an alternative to the Wilcoxon Signed Ranks test. The two tests are quite similar except that the Sign test focuses only on the sign of difference and is not interested in the value of the difference. As a result, the Sign test loses a lot of detail and is less likely to find significant effects. However, on some (rare) occasions you may have recorded only whether a change was positive or negative. For instance, if you were a doctor you could say whether a patient's health

Table 16.17 SPSS output for Sign test

Hypothesis Test Summary

	Null Hypothesis	Test	Sig.	Decision
1	The median of differences between Behaviour rating after using time-out technique and Behaviour rating before using time-out technique equals 0.	Related-Samples Sign Test	.227[1]	Retain the null hypothesis.

Asymptotic significances are displayed. The significance level is .05.

[1]Exact significance is displayed for this test.

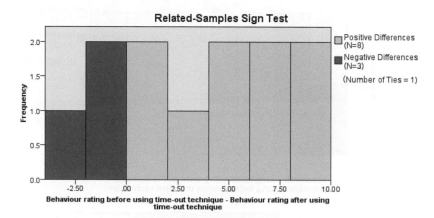

Related-Samples Sign Test

Positive Differences (N=8)
Negative Differences (N=3)
(Number of Ties = 1)

Behaviour rating before using time-out technique - Behaviour rating after using time-out technique

Total N	12
Test Statistic	8.000
Standard Error	1.658
Standardized Test Statistic	1.206
Asymptotic Sig. (2-sided test)	.228
Exact Sig. (2-sided test)	.227

1. The exact p-value is computed based on the binomial distribution because there are 25 or fewer cases.

Sign test
Non-parametric test used to compare changes in sign (positive versus negative) between two paired conditions; alternative to Wilcoxon Signed Ranks test.

was improving or not, but this would be difficult to quantify using a precise score. A **Sign test** would be suitable on this occasion.

The SPSS output will consist of a table, which tells you whether you should retain or reject the null hypothesis, and, if you double-click, you will get more detailed information (Table 16.17). Take a note of the number of positive and negative differences, as well as the Sig. Value. Notice here that no significant difference was found using the Sign test, even though the same data gave a significant result using the Wilcoxon Signed Ranks test.

Summary

In this chapter, you were introduced to the methods used to compare two averages. There are two questions you need to consider when deciding on which test to select: (1) whether you should use a parametric test or not, and (2) whether you are comparing independent or paired samples. If your answer to question (1) is parametric, you will use one of the t-tests: independent samples if you are comparing two separate groups, and paired samples if you are comparing the same or paired/matched) groups. In each case, a t-value is calculated, its probability obtained and a decision made about the null hypothesis based on this. If the p-value is less than .05, we can conclude that there is a significant difference between the means.

However, if you need to use a non-parametric test (e.g. because you have ordinal data, the data are not normally distributed), then you cannot use a t-test. Non-parametric tests tend to have less power than parametric tests, but can be used in more situations. The non-parametric equivalent of the independent-samples t-test is the Mann-Whitney U-test, and the non-parametric equivalent of the paired-samples t-test is the Wilcoxon Signed Ranks test. The Sign test is sometimes used as an alternative to the Wilcoxon Signed Ranks test.

Questions

1 Under what conditions would you select a non-parametric test over its parametric equivalent?

2 What information needs to be included when reporting the results of a t-test? Why?

3 Why do we need to know the degrees of freedom when analysing a t-test?

4 What is a directional hypothesis and why are you advised against using this type of hypothesis?

5 Which of the following set of conditions is likely to generate the highest t-value? (1) large difference between means, large variability about means; (2) large difference between means, small variability about means; (3) small difference between means, large variability about means; (4) small difference between means, small variability about means.

6 What does a significant Levene's test tell us?

7 What are the assumptions of t-tests?

8 In a paired-samples t-test SPSS output table, the 95% confidence interval of the difference is between 1.23 and 4.36. Is there likely to be a significant difference?

Activities

1 A researcher conducts an experiment comparing two methods of teaching young children to read. An older method is compared with a newer one and the mean performance of the new method was found to be greater than that of the older method. The results are reported as, $t(120) = 2.10, p = .04 (d = .34)$.

   (a) Is the result statistically significant?

   (b) What type of test was used?

   (c) What is the non-parametric equivalent of this test?

   (d) Based on the effect size measure, d, what may we say about the size of the effect found in this study?

   (e) The researcher states that on the basis of this result the newer method is clearly of practical significance when teaching children to read and should be implemented right away. How would you respond to this statement?

   (f) What would the construction of confidence intervals add to our understanding of these results?

2 A paired-samples t-test had generated the following values: $t = 2.45$, $df = 28$. Calculate Cohen's d and state whether there is a small, medium or large effect.

3 In an experiment conducted by Professor Dre, the average number of errors in the two groups was 38.4 and 13.2; this difference was not statistically significant. When Professor Seuss conducted the same experiment, the means of the two groups were 21.1 and 14.7, but the difference was statistically significant. Explain how this could happen.

Comparing Differences between More than Two Conditions: Part 1 – One-way Designs

OVERVIEW

In this chapter, you will be introduced to another type of statistical test – analysis of variance (or ANOVA for short). ANOVA is used when you want to compare means from more than two conditions. It is an extremely flexible method and consequently is the most widely used test for analysing psychological experiments. Here, we will discuss the use of ANOVA for analysing one-way (single-factor) designs; the next chapter will cover how ANOVA is used with more complex factorial designs. You may find it helpful to review content from Chapters 11 and 12 before reading this chapter.

OBJECTIVES

After studying this chapter and working through the exercises, you should be able to:

- Describe why ANOVA is preferable to multiple *t*-tests when comparing more than two means

- Define the *F*-ratio and explain the logic behind it

- Describe how ANOVA can be used to test null hypotheses

- Distinguish between the one-way between-subjects ANOVA, one-way within-subjects ANOVA, Kruskal-Wallis test and Friedman test

- Calculate and determine an effect size measure for ANOVA

- Distinguish between *a priori* and *post hoc* comparisons

- Conduct analysis, interpret output and write up results for the one-way between-subjects ANOVA, one-way within-subjects ANOVA, Kruskal-Wallis test and Friedman test

Comparing more than two conditions: why not just use *t*-tests?

In the previous chapter we looked at ways in which you can compare means from two conditions using *t*-tests (or their non-parametric equivalents). But what do you do if you want to look at differences between *more than two* conditions? Can't you just use lots of *t*-tests between all the possible pairs of conditions (e.g. A versus B; A versus C; B versus C)? The simple answer is no.

When you run a *t*-test with an alpha level of .05 (5%), you accept that a *t*-value with a probability of less than 5% is statistically significant and unlikely to occur under the null hypothesis. However, note the use of the word "unlikely" in the previous sentence. That tells you that your result is not 100% certain. It is not. We are dealing with probability here and not certainty, so there is still a chance that you might get a significant *t*-value when there is in fact no difference in the population. This is what we refer to as a Type I error and the probability of this type of error is equal to your alpha level. So, if you do find a significant result (and you've used a significance level of .05), then there's a 5% chance that your result is a fluke that has happened even though the null hypothesis is indeed true (i.e. a Type I error). The .05 (5%) level is used because it represents a good balance between finding significant results and the chance of committing Type I errors, but there is still a 5% chance that you will have made a **Type I error** in any test in which you reject the null hypothesis using an alpha level of .05.

ch. 15
pp.335–338

When you run multiple *t*-tests on the same data, you increase the chance of a Type I error and this is not a good thing. Consider a simple experiment where a researcher is comparing performance under three conditions: condition A, condition B and a control condition. If you wanted to examine differences between these conditions using *t*-tests, you would need to run the following comparisons:

- Condition A versus Condition B
- Condition A versus Control
- Condition B versus Control

> **Familywise error rate**
> The likelihood of making a Type I error across a number of comparisons; increases as number of comparisons increases.

For *each* of these *t*-tests there would be a 5% chance of committing a Type I error and obtaining a false significant result. However, across all of the *t*-tests the *overall* Type I error rate, which is known as the "**familywise error rate**", has increased to 14%.[1] If there had been four conditions rather than three, this would have meant six comparisons and a familywise error rate of 26.5%. This means that by running multiple *t*-tests on the same data, the likelihood of obtaining a false significant result is greatly increased.

If this concept does not make sense, imagine that you have a drawer filled with 20 socks, 19 of which are black and one which is white (for the moment just ignore the fact that you have odd socks). If you closed your eyes and just picked out any sock from the drawer, the probability of you picking up the white sock would be 1/20, or 5%. However, if you keep on blindly picking out socks (and put back the socks you have already taken out), the likelihood of you eventually picking out the white sock increases. In other words, the more times you have a go at picking out a sock, the more likely you are to find the white one.

The same principle applies to running multiple *t*-tests, except we are dealing with significant and non-significant results rather than white and black socks, respectively. A significant result is like a white sock – the more you fish about for one, the more likely you are to find one. If you use the 5% level of significance, then this essentially means that 1 in 20 results that you interpret as significant will be "false" (i.e. will be a Type I error). These are pretty good odds. We can live with them. But what this also means is that, the more tests you do on the same data using the 5% significance level, the more likely it is that you will find a "false" significant result. If you do 20 tests using this 5% (1 in 20) level, then, by definition, one of them will be falsely significant. The bottom line is that if you want to compare more than two conditions, you cannot use lots of *t*-tests because this increases the chances of getting a false significant result and you will be committing a Type I error.

Analysis of variance

So, if you cannot use *t*-tests, what do you do? This is where a set of tests called **analysis of variance** (**ANOVA** – from ANalysis Of VAriance) comes into play. ANOVA is simply an extension of *t*-tests – they are both parametric and used to test for differences, but ANOVA does it on a bigger scale and can be used to compare more than two conditions.

> **Analysis of variance (ANOVA)**
> Set of parametric inferential statistical tests used to test for differences between more than two means by comparing variances between and within groups.

> **F statistic**
> The test statistic calculated when using ANOVA; the ratio of the between-groups variance to the within-groups variance.

ch. 16

Recall that a *t*-**test** involves the calculation of a *t* statistic, which is a ratio of the differences between two means and the variability around those means. ANOVA works in a similar way by calculating an *F* **statistic**, which tells us about the variance in the data (hence the name analysis of variance). The *F* statistic is a ratio of two types of variance: between-groups variance and within-groups variance.

---

1 You can calculate the familywise error rate using this formula: $1 - .95^n$ (where *n* is the number of comparisons). Thus, for three comparisons the error rate $= 1 - .95^3 = 1 - .857 = .143 = 14.3\%$, and for six comparisons, the error rate $= 1 - .95^6 = 1 - .735 = .265 = 26.5\%$.

Between-groups variance
The variability of each group mean from the grand mean; attributed to effects of independent variable, plus measurement error and individual differences; also known as systematic variance.

Within-groups variance
The variability of each score from its group mean; attributed to error in measurement and individual differences; also known as error variance.

Between-groups variance refers to the deviation of the group means from what is called the grand mean (i.e. the mean score of all individuals in all groups). If there is no real difference between the groups, then their means will be similar, and will be close to the grand (overall) mean. In this case, the between-groups variance will be small (because the groups do not vary much from each other). As differences between group means increase, so too will the between-groups variance.

Within-groups variance, on the other hand, is the deviation of the individual scores *within* each group from their respective group means. (You may sometimes see between-groups variance referred to as systematic variance and within-groups variance as error variance.) What this means is that, if you have three groups, then the scores in group 1 will vary from *each other*, as will the scores in groups 2 and 3. When you look at the variation of scores *within* a group, this is within-group variance.

The concepts of between- and within-groups variances can be illustrated using an example. The data in Table 17.1 show the number of words correctly recalled (out of a possible 20) on a test in an experiment investigating memory training techniques. Five participants were randomly assigned to each of four conditions: (1) a control condition with no specific instructions; (2) a story condition, in which participants were instructed to make up a story using the to-be-remembered words; (3) an imagery condition, in which participants used visual imagery to aid their memory; and (4) a rhyme condition, in which participants were asked to use rhymes to remember the words.

To get an idea of the between-groups variance, we need to calculate the grand mean, the average of all the group means: $(10 + 13.2 + 14.4 + 13.4)/4 = 51/4 = 12.75$. Between-groups variance refers to the deviation of each of the group means from this grand mean. For example, we have group means of 10.0, 13.2, 14.4 and 13.4 – how do these compare with the grand mean of 12.75? Is there a large degree of variability in the means, or are they all close to the grand mean? How do the group means compare with one another?

Within-groups variance focuses on each group individually by looking at the deviation of each individual score from its group mean. For example, the control group has scores ranging from 8 to 12, and the group mean is 10.0. Is there a similar degree of deviation from the group mean in the other groups? Are there very large differences within individual groups?

Table 17.1 Data from memory experiment

				Instruction condition			
Control		Story		Imagery		Rhyme	
Participant	Score	Participant	Score	Participant	Score	Participant	Score
1	12	6	15	11	16	16	14
2	10	7	14	12	16	17	14
3	9	8	13	13	13	18	15
4	11	9	12	14	12	19	12
5	8	10	12	15	15	20	12
Mean	10.0		13.2		14.4		13.4

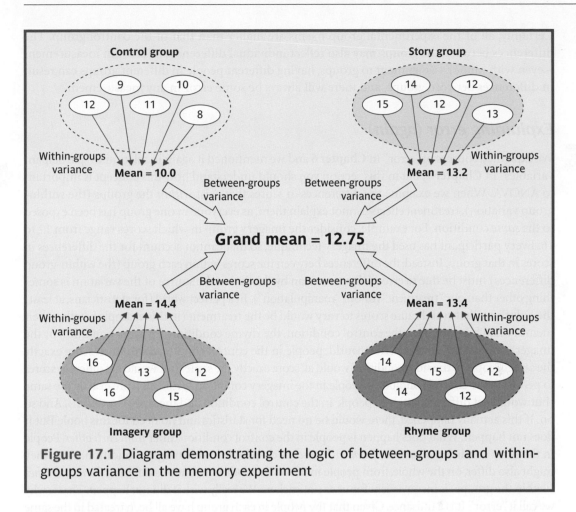

Figure 17.1 Diagram demonstrating the logic of between-groups and within-groups variance in the memory experiment

Figure 17.1 shows the different comparisons that are made when we look at between-groups and within-groups variance. The within-groups variance is represented by the differences between the scores within each group. The between-groups variance is the difference between scores in different groups. This can be represented by the differences between the means of each group.

STOP & Think

What factors might account for differences between groups in the memory experiment? How could you explain differences within groups?

What factors contribute towards between- and within-groups variance? One of the reasons why there may be differences between groups is that the treatment (the effect of being in a particular condition) has had an effect. In our example, the group means are not equal and this may reflect the fact that the different memory techniques have actually had an effect on memory performance.

Certainly, all of the experimental group means are higher than that of the control group. The differences between the groups may also reflect individual differences or error in measurement – even with random assignment to groups, having different people in different groups can result in differences between groups, and there will always be some error in any measurement.

Explaining error (again)

ch. 6
pp.106–111

We explained sources of "error" in **Chapter 6** and we mentioned it again in relation to "participant variables" in **Chapter 7**, but in this section you should understand how this concept is important to ANOVA. When we examine the differences in scores that exist *within* the groups (the within-group variation), treatment effects cannot explain them, as everyone in one group has been exposed to the *same* condition. For example, consider the imagery group in which scores range from 12 to 16. Every participant has used the imagery technique, so that cannot account for the differences in scores in that group. Instead, the differences between the scores within each group (the within-group differences) must be due to error. What we mean by this is that the source of the variation is something other than our "treatment" (or our "manipulation"). In a perfect world (for statisticians, at least) the *only* thing that could cause scores to vary would be the treatment (in this example whether their memory had been tested in the control condition, the rhyme condition, the story condition or the imagery condition). In this perfect world, people in the control condition would all score exactly the same. People in the story condition would all score exactly the same (but would get different scores to people in the control condition). People in the imagery condition would all score exactly the same (but would get different scores to people in the control condition and the story condition). And so on. If this actually happened, there would be no need for statistics and no need for this book. But it does not happen. What does happen is people in the control condition differ *from each other*. People in the story condition also differ *from each other* as do people in the imagery condition. Now, they might also differ, on the whole, from people in the other conditions, but this differing *from each other* (within the groups) is inconvenient for us as statisticians. We really wish it did not happen. That is why we call it "error". It is a nuisance. Given that the people in each group have all been treated in the same way and taken the test under the same conditions, it would be best all round if they all got the same scores. So why this error? It must come from somewhere. It does – it comes from errors of measurement (which are usually unpredictable and unavoidable) and individual differences. It is just a fact of life (and statistics) that people are different to each other. These differences will cause them to obtain different scores, even when they have been tested under the same conditions. So, we call this unwanted variation "error". (This explains why the within-groups variance is sometimes referred to as "error variance" or the "error term" as it tells us about the degree of error.)

ch. 7
pp.115–11

Getting back to F

As we mentioned earlier, the *F* statistic is the ratio between the between-groups variance and within-groups variance:

$$F = \frac{\text{between-groups variance}}{\text{within-groups variance}} = \frac{\text{treatment effect} + \text{error}}{\text{error}}$$

STOP & Think

Under what circumstances would you expect to find a large *F*-value?

Notice that error features both on the numerator (the top part) and on the denominator (the bottom part) of the ratio. We would expect the between-groups error and within-groups error to be roughly equal, effectively cancelling each other out (although they may be different in some circumstances, there is generally no reason to expect that measurement error will be different in one condition compared to another, especially if the measurements are taken in the same way). Therefore, if there is a treatment effect, we would expect to find that the between-groups variance is greater than the within-groups variance, resulting in a large *F*-value.

On the other hand, if there is little or no treatment effect, the between-groups variance would be about the same as the within-groups variance. If there was absolutely no treatment effect, we would have an *F*-value of 1:

$$F = \frac{\text{treatment effect} + \text{error}}{\text{error}} = \frac{0 + \text{error}}{\text{error}} = \frac{\text{error}}{\text{error}} = 1$$

Thus, the larger your *F*-value, the more likely it is that your treatment is having an effect. But how large does your *F*-value need to be before you can conclude that there is a treatment effect?

F-distributions and degrees of freedom

Recall that when working out the probability – and therefore significance – of *t*-values, we can consult a frequency distribution of *t*-values; which one we choose depends on the degrees of freedom (*df*). It is the same idea for *F*-values except the choice of frequency distribution depends on *two* separate degrees of freedom: one related to the number of conditions that we have in our experiment and one related to the number of participants that we have in each condition. This is because, in order to understand the design of a study with more than two conditions, we need to know these two separate characteristics. (With *t*-tests, we already know that there are two conditions so only one *df*-value is needed, related to sample size.)

The *df*-value related to the number of conditions in ANOVA is called the between-groups *df* and is simply the number of conditions minus 1. So in our memory experiment example with four conditions, *df* = 4 − 1 = 3. If we know the grand mean and know three of the group means, we can work out what the fourth group mean is. In other words, three of the group means are free to vary – there are three degrees of freedom.

The other *df*-value is called the within-groups or error *df*, and refers to differences within individual groups or conditions. In our memory experiment, there were five participants in each condition. If we know the group mean for a given condition and know four of the participants' scores, we can determine the remaining score. In this condition, there are four degrees of freedom. The same would apply to the other groups, giving an overall within-groups *df* of 16 (= 4 + 4 + 4 + 4). A quick way of calculating the within-groups *df* is by subtracting the

ch. 16
pp.347–348

ch. 16
pp.345–346

number of conditions from the overall number of participants ($20 - 4 = 16$). Coupled with the between-groups *df*, we can report the *df* for the memory experiment as $df = 3, 16$.

STOP & Think

What would the degrees of freedom be for a study with three conditions and 20 participants in each condition?

Please do not worry if this talk of degrees of freedom confuses you – it is quite an abstract concept and if you use a statistical computer package, it will calculate the *df*-values for you anyway. All that matters is that you appreciate the fact that you need to know the two *df*-values – between-groups *df* and within-groups *df* – when dealing with ANOVA.

Once the *df*-values have been obtained, we can find out the probability of our *F*-value. As with *t*-tests, we work out the significance of the *F*-value that we have obtained in our analyses by referring to a distribution. Again, as with *t*-tests, there are many different *F*-distributions. The shape of the distribution of *F*-values is not the same as that of *t*-values – the *F*-distribution is not symmetrical and the values are all positive. Furthermore, the shape of the distribution varies greatly according to the *df*-values (Figure 17.2).

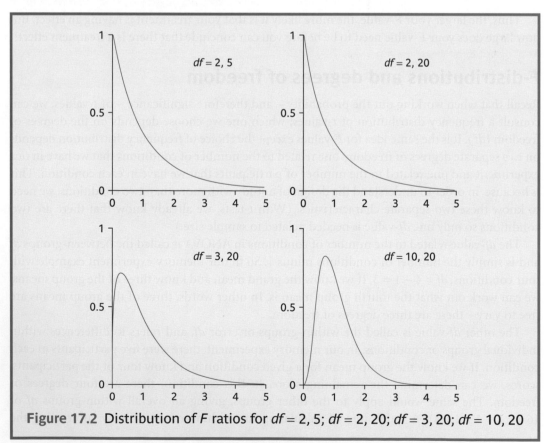

Figure 17.2 Distribution of *F* ratios for $df = 2, 5$; $df = 2, 20$; $df = 3, 20$; $df = 10, 20$

Despite the differences in the shape of the *F* distributions, the main thing to note is that across all distributions, high *F*-values have low probabilities. If a specific *F*-value is high enough to have a probability less than .05, we can say that it is significant.

Using ANOVA to test null hypotheses

The principle behind using ANOVA to **test null hypotheses** is the same as with other inferential statistical methods: we formulate hypotheses, calculate a statistic (i.e. *F*) and obtain its probability (*p*). If *p* is less than .05, we have a significant result and so reject the **null hypothesis** and accept the alternative hypothesis as the best available explanation. If *p* is greater than .05, we have a non-significant result and so cannot reject the null hypothesis.

ch. 15
pp.330–332

In ANOVA, the null hypothesis is that there is no difference between the means (i.e. the differences between the means is 0); the alternative hypothesis is that there is a difference between the means. Note that the alternative hypothesis is not making predictions about the direction of any differences – it merely states that there is a difference.

Consequently, if you have a significant *F*-value, the null hypothesis – that there is no difference between the means – is rejected and you can conclude that there is a difference in the means. If the *F*-value is non-significant, you would have to retain the null hypothesis and conclude that there was no difference between the means.

You may have spotted a slight problem here – ANOVA only tells us if there is a difference between means; it does not tell us where those differences actually lie and which groups differ from which. All it does is tell us that there is a difference "somewhere". However, some clever little tests can help us make sense of it all.

Test yourself[2]

1 In an ANOVA model, which of the following is considered "error"?

  (a) Within-groups variation

  (b) Between-groups variation

  (c) Treatment effect

  (d) Both (b) and (c)

2 In a between-subjects ANOVA, which of the following will be large if there is a significant effect?

  (a) Within-groups variation

  (b) Between-groups variation

  (c) *F*-value

  (d) Both (b) and (c)

---

2   Answers: 1 = a; 2 = d.

A priori comparisons and post hoc tests

A priori comparisons
Also called planned comparisons; hypothesis-directed statistical tests used to compare differences between two conditions when a significant ANOVA has been obtained; the comparisons to be made are determined before any analysis has been conducted.

When you run an ANOVA and obtain a significant result, you need to do some further investigation to work out where the differences are. If you have specific hypotheses about differences between conditions which were formulated *before* the experiment, you can use *a priori* **comparisons** (or planned comparisons). For example, in our memory experiment example, based on previous theory and research you may predict that the imagery, story and rhyme groups will perform better than the control group. Using new ANOVAs or *t*-tests you could run three planned comparisons between imagery versus control, story versus control and rhyme versus control to find out if your predictions were correct.

However, you may have noticed a problem with this approach. Right at the beginning of the chapter we warned you about the problems of conducting multiple comparisons using *t*-tests as this increases the familywise error rate. Surely it is a bit contradictory to say you cannot use lots of *t*-tests and then go and use them anyway? Well, yes and no. First, you only run *a priori* comparisons if you have a significant *F*-value, so it is not as though you would do this for every possible ANOVA. Second, because you run only the comparisons that you have *planned*, you will not be doing every single possible comparison and so do not increase the familywise error rate quite so much. For the memory experiment, if you did not use ANOVA to begin with, you would need to run six separate *t*-tests to cover all possible comparisons to determine if there were actually any differences. This is in contrast to the three *a priori* comparisons. Last, if you are really worried about the number of *a priori* comparisons you are making and the familywise Type I error rate, you can adjust your alpha (significance) level[3] to reflect this by dividing it by the number of comparisons being made. Thus, for three comparisons with an alpha level of .05, the new alpha level would be .0167 (.05 ÷ 3 = .0167). For a result to be significant, it would now have to have a probability of less than .0167. This method of adjusting the alpha level by dividing by the number of comparisons is called the **Bonferroni method**.

Bonferroni method
Method of controlling familywise Type I error rates by dividing alpha level by the number of comparisons to be made.

STOP & Think

What would the alpha (significance) level need to be when making six planned comparisons?

As you may have worked out, though, if you use the Bonferroni method, you may end up with a very low alpha level. The more planned comparisons you make, the lower the new alpha level and the less likely you are to find a significant result (because making the significance level that low means that the region of the curve in which a value you will interpret as significant becomes vanishingly small – and values in that region are extremely rare). Not only that, but *a priori* comparisons often do not tell you the whole story – perhaps there are some interesting differences

---

3   Remember that the alpha level is another word for your "critical" level of significance. Usually, when you do a single test, this is the magical .05 level.

which you did not predict prior to the analysis. And what do you do if there is no previous theory or research to help you make specific predictions and planned comparisons in the first place?

It is for these reasons that some researchers prefer not to use *a priori* comparisons and instead use a set of tests called **post hoc comparisons** (*post hoc* means after the event). *Post hoc* tests work in a similar way to multiple *t*-tests but have already made adjustments to control the familywise error rate – you do not have to recalculate alpha levels as you would do with the Bonferroni method. Furthermore, *post hoc* tests make every single possible comparison and therefore give a very complete picture of what is going on in your data.

There are a number of different *post hoc* tests available, including ones with exotic names such as Tukey's HSD, Fisher's LSD and the Scheffé test. Some of these tests are more conservative (less likely to find a significant result, but control error rate) whereas others are more liberal (more likely to find significant results but at the expense of error rate). We will come back to some of these *post hoc* tests later in chapter, but for a fuller discussion, please see Howell (2007).

It is very much up to you whether you use planned comparisons or *post hoc* tests to help you interpret your ANOVA result. You should think carefully about whether you are only interested in comparisons between specific conditions or if you want to look at all possible comparisons. You should also bear in mind that planned comparisons are generally more sensitive at detecting differences than *post hoc* tests, due to the smaller number of comparisons being made. And you most definitely should not have a go at both *a priori* and *post hoc* and just choose the one that gives you the best results! You should make your decision *before* you have run your ANOVA.

> **Post hoc comparisons**
> Statistical tests used to compare all possible differences between two conditions *after* a significant ANOVA has been obtained; usually involve adjustments to control familywise error rate.

Effect size measures for ANOVA

You might remember that effect size measures can be used to give us an indication of the size of the effect of the independent variable. This is useful because *p*-values tell you only about the probability of a result occurring under the null hypothesis – they do not tell us if differences are particularly large or important.

The most popular measure of **effect size** for ANOVA is **eta squared (η^2)**, which indicates the amount of variance in the dependent variable that can be explained by the independent variable. Eta squared values can range between 0 and 1 – the higher the value, the more of an effect the independent variable is having. You can calculate eta squared by hand using the following formula:

> **Eta squared (η^2)**
> Effect size measure for ANOVA; indicates amount of variance in dependent variable that is attributable to independent variable.

ch. 15 pp.334–335

$$\text{Eta squared} = \frac{\text{Between-groups sum of squares}}{\text{Total sum of squares}}$$

In the Know

What is "sum of squares"?
Sum of squares (SS) is a term that will pop up frequently in the next couple of chapters. It basically means the sum of the squared deviations. In other words, you find out how much each square deviates from the mean (some will be positive, some negative) and then square these values (to get rid of the negatives). Then you add them all up. Hence: sum of squares.

Partial eta squared (η_p^2)
Effect size measure for ANOVA commonly calculated in statistical computer packages; differs from eta squared only in the denominator of its formula

The between-groups sum of squares and total sum of squares are values that are used in the calculation of the F-ratio (we will come to this later) and can also be found in ANOVA output tables from statistical computing packages.

However, most statistical computing packages will calculate a slightly different effect size, **partial eta squared (η_p^2)**, for you. The difference lies in the denominator (lower part) of the formula:

$$\text{Partial eta squared} = \frac{\text{Between-groups sum of squares}}{\text{Between-groups sum of squares} + \text{within-groups sum of squares}}$$

For the ANOVAs discussed in this chapter, eta squared and partial eta squared will be the same, but it is when you have more complex ANOVA designs (see next chapter) that they will differ. Most people are happy to let the computer do the hard work and report partial eta squared, so just make sure that you make it clear when reporting results that you are using *partial* eta squared.

One-way between-subjects ANOVA

One-way between-subjects ANOVA
Parametric inferential statistical test used to compare differences in means from two or more groups in a single factor design.

So far, we have been discussing the general principles of ANOVA, but there are a number of different ANOVAs. The first we will cover is the **one-way between-subjects ANOVA**. One-way just means that one independent variable (or factor) is being investigated and between-subjects refers to designs with separate groups in each condition (see **Chapter 7**). Therefore, this test is equivalent to the independent-samples t-test as it is used to compare differences in means from two or more independent groups.

ch. 7
pp.114–11⁹

The memory experiment we have been using as an example throughout this chapter is suitable for analysis for a one-way between-subjects ANOVA. There is one factor (memory technique) with four levels (imagery, story, rhyme and control), and participants have been randomly assigned to one of these four conditions. We can therefore use one-way between-subjects ANOVA to determine if there is a significant difference between the means.

However, before progressing with any ANOVA, you must first check that its parametric assumptions have been met. The assumptions for the one-way between-subjects ANOVA are the same as for the independent-samples t-test: data should be interval/ratio and normally distributed, and there should be homogeneity of variance (i.e. the samples should have equal variances). Histograms and boxplots can be used to make decisions about data distribution (e.g. a histogram

ch. 16
pp.351–352

representing the frequency of scores should look symmetrical and a "normal curve" could be easily fitted over it), and Levene's test can confirm whether there is homogeneity of variance.

An example of selected SPSS output is shown in Table 17.2 and Figure 17.3. Note that the standard deviations of the groups do not differ hugely, suggesting homogeneity of variance, and there is no evidence of outliers or extreme scores in the boxplots. (However, with only five participants in each group, it is very difficult to determine anything about the shape of the distribution of population data from boxplots or histograms.)

Table 17.2 Descriptive statistics for memory experiment

Report

Number of words correctly recalled

Instruction condition	Mean	N	Std. Deviation
Control	10.00	5	1.581
Story	13.20	5	1.304
Imagery	14.40	5	1.817
Rhyme	13.40	5	1.342
Total	12.75	20	2.197

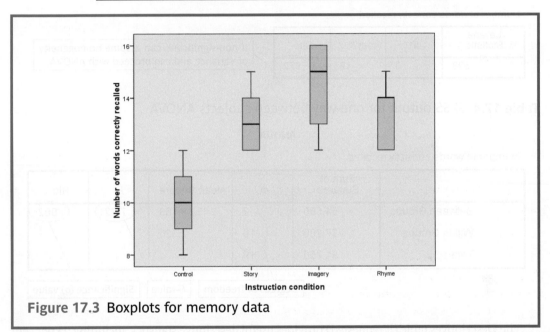

Figure 17.3 Boxplots for memory data

STOP & Think

Look at the means and the boxplot. Can you make any preliminary predictions about the results of the ANOVA?

One-way between-subjects ANOVA using SPSS

The SPSS output for a one-way between-subjects ANOVA is shown in Table 17.3 and Table 17.4. Please remember that you can find detailed instructions on how to run the test on our website.

Table 17.3 SPSS output for analysis of memory data

Descriptives

Number of words correctly recalled

	N	Mean	Std. Deviation	Std. Error	95% Confidence Interval for Mean		Minimum	Maximum
					Lower Bound	Upper Bound		
Control	5	10.00	1.581	.707	8.04	11.96	8	12
Story	5	13.20	1.304	.583	11.58	14.82	12	15
Imagery	5	14.40	1.817	.812	12.14	16.66	12	16
Rhyme	5	13.40	1.342	.600	11.73	15.07	12	15
Total	20	12.75	2.197	.491	11.72	13.78	8	16

Test of Homogeneity of Variances

Number of words correctly recalled

Levene Statistic	df1	df2	Sig.
.523	3	16	.672

If non-significant, can assume homogeneity of variance and can proceed with ANOVA.

Table 17.4 SPSS output for one-way between-subjects ANOVA

ANOVA

Number of words correctly recalled

	Sum of Squares	df	Mean Square	F	Sig.
Between Groups	54.550	3	18.183	7.821	.002
Within Groups	37.200	16	2.325		
Total	91.750	19			

Degrees of freedom | F-value | Significance (p) value

ch. 15
pp.326–330
The Descriptives table (if requested) provides useful descriptive statistics, including 95 per cent **confidence intervals** for the mean. The next table in our output presents the result of Levene's test for homogeneity of variance. It is non-significant (i.e. there are no significant differences in the variances of the groups), so the assumption of the test has been met. The ANOVA table presents the results of the ANOVA itself. Note the *df*-values for between groups (3) and within groups (16), the *F*-value (7.821) and the Sig. value (.002). We have a significant result and can conclude that there is a difference between the means (i.e. reject the null hypothesis). You can also calculate eta squared based on the values in the sum of squares column: eta squared = between-groups sum of squares/total sum of squares = 54.550/91.750 = .595.

If you have requested *post hoc* comparisons, they will need to be inspected to identify any significant differences. The Multiple Comparisons table (Table 17.5) presents every single possible comparison. Each row of results presents a comparison between the condition in the first column (I) and the condition in the relevant row of the second column (J). For example, the first row gives us the result of the *post hoc* comparison between the control and story conditions:

Table 17.5 SPSS output showing *post hoc* comparisons

> If there is an asterisk (*), then a significant difference between means.

Multiple Comparisons

Number of words correctly recalled
Tukey HSD

(I) Instruction condition	(J) Instruction condition	Mean Difference (I-J)	Std. Error	Sig.	95% Confidence Interval	
					Lower Bound	Upper Bound
Control	Story	-3.200*	.964	.020	-5.96	-.44
	Imagery	-4.400*	.964	.002	-7.16	-1.64
	Rhyme	-3.400*	.964	.013	-6.16	-.64
Story	Control	3.200*	.964	.020	.44	5.96
	Imagery	-1.200	.964	.609	-3.96	1.56
	Rhyme	-.200	.964	.997	-2.96	2.56
Imagery	Control	4.400*	.964	.002	1.64	7.16
	Story	1.200	.964	.609	-1.56	3.96
	Rhyme	1.000	.964	.731	-1.76	3.76
Rhyme	Control	3.400*	.964	.013	.64	6.16
	Story	.200	.964	.997	-2.56	2.96
	Imagery	-1.000	.964	.731	-3.76	1.76

*. The mean difference is significant at the 0.05 level.

> Significance (*p*) value

the difference between the group means was −3.2, which has a *p* value of .020 (significant). Note that SPSS helpfully highlights significant mean differences with an asterisk (*).

You will notice that there are lots of comparisons here, but you do not need to look at all of them as there's quite a bit of repetition going on (e.g. we have separate results for control versus story and story versus control, even though they are effectively the same thing). What you can see from this particular study is that there were a number of significant differences: control versus story, control versus imagery, control versus rhyme. If you go back to the table of descriptive statistics, you will see that in each case the control condition has the lower mean. Therefore, the control condition had a significantly lower mean than the story, imagery and rhyme conditions. It is also interesting to note that there were no significant differences between the experimental conditions – they appeared to be equally effective at aiding memory.

If you are having difficulty understanding the *post hoc* comparisons, you may find it helpful to also consult the table under the Homogeneous Subsets heading in your output. This splits conditions into separate subsets according to whether there are significant differences between the group means. For the memory experiment, there were two subsets: one that contained the control group only, and another that included the three experimental conditions (Table 17.6). This makes it easy to see that there were no significant differences between the experimental conditions (they are in the same subset), but they all differ significantly from the control condition (in a different subset). If requested, a line graph can also help you with interpretation (see Figure 17.4).

Alternative one-way between-subjects ANOVA in SPSS

There is an alternative method of obtaining the one-way between-subjects ANOVA in SPSS, which is slightly more fiddly, but you get a lot more detail in your results, including partial eta

Table 17.6 SPSS homogeneous subsets output table

Number of words correctly recalled

Tukey HSD[a]

Instruction condition	N	Subset for alpha = 0.05	
		1	2
Control	5	10.00	
Story	5		13.20
Rhyme	5		13.40
Imagery	5		14.40
Sig.		1.000	.609

> Significant differences between conditions in different subsets.
> No differences between conditions in same subset.

Means for groups in homogeneous subsets are displayed.

a. Uses Harmonic Mean Sample Size = 5.000.

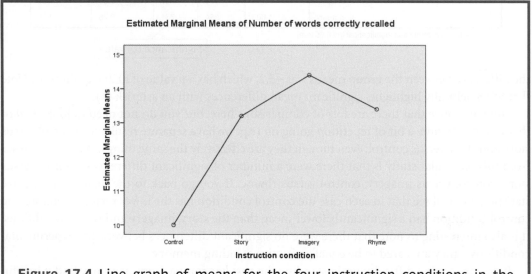

Figure 17.4 Line graph of means for the four instruction conditions in the memory experiment

squared. This procedure is also used for more advanced ANOVAs, so you may as well get to grips with it now. For details on how to run this procedure, please go to our website.

The output for this method is shown in Table 17.7 and Table 17.8. The Between-subjects factors table just summarizes the conditions and number of participants in each group (N). The Descriptive statistics table is self-explanatory. The Levene's test of equality of error variances is the test we use to check the assumption of homogeneity of variance by inspecting the Sig. value. The Tests of Between-Subjects Effects presents the ANOVA results. Ignore the first two rows of results and go to the row labelled with the name of your grouping variable (e.g. condition) and the Error row. These are equivalent to the Between-groups and Within-groups rows from the

Table 17.7 SPSS output for between-subjects ANOVA

Between-Subjects Factors

		Value Label	N
Instruction condition	1	Control	5
	2	Story	5
	3	Imagery	5
	4	Rhyme	5

Descriptive Statistics

Dependent Variable:Number of words correctly recalled

Instruction condition	Mean	Std. Deviation	N
Control	10.00	1.581	5
Story	13.20	1.304	5
Imagery	14.40	1.817	5
Rhyme	13.40	1.342	5
Total	12.75	2.197	20

Table 17.8 SPSS output for alternative one-way between-subjects ANOVA

Levene's Test of Equality of Error Variances[a]

Dependent Variable:Number of words correctly recalled

F	df1	df2	Sig.
.523	3	16	.672

If non-significant, can assume homogeneity of variance and can proceed with ANOVA.

Tests the null hypothesis that the error variance of the dependent variable is equal across groups.

a. Design: Intercept + Condition

Tests of Between-Subjects Effects

Dependent Variable:Number of words correctly recalled

Source	Type III Sum of Squares	df	Mean Square	F	Sig.	Partial Eta Squared
Corrected Model	54.550[a]	3	18.183	7.821	.002	.595
Intercept	3251.250	1	3251.250	1398.387	.000	.989
Condition	54.550	3	18.183	7.821	.002	.595
Error	37.200	16	2.325			
Total	3343.000	20				
Corrected Total	91.750	19				

a. R Squared = .595 (Adjusted R Squared = .519)

Degrees of freedom | F-value | Significance (p) value | Effect size output shown in the previous section. As before, make a note of the values of *df* (remember the two values), *F* and Sig. (*p*). There is an additional column – Partial eta squared – which gives the effect size. Make a note of this too.

The output for the *post hoc* comparisons is exactly the same as before, so there is no point in presenting it again.

One-way between-subjects ANOVA by hand

ch. 14
pp.293–294

Recall from earlier that the *F*-statistic is the ratio of between-groups variance to within-groups variance. As discussed in Chapter 14, the formula for the variance is:

$$s_2 = \frac{\sum (X - \bar{X})^2}{N - 1}$$

To obtain the variances we need for the *F*-statistic, the first thing to do is calculate something called the sums of squares, which is the *top* part of the variance formula – the difference between each score and the mean is squared, and these squares are added together (hence "sums" of "squares").

First, we calculate the sum of squares total (SS_{total}), which uses all of the scores and the grand mean (i.e. the mean of all the group means). Using our memory technique experiment example, we know that our grand mean is 12.75, so you would find the difference between each score and 12.75, square these differences and add them together. Table 17.9 gives you an idea of how the first step of this is done.

As you can imagine, this is quite time-consuming and you end up with lots of decimal places, which can lead to inaccuracies. Fortunately, there is a quick way around this if you use the formula in Figure 17.5.

Table 17.9 First step in working out sums of squares

Participant	1	2	3	4	...	18	19	20
Score	12	10	9	11	...	15	12	12
Difference from grand mean (12.75)	−0.75	−2.75	−3.75	−1.75	...	2.25	−0.75	−0.75
Squared difference	0.5625	7.5625	14.0625	3.0625	...	5.0625	0.5625	0.5625

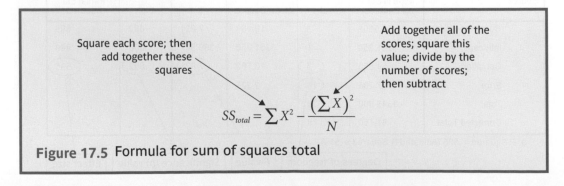

Square each score; then add together these squares

Add together all of the scores; square this value; divide by the number of scores; then subtract

$$SS_{total} = \sum X^2 - \frac{(\sum X)^2}{N}$$

Figure 17.5 Formula for sum of squares total

So, for our example:

$$\sum X^2 = 12^2 + 10^2 + 9^2 + 11^2 + 8^2 + 15^2 + 14^2 + 13^2 + 12^2 + 12^2 + 16^2 + 16^2 + 13^2 + 12^2$$
$$+ 15^2 + 14^2 + 14^2 + 15^2 + 12^2 + 12^2 = 3343$$

$$\sum X = 12 + 10 + 9 + 11 + 8 + 14 + 13 + 12 + 12 + 16 + 16 + 13 + 12 + 15 + 14$$
$$+ 104 + 15 + 12 + 12 = 255$$

Therefore,

$$SS_{total} = \sum X^2 - \frac{(\sum X)^2}{N} = 3\ 343 - \frac{255^2}{20} = 3\ 343 - \frac{65\ 025}{20} = 3\ 343 - 3\ 251.25 = 91.75$$

The next stage is calculating the $SS_{between}$, which uses the differences between the group means and the grand mean in calculating the sum of squares. So, rather than using individual scores, you use the values of the group means (Figure 17.6).

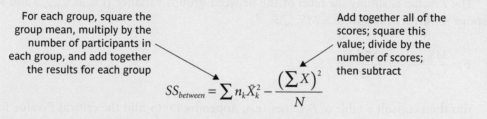

For each group, square the group mean, multiply by the number of participants in each group, and add together the results for each group

Add together all of the scores; square this value; divide by the number of scores; then subtract

$$SS_{between} = \sum n_k \bar{X}_k^2 - \frac{(\sum X)^2}{N}$$

Figure 17.6 Formula for sum of squares between subjects

We know that our group means are 10, 13.2, 14.4 and 13.4, so:

$$\sum n_k \bar{X}_k^2 = (5 \times 10^2) + (5 \times 13.2^2) + (5 \times 14.4^2) + (5 \times 13.4^2) = 3\ 305.8$$

Therefore,

$$SS_{between} = \sum n_k \bar{X}_k^2 - \frac{(\sum X)^2}{N} = 3\ 305.8 - 3\ 251.25 = 54.55$$

The final sum of squares we need to work out is SS_{error}. We know that $SS_{total} = SS_{between} + SS_{error}$, so all we have to do is subtract $SS_{between}$ from SS_{total}:

$$SS_{error} = SS_{total} - SS_{between} = 91.75 - 54.55 = 37.2$$

Now that we have calculated the sums of squares, the next stage in calculating the variances is to divide each sum of square by its corresponding df. Recall from earlier that the between-groups df ($df_{between}$) is equal to the number of conditions minus 1 and the within-groups (or error) df

(df_{error}) is equal to the number of case minus the number of conditions. So, for our example data, $df_{between} = 3$ (i.e. $4 - 1$) and $df_{error} = 16$ (i.e. $20 - 4$). To calculate the total df (df_{total}), just add together $df_{between}$ and df_{error}; in our example this would be 19 ($3 + 16$). The df_{total} can also be calculated by subtracting 1 from the total number of cases.

Now that we have got the df values, we can (finally) work out the variances, or mean sum of squares (MS), as they're called in ANOVA-speak. To do this, we divide each SS by its corresponding df:

$$MS_{between} = \frac{SS_{between}}{df_{between}} = \frac{54.55}{3} = 18.183$$

$$MS_{error} = \frac{SS_{error}}{df_{error}} = \frac{37.2}{16} = 2.325$$

$$MS_{total} = \frac{SS_{total}}{df_{total}} = \frac{91.75}{19} = 4.829$$

The F-value is simply the ratio of the between-groups variance (i.e. $MS_{between}$) and within-groups (or error) variance (i.e. MS_{error}):

$$F = \frac{MS_{between}}{MS_{error}} = \frac{18.183}{2.325} = 7.821$$

You then consult a table of F-values (e.g. Appendix D) to find the critical F-value for your two given df values and your chosen alpha (significance) level. If your obtained F-value is greater than the critical F-value, you have a significant result.

Reporting results from a one-way between-subjects ANOVA

As with t-tests, there is a standard format for reporting the results of ANOVA, including the values of F, df (remember there are two!) and p (Figure 17.7).

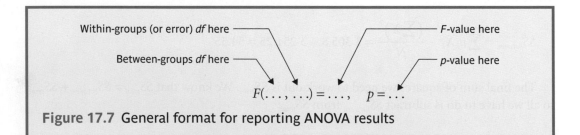

Figure 17.7 General format for reporting ANOVA results

For the memory experiment, this would give you: $F(3, 16) = 7.821$, $p = .002$ (or $F(3, 16) = 7.821$, $p < .05$ if you calculated it by hand).

You should also remember to report an effect size and the results of any *post hoc* analyses (if needed). The results of the memory experiment could be written up like this:

A one-way between-subjects ANOVA revealed a significant difference between the group means, $F(3, 16) = 7.821$, $p = .002$, $\eta_p^2 = .595$. *Post hoc* Tukey's HSD tests revealed that the Control group ($M = 10.0$, $SD = 1.58$) had a significantly lower mean number of words remembered than the Story group ($M = 13.20$, $SD = 1.30$; $p = .020$), Imagery group ($M = 14.40$, $SD = 1.82$; $p = .002$) and Rhyme group ($M = 13.40$, $SD = 1.34$; $p = .013$). There were no significant differences between the Story, Imagery and Rhyme groups (all $ps > .05$).

One-way within-subjects (repeated measures) ANOVA

Just as the one-way between-subjects ANOVA was an extension of the independent-samples *t*-test, there is also an ANOVA equivalent of the paired-samples *t*-test: the **one-way within-subjects ANOVA** (sometimes referred to as one-way repeated measures ANOVA). This test, therefore, is used to compare means from two or more conditions from the **same group of participants**.

One-way within-subjects ANOVA works in a very similar way to one-way between-subjects ANOVA. First, you should state your null hypothesis – there will be no difference between the means – and your alternative hypothesis – there will be a difference between the means. Next, an *F* value is calculated and its probability (*p*-value) obtained. If the *p*-value is less than .05, the null hypothesis is rejected and we conclude that there is a significant difference between the means. Planned comparisons or *post hoc* tests can then be used to identify where any differences lie. If the *p*-value is greater than .05, the null hypothesis is retained and we conclude that there is no difference between the means.

Recall that *F* ratios examine whether the differences between groups (or conditions) are greater than the differences within them:

$$F = \frac{\text{between-groups variance}}{\text{within-groups variance}} = \frac{\text{treatment effect} + \text{error}}{\text{error}}$$

In a between-subjects ANOVA, the "error" in the *F*-ratio comes from error in measurement and individual differences. However, individual differences are not an issue in a within-subjects ANOVA as the same group of people take part in each condition. Think about it like this: in a between-subjects experiment, you have *completely different* people in each condition. This means that there's more opportunity for their scores to vary (because people are different). However, in a within-subjects ANOVA, it's the *same people* who take part in each condition. This means that any difference in scores between conditions cannot be due to individual differences (because the individuals in each condition are the same). As it is the same people in each condition, then any differences in one person's score are more likely to be a result of the "treatment" (i.e. the different conditions that he is being measured in). This means that we can essentially remove the individual differences contribution from the error part of the *F*-ratio. The consequence of this is that the amount of error in ratio is greatly reduced – the within-groups variance now includes only measurement error – and a large *F*-value is more likely to

ch. 7
p.125 – 135

One-way within-subjects ANOVA
Parametric inferential statistical test used to compare means from the same group of participants under two or more conditions; also called repeated measures ANOVA.

be obtained. This means that a within-subjects ANOVA is more sensitive to the effects of the independent variable and is more likely to produce a significant result.

Sphericity
Also called homogeneity of covariance; an assumption of within-subjects ANOVA; similar to homogeneity of variance, but refers to difference scores.

Mauchly's test of sphericity
Statistical test used to test the assumption of sphericity.

ch. 7
pp.132–134

The one-way within-subjects ANOVA also makes the same assumptions as the one-way between-subjects ANOVA: interval/ratio data, normally distributed and homogeneity of variance across conditions. There is also an additional assumption called homogeneity of covariance, or **sphericity**. This is a complex concept and goes beyond the scope of this book. However, put simply, it is similar to homogeneity of variance but refers to difference scores (i.e. the difference between participants' scores in one condition compared with another). A within-subjects ANOVA assumes that the variance in these difference scores is equivalent. Thankfully, there is a test for this – **Mauchly's test of sphericity** – which can be calculated using SPSS.

We can use our memory experiment data to demonstrate a one-way within-subjects ANOVA. Assume that rather than having four separate groups of five participants, the experiment involved just five participants who took part under all four conditions. Remember that the order in which the conditions were presented would need to be **counterbalanced** and that different words would have to be used in each condition to avoid any practice effects. Table 17.10 presents the same data as before, but for a within-subjects design.

Before proceeding with analysis, be sure to check that the ANOVA assumptions have been met.

One-way within-subjects ANOVA in SPSS

For full details on the SPSS procedure for the one-way within-subjects ANOVA, please go to our website. SPSS will give you lots of output for the ANOVA – you can delete or disregard the tables labelled Multivariate Tests, Tests of Within-Subject Contrasts and Tests of Between-Subject Effects as they are not relevant here. The first table, Within-Subjects Factors, just gives you the names of the variables you identified as the different levels (i.e. conditions) of the independent variable – check that these are correct! The Descriptive Statistics table is self-explanatory (Table 17.11).

Mauchly's test of sphericity is the next important table and confirms whether the assumption of sphericity has been met or not. If Mauchly's test is non-significant (Sig. value greater than .05),

Table 17.10 Data from within-subjects memory experiment

Participant	Instruction condition			
	Control	Story	Imagery	Rhyme
1	12	15	16	14
2	10	14	16	14
3	9	13	13	15
4	11	12	12	12
5	8	12	15	12

Table 17.11 SPSS output for within-subjects ANOVA

Within-Subjects Factors

Measure:Number_of_words

Memory_condition	Dependent Variable
1	Contol
2	Story
3	Imagery
4	Rhyme

Descriptive Statistics

	Mean	Std. Deviation	N
Control condition - number of words recalled	10.00	1.581	5
Story condition - number of words recalled	13.20	1.304	5
Imagery condition - number of words recalled	14.40	1.817	5
Rhyme condition - number of words recalled	13.40	1.342	5

Table 17.12 SPSS output for Mauchly's test of sphericity

Mauchly's Test of Sphericity[b]

If greater than .05 → Sphericity assumed
If less than .05 → Greenhouse-Geisser

Measure:Number_of_words

Within Subjects Effect	Mauchly's W	Approx. Chi-Square	df	Sig.	Epsilon[a]		
					Greenhouse-Geisser	Huynh-Feldt	Lower-bound
Memory_condition	.082	6.799	5	.262	.654	1.000	.333

Tests the null hypothesis that the error covariance matrix of the orthonormalized transformed dependent variables is proportional to an identity matrix.

a. May be used to adjust the degrees of freedom for the averaged tests of significance. Corrected tests are displayed in the Tests of Within-Subjects Effects table.

b. Design: Intercept
Within Subjects Design: Memory_condition

we can assume sphericity and so consult the Sphericity Assumed row of results in the Tests of Within-Subjects Effects table. If Mauchly's test is significant (Sig. less than .05), the assumption has been violated and you should consult the Greenhouse-Geisser row of results, which makes adjustments to the degrees of freedom (Table 17.12). Please remember that Mauchly's test does *not* tell us anything about differences between the means – it just tells us which row of results to consult. The "default" row is Sphericity Assumed, so if Mauchly's test is significant, this should tell you that something unusual is going on and you should consult the non-default row.

Table 17.13 SPSS output showing within-subjects effects

Tests of Within-Subjects Effects

Measure:Number_of_words

Source		Type III Sum of Squares	df	Mean Square	F	Sig.	Partial Eta Squared
Memory_condition	Sphericity Assumed	54.550	3	18.183	12.328	.001	.755
	Greenhouse-Geisser	54.550	1.962	27.805	12.328	.004	.755
	Huynh-Feldt	54.550	3.000	18.183	12.328	.001	.755
	Lower-bound	54.550	1.000	54.550	12.328	.025	.755
Error(Memory_condition)	Sphericity Assumed	17.700	12	1.475			
	Greenhouse-Geisser	17.700	7.847	2.256			
	Huynh-Feldt	17.700	12.000	1.475			
	Lower-bound	17.700	4.000	4.425			

STOP & Think

Which row of results should you consult if Mauchly's test had the following Sig. values: (1) .001, (2) .500, (3) .04?

The tests of Within-Subjects Effects table (Table 17.13) presents the really important information – the values of *df*, *F*, *p* and effect size. You should consult only the appropriate row of results (i.e. Sphericity Assumed or Greenhouse-Geisser) and just ignore anything in the other rows. For our memory experiment, we can use the Sphericity Assumed rows as Mauchly's test was non-significant.

As we have a significant result ($p = .001$), we need to inspect *post hoc* tests to find out where the differences lie. (Note that our *p* value is less than when we ran the one-way between-subjects ANOVA using the same data, thus indicating the increased sensitivity of the test.) *Post hoc* results are found the Pairwise Comparisons table (Table 17.14).

Any significant differences are highlighted with an asterisk (*) in the Mean Difference column. Therefore, the only significant difference is between condition 1 (Control) and condition 2 (Story).[4]

One-way within-subjects ANOVA by hand

To calculate the one-way within-subjects ANOVA by hand, you will need to calculate four different sums of squares: total, between-subjects, between-treatments and error (Figure 17.8).

SS_{total} is calculated as before:

---

4 Perceptive readers may be wondering why, if we had a more significant *F*-value with the within-subjects than between-subjects ANOVA, we have only one significant *post hoc* difference here and not three, as with the between-subjects ANOVA. The reason is that different *post hoc* tests were used – Tukey's HSD was used earlier and is not available for within-subjects ANOVA. Compared to Tukey's HSD, Bonferroni is a much stricter and more conservative test and is less likely to find a significant result.

Table 17.14 SPSS output showing pairwise comparison *post hoc* results

Pairwise Comparisons

Measure:Number_of_words

(I) Memory_condition	(J) Memory_condition	Mean Difference (I-J)	Std. Error	Sig.a	95% Confidence Interval for Differencea	
					Lower Bound	Upper Bound
1	2	-3.200*	.583	.032	-6.029	-.371
	3	-4.400	1.030	.077	-9.394	.594
	4	-3.400	.872	.105	-7.629	.829
2	1	3.200*	.583	.032	.371	6.029
	3	-1.200	.583	.652	-4.029	1.629
	4	-.200	.490	1.000	-2.576	2.176
3	1	4.400	1.030	.077	-.594	9.394
	2	1.200	.583	.652	-1.629	4.029
	4	1.000	.894	1.000	-3.339	5.339
4	1	3.400	.872	.105	-.829	7.629
	2	.200	.490	1.000	-2.176	2.576
	3	-1.000	.894	1.000	-5.339	3.339

Based on estimated marginal means

*. The mean difference is significant at the .05 level.

a. Adjustment for multiple comparisons: Bonferroni.

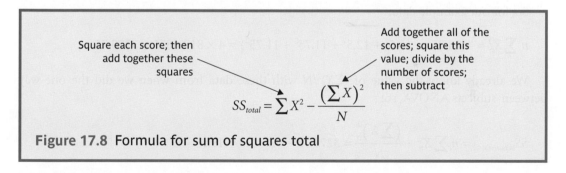

Figure 17.8 Formula for sum of squares total

Note that *N* refers to the number of scores, not the number of participants. As we are using the same scores as in the one-way between-subjects example, there is no need to repeat the calculations here: $SS_{total} = 91.75$.

$SS_{between\ subj}$ is the variation in participants' mean scores. For the five participants in our example, we can work out their average score across all conditions (Table 17.15).

When calculating $SS_{between\ subj}$ we use these participant means (Figure 17.9).

Table 17.15 Data for memory experiment with individual participant means

| Participant | Instruction condition | | | | Mean |
	Control	Story	Imagery	Rhyme	
1	12	15	16	14	14.25
2	10	14	16	14	13.5
3	9	13	13	15	12.5
4	11	12	12	12	11.75
5	8	12	15	12	11.75

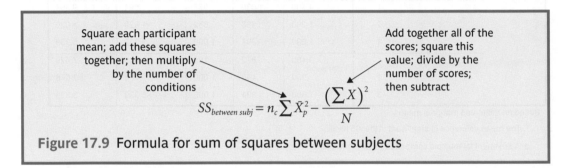

Square each participant mean; add these squares together; then multiply by the number of conditions

Add together all of the scores; square this value; divide by the number of scores; then subtract

$$SS_{between\ subj} = n_c \sum \bar{X}_p^2 - \frac{(\sum X)^2}{N}$$

Figure 17.9 Formula for sum of squares between subjects

So, for our example data:

$$n_c \sum \bar{X}_p^2 = 4(14.25^2 + 13.5^2 + 12.5^2 + 11.75^2 + 11.75^2) = 4 \times 817.6875 = 3270.75$$

We already know the value of $(\Sigma X)^2/N$ with these data from when we did the one-way between-subjects ANOVA, so:

$$SS_{between\ subj} = n_c \sum \bar{X}_p^2 - \frac{(\sum X)^2}{N} = 3270.75 - 3251.25 = 19.5$$

Next, we calculate $SS_{treatments}$, which tells us about the variation between the means for each treatment condition (Table 17.16).

The formula is similar to before, but uses the number of cases in each condition and the treatment means (Figure 17.10).

Table 17.16 Data from memory experiment with condition means

| Participant | Instruction condition | | | |
	Control	Story	Imagery	Rhyme
1	12	15	16	14
2	10	14	16	14
3	9	13	13	15
4	11	12	12	12
5	8	12	15	12
Mean	10.0	13.2	14.4	13.4

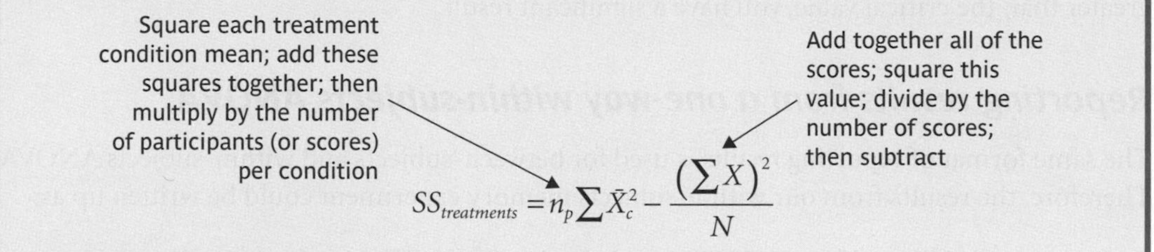

Square each treatment condition mean; add these squares together; then multiply by the number of participants (or scores) per condition

Add together all of the scores; square this value; divide by the number of scores; then subtract

$$SS_{treatments} = n_p \sum \bar{X}_c^2 - \frac{(\sum X)^2}{N}$$

Figure 17.10 Formula for sum of squares treatments

For our example data:

$$n_p \sum \bar{X}_c^2 = 5(10.0^2 + 13.2^2 + 14.4^2 + 13.4^2) = 5 \times 661.16 = 3\ 305.8$$

So,

$$SS_{treatments} = n_p \sum \bar{X}_c^2 - \frac{(\sum X)^2}{N} = 3\ 305.8 - 3\ 251.25 = 54.55$$

SS_{error} is whatever variation is left over, so subtract $SS_{treatments}$ and $SS_{between\ subj}$ from SS_{total}. For our example data:

$$SS_{error} = SS_{total} - SS_{between\ subj} - SS_{treatments} = 91.75 - 19.5 - 54.55 = 17.7$$

The next stage is calculating the df-values: df_{total} is the number of scores minus 1, $df_{between\ subj}$ is the number of scores per treatment condition minus 1, $df_{treatments}$ is the number of treatment conditions minus 1, and df_{error} is what's left after subtracting the other two df-values from df_{total}. Therefore, for our example data, $df_{total} = 19$ (i.e. $20 - 1$), $df_{between\ subj} = 4$ (i.e. $5 - 1$), $df_{treatments} = 3$ (i.e. $4 - 1$) and $df_{error} = 12$ (i.e. $19 - 4 - 3$).

Next, we calculate the mean sum of squares for the treatment conditions ($MS_{treatments}$) and the error (MS_{error}) by dividing the SS value by the appropriate df-value.

$$MS_{treatments} = \frac{SS_{treatments}}{df_{treatments}} = \frac{54.55}{3} = 18.183$$

$$MS_{error} = \frac{SS_{error}}{df_{error}} = \frac{17.7}{12} = 1.475$$

All that remains is to calculate the F-statistic:

$$F = \frac{MS_{treatments}}{MS_{error}} = \frac{18.183}{1.475} = 12.327$$

Check this value against the critical F-value for your df-values and alpha level; if your F-value is greater than the critical value, you have a significant result.

Reporting results from a one-way within-subjects ANOVA

The same format of reporting results is used for between-subjects and within-subjects ANOVA. Therefore, the results from our within-subjects memory experiment could be written up as:

A one-way within-subjects ANOVA revealed a significant difference between the group means, $F(3, 12) = 12.33$, $p = .001$, $\eta_p^2 = .755$. *Post hoc* Bonferroni tests revealed that the Control group ($M = 10.0$, $SD = 1.58$) had a significantly lower mean number of words remembered than the Story group ($M = 13.20$, $SD = 1.30$; $p = .032$). No other comparisons were significant (all $ps > .05$).

Non-parametric equivalents of one-way ANOVA

If you have only ordinal data or your interval/ratio data are not normally distributed, the assumptions of ANOVA have not been met and you need to use a non-parametric equivalent. Remember that non-parametric tests use less detail from the data and so are usually less likely to find a significant result.

Kruskal-Wallis test

Kruskal-Wallis test
Non-parametric equivalent of one-way between-subjects ANOVA; used to compare differences in scores for two or more groups.

The non-parametric equivalent of the one-way between-subjects ANOVA is the **Kruskal-Wallis test**. That is, the Kruskal-Wallis test is used to compare scores from two or more groups. In that respect, it is an extension of the **Mann-Whitney U test**, which compares scores from just two groups. It works by ranking all of the scores and then comparing the total ranks for each group. If one group's sum of ranks is much higher than the other group's, this suggests that there may be differences between the groups.

ch. 16
pp.367–37

SPSS output for Kruskal-Wallis test

Please see our website for full details on how to run the Kruskal-Wallis test in SPSS. The SPSS output for the test using our memory experiment data is shown in Table 17.17.

Table 17.17 SPSS output for Kruskal-Wallis analysis

Hypothesis Test Summary

	Null Hypothesis	Test	Sig.	Decision
1	The distribution of Number of words correctly recalled is the same across categories of Instruction condition.	Independent-Samples Kruskal-Wallis Test	.013	Reject the null hypothesis.

Asymptotic significances are displayed. The significance level is .05.

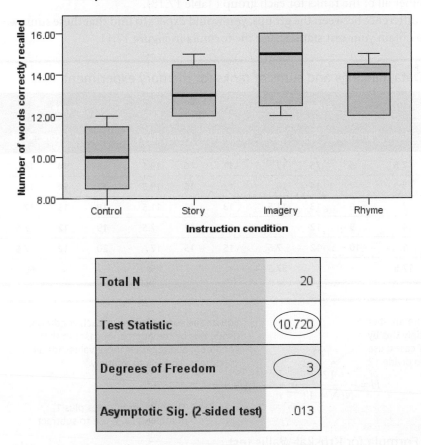

Independent-Samples Kruskal-Wallis Test

Total N	20
Test Statistic	10.720
Degrees of Freedom	3
Asymptotic Sig. (2-sided test)	.013

1. The test statistic is adjusted for ties.

The *Test Statistics* table is where you find the important results. Chi-square (χ^2) is the test statistic used for Kruskal-Wallis, so make a note of it. You should also note the values for *df* and Exact Sig.

Here we have a significant result, so we need to follow it up to understand where the differences lie. However, there is no *post hoc* option available for Kruskal-Wallis, so you are recommended to use multiple Mann-Whitney *U*-tests. To control for Type I errors, use the Bonferroni correction method. Therefore, if you wanted to make all possible comparisons for the memory experiment, you would need to divide your alpha level by 6, to give you .05/6 = .008, which is pretty low and means you are very unlikely to find anything significant. However, if you had planned beforehand to use *a priori* comparisons between the Control group and each of the three experimental conditions, the adjusted *p*-value would only be .05/3 = .016. Remember, you should decide on *a priori* or *post hoc* comparisons before doing any analysis – you cannot run *post hoc* comparisons and then change to planned just to get a significant result!

Kruskal-Wallis test by hand

Like other non-parametric tests, the Kruskal-Wallis test is fairly straightforward and satisfying to do by hand. The first step is to rank all scores from lowest to highest regardless of group. Next, you add together all of the ranks for each group (Table 17.18).

If there was no difference between the groups, you would expect to find that these sums were roughly similar. To obtain your test statistic, use the formula in Figure 17.11.

Table 17.18 Data, rankings and sums of ranks for memory experiment

| | Control | | | Story | | | Imagery | | | Rhyme | |
Participant	Score	Rank	Participant	Score	Rank	Participant	Score	Rank	Participant	Score	Rank
1	12	7.5	6	15	17	11	16	19.5	16	14	14
2	10	3	7	14	14	12	16	19.5	17	14	14
3	9	2	8	13	11.5	13	13	11.5	18	15	17
4	11	4	9	12	7.5	14	12	7.5	19	12	7.5
5	8	1	10	12	7.5	15	15	17	20	12	7.5
Sum		17.5			57.5			75			60

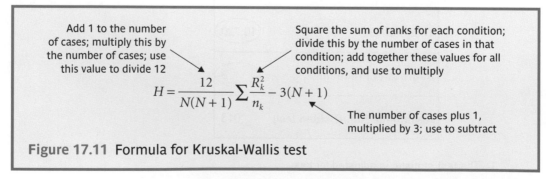

Figure 17.11 Formula for Kruskal-Wallis test

Therefore, for our sample data:

$$H = \frac{12}{20(20+1)} \left(\frac{17.5^2}{5} + \frac{57.5^2}{5} + \frac{75^2}{5} + \frac{60^2}{5} \right) - 3(20+1)$$

$$= \frac{12}{420} \left(\frac{306.25}{5} + \frac{3\,306.25}{5} + \frac{5\,625}{5} + \frac{3\,600}{5} \right) - 3(21)$$

$$= 0.0286(61.25 + 661.25 + 1\,125 + 720) - 63 = (0.0286 \times 2\,567.5) - 63$$

$$= 73.4305 - 63 = 10.4305$$

You treat this H statistic as χ^2 and inspect the table of critical χ^2 values (Appendix B) for your appropriate df-value (i.e. number of conditions minus 1). If your test statistic is more extreme than the critical value, you have a significant result.

Reporting results of a Kruskal-Wallis test

As with many other non-parametric tests, the guidelines about reporting the results for a Kruskal-Wallis test are not as strict as for their parametric equivalents. However, you should at least include the values of chi-square, df and p. The results for the memory experiment could be written up as:

A Kruskal-Wallis test revealed a significant difference between the groups, χ^2 (3) = 10.72, $p = .005$. *Post hoc* multiple Mann-Whitney U-tests were used to compare pairs of groups, with an adjusted alpha level of .008 to control for Type I errors. However, with this strict criterion, no significant differences were found.

Friedman test

The **Friedman test** is the non-parametric equivalent of the one-way within-subjects ANOVA, and so is used to compare scores from two or more conditions when the same group have taken part under all conditions. It can also be thought of as an extension of the **Wilcoxon Signed Ranks test**, which deals with only two conditions.

The Friedman test works by looking at each individual participant's scores across all conditions, and then summing these ranks for each condition. The sum of ranks for each condition are then compared. If one condition has a much higher sum of ranks than other conditions, this indicates that that particular condition has higher scores.

Friedman test
Non-parametric equivalent of one-way within-subjects ANOVA; compares differences in scores from two or more conditions from the same group of participants.

SPSS output for Friedman test

The SPSS output for the Friedman test for the within-subjects version of our memory experiment is shown in Table 17.19. (Please see our website for details of the procedure.) The Hypothesis Test Summary table provides you with the p-value and tells you if the null

ch. 16
p.372–375

Table 17.19 SPSS output for Friedman test

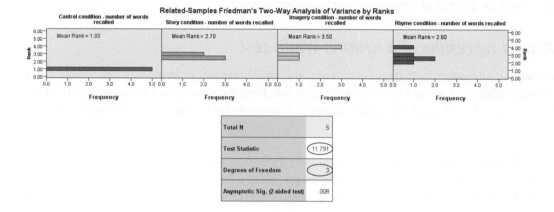

hypothesis should be rejected or retained. If you double-click on this table in SPSS, you will get further output, which gives you the mean ranks for each condition as well as the values of the test statistic and *df*.

With a significant result, we would need to use planned or *post hoc* comparisons to determine where the differences lie. Either way, you should use multiple Wilcoxon Signed Ranks tests and adjust the alpha level by dividing by the number of comparisons. Remember that the more comparisons you make, the lower the alpha level will become and the more difficult it will be to find a significant result.

Friedman test by hand

To do the Friedman test by hand, you rank the scores *for each participant* across all conditions and then find the sum of the ranks for each condition. In other words, you look at a single participant's scores across all the conditions and put them in rank order, before adding together the ranks of different participants in the same condition. Thus, for our memory experiment example see Table 17.20.

To calculate the test statistic, use the formula in Figure 17.12.

Table 17.20 Data, ranks and sums of ranks for memory experiment

Participant	Control		Story		Imagery		Rhyme	
	Score	Rank	Score	Rank	Score	Rank	Score	Rank
1	12	1	15	3	16	4	14	2
2	10	1	14	2.5	16	4	14	2.5
3	9	1	13	2.5	13	2.5	15	4
4	11	1	12	3	12	3	12	3
5	8	1	12	2.5	15	4	12	2.5
Sum		5		13.5		17.5		14

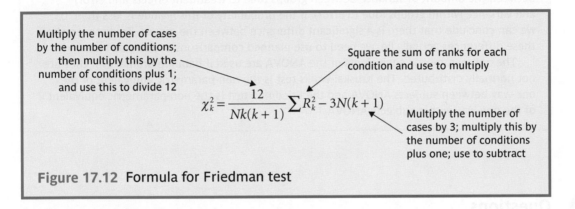

Multiply the number of cases by the number of conditions; then multiply this by the number of conditions plus 1; and use this to divide 12

Square the sum of ranks for each condition and use to multiply

$$\chi_k^2 = \frac{12}{Nk(k+1)} \sum R_k^2 - 3N(k+1)$$

Multiply the number of cases by 3; multiply this by the number of conditions plus one; use to subtract

Figure 17.12 Formula for Friedman test

Therefore, for our sample data:

$$\chi_k^2 = \frac{12}{5 \times 4(4+1)} (5^2 + 13.5^2 + 17.5^2 + 14^2) - (3 \times 5)(4+1)$$

$$= \frac{12}{20(5)} (25 + 182.25 + 306.25 + 196) - 15(5) =$$

Inspect the table of critical χ^2 values (Appendix B) for your appropriate df-value (i.e. number of conditions minus 1). If your test statistic is more extreme than the critical value, you have a significant result.

Reporting results of a Friedman test

As with the Kruskal-Wallis test, there is no agreed standard format for reporting Friedman test results, but you should include chi-square, df and p somewhere. The results for the memory experiment when analysed using the Friedman test could be written up as:

A Friedman test revealed a significant difference between the conditions, χ^2 (3) = 11.79, $p = .002$. *Post hoc* multiple Wilcoxon Signed Ranks tests were used to compare pairs of groups, with an adjusted alpha level of .008 to control for Type I errors. However, with this strict criterion, no significant differences were found between the conditions.

Summary

In this chapter, you were introduced to the methods used to compare two or more conditions from a single factor design. Multiple *t*-tests cannot be used for comparing more than two conditions because of the risk of increasing the Type I error rate.

The parametric tests used to compare two or more conditions are called ANOVAs; we use the one-way between-subjects ANOVA when we have different groups in each condition and the one-way within-subjects (or repeated measures) ANOVA when the same group contributes to each condition. In both cases, an *F*-value is calculated, which is the ratio between the amount of variance between groups (due to treatment effects and error) and variance within groups (due to error). If the probability of this *F*-value is less than .05, we can conclude that there is a significant difference between the means. To discover where these differences actually lie, we need to use planned comparisons or *post hoc* tests.

The non-parametric equivalents of the ANOVA are used if data are ordinal or if they are not normally distributed. The Kruskal-Wallis test is the non-parametric equivalent of the one-way between-subjects ANOVA and the Friedman test is the non-parametric equivalent of the one-way within-subjects ANOVA.

Questions

1 Why can we not just use multiple *t*-tests instead of ANOVA when comparing differences between two or more conditions?

2 What are the two sources of variance in the *F*-ratio, and what factors contribute to these variances?

3 Which of the following set of conditions is likely to produce the highest *F*-value?

(a) strong treatment effect, high error

(b) strong treatment effect, low error

(c) weak treatment effect, high error

(d) weak treatment effect, low error

4 Why is a within-subjects ANOVA more sensitive than a between-subjects ANOVA?

5 Why do we need to use *a priori/post hoc* comparisons?

6 Under which circumstances would you select *post hoc* comparisons over *a priori* (planned) comparisons?

7 An SPSS data file is set up with a grouping variable and a score variable. The data were measured on an ordinal scale. What is the most appropriate method of analysing these data?

8 In an SPSS output table, the p-value for Mauchly's test of sphericity is .035. Which row of results should be consulted in the tests of within-subjects effects table?

9 What is the Bonferroni method and why is it used?

10 What are the assumptions of one-way between-subjects ANOVA and one-way within-subjects ANOVA, and how can they be checked?

 ## Activities

1 A social psychologist compares three kinds of propaganda messages on college students' attitudes towards the war on terrorism. Ninety ($N = 90$) students are randomly assigned in equal numbers to the three different communication conditions. A paper-and-pencil attitude measure is used to assess students' attitudes towards the war after they are exposed to the propaganda statements. An ANOVA is carried out to determine the effect of the three messages on student attitudes. The ANOVA summary table is shown in Table 17.21.

● What are the null and alternative hypotheses here?

● Explain whether there is a significant result or not, and what this means in relation to the null hypothesis.

● Calculate an appropriate effect size measure for this study.

● Report the result in the correct format.

Table 17.21 ANOVA summary table

Source	Sum of squares	df	Mean square	F	p
Communication	180.10	2	90.05	17.87	0.000
Error	438.50	87	5.04		

2 Analyse, interpret and write up the findings for the following study:

Imagine you have conducted an experiment on how well participants can detect a signal against a background of noise, measured in decibels (db). Fifteen participants were exposed to different levels of background noise (no noise, 20 db, or 40 db) and asked to indicate whether or not they heard a tone. The number of times that the participant correctly stated that a tone was present represents your dependent variable. You found that participants in the no-noise group detected more of the tones (36.4) than participants in either the 20-db (23.8) or 40-db (16.0) groups. Table 17.22 shows the scores for each group.

Table 17.22 Scores for each group			
	No noise	20 decibels	40 decibels
	33	22	17
	39	24	14
	41	25	19
	32	21	11
	37	27	19
M	36.4	23.8	16.0

3 Imagine the study in the previous activity was conducted on five participants rather than 15, and that each participant was exposed to each condition. Assuming the same scores, analyse, interpret and write up the findings for this version of the study.

Chapter 18

Comparing Differences between More than Two Conditions: Part 2 – Factorial Designs

OVERVIEW

In the last chapter you were introduced to **analysis of variance** (**ANOVA**) and how it can be used to compare means from more than two conditions in a single-factor design. However, ANOVA is remarkably flexible and can be used to analyse more complex designs involving more than one independent variable. ANOVA can not only tell us about the overall effects of the independent variables, but also how they interact. The techniques covered in this chapter – between-subjects factorial ANOVA, within-subjects factorial ANOVA and mixed factorial ANOVA – build on the techniques discussed in the previous chapter, so it is worth revising that content before moving on. (If you have a factorial design in which the dependent measure is nominal, please go to **Chapter 20**.)

ch. 17

ch. 20

OBJECTIVES

After studying this chapter and working through the exercises, you should be able to:

● Identify the characteristics of a factorial design

● Distinguish between between-subjects, within-subjects and mixed factorial designs

● Define main effect and interaction in factorial designs

● Interpret the main effects and interactions of a factorial design

● Conduct analysis, interpret output and write up results for the between-subjects factorial ANOVA, within-subjects factorial ANOVA and mixed factorial ANOVA

Factorial designs

Factorial design
Research design that has more than one independent variable; every level of one independent variable is combined with every level of every other independent variable.

Factor
Another name for independent variable, commonly used when discussing factorial designs.

Level
A condition in an independent variable (factor).

Main effect
In a factorial design, the overall effect of a factor on the dependent variable.

Interaction
The differing effect of one factor on the dependent variable, depending on the particular level of another factor.

Before we move on to the statistical content of this chapter, it is time for a little revision. In Chapter 7 we introduced you to **factorial designs**, where there is more than one independent variable, or **factor**, each with two or more **levels**. Note, however, that there is still *one* dependent variable. This type of design is very popular with researchers because it is a bit like combining several experiments into one, meaning that they are usually quicker and cheaper than running lots of individual one-factor experiments.

Another reason why factorial designs are so popular is that they generate more information than simple one-factor experiments. Specifically, factorial designs give you two kinds of information. The first is information about the effect of each independent variable by itself: we call this the **main effect** of a factor. We can think of this in the same way as separate one-way ANOVAs for each factor. In a design with two factors, there are two main effects – one for each factor. The second type of information is called an **interaction**. If there is an interaction between two factors, the effect of one factor on the dependent variable depends on the particular level of the other factor – they interact. Interactions are a new source of information that cannot be obtained in a simple one-factor experimental design.

The variables in a factorial design can be entirely between-subjects (i.e. different samples in each condition), entirely within-subjects (i.e. same sample in each condition) or can consist of a mixed design, which incorporates at least one between-subjects variable and at least one within-subjects variable. Thus, we can describe a factorial design as a **between-subjects factorial design**, a **within-subjects factorial design** or a **mixed factorial design**. For example, recall the study first introduced in **Chapters 6 and 7** which examined the effect of exercise on mood ratings. We could design a factorial experiment to look at this by using two factors, each with two levels: level of exercise (30 minutes of exercise, 30 minutes of non-strenuous activity) and time of testing (day, night). Combining these two factors would result in four individual conditions: exercise/day, exercise/night, no exercise/day and no exercise/night. The four possible designs for this 2 × 2 factorial experiment are shown in Table 18.1.

ch. 7
pp.137–1

chs 6, 7

Table 18.1 Possible designs for a 2 × 2 factorial experiment looking at effects of exercise and time of testing on mood ratings

Between-subjects factorial design

		Level of exercise (between-subjects)	
		Exercise	No exercise
Time of testing (between-subjects)	Day	Group 1	Group 2
	Night	Group 3	Group 4

Within-subjects factorial design

		Level of exercise (within-subjects)	
		Exercise	No exercise
Time of testing (within-subjects)	Day	Group 1	Group 1
	Night	Group 1	Group 1

Mixed factorial design

		Level of exercise (within-subjects)	
		Exercise	No exercise
Time of testing (between-subjects)	Day	Group 1	Group 1
	Night	Group 2	Group 2

Mixed factorial design

		Level of exercise (between-subjects)	
		Exercise	No exercise
Time of testing (within-subjects)	Day	Group 1	Group 2
	Night	Group 1	Group 2

Between-subjects factorial design
Factorial design in which every factor is a between-subjects variable; a different group takes part in each condition.

Within-subjects factorial design
Factorial design in which every factor is a within-subjects variable; the same group takes part under all conditions.

Mixed factorial design
Factorial design in which one or more factors are between-subjects variables and one or more are within-subjects variable.

In the first design in Table 18.1, both factors are between-subjects. This means that a different sample of people is assigned to each of the four conditions. In the second design, both factors are within-subjects, meaning that the same sample of people takes part in all four conditions. The other designs show a mixed factorial design where one factor is between-subjects and the other within-subjects. For the between-subjects factor, different samples are assigned to each level, but they take part under all levels of the within-subjects factor. This sounds complicated, so let us give an example. If "time of testing" was between-subjects and "level of exercise" was within-subjects, one group of participants would be tested during the day and another group at night, but *all* participants would take part in both the exercise and the no-exercise conditions. Alternatively, another example of a mixed-factorial design would be if "time of testing" was within-subjects and "level of exercise" was between-subjects. In this case, one group of participants would be tested in the "exercise" condition and another in the "no-exercise condition" but *both* of these groups would take part in their respective conditions during the day and at night.

> ## STOP & Think
>
> What are the practical advantages and disadvantages associated with each type of factorial design? Which design do you think is best for the exercise and mood study? Why?

In the exercise and mood study, you could choose any of the possible designs. Of course, sometimes you are more restricted in your choice of factorial design. If you wanted to conduct a study, for example, in which age (younger versus older) and gender (male versus female) were the factors, this would require a between-subjects factorial design – it would not be possible to have participants take part under all possible conditions (think about it). But if you do have some choice, bear in mind that when using within-subjects factors you do not have to worry about individual differences and you generally need fewer participants compared with between-subjects factors. On the other hand, a within-subjects design may result in order effects, thus requiring counterbalancing. You need to think very carefully about these issues when designing a factorial study.

Increasing the number of levels or factors in a factorial design

The 2×2 is the simplest factorial design. One way to increase the complexity is to increase the number of levels of one or more of the factors. A 2×3 design, for example, contains two factors: the first has two levels and the second has three levels. Therefore, a 2×3 has six conditions. In the exercise and mood study, the exercise factor could be changed to have three levels: strenuous exercise, mild exercise and no exercise. If the time of testing factor still had two levels, this would produce a 2×3 design (see Table 18.2).

As well as increasing the number of levels of a factor, we can also increase the number of factors in the design. A $2 \times 2 \times 2$ factorial design contains three factors, each with two levels. Thus, there are eight conditions in this design. In a $2 \times 2 \times 3$ design, there are 12 conditions; in a $2 \times 2 \times 2 \times 2$ design, there are 16, and so on. We could extend the exercise–mood study by adding an extra factor: gender. The design would then be a $2 \times 2 \times 3$ design (see Table 18.3).

Table 18.2 2×3 factorial experiment looking at effects of time of testing and exercise on mood ratings

		Level of exercise		
		Strenuous exercise	Mild exercise	No exercise
Time of testing	Day	Condition 1	Condition 2	Condition 3
	Night	Condition 4	Condition 5	Condition 6

Table 18.3 $2 \times 2 \times 3$ factorial design looking at effects of time of testing, sex and exercise on mood ratings

		Male		
		Level of exercise		
		Strenuous exercise	Mild exercise	No exercise
Time of testing	Day	Condition 1	Condition 2	Condition 3
	Night	Condition 4	Condition 5	Condition 6
		Female		
		Level of exercise		
		Strenuous exercise	Mild exercise	No exercise
Time of testing	Day	Condition 7	Condition 8	Condition 9
	Night	Condition 10	Condition 11	Condition 12

Students often get overexcited with factorial designs and are tempted to include in a study as many factors as they can think of. Do not do the same. One problem with this is that the design may become incredibly complex and require large numbers of participants, particularly if the design is between-subjects. The $2 \times 2 \times 3$ design discussed above had 12 conditions; a $2 \times 2 \times 2 \times 3$ design would have 24 conditions; adding another factor with two levels would result in 48 conditions. If your design was entirely between-subjects and you planned on having 10 participants in each condition, this would mean getting hold of 480 willing volunteers!

So, although factorial designs allow for great flexibility in design and can produce more information than multiple one-factor experiments, this also means that analysing and interpreting data can be more complex. While it is theoretically possible to have a factorial design with any number of factors, you are strongly advised to stick to designs with no more than three factors – any more and you will find it almost impossible to interpret.

Main effects and interactions

ch. 7
pp.137–138

So, how do we identify main effects and interactions, and interpret results from factorial designs? The easiest way to demonstrate this is through another example. Recall the 2×2 experiment outlined in **Chapter 7** in which Smith and Ellsworth (1987) looked at the effects of misleading questions on eyewitness testimony accuracy. After watching a video of a crime, participants were asked a number of questions. One of the factors in the experiment was the type of question – misleading or unbiased – and the other factor was whether the person asking the questions was naive (i.e. had only seen the video once) or knowledgeable (i.e. had seen the video several times). Thus, there were two factors, each with two levels, producing four individual conditions (see Table 18.4).

To illustrate main effects and interactions, we can look at results based on the Smith and Ellsworth study on accuracy of eyewitness testimony. Table 18.5 illustrates a common method of presenting outcomes for the various groups in a factorial design. The number in each cell in Table 18.5 (these boxes with numbers are called "cells") represents the mean percentage errors made in the four conditions.

Main effects

A main effect is the overall effect that each factor has by itself on the dependent variable. We can learn about main effects by looking at the overall means in the right-hand column and bottom row (also called the margin means as they are in the margins of the figure) of Table 18.5. In the "misleading questions" condition, participants make, on average, 29.5 errors when tested in the

Table 18.4 The 2×2 factorial design of Smith and Ellsworth's (1987) experiment

		Question	
		Unbiased	Misleading
Questioner	Knowledgeable	Condition 1	Condition 2
	Naive	Condition 3	Condition 4

Table 18.5 2×2 factorial design: results of the eyewitness testimony experiment

		Question (factor A)		Overall mean (main effect of factor B)
		Unbiased	Misleading	
Questioner (factor B)	Knowledgeable	13	41	27.0
	Naive	13	18	15.5
Overall mean (main effect of factor A)		13.0	29.5	

recall task. For the "unbiased questions" condition it is 13.0. It would therefore appear that more errors are being made in the misleading condition than in the unbiased condition.

Note that these means are calculated by averaging across all participants in the unbiased group and all participants in the misleading group, *irrespective* of the type of questioner (knowledgeable or naive). For example, the mean of 29.5 for the misleading group is the average of 41 from the knowledgeable-misleading group and 18 from the naive-misleading group. The main effect of type of questioner can also be examined by comparing the overall mean for the knowledgeable group (27) with the overall mean for the naive group (15.5). Thus, in general, more errors result when the questioner is knowledgeable *and* when the questions are misleading.

Interactions

While the main effects in Table 18.5 tell us that, overall, people make more errors in the recall task when the questioner is knowledgeable and when the questions are misleading, they do not tell us the whole picture – what about the pattern evident in the group means? We can see that when the questions are unbiased, having a knowledgeable or naive questioner does not really make much of a difference (means of 13 for both conditions), but when the questions are misleading, more errors are reported with a knowledgeable questioner compared to a naive questioner (means of 41 and 18.5, respectively). This suggests that there is an interaction – the level of knowledge of the questioner appears to have no effect when the questions are unbiased, but *does* make a difference when the questions are misleading. We can also look at the interaction from the other point of view – when the questioner is naive, the type of question has little effect (means of 13 for unbiased questions and 18 for misleading questions), but when the questioner is knowledgeable, misleading questions result in more errors (means of 13 for unbiased question and 41 for misleading questions).

Whichever way you look at it, there is clearly an interaction and the effect of one of the factors depends on the level of the other factor. Therefore, when considering the effects of type of question and level of knowledge of questioner on recall errors, we must consider both variables. Just looking at the main effects does not tell us this, and our interpretation of the main effects must also be informed by the interaction.

Interactions can easily be seen when the means for all conditions are presented in a graph. Figure 18.1 shows a bar graph of the results of the eyewitness testimony experiment. Note that all four means have been graphed. Two bars compare the types of questioner in the unbiased question condition; the same comparison is shown for the misleading question condition. You can see that questioner knowledge is not a factor when an unbiased question is asked; however, when the question is misleading, the knowledgeable questioner has a greater ability to create bias than does the naive questioner.

Bar graphs are helpful, but you will often see line graphs of means used to interpret interactions. In such line graphs, the dependent variable is placed on the y-axis (vertical), one of the factors is placed on the x-axis (usually the factor with the most levels), and the other is identified by different lines on the graph. If you have a third factor, this would require a separate graph for each level of that third factor. The means from the eyewitness testimony experiment can be presented in a line graph (see Figure 18.2). When the lines diverge in this way in a line graph of means, it usually indicates the presence of an interaction.

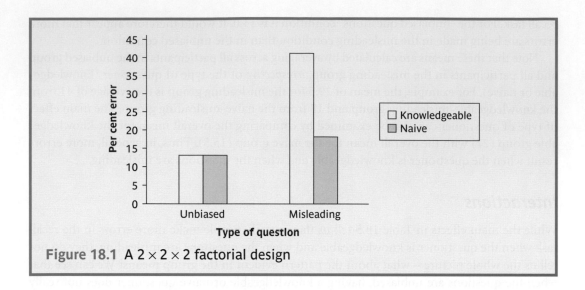

Figure 18.1 A 2 × 2 × 2 factorial design

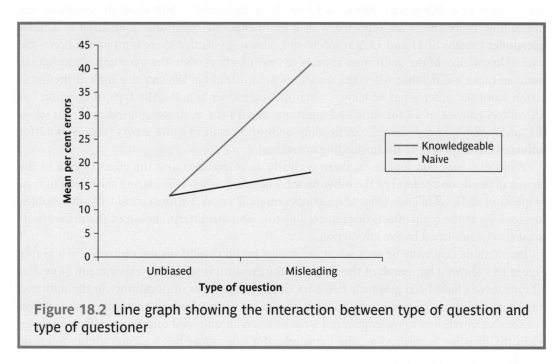

Figure 18.2 Line graph showing the interaction between type of question and type of questioner

The concept of interaction is a relatively simple one that you probably use all the time. When we say "it depends," we are usually indicating that some sort of interaction is operating – it depends on some other variable. Suppose, for example, that a friend has asked you if you want to go to the cinema. Whether you go may reflect an interaction between two variables: (1) is an examination coming up? and (2) who stars in the film? If there is an examination coming up, you would not go under any circumstance (obviously . . . right?). If you do not have an examination to worry about, your decision will depend on whether you like the actors in the film; that is, you will go only if a favourite star is in the film.

Interpreting 2 × 2 factorial designs

There are several possibilities when analysing the results of a 2 × 2 factorial design: (1) there may or may not be a main effect of factor A, (2) there may or may not be a main effect of factor B, and (3) there may or may not be an interaction between factor A and factor B.

Table 18.6 presents the means from four 2 × 2 factorial experiments; these data are also illustrated graphically in Figure 18.3. In each experiment the two factors, labelled A and B, have two levels, identified by using subscript numbers $_1$ and $_2$. We are using generic terminology here so that you can apply the results and interpretation to any 2 × 2 design, but if you find it too abstract you may find it easier to use more concrete labels. For example, perhaps the experiment is looking at the influence of crowding (factor A, low crowding versus high crowding) and presence of windows (factor B, no windows versus room with windows) on performance on a cognitive task. If you can think of your own 2 × 2 design, then feel free to use that.

To determine whether there is an interaction in the examples, you should look at the cell means (i.e. the means for each individual condition). If the changes that occur in the means of one row of the figure are similar to the changes in the other row, the two factors are not interacting. However, if the changes in one row are greater, lesser or reversed from those in the other row, this suggests an interaction. Interactions are also easy to spot in line graphs as the lines will often cross or diverge from each other; parallel lines suggest no interaction.

In contrast, it is more difficult to determine main effects from looking at line graphs. Instead, you should consult the overall margin means in the tables. As you will see, you need to be careful when interpreting main effects when there is an interaction.

Table 18.6 Four different 2 × 2 factorial designs

Example 1	A_1	A_2	Margin M		Example 2	A_1	A_2	Margin M
B_1	20	30	25		B_1	20	30	25
B_2	30	20	25		B_2	30	40	35
Margin M	25	25			Margin M	25	35	

Example 3	A_1	A_2	Margin M		Example 4	A_1	A_2	Margin M
B_1	20	30	25		B_1	10	20	15
B_2	20	20	20		B_2	30	50	40
Margin M	20	25			Margin M	20	35	

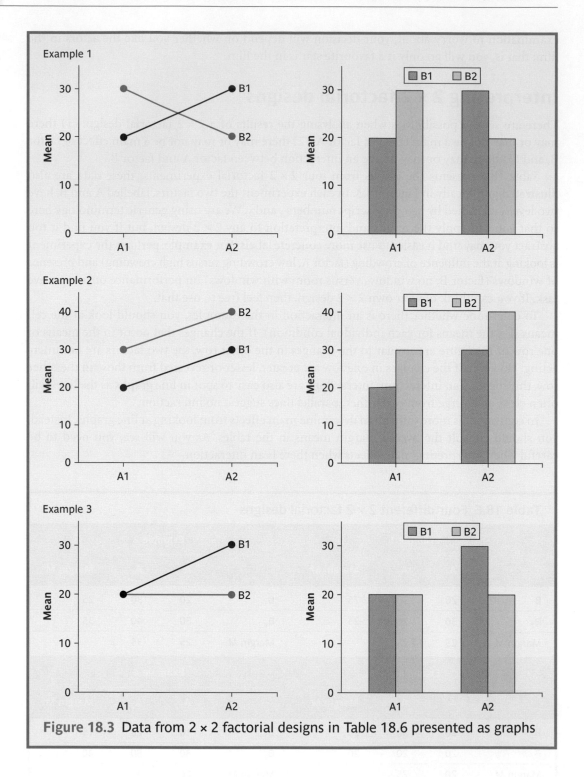

Figure 18.3 Data from 2 × 2 factorial designs in Table 18.6 presented as graphs

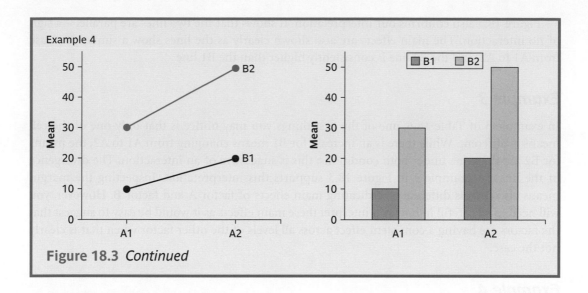

Figure 18.3 *Continued*

STOP & Think

Before proceeding, go through the examples in Figure 18.3 and try to determine if there are main effects and/or interactions.

Example 1

The first thing you will probably notice from example 1 in Table 18.6 is that there is no difference between the margin means for A1 and A2 or between B1 and B2, indicating that there is no main effect of factor A and no main effect of factor B. However, in B1, changing from A1 to A2 leads to an increase in the mean score by 10 points (i.e. 20 to 30). This pattern is reversed for B2, with a 10-point *decrease* when changing from A1 to A2 (i.e. 30 to 20). This suggests that there may be an interaction.

The interaction is obvious in the line graph for example 1 shown in Figure 18.3. The lines are crossing, strongly suggesting an interaction. Interactions such as this are often referred to as crossed interactions.

Example 2

In example 2 in Table 18.6, we can see that there appears to be a difference in the margin means for factor A and factor B, indicating main effects. However, when we look at the cell means, the means for B1 and B2 increase by the *same amount* when changing from A1 to A2 (20 to 30; 30 to 40 respectively). This would suggest that there is no interaction. In terms of the interaction, it does not matter that the B1 means are lower than the B2 means – it is the direction and amount of change that we are interested in.

Figure 18.3 also confirms our interpretation. It shows that the two lines are parallel – a sign of no interaction. The main effects are also shown clearly as the lines show a similar increase from A1 to A2, and the B2 line is consistently higher than the B1 line.

Example 3

In example 3 of Table 18.6, one of the first things you may notice is that only one of the cell means is different. While there is an increase for B1 means changing from A1 to A2, the means for B2 are the same under both conditions; this is suggestive of an interaction. The divergence of the lines in example 3 in Figure 18.3 supports this interpretation. Inspecting the margin means also reveals differences, indicating main effects of factor A and factor B. However, you will need to be careful in how you interpret these main effects as it would be easy to suggest that the factors are having a consistent effect across all levels of the other factor when that is clearly not the case.

Example 4

From example 4 in Figure 18.4, it is clear that the lines diverge and that there may be an interaction. The lines are not parallel but they do not cross each other; this type of interaction is sometimes referred to as an uncrossed interaction. As well as the interaction, there also appear to be main effects as the margin means in example 4 in Figure 18.3 show differences for both factor A and factor B.

Some writers recommend that you should ignore main effects altogether if you have any interaction, since stating that you have an interaction suggests that factors are not actually acting independently on the dependent variable. However, Howell (2007) argues that this is unreasonable as some main effects can be meaningful even in the presence of an interaction. You are therefore advised to interpret main effects when they make sense in the context of the data. In example 4 it is a good idea to discuss main effects as there is a clear increase from A1 to A2 across both levels of factor B, and an increase from B1 to B2 across both levels of factor A. If you ignored the main effects here you would not be getting the full picture from the data and could be missing out on some important information.

We have discussed four possible outcomes of a 2 × 2 design, but there are eight possible outcomes for this type of design (see Figure 18.4). For each outcome, the means are given and then presented as a line graph. You should go through each and try to explain why there is or is not a main effect of factor A, a main effect of factor B and an A × B interaction.

Interpreting more complex factorial designs

So far, we have focused on interpreting 2 × 2 factorial designs as these are the most simple and easiest to interpret. Other two-factor designs (e.g. 2 × 3, 2 × 4, 3 × 3) can be interpreted in exactly the same way as a 2 × 2 design: as there are still two factors, you have only two main effects and an interaction between the two factors. Table 18.7 shows a 2 × 3 factorial design with the factors of task difficulty (easy, hard) and anxiety level (low, moderate, high). The dependent variable is performance on the task. The numbers in each of the six cells of the design indicate

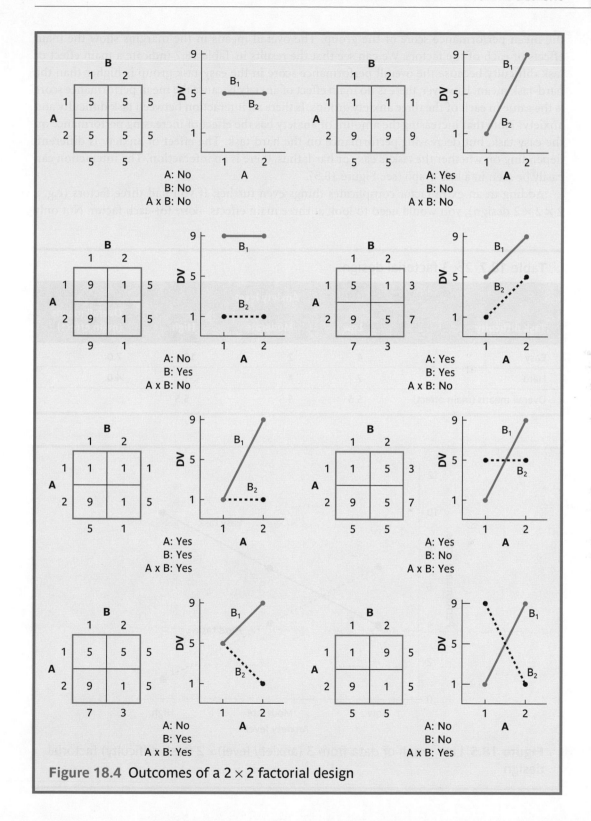

Figure 18.4 Outcomes of a 2 × 2 factorial design

the mean performance score of the group. The overall means in the margins show the main effects of each of the factors. We can see that the results in Table 18.7 indicate a main effect of task difficulty because the overall performance score in the easy-task group is higher than the hard-task mean. However, there is no main effect of anxiety because the mean performance score is the same in each of the three anxiety groups. Is there an interaction between task difficulty and anxiety? Note that increasing the amount of anxiety has the effect of increasing performance on the easy task, but decreasing performance on the hard task. The effect of anxiety is different, depending on whether the task is easy or hard; thus, there is an interaction. The interaction can easily be seen in a line graph (see Figure 18.5).

Adding in an extra factor complicates things even further. If you had three factors (e.g. a $2 \times 2 \times 2$ design), you would need to look at three main effects – one for each factor. Not only

Table 18.7 2×3 factorial design

Task difficulty	Anxiety level			Overall means (main effect)
	Low	Moderate	High	
Easy	4	7	10	7.0
Hard	7	4	1	4.0
Overall means (main effect)	5.5	5.5	5.5	

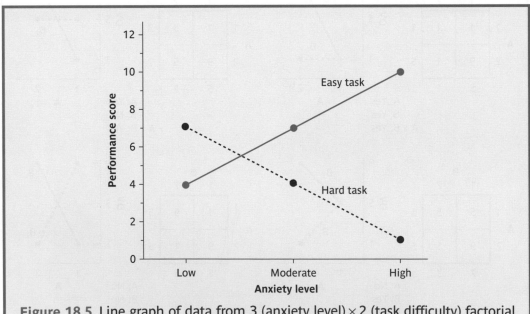

Figure 18.5 Line graph of data from 3 (anxiety level) $\times$ 2 (task difficulty) factorial design

Table 18.8 Example of 2 × 2 × 2 factorial design

	Class size	
	10	40
Instruction method	Male	
Lecture	Condition 1	Condition 2
Discussion	Condition 3	Condition 4
	Female	
Lecture	Condition 5	Condition 6
Discussion	Condition 7	Condition 8

that, but you would also need to look at more than one interaction. This is because the three factors (A, B and C) could interact with each other in a number of ways. For a three-factor design, there are three possible two-way interactions: A × B, A × C and B × C, and one three-way interaction: A × B × C. A **three-way interaction** occurs when the nature of the interaction between two of the factors differs depending on the particular level of the other variable. Three-way interactions are rather complicated, but you will be glad to hear that they are rare in psychological research.

A 2 × 2 × 2 factorial design is shown in Table 18.8. The factors are: (1) instruction method (lecture, discussion), (2) class size (10, 40), and (3) student gender (male, female). The dependent variable is performance on a standard test.

Notice that the 2 × 2 × 2 design can be seen as two 2 × 2 designs, one for males and one for females. To work out whether there is a main effect of instruction method, you would obtain the overall lecture mean by considering all participants who experienced the lecture method, and compare this with the overall discussion mean, derived from all participants in this condition. You would do something similar to look at the main effects of sex and class size (i.e. look at the overall differences between males and females and classes of 10 and classes of 40).

We can also look at the interactions between (1) method and class size, (2) method and gender, (3) class size and gender, and (4) method, class size and gender. To examine a two-way interaction, you need to ignore the third factor and work out the means as if you were just looking at a two-factor design. Therefore, for the method × class size interaction, you would calculate means for the four conditions resulting from the combination of these factors: lecture/class size of 10, lecture/class size of 40, discussion/class size of 10 and discussion/class size of 40, and interpret as you would do for a normal 2 × 2 interaction. Interpreting the three-way interaction involves looking at the cell means and identifying the two-way interaction for each level of the third variable. For example, you could examine the method × class size interaction for males and for females. If it appears that the two-way interaction is not consistent across all levels of the third variable, then you have a three-way interaction.

Three-way interaction
The differing interaction of two factors, depending on the particular level of a third factor.

Using ANOVA to analyse data from factorial designs

You should now have a fairly good idea of factorial designs and how to interpret findings. However, you may have noticed that it is not always clear whether you have main effects or interaction – how different do the means actually need to be? As you will probably have guessed, we can use a statistical test to tell us when these differences between means are or are not significant, and the appropriate test (or set of tests) is factorial ANOVA.

Between-subjects factorial ANOVA
NHST method used to analyse data from a between-subjects factorial design.

Within-subjects factorial ANOVA
NHST method used to analyse data from a within-subjects factorial design.

Mixed factorial ANOVA
NHST method used to analyse data from a mixed factorial design.

There are three different factorial ANOVAs to choose from, and which one you use depends on the design of the study: **between-subjects factorial ANOVA** is used for entirely between-subjects designs, **within-subjects factorial ANOVA** is for entirely within-subjects designs and **mixed factorial ANOVA** is used when you have at least one between-subjects factor and at least one within-subjects factor. It is therefore vital that you can identify the different types of factorial designs before moving on to any analysis.

The factorial ANOVAs are just extensions of the corresponding one-way ANOVAs and consequently make the same **assumptions about data**. However, unlike one-way ANOVAs, there are no non-parametric equivalents to factorial ANOVAs, so if you are planning on designing a factorial design in which you are collecting ordinal data, you may need to think again.

ch. 17
pp.390, 4C

Whichever method of factorial ANOVA is used, it will provide you with separate F-values for each of the main effects and interactions. Therefore, for a 2×2 factorial design you would obtain three F-values – one relating to the main effect of factor A, one relating to the main effect of factor B and one relating to the $A \times B$ interaction. For a $2 \times 2 \times 2$ design you would have seven separate F-values – three for the main

ch. 17
pp.389, 395 –
396, 402

effects, three for the two-way interactions and one for the three-way interaction. You inspect and interpret factorial ANOVA results in a similar way to results for one-way ANOVA – if the p-value is less than .05, you have a significant difference, and if the p-value is greater, there is no significant difference. Thus, a significant result indicates the presence of a significant main effect or interaction. Remember to obtain **effect sizes** too.

For a 2×2 factorial ANOVA, inspecting matrices and graphs is usually sufficient to help you interpret results, but you may find additional analysis helpful, particularly for more complex

Simple main effect
In a factorial design, the effect of one factor at a particular level of another factor.

factorial designs. If you have a significant main effect of a factor with three or more levels, you can run *post hoc* tests just as you do for a one-way ANOVA. To interpret a significant interaction, you can look at the simple main effects. A **simple main effect** analysis examines mean differences at each level of the factor. For example, if you wanted to interpret a significant interaction from our earlier difficulty (easy, hard) and anxiety level (low, medium, high) example, you could do a comparison between the easy and hard tasks for each of the three levels of anxiety. Alternatively, you could compare low, medium and high anxiety in the easy task condition and in the hard task condition. In this way, you can think of simple main effects as running separate t-tests or ANOVAs for each level of a factor. In fact, using t-tests or ANOVAs (and making appropriate corrections to the alpha level) is probably the easiest way for you to interpret significant interactions.

We will now go through a further worked example of each type of design, using SPSS output and details on how to calculate the F-values by hand. Remember that full details of the

SPSS procedure for factorial ANOVA can be found on our website.

Between-subjects factorial ANOVA

Table 18.9 presents the results from a between-subjects factorial design looking at the effects of gender and personality on a measure of subjective (e.g. the satisfaction with life scale; Diener et al., 1985). The personality factor had two levels: extrovert (i.e. outgoing, talkative, sociable) and introvert (i.e. reserved, serious, organized), which were determined by administering a personality test and categorizing participants. The gender factor obviously also has two levels. We are therefore looking at a 2 × 2 design.

To get an idea of whether there may be main effects or interactions, we can consult the table of means (Table 18.10).

Table 18.9 Life satisfaction scores for women and men who are extroverts or introverts

		Men	Women
	Extroverts	33	32
		31	27
		30	23
		26	22
		25	16
		23	24
Personality type	Introverts	26	26
		25	25
		23	23
		21	21
		19	19
		18	18

Table 18.10 Cell means and margin means for the data in Table 18.9

Personality	Gender		Margin M
	Men	Women	
Extroverts	28	24	26
Introverts	22	22	22
Margin *M*	25	23	Grand *M* = 24

> ## STOP & Think
>
> Look at Table 18.10 and draw some preliminary interpretations. Does it look as though there are main effects and/or interactions?

Looking at the margin means, it seems as though there may be a main effect of personality as the overall mean for extroverts is higher than that for introverts. The overall mean for men is also higher than the overall mean for women, but this difference is not as large. If we inspect the cells means we can see that there is no difference between the mean for male introverts and female introverts, but male extroverts have a higher mean than female extroverts. This therefore suggests the presence of an interaction.

Of course, inspecting the means can only give us a preliminary indication of whether there are likely to be main effects or interactions, but the only way to be sure is to run an ANOVA, which looks at variability in scores to determine if differences between means are significant.

Between-subjects factorial ANOVA using SPSS

Table 18.11 and Figure 18.6 are some examples of SPSS output from an exploratory analysis of the data. As can be seen, there is no evidence of outliers or skewed distributions – the parametric assumptions have been met and we can proceed with the ANOVA.

The SPSS output for a between-subjects factorial ANOVA is similar to that for a one-way ANOVA, except that there are a few more rows in the ANOVA table to report the F-values for the main effects and interactions.

The first table is the *between-subjects factors* table. Check this to ensure that you have used the correct factors and that you have the right number of participants in each group. The next table (if requested) will provide you with descriptive statistics.

Table 18.11 SPSS output for the "satisfaction with life" data

Between-Subjects Factors

		Value Label	N
Personality type	1	Extravert	12
	2	Introvert	12
Gender	1	Male	12
	2	Female	12

Report

Life Satisfaction score

Gender	Personality type	Mean	N	Std. Deviation
Male	Extravert	28.00	6	3.899
	Introvert	22.00	6	3.225
	Total	25.00	12	4.632
Female	Extravert	24.00	6	5.329
	Introvert	22.00	6	3.225
	Total	23.00	12	4.328
Total	Extravert	26.00	12	4.918
	Introvert	22.00	12	3.075
	Total	24.00	24	4.501

The results of Levene's test for homogeneity of variances are presented in Table 18.12. We have seen **Levene's test** before, when we covered the independent-samples t-test (Chapter 16). Remember, that homogeneity of variance is an assumption of ANOVA, and if Levene's test is significant (i.e. p-value less than .05), this assumption has been violated. In our current example, it is non-significant and we can proceed.

ch. 16 pp.352, 355–356

Next we come to the all-important tests of *between-subjects effects ANOVA* table (Table 18.13). It looks scary, but it is actually very easy to interpret. First, ignore the Corrected model and Intercept rows, and focus on the rows labelled with the factor names and the interaction – these are where you find the relevant results (i.e. *df*, *F*, *p*-value and partial eta squared).

In our example, we are interested in the main effect of gender (i.e. whether males and females differ in their life satisfaction), the main effect of personality (i.e. whether people with different personalities report differences in life satisfaction) and also how these two things interact with each other (for example, we might find that female extroverts score high on life satisfaction, while male extroverts score low). If we look along the row labelled "personality", this tells us about the main effect of personality, the row labelled "gender" gives us the results for the main effect of gender, and the row labelled "gender * personality" should be consulted to find the results for the interaction. If you had a three-factor ANOVA, there would be additional rows of results to reflect the extra main effect and interactions.

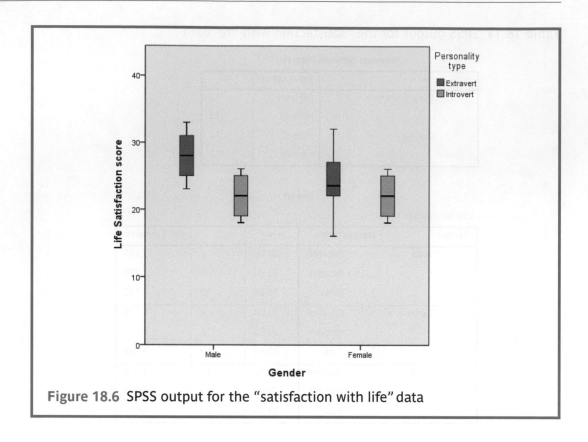

Figure 18.6 SPSS output for the "satisfaction with life" data

Table 18.12 SPSS output showing Levene's test of equality of variances

Levene's Test of Equality of Error Variances[a]

Dependent Variable:Life Satisfaction score

F	df1	df2	Sig.
.336	3	20	.800

Tests the null hypothesis that the error variance of the dependent variable is equal across groups.

a. Design: Intercept + Personality + Gender + Personality * Gender

> If this is significant, one of the assumptions of ANOVA has been violated.

Table 18.13 SPSS output for between subjects effects

Consult this row for main effect of personality

Consult this row for main effect of gender

Consult this row for gender × personality interaction

Tests of Between-Subjects Effects

Dependent Variable:Life Satisfaction score

Source	Type III Sum of Squares	df	Mean Square	F	Sig.	Partial Eta Squared
Corrected Model	144.000ª	3	48.000	2.981	.056	.309
Intercept	13824.000	1	13824.000	858.634	.000	.977
Personality	96.000	1	96.000	5.963	.024	.230
Gender	24.000	1	24.000	1.491	.236	.069
Personality * Gender	24.000	1	24.000	1.491	.236	.069
Error	322.000	20	16.100			
Total	14290.000	24				
Corrected Total	466.000	23				

df-values | *F*-values | *p*-values | Effect size

a. R Squared = .309 (Adjusted R Squared = .205)

STOP & Think

Before moving on, write up and interpret the findings from the ANOVA. Are there significant main effects or interactions? Do these confirm your preliminary interpretations of the data from earlier?

We can see that the main effect of gender is non-significant (the *p*-value in the Sig. column is .236, which is greater than .05) and the gender × personality interaction is also non-significant ($p = .236$). However, the main effect of personality is significant ($p = .024$) and this requires further investigation. If you requested marginal means, you can inspect the tables that follow the main ANOVA table, or you can look back at earlier tables of descriptive statistics (just be sure that you are using the correct means). In our example, we are only interested in the personality-type table (Table 18.14) and can see that the overall extrovert group mean is higher than the overall introvert group mean. Therefore, extroverts had a significantly higher life satisfaction rating that introverts.

The profile plots line graph also helps us with our interpretation (Figure 18.7). The extroverts line is consistently higher than the introverts line, suggesting a main effect of personality. And although it looks as though differences are large and the lines diverge from each other, notice that the scale of the *y*-axis only covers a range of 22 to 28 – any differences are therefore magnified.

Table 18.14 SPSS output showing descriptive statistics

1. Personality type

Dependent Variable:Life Satisfaction score

Personality type			95% Confidence Interval	
	Mean	Std. Error	Lower Bound	Upper Bound
Extravert	26.000	1.158	23.584	28.416
Introvert	22.000	1.158	19.584	24.416

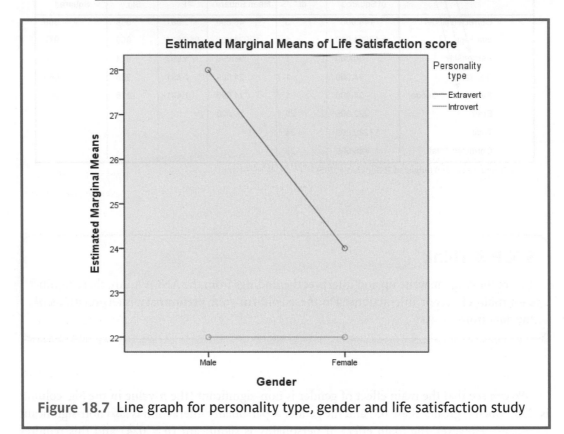

Figure 18.7 Line graph for personality type, gender and life satisfaction study

Between-subjects factorial ANOVA by hand

First, it is very unlikely that you will ever have to conduct a factorial ANOVA by hand. Most of the time, you will be conducting them on statistical computer packages. We have included it here because some tutors and lecturers like their students to do these tests manually in the first instance, to get familiar with what the test is doing with the data. There is a lot of number-crunching, but try not to let that put you off – it is really just a series of small calculations joined together.

ch. 17
pp.396–398,
402–406

The calculations required for a between-subjects factorial ANOVA are similar to those for a one-way ANOVA; there are just more of them. It takes a bit of time to do, but can be strangely satisfying once you get to the end. With the one-way ANOVA we calculated three different sums

Table 18.15 Data and means for personality/gender and satisfaction with life study

	Men	Women	Mean
Extroverts	33	32	
	31	27	
	30	23	
	26	22	
	25	16	
	23	24	
Mean	28	24	**26**
Introverts	26	26	
	25	25	
	23	23	
	21	21	
	19	19	
	18	18	
Mean	22	22	**22**
Mean	**25**	**23**	**24**

$\Sigma X = 576$
$\Sigma X^2 = 14290$
$(\Sigma X)^2 = 331776$
$N = 24$

of squares: SS_{total}, $SS_{between}$ and SS_{error}. With a factorial ANOVA we go further and break down the $SS_{between}$ – now called SS_{cells} – into variance related to the first factor (factor A; SS_A), to the second factor (factor B; SS_B) and to the interaction between the two factors (A × B; $SS_{A\times B}$). We can then use these sums of squares to produce the F-values for the main effects and interaction.

Table 18.15 contains the data for our gender and personality example. Note that we have already calculated means and other useful values that will be used in the calculation of the sums of squares.

The first stage of analysis is to calculate the SS_{total} using the formula that we used for the one-way ANOVA (Figure 18.8).

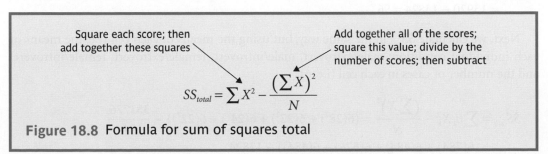

Square each score; then add together these squares

Add together all of the scores; square this value; divide by the number of scores; then subtract

$$SS_{total} = \sum X^2 - \frac{(\sum X)^2}{N}$$

Figure 18.8 Formula for sum of squares total

With the values from our table, we can calculate SS_{total} for our example data:

$$SS_{total} = \sum X^2 - \frac{(\sum X)^2}{N} = 14290 - \frac{331776}{24} = 14290 - 13824 = 466$$

Next, we calculate SS_A – the sum of squares for factor A (gender). We are interested in the main effect of gender and so look at the overall means for males and females, regardless of personality type. The formula we use is shown in Figure 18.9.

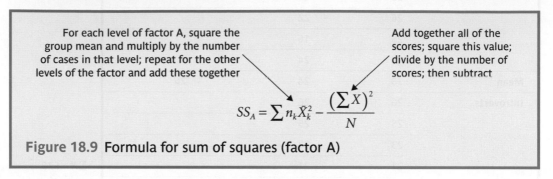

For each level of factor A, square the group mean and multiply by the number of cases in that level; repeat for the other levels of the factor and add these together

Add together all of the scores; square this value; divide by the number of scores; then subtract

$$SS_A = \sum n_k \bar{X}_k^2 - \frac{(\sum X)^2}{N}$$

Figure 18.9 Formula for sum of squares (factor A)

Note that this formula uses both n (the number of cases in each level of the factor), and N (the total number of cases). For the gender factor, there were 12 cases in each level of the factor (12 males, 12 females); therefore, $n = 12$. So the SS_A for the gender factor in our example would be:

$$SS_A = \sum n_k \bar{X}_k^2 - \frac{(\sum X)^2}{N} = (12(25^2) + 12(23^2)) - \frac{331776}{24}$$
$$= (12(625) + 12(529)) - 13824 = (7500 + 6348) - 13824$$
$$= 13848 - 13824 = 24$$

You repeat the same process for SS_B – the sum of squares for factor B (personality) – but this time using the overall means for extraverts and introverts (i.e. the group means for factor B). There are 12 cases in each level of this factor, so our value of n will be 12 again.

$$SS_B = \sum n_k \bar{X}_k^2 - \frac{(\sum X)^2}{N} = (12(26^2) + 12(22^2)) - \frac{331776}{24}$$
$$= (12(676) + 12(484)) - 13824 = (8112 + 5808) - 13824$$
$$= 13920 - 13824 = 96$$

Next, we calculate SS_{cells} in the same way, but using the means of each cell (i.e. the means of each individual condition: male/extrovert, male/introvert, female/extrovert, female/introvert) and the number of cases in each cell (i.e. 6).

$$SS_{cells} = \sum n_k \bar{X}_k^2 - \frac{(\sum X)^2}{N} = (6(28^2) + 6(22^2) + 6(24^2) + 6(22^2)) - \frac{331776}{24}$$
$$= (6(784) + 6(484) + 6(576) + 6(484)) - 13824$$
$$= (4704 + 2904 + 3456 + 2904) - 13824 = 13968 - 13824 = 144$$

Although SS_{cells} does not appear in ANOVA summary tables, it helps us to calculate our other sums of squares. Recall that we can break SS_{cells} down into SS_A, SS_B and $SS_{A\times B}$. So, to calculate $SS_{A\times B}$ we use:

$$SS_{A\times B} = SS_{cells} - SS_A - SS_B$$

For our example data, this would be:

$$SS_{AB} = SS_{cells} - SS_A - SS_B = 144 - 24 - 96 = 24$$

The final sum of squares to be calculated is SS_{error}, which is the error that is not explained by SS_{cells}. Therefore:

$$SS_{error} = SS_{total} - SS_{cells}$$

For our example data, this would be:

$$SS_{error} = SS_{total} - SS_{cells} = 466 - 144 = 322$$

Now that we have the sums of squares, we need to calculate the degrees of freedom (df) so that we can calculate the variances. For the main effects, df is the number of levels in that factor minus 1; for the interaction, you multiply together the df values for each factor; and the error df is calculated by subtracting the main effect and interaction df values from $N - 1$ (i.e. total number of cases minus 1). Therefore, for our example, we would have: $df_A = 1$, $df_B = 1$, $df_{A\times B} = 1$, $df_{error} = 20$ (i.e. $23 - 1 - 1 - 1$).

We are finally ready to calculate our variances (mean sum of squares, MS) and our F-values. Remember from **Chapter 17** that MS is calculated by dividing the SS by the appropriate df, and F is calculated by dividing the appropriate MS by SS_{error}. The results for our example data can be presented in a summary table (Table 18.16).

ch. 17
pp.397–398,
405–406

Table 18.16 Table showing *SS, df, MS* and *F* for factors

	SS	df	MS	F
Gender (factor A)	24	1	24.0	1.491
Personality (factor B)	96	1	96.0	5.963
Gender × Personality (A × B)	24	1	24.0	1.491
Error	322	20	16.1	

All that remains is to check the critical F-values (Appendix D) for the appropriate df (remember that there will be two). If your calculated F-value is more extreme than the critical value, you have a significant result.

Reporting result from a between-subjects factorial ANOVA

You use the same format for reporting your ANOVA results as described in Chapter 13, the only difference is that you now have more results to report. Remember to include measures of effect size and any *post hoc* analyses (where applicable). The results from our example could therefore be written up as:

> A 2 × 2 between-subjects factorial ANOVA was used to analyse the data. There was no significant main effect of gender, $F(1, 20) = 1.491, p = .236, \eta_p^2 = .069$, and no significant interaction between gender and personality, $F(1, 20) = 1.491, p = .236, \eta_p^2 = .069$. However, there was a significant main effect of personality, $F(1, 20) = 5.963, p = .024, \eta_p^2 = .230$, with the mean life satisfaction score for the extrovert group ($M = 26.33, SD = 4.91$) being significantly higher than the introvert group ($M = 22.00, SD = 3.08$).

Within-subjects factorial ANOVA

We will illustrate the within-subjects factorial ANOVA using another example. The experiment was looking at estimation of time, and had two factors: time interval (12, 24 and 36 seconds) and noise condition (quiet, noisy). Therefore, this was a 3 × 2 experiment. Participants experienced a randomly determined time interval (e.g. 24 seconds), indicated by the appearance of the words "start" and "stop" on a computer screen, and then were asked to estimate the duration of that interval. In each trial, participants would hear through their headphones either noise (in the form of a recording of sound from a city centre) or complete silence.

Table 18.17 presents the participants' median estimates for each condition, and the overall mean for each condition. (A median was used rather than a mean because means are influenced by extreme scores, and extreme scores occur quite frequently in this type of research, for example, due to momentary loss of attention.)

> ### STOP & Think
>
> Can you make any preliminary interpretations based on the results in Table 18.8?

 Two-way factorial within-subjects ANOVA in SPSS

Figure 18.10 and Table 18.18 are some examples of output from exploratory data analysis. Although there are two outliers in the boxplot, they are not too troublesome – with a small sample size it is quite common to get outliers, and ANOVA can withstand some violation of its assumptions. Remember that the details on the ANOVA procedure can be found on our website.

The SPSS output for a within-subjects factorial ANOVA begins with the Within-subjects factors table (Table 18.19), which specifies the variables that have been matched with each condition. It is really important that you check this to see if you have set up the analysis correctly.

Table 18.20 provides descriptive statistics; you can ignore the multivariate tests table. We consult Mauchly's test of sphericity to check that the assumption of sphericity has not been violated. Remember that this does not tell us if we have significant differences, but just tells us which row of results to look at. If Mauchly's test is significant (p less than .05), we consult the Greenhouse-Geisser row of results in the ANOVA table; if it is non-significant (p greater

Table 18.17 Data for a 3×2 within-subjects factorial time estimation experiment

| Participant | Time interval/noise condition | | | | | |
| | 12 seconds | | 24 seconds | | 36 seconds | |
	Quiet	Noisy	Quiet	Noisy	Quiet	Noisy
1	13	14	21	25	30	40
2	10	12	15	20	35	47
3	12	10	23	30	35	39
4	12	11	15	25	29	32
5	16	8	36	40	50	56
6	10	13	25	24	39	37
7	11	16	24	26	30	39
8	12	15	22	21	38	35
9	14	12	30	28	31	41
10	15	10	31	34	54	60
Mean	12.5	12.1	24.2	27.3	37.1	42.6

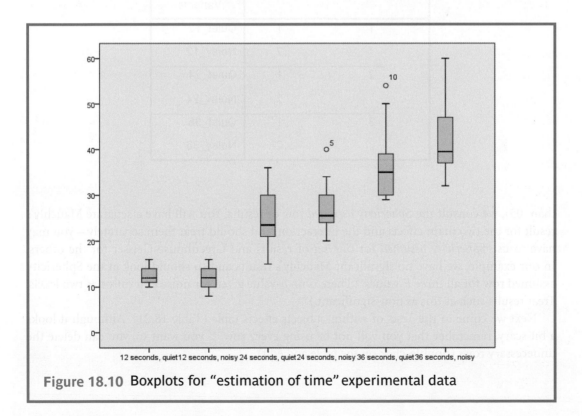

Figure 18.10 Boxplots for "estimation of time" experimental data

Table 18.18 Descriptive statistics for "estimation of time" experimental data

Descriptive Statistics

	N	Minimum	Maximum	Mean	Std. Deviation
12 seconds, quiet	10	10	16	12.50	2.014
12 seconds, noisy	10	8	16	12.10	2.470
24 seconds, quiet	10	15	36	24.20	6.713
24 seconds, noisy	10	20	40	27.30	6.056
36 seconds, quiet	10	29	54	37.10	8.621
36 seconds, noisy	10	32	60	42.60	9.058
Valid N (listwise)	10				

Table 18.19 SPSS table specifying variables and conditions

Within-Subjects Factors

Measure:Estimate

Time	Noise	Dependent Variable
1	1	Quiet_12
	2	Noisy_12
2	1	Quiet_24
	2	Noisy_24
3	1	Quiet_36
	2	Noisy_36

than .05), we consult the *Sphericity assumed* row of results. You will have a separate Mauchly's result for the two main effects and the interaction, and should treat them separately – you may have to use *Sphericity assumed* for one set of results and Greenhouse-Geisser for the others. In our example, we have no significant Mauchly's results and so should look at the Sphericity assumed row for all three *F*-values. (There is no *p*-value given for noise as it only has two levels. Treat results such as this as non-significant.)

Next we come to the Tests of within-subjects effects table (Table 18.21). Although it looks a bit scary, remember that you will not be using every row. If you want to, you can delete the unnecessary rows (double-click on the table and edit).

Table 18.20 SPSS table showing Mauchly's test of sphericity

Descriptive Statistics

	Mean	Std. Deviation	N
12 seconds, quiet	12.50	2.014	10
12 seconds, noisy	12.10	2.470	10
24 seconds, quiet	24.20	6.713	10
24 seconds, noisy	27.30	6.056	10
36 seconds, quiet	37.10	8.621	10
36 seconds, noisy	42.60	9.058	10

If significant → consult Greenhouse-Geisser row
If non-significant → consult Sphericity assumed row

Mauchly's Test of Sphericity[b]

Measure:Estimate

Within Subjects Effect	Mauchly's W	Approx. Chi-Square	df	Sig.	Greenhouse-Geisser	Huynh-Feldt	Lower-bound
					Epsilon[a]		
Time	.702	2.826	2	.243	.771	.899	.500
Noise	1.000	.000	0	.	1.000	1.000	1.000
Time * Noise	.957	.351	2	.839	.959	1.000	.500

Tests the null hypothesis that the error covariance matrix of the orthonormalized transformed dependent variables is proportional to an identity matrix.

a. May be used to adjust the degrees of freedom for the averaged tests of significance. Corrected tests are displayed in the Tests of Within-Subjects Effects table.

b. Design: Intercept
Within Subjects Design: Time + Noise + Time * Noise

STOP & Think

Before moving on, write up and interpret the findings from the ANOVA. Are there significant main effects or interactions? Do these confirm your preliminary interpretations of the data from earlier?

Going through the table, we can see that we have significant main effects of time and noise. We will need to consult *post hoc* tests to make sense of what's going on here. (Note that when you see .000 in SPSS, this does *not* mean that the p-value is equal to exactly 0 – it has just been rounded down to three decimal places. You should report this as $p < .001$.) There is also a significant interaction.

Next are the tables of Tests of within-subjects contrasts and Tests of between-subject effects; you can ignore or delete these. The next few tables (Table 18.22) help us to interpret our main effects as they provide the overall means for each level and *post hoc* tests. For example, we can see that there are significant differences between every pair of levels for the time factor, with 12 seconds

Table 18.21 SPSS output displaying within subjects effects

Tests of Within-Subjects Effects

Measure:Estimate

Source		Type III Sum of Squares	df	Mean Square	F	Sig.	Partial Eta Squared
Time	Sphericity Assumed	7591.433	2	3795.717	78.511	.000	.897
	Greenhouse-Geisser	7591.433	1.541	4925.304	78.511	.000	.897
	Huynh-Feldt	7591.433	1.798	4221.396	78.511	.000	.897
	Lower-bound	7591.433	1.000	7591.433	78.511	.000	.897
Error(Time)	Sphericity Assumed	870.233	18	48.346			
	Greenhouse-Geisser	870.233	13.872	62.734			
	Huynh-Feldt	870.233	16.185	53.768			
	Lower-bound	870.233	9.000	96.693			
Noise	Sphericity Assumed	112.067	1	112.067	13.400	.005	.598
	Greenhouse-Geisser	112.067	1.000	112.067	13.400	.005	.598
	Huynh-Feldt	112.067	1.000	112.067	13.400	.005	.598
	Lower-bound	112.067	1.000	112.067	13.400	.005	.598
Error(Noise)	Sphericity Assumed	75.267	9	8.363			
	Greenhouse-Geisser	75.267	9.000	8.363			
	Huynh-Feldt	75.267	9.000	8.363			
	Lower-bound	75.267	9.000	8.363			
Time * Noise	Sphericity Assumed	88.033	2	44.017	4.460	.027	.331
	Greenhouse-Geisser	88.033	1.918	45.904	4.460	.029	.331
	Huynh-Feldt	88.033	2.000	44.017	4.460	.027	.331
	Lower-bound	88.033	1.000	88.033	4.460	.064	.331
Error(Time*Noise)	Sphericity Assumed	177.633	18	9.869			
	Greenhouse-Geisser	177.633	17.260	10.292			
	Huynh-Feldt	177.633	18.000	9.869			
	Lower-bound	177.633	9.000	19.737			

producing significantly shorter estimated times than 24 or 36 seconds (obviously!), and 24 seconds having significantly shorter estimates than 36 seconds. As the factor of noise only has two levels, we just need to look at the means to interpret the main effect – the overall mean for the quiet conditions (24.60) was therefore significantly lower than that for the noisy conditions (27.33).

To interpret the significant interaction, you can consult tables of means and the line graph (Figure 18.11[1]). You could also investigate the simple main effects by running paired-samples t-tests, comparing the quiet and noisy condition for each time interval. If you do this, you should consider adjusting your alpha level (e.g. .05/3 = .0167) to reduce the chance of a Type I error. Whichever method(s) you use to interpret the interaction, you should be able to determine in our example that there was little difference between the estimates in the quiet and noisy conditions for the 12-second time interval, but the difference increased as the time interval increased.

Within-subjects factorial ANOVA by hand

You will spot similarities in the calculations used for the within-subjects factorial ANOVA and those used for the one-way within-subjects ANOVA and two-way between-subjects ANOVA.

---

[1]   You will notice that SPSS labels the line graph with numbers rather than words. These refer to the level of the factor, and these can be found in the within-subjects factor table.

Table 18.22 SPSS output showing descriptive statistics and post-hoc pairwise comparisons

Estimates

Measure:Estimate

Time	Mean	Std. Error	95% Confidence Interval	
			Lower Bound	Upper Bound
1	12.300	.327	11.561	13.039
2	25.750	1.931	21.382	30.118
3	39.850	2.678	33.792	45.908

Pairwise Comparisons

Measure:Estimate

(I) Time	(J) Time	Mean Difference (I-J)	Std. Error	Sig.[a]	95% Confidence Interval for Difference[a]	
					Lower Bound	Upper Bound
1	2	-13.450[*]	1.924	.000	-19.094	-7.806
	3	-27.550[*]	2.732	.000	-35.564	-19.536
2	1	13.450[*]	1.924	.000	7.806	19.094
	3	-14.100[*]	1.827	.000	-19.459	-8.741
3	1	27.550[*]	2.732	.000	19.536	35.564
	2	14.100[*]	1.827	.000	8.741	19.459

Based on estimated marginal means

*. The mean difference is significant at the .05 level.

a. Adjustment for multiple comparisons: Bonferroni.

Estimates

Measure:Estimate

Noise	Mean	Std. Error	95% Confidence Interval	
			Lower Bound	Upper Bound
1	24.600	1.641	20.887	28.313
2	27.333	1.304	24.383	30.284

The main difference is that you will need to calculate an additional SS_{error} for each main effect/interaction. The data for our example are presented in Table 18.23, with means, including means for each participant. Notice that we have organized the data in two different ways, to demonstrate the different types of means that will be used in our calculations. We've also stated some of the means with four decimal places – this is to ensure that our values are close to those calculated using SPSS; four decimal places is normally a bit excessive for a table of means.

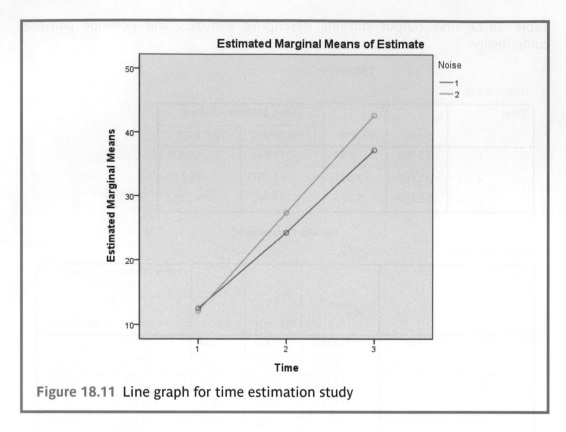

Figure 18.11 Line graph for time estimation study

First we calculate SS_{total} in the usual manner, remembering that in within-subjects ANOVA, N is the number of scores:

$$SS_{total} = \sum X^2 - \frac{\left(\sum X\right)^2}{N} = 50482 - \frac{2427364}{60} = 50482 - 40456.0667 = 10025.9333$$

Next we calculate $SS_{between\ subj}$ using the means for each participant (i.e. their mean across all conditions; Figure 18.12).

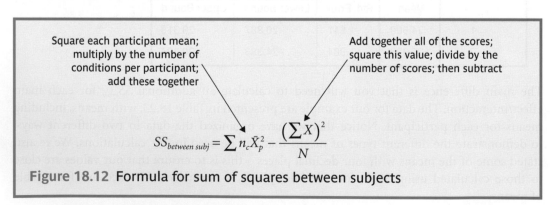

Square each participant mean; multiply by the number of conditions per participant; add these together

Add together all of the scores; square this value; divide by the number of scores; then subtract

$$SS_{between\ subj} = \sum n_c \bar{X}_p^2 - \frac{\left(\sum X\right)^2}{N}$$

Figure 18.12 Formula for sum of squares between subjects

Table 18.23 Data and means for time estimation experiment presented in two different ways

	Time interval/noise condition								
	12 seconds			24 seconds			36 seconds		
Pt	Quiet	Noisy	Mean	Quiet	Noisy	Mean	Quiet	Noisy	Mean
1	13	14	13.50	21	25	23.00	30	40	35.00
2	10	12	11.00	15	20	17.50	35	47	41.00
3	12	10	11.00	23	30	26.50	35	39	37.00
4	12	11	11.50	15	25	20.00	29	32	30.50
5	16	8	12.00	36	40	38.00	50	56	53.00
6	10	13	11.50	25	24	24.50	39	37	38.00
7	11	16	13.50	24	26	25.00	30	39	34.50
8	12	15	13.50	22	21	21.50	38	35	36.50
9	14	12	13.00	30	28	29.00	31	41	36.00
10	15	10	12.50	31	34	32.50	54	60	57.00
Mean	12.5	12.1		24.2	27.3		37.1	42.6	
			12.30			25.75			39.85

	Noise condition/time interval								
	Quiet				Noisy				Participant mean
Pt	12 secs	24 secs	36 secs	Mean	12 secs	24 secs	36 secs	Mean	
1	13	21	30	21.3333	14	25	40	26.3333	23.8333
2	10	15	35	20.0000	12	20	47	26.3333	23.1667
3	12	23	35	23.3333	10	30	39	26.3333	24.8333
4	12	15	29	18.6667	11	25	32	22.6667	20.6667
5	16	36	50	34.0000	8	40	56	34.6667	34.3333
6	10	25	39	24.6667	13	24	37	24.6667	24.6667
7	11	24	30	21.6667	16	26	39	27.0000	24.3333
8	12	22	38	24.0000	15	21	35	23.6667	23.8333
9	14	30	31	25.0000	12	28	41	27.0000	26.0000
10	15	31	54	33.3333	10	34	60	34.6667	34.0000
Mean	12.5	24.2	37.1		12.1	27.3	42.6		
				24.6000				27.3333	25.9667

$\sum X = 1558$
$\sum X^2 = 50\ 482$
$(\sum X)^2 = 2\ 427\ 364$

So, for our example data, this would be:

$$SS_{between\ subj} = \sum n_c \bar{X}_p^2 - \frac{(\sum X)^2}{N}$$

$$= 6(23.8333^2) + 6(23.1667^2) + \cdots + 6(26.0000^2) + 6(34.0000^2) - \frac{2427364}{60}$$

$$= (3408.1667 + 3220.1667 + \cdots + 4056 + 69366) - 40456.0667$$

$$= 41567.3334 - 40456.0637 = 1111.2697$$

Next, we find the sum of squares for factor A (time), using the overall means for each level of the factor (i.e. the overall means for 12 seconds, 24 seconds and 36 seconds); $n = 20$ as each of these means was calculated using 20 scores:

$$SS_A = \sum n_k \bar{X}_k^2 - \frac{(\sum X)^2}{N} = (20(12.30^2) + 20(25.75^2) + 20(39.85^2)) - \frac{2427364}{60}$$

$$= (20(151.29) + 20(663.0625) + 20(1588.0225)) - 40456.0667$$

$$= (3025.8 + 13261.25 + 31760.45) - 40456.0667$$

$$= 48047.5 - 40456.0667 = 7591.4333$$

In order to find the SS_{error} for factor A ($SS_{error\ A}$), we first need to calculate SS_{cells} for factor A ($SS_{cells\ A}$). This time, we use the means for each participant at each level of factor A (i.e. the means for each participant at 12 seconds, 24 seconds and 36 seconds); $n = 2$ as two scores make up each of these means. The calculation is shown below:[2]

$$SS_{cells\ A} = \sum n_k \bar{X}_k^2 - \frac{(\sum X)^2}{N}$$

$$= (2(13.50^2) + 2(11.00^2) + \cdots + 2(36.00^2) + 2(57.00^2)) - \frac{2427364}{60}$$

$$= (2(182.25) + 2(121) + \cdots + 2(1296) + 2(3249)) - 40456.0667$$

$$= (364.5 + 242 + \cdots + 2592 + 6498) - 40456.0667$$

$$= 50029 - 40456.0667 = 9572.9333$$

We can now calculate $SS_{error\ A}$:

$$SS_{error\ A} = SS_{cells\ A} - SS_A - SS_{between\ subj} = 9572.9333 - 7591.4333 - 1111.2667 = 870.2333$$

We repeat the same process for factor B (noise). We calculate SS_B using the overall means for each level of the factor (i.e. quiet, noisy); $n = 30$ as 30 scores were used to calculate each of these means:

---

[2]   Don't worry about the " . . . " in the calculation below – it's just there to indicate that we're not showing you the whole set of calculations. There are quite a few participants and the calculations would take up a lot of space if we showed you everything!

$$SS_B = \sum n_k \bar{X}_k^2 - \frac{(\sum X)^2}{N} = (30(24.6000^2) + 30(27.3333^2)) - \frac{2427364}{60}$$

$$= (30(605.1600) + 30(747.1093)) - 40456.0667$$
$$= (18154.8000 + 22413.2790) - 40456.0667$$
$$= 40568.0790 - 40456.0667 = 112.0123$$

(This value is slightly different to that in the SPSS output table simply due to rounding down.)

Next, we calculate $SS_{cells\ B}$ using the means for each participant at each level of factor B (i.e. the mean for each participant in the quiet and noisy conditions); $n = 3$ as three scores make up each of these means:

$$SS_{cells\ B} = \sum n_k \bar{X}_k^2 - \frac{(\sum X)^2}{N}$$

$$= (3(21.3333^2) + 3(20.0000^2) + \cdots + 3(27.0000^2) + 3(34.6667^2)) - \frac{2427364}{60}$$

$$= (3(455.1097) + 3(400.0000) + \cdots + 3(729.0000) + 3(1201.7801)) - 40456.0667$$
$$= (1365.3291 + 1200 + \cdots + 2187 + 3605.3403) - 40456.0667$$
$$= 41754.6763 - 40456.0667 = 1298.6096$$

We can now calculate $SS_{error\ B}$:

$$SS_{error\ B} = SS_{cells\ B} - SS_B - SS_{between\ subj} = 1298.9096 - 112.0123 - 1111.2667 = 75.6306$$

Again, because of rounding of values in the calculations, this value is slightly greater than that in the SPSS table.

Recall from two-way between-subjects ANOVA, that we calculate the sum of square for the interaction by subtracting SS_A and SS_B from SS_{cells}. It's a similar process in two-way within-subjects ANOVA. We calculate $SS_{cells\ A\times B}$ and subtract SS_A and SS_B, leaving us with $SS_{A\times B}$. To calculate $SS_{cells\ A\times B}$ we use the means from each individual condition, made up of the different combinations of the levels of the factors (i.e. 12 seconds/quiet, 12 seconds/noisy, 24 seconds/ quiet etc.); $n = 10$ as 10 scores were used to calculate each of the means:

$$SS_{cells\ A\times B} = \sum n_k \bar{X}_k^2 - \frac{(\sum X)^2}{N}$$

$$= (10(12.5^2) + 10(24.2^2) + 10(37.1^2) + 10(12.1^2) + 10(27.3^2) + 10(42.6^2)) - \frac{2427364}{60}$$

$$= (10(156.25) + 10(585.64) + 10(1376.41) + 10(146.41) + 10(745.29)$$
$$+ 10(1814.76)) - 40456.0667$$
$$= (1562.5 + 5856.4 + 13764.1 + 1464.1 + 7452.9 + 18147.6) - 40456.0667$$
$$= 48247.6 - 40456.0667 = 7791.5333$$

Table 18.24 ANOVA summary table

	SS	df	MS	F
Time (factor A)	7591.4333	2	3795.7167	78.5110
Error (time) (factor A)	870.2333	18	48.3463	
Noise (factor B)	112.0123	1	112.0123	13.3294
Error (noise) (factor B)	75.6306	9	8.4034	
Time × Noise (A × B)	88.0877	2	44.0438	4.4723
Error (Time × Noise) (A × B)	177.2664	18	9.8481	

Therefore, $SS_{A\times B}$ for our example data would be:

$$SS_{A\times B} = SS_{cells\ A\times B} - SS_A - SS_B = 7791.5333 - 7591.4333 - 112.0123 = 88.0877$$

We calculate SS_{error} for the interaction (i.e. $SS_{error\ A\times B}$) by subtracting all of the other SS values from SS_{total}:

$$
\begin{aligned}
SS_{error\ A\times B} &= SS_{total} - SS_{between\ subj} - SS_A - SS_{error\ A} - SS_B - SS_{error\ B} - SS_{A\times B} \\
&= 10025.9333 - 1111.2697 - 7591.4333 - 870.2333 - 112.0123 - 75.6306 - 88.0877 \\
&= 177.2664
\end{aligned}
$$

All that remains is to calculate the df-values. For the main effects, df is the number of levels in that factor minus 1; for the interaction, you multiply together the df-values for each factor; and the error df-values are calculated by multiplying the number of participants minus 1 by df-value for the appropriate main effect/interaction. Therefore, for our example data the df-values would be: $df_A = 2$ (i.e. $3 - 1$), $df_B = 1$ (i.e. $2 - 1$), $df_{A\times B} = 2$ (i.e. 2×1), $df_{error\ A} = 18$ (i.e. $(10 - 1) \times 2$), $df_{error\ B} = 9$ (i.e. $(10 - 1) \times 1$), $df_{error\ A\times B} = 18$ (i.e. $(10 - 1) \times 2$).

Putting all of these values into an ANOVA summary table (Table 18.24), we can calculate our F-values and compare them with critical values of F (Appendix D).

Our hand-calculated F-values are not exactly the same as those in the SPSS – this is almost inevitable given the number of steps in the calculations and rounding to a sensible number of decimal places. If you really want to obtain precise F-values but do not want to use SPSS, you should consider using a spreadsheet package such as MS Excel to do your calculations.

Reporting result from a within-subjects factorial ANOVA

The same ANOVA format as before should be used when reporting results. The results from our example could therefore be written up as:

A 2×2 within-subjects factorial ANOVA was used to analyse the data. There was a significant main effect of time interval, $F(2, 18) = 78.511$, $p < .001$, $\eta_p^2 = .897$. *Post hoc* Bonferroni tests revealed that overall mean estimates were significantly lower in the 12 seconds condition ($M = 12.30$) than in the 24 or 36 seconds conditions ($M = 25.75$, $M = 39.85$, respectively, both $ps < .001$), and significantly lower in the 24 seconds condition than the 36 seconds condition ($p < .001$). There was also a significant main effect of noise condition, $F(1, 9) = 13.40$, $p = .005$, $\eta_p^2 = .598$, with the overall estimate for the quiet condition ($M = 24.60$) being significantly lower than that for the noisy condition ($M = 27.33$). Furthermore, there was a significant time × noise interaction, $F(2, 18) = 4.46$, $p = .027$, $\eta_p^2 = .331$. Paired-samples t-tests were used to help interpret the interaction and to investigate the simple main effects. The alpha level was adjusted using the Bonferroni correction to minimize Type I errors ($.05/3 = .0167$). Using this stricter alpha level, there were no significant differences in the mean estimates for the quiet and noisy conditions for the 12-second interval, $t(9) = 0.32$, $p = .759$, or for the 24-second interval, $t(9) = -2.59$, $p = .029$. However, the mean estimate for the quiet condition was significantly lower than that of the noisy condition for the 36-second interval, $t(9) = -3.42$, $p = .008$.

Mixed factorial ANOVA

To illustrate a mixed factorial ANOVA, we will be using data from a study in which participants judged how often they had heard certain songs (see Table 18.25). The participants listened to a number of different songs and were asked to judge how many times they had heard each song. Some songs had been presented once, some twice and others three times. This was a within-

Table 18.25 Data from 3 × 2 mixed factorial design study looking at frequency judgements of songs

Group	Participant	Presentation frequency		
		1 time	2 times	3 times
Incidental group	1	1.20	2.20	3.00
	2	0.80	2.00	3.20
	3	1.20	1.80	2.80
	4	1.50	2.00	2.50
	5	1.20	2.50	3.20
	M (SD)	1.18 (0.25)	2.10 (0.26)	2.94 (0.30)
Intentional group	6	1.20	1.50	2.00
	7	1.00	2.00	2.50
	8	1.00	1.20	3.20
	9	1.20	2.20	2.80
	10	1.00	2.20	3.50
	M (SD)	1.08 (0.11)	1.82 (0.45)	2.80 (0.59)

subjects factor. Half of the participants did not expect this frequency judgement test (incidental group), and the other half of the participants did expect this test (intentional group). Group therefore was a between-subjects factor.

STOP & Think

What preliminary interpretations can you make based on the results in Table 18.14?

Mixed factorial ANOVA in SPSS

The first two tables of SPSS output (see Table 18.26) – Within-subjects factors and Between-subjects factors – confirm what the levels of each factor are. Check that these are correct.

Table 18.26 SPSS output showing factors and descriptive statistics

Within-Subjects Factors

Measure:Judged_frequency

Frequency	Dependent Variable
1	One_time
2	Two_times
3	Three_times

Between-Subjects Factors

		Value Label	N
Group	1	Incidental	5
	2	Intentional	5

Descriptive Statistics

	Group	Mean	Std. Deviation	N
One time	Incidental	1.1800	.24900	5
	Intentional	1.0800	.10954	5
	Total	1.1300	.18886	10
Two times	Incidental	2.1000	.26458	5
	Intentional	1.8200	.44944	5
	Total	1.9600	.37771	10
Three times	Incidental	2.9400	.29665	5
	Intentional	2.8000	.58737	5
	Total	2.8700	.44485	10

The next table is Descriptive statistics. Again, check that everything looks OK here and that things have been labelled correctly.

Box's test of equality of covariance matrices (if requested) is useful to check an additional assumption of the mixed factorial ANOVA (Table 18.27): that there should be a similar pattern of inter-correlations among the levels of the within-subjects factor for each level of the between-subjects factor. Do not worry if you did not understand this – all you need to concentrate on is that Box's test shouldn't be significant. Pallant (2010) recommends that you use an alpha level of .001 (i.e. it is significant if the p-value is less than .001) as the test is quite sensitive.

The next table, Multivariate statistics, can be ignored or deleted. We then come to Mauchly's test of sphericity (Table 18.28). If it is significant, we consult the Greenhouse-Geisser row of

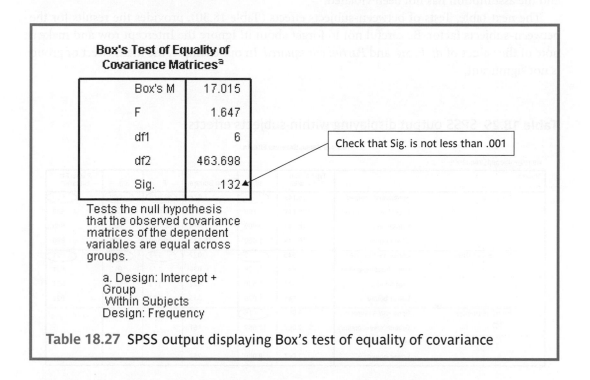

Box's Test of Equality of Covariance Matrices[a]

Box's M	17.015
F	1.647
df1	6
df2	463.698
Sig.	.132

Check that Sig. is not less than .001

Tests the null hypothesis that the observed covariance matrices of the dependent variables are equal across groups.

a. Design: Intercept + Group
Within Subjects
Design: Frequency

Table 18.27 SPSS output displaying Box's test of equality of covariance

Table 18.28 SPSS output displaying Mauchly's test of sphericity

Mauchly's Test of Sphericity[b]

If Sig. < .05 → Greenhouse-Geisser
If Sig. > .05 → Sphericity assumed

Measure:Judged_frequency

Within Subjects Effect	Mauchly's W	Approx. Chi-Square	df	Sig.	Epsilon[a]		
					Greenhouse-Geisser	Huynh-Feldt	Lower-bound
Frequency	.829	1.314	2	.518	.854	1.000	.500

Tests the null hypothesis that the error covariance matrix of the orthonormalized transformed dependent variables is proportional to an identity matrix.

a. May be used to adjust the degrees of freedom for the averaged tests of significance. Corrected tests are displayed in the Tests of Within-Subjects Effects table.

b. Design: Intercept + Group
Within Subjects Design: Frequency

results in the ANOVA table; if it is non-significant, we use the Sphericity assumed row. In our example, we therefore would use the Sphericity assumed row.

Then we come to the Tests of within-subjects effects table (Table 18.29), which provides the results for the within-subjects factor and the interaction, but not the between-subjects factor. Follow the appropriate row of results (i.e. Sphericity assumed or Greenhouse-Geisser) and take a note of the values of df, F, p and effect size. In our example, we can see that there is a significant main effect of frequency, but the frequency × group interaction is non-significant.

You can ignore the Tests of within-subjects contrasts table, so just move on to Levene's test for equality of error variances, which is testing for homogeneity of variance (one of the assumptions of ANOVA). A non-significant result means that there is homogeneity of variance and the assumption has not been violated.

The next table, Tests of between-subjects effects (Table 18.30), provides the results for the between-subjects factor. Be careful not to forget about it! Ignore the Intercept row and make a note of the values of df, F, $Sig.$ and $Partial\ eta\ squared$. In our example, the main effect of group is not significant.

Table 18.29 SPSS output displaying within-subjects effects

Tests of Within-Subjects Effects

Measure:Judged_frequency

Source		Type III Sum of Squares	df	Mean Square	F	Sig.	Partial Eta Squared
Frequency	Sphericity Assumed	15.149	2	7.574	58.640	.000	.880
	Greenhouse-Geisser	15.149	1.708	8.870	58.640	.000	.880
	Huynh-Feldt	15.149	2.000	7.574	58.640	.000	.880
	Lower-bound	15.149	1.000	15.149	58.640	.000	.880
Frequency * Group	Sphericity Assumed	.045	2	.022	.173	.843	.021
	Greenhouse-Geisser	.045	1.708	.026	.173	.810	.021
	Huynh-Feldt	.045	2.000	.022	.173	.843	.021
	Lower-bound	.045	1.000	.045	.173	.688	.021
Error(Frequency)	Sphericity Assumed	2.067	16	.129			
	Greenhouse-Geisser	2.067	13.662	.151			
	Huynh-Feldt	2.067	16.000	.129			
	Lower-bound	2.067	8.000	.258			

Table 18.30 SPSS output displaying between-subjects effects

Tests of Between-Subjects Effects

Measure:Judged_frequency
Transformed Variable:Average

Source	Type III Sum of Squares	df	Mean Square	F	Sig.	Partial Eta Squared
Intercept	118.405	1	118.405	902.709	.000	.991
Group	.225	1	.225	1.718	.226	.177
Error	1.049	8	.131			

Table 18.31 SPSS output showing descriptive statistics (a) and pairwise comparisons (b)

(a)

Estimates

Measure:Judged_frequency

Frequency	Mean	Std. Error	95% Confidence Interval	
			Lower Bound	Upper Bound
1	1.130	.061	.990	1.270
2	1.960	.117	1.691	2.229
3	2.870	.147	2.531	3.209

(b)

Pairwise Comparisons

Measure:Judged_frequency

(I) Frequency	(J) Frequency	Mean Difference (I-J)	Std. Error	Sig.ª	95% Confidence Interval for Differenceª	
					Lower Bound	Upper Bound
1	2	-.830*	.129	.001	-1.220	-.440
	3	-1.740*	.188	.000	-2.306	-1.174
2	1	.830*	.129	.001	.440	1.220
	3	-.910*	.160	.001	-1.392	-.428
3	1	1.740*	.188	.000	1.174	2.306
	2	.910*	.160	.001	.428	1.392

Based on estimated marginal means

*. The mean difference is significant at the .05 level.

a. Adjustment for multiple comparisons: Bonferroni.

The rest of the output is composed of tables designed to help you interpret your results – marginal means, *post hoc* pairwise (Table 18.31) comparisons and a plot of the means (Figure 18.13). In the current example, there was only a main effect of frequency and the *post hoc* tests revealed that there were significant differences between all of the three levels.

The plot of the means (Figure 18.13) also confirms the results – the lines are parallel (no interaction), there is very little difference between the means for Incidental and Intentional (no main effect of group), but there is a clear increase in judged frequency as actual frequency of presentation increases.

Mixed factorial ANOVA by hand

As you may have guessed, calculating a mixed factorial ANOVA by hand is a mixture of the methods we used when calculating the two-way between-subjects and two-way within-subjects ANOVAs. We treat every effect that involves the within-subjects factor as "within-subjects" (i.e.

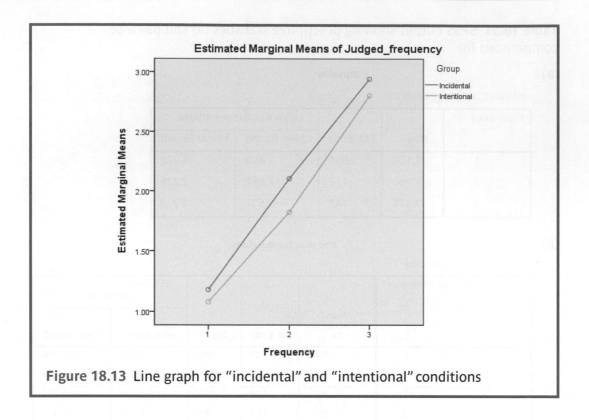

Figure 18.13 Line graph for "incidental" and "intentional" conditions

the within-subjects factor main effect and the interaction). We will be using the data from our frequency judgement study (we have omitted the standard deviations as they do not play a part in this calculation; they are in Table 18.24 if you want to see them; see Table 18.32).

As usual, we first calculate SS_{total}, using $N = 30$ (there are 30 scores):

$$SS_{total} = \sum X^2 - \frac{\left(\sum X\right)^2}{N} = 136.94 - \frac{3552.16}{30} = 136.94 - 118.4053 = 18.5347$$

Next, we calculate $SS_{between\ subj}$ using the means for each participant (i.e. their mean across all conditions); $n = 3$ since three scores were used to calculate each mean:

$$SS_{between\ subj} = \sum n_c \bar{X}_p^2 - \frac{\left(\sum X\right)^2}{N}$$

$$= (3(2.1333^2) + 3(2.0000^2) + \cdots + 3(2.0667^2) + 3(2.2333^2)) - \frac{3552.16}{30}$$

$$= (13.6529 + 12.0000 + \cdots + 12.8137 + 14.9629) - 118.4053$$

$$= 119.6758 - 118.4053 = 1.2705$$

We calculate the sum of squares for the between-subjects factor (group, SS_A) using the overall means for the groups; $n = 15$ since 15 scores were used to calculate these means:

Table 18.32 Data from 3×2 mixed factorial design study looking at frequency judgements of songs with means

Group	Participant	Presentation frequency			Mean
		1 time	2 times	3 times	
Incidental group	1	1.20	2.20	3.00	2.1333
	2	0.80	2.00	3.20	2.0000
	3	1.20	1.80	2.80	1.9333
	4	1.50	2.00	2.50	2.0000
	5	1.20	2.50	3.20	2.3000
	Mean	1.18	2.10	2.94	2.0733
Intentional group	6	1.20	1.50	2.00	1.5667
	7	1.00	2.00	2.50	1.8333
	8	1.00	1.20	3.20	1.8000
	9	1.20	2.20	2.80	2.0667
	10	1.00	2.20	3.50	2.2333
	Mean	1.08	1.82	2.80	1.9000
	Overall mean	1.13	1.96	2.87	1.9867

$\sum X = 59.6$
$\sum X^2 = 136.94$
$(\sum X)^2 = 3552.16$

$$SS_A = \sum n_k \bar{X}_k^2 - \frac{(\sum X)^2}{N} = (15(2.0733^2) + 15(1.9000^2)) - \frac{3552.16}{30}$$
$$= (15(4.2986) + 15(3.6100)) - 118.4053$$
$$= (64.4790 + 54.1500) - 118.4053 = 118.6290 - 118.4053 = 0.2337$$

We find $SS_{error\ A}$ (i.e. SS_{error} for the group factor), but subtracting SS_A from $SS_{between\ subj}$:

$$SS_{error\ A} = SS_{between\ subj} - SS_A = 1.2705 - 0.2337 = 1.0368$$

The within-subjects factor (frequency) is dealt with next, using the overall means for each level of the frequency factor, $n = 10$ since 10 scores were used to calculate the means:

$$SS_B = \sum n_k \bar{X}_k^2 - \frac{(\sum X)^2}{N} = (10(1.13^2) + 10(1.96^2) + 10(2.87^2)) - \frac{3552.16}{30}$$
$$= (10(1.2769) + 10(3.8416) + 10(8.2369)) - 118.4053$$
$$= (12.769 + 38.416 + 82.369) - 118.4053 = 133.554 - 118.4053 = 15.1487$$

Table 18.33 ANOVA summary table

	SS	df	MS	F
Group (factor A – between-subjects)	0.2337	1	0.2337	1.80
Error (Group) (factor A – between-subjects)	1.0368	8	0.1296	
Frequency (factor B – within-subjects)	15.1487	2	7.5744	58.31
Group × Frequency (A × B)	0.0363	2	0.0182	0.14
Error (Group × Frequency) (A × B)	2.0792	16	0.1299	

Now we calculate SS_{cells}, using the means for each individual condition; $n = 5$:

$$SS_{cells} = \sum n_k \bar{X}_k^2 - \frac{\left(\sum X\right)^2}{N}$$

$$= (5(1.18^2) + 5(2.10^2) + 5(2.94^2) + 5(1.08^2) + 5(1.82^2) + 5(2.80^2)) - \frac{3552.16}{30}$$

$$= (5(1.3924) + 5(4.41) + 5(8.6436) + 5(1.1664) + 5(3.3124) + 5(7.84)) - 118.4053$$

$$= (6.962 + 22.05 + 43.218 + 5.832 + 16.562 + 39.2) - 118.4053$$

$$= 133.824 - 118.4053 = 15.4187$$

The SS for the interaction ($SS_{A \times B}$) is calculated by subtracting the SS for the main effects from SS_{cells}:

$$SS_{A \times B} = SS_{cells} - SS_A - SS_B = 15.4187 - 0.2337 - 15.1487 = 0.0363$$

We now need to calculate SS_{within}, as this will help us find the remaining SS value. To calculate SS_{within}, you subtract $SS_{between\ subj}$ from SS_{total}:

$$SS_{within} = SS_{total} - SS_{between\ subj} = 18.5347 - 1.2705 = 17.2642$$

To obtain the $SS_{error\ A \times B}$, you subtract the SS for the within-subjects main effect and the SS for the interaction from the SS_{within}:

$$SS_{error\ A \times B} = SS_{within} - SS_B - SS_{A \times B} = 17.2642 - 15.1487 - 0.0363 = 2.0792$$

We can then put the appropriate values into the ANOVA summary table (Table 18.33) and calculate the F-values. (The calculated values vary slightly from those in the SPSS output table due to rounding down decimal places.) Remember, that if the F-value is greater than the critical F-value in the critical value table, then it is significant.

Reporting results of a mixed factorial ANOVA

The same format as before should be used. Therefore, the results from the current study could be written up as:

A mixed factorial ANOVA was used to analyse the data. There was no significant main effect of group, $F(1, 8) = 1.72$, $p = .226$, $\eta_p^2 = .177$, and there was no significant group × frequency interaction, $F(2, 16) = 0.17$, $p = .843$, $\eta_p^2 = .021$. However, there was a significant main effect of frequency of presentation, $F(2, 16) = 58.64$, $p < .001$, $\eta_p^2 = .880$. *Post hoc* Bonferroni tests revealed that the overall mean judged frequency for songs that were presented once ($M = 1.13$) was significantly lower than that for songs presented twice ($M = 1.96$) or three times ($M = 2.87$). Additionally, the mean judged frequency for songs that were presented twice was significantly lower than that for songs presented three times ($p < .001$).

Analysing three-way factorial designs

Using the principles covered in this chapter, you can go on to analyse designs with any number of factors. However, in reality you will probably come across only three-way factorial designs, and, even then, very rarely.

In terms of the SPSS output for three-way factorial designs, this is very similar to the output for the two-way ANOVAs apart from the fact that there will be an extra main effect to look for and three further interactions. Just stick to the advice here and do not be put off by the huge tables of results.

However, perhaps the most difficult part of a three-way factorial ANOVA is interpreting significant interactions. Inspecting graphs of means can help. You will be given a different plot for each level of the third factor and have to compare the pattern shown in each plot. If this does not clarify things, you could always go back and produce new graphs – sometimes switching around which variables appear on the horizontal axis, as separate lines or separate plots can make a big difference. You could also run two-way ANOVAs for each level of the third variable, similar to simple main effects analysis.

Summary

In this chapter, we discussed the ways in which we can analyse data from designs involving two or more factors. Depending on the overall design, three different ANOVAs are available to choose from: the between-subjects factorial ANOVA, in which all factors are altered between-subjects (i.e. different groups for each condition); the within-subjects factorial ANOVA, in which all factors are altered within-subjects (i.e. same participants in each condition); and the mixed factorial ANOVA, in which at least one factor is between-subjects and at least one factor is within-subjects. There are no non-parametric equivalents for these tests.

In factorial ANOVA, you are given results for the overall effects of each factor – main effects – plus the interaction between the factors. For a two-factor design, this would mean two main effects and one interaction. Each of these results is indicated by an *F*-value with an associated *p*-value – if it is significant, there is a significant main effect or interaction. Significant results can be interpreted through the use of tables of means, *post hoc* tests and plots of means. If lines diverge or cross in a means plot, this normally suggests the presence of an interaction.

Questions

 1 What is a main effect?

 2 What is an interaction, and how does it differ from main effects?

 3 How many F-values does a 2×2 factorial ANOVA produce?

 4 How many F-values does a $3 \times 2 \times 2$ factorial ANOVA produce?

 5 How many independent variables does a $2 \times 4 \times 6$ factorial experiment have?

 6 How many factors with three levels are there in a $2 \times 4 \times 6$ factorial experiment?

 7 How many conditions does a $2 \times 3 \times 4$ factorial design have?

 8 Why are *post hoc* tests not necessary in a 2×2 factorial design?

 9 What does a means plot in which the lines are parallel suggest?

10 What would you do to interpret a significant interaction?

 Activities

 1 The numbers in the 2×2 factorial matrix (Figure 18.14) are cell means but one cell entry is missing. Identify which number should be put in the empty cell so that

   (a) there is no indication of a main effect of A

   (b) there is no indication of a main effect of B

   (c) there is no indication of an interaction effect

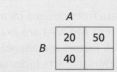

 Figure 18.14 Factorial matrix

 2 The numbers in the 2×2 factorial matrices (Figure 18.15) are cell means. Match the bold-faced letter with the description.

   (a) There is a main effect for A but not for B; no interaction

   (b) There is a main effect for B but not for A; no interaction

   (c) There is a main effect for A and for B; no interaction

   (d) No main effect for A or B; interaction is present

W

	A	
B	25	25
	10	10

X

	A	
B	5	15
	5	15

Y

	A	
B	5	20
	20	5

Z

	A	
B	5	10
	15	20

Figure 18.15 Factorial matrices

3 Participants learned a list of words and recalled them 20 minutes later. Words were learned while sitting on the beach or underwater (using scuba gear). The words were recalled in either the same place or the other place. The four group means are shown in the cells of the 2×2 matrix (Table 18.34). Write out an interpretation of the results. (Based on Godden and Baddeley, 1975.)

Table 18.34 Group means of words learned and recalled

		Words learned	
		On land	Underwater
Words recalled	On land	14	9
	Underwater	9	11

4 In a study by Chaiken and Pliner (1987), research participants read an "eating diary". Participants were told that the diary was that of either a male or female stimulus person. The information in the diary indicated that the person ate either large meals or small meals. After reading this information, participants rated the person's femininity and masculinity.

(a) Identify the design of this experiment.

(b) How many conditions are in the experiment?

(c) Identify the independent variable(s) and dependent variable(s).

Chaiken and Pliner reported the following mean femininity ratings (higher numbers indicate greater femininity): male – small meals (2.02), male–large meals (2.05), female – small meals (3.90), and female – large meals (2.82). Assume there are equal numbers of participants in each condition.

▶

(d) Are there any main effects?

(e) Is there an interaction?

(f) Graph the means.

(g) Describe the results in a brief paragraph.

5 A developmental psychologist gives two types of critical thinking tests to children aged 10 years, 12 years and 14 years. There are 28 children tested at each age level; 14 received one form (A or B) of the test. The dependent measure is the percentage correct on the tests. The mean percentage correct for the children at each age level and for the two tests is as shown in Table 18.35.

Table 18.35 Mean percentage correct for two types of critical thinking tests

Test	10 years	12 years	14 years
Form A	38.14	63.64	80.21
Form B	52.29	68.64	80.93

The ANOVA summary table for this experiment is as shown in Table 18.36.

Table 18.36 ANOVA summary table

Source	Sum of squares	df	Mean square	F	p
Age	17698.95	2	8849.48	96.72	.000
Test	920.05	1	920.05	10.06	.002
Age × Test	658.67	2	329.33	3.60	.032
Error	7136.29	78	91.49		

(a) Draw a graph showing the mean results for this experiment. Based on your examination of the graph, would you suspect a statistically significant interaction effect between the variables? Explain why or why not.

(b) What variables would be created in SPSS in order to analyse these data?

(c) What type of ANOVA has been used?

(d) Which effects were statistically significant? Describe verbally each of the statistically significant effects.

(e) What further analyses could you do to determine the source of the interaction effect?

(f) What is the simple main effect of form for each level of age?

Chapter 19

Testing for Relationships and Making Predictions

chs 16–18

ch. 20

OVERVIEW

In Chapters 16–18, the focus was on methods used to compare *differences* between groups or conditions. However, as you will be well aware by now, not all research is interested in comparing differences; correlational research instead concentrates on investigating *relationships* between variables. In this chapter you will be introduced to the main techniques used to analyse relationships and make predictions – correlation and regression. (If you want to analyse relationships between two **nominal variables**, have a look at Chapter 20.)

OBJECTIVES

After studying this chapter and working through the exercises, you should be able to:

- Identify characteristics of a relationship from the magnitude and sign of a correlation coefficient
- Identify factors that can influence the value of a correlation coefficient
- Distinguish between Pearson's correlation, Spearman's correlation and Kendall's tau
- Calculate and interpret the coefficient of determination (r^2)
- Describe the point-biserial correlation and biserial correlation and their uses

- Explain partial correlation and its uses

- Conduct analysis, interpret output and write up results for Pearson's correlation, Spearman's correlation, Kendall's tau and partial correlation

- State the regression equation and explain how it can be used to predict scores on a criterion variable

- Distinguish between simple, hierarchical and stepwise multiple regression

- Conduct analysis, interpret output and write up results for simple bivariate regression, simple (simultaneous) multiple regression, hierarchical multiple regression and stepwise multiple regression

- Identify the assumptions of correlation and regression and how you might check for them

Correlation

In Chapter 5, you were introduced to **correlational research**, in which the focus is on examining the relationship between variables. There is no manipulation of variables as there is in experimental research; instead, variables are measured "as is". This type of design is useful in real-world research where variables are measured as they exist naturally, or in research where it is impossible or unethical to manipulate variables.

ch. 5
pp.86–89

Students often get confused about whether a study is looking at differences or relationships. For example, it is not uncommon for people to talk about the "relationship" between gender (male or female, obviously) and a dependent variable (say, verbal ability), when the most appropriate statistical method for such a study would be a test that looks for *differences between groups*, and not for relationships. Usually, in correlational research we are interested in looking at the relationship between two (or more) continuous variables.[1] So, if you are unsure whether you are testing for differences or relationships, check your variables – if one of the variables is a grouping variable or an independent variable with different levels (usually categorical in nature),[2] and the other is a dependent or score variable, you will be testing for differences; if you do not have an independent variable and are interested in two continuous score variables, you will be testing for relationships.

Correlation
When scores on one variable covary with scores on another.

Correlation coefficient
A statistic which indicates the degree of covariation between two variables; ranges between −1.00 and +1.00.

A **correlation** exists when two different measures of the same people, events or things vary together – that is, when scores on one variable covary with scores on another variable. Correlation is also the general name given to techniques used to calculate a statistic called a **correlation coefficient**, which gives us a quantitative measure of the degree of this covariation. The correlation coefficient is a very useful statistic as it tells us a number of useful things about a relationship. First, the *magnitude* of the coefficient gives an indication of the strength of a relationship.

---

1 Continuous variables are those that are scored in a numerically continuous (e.g. 1, 2, 3) way.

2 For example "gender" would be a grouping variable as it groups people into two categories – male and female

The value of a correlation coefficient can range from +1.00 through 0 to −1.00. A coefficient of 0 indicates that no linear relationship exists,[3] but the closer a correlation coefficient is to +1.00 or −1.00, the stronger the relationship between the two variables. Both +1.00 and −1.00 indicate what we call a **perfect relationship**. This just means that changes in the scores of one variable are accompanied by perfectly predictable changes in the scores of the other variable.

As well as looking at the magnitude of the correlation coefficient, we can also look at its *sign* (i.e. whether it is a positive or negative number) to tell us about the direction of the relationship. A **positive relationship** is one in which, as scores on one variable increase, scores on the other variable also increase. For example, there is a positive relationship between hours of study and exam grades – as hours of study increase, so too do grades. A **negative relationship** is one in which, as scores on one variable increase, scores on the other variable *decrease* (i.e. an inverse relationship). An example is the age of a car and its monetary value – as a car gets older, its value decreases. As you may have guessed, a positive correlation coefficient indicates a positive relationship and a negative coefficient indicates a negative relationship. Students sometimes mistakenly interpret a negative correlation coefficient as indicating the absence of a relationship. The sign of a correlation coefficient only tells us about the *direction* of a relationship and is not related to the strength of a relationship. For example, a correlation coefficient of −.46 indicates a stronger relationship than one that is .20, but the relationships are in a different direction.

Perfect relationship
Occurs when changes in scores in one variable are related to perfectly predictable changes in scores in another variable; indicated by correlation coefficient of +1.00 and −1.00.

Positive relationship
A relationship in which increases in scores on one variable are associated with increases in scores on another variable.

STOP & Think

Identify three of your own examples for positive and negative relationships that you have come across.

ch. 14
p.306–308

The nature of a correlation can be represented graphically using a **scatterplot** (see **Chapter 14**). One of the variables is plotted on the x-axis and the other on the y-axis. Each dot of a scatterplot represents a pair of scores, one for the *x* variable and one for the *y* variable. The magnitude or degree of correlation is seen in a scatterplot by determining how well the points correspond to a straight line; stronger correlations more clearly resemble a straight line of points. The sign of a correlation can also be determined by looking at the general direction of the cloud of points on a scatterplot – if the cloud goes from the bottom-left to the top-right of the scatterplot, then the correlation will be positive; if the cloud of points goes from top-left to bottom-right, the correlation will be negative. Figure 19.1 shows several scatterplots, which present different correlations. In the first scatterplot ($r = .00$), there is no discernible pattern in the data – the points do not resemble a straight

Negative relationship
A relationship in which increases in scores on one variable are associated with decreases in scores on another variable.

Scatterplot
Graph in which pairs of scores on two variables are represented by separate points.

---

3   Although a correlation of 0 sometimes indicates that a curvilinear relationship exists; for example, one that looks like a "U", either the right way up or upside down.

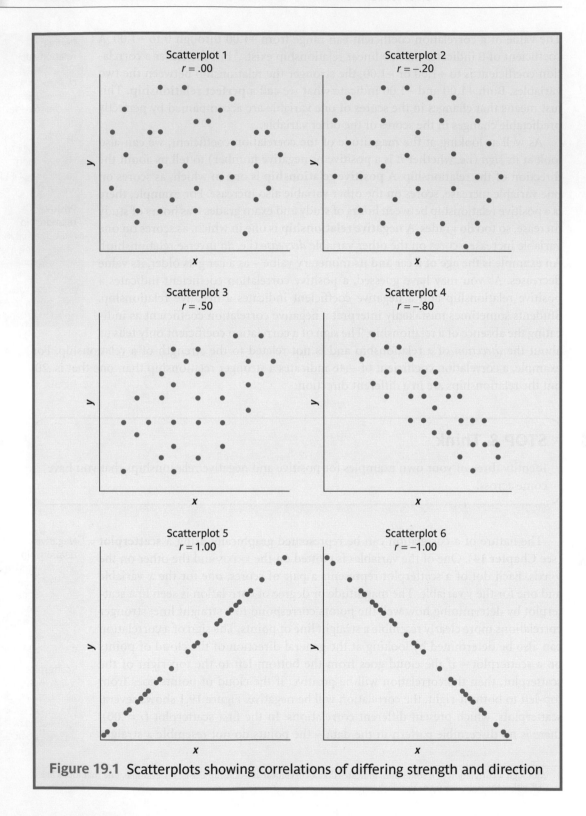

Figure 19.1 Scatterplots showing correlations of differing strength and direction

line and there is no general positive or negative trend. Scatterplot 2 ($r = -.20$) shows a low negative correlation – there is a general trend for y scores to decrease as x scores increase, but the points do not fit closely to a straight line. Scatterplot 3 ($r = .50$) shows a slightly stronger positive correlation, with the points closer to forming a straight line. Scatterplot 4 ($r = -.80$) shows a strong correlation, but notice the direction of the cloud of points, indicative of a negative relationship. Scatterplots 5 and 6 ($r = 1.00$ and $r = -1.00$, respectively) both show perfect relationships, with the points forming a perfect straight line; the only difference is in the direction of the relationship.

STOP & Think

Sketch a scatterplot for each of the following correlations: $r = .30$, $r = -.50$, $r = .90$.

Interpreting correlations

If you find a correlation between two variables it is very tempting – but very wrong! – to conclude that one variable causes changes in the other. You cannot draw any conclusions about cause-and-effect from correlational research. Instead, all you can conclude is that the variables are related in some way. You could put forward some potential explanations for the relationship, but correlation cannot tell you which, if any, of the possible explanations is correct.

In **Chapter 5** we discussed the positive relationship between self-rated level of aggression and amount of exposure to violent video games. While it is common for the media to jump on a result like this and conclude that watching video games causes aggression, you need to be a little more cautious when interpreting correlations. It is possible that watching video games does indeed lead to higher levels of aggression. But it is equally valid to argue that being aggressive makes an individual more likely to watch violent video games.

ch. 5
pp.86 – 87

There is also the problem of the "third variable", when an unobserved variable influences both of the observed variables to create a correlation between them, even though there is no direct relationship. One frequently used illustration of this point is the fact that there is a positive correlation between the number of ice creams sold in a city and the number of violent crimes (murder, rape, assault, etc.). On one hand, you could argue that eating ice cream causes people to commit violent crimes, or that committing violent crimes makes people want to eat ice creams. Obviously neither of these explanations is likely to be true – just because two variables are related does not tell us that there is a direct relationship between the variables. It is much more likely that a third variable – temperature – is the likely culprit for this relationship.

Another favourite example was discussed by Matthews (2001), who examined data for a number of European countries and found that there is a correlation of 0.62 between number of pairs of storks and birth rate in each country. Does this mean that storks bring babies? No. There is a relationship, but it is thought to be due to the size of the country – the larger the country, the larger the population of humans and storks. The message from all of this is to exercise a bit of caution when interpreting correlations as it may be more complex than it first appears.

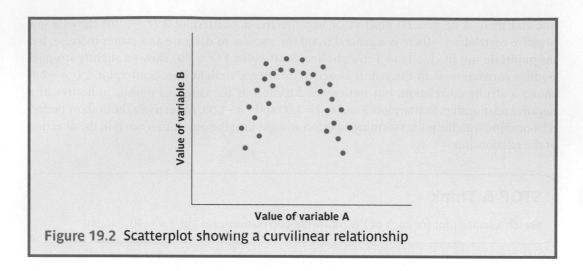

Figure 19.2 Scatterplot showing a curvilinear relationship

Pearson's correlation coefficient

Pearson correlation coefficient
Correlation coefficient which describes degree of linear relationship between two interval/ratio variables; denoted by r.

The most commonly used test for correlations is Pearson's product-moment correlation coefficient, more commonly called the **Pearson correlation coefficient** (symbolized by r). This method is used to investigate the degree of the relationship between two interval/ratio variables. Specifically, it looks at *linear* relationships between variables. This means that the value of Pearson's correlation tells us how well the data fit a straight line: a Pearson r of +1.00 or −1.00 therefore indicates that the data fall perfectly on a straight line in a scatterplot.

If the relationship between variables is non-linear, the Pearson correlation underestimates the degree of the relationship between the variables. For example, the Pearson correlation between the variables in Figure 19.2 is zero, even though there is a clear – but non-linear – relationship. Thus, if points on a scatterplot show a clear non-linear relationship, you should *not* use Pearson's correlation.

As well as inspecting scatterplots for the shape of the relationship, you should also inspect the shape of the frequency distributions for the scores – the scores should be relatively normally distributed. This is because a mean represents data well only when they are normally distributed, and the calculation of Pearson's correlation involves standard deviations, which, as you may recall, are calculated using the mean. (We will cover how to calculate Pearson's r later in the chapter.) You should therefore inspect the frequency distributions of each set of scores to ensure that they are normal (or nearly normal) before using the Pearson r. (Do not confuse the scatterplots we have been using in this chapter with frequency distributions. They are showing different things – the scatterplot shows how scores on one variable are related to scores on another. A frequency distribution shows how frequent scores are for one variable only.)

There are a number of other factors which could affect Pearson's correlation. The first is the presence of outliers. An outlier[4] can drastically change your correlation coefficient and affect the

---

4   We mentioned outliers in Chapter 14. An outlier is a score that is far away in value from the rest of the data-set that it belongs to.

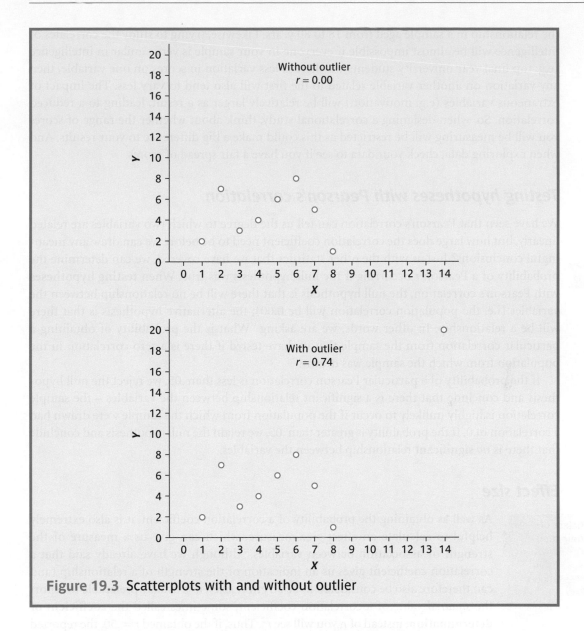

Figure 19.3 Scatterplots with and without outlier

magnitude of your correlation, its sign or both. This is especially true if you use a small number of pairs of scores to compute the Pearson *r*. In Figure 19.3, two sets of data are presented in scatterplots – one which includes an outlier and one which excludes the outlier. As you can see, the presence of one outlier makes a massive difference to the value of the correlation coefficient (*r*). Both sets of data are exactly the same except for the one outlier (it is in the top right of the lower scatterplot). This one outlier greatly increases the correlation coefficient, which is 0 without it, but .74 with it.

Restricting the range over which the variables vary can also affect Pearson *r*. For example, if you were to examine the relationship between age and another variable (e.g. reaction time) in a sample aged 18–24 years, you would probably find a weaker correlation than if you examined the relationship in a sample aged from 18 to 80 years. Likewise, trying to study the correlates of intelligence will be almost impossible if everyone in your sample is very similar in intelligence (e.g. top final year university students). If there is less variation in scores on one variable, then any variation on another variable related to the first will also tend to vary less. The impact of extraneous variables (e.g. motivation) will be relatively larger as a result, leading to a reduced correlation. So, when designing a correlational study, think about whether the range of scores you will be measuring will be restricted as this could make a big difference to your results. And when exploring data, check your data to see if you have a fair spread of scores.

Testing hypotheses with Pearson's correlation

ch. 15
pp.330–332

We have seen that Pearson's correlation can tell us the degree to which two variables are related linearly, but how large does the correlation coefficient need to be before we can draw any meaningful conclusions? Just as with the other statistics that we have covered, we can determine the probability of a Pearson r occurring if the null hypothesis was true. When **testing hypotheses** with Pearson's correlation, the null hypothesis is that there will be no relationship between the variables (i.e. the population correlation will be 0.00); the alternative hypothesis is that there will be a relationship. In other words, we are asking "What is the probability of obtaining a particular correlation from the sample that we have tested if there is a zero correlation in the population from which the sample was drawn?"

If the probability of a particular Pearson correlation is less than .05, we reject the null hypothesis and conclude that there is a significant relationship between the variables – the sample correlation is highly unlikely to occur if the population from which the sample were drawn had a correlation of 0. If the probability is greater than .05, we retain the null hypothesis and conclude that there is *no* significant relationship between the variables.

Effect size

Coefficient of determination
Measure of strength of a relationship; describes amount of variance explained; denoted by r^2.

As well as obtaining the probability of a correlation coefficient, it is also extremely helpful to calculate an effect size measure, which can give us a measure of the strength of association between variables. Although we have already said that a correlation coefficient gives us an indication of the strength of a relationship (and can therefore also be considered to be an effect size), it is usually preferable to report the *squared* value of a correlation coefficient, sometimes called the **coefficient of determination**; instead of r, you will see r^2. Thus, if the obtained $r = .50$, the reported $r^2 = .25$.

Why transform the value of r? The reason is that the transformation changes the obtained r to a percentage. The percentage value represents the percentage of variance in one variable that is accounted for by the second variable. The range of r^2 values can range from 0.00 (0%) to 1.00 (100%). The r^2 value is sometimes referred to as the percentage of shared variance between the two variables. What does this mean, exactly?

Recall the concept of variability in a set of scores – if you looked at a class of students' examination performance, you would see that their scores range from low to high marks. If you were studying factors that are related to examination performance, you could look at the relationship between examination marks and a number of different variables. One such variable might be time spent revising. If the correlation was .60, that means that 36% ($.60^2 = .36$) of the variability in examination grades can be accounted for by time spent revising. This still leaves 64 per cent of the variability in examination grades unexplained. This variability might be accounted for by other variables, such as anxiety levels, attendance at class, quality of lecturing, class size, etc. In an ideal world, you could account for 100% of the variability if you had enough information on all other variables that contribute to people's weights: each variable would make an incremental contribution until all the variability is accounted for.

There have been some attempts to label effect sizes for correlations. For example, Cohen (1969) proposed that r values of .10, .30 and .50 represented small, medium and large effect sizes, respectively. The corresponding r^2 values would therefore be .01 (small), .09 (medium) and .25 (large). However, these values are not always appropriate. For example, if you are testing the test–retest **reliability** of a measure, an r value of .80 or above is considered to indicate a reliable measure; an r-value of .50 is very small, not large. At the other end of the scale, an r-value of .03 is enough for the widespread recommendation to take a low dose of aspirin to prevent heart attacks (Rosnow & Rosenthal, 1989). Part of the problem is that r is used in such a wide variety of ways. Whether an r is considered small, medium or large depends on the reason it was calculated and the researcher's experience with the two variables. Nevertheless, Cohen's classification is useful.

ch. 4
pp.69–73

Hemphill (2003) addressed the question of establishing adjectives for r by cataloguing thousands of correlation coefficients that were reported in hundreds of studies. Dividing the distribution of r-values into thirds, he found:

Lowest third rs were less than .20
Middle third r-values of .20 to .30
Highest third rs were greater than .30

We will return to r^2 and the idea of explaining variability in scores on a variable later in the chapter, in our discussion of regression.

Example of the Pearson correlation

We can illustrate the Pearson correlation with an example. Suppose you want to know whether travel experiences are related to knowledge of geography. In your study, you give a 15-item quiz on geography to 10 university students, and you also ask how many different countries participants have visited. After obtaining the pairs of observations from each participant, a Pearson r can be computed to measure the strength of the relationship between travel experience and knowledge of geography. Data for the study are shown in Table 19.1.

Pearson correlation using SPSS

As always, before conducting any analysis in SPSS, you should ensure that the data have been explored. It is important that you check the scatterplot to determine if the relationship appears to be linear or not. The scatterplot for the geography data is shown in Figure 19.4. There appears to be no strong evidence of a non-linear relationship, so we can proceed with analysis using the Pearson correlation.

SPSS

The SPSS output for the Pearson correlation is in the form of a table – or matrix – with one column and one row representing each of the variables being correlated. To find the correlation,

Table 19.1 Data for correlation study

Participant	Number of countries visited	Geography test score
1	1	10
2	3	15
3	4	8
4	5	9
5	5	7
6	9	10
7	11	15
8	12	13
9	12	15
10	14	14

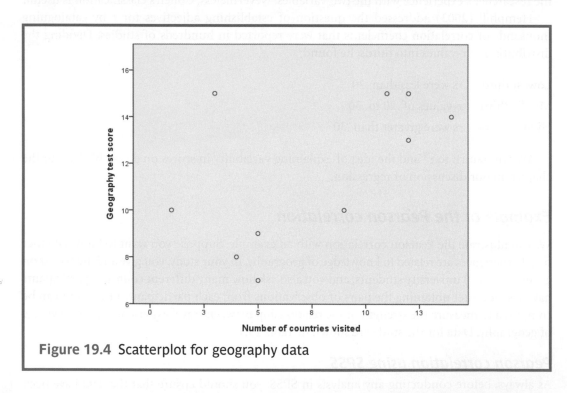

Figure 19.4 Scatterplot for geography data

look where the row of one variable and the column of the other variable intersect. (Do not worry about the correlations of 1.00 – they are just the correlations between a variable and itself.) Three values are reported – the Pearson correlation (if significant, this will have a * next to it), the Sig. value and N (number of cases). As you can see, in our example (Table 19.2) the Pearson correlation is .567, but it is not significant ($p = .087$). We would therefore have to conclude that there was no relationship between the number of countries visited and geography test scores.

Table 19.2 SPSS output displaying correlation coefficient and significance

Correlations

		Number of countries visited	Geography test score
Number of countries visited	Pearson Correlation	1	.567
	Sig. (2-tailed)		.087
	N	10	10
Geography test score	Pearson Correlation	.567	1
	Sig. (2-tailed)	.087	
	N	10	10

People can sometimes get confused with non-significant correlations and mistakenly report that there is a relationship between the variables but it was not significant – based on the results of your Pearson correlation, you can conclude that there is a relationship in the population (significant) *or* no relationship (non-significant). Remember that you are testing whether the correlation obtained from your sample data would be likely to occur if the population correlation was 0.00, so if your p value is greater than .05 this indicates that your sample correlation is a result of error and not due to a systematic relationship in the population.

Pearson's correlation by hand

To calculate Pearson's correlation by hand, you use the formula in Figure 19.5.

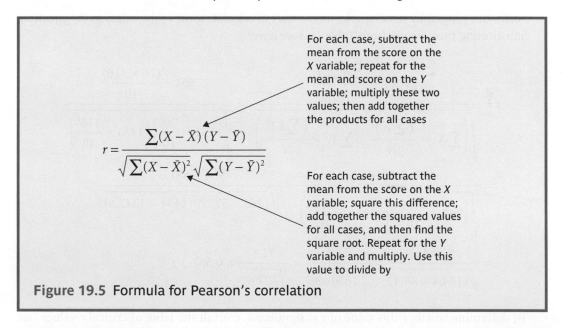

$$r = \frac{\sum (X - \bar{X})(Y - \bar{Y})}{\sqrt{\sum (X - \bar{X})^2}\sqrt{\sum (Y - \bar{Y})^2}}$$

For each case, subtract the mean from the score on the X variable; repeat for the mean and score on the Y variable; multiply these two values; then add together the products for all cases

For each case, subtract the mean from the score on the X variable; square this difference; add together the squared values for all cases, and then find the square root. Repeat for the Y variable and multiply. Use this value to divide by

Figure 19.5 Formula for Pearson's correlation

The top part of the formula tells us the degree of covariance between the two variables – as scores on the X variable vary, do scores on the Y variable vary in a consistent way? The bottom part of the formula represents the maximum possible value of the covariance (i.e. if the points fell on a perfect straight line through the points on a scatterplot).

As you can imagine, calculating Pearson's correlation can get quite time-consuming with large numbers of cases. Thankfully, the formula can be rearranged so that you do not need to use the mean in your calculations (Figure 19.6).

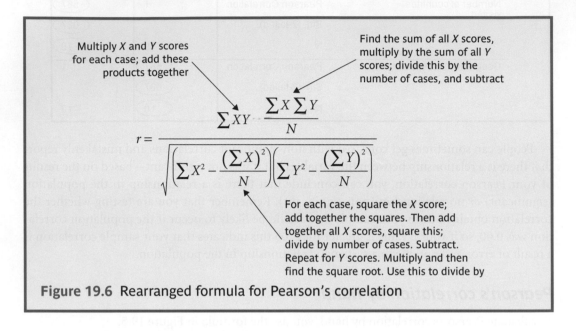

Figure 19.6 Rearranged formula for Pearson's correlation

So, for our geography test example, we can start to calculate some of the values in the equation. Substituting these values from Table 19.3 we have:

$$r = \frac{\sum XY - \dfrac{\sum X \sum Y}{N}}{\sqrt{\left(\sum X^2 - \dfrac{(\sum X)^2}{N}\right)\left(\sum Y^2 - \dfrac{(\sum Y)^2}{N}\right)}} = \frac{954 - \dfrac{(76 \times 116)}{10}}{\sqrt{\left(762 - \dfrac{76^2}{10}\right)\left(1434 - \dfrac{116^2}{10}\right)}}$$

$$= \frac{954 - 8816/10}{\sqrt{\left(762 - \dfrac{5776}{10}\right)\left(1434 - \dfrac{13456}{10}\right)}} = \frac{954 - 881.6}{\sqrt{(762 - 577.6)(1434 - 1345.6)}}$$

$$= \frac{72.4}{\sqrt{(184.4 \times 88.4)}} = \frac{72.4}{\sqrt{16300.96}} = \frac{72.4}{\sqrt{127.67}} = 0.567$$

To determine whether this value of r is significant, consult the table of critical r values (see Appendix F) and find the critical r value for your chosen level of significance and the number of

Participant	Number of countries visited (X)	Geography test score (Y)	X^2	Y^2	XY
1	1	10	1	100	10
2	3	15	9	225	45
3	4	8	16	64	32
4	5	9	25	81	45
5	5	7	25	49	35
6	9	10	81	100	90
7	11	15	121	225	165
8	12	13	144	169	156
9	12	15	144	225	180
10	14	14	196	196	196
Total	$\Sigma X = 76$	$\Sigma Y = 116$	$\Sigma X^2 = 762$	$\Sigma Y^2 = 1434$	$\Sigma XY = 954$

Table 19.3 Conducting a Pearson's correlation

degrees of freedom (= number of cases – 2). So, for our example, the critical value for 8 degrees of freedom and a .05 significance level is .632; our calculated r value is not significant.

Reporting results of Pearson's correlation

To report the results of Pearson's correlation in a research report, you should give the value of r, the df (or N) and the p value. You can also report the effect size, r^2. For example:

There was no significant correlation between number of countries visited and geography test score, $r (8) = .567, p = .087$.
Or
Pearson's correlation revealed no significant relationship between geography test scores and number of countries visited, $r = .567, n = 10, p = .087; r^2 = .321$.

Non-parametric correlation

While the Pearson correlation is by far the most commonly used correlational technique, it assumes that you are testing for a linear relationship and have interval/ratio data. But what do you do if you do not meet these assumptions? Thankfully there are other correlations that can deal with ordinal data or non-linear relationships. The most common of these non-parametric correlations is the **Spearman correlation** (r_s or rho). Spearman's correlation can be used to look at the relationship between variables when one or both of the variables are ordinal. You should also use

Spearman correlation
Non-parametric correlation technique used to describe relationship between two interval/ratio/ordinal variables; relationship should be monotonic, but not necessarily linear; denoted by r_s or rho.

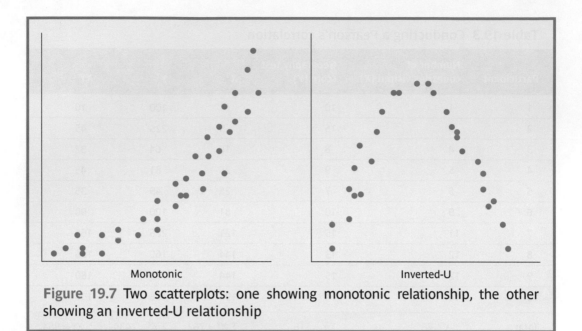

Figure 19.7 Two scatterplots: one showing monotonic relationship, the other showing an inverted-U relationship

Monotonic relationship
A relationship that goes in one direction, but is not necessarily linear.

Spearman's correlation if your data are interval/ratio but there appears to be a monotonic non-linear relationship. A **monotonic relationship** is simply a relationship that goes in one direction. Figure 19.7 shows a scatterplot with a non-linear monotonic relationship, suitable for Spearman's correlation, and a scatterplot with a non-linear relationship that is not monotonic, and would therefore not be suitable for Spearman's correlation.

Spearman's correlation can deal with non-linear relationships because it converts scores into ranks (if they are not already ranked) and works out the linear correlation between the ranks. The use of ranks is based on the assumption that, if two variables are correlated, then they will be ranked similarly. For example, if you are correlating height and shoe size, you might expect the people with the highest (and lowest) rank in the sample for height would also have a similar rank when their shoe size is measured. In other words, the people ranked tallest on the height measure would also be ranked as having the largest feet on the shoe-size measure. The use of ranks also means that if you have non-normal distributions and outliers, they will not exert as much of an influence as they do on Pearson's correlation.

Kendall's tau
Non-parametric correlation technique used in same way as Spearman correlation, but recommended for small samples and tied ranks; denoted by τ.

An alternative to Spearman's correlation is **Kendall's tau** (τ). Field (2009) recommends that Kendall's tau is used when you have small samples and large numbers of tied ranks (i.e. lots of scores that are the same), and some authors recommend the general use of Kendall's tau over Spearman's correlation (see Howell, 2007). Nevertheless, Spearman's correlation is still more frequently used than Kendall's when a non-parametric correlation technique is needed.

Spearman's correlation and Kendall's tau in SPSS

 Details of SPSS procedures for non-parametric correlations can be found on the website that accompanies this book. The SPSS output for Spearman's correlation and Kendall's tau is similar

Table 19.4 SPSS output displaying Pearson's correlation (a) and Kendall's tau (b)

Correlations

			Number of countries visited	Geography test score
Kendall's tau_b	Number of countries visited	Correlation Coefficient	1.000	.310
		Sig. (2-tailed)	.	.232
		N	10	10
	Geography test score	Correlation Coefficient	.310	1.000
		Sig. (2-tailed)	.232	.
		N	10	10
Spearman's rho	Number of countries visited	Correlation Coefficient	1.000	.390
		Sig. (2-tailed)	.	.265
		N	10	10
	Geography test score	Correlation Coefficient	.390	1.000
		Sig. (2-tailed)	.265	.
		N	10	10

to that for Pearson's correlation. Table 19.4 shows the results for Spearman's correlation and Kendall's tau (if you requested both of these correlations at the same time, you will have a larger table which combines both of these tables). As you can see, the correlation coefficients are much lower and the *p* values higher than for the Pearson's correlation. This partly reflects the loss of detail that results from ranking data when calculating these correlations.

Spearman's correlation by hand

It is easy to calculate Spearman's correlation by hand if you know how to calculate Pearson's correlation – they use the same formula. The only difference is that Spearman's uses the ranks rather than the actual scores (these can be distinguished from actual scores through the use of a subscript r (i.e. $_r$), to indicate that they are ranks rather than scores). So, for our example data, the values we need for our calculation are as shown in Table 19.5.

We can now put these values into the equation:

$$r_s = \frac{\sum X_r Y_r - \dfrac{\sum X_r \sum Y_r}{N}}{\sqrt{\left(\sum X_r^2 - \dfrac{(\sum X_r)^2}{N}\right)\left(\sum Y_r^2 - \dfrac{(\sum Y_r)^2}{N}\right)}} = \frac{334 - \dfrac{(55 \times 55)}{10}}{\sqrt{\left(384 - \dfrac{55^2}{10}\right)\left(382.5 - \dfrac{55^2}{10}\right)}}$$

$$= \frac{334 - 3025/10}{\sqrt{\left(384 - \dfrac{3025}{10}\right)\left(382.5 - \dfrac{3025}{10}\right)}} = \frac{334 - 302.5}{\sqrt{(384 - 302.5)(382.5 - 302.5)}}$$

$$= \frac{31.5}{\sqrt{(81.5 \times 80)}} = \frac{31.5}{\sqrt{6520}} = \frac{31.5}{80.76} = 0.390$$

Table 19.5 Conducting a Spearman's rho correlation

| | Original scores | | Ranks | | | | |
Participant	Number of countries visited (X)	Geography test score (Y)	X_r	Y_r	X_r^2	Y_r^2	$X_r Y_r$
1	1	10	1	4.5	1	20.25	4.5
2	3	15	2	9	4	81	18
3	4	8	3	2	9	4	6
4	5	9	4.5	3	20.25	9	13.5
5	5	7	4.5	1	20.25	1	4.5
6	9	10	6	4.5	36	20.25	27
7	11	15	7	9	49	81	63
8	12	13	8.5	6	72.25	36	51
9	12	15	8.5	9	72.25	81	76.5
10	14	14	10	7	100	49	70
Total			$\sum X_r = 55$	$\sum Y_r = 55$	$\sum X_r^2 = 384$	$\sum Y_r^2 = 382.5$	$\sum X_r Y_r = 334$

Once you have calculated your value of r_s, check it against the tables of critical values for your number of cases and chosen level of significance. For our example, the critical value of r_s with a .05 significance level is 0.648; our calculated value is less than this and is therefore not significant.

Reporting results of non-parametric correlation

When reporting the result of a non-parametric correlation, you should report the correlation coefficient (r_s or τ), the number of cases (n) and the p value. For example:

Spearman's correlation revealed no significant correlation between number of countries visited and geography test scores, $r_s = .390$, $n = 10$, $p = .265$.

Point-biserial correlation

Point-biserial correlation Correlation technique used to test for relationship between a truly dichotomous variable and a continuous variable.

Although we have said that correlation is suitable for continuous variables, there are types of correlation that can be used when one of the variables is dichotomous (i.e. consists of two categories). One of these correlations is called the **point-biserial correlation**. So, if you want to look at the correlation between a dichotomous variable (e.g. gender, yes/no responses) and a continuous variable, you could use this test (you just run the Pearson correlation, but with the dichotomous variable coded as 0s and 1s to represent the two groups). You may have realized that you could run an independent-samples *t*-test on the same data, and you would be correct. The crucial difference is the focus of the test – the point-biserial correlation looks at the relationship between the variables, whereas the *t*-test looks at the differences between the groups. The point-biserial correlation would also allow for easy calculation of an effect size (r^2). However, people usually prefer using the *t*-test rather than the point-biserial correlation, and you are probably best advised to stick with the *t*-test as well.

You should be aware of a couple of things about the point-biserial correlation. First, its magnitude depends partly on the proportion of participants falling into each of the dichotomous categories. If the number of participants in each category is equal, then the maximum value the point-biserial can attain is 1.0 (just as with the Pearson *r*). However, if the number of participants in each category is *not* equal, then the maximum attainable value for the point-biserial correlation is less than 1.0. Consequently, the degree of relationship between the two variables may be underestimated. You should examine the proportion of participants using each category of the dichotomous variable and, if the proportions differ greatly, temper your conclusions accordingly.

There is another type of correlation that involves dichotomous variables – the **biserial correlation**. We are telling you about it as you may come across this in the literature, but it is actually unlikely that you will use it yourself. What makes this correlation different from the point-biserial correlation relates to the nature of the dichotomous variable involved. In the point-biserial correlation, the variable represents a true dichotomy (e.g. male/female) in which the categories are truly discrete and distinct from one another. In the biserial correlation, the dichotomy is more arbitrary. For example, consider the pass/fail dichotomy: although people either pass or fail, they can do so at different levels, with some people only just failing or passing, others failing spectacularly or passing with flying colours. In other words there is an underlying continuum and the two categories, pass and fail, are not truly discrete. The biserial correlation is used when it is assumed that the dichotomous variable is continuous in nature, and as a result, a different formula is used. If you used the point-biserial correlation with a continuous variable, the true strength of the relationship will tend to be underestimated.

> **Biserial correlation**
> Correlation technique used to test for relationship between an artificially dichotomous variable and a continuous variable.

Partial correlation

We have seen that interpreting correlations can be difficult due to the "third variable" where an uncontrolled variable may be responsible for the relationship between the two variables of interest. A technique called **partial correlation** provides us with a way of statistically controlling third variables. A partial correlation is a correlation between the two variables of interest, but with the influence of the third variable removed from, or "partialled out" of, the original correlation. This gives us an idea of what the correlation between the primary variables would be if the third variable were held constant.

> **Partial correlation**
> Correlation technique which tests for the relationship between two variables, while removing the influence of another.

Imagine you were interested in the relationship between age and performance on a reasoning test and found a significant correlation of $r = -.471$. However, one factor which could account for this relationship is years of education – older adults tend to have fewer years of education than younger adults and so may be less familiar with a reasoning test.

By partialling out years of education, you can get an indication of the relationship between age and reasoning if everybody had the same number of years of education.

SPSS

It's quite straightforward to run a partial correlation in SPSS (details are on our website). The output table (Table 19.6) consists of two parts: one section with the zero-order correlations (i.e. the original correlations, without any partialling out), and one with the partial correlations. If we look at the zero-order correlations below, we can see that there are significant correlations between age and reasoning ($r = -.471, p = .018$), age and years of education ($r = -.465, p = .019$), and reasoning and years of education ($r = .406, p = .044$). It therefore looks likely that years of education may play a role in explaining the age–reasoning relationship. To determine this, look at the partial correlations in the lower part of Table 19.6. You can see that once years of education has been controlled for, there is no longer a significant relationship between age and reasoning ($r = -.348, p = .095$).

As you can imagine, partial correlation can be a very useful technique. However, it still does not answer the question of causality, and you still need to identify a potential third variable and measure it before you can partial it out.

Regression

Linear regression
Statistical technique used to make predictions about scores on one variable based on scores on other variable(s).

Knowing that there is a correlation between two variables can help us to make predictions. For example, if we know that there is a consistent negative linear relationship between examination anxiety and examination performance, and we know someone's examination anxiety score, we can make a fairly good prediction of what their exam mark will be.

Linear regression is a technique that helps us to make predictions about scores on one variable based on knowledge of the values of others. For example, we might want to predict scores on a measure of suggestibility based on "units of alcohol drunk".

Table 19.6 SPSS output for partial correlation

Correlations

Control Variables			Participant age	Reasoning score	Years of education
-none-[a]	Participant age	Correlation	1.000	-.471	-.465
		Significance (2-tailed)	.	.018	.019
		df	0	23	23
	Reasoning score	Correlation	-.471	1.000	.406
		Significance (2-tailed)	.018	.	.044
		df	23	0	23
	Years of education	Correlation	-.465	.406	1.000
		Significance (2-tailed)	.019	.044	.
		df	23	23	0
Years of education	Participant age	Correlation	1.000	-.348	
		Significance (2-tailed)	.	.095	
		df	0	22	
	Reasoning score	Correlation	-.348	1.000	
		Significance (2-tailed)	.095	.	
		df	22	0	

a. Cells contain zero-order (Pearson) correlations.

In its simplest form, regression works out the best-fitting line for the data on a scatterplot and uses this as the basis for prediction. Consider a simple data set with two variables, *X* and *Y*. The data are presented in Table 19.7 and in scatterplots in Figure 19.8.

So, if we knew that someone had scored 5 on *X*, what would their score on *Y* be? We find where our *X* value meets the best-fitting line and use the corresponding *Y* value of that point as

Table 19.7 Data for linear regression

X	7	3	2	10	8	7	9	6	3	1
Y	8	4	4	9	9	7	8	8	4	6

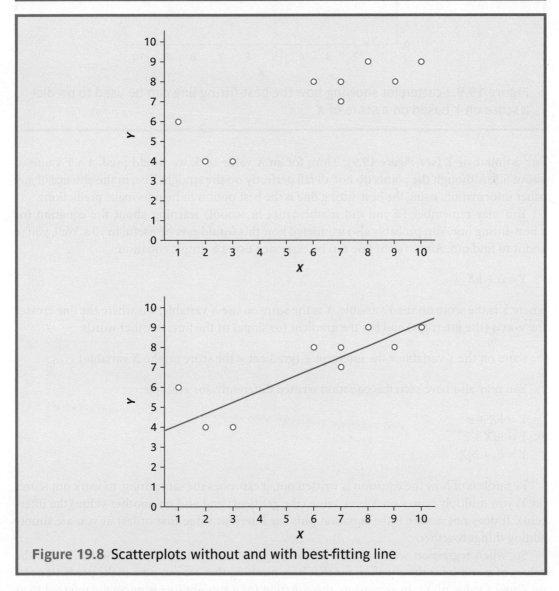

Figure 19.8 Scatterplots without and with best-fitting line

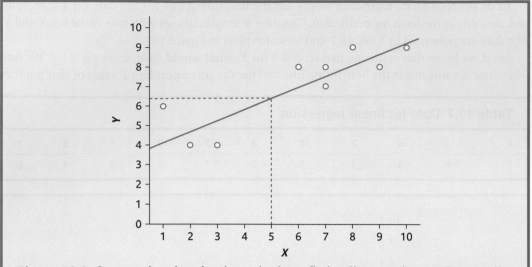

Figure 19.9 Scatterplot showing how the best-fitting line can be used to predict a score on *Y* based on a score of *X*

our estimate of *Y* (see Figure 19.9). Thus, for an *X* value of 5, we would predict a *Y* value of about 6.3. Although the points do not all fall perfectly on the straight line, in the absence of any other information, using the best-fitting line is the best option to help us make predictions.

You may remember (if you did mathematics in school) learning about the equation for a best-fitting line. You probably also wondered how this would ever be useful to you. Well, you're about to find out. Any straight line can be expressed using a simple equation:

$Y = a + bX$

where *Y* is the score on the *Y* variable, *X* is the score on the *X* variable, *a* is where the line crosses the y-axis (the intercept) and *b* is the gradient (or slope) of the line. In other words:

score on the *Y* variable = the intercept + (gradient × the score on the *X* variable)

You may also have seen this equation written differently, for example:

$Y = bX + a$
$Y = mX + c$
$Y = b_0 + b_1 X$

Regardless of how the equation is written out, it expresses the same thing: to work out scores on *Y*, you multiply scores on *X* by a value (the gradient) and add on another value (the intercept). It does not matter if the equation puts the intercept value first or last as you are simply adding things together.

So, when regression works out the best-fitting line for a set of data, it also works out the values of *a* and *b* for the equation for that line, meaning that we can now make predictions (if we know a value of *X*). In regression, the equation for a straight line is normally referred to as a regression equation, and the X variable is sometimes called the predictor variable and the Y variable, the criterion variable.

Testing hypotheses with linear regression

We can test hypotheses by determining the significance of a regression equation. In linear regression involving two variables, the null hypothesis is that the equation does not explain a significant amount of the variability in Y scores. In other words, there is no relationship between the two variables and the values in the regression equation are merely a result of error or chance (Gravetter & Wallnau, 2007).

Analysis of regression is similar to ANOVA in that it calculates an F-value. This value is a ratio of the degree of variability in y scores that can be accounted for by the regression equation and the degree of variability that would be expected by chance alone. If the regression equation accounts for a relatively high proportion of the variability, then the F-value will be higher and therefore more significant.

Example of simple linear regression

To illustrate linear regression with two variables, we can consider an example looking at the relationship between lecture attendance and exam performance for a specific module. Table 19.8 is a table of data for 15 students.

Table 19.8 Data for examination mark and lecture attendance study		
Student	Number of lectures attended	Examination mark (%)
1	10	72
2	12	52
3	12	64
4	11	54
5	8	38
6	5	66
7	8	62
8	9	58
9	10	57
10	2	35
11	4	46
12	6	51
13	12	80
14	11	62
15	5	57

Simple linear regression in SPSS

Figure 19.10 is a scatterplot for our example data; as you can see, there appears to be a general positive relationship.

If you follow the SPSS procedure for linear regression, you will be greeted by a number of tables (Tables 19.9 – a–g). The Descriptive statistics and Correlations tables (Tables 19.9 – a and b)

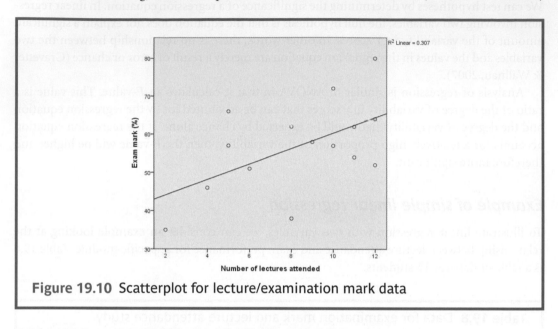

Figure 19.10 Scatterplot for lecture/examination mark data

Tables 19.9a and b SPSS output for linear regression

Descriptive Statistics

	Mean	Std. Deviation	N
Exam mark (%)	56.93	11.865	15
Number of lectures attended	8.33	3.244	15

Correlations

		Exam mark (%)	Number of lectures attended
Pearson Correlation	Exam mark (%)	1.000	.554
	Number of lectures attended	.554	1.000
Sig. (1-tailed)	Exam mark (%)	.	.016
	Number of lectures attended	.016	.
N	Exam mark (%)	15	15
	Number of lectures attended	15	15

Table 19.9c SPSS output for linear regression showing independent variables entered

Variables Entered/Removed[b]

Model	Variables Entered	Variables Removed	Method
1	Number of lectures attended[a]	.	Enter

a. All requested variables entered.

b. Dependent Variable: Exam mark (%)

Table 19.9d SPSS output for regression showing model summary

Model Summary[b]

Model	R	R Square	Adjusted R Square	Std. Error of the Estimate
1	.554[a]	.307	.253	10.254

a. Predictors: (Constant), Number of lectures attended

b. Dependent Variable: Exam mark (%)

Table 19.9e SPSS output for regression showing significance of regression equation

ANOVA[b]

Model		Sum of Squares	df	Mean Square	F	Sig.
1	Regression	604.091	1	604.091	5.745	.032[a]
	Residual	1366.842	13	105.142		
	Total	1970.933	14			

a. Predictors: (Constant), Number of lectures attended

b. Dependent Variable: Exam mark (%)

are self-explanatory, but note that the Correlations table is laid out differently to what you are used to. As you can see, there is a significant correlation between examination marks and lecture attendance ($r = .554$, $p = .016$).

The next tables give you the results of the regression analysis. The Variables entered/removed table (Table 19.9 – c) just confirms what your dependent and independent variables are – check that this is correct.

The Model summary table (Table 19.9 – d) is important as this is where you obtain R (the correlation coefficient) and R^2. These are exactly the same as the r and r^2 that saw when we discussed correlation, the only difference being that we use the upper case R and R^2, which indicate that we're referring to regression rather than correlation here. It also provides Adjusted R Square which is thought to be a better measure. Thus, 25.3 per cent (.253) of the variance in examination marks can be explained by looking at lecture attendance.

The ANOVA table tells us if the regression equation is a significantly better predictor of scores than if we just used the mean. In our example (Table 19.9 – e), $F = 5.745$ and is significant ($p = .032$).

Table 19.9f SPSS output for regression: coefficients table

Coefficients[a]

Model		Unstandardized Coefficients		Standardized Coefficients	t	Sig.
		B	Std. Error	Beta		
1	(Constant)	40.059	7.521		5.326	.000
	Number of lectures attended	2.025	.845	.554	2.397	.032

a. Dependent Variable: Exam mark (%)

Table 19.9g SPSS output for regression: residuals table

Residuals Statistics[a]

	Minimum	Maximum	Mean	Std. Deviation	N
Predicted Value	44.11	64.36	56.93	6.569	15
Residual	-18.258	15.816	.000	9.881	15
Std. Predicted Value	-1.952	1.130	.000	1.000	15
Std. Residual	-1.781	1.542	.000	.964	15

a. Dependent Variable: Exam mark (%)

The Coefficients table (Table 19.9 – f) is where you find the values for the regression equation – look under Unstandardized coefficients column B. The value in the (Constant) row is the intercept or a in the equation; the other value is the gradient, or what we multiply the independent variable by. Thus, the regression equation would be:

> **Residual**
> The difference between an actual score and the score that would be predicted based on the regression equation.

$$Y = a + bX$$
$$\text{Examination mark} = 40.059 + (2.025 \times \text{Number of lectures attended})$$

Using this equation you could then predict someone's examination mark based on the number of lectures they had attended.

The Residual statistics table (Table 19.9 – g) gives you details on the residuals. A **residual** is the difference between an actual score and a predicted score, so in this case the residuals represent the differences between *Y* scores in our actual data set (i.e. the data that we have collected from our sample) and the values of *Y* that would be predicted using the regression equation (i.e. predicted values that do not actually exist). These values are then standardized into **z-scores**. Small residuals mean that the predicted values are close to the actual values, and the regression equation is a good predictor.

> **Homoscedasticity**
> An assumption of regression and multivariate statistics; occurs when scores on one variable have same degree of variation across the full range of scores on another variable (e.g. in regression, residuals would have a similar degree of variation across the full range of predictor variable scores).

ch. 15
pp.322 –

The rest of the output consists of graphs to help you determine if some assumptions have been met. One of these assumptions is that the relationship between the variables in the regression analysis should be linear. The second assumption is something called **homoscedasticity**, which means that the residuals should have the same degree of variation across the full range of scores on the predictor variable.

If, for example, the regression equation was accurate at predicting low *y*-values but not higher *y*-values, then you would see small residuals for low predicted values, but higher residuals as predicted values increase. In other words, the assumption of homoscedasticity has been violated. This pattern of unequal variances in the residuals across the range of predicted values is called **heteroscedasticity**.

A relatively normal distribution curve in the histogram (Figure 19.11 – a) in your output indicates homoscedasticity and that you have a range of residuals, with

Heteroscedasticity
Occurs when degree of variation in scores in one variable is not the same across the full range of scores of another variable (e.g. in regression, degree of variation in residuals would increase or decrease consistently across the full range of predictor variable scores).

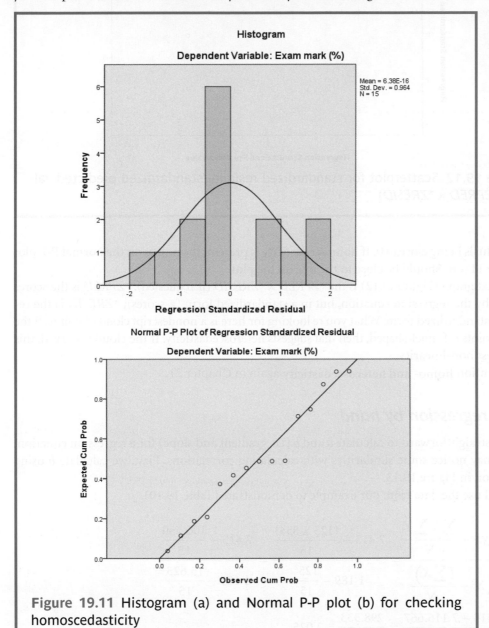

Figure 19.11 Histogram (a) and Normal P-P plot (b) for checking homoscedasticity

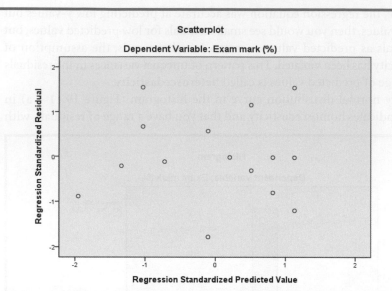

Figure 19.12 Scatterplot for standardized residual/standardized values (*ZPRED* × *ZRESID*)

most residuals being close to 0. If homoscedasticity is present, the points on the normal P-P plot (Figure 19.11 – b) should be close to the line on the plot.

The next graph (Figure 19.12) is the *ZPRED* × *ZRESID* (if requested). *ZPRED* is the scores predicted by the regression equation, but in a standardized form (z-scores); *ZRESID* is the residuals in standardized form. What you're looking for here is a nondescript cloud of points. If the cloud of points is funnel-shaped, then that suggests heteroscedasticity. If the cloud is curved, this may suggest non-linearity.

We mention **homo- and heteroscedasticity** again in Chapter 21.

ch. 21
pp.527–528

Simple regression by hand

It is quite straightforward to calculate a and b (i.e. gradient and slope) for a regression equation, and you may notice some similarities with calculating correlations. First, we calculate b using the equation in Figure 19.13.

We will use the data from our example to demonstrate (Table 19.10).

$$b = \frac{\sum XY - \dfrac{\sum X \sum Y}{N}}{\sum X^2 - \dfrac{\left(\sum X\right)^2}{N}} = \frac{7\ 415 - \dfrac{(125 \times 854)}{15}}{1\ 189 - \dfrac{125^2}{15}} = \frac{7\ 415 - \dfrac{106\ 750}{15}}{1\ 189 - \dfrac{15\ 625}{15}}$$

$$= \frac{7\ 415 - 7\ 116.667}{1\ 189 - 1\ 041.667} = \frac{298.333}{147.333} = 2.025$$

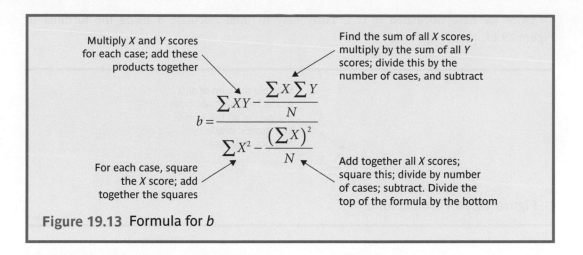

Figure 19.13 Formula for *b*

Table 19.10 Data for lectures/examination mark study for regression calculation

Participant	Number of lectures attended (X)	Examination mark (%) (Y)	X²	Y²	XY
1	10	72	100	5184	720
2	12	52	144	2704	624
3	12	64	144	4096	768
4	11	54	121	2916	594
5	8	38	64	1444	304
6	5	66	25	4356	330
7	8	62	64	3844	496
8	9	58	81	3364	522
9	10	57	100	3249	570
10	2	35	4	1225	70
11	4	46	16	2116	184
12	6	51	36	2601	306
13	12	80	144	6400	960
14	11	62	121	3844	682
15	5	57	25	3249	285
	$\sum X = 125$	$\sum Y = 854$	$\sum X^2 = 1189$	$\sum Y^2 = 50\,592$	$\sum XY = 7\,415$

Once we have calculated b, it is fairly easy to then calculate a using the formula in Figure 19.14.

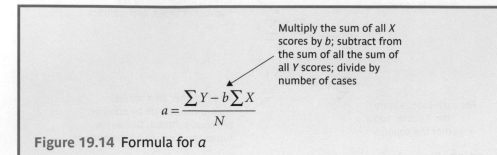

Multiply the sum of all X scores by b; subtract from the sum of all the sum of all Y scores; divide by number of cases

$$a = \frac{\sum Y - b\sum X}{N}$$

Figure 19.14 Formula for a

So, for our example data, this would be:

$$a = \frac{\sum Y - b\sum X}{N} = \frac{854 - (2.025 \times 125)}{15} = \frac{854 - 253.125}{15} = \frac{600.875}{15} = 40.058$$

(This value is slightly less than that in the SPSS output as a result of rounding down/up to three decimal places.)

Multiple regression

Multiple regression
Statistical technique used to predict scores on a criterion variable based on scores on several predictor variables.

In the last section, we discussed simple bivariate (two-variable) linear regression in which we use one variable to help us to predict scores on another. However, it is more common in research to look at how several variables can help us to predict scores on an outcome variable using a technique called **multiple regression**. Using several variables at once may help improve overall prediction and can also tell us about the relative contribution of each variable to the prediction. To account for the extra variables, the regression equation produced by multiple regression is an extended version of the equation we introduced in the previous section:

Bivariate linear regression:　$Y = a + bX$
Multiple regression:　　　　$Y = a + b_1X_1 + b_2X_2 + b_3X_3 + \cdots$

Remember that Y is the criterion score, or the score that is being predicted, X is a score on a predictor variable, a is a constant, and b is a coefficient (or regression weight). You will notice that the multiple regression equation has several predictor variables, each indicated by an X with a subscript number (i.e. X_1 = first predictor, X_2 = second predictor, and so on), and each with its own coefficient (i.e. b_1 = coefficient for X_1, b_2 = coefficient for X_2, and so on). Thus, if we know an individual's scores on all predictor variables, we can predict their score on the Y variable.

Once we have predicted scores, we can obtain the correlation between these and the actual scores. This correlation is called the **multiple correlation coefficient** (**multiple R**) as it is based on a regression equation with multiple predictors rather than just one. As with R, the larger the value of multiple R, the higher the correlation between predicted and actual scores, and the more accurately the regression equation is predicting scores. Therefore, a multiple R of 1 indicates that the multiple regression equation has predicted the scores perfectly. We can also square multiple R to give us multiple R^2, a measure of the amount of variance being explained by the regression equation. However, because of sampling error, **R-square** tends to overestimate the variance accounted for, especially with small samples (Tabachnick & Fidell, 2001). **Adjusted R-square** compensates for this overestimation. You should use the adjusted R-square as a measure of variance accounted for rather than the unadjusted R-square.

Multiple regression therefore is the process by which we determine the values of the a and b coefficients, and test how well the resulting regression equation can predict scores on the Y variable. Multiple regression uses detailed information about the correlations between the variables to identify the unique contribution made by each one. Previously, we have mentioned partial correlation where we can separate out the contributions of individual variables. Multiple regression does something similar and gives us coefficients which indicate the independent contribution of each variable.

Methods of multiple regression

Some people get carried away when they first hear about multiple regression, and think that they can include hundreds of variables and see what happens. This is not a sensible approach – there should always be some logic behind the variables that you use in a multiple regression. For example, you may be testing a specific theory or there is another conceptual reason for including a variable. Ultimately, the aim of multiple regression is to find the simplest regression equation to predict scores accurately.

As well as deciding which predictor variables to include in the regression, researchers also have to decide on the type of multiple regression. There are several types of multiple regression analysis, including simple (or simultaneous), hierarchical and stepwise analyses. The main difference between these types is how the predictor variables are entered into the regression equation, and this may affect the final result.

In **simple (simultaneous) regression** analysis, all variables are entered simultaneously, regardless of whether they are actually good predictors or not. Each predictor variable is assessed as if it had been entered after each of the other predictors had been entered. In contrast, the other methods of analysis go through various stages before arriving at a final solution.

In **hierarchical regression**, the researcher specifies the order in which the variables are entered into the regression equation. This is commonly used if you have a well-developed theory or model suggesting a certain causal order. For example, you could enter known predictors into the regression model and then add in new predictors in the next stage of analysis to see if they make a significant contribution.

Multiple correlation coefficient
The correlation between actual scores and scores predicted using multiple regression equation.

R-square
The square of the multiple R in a multiple regression analysis. Provides a measure of the amount of variability in the dependent measure accounted for by the best linear combination of predictor variables.

Adjusted R-square
Measure of amount of variance in criterion variable predicted by multiple regression equation.

Simple (simultaneous) regression
Multiple regression method in which all variables are entered into the equation in one step.

Hierarchical regression
Multiple regression method in which the order in which variables are entered into the equation is determined by the researcher, usually based on theory or previous research.

Stepwise regression
Set of multiple regression methods in which the order in which variables are entered into the equation is determined by statistical criteria.

In **stepwise regression**, the order in which variables are entered is based on a mathematical decision, not on a theory. In the forward method of stepwise regression, predictor variables are entered one at a time, starting with the variable calculated as accounting for the most variance in the criterion variable. If including this predictor means that the regression equation is significantly better at predicting scores than if you were just using the constant (a), the variable is kept in. The next variable that predicts the highest proportion of the remaining variance is then entered, and then the next best predictor, and so on until adding further variables does not significantly improve how good the regression equation is at predicting scores. The backward method is the opposite of the forward method: it starts with all variables being entered into the regression equation and then goes through stages removing the worst predictor variables. SPSS has another method called stepwise, which adds the best predictor variables one at a time (like the forward method), but also allows for the worst predictors to be removed at each stage (like the backward method). As variables are entered into the equation, it may be the case that other predictors become redundant and unnecessary. These stepwise methods mean that the final regression equation may include any number of possible predictor variables.

Your choice of regression strategies should be based on your research questions or underlying theory. If you have a theoretical model suggesting a particular order of entry, use hierarchical regression. In the absence of any well-specified theory, you should usually choose simultaneous regression. Stepwise regression is used infrequently because it tends to capitalize on chance. Sampling and measurement error tend to make unstable correlations among variables in stepwise regression. Thus, the statistical decisions used to determine order of entry may vary considerably from sample to sample. The resulting regression equation may be unique to a particular sample.

Example of multiple regression

Following on from our earlier example of predicting examination marks based on number of lectures attended, we can extend it to include some additional variables. Perhaps the number of hours spent revising the day before the examination could have some influence on the examination mark. Or what about the perceived amount of effort put in during the entire module? Table 19.11 contains a set of data for a module with 30 students, with their examination marks, number of lectures attended, number of hours spent revising the day before the examination, and each student's rating of the effort they had put into the module (1 = low effort, 10 = high effort).

 ## Multiple regression in SPSS

Before you proceed with any multiple regression, it is helpful to explore the data and look at the correlations between the variables.

First, check the correlations between your predictor variables and criterion variable. For our example (Table 19.12), we can see that both number of lectures attended and perceived effort are positively related to examination marks, but hours spent revising shows no significant relationship with examination marks, suggesting that hours spent revising is unlikely to be a good predictor.

Table 19.11 Data for multiple regression

Student	Examination mark	No. of lectures attended	No. of hours spent revising day before examination	Perceived effort during module
1	70	9	12	7
2	56	12	9	8
3	62	8	7	9
4	50	11	1	4
5	38	8	5	6
6	58	5	6	5
7	66	10	2	5
8	52	8	8	5
9	57	11	9	6
10	34	2	3	2
11	46	4	8	3
12	53	7	7	4
13	81	12	6	8
14	62	9	6	7
15	55	5	8	10
16	25	2	2	1
17	41	9	9	8
18	61	10	5	6
19	48	7	7	2
20	55	8	8	7
21	57	12	3	3
22	64	8	6	7
23	32	4	6	5
24	47	11	10	10
25	59	9	6	3
26	60	7	11	5
27	67	12	7	7
28	69	11	4	8
29	53	9	10	5
30	35	8	8	6

Table 19.12 SPSS correlation output for multiple regression data

Correlations

		Exam mark (%)	Number of lectures attended	Number of hours spent revising on day before exam	Perceived effort
Exam mark (%)	Pearson Correlation	1	.631**	.154	.435*
	Sig. (2-tailed)		.000	.416	.016
	N	30	30	30	30
Number of lectures attended	Pearson Correlation	.631**	1	.102	.457*
	Sig. (2-tailed)	.000		.591	.011
	N	30	30	30	30
Number of hours spent revising on day before exam	Pearson Correlation	.154	.102	1	.442*
	Sig. (2-tailed)	.416	.591		.014
	N	30	30	30	30
Perceived effort	Pearson Correlation	.435*	.457*	.442*	1
	Sig. (2-tailed)	.016	.011	.014	
	N	30	30	30	30

**. Correlation is significant at the 0.01 level (2-tailed).

*. Correlation is significant at the 0.05 level (2-tailed).

> **Multicollinearity**
> Occurs when variables are highly correlated with each other.

You should also check the correlations between the predictor variables. **Multicollinearity** occurs when predictor variables are highly correlated *with each other* and this is undesirable for multiple regression. If two predictor variables are very closely correlated, then once one predictor has been entered into the regression equation, adding the second will not improve the prediction and the value of R will not increase by much. Multicollinearity also means that the results of multiple regression can be difficult to interpret (which of the variables is the most important?) and that you can be less certain that your regression coefficients represent the population (Field, 2009). The presence of very high correlations between predictor variables ($r = .80$ or higher) is indicative of multicollinearity; in our example, there are some significant correlations between predictor variables, but the coefficients are no higher than .50.

Simultaneous multiple regression in SPSS

Please follow the instructions on the website for this text to guide you through running simultaneous multiple regression (and the other forms of multiple regression) in SPSS. The first table in your output will be some descriptive statistics (if requested). Next, you have a table of correlations (Table 19.13 – a). Note that it is laid out differently to a usual correlation table.

The next table summarizes the variables that have been entered into the regression equation (Table 19.13 – b) – it is always worth checking this to see if you have done this the right way.

The Model summary table (Table 19.13 – c) gives us R and adjusted R square, which tells us that 35.9 per cent of the variance in the criterion variable can be explained by the predictor variables.

The ANOVA table (Table 19.13 – d) confirms that the regression model significantly fits the data.

Table 19.13a SPSS output for multiple regression displaying correlations

Correlations

		Exam mark (%)	Number of lectures attended	Number of hours spent revising on day before exam	Perceived effort
Pearson Correlation	Exam mark (%)	1.000	.631	.154	.435
	Number of lectures attended	.631	1.000	.102	.457
	Number of hours spent revising on day before exam	.154	.102	1.000	.442
	Perceived effort	.435	.457	.442	1.000
Sig. (1-tailed)	Exam mark (%)	.	.000	.208	.008
	Number of lectures attended	.000	.	.295	.006
	Number of hours spent revising on day before exam	.208	.295	.	.007
	Perceived effort	.008	.006	.007	.
N	Exam mark (%)	30	30	30	30
	Number of lectures attended	30	30	30	30
	Number of hours spent revising on day before exam	30	30	30	30
	Perceived effort	30	30	30	30

Table 19.13b SPSS output for multiple regression showing variables entered

Variables Entered/Removed[b]

Model	Variables Entered	Variables Removed	Method
1	Perceived effort, Number of hours spent revising on day before exam, Number of lectures attended[a]	.	Enter

a. All requested variables entered.

b. Dependent Variable: Exam mark (%)

The Coefficients table (Table 19.13 – e) provides the values for the regression equation. Note that each of the predictor variables has its own coefficient. The equation would therefore be:

$$Y = a + b_1X_1 + b_2X_2 + b_3X_3$$

Table 19.13c SPSS output for multiple regression showing model summary

Model Summary[b]

Model	R	R Square	Adjusted R Square	Std. Error of the Estimate
1	.652[a]	.426	.359	10.059

a. Predictors: (Constant), Perceived effort, Number of hours spent revising on day before exam, Number of lectures attended

b. Dependent Variable: Exam mark (%)

Table 19.13d SPSS output for multiple regression showing significance of the model

ANOVA[b]

Model		Sum of Squares	df	Mean Square	F	Sig.
1	Regression	1950.475	3	650.158	6.425	.002[a]
	Residual	2630.892	26	101.188		
	Total	4581.367	29			

a. Predictors: (Constant), Perceived effort, Number of hours spent revising on day before exam, Number of lectures attended

b. Dependent Variable: Exam mark (%)

Table 19.13e SPSS output for multiple regression showing coefficients

Coefficients[a]

Model		Unstandardized Coefficients		Standardized Coefficients	t	Sig.
		B	Std. Error	Beta		
1	(Constant)	27.723	7.030		3.944	.001
	Number of lectures attended	2.418	.742	.549	3.258	.003
	Number of hours spent revising on day before exam	.095	.775	.021	.123	.903
	Perceived effort	.946	1.006	.176	.940	.356

a. Dependent Variable: Exam mark (%)

$$\text{Examination mark} = \text{Constant} + (b_1 \times \text{Number of lectures}) + (b_2 \times \text{Hours revising})$$
$$+ (b_3 \times \text{Perceived effort})$$
$$= 27.723 + (2.418 \times \text{Number of lectures}) + (.095 \times \text{Hours revising})$$
$$+ (.946 \times \text{Perceived effort})$$

Another thing to note from the Coefficients table is the Standardized coefficients column in which the coefficients have been converted into a standard format, thus allowing for direct comparisons. We can see from this that hours spent revising has much less of an influence than the other variables. The results of the *t*-tests also confirm this.

You should check the Residuals statistics (Table 19.13 – f) for anything unusual.

Table 19.13f SPSS output for multiple regression showing residual statistics

Residuals Statistics[a]

	Minimum	Maximum	Mean	Std. Deviation	N
Predicted Value	33.70	65.16	53.77	8.201	30
Residual	-18.504	16.123	.000	9.525	30
Std. Predicted Value	-2.447	1.390	.000	1.000	30
Std. Residual	-1.840	1.603	.000	.947	30

a. Dependent Variable: Exam mark (%)

Then we have graphs (Figure 19.15) which we should use to check for homoscedasticity, which seems to be evident.

Stepwise multiple regression in SPSS

The output for stepwise multiple regression will look very similar to that for simultaneous multiple regression, but may include several models[5] rather than just one, to show you the process that the regression has gone through to arrive at the best model. If you are presented with several models in your output, select the last one.

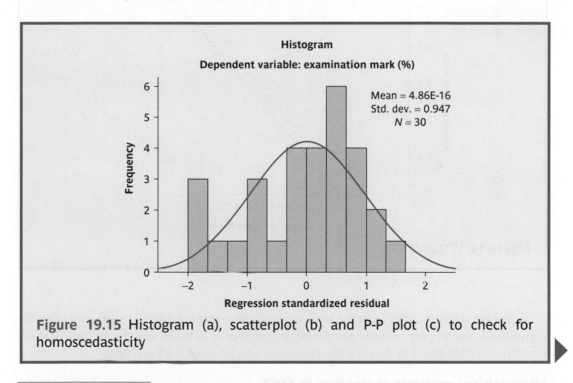

Figure 19.15 Histogram (a), scatterplot (b) and P-P plot (c) to check for homoscedasticity

5   When we talk about a "model" we are referring to the way in which our analysis is explaining the data. A simple regression gives you one "model" – i.e. it explains the data in one way. A stepwise multiple regression gives you many models, because you will get a different explanation each time you add in a new variable to consider. Each new variable will mean that the explanation (model) has to take this into account. Roughly speaking, the best model is the one that explains the data most efficiently.

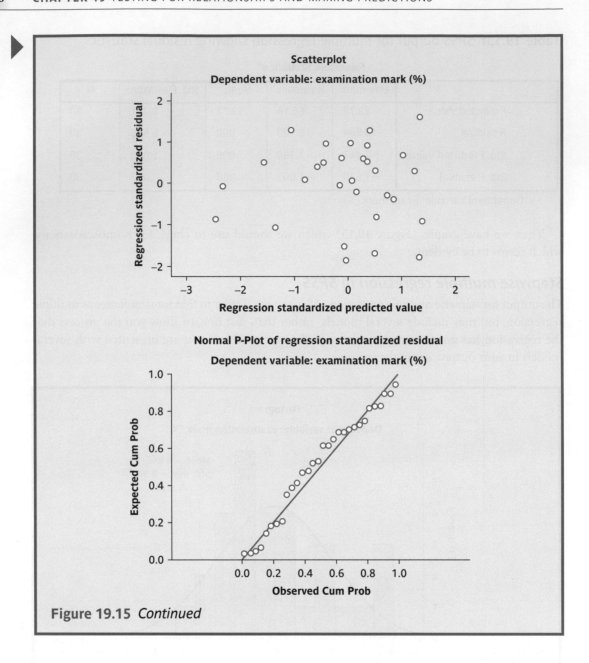

Scatterplot

Dependent variable: examination mark (%)

Normal P-Plot of regression standardized residual

Dependent variable: examination mark (%)

Figure 19.15 *Continued*

Below are selected tables from the stepwise multiple regression (Table 19.14). Note that the regression equation only includes one predictor (number of lectures) and the multiple *R* is still very close to what it was in the previous regression which included all variables.

Hierarchical multiple regression in SPSS

Hierarchical multiple regression involves the researcher selecting the order in which variables enter the regression equation – please see our website for guidance on how to do this in SPSS.

Table 19.14 SPSS output for multiple regression

Variables Entered/Removed[a]

Model	Variables Entered	Variables Removed	Method
1	Number of lectures attended	.	Stepwise (Criteria: Probability-of-F-to-enter <= .050, Probability-of-F-to-remove >= .100).

a. Dependent Variable: Exam mark (%)

Model Summary[b]

Model	R	R Square	Adjusted R Square	Std. Error of the Estimate
1	.631[a]	.398	.377	9.924

a. Predictors: (Constant), Number of lectures attended

b. Dependent Variable: Exam mark (%)

Coefficients[a]

Model		Unstandardized Coefficients		Standardized Coefficients	t	Sig.
		B	Std. Error	Beta		
1	(Constant)	30.780	5.641		5.457	.000
	Number of lectures attended	2.781	.646	.631	4.303	.000

a. Dependent Variable: Exam mark (%)

Excluded Variables[b]

Model		Beta In	t	Sig.	Partial Correlation	Collinearity Statistics Tolerance
1	Number of hours spent revising on day before exam	.091[a]	.608	.548	.116	.990
	Perceived effort	.186[a]	1.133	.267	.213	.791

a. Predictors in the Model: (Constant), Number of lectures attended

b. Dependent Variable: Exam mark (%)

Table 19.15 comprises some selected tables from the hierarchical regression output in SPSS. The variables were entered in two steps, so the results include two models to reflect this. The Model summary table shows just how much additional variance can be explained by the addition of the other variables in the second model.

Table 19.15 SPSS output for hierarchical multiple regression

Variables Entered/Removed[b]

Model	Variables Entered	Variables Removed	Method
1	Number of lectures attended	.	Stepwise (Criteria: Probability-of-F-to-enter <= .050, Probability-of-F-to-remove >= .100).
2	Number of hours spent revising on day before exam, Perceived effort[a]	.	Enter

a. All requested variables entered.

b. Dependent Variable: Exam mark (%)

Model Summary[c]

Model	R	R Square	Adjusted R Square	Std. Error of the Estimate
1	.631[a]	.398	.377	9.924
2	.652[b]	.426	.359	10.059

a. Predictors: (Constant), Number of lectures attended

b. Predictors: (Constant), Number of lectures attended, Number of hours spent revising on day before exam, Perceived effort

c. Dependent Variable: Exam mark (%)

ANOVA[c]

Model		Sum of Squares	df	Mean Square	F	Sig.
1	Regression	1823.747	1	1823.747	18.518	.000[a]
	Residual	2757.620	28	98.486		
	Total	4581.367	29			
2	Regression	1950.475	3	650.158	6.425	.002[b]
	Residual	2630.892	26	101.188		
	Total	4581.367	29			

a. Predictors: (Constant), Number of lectures attended

b. Predictors: (Constant), Number of lectures attended, Number of hours spent revising on day before exam, Perceived effort

c. Dependent Variable: Exam mark (%)

Table 19.15 *Continued*

Coefficients[a]

Model		Unstandardized Coefficients		Standardized Coefficients		
		B	Std. Error	Beta	t	Sig.
1	(Constant)	30.780	5.641		5.457	.000
	Number of lectures attended	2.781	.646	.631	4.303	.000
2	(Constant)	27.723	7.030		3.944	.001
	Number of lectures attended	2.418	.742	.549	3.258	.003
	Number of hours spent revising on day before exam	.095	.775	.021	.123	.903
	Perceived effort	.946	1.006	.176	.940	.356

a. Dependent Variable: Exam mark (%)

Excluded Variables[b]

Model		Beta In	t	Sig.	Partial Correlation	Collinearity Statistics Tolerance
1	Number of hours spent revising on day before exam	.091[a]	.608	.548	.116	.990
	Perceived effort	.186[a]	1.133	.267	.213	.791

a. Predictors in the Model: (Constant), Number of lectures attended

b. Dependent Variable: Exam mark (%)

Reporting results of regression analysis

Regression is used in lots of different ways and there are lots of different statistics to report, so it is unsurprising that there is no one specified format for reporting the results of regression analyses. However, it is common to report some or all of: R; R^2; adjusted R^2; the ANOVA results (F, df, p); the unstandardized b coefficients and intercept a; the standardized beta coefficients and their associated p-values; plus correlations and semi-partial correlations between variables. You rarely see the actual regression equation written out in full.

It is often helpful to present your regression results in a table, particularly if you have a number of predictor variables or have run a number of different regression analyses. Have a look at examples in relevant studies in journals to get an idea of how to summarize all of the necessary information. Also, do not forget to tell the reader what method of regression you used.

Summary

In this chapter we discussed the statistical methods used to analyse relationships and to make predictions. A correlation coefficient can tell us about the direction and magnitude of a relationship and varies between −1.00 and +1.00; squaring the correlation coefficient will give an indication of the amount of variance being explained. Pearson's correlation is the most commonly used correlation technique and is suitable for linear relationships. If data are ordinal or the relationship is non-linear but monotonic, Spearman's correlation or Kendall's tau are suitable alternatives. The point-biserial correlation and biserial correlation can be used if one of the variables is dichotomous. Partial correlation enables researchers to examine the relationship between two variables while simultaneously controlling for the influence of a third.

Regression is the name given to techniques which are used to help predict scores on one variable based on scores on another or several other variables. Simple linear regression is used with two variables – one predictor and one criterion variable; multiple regression uses several predictor variables, but still only one criterion variable. The outcome of regression is the regression equation, which expresses the best model for predicting scores on the criterion variable based on the predictor variable(s). Using ANOVA, we can test the significance of this equation to determine if it predicts scores significantly better than if we just used the mean. As well as calculating the coefficients (b) and constant for the regression equation (a), we can also calculate R (the correlation between actual criterion scores and predicted scores), multiple R (the multiple correlation between actual and predicted scores) and R^2, which expresses the proportion of variability in criterion scores that can be accounted for by the regression equation. There are a number of different multiple regression methods, which specify the order in which variables are entered into or removed from the regression equation. These methods include simple (simultaneous), hierarchical and stepwise (forward, backward).

Questions

1 What affects the magnitude and direction of a correlation coefficient?

2 What can you say about a relationship with a significant correlation coefficient of −.20?

3 For a correlation of .60, what amount of variance has been explained?

4 Under what circumstances would you use Kendall's tau?

5 What is the main difference between the point-biserial correlation and the biserial correlation?

6 Why is it helpful to use partial correlation?

7 In multiple regression, what part of the SPSS output should you consult to determine the relative contribution of each predictor variable?

8 What are the different methods of multiple regression and how do they differ?

9 What is heteroscedasticity and how can we check for it?

10 What is multicollinearity and why is it a problem for multiple regression?

Activities

1   A researcher observed schoolchildren during their break-time for a month, recording for each child the number of aggressive acts. He also had access to each family's report of the average number of hours of television the child watched each week. The correlation coefficient was .40 and was significant. How could you interpret this result?

2   A social psychologist seeks to determine the relationship between a paper-and-pencil measure of prejudice and people's attitudes towards racial profiling as a crime deterrent. At the beginning of the semester students in a psychology class are asked to complete six different questionnaires. Among the questionnaires is a measure of prejudice. Later in the semester students are invited to take part in an experiment examining attitudes about criminal behaviour and law enforcement tactics. As part of the experiment students complete a questionnaire asking about attitudes towards racial profiling as a crime deterrent. The researcher wishes to find out if scores on the prejudice measure obtained earlier will predict people's attitudes about racial profiling. Higher scores on the prejudice measure indicate greater prejudice and higher scores on the profiling scale indicate greater support for racial profiling. Scores on both measures are obtained for 22 students, as shown in Table 19.16.

Table 19.16 Score obtained for 22 students																						
Student	1	2	3	4	5	6	7	8	9	10	11	12	13	14	15	16	17	18	19	20	21	22
Prejudice	19	15	22	12	9	19	16	21	24	13	10	12	17	23	19	23	18	11	10	19	24	22
Profiling	7	6	9	6	4	7	8	9	5	5	7	4	8	9	10	10	5	6	4	8	8	7

(a)   Draw a scatterplot showing the relationship between these two measures.

(b)   Inspect the scatterplot and comment on the presence or absence of a linear trend in the data.

(c)   Calculate a correlation coefficient for these data and comment on the direction and strength of the relationship.

(d)   On the basis of the correlational analysis the researcher concludes that prejudicial thinking causes people to support racial profiling by law enforcement agencies. Comment on this conclusion based on what you know about the nature of correlational evidence.

(e)   Using the same data, construct a regression equation which can be used to predict racial profiling scores based on prejudice scores.

20

Analysing Nominal Data

OVERVIEW

Up until now, we have considered statistical tests that are used when the dependent (or outcome) variable is measured on an interval/ratio or ordinal scale. However, sometimes we can have a nominal outcome, which would be unsuitable for the tests we have looked at so far. However, there is a set of tests that you can use based on a statistic called chi-square, and these will be the focus of this chapter. You will be introduced to the chi-square test of goodness-of-fit, used to compare differences in proportions in a nominal variable, and the chi-square test of association, used to test for associations between two nominal variables. We will also discuss the binomial test, which is used to compare proportions in dichotomous variables.

OBJECTIVES

After studying this chapter and working through the exercises, you should be able to:

- State the null hypothesis for a chi-square test and calculate expected frequencies appropriate to that null hypothesis

- Distinguish between the chi-square test of goodness-of-fit, the chi-square test of association and the binomial test

- Identify assumptions of the chi-square tests

- Distinguish between two measures of strength of association between two nominal variables: the phi coefficient and Cramér's V

- Conduct analysis, interpret output and write up results for the chi-square test of goodness-of-fit, chi-square test of association and the binomial test

Nominal data: a reminder

In **Chapter 4** we discussed the differences between interval/ratio, ordinal and nominal data. (If you still are not clear on the distinctions between them, it is probably a good idea to go back over it before reading this chapter.) What you should notice is that nominal data are quite different to interval/ratio and ordinal data. Nominal data represent named discrete categories, so rather than achieving a certain score on a variable as you would do with interval/ratio or ordinal scales, people belong to a group (e.g. male/female) or achieve a certain outcome (e.g. pass/fail). All you can do with this type of data is count it – there is no real measurement of it and so you cannot calculate means or standard deviations, and so are restricted in your choice of statistical test.

 ch. 4
pp.62–68

We have already looked at nominal variables in **previous chapters**, for example, when comparing groups using an independent-samples *t*-test or between-subjects ANOVA. In those cases, the nominal variable was the *independent* variable or the variable which told us about different groups; the *dependent* variable was interval/ratio (for *t*-tests and ANOVA) or ordinal (for non-parametric equivalents). So what we were basically doing was splitting people up on the basis of what category they were in, and then seeing if there was a difference on some measured (dependent) variable between the categories. However, when the *dependent* variable is also nominal (e.g. yes/no/do not know, pass/fail, option a/b/c/d), you cannot calculate means or rankings, and so cannot run *t*-tests, ANOVAs or their non-parametric equivalents. Instead, you can use chi-square tests (chi is pronounced with a hard k and rhymes with "eye" – "ki"). There are two main chi-square tests that you will come across:

 chs 16, 17

1 The *chi-square test of goodness-of-fit* is used when you want to examine *differences* between categories within *one* nominal variable.

2 The *chi-square test of association* (sometimes also called the test of independence) is used when you want to examine the *relationship* between *two* nominal variables.

Chi-square test of goodness-of-fit

Imagine you had designed a questionnaire for students which included a question about the main method of transport usually used to travel to university. Participants had to select one of five options: (1) car, (2) bus, (3) train, (4) bicycle, (5) on foot. A summary of the frequency of responses is shown in Table 20.1.

What can you say about the proportion of cases who have selected the different types of transport? Does it look as though one (or more) of the options is more popular than others?

Table 20.1 Frequencies for main method of transport used to get to university

Mode of transport	Car	Bus	Train	Bicycle	On foot
Frequency	14	18	3	5	10

Chi-square test of goodness-of-fit
Non-parametric statistical test used to compare proportions of cases in categories of a single nominal variable with proportions expected under null hypothesis.

Expected frequencies
Frequencies expected if the null hypothesis were true; may reflect no preference or no difference from a comparison population.

Observed frequencies
Frequencies that have been actually obtained in a sample.

The **chi-square test of goodness-of-fit** can help you to answer these questions. This test is used when you are examining one nominal variable and you want to compare the proportion of cases that fall into each category.

The chi-square test of goodness-of-fit works by calculating the proportions you would expect if the null hypothesis was true and then comparing these **expected frequencies** with the actual **observed frequencies**. The expected frequencies therefore depend on what your null hypothesis is and, with this type of chi-square test, there are two possible options. The first is the one that you will probably use the most – it states that there is no preference. In other words, the population is evenly distributed across the categories. Therefore, in our example, our null hypothesis would state that participants show no preference for type of transport and we would expect the same proportion[1] of participants to select each of the five types of transport. With 50 participants in total, we would expect 10 participants (one-fifth of the sample) to select each type of transport if the null hypothesis was true (see Table 20.2).

The other type of null hypothesis that you can use with this type of chi-square test states that the proportions do not differ from a comparison population. For example, you may want to compare your sample proportions with a set of national statistics or proportions obtained in previous research. In this instance, your expected frequencies would depend on the proportions in the comparison population. In our example, we could compare our sample proportions with proportions from a national survey of students. Therefore, if the national survey found that 24 per cent of respondents used a car as their main mode of transport to get to university, this would mean that we would expect 24 per cent of our sample of 50 to also select car, giving us an expected frequency of 12 ($50 \times .24 = 12$). This and the other expected frequencies are shown in Table 20.3. Do not worry that some of the expected frequencies are not whole numbers – expected frequencies are hypothetical values and just represent what you would find if the data fitted the null hypothesis perfectly.

As you can see, the expected frequencies differ depending on which null hypothesis you are using, so it is really important that you are clear which null hypothesis is appropriate for a given study. In most cases though, you will use the "no preference" hypothesis and will expect equal proportions.

Table 20.2 Observed and expected frequencies for main method of transport used to get to university, with "no preference" null hypothesis

Mode of transport	Car	Bus	Train	Bicycle	On foot
Observed frequency	14	18	3	5	10
Proportion based on null hypothesis	1/5	1/5	1/5	1/5	1/5
Expected frequency	10	10	10	10	10

---

1   A common mistake that students often make is to confuse "proportion" with "number". The null hypothesis for a chi-square does not say that the same number of people will prefer each mode of transport, but that there will be an equal proportion.

Table 20.3 Observed and expected frequencies for main method of transport used to get to university, with "no difference from comparison population" null hypothesis

Mode of transport	Car	Bus	Train	Bicycle	On foot
Observed frequency	14	18	3	5	10
Proportion based on null hypothesis	24%	30%	10%	11%	25%
Expected frequency	12	15	5	5.5	12.5

Once you have identified the appropriate null hypothesis, the chi-square test of goodness-of-fit compares the expected frequencies with the observed frequencies to produce a statistic called chi-square (χ^2; we will cover how this is calculated later – it is very straightforward). If the value of chi-square is sufficiently large, it will produce a significant result and we can conclude that the expected frequencies are significantly different from the observed frequencies. If the value of chi-square is low, the result will not be significant and so we would conclude that the expected and observed frequencies do not differ. Essentially, what we are doing with this test is testing whether our data fit the expected pattern of results, hence the name: goodness-of-fit. A significant chi-square indicates a poor fit; a non-significant chi-square indicates a good fit.

In order to determine what represents high and low chi-square values, we need to consult a chi-square distribution. It's different to the **_t_-value frequency distribution** we saw in Chapter 16 in that the chi-square distribution is positively skewed rather than symmetrical, meaning that low chi-square values are more likely and high chi-square values less likely. If a chi-square statistic has a probability of less than 5 per cent (i.e. .05), it is significant. Another thing to bear in mind is that the shape of the chi-square distribution changes depending on the degrees of freedom, which, for chi-square, is equal to the number of categories – 1. Thus, the chi-square values in the extreme 5 per cent of the distribution will depend on the degrees of freedom. Figure 20.1 shows how the critical values and shape of the chi-square distribution change for 1 and 10 degrees of freedom.

ch. 16
pp.345 – 346

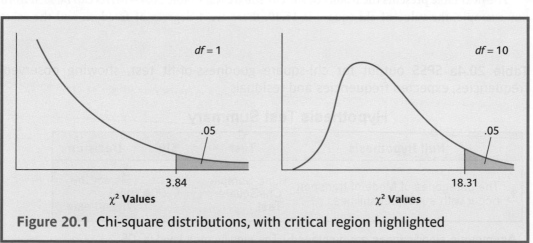

Figure 20.1 Chi-square distributions, with critical region highlighted

So, the chi-square test of goodness-of-fit compares proportions that we would expect under the null hypothesis with the proportions that have actually been obtained. If the resulting chi-square statistic is large enough, we have a significant result and can conclude that our observed frequencies do not fit the expected pattern.

Assumptions of chi-square

Before moving any further, you should be aware of two important assumptions of chi-square tests:

1 *Independent observations*: each participant should contribute to only one category. The total frequency in a chi-square test should be the same as the number of participants. If the transport survey, for example, had asked participants to tick *all* modes of transport that they use rather than just the main mode of transport, the resulting data would not be suitable for a chi-square test as participants would have contributed to more than one category. You should think about this when designing a study if you plan on using chi-square.

2 *Expected frequencies*: chi-square tests assume that expected counts will be greater than 5. The reason for this is that the value of chi-square can become distorted with small expected frequencies. To get round this problem, try to use large samples when collecting data suitable for chi-square analysis.

Chi-square test of goodness-of-fit in SPSS

Details of how to run the chi-square test of goodness-of-fit in SPSS, for both the "no preference" and "comparison" population proportions null hypotheses, can be found on our website. We will go through the output separately for the tests with different null hypotheses, beginning with the null hypothesis of no preference (assumes equal proportions). The first table in the output is the table of expected and observed frequencies (Table 20.4 – a), which includes the residuals (or differences between the two frequencies). Large residuals would suggest that your data do not fit the expected pattern.

The next table presents the results of the chi-square test (Table 20.4 – b). As can be seen from our example, the value of chi-square is 15.40, there are 4 degrees of freedom and the exact

Table 20.4a SPSS output for chi-square goodness-of-fit test, showing observed frequencies, expected frequencies and residuals

Hypothesis Test Summary

	Null Hypothesis	Test	Sig.	Decision
1	The categories of Mode of transport occur with equal probabilities.	One-Sample Chi-Square Test	.004	Reject the null hypothesis.

Asymptotic significances are displayed. The significance level is .05.

Table 20.4b SPSS output for chi-square goodness-of-fit test displaying test statistics

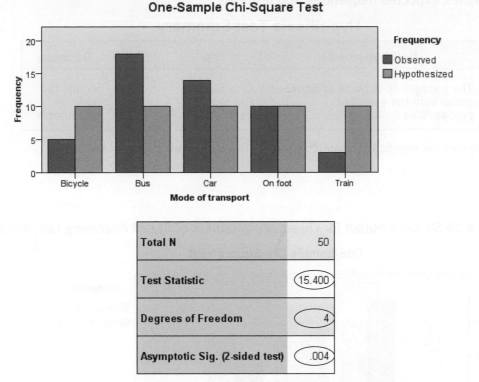

One-Sample Chi-Square Test

Total N	50
Test Statistic	15.400
Degrees of Freedom	4
Asymptotic Sig. (2-sided test)	.004

1. There are 0 cells (0%) with expected values less than 5. The minimum expected value is 10.

significance is .004, thus indicating that the observed frequencies differ significantly from the expected frequencies. In other words, there were significant preferences among the categories. Note the message underneath the table – if you have some cells with expected frequencies less than 5, you have violated one of the assumptions of chi-square.

The output for the chi-square test of goodness-of-fit when the null hypothesis states no difference from a comparison population is in the same format as before. However, this time we can see that the residuals are smaller and there is no significant result, indicating that our sample proportions fit the expected proportions – there were no preferences among the categories (Tables 20.5 – a and b).

Chi-square test of goodness-of-fit by hand

To run the chi-square test of goodness-of-fit by hand, the first thing you do is calculate the expected frequencies based on your null hypothesis. As discussed earlier, if your null hypothesis is no preference, your expected frequencies are simply the total number of cases divided by the number of conditions; if your null hypothesis is based on population proportions, you apply those proportions to the total number of cases.

Table 20.5a SPSS output for chi-square goodness-of-fit test, showing observed frequencies, expected frequencies and residuals

Hypothesis Test Summary

	Null Hypothesis	Test	Sig.	Decision
1	The categories of Mode of transport occur with the specified probabilities.	One-Sample Chi-Square Test	.685	Retain the null hypothesis.

Asymptotic significances are displayed. The significance level is .05.

Table 20.5b SPSS output for chi-square goodness-of-fit test displaying test statistics

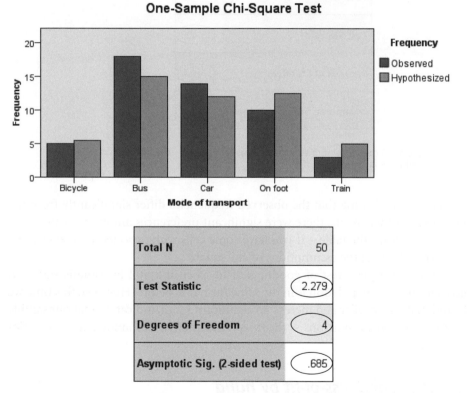

One-Sample Chi-Square Test

Total N	50
Test Statistic	2.279
Degrees of Freedom	4
Asymptotic Sig. (2-sided test)	.685

1. There are 0 cells (0%) with expected values less than 5. The minimum expected value is 5.

You then use the observed frequencies and expected frequencies to calculate χ^2 (Figure 20.2).

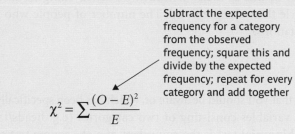

Subtract the expected frequency for a category from the observed frequency; square this and divide by the expected frequency; repeat for every category and add together

$$\chi^2 = \sum \frac{(O - E)^2}{E}$$

Figure 20.2 Formula for chi-square

So, for the equal proportions example, the calculation would be:

$$\chi^2 = \sum \frac{(O - E)^2}{E} = \frac{(14 - 10)^2}{10} + \frac{(18 - 10)^2}{10} + \frac{(3 - 10)^2}{10} + \frac{(5 - 10)^2}{10} + \frac{(10 - 10)^2}{10}$$

$$= \frac{4^2}{10} + \frac{8^2}{10} + \frac{(-7)^2}{10} + \frac{(-5)^2}{10} + \frac{0^2}{10} = \frac{16}{10} + \frac{64}{10} + \frac{49}{10} + \frac{25}{10} + \frac{0}{10}$$

$$= 1.6 + 6.4 + 4.9 + 2.5 + 0 = 15.4$$

And for the comparison population proportions example:

$$\chi^2 = \sum \frac{(O - E)^2}{E} = \frac{(14 - 12)^2}{12} + \frac{(18 - 15)^2}{15} + \frac{(3 - 5)^2}{5} + \frac{(5 - 5.5)^2}{5.5} + \frac{(10 - 12.5)^2}{12.5}$$

$$= \frac{2^2}{12} + \frac{3^2}{15} + \frac{(-2)^2}{5} + \frac{(-0.5)^2}{5.5} + \frac{(-2.5)^2}{12.5} = \frac{4}{12} + \frac{9}{15} + \frac{4}{5} + \frac{0.25}{5.5} + \frac{6.25}{12.5}$$

$$= 0.333 + 0.600 + 0.800 + 0.045 + 0.5 = 2.278$$

(This value is very slightly different to that calculated using SPSS as we rounded up/down to three decimal places.)

Once you have the value of χ^2, you should inspect the table of critical χ^2 values (see Appendix B). Find your chosen significance level and your degrees of freedom (i.e. number of categories minus 1). For a significance level of .05 and 4 degrees of freedom, the critical value is 9.49 – the χ^2 for the no preference null hypothesis is more extreme than this and is therefore significant, but the χ^2 for the comparison population proportions null hypothesis is less than the critical value and so is not significant.

Reporting the result of a chi-square test of goodness-of-fit

When reporting the results of a chi-square test of goodness-of-fit, you should report the chi-square value, *df*, sample size (*n*) and *p*-value. The results for the transport study (null hypothesis = no preference) could be written up like this:

There was a significant preference for certain modes of transport, χ^2 (4, $n = 50$) = 15.40, $p = .004$. Compared to the frequencies expected under the null hypothesis, more participants reported taking the car or bus as their main method of travelling to university and fewer took the train or bicycle than was predicted. The number of people who travelled on foot was in line with expectations.

Binomial test

Binomial test
Non-parametric statistical test used to compare proportions in a dichotomous (two-category) variable.

There is a test that you should be aware of, which has been specifically designed to deal with nominal variables consisting of two categories (e.g. heads/tails, male/female, yes/no). The **binomial test** is the equivalent of a chi-square test of goodness-of-fit for dichotomous (two-category) variables and will give you the same statistical outcome as the chi-square. Having a dichotomous variable, however, does not necessarily mean that there are only two possible outcomes, only that the outcomes can be classified into two categories. For example, in our transport example, we may ask the question of whether people used public transport (i.e. bus and train) or not. Although there are five possible outcomes, we are condensing them down to two (used public transport, did not use public transport), to give us a dichotomous variable.

As with the chi-square test of goodness-of-fit, you need to be clear on the null hypothesis being used with the binomial test. The null hypothesis could be that there is no preference or that there is no difference from a comparison population. In most cases, the "no preference" null hypothesis would result in a probability of 1/2 for each of the two categories (i.e. participants have a 50–50 chance of belonging to each category). But in cases where there are more than two outcomes, the probabilities may be different. In our transport example, the probability of selecting public transport is 2/5 and not 1/2, and the probability of walking to university is 1/5. If the null hypothesis instead states that there is no difference from a comparison population, the probabilities will come from the existing data.

Example of binomial test

In a university psychology class, there were 55 females and 22 males. If we wanted to determine if there were statistically more females than males in the class than would be expected by chance, we can use the binomial test.

The SPSS output consists of just one table. Check that the values in N, Observed prop. (observed proportion; i.e. what proportion exists in your data) and Test prop. (the proportion you're testing against; in this case .50 because you would expect a 50–50 split between males and females in the class) look correct. Then check the Exact Sig. value. As you can see, in our example (Table 20.6) we have significantly more females in the class than we would expect by chance.

To write up the result, you need only to report the p-value, but it is also useful to report the observed proportions or frequencies:

The class consisted of 71% females and 29% males. A binomial test revealed that this was a statistically significant difference, $p < .001$.

Table 20.6 SPSS output for binomial test

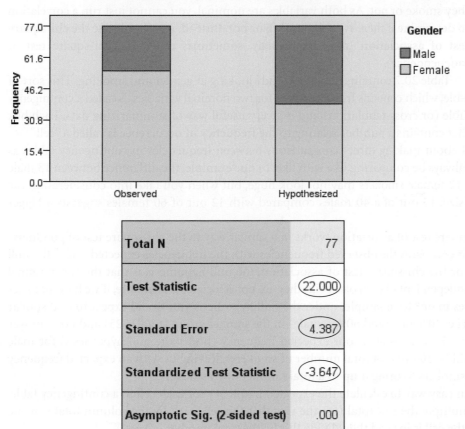

Hypothesis Test Summary

	Null Hypothesis	Test	Sig.	Decision
1	The categories defined by Gender = Male and Female occur with probabilities 0.5 and 0.5.	One-Sample Binomial Test	.000	Reject the null hypothesis.

Asymptotic significances are displayed. The significance level is .05.

One-Sample Binomial Test

Total N	77
Test Statistic	22.000
Standard Error	4.387
Standardized Test Statistic	-3.647
Asymptotic Sig. (2-sided test)	.000

Chi-square test of association

Whereas the chi-square test of goodness-of-fit is used to look at differences between categories in one nominal variable, we are more often interested in determining whether two nominal variables are associated. Suppose you want to know whether there is a relationship between gender and smoking. To do this, you sample 100 adults (44 males and 56 females) and ask whether

Table 20.7 Contingency table for gender and smoking status study

Gender	Smoking status		Total
	Smoker	Non-smoker	
Male	13	27	40
Female	12	48	60
Total	25	75	100

Chi-square test of association
Non-parametric statistical test used to analyse associations between two nominal variables.

they smoke or not. As both variables are nominal, you cannot just run a correlation to determine if there is a relationship or not. Instead, you should use the **chi-square test of association** (also, confusingly, sometimes called the chi-square test of independence).

Table 20.7 contains data for a study looking at gender and smoking. This sort of table, which contains frequency data for two nominal variables, is called a contingency table (or cross-tabulation) and is a very useful way of summarizing data. Each box that contains a number relating to the frequency of occurrence is called a "cell".

Be careful about making direct comparisons between frequencies in contingency tables as you may not always be comparing like with like. In our example, the difference between 13 male smokers and 12 female smokers may not look huge, but when you take into consideration the total sample size, 13 out of a 40 males compared with 12 out of 60 females suggests a bigger difference.

The chi-square test of association works in a similar way to the chi-square test of goodness-of-fit in that it compares the observed frequencies with the frequencies expected under the null hypothesis. For the chi-square test of association, the null hypothesis is that the two nominal variables are independent of each other (i.e. they are not associated). Therefore, if we have 40 males and 60 females in our total sample, under the null hypothesis you would expect to find similar proportions (i.e. 40% male and 60% female) in the smoker group (total = 25) and non-smoker group (total = 75). For instance, our expected frequency (under the null hypothesis) for male smokers would be 10 (40% of total number of smokers), leaving us with an expected frequency of 15 female smokers to bring it up to a total number of 25 smokers.

There is an easy way to calculate the expected frequency for each cell in a contingency table. You simply multiply the row total (for the row that the cell is in) by the column total (for the column that the cell is in) and then divide this by the total number of cases:

$$E = \frac{row\ total \times column\ total}{N}$$

For example, for the first cell (male smokers) we can work out the expected frequency by taking the total of the row that the cell belongs to (40), multiplying by the total of the column that the cell belongs to (25) and then dividing by the total number of cases (100). This would give us our expected frequency of 10.

Table 20.8 Contingency table for gender and smoking status study, with observed and expected frequencies

Gender		Smoking status Smoker	Smoking status Non-smoker	Total
Male	Observed frequency	13	27	40
	Expected frequency	10	30	
Female	Observed frequency	12	48	60
	Expected frequency	15	45	
Total		25	75	100

Although SPSS (or other statistical programs) can work out expected frequencies for you, it is a good idea to have a go yourself to get an understanding of where these expected frequencies come from.

Test yourself

Before moving on, work out the rest of the expected frequencies for male and female non-smokers in our smoking example (answers are in Table 20.4).

Table 20.8 is the contingency table for gender and smoking status with observed and expected frequencies. The presence of any large differences between observed and expected frequencies suggests that there may be a significant chi-square statistic. If chi-square is significant, we can conclude that the two nominal variables are associated; if it is not significant, we can conclude that the variables are independent.

Measures of strength of association

As with other statistical tests, looking at the *p*-value for the chi-square test of association tells us only about the probability of obtaining a given statistic – it does not tell us anything about the strength of the association. For this reason, you are recommended to report an effect size. The two most commonly used measures of strength of association are the **phi coefficient** and **Cramér's V**. These effect size measures can range between 0 and 1, much like a correlation coefficient: the closer the value is to 1, the stronger the association; the closer the value is to 0, the weaker the association. The phi coefficient is suitable only for 2 × 2 contingency tables (i.e. two nominal variables each with two categories), whereas Cramér's V can be used for larger contingency tables, with more categories. For 2 × 2 tables, the phi coefficient and Cramér's V are the same.

Phi coefficient
Measure of strength of association between two nominal variables; suitable for 2 × 2 contingency tables.

Cramér's V
Measure of strength of association between two nominal variables; suitable for any size of contingency table.

Chi-square test of association in SPSS

The first main table of the SPSS output is the cross-tabulation (or contingency table). If you selected only Observed and Expected counts (see our website for details on the SPSS procedure), your table will look something like Table 20.9 – a.

If you selected Percentages and Residuals, the table will look like Table 20.9 – b.

As you can see, there does not appear to be much difference between the observed and expected counts. Make sure that you check the table carefully to see that you have the correct observed counts.

Table 20.9 – c is the chi-square tests table, where you should note the value of Pearson chi-square, the number of degrees of freedom (*df*) and the Exact Sig. (2-tailed). In this example, we have a non-significant result ($p = .238$), and so cannot reject the null hypothesis and conclude that the two variables, gender and smoking behaviour, are not associated.

You will also notice the notes at the bottom Table 20.9 – c. One to pay close attention to is note a, which tells you about the number of expected counts that are less than 5. If you have expected counts less than 5, this can cause problems for chi-square and you are recommended to consult the result for Fisher's exact test instead.

Next we have the table with measures of strength of association (Table 20.9 – d). As already discussed, the phi coefficient and Cramér's V can both be used with 2×2 contingency tables such as that in our example. As would be expected with a non-significant result, the value of the effect size measures is low.

Finally, we have a bar chart (Figure 20.3), if requested earlier. It makes the overall pattern very clear – more non-smokers than smokers in both males and females, and therefore no association.

Chi-square test of association by hand

The procedure for calculating the chi-square test of association by hand is exactly the same as for the chi-square test of goodness-of-fit; the only difference is in the way that you calculate the expected frequencies:

$$E = \frac{row\ total \times column\ total}{N}$$

Once you have calculated your expected frequencies, you use the same formula as before to calculate χ^2 (Figure 20.4).

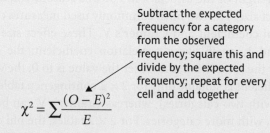

Subtract the expected frequency for a category from the observed frequency; square this and divide by the expected frequency; repeat for every cell and add together

$$\chi^2 = \sum \frac{(O - E)^2}{E}$$

Figure 20.4 Formula for chi-square

Table 20.9a SPSS output showing contingency table (cross-tabulation)

Gender * Smoker Crosstabulation

			Smoker		
			Smoker	Non-smoker	Total
Gender	Male	Count	13	27	40
		Expected Count	10.0	30.0	40.0
	Female	Count	12	48	60
		Expected Count	15.0	45.0	60.0
Total		Count	25	75	100
		Expected Count	25.0	75.0	100.0

Table 20.9b SPSS output showing contingency table (cross-tabulation), with percentages and residuals

Gender * Smoker Crosstabulation

			Smoker		
			Smoker	Non-smoker	Total
Gender	Male	Count	13	27	40
		Expected Count	10.0	30.0	40.0
		% within Gender	32.5%	67.5%	100.0%
		% within Smoker	52.0%	36.0%	40.0%
		% of Total	13.0%	27.0%	40.0%
	Female	Count	12	48	60
		Expected Count	15.0	45.0	60.0
		% within Gender	20.0%	80.0%	100.0%
		% within Smoker	48.0%	64.0%	60.0%
		% of Total	12.0%	48.0%	60.0%
Total		Count	25	75	100
		Expected Count	25.0	75.0	100.0
		% within Gender	25.0%	75.0%	100.0%
		% within Smoker	100.0%	100.0%	100.0%
		% of Total	25.0%	75.0%	100.0%

Table 20.9c SPSS output showing chi-square tests

Chi-Square Tests

	Value	df	Asymp. Sig. (2-sided)	Exact Sig. (2-sided)	Exact Sig. (1-sided)
Pearson Chi-Square	2.000ᵃ	1	.157		
Continuity Correctionᵇ	1.389	1	.239		
Likelihood Ratio	1.972	1	.160		
Fisher's Exact Test				.167	.120
Linear-by-Linear Association	1.980	1	.159		
N of Valid Cases	100				

a. 0 cells (.0%) have expected count less than 5. The minimum expected count is 10.00.

b. Computed only for a 2x2 table

Table 20.9d SPSS output showing contingency table (cross-tabulation), with percentages and residuals

Symmetric Measures

		Value	Approx. Sig.
Nominal by Nominal	Phi	.141	.157
	Cramer's V	.141	.157
N of Valid Cases		100	

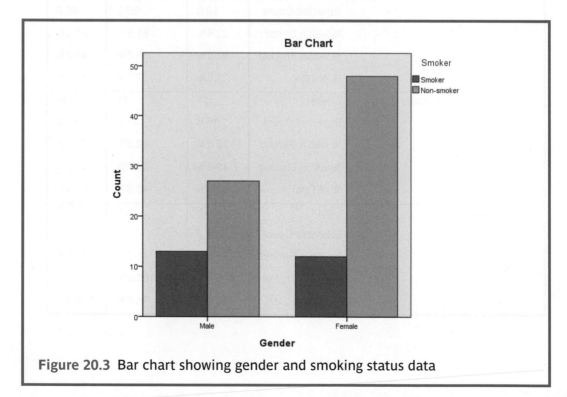

Figure 20.3 Bar chart showing gender and smoking status data

So, for our example data, the calculations would be:

$$\chi^2 = \sum \frac{(O-E)^2}{E} = \frac{(13-10)^2}{10} + \frac{(27-30)^2}{30} + \frac{(12-15)^2}{15} + \frac{(48-45)^2}{45}$$

$$= \frac{3^2}{10} + \frac{3^2}{30} + \frac{(-3)^2}{15} + \frac{3^2}{45} = \frac{9}{10} + \frac{9}{30} + \frac{9}{15} + \frac{9}{45} = 0.9 + 0.3 + 0.6 + 0.2$$

$$= 2$$

For 3 degrees of freedom and a significance level of .05, the critical value of χ^2 is 7.82; the value of χ^2 for our example data is less than this and is therefore not significant. We can conclude that there is no association between the variables.

Reporting the result of a chi-square test of association

The format of reporting this chi-square test is the same as for the chi-square test of goodness-of-fit: you should report the values of chi-square, *df*, *n* and *p*. You should also report phi or Cramér's V where appropriate. The results of the gender and smoking study could be written up as:

A chi-square test of association revealed that gender and smoking behaviour were not significantly associated, $\chi^2 (1, n = 100) = 2.00$, exact $p = .238$.

More complex designs with nominal data

If you have designed a study that collects nominal data, but is more complex than those included here (e.g. you are examining three independent variables in a three-way design), please have a look at Chapter 21, which includes details of more **advanced statistical methods**.

ch. 21
pp.533 – 534,
536 – 537

> ### Summary
>
> This chapter covered the main tests used to analyse nominal data, based on the chi-square statistic. Chi-square tests assume independent observations and expected frequencies greater than 5. The chi-square test of goodness-of-fit is used when you want to look at differences between proportions of cases in each category. It compares the observed frequencies with frequencies based on the null hypothesis, which either states no preference or no difference from a comparison population. A significant chi-square statistic indicates that the observed data do not fit the expected pattern. The binomial test was discussed as an alternative to the chi-square test of goodness-of-fit when you are dealing with a dichotomous variable.
>
> The chi-square test of association is used to test for associations between two nominal variables. Expected frequencies are calculated based on row and column totals in a contingency table. A significant chi-square statistic indicates that the variables are associated in some way; a non-significant result indicates that they are independent. To get an indication of the strength of the relationship, we can look at effect size measures such as phi and Cramér's V. For 2 × 2 contingency tables, phi is preferred; for other sizes of tables, use Cramér's V.

Questions

1 Why is it not possible to run tests such as *t*-tests, ANOVAs, correlations and their non-parametric equivalents on nominal data?

2 What are the two possible types of null hypotheses that can be used with the chi-square test of goodness-of-fit?

3 A chi-square test of goodness-of-fit has produced a significant result ($p < .05$). Do the data fit the expected pattern?

4 What are the two main assumptions of chi-square tests and how can you check for them?

5 What is the appropriate measure of strength of association for a 3×2 contingency table?

6 A chi-square test of association has produced a non-significant result ($p > .05$). Are the variables associated?

7 Under what circumstances would you use the binomial test?

 Activities

1 Draw a contingency table for the following data-set and calculate expected frequencies:

Participant	Gender	Pass or fail	Participant	Gender	Pass or fail
1	Male	Pass	11	Female	Pass
2	Female	Fail	12	Male	Fail
3	Male	Pass	13	Female	Fail
4	Female	Fail	14	Male	Pass
5	Male	Pass	15	Female	Pass
6	Male	Fail	16	Male	Fail
7	Female	Pass	17	Male	Pass
8	Male	Pass	18	Female	Fail
9	Female	Fail	19	Female	Pass
10	Female	Pass	20	Male	Fail

(a) Does it look as though the variables are associated? Why/why not?

(b) Run a chi-square test of association and, report and interpret the results.

2 A study was interested in participants' preferences for cola drinks and 80 participants were asked to blind taste four different cola drinks and select their favourite. The data are summarized in Table 20.10.

Table 20.10 Data for the study				
Cola	Cola A	Cola B	Cola C	Cola D
Observed frequency	25	10	17	28

(a) The null hypothesis states that there will be no preference. Calculate the expected frequencies. Does it look as though the data fit the expected pattern?

(b) The researchers conduct a follow-up study and want to compare the findings of the follow-up study with the original research. The data for the follow-up study are summarized in Table 20.11.

Table 20.11 Data for the further study				
Cola	Cola A	Cola B	Cola C	Cola D
Observed frequency	30	14	18	38

(c) Calculate the expected frequencies for this study (based on the original preferences). Does it look as though the data fit the expected pattern?

(d) Now run the chi-square test of goodness-of-fit for both sets of data and write up and interpret the results.

Chapter 21

Advanced Statistical Methods

OVERVIEW

You may think that we have already covered lots of different statistical methods, and you would be correct, but there are also many other, more advanced statistical techniques that can be used. These techniques are all based on multivariate designs – they all involve multiple dependent or outcome measures. Thanks to statistical computer programs, these advanced statistical methods are becoming easier to use and are used more frequently in research. Even if you will not necessarily use all of the techniques presented in this chapter, you will almost certainly come across them in research literature, so it is important that you understand what you are reading about.

Providing you with a full, in-depth discussion on these techniques is beyond the scope of one chapter. Although we are only touching the tip of the iceberg here, you will find that this chapter is different to the others in this book in terms of its complexity. There is a lot in here, so take it slowly and persist. Should you require a more detailed discussion, please consult Tabachnik and Fidell's (2007) *Using Multivariate Statistics* or another similar advanced statistics textbook. The purpose of this chapter, therefore, is to provide you with an introduction to the advanced statistical methods you are mostly likely to encounter and, hopefully, use.

OBJECTIVES

After studying this chapter and working through the exercises, you should be able to:

- Identify assumptions and requirements of multivariate statistical tests and describe how they should be dealt with before analysis
- Identify situations in which multivariate statistical analysis would be appropriate
- Describe uses of factor analysis techniques

- Interpret factor loadings
- Distinguish between logistic regression and discriminant function analysis, and explain their uses
- Discuss why MANOVA is preferable to multiple univariate ANOVAs
- Describe why ANCOVA and MANCOVA can be useful in experimental research
- Identify applications of loglinear analysis
- Explain how path analysis and structural equation modelling can be used to test causal models

Multivariate statistical analysis

In previous chapters we have considered research in which there is one independent variable and one dependent variable, or where multiple dependent variables are dealt with separately in any statistical tests. This approach is called a **univariate strategy**. Although many research questions can be addressed with a univariate strategy, others are best addressed by considering variables together in a single analysis. When you include two or more dependent measures in a single analysis, you are using a **multivariate strategy**. A **multivariate design** is a research design in which multiple dependent or multiple predictor and/or criterion variables are included.

In **Chapter 19** you were introduced unsuspectingly to multivariate design when we discussed **multiple regression**. To remind you, the goal of multiple regression is to explain the variation in one variable (the dependent or criterion variable) based on variation in a set of others (the predictor variables). Thus, multiple regression can be considered to be a multivariate statistical technique as there are several variables being measured and analysed at the same time.

Correlational multivariate techniques

A number of other multivariate techniques also adopt a correlational multivariate design and are used to evaluate relationships between variables. Such techniques include logistic regression, discriminant function analysis and factor analysis, all of which will be discussed in more detail later in this chapter. Logistic regression and discriminant function analysis are similar to multiple regression, except that the criterion variable (the variable being predicted) is categorical rather than continuous. Factor analysis is a technique used to reduce large numbers of variables into smaller groups, or factors, that consist of variables relating to one another and sharing a common underlying dimension.

Path analysis is another correlational multivariate technique that will be covered, and is useful in investigating possible causal relationships among variables. Path analysis is based on multiple regression, and begins with a theory or model about a causal chain of events involving

ch. 19
pp.490–501

Univariate strategy
Research design which involves one dependent variable.

Multivariate strategy
Research design which involves multiple dependent measures.

Multivariate design
A research design in which multiple dependent measures are analysed with a single, multivariate statistical test.

Multiple regression
Multivariate linear regression when you have a single criterion variable and multiple predictor variables.

several variables and a behaviour. Based on the results of a series of multiple regression analyses, the validity of the theory or model can be tested and you can begin to form some *tentative* conclusions about possible causal relationships among your variables. Note that the word tentative has been emphasized – you must exercise caution when interpreting causal connections from multivariate correlational data. Remember that it is very difficult to draw any conclusions about cause and effect from correlational data, but multivariate correlational techniques, at the very least, allow you to have greater confidence in possible causal connections among variables.

Indeed, this is one of the main advantages of using correlational multivariate techniques: they can help us with the "third variable" problem and can examine complex relationships between several variables rather than having to look at just two variables at a time. The other main advantage of these techniques is that they allow you to look at relationships between several variables while also controlling for Type I errors. The alternative to multivariate correlational analyses would be to run lots of correlations between all possible pairs of variables. Recall from Chapter 17, when we discussed why we use ANOVAs, that running multiple analyses on the same data increases the likelihood of obtaining **false positive results** (Type I errors). Running multiple correlations between pairs of variables therefore would increase the likelihood of finding a significant relationship that actually did not exist in the population.

ch. 17 pp.380–381

Experimental multivariate techniques

Multivariate statistical methods can also be used with experimental designs – you can manipulate one or more independent variable(s) and look for changes in the dependent variables. These dependent variables are then combined statistically (based on correlations among them) and analysed using a single statistical test, rather than using lots of separate analyses. The two most commonly used multivariate statistical methods to analyse multiple dependent variables in an experimental design are multivariate analysis of variance (MANOVA) and multivariate analysis of covariance (MANCOVA). These tests are an extension of **ANOVA** and are used to compare different groups or conditions on several dependent measures; they will be discussed in more depth later.

chs 17–18

Using a multivariate experimental strategy has several advantages over a univariate strategy. First, collecting several dependent measures and treating them as a correlated set may reveal relationships that might be missed if a traditional univariate approach were taken. Because multivariate statistical tests consider the correlations among dependent variables, they tend to be more powerful than separate univariate tests of those same dependent variables. Second, because all of your dependent variables are handled in a single analysis, complex relationships among variables can be studied with less chance of making a Type I error than when using multiple univariate tests (Bray & Maxwell, 1982).

A third advantage of the multivariate strategy applies when you have used a within-subjects (repeated measures) design. A fairly restrictive set of assumptions underlies the univariate within-subjects ANOVA which is often difficult to satisfy (e.g. homogeneity of covariance). Using MANOVA allows you to analyse your data with less concern over these restrictive assumptions.

In summary, multivariate analysis is a family of analytic techniques designed to analyse research in which multiple dependent measures are used. These analytic techniques can be used with experiments or correlational studies that have multiple dependent measures. In most cases, using a multivariate analysis is more informative than using several univariate analyses.

Assumptions and requirements of multivariate statistics

Before using multivariate statistics, you must check to see that your data meet the assumptions and requirements underlying the statistic to be used. We have already discussed some of these **assumptions** in the section on multiple regression (Chapter 19) and when we discussed parametric tests. These assumptions include linearity, normality and homoscedasticity. In addition, you must evaluate your data for the presence of outliers and measurement error, and for sufficient sample size. (Note that these assumptions do not apply to loglinear analysis as the variables there are nominal.)

ch.19
pp.486 – 488,
494

Linearity

We saw in Chapter 19 that one assumption underlying Pearson's correlation is that the relationship between the two variables is **linear**. The presence of a non-linear relationship between variables could lead to an underestimation of the degree of relationship between variables. Multivariate statistics, which are based on correlations (even MANOVA and MANCOVA), therefore also assume that the relationships between variables are linear. The easiest way to check for linearity is to inspect scatterplots of pairs of variables – if the data are linear, the cloud of points in the scatterplot should be oval-shaped; if the data are non-linear, it will be U-shaped (or an inverted U shape; Tabachnick & Fidell, 2001).

ch. 19
pp.465 – 468

Although mild deviations from linearity will not lead to a serious underestimation of a relationship with multivariate statistics, moderate to serious deviations can cause more problems. If your data are non-linear, you may be able to correct the problem by transforming the data (please see Tabachnick & Fidell, 2007, for advice on data transformation). You may have to transform both offending variables in order to restore linearity. After any transformation, you should check the scatterplots again to see if the transformation had its intended effect.

Outliers

Again, in Chapter 19 we saw the problem of **outliers** in relation to correlation. As bivariate correlation works by fitting the best-fitting straight line to the data, the presence of outliers or extreme scores can change the slope of the straight line. You therefore have to check for the presence of outliers when using multivariate statistics.

ch. 19
pp.468 – 469

Identifying outliers

There are two types of outliers that you should consider in multivariate statistics: univariate outliers and multivariate outliers. A **univariate outlier** is a deviant score on one variable from a given source, whereas a **multivariate outlier** is a deviant score on a combination of variables from a single source.

A score is considered to be a univariate outlier if it is more than 3 standard deviations above or below the mean (Tabachnick & Fidell, 2007). If this is the case, then the score can be said to be significantly different to the rest of the population of scores. You can easily identify outliers by converting raw scores to **z-scores** or by checking **boxplots**.

Univariate outlier
A deviant score on one variable.

Multivariate outlier
A deviant score on a combination of variables from a single source.

ch. 14
p.300 – 302
ch. 15
p.322 – 323

Detecting multivariate outliers is more difficult than detecting univariate outliers, but they can be detected either statistically or graphically (Tabachnick & Fidell, 2001). Using the statistical method, you obtain a statistic called the *Mahalanobis Distance* from a statistical program such as SPSS. The Mahalanobis Distance represents the distance between a particular case and the centroid (the point created by the means of all the variables in the analysis) of other cases. A large Mahalanobis Distance indicates that a case has extreme values on one or more of the independent variables.

There are other statistical techniques that you can use to detect multivariate outliers (see, e.g. Tabachnick & Fidell, 2007). You also can detect multivariate outliers by inspecting plots of residuals provided by multiple regression programs. Any point on the plot that is distant from other points is a multivariate outlier. Screening for multivariate outliers should be done again after the data are cleaned up because some outliers may "hide" behind others (Tabachnick & Fidell, 2007).

Dealing with outliers

Identifying outliers is all very well and good, but what can you do if you have them in your data? First, double-check that the outliers are actually genuine and are not just errors in entering data. If the outliers are indeed genuine, you have two options. The first option is to normalize the distribution by transforming data from the variable in question. Students often think that transforming data is the same as manipulating data and should therefore be seen as bad. Yes, manipulating your data until you get your desired result is most definitely *not* a good thing, but the point of transforming is that all cases will be affected in the same way. You can think of it as a bit like "translating" data that is in a "foreign language" – you are changing it into a format that can be used and understood, but the actual underlying content remains the same.

If your data have a moderate positive skew, they could be transformed with a square root transformation (you can do this easily in SPSS using the Compute procedure, e.g. new_score = SQRT score). You should use a logarithmic transformation if your data have a more serious positive skew. Again, transformations such as these reduce the impact of outliers if they are found only in one tail of your distribution. If outliers exist in both tails, transformations may not help (Tabachnick & Fidell, 2007).

If your data are negatively skewed, you need to first transform them so that they are positively skewed. This can be done by subtracting each score from the highest score in the distribution and adding 1. The resulting positively skewed data are then transformed as before with either a square root or log transformation, depending on the degree of skewness. This can all be done in one step with the SPSS Compute procedure (e.g. new_score = SQRT ((100 − score) + 1)).

The second (and much simpler) way to deal with outliers is to delete from the analysis either all data from the participant with the outlying scores or the entire variable. The disadvantage to this procedure is that you lose data, and multivariate statistics often require large sample sizes.

Of all the requirements of multivariate statistics, detecting outliers is probably the most important. The presence of just a single multivariate outlier can change the results of your analysis and affect your conclusions, so be sure to check and correct for both univariate and multivariate outliers. However, do not get carried away and remove all the scores you do not like the look of. You should be clear about what constitutes an outlier or not and have very good reasons for removing scores or manipulating data. Think carefully, too, about why you have got an outlier and what that is telling you – perhaps it is nothing to do with the participant, but might be an error on your part (e.g. poorly designed measure). It might also be telling you something interesting about a particular case, or it might even belong to a different population. Not all outliers are bad, and the trick is to hone your skills in recognizing when and how to deal with them.

Normality and homoscedasticity

Another assumption of multivariate statistics, as with the parametric methods we have discussed in previous chapters, is that of normality: it is assumed that the population distribution underlying your sample distribution is normally distributed on the measure that you are taking. You should therefore check histograms and transform skewed data for multivariate statistics, just as you would do for any other parametric test.

A further assumption of multivariate statistics is **homoscedasticity**. We have already discussed this in **Chapter 19**, where it was mentioned in relation to multiple regression. Put generally, homoscedasticity is the assumption that "the variability in scores for one continuous variable is roughly the same at all values of the another continuous variable" (Tabachnick & Fidell, 2007, p. 85). Figure 21.1 shows two scatterplots of two hypothetical variables. Panel (a) shows the pattern of data indicating homoscedasticity. Notice that the shape of the scatterplot created by the data points is elliptical. If both variables are normally distributed, homoscedasticity results.

Homoscedasticity
An assumption of regression and multivariate statistics; occurs when scores on one variable have the same degree of variation across the full range of scores on another variable (e.g. in regression, residuals would have a similar degree of variation across the full range of predictor variable scores).

ch. 19
p.486–488

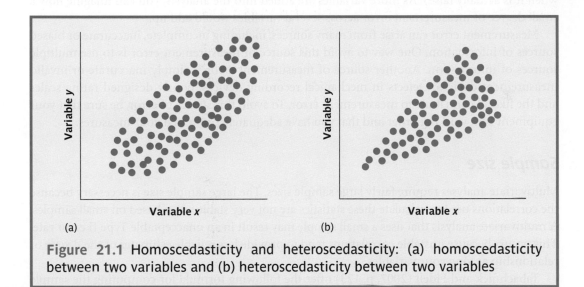

Figure 21.1 Homoscedasticity and heteroscedasticity: (a) homoscedasticity between two variables and (b) heteroscedasticity between two variables

Contrast the scatterplot shown in panel (b) of Figure 21.1 with the one shown in panel (a). Notice how the shape of the scatterplot has changed from elliptical to conical. The conical pattern

Heteroscedasticity
Occurs when degree of variation in scores in one variable is not the same across the full range of scores of another variable (e.g. in regression, degree of variation in residuals would increase or decrease consistently across the full range of predictor variable scores).

Multicollinearity
Occurs when variables are highly correlated with each other.

of data points indicates that **heteroscedasticity** is present. Heteroscedasticity usually occurs because the distribution of one or more variable(s) included in the analysis is skewed. To eliminate heteroscedasticity, apply one of the data transformations previously discussed.

Multicollinearity

As we discussed in **Chapter 19**, **multicollinearity** results when variables in your analysis are highly correlated (Tabachnick & Fidell, 2007), and this is a further assumption of multivariate statistics. If two variables are highly correlated (around $r = .80$ or more), one of them should be eliminated from the analysis. The high correlation means the two variables are measuring essentially the same thing, so little is lost by eliminating one of them.

ch. 19
p.494

Error of measurement

Another issue that you need to be aware of when using multivariate statistics is error in measurement. Drawing valid conclusions relies on the fact that variables are being measured accurately. However, even with the very best measures there will always be some degree of error in measurement, and the best we can hope for is that the values that are measured are a good estimate of the true values. Error of measurement can be particularly troublesome in multivariate research because it leads to an underestimation of the correlations among variables that are used to compute the various multivariate statistics (Asher, 1976; Hunter, 1987), and this in turn leads to Type II errors (i.e. accepting the null hypothesis when it is actually false). As more variables are added into the analysis, you can imagine how a small degree of measurement error across several variables would add up.

Measurement error can arise from many sources, including incomplete, inaccurate or biased sources of information. One way to avoid this source of measurement error is to use multiple sources of information. Another source of measurement error is simply inaccurate or invalid measurement devices. Defects in mechanical recording devices, poorly designed rating scales and the like all contribute to measurement error. To avoid this source of error, be sure that your equipment is in working order and that you have adequately pre-tested your measures.

Sample size

Multivariate analyses require fairly large sample sizes. The large sample size is necessary because the correlations used to calculate these statistics are not very stable when based on small samples. A multivariate analysis that uses a small sample may result in an unacceptable Type II error rate. This occurs because unstable correlations tend to provide less reliable estimates of the degree of relationship among your variables.

Tabachnick and Fidell (2007, p. 123) offer the following formula for computing the sample size required for a multiple regression analysis:

$$N \geq 50 + 8m$$

where m = the number of predictor variables. So, if you have five predictor variables, you would need a minimum of 90 participants in your sample. Larger samples may be needed if your data are skewed, there is substantial measurement error, or you anticipate weak relationships among variables (Tabachnick & Fidell, 2007). Tabachnick and Fidell also caution that you can have *too large* a sample. With overly large samples, very weak relationships that may have neither theoretical nor practical value can achieve statistical significance.

To summarize, several factors should be considered before using multivariate statistics. Make sure that your data meet the assumptions of the test you are going to use (i.e. normality, linearity and homoscedasticity), that you have removed any outliers or minimized their effects through transformation, that you have considered error of measurement, and that you have gathered a sufficiently large sample. If you violate the assumptions of the test or fail to take into account the other important factors, the results that you obtain may not be valid.

Multivariate statistical tests

Now that you are familiar with the general logic behind multivariate statistics and understand (hopefully) the assumptions and requirements of these tests, we can explore some of the more popular multivariate data analysis techniques. This discussion begins with an examination of factor analysis, logistic regression and discriminant function analysis, then moves on to look at the techniques used to analyse multivariate data from experimental designs (e.g. MANOVA and multiway frequency analysis) and, finally, techniques for causal modelling.

Factor analysis

Imagine that you are interested in measuring the degree to which males conform to male social norms. Before you conduct your study, you need to find a way to define just what those norms are. While reviewing the literature, you discover that there are several male social norms that are relevant to male social behaviour. You decide to design a questionnaire including 100 items to measure male social norms and administer it to a sample of male participants.

After all your participants have completed the questionnaire, you now face the task of determining the underlying nature of male social norms. One question that interests you is whether all the questions on your questionnaire measure a single dimension (such as aggressiveness) or several dimensions (such as aggressiveness, competitiveness and dominance). Your search for the dimensions underlying male social norms lends itself perfectly to factor analysis.

Factor analysis operates by extracting as many significant factors from your data as possible, based on the correlations between your measures. A **factor** is a dimension that consists of any number of variables. In your study of male social norms, for example, you may find that your 100 questions actually measure three underlying dimensions (e.g. aggressiveness, competitiveness and dominance). Factor analysis involves extracting one factor (such as aggressiveness) and then evaluating your data for the existence of additional factors.

The factors extracted in factor analysis are not of equal strength. Each successive factor accounts for less and less variance. Typically, the first two or three factors

Factor analysis
Multivariate statistical technique used to identify underlying dimensions based on correlations between variables.

Factor
An underlying dimension that cannot be measured directly, but which can be identified during factor analysis.

will be the strongest (i.e. account for the most variance). The strength of a factor is indicated by its eigenvalue (for a more complete discussion of eigenvalues, see Tatsuoka, 1971, or Tabachnick & Fidell, 2007). Factors with eigenvalues less than 1.0 usually are not interpreted.

Factor loadings

Factor loading
The correlation between a variable and an underlying factor.

To determine the dependent variables constituting a common factor, **factor loadings** are computed. Each factor loading is the correlation between a single variable and the underlying factor. If the variable and underlying factor are positively related, this will result in a positive factor loading; a negative factor loading means that there's a negative correlation between the variable and underlying factor. Loadings are usually interpreted only if they are equal to or exceed ±.30. By looking at the variables that load onto different factors, you should get an idea of what the underlying dimensions might be.

Rotation of factors

After you have obtained your factor loadings, you must interpret them. This is the part that is often the most difficult – factor analysis will tell you which variables load onto different factors, but it will not tell you what the underlying dimensions actually are or what they mean. That is up to you.

To aid in interpretation of factor loadings, we can use factor rotation to make the factors distinct. Figure 21.2 shows a plot of some factor loadings. The factor loadings for each variable are used as coordinates on the graph. Panel (a) of Figure 21.2 shows the plot of the unrotated factor loadings. Panel (b) of Figure 21.2 shows the axes after rotation, where the axes of the graph have been rotated so that the best factor structure is produced. In other words, rotation is a technique used to help make the factor structure easier to interpret.

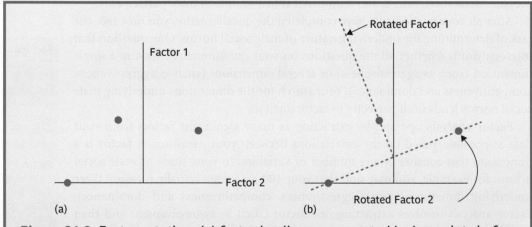

Figure 21.2 Factor rotation: (a) factor loadings represented by large dots before rotation and (b) the same loadings after rotation of the axis

Two types of rotation are orthogonal rotation and oblique rotation. In **orthogonal rotation**, the axes remain perpendicular. Orthogonal rotation assumes that your measures are uncorrelated and consequently that the factors extracted are un-related. Generally, orthogonal rotation is preferred over oblique rotation because it makes the results easier to interpret. The most popular orthogonal rotation method is **varimax**, which maximizes the variance of loadings on each factor and simplifies factors (Tabachnick & Fidell, 2007). In **oblique rotation**, the angle between the axes, as well as the orientation of the axes in space, may change. Oblique rotation assumes that your measures and factors are correlated. If you have good reason to believe that your measures are correlated, oblique rotation might be a better choice than orthogonal rotation. Figure 21.3 illustrates the difference between the two rotation strategies. Panel (a) shows orthogonal rotation, and panel (b) shows oblique rotation.

Principal components and principal factors analysis

Two types of factor analysis are **principal components analysis** and **principal factors analysis**. Panel (a) of Table 21.1 shows a standard three-variable correlation matrix. Remember, such correlations are used to calculate factor loadings. Panel (b) shows the same correlation matrix completed by filling in the correlations missing from the matrix in panel (a). Notice that the values on the diagonal of the matrix are all 1s. In principal components analysis, the diagonal of the completed correlation matrix is filled with 1s. In contrast, principal factors analysis completes the correlation matrix by entering *communalities* along the diagonal. Essentially, communality is a measure of a variable's reliability and is fairly easy to obtain after factor analysis. In practice, however, you need these values before analysis. Various techniques have been proposed for estimating communalities (see Bennett & Bowers, 1976), none of which is much better than any other.

Your choice between principal components and principal factors analysis rests on the goals of the analysis. If your goal is to reduce a large number of variables down to a smaller set and to obtain an empirical summary of the data, then principal components analysis is most appropriate. If your research is driven by empirical or theoretical predictions, then principal factors analysis is best (Tabachnick & Fidell, 2007). In the absence of any clear information on which technique is best, you should probably use principal components in those situations in which you do not have any empirical or theoretical guidance on the values of the communalities.

Exploratory versus confirmatory factor analysis

Another distinction is between exploratory factor analysis and confirmatory factor analysis. **Exploratory factor analysis** is used when you have a large set of variables that you want to describe in simpler terms and you have no reason to predict which variables will cluster together. Exploratory factor analysis is therefore useful in the early stages of research to identify the variables that cluster together. From such an analysis, research hypotheses can be generated and tested (Tabachnick & Fidell, 2007).

Orthogonal rotation
Factor rotation technique which considers factors to be independent.

Varimax
Popular method of orthogonal rotation.

Oblique rotation
Factor rotation technique which considers factors to be correlated.

Principal components analysis
Type of factor analysis, mainly used to reduce number of variables to summary of components.

Principal factors analysis
Type of factor analysis, mainly used to confirm empirical or theoretical predictions.

Exploratory factor analysis
Factor analysis technique in which there is no *a priori* reason to predict which variables will cluster together.

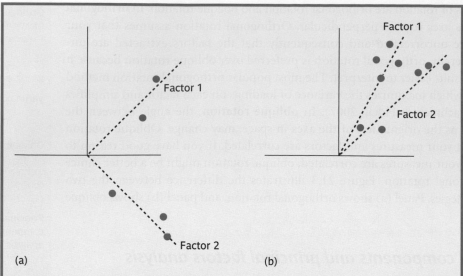

Figure 21.3 Orthogonal and oblique factor rotation: (a) in orthogonal rotation, the rotated axes remain at right angles; (b) in oblique rotation, the angle of the axes changes

Table 21.1 Two correlation matrices for three variables

(a) Hypothetical correlation matrix			
	Variable 1	**Variable 2**	**Variable 3**
Variable 1			
Variable 2	.71		
Variable 3	.61	.74	

(b) Completed correlation matrix			
	Variable 1	**Variable 2**	**Variable 3**
Variable 1	1.00	.71	.61
Variable 2	.71	1.00	.74
Variable 3	.61	.74	1.00

Confirmatory factor analysis is used in later stages of research where you can specify how variables might relate given some underlying psychological process (Tabachnick & Fidell, 2007).

 For further details of how to run factor analysis using SPSS, please visit our website.

> **Confirmatory factor analysis**
> Factor analysis technique in which the goal is to test theory and confirm predictions.

Logistic regression and discriminant function analysis

ch. 19
pp.490 – 501

As you may have gathered from Chapter 19, **multiple regression** can be a very useful technique. However, what can you do if the variable you want to predict is nominal? Fortunately, there are multivariate techniques, based on multiple regression, which can deal with this sort of situation.

Logistic regression is a special case of multiple regression in which you have several predictor variables, but the criterion variable is nominal. Thus, logistic regression can help us to predict which category someone may be assigned to. **Binary logistic regression** is used when the outcome variable is dichotomous; **multinominal logistic regression** is used when there are more than two categories.

Logistic regression has many real-world applications. For example, imagine you wanted to predict whether giving a patient a certain treatment would be successful. There may be a number of variables to consider, such as their age, gender, length of illness, whether they are on other medication or not, whether they smoke or not etc. Logistic regression would tell you whether these variables were good predictors or not, and would produce an equation which would allow you to predict the likelihood of whether a patient's treatment would be successful.

We saw in Chapter 19 that the multiple regression equation could be written as:

$$Y = a + b_1 X_1 + b_2 X_2 + b_3 X_3 + \ldots$$

where a is a constant, b is a coefficient (or regression weight), Y is the criterion variable, and X is a predictor variable.

In logistic regression the regression equation is:

$$logit = a + b_1 X_1 + b_2 X_2 + b_3 X_3 + \ldots$$

As with multiple regression, logistic regression provides b coefficients for the predictor variables and a constant. But the main difference is that, rather than predicting a score on a certain variable Y, the equation provides a value called *logit*. There is not space to explain here why *logit* is used (and we are sure you do not want to spend ages reading about it), but essentially *logit* represents the natural logarithm of odds of a certain outcome. You may have come across the natural logarithm (*ln* or *log* e) in mathematics, but do not worry too much if it is not familiar – all you need to realize is that the outcome has been changed into a different format. Therefore, if you intend to use logistic regression to help you predict an outcome, you need to change the outcome back into normal odds. If you have a scientific calculator, this can be done easily by finding the *ex* button (now you know what it's used for!) and then entering the value of *logit*. For instance, in our medical example, if we had entered into the equation values for a particular patient and the value of *logit* = −0.443, $e^{-0.443}$ = 0.642, meaning that the odds of successful treatment are 0.642 (or 0.642 times more likely to be successful than unsuccessful).

There are a number of important statistics in logistic regression which are equivalent to statistics we saw in multiple regression. The multiple correlation coefficient R and R^2 indicate how well a multiple regression model fits the data; in logistic regression, we use something

Logistic regression
Multiple regression technique in which outcome variable is categorical.

Binary logistic regression
Logistic regression in which outcome variable is dichotomous.

Multinomial logistic regression
Logistic regression in which outcome variable consists of more than two categories.

called the log-likelihood statistic. In SPSS, this is multiplied by −2 to produce a statistic called −2LL, which provides a measure of the degree of variability in the data. −2LL behaves in a similar way to chi-square. (Remember, that in the chi-square test of goodness-of-fit, large chi-square values are more likely to be significant, and therefore indicate that the observed frequencies do not fit the expected pattern.) Low values of −2LL therefore indicate that the regression model is predicting the criterion variable well, whereas high values suggest a poor fit. Note that this is different to R and R^2, where a higher value suggests better prediction.

Discriminant function analysis
Multivariate statistical technique used when you have multiple predictor variables and a categorical criterion variable.

Another important statistic to note in logistic regression is Wald's chi-square. This tells us whether a predictor variable is making a significant contribution to the model. In this way, it is equivalent to the t-values provided in multiple regression.

Discriminant function analysis is similar to logistic regression, but seems to have been overtaken in popularity by logistic regression, partly because discriminant function analysis assumes that predictor variables exhibit normality (and are therefore continuous), whereas logistic regression allows categorical predictor variables to be included (Howell, 2007; Kinnear & Gray, 2009). Discriminant function analysis can be used to identify a simple rule for classifying participants into groups or to determine which of your predictor variables contributes most heavily to the separation of groups. The analysis works by forming **discriminant functions**, which look similar to multiple regression equations. For each group of dependent variables, a discriminant function score (D) is calculated, which represents the best linear combination of predictor variables, just as in multiple regression.

Discriminant function
A combination of predictor variables, presented in the form of a linear equation.

More than one discriminant function can link your predictors with your dependent variable. However, the number of functions is limited to the number of predictors or to the number of levels of the dependent variable minus 1, whichever is smaller. For example, if you had seven predictors and three levels of the dependent variable, the number of possible functions is 2 (or 3 − 1). Each discriminant function represents a different linkage between the predictors and dependent variable. The first calculated maximizes the separation between levels of the dependent variable. Subsequent functions represent progressively weaker linkages between the predictors and the dependent variable.

 SPSS

Discriminant function analysis can be run in SPSS (see our website for details). The output of the SPSS analysis gives you several important pieces of information. First, the output will indicate the number of discriminant functions extracted, along with tests of statistical significance. Second, you can request several other statistics needed to interpret your results.

Beta weight
Standardized regression weight used to interpret the results of a linear regression analysis. A beta weight can be interpreted as a partial correlation coefficient.

These include the standardized discriminant function coefficients (analogous to **beta weights**), canonical discriminant function coefficients (analogous to b coefficients) and pooled within-groups correlations between the discriminant functions and predictor variables (structure correlations), which can be interpreted much like factor loadings. By convention, you typically consider those structure correlations that exceed .30. The structure correlations can help you determine what each discriminant function represents.

Although discriminant function analysis is not quite as popular as logistic regression, it is often used as a follow-up to multivariate analysis of variance, to which it is closely related and which we will now discuss.

Multivariate analysis of variance (MANOVA)

ch. 5
p.94 – 99

ch. 17
p.380 – 381

As you may have guessed from the name, **multivariate analysis of variance (MANOVA)** is related to analysis of variance, and is used when you have multiple dependent variables. It is often a good idea to measure more than one type of outcome in a study, to improve validity. For example, if you were conducting an experiment looking at stress, you might want to record more than one measure of stress (e.g. heart rate, respiration rate and a questionnaire designed to assess perceived stress). Of course, you could run separate univariate ANOVAs on each of those measures, but remember in **Chapter 17** when we discussed why ANOVA was preferable to running multiple *t*-tests? Well, the same logic applies here – running multiple univariate ANOVAs increases the risk of committing a Type I error, but MANOVA controls for this by considering the dependent variables in the same analysis.

> **Multivariate analysis of variance (MANOVA)** Multivariate statistical technique which is an extension of ANOVA to analyse more than one dependent variable.

MANOVA also has some other advantages over multiple univariate ANOVAs. Univariate ANOVAs consider dependent variables in isolation and so cannot tell us about the relationship between those variables, whereas MANOVA can provide us with useful information about correlations between dependent variables. MANOVA can also tell us whether we can distinguish between groups of cases based on scores across a combination of variables, in a similar way to discriminant function analysis. As this would not be possible with several univariate ANOVAs, MANOVA can be considered to be more powerful than conducting multiple ANOVAs.

You may be thinking to yourself: so why do we bother with ANOVAs at all if MANOVA is so great and has all these advantages? It is because there has to be sound reasoning behind why you are using multiple dependent measures and why you think they should be considered all together in the same analysis. Basically, this means that it is not a good idea to measure hundreds of dependent variables and throw them into a MANOVA, hoping for the best, as you will get nothing meaningful out of it.

We will not go into the theory behind MANOVA just now, as it is fairly complex. However, it involves converting the dependent variables into discriminant functions which are then entered into a ratio similar to the *F*-ratio in univariate ANOVA. In univariate ANOVA we used the *F*-ratio to tell us whether we had a significant difference or not, but in MANOVA you have the option of four different statistics, all with quite exotic names: Pillai's Trace (V), Wilks' Lambda (λ), Hotelling's Trace (T^2) and Roy's Largest Root. When there is only one discriminant function in the analysis, these statistics will not differ, but otherwise you will need to select one. Unfortunately, there is no consensus on which of these statistics you should use, but Pillai's Trace and Wilks' Lambda seem to be the most commonly reported. If you need a fuller discussion, please see Field (2009).

SPSS can be used to run MANOVA. Output will include a table of Multivariate Statistics, which presents the values of different statistics, those values converted into *F*-values, and their probabilities. If your chosen statistic is significant, this indicates that the groups differ significantly on the dependent variables. You will also get the usual univariate ANOVA output, which you can use to help with interpretation of your results. However, some people recommend that you use discriminant function analysis rather than univariate ANOVAs to help you interpret your MANOVA results (e.g. Field, 2009).

We have been discussing MANOVA as an extension to between-subjects ANOVA, but you can also use MANOVA with within-subjects designs. Here, the repeated measures (i.e. scores under different conditions) are treated as correlated dependent variables and are analysed accordingly. In doing so, this eliminates the problem of the assumption of homogeneity associated with univariate within-subjects (repeated measures) ANOVA.

ANCOVA and MANCOVA

Analysis of covariance (ANCOVA)
Statistical technique which compares means on a dependent variable, once the influence of covariates has been controlled for.

Multivariate analysis of covariance (MANCOVA)
Multivariate statistical technique which compares difference on multiple dependent variables, once the influence of covariates has been controlled for.

There are even more variations on ANOVA that you may come across: **analysis of covariance (ANCOVA)** and **multivariate analysis of covariance (MANCOVA)**. These techniques work in the same way as their ordinary ANOVA and MANOVA counterparts, but the important difference is that they allow you to control for covariates. A covariate is a continuous variable which is not part of the actual experimental design, but which may be related to the dependent variable(s) in question and may consequently confound the results. For example, in an experiment looking at the effects of different imagery techniques on memory test performance, age could be entered as a covariate – it could be related to memory performance, but is not the focus of the experiment. ANCOVA and MANCOVA allow you to remove the influence of covariates, thus providing you with a "purer" result.

It is easy to run ANCOVA or MANCOVA in SPSS (see our website for detailed instructions). The output is presented in the same way as for other ANOVAs, but will include a row of results for each covariate. You should inspect the F- and p-values for the covariates – a significant result indicates that the covariate significantly predicts the dependent variable(s). The other results should be interpreted in the same way as before, but remembering that the values have been adjusted to remove the influence of the covariate(s).

SPSS

A word of warning though – remember that you will have to identify and measure potential covariates before you can use these techniques, and you should have sound reasons for including them in the analysis.

Multiway frequency analysis

Multiway frequency analysis
A set of techniques used to analyse nominal data.

Loglinear analysis
A type of multiway frequency analysis; an extension to the chi-square test of association, considering more than two categorical variables.

The multivariate statistical techniques we have been discussing all require same interval/ratio data. However, there are also situations where you are only measuring multiple nominal variables. For these cases, **multiway frequency analysis** is an alternative. A specific type of multiway frequency analysis used for categorical or qualitative variables is loglinear analysis.

Loglinear analysis is analogous to **chi-square** (see Chapter 20) in that you use observed and expected frequencies to evaluate the statistical significance of your data. An important difference between chi-square and loglinear analysis is that loglinear analysis can easily be applied to experimental research designs that include more than two independent variables, whereas chi-square is normally limited to the two-variable case.

ch. 20

Loglinear analysis has a wide range of applications. You can use loglinear analysis if you conducted a correlational study with several categorical variables; loglinear analysis is well suited to this task. You also can use loglinear analysis if you conducted an experiment including a categorical dependent variable (e.g. guilty/not guilty) even if your independent variables were quantitative.

Loglinear analysis is also a useful tool for testing and building theoretical models. In this application, you specify how variables should be entered into the analysis for the models that you wish to test. Loglinear analysis is then used to test the relative adequacy of each model.

Finally, because loglinear analysis is a non-parametric statistic, you can use it if your data violate the assumptions of parametric statistics. In this instance, you can use loglinear analysis even if your dependent variable was measured along an interval or ordinal scale (Tabachnick & Fidell, 2007).

However, one important requirement must still be met. Like chi-square, loglinear analysis uses observed and expected cell frequencies to compute your test statistic. To obtain valid results, your expected cell frequencies must be relatively large. Tabachnick and Fidell (2007) recommend having five times as many subjects as cells to ensure adequate expected frequencies. So, for example, if you have a $2 \times 2 \times 2$ design, you should have $2 \times 2 \times 2 \times 5 = 40$ participants to ensure sufficiently large expected cell frequencies.

You should inspect all expected frequencies to ensure that they are all larger than 1 and that no more than 20 per cent of them fall below 5 (Tabachnick & Fidell, 2007). If you find small expected frequencies, Tabachnick and Fidell suggest several remedies. First, you could accept and live with the reduced power of the analysis caused by low expected frequencies. Second, categories can be collapsed or combined to increase frequencies within each category. Third, you could delete variables to reduce the number of categories in your analysis. This latter strategy should be done with caution, and you should not delete variables that are correlated with other variables in the analysis (Tabachnick & Fidell, 2007).

When you use ANOVA or multiple regression to analyse your data, your analysis uses group means as a basis for analysis. When you have categorical data, however, you must deal with proportions instead of means. For example, if you used a three-factor design with a categorical dependent variable (e.g. yes/no), you would summarize your data according to the proportion of subjects falling into each category.

Whereas chi-square is used to compare observed and expected frequencies in the chi-square tests, for loglinear analysis we use something called the likelihood ratio (G_2). This is similar to the logit value we saw in logistic regression, in that the likelihood ratio involves taking the natural log of the ratio of observed cell frequency to the expected cell frequency. A G_2 is computed for each main effect and interaction in your design and is interpreted in the same way as chi-square (using the chi-square tables to establish statistical significance). The analysis involves looking at the main effects and interactions and determining whether removing them from the model significantly affects the overall fit of the model.

Loglinear analysis can be run using SPSS (see our website for details) and will present you with a table of observed and expected frequencies. You should also inspect the table labelled K-Way and Higher Order Effects, which will tell you which main effects and interactions have been kept in the final model. SPSS will also give you goodness-of-fit statistics – remember that a *non*-significant result indicates that the final model provides a good fit.

SPSS

Path analysis

Path analysis
Application of multiple regression techniques used to test causal models.

Unlike the other analytic techniques already discussed, **path analysis** is not a statistical procedure in and of itself. Instead, it is an application of multiple regression techniques to the testing of causal models. Path analysis allows you to test a model specifying the causal links among variables by applying simple multiple regression techniques.

It is important to remember that path analysis is designed to test causal models, and not to sift through data trying to find interesting relationships among variables. It is therefore essential that the causal model used in path analysis is clearly articulated and has a strong theoretical or empirical base.

Translating theoretical propositions into a clearly defined path model can be tricky. You are always tempted to determine how to measure your variables first and then derive the model. This method may not be the best. It may limit the possible causal relationships within your model and consequently may not allow you to test your theory adequately. Instead, first develop a list of the causal links among variables as suggested by your theory (Hunter & Gerbing, 1982). Then show these links among variables in a path diagram. After developing the path model and diagram, you can then decide how to measure your variables.

Causal relationships

The heart of path analysis is developing a causal model and identifying causal relationships. Causal relationships among variables can take many forms. The simplest of these is shown in panel (a) of Figure 21.3, where variable *A* (independent variable) causes changes in variable *B* (dependent variable). Another possible causal relationship is shown in panel (b). Here, two variables independently influence variable *B*. This model suggests that variation in the dependent variable has multiple causes. These causal variables can be uncorrelated, as shown in panel (b). Panel (c) shows a situation in which two variables believed to cause changes in the dependent variable are correlated. In Figure 21.4 (and in path analysis, in general), straight arrows denote causal relationships and are called *paths*. Curved, double-headed arrows denote correlational relationships.

The simple causal relationships just described can be combined to form more complex causal models. One such model is the causal chain in which a sequence of events leads ultimately to variation in the dependent variable. To illustrate a simple causal chain, consider trying to determine what variables correlated with examination grades.

Suppose you believe that parental education (PE) and student motivation (SM) relate to variation in examination grades. You have reason to believe that a causal relationship exists. So you develop a causal model like the one illustrated in panel (a) of Figure 21.5. Your model suggests that PE causes changes in SM, which then causes changes in examination grades. Notice that you are proposing that PE does not directly cause changes in examination grades but rather operates through SM.

When developing simple causal chains (and more complex causal models), keep in mind that the validity of your causal model depends on how well you have done your homework and conceptualized your model. Perhaps SM does not directly cause changes in examination grades as predicted but rather operates through yet another variable, such as working hard (WH) in class. Panel (b) of Figure 21.5 shows a causal chain including WH. If you excluded WH from your model, the causal relationships and the model you develop may not be valid.

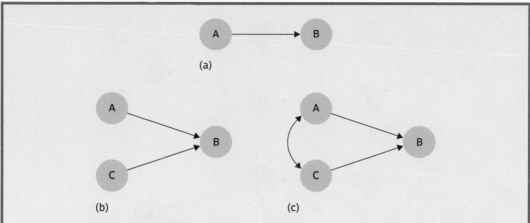

Figure 21.4 Three possible causal relationships: (a) variable *A* causes changes in *B*; (b) uncorrelated variables *A* and *C* contribute to changes in the value of *B*; (c) correlated variables *A* and *C* cause changes in the value of *B*

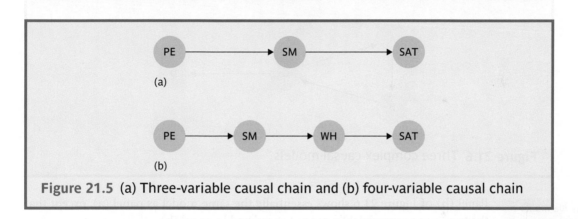

Figure 21.5 (a) Three-variable causal chain and (b) four-variable causal chain

You can progress from simple causal chains to more complex models quite easily. Figure 21.6 shows three examples of more complex causal models. In panel (a), the causal model suggests variables *A* and *B* are correlated (indicated by the curved arrow). Variable *A* is believed to exert a causal influence on variable *C*, and *B* on *D*. Variable *D* is hypothesized to cause changes in *C*, and both *D* and *C* are believed to cause changes in *E*.

Types of variables and causal models

Variables *A* and *B* in panel (a) of Figure 21.6 are called **exogenous variables**. Exogenous variables begin the causal sequence. Notice that no causal paths lead to variable *A* or *B*. All the other variables in the model shown in panel (a) are **endogenous variables**. These variables are internal to the model, and changes in them are believed to be caused by other variables. Variables *C*, *D* and *E* are all endogenous variables.

Exogenous variable
A variable which begins a causal sequence in path analysis.

Endogenous variable
An internal variable in a path analysis model, changes in which are caused by other variables.

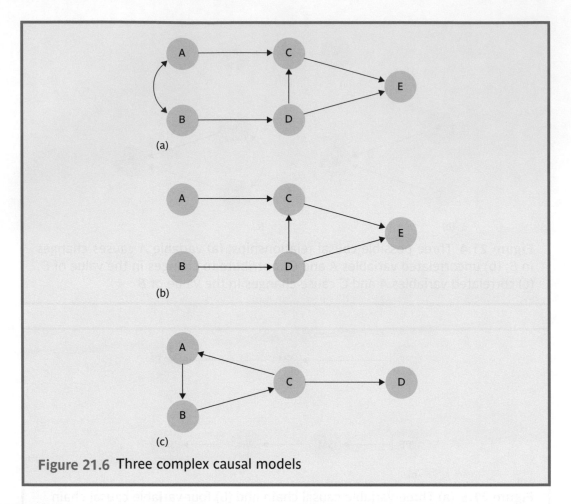

Figure 21.6 Three complex causal models

Recursive model
A path analysis
model which
includes no loops.

**Non-recursive
model**
A path analysis
model which
includes loops.

Path coefficient
Estimate of
relationship
between variables
in path analysis
model.

Panel (b) of Figure 21.6 shows essentially the same model as panel (a), except that the two exogenous variables are not correlated in panel (b).

The models in panels (a) and (b) are both known as **recursive models**. Notice that there are no loops of variables. That is, causal relationships run in only one direction (e.g. *D* causes *C*, but *C* does not cause *D*). In contrast, panel (c) of Figure 21.6 shows a **non-recursive model**, which has a causal loop. In this case, variable *A* is believed to be a cause of *C* (operating through *B*), but *C* also can cause *A*. In general, recursive models are much easier to deal with conceptually and statistically (Asher, 1976).

Estimating the degree of causality

After you have developed your causal models and measured your variables, you then obtain estimates of the causal relationships among your variables. These estimates are called **path coefficients**. Figure 21.7 shows a causal model with the path coefficients indicated for each causal path.

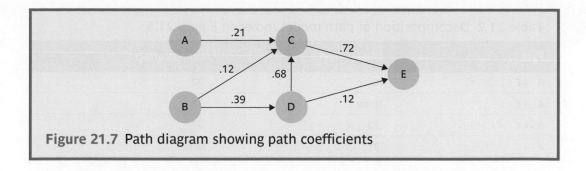

Figure 21.7 Path diagram showing path coefficients

Path coefficients are determined by using a series of multiple regression analyses. Each *endogenous* variable is used as a dependent variable in the regression analysis. All the variables in the model that are assumed to influence the dependent variable are used as predictors. For example, the path coefficients for *A–C* and *D–C* in Figure 21.7 are obtained by using *C* as the dependent variable and *A*, *B* and *D* as predictors. The path coefficients are the standardized regression weights (beta weights) from these analyses.

Interpreting path analysis

Path analysis is used to test the validity of a presumed causal model. So, you should look at the path coefficients and determine whether the pattern expected by the model has emerged. In addition to looking at the path coefficients (which give you estimates of the direct effects of variables on other variables), you also decompose the paths into indirect effects. Decomposition can be done according to Wright's rules (cited in Asher, 1976).

Wright's rules state that the correlation between any two variables can be broken down into simple and compound paths. The compound path is the product of the simple paths that it comprises (Asher, 1976). The simple path is the direct link between the two variables, and the compound path consists of all indirect routes from one variable to another. The following are three general instructions given by Wright to guide the decomposition of a path (Asher, 1976, p. 33):

1 No path may pass through the same variable more than once.
2 No path may go backward on (against the direction of) an arrow after the path has gone forward on a different arrow.
3 No path may pass through a double-headed curved arrow . . . more than once in any single path.

In Figure 21.5, the relationship between variables *B* and *C* consists of the simple path linking *B* with *C*, plus the product of the path coefficients linking *B*, *D* and *C*. Table 21.2 shows the decomposition of the model shown in Figure 21.5.

Interpretation of the path coefficients themselves can be tricky. In most cases, the beta weights cannot be interpreted as representing the unique contribution of one variable to variance in another. Remember that a beta weight not only has components of the degree of relationship between two variables but also includes components of any other predictors. For example, in

Table 21.2 Decomposition of path model shown in Figure 21.5		
Path	Direct effect	Indirect effect
$B \rightarrow E$	None	.32
$A \rightarrow E$	None	.15
$B \rightarrow C$	.12	.27
$A \rightarrow C$	.21	None

Semi-partial correlation
Multivariate correlational statistic used to examine the relationship between two variables with the effects of a third variable removed from only one of them; also called part correlation.

Structural equation modelling (SEM)
Version of path analysis which allows for existence of latent variables.

Latent variable
Variables in a structural equation model which cannot be observed or measured directly.

Figure 21.5, the path coefficient linking variables C and E does not represent the unique contribution of C to E. Rather, variables A, B and D also contribute to E, and these contributions may be reflected in the C to E path coefficient.

There is no easy way around this conceptual difficulty. One possible solution is to use **semi-partial correlation** coefficients in place of beta weights. As we indicated, these can be obtained from SPSS or calculated easily by hand. These semi-partial correlations provide a better estimate of the degree of impact of one variable on another (with others held constant) than do the beta weights.

Structural equation modelling

Structural equation modelling (SEM) is a variant of path analysis. With path analysis, variables that are directly observed and measured are included in the analysis (Streiner, 2006). Sometimes, however, you deal with constructs that are not directly observable but are evident in a number of behaviours (Streiner, 2006). For example, depression is a hypothetical construct that cannot be observed directly. Instead, we can measure several behaviours that relate to depression (e.g. suicidal thoughts, loss of energy and sleep disturbances). One advantage of SEM over path analysis is that it allows you to evaluate hypothetical constructs within the models that you test (Streiner, 2006). In the language of SEM, those variables in a model that are not directly observable or measurable are called **latent variables**.

Structural equation modelling is normally used as a confirmatory procedure and not an exploratory one (Garson, 2009). Garson suggests that there are three confirmatory applications of SEM:

1 *Strictly confirmatory approach.* You test a model to see if data that you collected are consistent with the predictions of the model.

2 *Alternative models approach.* You test two or more alternative models to see which one (if any) best fits the data collected.

3 *Model development approach.* You use SEM to develop a model by combining exploratory and confirmatory approaches. You then test the model, and if you find that it does not fit the data very well, you make modifications to the model and retest it. You keep doing this until you find the model that best fits the data.

An important fact to keep in mind about SEM is that it requires you to develop a model for testing that is based on existing theory and research. You do not go on a "fishing expedition" by throwing variables into an SEM analysis and hope to find meaningful relationships and causal connections. However, as noted above, SEM can serve an exploratory function, but even here, you need to specify a coherent model to be tested.

Developing a model for SEM analysis starts with a verbal statement of how variables relate (e.g. according to a theory; Hershberger et al., 2003). Next, you draw out the model using boxes, ovals and arrows. Boxes represent variables that you will measure or have measured; their names are written inside the boxes. Circles denote latent variables. Arrows specify the relationships among variables: straight arrows for causal relationships and curved arrows for correlational relationships (Hershberger et al., 2003).

As you saw in our discussion of path analysis, path coefficients are derived by using multiple regression analysis. Thankfully, there are specialized SEM computer programs which can do all the statistical analysis for you. The most popular programs used for this purpose are LISREL, published by Scientific Software International (http://www.ssicentral.com), and AMOS, published by SPSS.

An example of SEM

For years social psychologists have been studying the effects of media exposure on behaviour. One area of concern is whether exposure to televised sexual content relates to a young adolescent's decision to engage in sexual behaviour at an early age. To investigate the variables that link exposure to television sexual content with sexual behaviour, Martino et al. (2005) used SEM. Based on previous research and theory, Martino et al. hypothesized that sexual messages seen on television might suggest that it is normative within the peer group to engage in sexual behaviour at a young age.

Participants in this study were male and female White, Black and Hispanic American adolescents between the ages of 12 and 17 years. Martino et al. (2005) obtained measures of three variables: exposure to sexual content on television (how often participants watched each of 23 television programmes), peer sexual norms (participants were asked how many of their friends had sexual intercourse) and sexual behaviour (whether the participant had or did not have sexual intercourse). In addition to these variables, they included two latent variables in the model: "Safe-sex self-efficacy" and "negative outcome expectancies" (Martino et al., 2005, p. 920), which they constructed from a set of measures that tapped into these constructs. For example, safe-sex self-efficacy included measures of condom use, talking to members of the opposite sex about sex, and obtaining condoms. The SEM model that they constructed is shown in Figure 21.8. Notice that the two latent variables are displayed in ovals and the other variables (directly measured) are shown in rectangles. The arrows indicate the directions and pathways of causal connections hypothesized.

Martino et al. (2005) found that their hypothesized model fitted the data reasonably well. As shown in Figure 21.8, they also found that there were significant causal paths between exposure to sex on television, perceived norms and sexual behaviour. There was no significant direct effect of exposure to sex on television and sexual behaviour. Additionally, the hypothesized relationships between the latent variables and sexual behaviour were also confirmed. Exposure

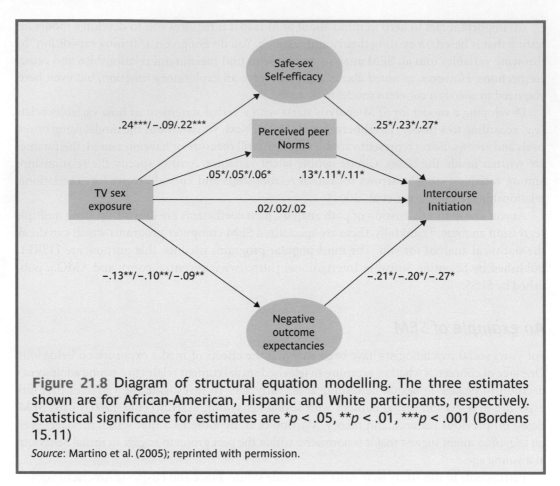

Figure 21.8 Diagram of structural equation modelling. The three estimates shown are for African-American, Hispanic and White participants, respectively. Statistical significance for estimates are *p < .05, **p < .01, ***p < .001 (Bordens 15.11)

Source: Martino et al. (2005); reprinted with permission.

to sex on television was positively related to safe-sex self-efficacy for African-Americans and Whites, which was in turn positively related to sexual behaviour. Exposure to sex on television reduced negative outcome expectancies, which in turn increased sexual behaviour.

Multivariate statistics: a final word

This chapter has briefly introduced you to a number of useful and potentially exciting techniques in this chapter. These are becoming increasingly popular in research and it is important that you can understand the basics behind each test. However, please remember that there simply was not enough space to discuss all topics in adequate depth and you should not undertake any multivariate analysis without reading further on the topic and familiarizing yourself with the debates surrounding the techniques. Thanks to SPSS and other computer packages, it is now easier than ever to run multivariate analysis, but it is essential that you understand what you are doing and why you are doing it. These computer programs will quite happily do whatever you tell them, so if you put in poor data or do not have a clue what you are doing, do not expect the output to make sense. Tabachnik and Fidell (2007) provide a very comprehensive discussion of multivariate methods, or, for a more psychology-focused discussion, have a look at Field (2009).

Summary

In this chapter, you were introduced to multivariate statistical methods, which are used when you have multiple dependent measures. Multivariate statistics assume that continuous variables exhibit linearity and normality, and that there is no evidence of heteroscedasticity or multicollinearity. Outliers and error of measurement are other issues that need to be considered before using multivariate statistical analysis methods.

Factor analysis was introduced as a method used to reduce a large set of variables to a smaller set, or to confirm that certain variables measure the same underlying dimensions. Two types of factor analysis are principal components and principal factors. Factor analysis extracts as many significant factors as possible. For each factor, a variable will have a certain loading, which is the correlation between the variable and the factor extracted. To aid interpretation of the factors, they are rotated; the most popular rotation method is varimax.

Logistic regression and discriminant function analysis are similar to multiple regression except that the variable to be predicted is categorical rather than continuous. Logistic regression tends to be more popular with researchers than discriminant function analysis because it allows for continuous predictor variables to be included, whereas discriminant function analysis does not.

MANOVA is closely related to discriminant function analysis and is used when you have an experiment with several related dependent measures. This is preferable to running multiple univariate ANOVAs and allows you to distinguish between groups based on a combination of variables. A significant result indicates that the groups differ significantly. ANCOVA and MANCOVA are other variations on ANOVA, and allow the researcher to control for the effects of covariates – variables which may be related to the dependent variable and which may confound the result. In this way, ANCOVA and MANCOVA provide "purer" results than their simple counterparts.

Multiway frequency analysis can be used to analyse categorical data from an experiment or categorical variables from a correlational study. It also can be used on interval or ratio data in instances in which your data do not meet the assumptions of the analysis of variance. Loglinear analysis is a form of multiway frequency analysis and is equivalent to an extension of the chi-square test of association.

Path analysis is used to test a clearly specified causal model. Using a theory, you develop a causal model, measure your variables, and then use a series of simple multiple regression analyses to derive path coefficients. The path coefficients are used as estimates of the magnitude of causal relationships among variables. Interpretation is facilitated by looking at both direct and indirect effects of variables. Structural equation modelling is a technique related to path analysis. It differs from path analysis in that it allows you to look at hypothetical variables called latent variables in your model.

Questions

1 What are the key assumptions and requirements of multivariate statistics?

2 How do various violations of the assumptions underlying multivariate statistics affect your data analysis? What can you do if these assumptions are violated?

3 When is factor analysis used?

4 Why are factors rotated in factor analysis?

5 What are logistic regression and discriminant function analysis used for, and what is the main difference between them?

6 When would you use a multivariate analysis of variance (MANOVA) to analyse your data?

7 How are the results of a MANOVA interpreted?

8 What is loglinear analysis, and when is it used?

9 What is path analysis, and how is it used in the research process?

10 Why is it important to develop a causal model when using path analysis?

11 When a structural model is diagrammed, what information is conveyed by the arrows leading from one variable to another?

12 What is structural equation modelling, and how does it differ from path analysis?

 Activities

1 Search through the results sections of recent journal articles to find examples of the techniques covered in this chapter. Make notes on how the results have been reported.

2 Select one (or more) of the topics covered in this chapter and make it your goal to read further on this topic. Consult other textbooks, journals and websites, with the aim of producing a two-page summary of your chosen test, its uses and how it should be interpreted.

3 Imagine a friend is planning on designing a study that will require analysis with multivariate statistical methods. What main advice would you give them? Write out a list of the main advantages and disadvantages associated with adopting a multivariate approach.

Chapter 22

Analysing Qualitative Data

OVERVIEW

The aim of this chapter is to introduce you to some of the main ways in which qualitative data can be analysed. We have already introduced you to some of the ideas underlying **qualitative research** and some of the methods of **qualitative data collection**. This chapter will look at what you do with qualitative data once it is collected. Techniques covered include content analysis, thematic analysis, Grounded Theory, Interpretative Phenomenological Analysis and discourse analysis. As you will see, each of these approaches makes different assumptions about the nature of knowledge and it is important that you recognize these fundamental differences as you read through the chapter. It is beyond the scope of this chapter to provide you with a full detailed discussion of the different approaches. If you require further information, you are recommended to consult one of the many texts on qualitative psychology (e.g. Banister et al., 1994; Parker, 2005; Richardson, 1996; Smith, 2003; Willig, 2008; Willig & Stainton-Rogers, 2008).

chs 10, 11

OBJECTIVES

After studying this chapter and working through the exercises, you should be able to:

- Discuss the role that epistemology plays in qualitative data analysis approaches
- Describe the aims and general analytic procedures of different qualitative data analysis approaches
- Distinguish between different qualitative data analysis approaches
- Critically evaluate different qualitative data analysis approaches
- Identify criteria that can be used to evaluate the quality of qualitative data analysis

Analysing qualitative data

Students often naively assume – based mainly on the fact that it is not statistics – that qualitative data analysis is an easy option. But if you think that this chapter is going to discuss wishy-washy, touchy-feely ways of summarizing data, then you are very much mistaken. Yes, qualitative data analysis does not involve calculating probabilities or producing regression equations, but what it does involve is rigorous analysis and interpretation of data. Qualitative data analysis most certainly is not easy and can often be extremely time-consuming and requires special skills that cannot be learnt overnight. However, it allows researchers to investigate areas which may be unsuitable for quantitative study (see **Chapter 10** for a discussion on this).

ch. 10 pp.186–190

Epistemology
A branch of philosophy that deals with the nature and origins of knowledge.

Epistemology plays an important role in qualitative data analysis. You were introduced to this in **Chapter 2** so there is no need to repeat everything here. However, you should be aware that different qualitative methodologies view knowledge in different ways and analysis reflects these different viewpoints. For example, some methods of analysis view language as reflecting an underlying truth or reality, whereas other approaches emphasize how language is used to construct reality. Some of the analytical techniques we will discuss, therefore, are allied to a particular epistemological or theoretical position and it is difficult to use such techniques effectively if you do not have a solid grounding in the appropriate theory.[1] For this reason, you are recommended to consult other qualitative psychology texts before conducting any of your own analysis (e.g. Banister et al., 1994; Parker, 2005; Richardson, 1996; Smith, 2003; Willig, 2008; much of what follows is based on these texts).

ch. 2 p.16

Despite theoretical and epistemological differences, the techniques covered in this chapter share some general similarities in analysis. Once transcription has taken place, data suitable for analysis are identified and coded. The coded material is then subjected to a particular analytic technique to identify patterns and themes. The analysis is then written up in the form of a report.

The techniques which we will discuss are some of the most popular methods for analysing qualitative data, but this is by no means an exhaustive list. The idea is to give you a flavour of the range of different methods and the particular focus of each method. The techniques discussed will be content analysis, thematic analysis, Grounded Theory, Interpretative Phenomenological Analysis and discourse analysis. Before reading any further, though, it is a good idea to refamiliarize yourself with the content of Chapter 11 and the different ways in which we can **collect qualitative data**.

ch. 11

Content analysis
Qualitative data analysis approach which converts qualitative data into categories which can then be quantified.

Content analysis

Content analysis is a technique which takes qualitative data and converts them into quantitative data, which can then be analysed statistically. Qualitative data are coded

---

1 In this chapter, and in qualitative research, "theory" can mean a number of things and is often used in a slightly different way to how we use it when talking about strictly scientific perspectives (such as those covered in Chapter 2). For example, in this chapter, when we talk about a "theoretical position" or "appropriate theory", we are referring to an epistemological position that is taken concerning the nature of knowledge. Some qualitative techniques will take a hard-line contructivist approach in which there is no such thing as "truth" and all knowledge is constructed. Others will take a less strict approach. The analysis techniques will reflect the underlying epistemological assumptions. Keep this in mind while going through this chapter.

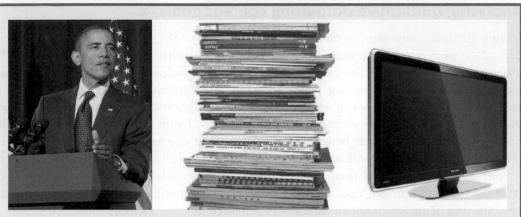

Figure 22.1 Content analysis can be used with a number of different media, e.g. political speeches, magazine articles, television programmes.
Source: © Vidura Luis Barrios/Alamy

according to (usually) predetermined categories, and the frequency of the categories can therefore be quantified and analysed.

The technique can be used with a number of different existing media, including writing, films, television, advertisements and political speeches (Figure 22.1). Occasionally, though, a researcher may collect new data specifically for the purpose of content analysis (e.g. diaries, verbal protocols). Although words are the most obvious type of item for investigation, content analysis can also be applied to other items, including characters, images or themes. For example, if you were interested in how weight was portrayed in the media, you could use content analysis in a number of ways. You could examine references in magazines to specific words such as "fat" or "skinny", or maybe you could look for certain themes in the magazines (e.g. someone being criticized for being overweight, or too thin), or even you could investigate the frequency of portrayal of characters who are significantly overweight or underweight in television drama programmes.

Sampling data

Before you do any analysis, however, you should think about how you will sample your data. Your research question will largely dictate what your sources will be, but you should aim to get a fairly representative sample. For instance, if you wanted to investigate the portrayal of older people in the media, you would need to identify which particular source(s) you will focus on (e.g. television, magazines, newspapers, radio) and the timescale you will be sampling (e.g. past month, past six months, past two years). If you opted for magazines, you would also need to consider what types of magazines you would choose in terms of topic, target readership, price, etc.

Analysing qualitative data using content analysis

Having identified your sources, the next stage is to consider the unit of analysis and this will depend on your research question, what is practicable and what will be most informative. In analysis involving magazines, for example, you could look at each article separately, or you could use a different unit of analysis (e.g. page, paragraph, line, sentence, word, every tenth page). If your research question focuses on whether a certain item exists within a unit or not, your choice of unit of analysis can make an important difference. So, if your unit of analysis is an article, no distinction would be made between an article with just one mention of a key word and an article with 30 mentions – both articles contain the key word and are coded as such. However, if your unit of analysis had been a paragraph or sentence, this difference would have been reflected. Of course, if your research question focuses on counting the frequency of use of an item, the unit of analysis is not an issue as you will be conducting a simple count.

Protocol analysis
Form of content analysis in which the data are verbal protocols.

A special version of content analysis is **protocol analysis** (e.g. Gilhooly & Green, 1996; Green & Gilhooly, 1996), which has been used predominantly in cognitive psychology to try to uncover thought processes while people are performing certain tasks. Participants are instructed to "think aloud" and say what they are thinking as they attempt the task. This verbal protocol is then transcribed and coded for analysis. For example, if the task in question was an anagram you may code for instances where participants rearrange letters, suggest a potential solution word, read out the letters in the anagram, discuss their own ability at anagrams, and so on. Once coded, you can then analyse the data and identify any similarities in how participants go about solving the problem.

Whatever type of material you decide to use, it is vital that you decide on clear categories with which to code the data. Some items will be easy to code (e.g. specific words), but others may be more difficult (e.g. a theme or character), so you should try to produce an unambiguous coding scheme. Categories are mutually exclusive – you should not have a section of data that could be coded in different ways – so your definitions should be clear and distinct enough to avoid this. This is especially important if you intend on having more than one person doing the coding.

Once you have coded the data you can do a number of different things with the analysis. You may want to simply present a table of frequencies for each category, or you may intend to use the quantitative data for subsequent analysis. Alternatively, you may want only to present categories and supporting examples from the data.

Critique of content analysis

A main benefit of using content analysis is that it is a useful way of summarizing qualitative data in a quantitative form, and thus allows for statistical analysis and comparison with other research. However, it has been criticized for not reflecting the detail and complexity of qualitative data, particularly if it consists of a simple word count. Content analysis also focuses on the overt meaning of items and tends to neglect the latent or hidden meaning of items. Nevertheless, content analysis has been a popular technique within psychology, but more researchers are now moving towards qualitative analysis of qualitative data.

In the Know

Example of content analysis in real-life research
Korr (2008) used content analysis to examine references to food in children's animated television programmes. He recorded 33 half-hour segments of children's programmes and coded the data for references to food. Verbal references were counted individually, but visual references were coded only once within each scene (e.g. a sandwich being eaten by a character throughout a scene would be counted only once). Each reference was coded as being a different food type (e.g. sweets, fruits and vegetables, meats, salty snacks), although Korr points out that this was often quite difficult to do in some instances (e.g. Krabby Patty sandwiches in *SpongeBob SquarePants*!).

Korr found that although sweets were referenced the most in the programmes (in 26.5% of the total references), fruits and vegetables were also referenced frequently (in 21.6% of all references). Compared to previous research, which found that adverts during children's television programmes referenced unhealthy foods, Korr concluded that the food referenced in children's television programmes was healthier than that shown in adverts. He recommends that parents should record their children's television viewing and fast forward through the advert breaks to ensure that their children see more positive nutritional messages.

Thematic analysis

Thematic analysis is sometimes confused with content analysis – true, the dividing line between them can be a bit hazy at times – but thematic analysis goes beyond the level of simple counts of items and instead looks for patterns, or themes, across whole sets of data. This identification, analysis and reporting of themes is part of the basic procedure of several other qualitative methodologies, so thematic analysis acts as a good foundation for qualitative researchers.

> **Thematic analysis**
> Qualitative data analysis approach which identifies and analyses patterns or themes across data-sets.

Another benefit of thematic analysis is that is flexible and versatile. Unlike some of the techniques we will discuss later in this chapter, thematic analysis is not allied to a specific theoretical framework and so can be applied to different frameworks and a number of different research topics. Coupled with the fact that it does not have one prescribed method, it is fairly accessible and easy to do.

You can use thematic analysis in a number of ways. For example, you could use it to provide a summary of the content of a set of qualitative data, or you may want to examine one theme, or a set of themes, in more detail. You may decide to use thematic analysis based on a particular existing theory, in which case you would probably already have some idea of the themes you would be investigating. Alternatively, the focus may not be on theory and you could adopt a more data-driven approach, letting the themes emerge directly from the data themselves.

The level at which you examine themes can vary too with thematic analysis. Braun and Clarke (2006) make a distinction between *semantic themes*, which are explicit in the data and focus on the surface meaning of what is being said or written, and *latent themes*, which are underlying and require more interpretation from the researcher. Usually, analysis focuses on one of these levels. This also touches on the issue of **epistemology** and means that thematic analysis can be conducted within a realist paradigm, where what is said or written is thought to

ch. 10
pp.178–185

reflect meaning and experience, or in a more constructionist paradigm, where meaning and experience are socially constructed.

Analysing qualitative data using thematic analysis

Although it is widely used, there is little agreement about how to do thematic analysis. However, Braun and Clarke (2006) have produced a helpful step-by-step guide which is well worth reading. What follows is based largely on this guide. Before any analysis can begin, you first need to collect your data. Usually this is in the form of written text or transcribed speech, and can be collected especially for the analysis, or can be pre-existing. The next stage is to familiarize yourself with the data through reading and rereading the data, making notes on any initial ideas or thoughts you may have. Once you are familiar with the data you can begin to start coding all the data in a systematic fashion, by noting important or interesting features of the data. This can be done in a variety of ways, including writing notes, highlighting, using Post-it notes, creating separate computer files, or you can use a computer program to help you. Note that you are not coding for themes just yet, so your codes do not need to be too broad. Just make sure that you identify anything of interest or which you may think is interesting.

Thematic map
Diagrammatic representation of the organization and relationships between themes and sub-themes; used in thematic analysis.

When the data have been coded thoroughly, you can move on to search for themes. To do this, you should collate all the codes and try to sort them into different themes and sub-themes. You may find it helpful to use some form of visual aid here to show how the codes, themes and any sub-themes are organized – for example, in a table or a **thematic map** (similar to a mind-map) (Figure 22.2), or even a pile of papers on the table. The end point for this part of the analysis is a set of themes and sub-themes, each with examples from the data to support them.

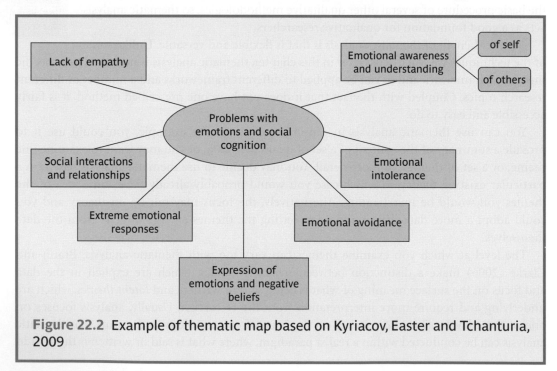

Figure 22.2 Example of thematic map based on Kyriacov, Easter and Tchanturia, 2009

The next phase of analysis is reviewing and refining the themes. You should look back over the coded data relating to a specific theme and decide whether you think the data fit the theme and form a consistent pattern. If not, you may need to amend the theme or reassign the data to a different theme. Once this has been done for all themes, you should consider your themes in relation to the whole data-set – do your themes and thematic map reflect your data-set? Again, there may need to be some revision of themes and recoding, and it is quite common for themes to be dropped or new themes to be created at this stage.

Now that you have a good idea of what your themes are and how they fit together, you are ready to define and name them. You need to think carefully about what the themes are about and the "story" that they tell. You should try to come up with a clear definition for each theme and a concise name.

The final stage of analysis is writing up the results. You should present a coherent analysis of the data, with sufficient evidence from the data. Importantly, your write-up should not just be a mere description of the data or a collection of extracts with little explanation, but should have an underlying argument that relates to the research question.

Critique of thematic analysis

As we have already mentioned, thematic analysis is a flexible technique, partly because it does not have ties to one particular epistemological or theoretical framework. However, this apparent lack of theory can also be seen as a disadvantage. There is no single agreed method of thematic analysis and, consequently, it does not have the same level of kudos as the "branded" forms of qualitative analysis (Braun & Clarke, 2006) that we will discuss later in this chapter. Thematic analysis can also be criticized for having limited interpretative power, and being unable to examine the complex and subtle ways in which language is used. Nonetheless, it offers an ideal starting point for those embarking on qualitative research for the first time.

In the Know

Example of thematic analysis in real-life research
Kyriacou et al. (2009) used thematic analysis to examine difficulties in emotions and social situations associated with anorexia nervosa (AN). They used focus groups and questionnaires to obtain data from patients with AN, carers and clinicians. Their analysis began by repeatedly going over each transcript and coding for references to emotion and social cognition. Constant comparison was then used to condense the emerging themes into the key themes.

Kyriacou et al. identified seven main themes: emotional awareness and understanding; emotional intolerance; emotional avoidance; emotional expression and negative beliefs; extreme emotional responses; social interactions and relationships; and lack of empathy. For example, under "emotional awareness and understanding", the authors identified that although patients lacked self-awareness of emotions, they were extremely sensitive to the emotions of others; this pattern was seen across all three groups of participants. Overall, Kyriacou et al. concluded that patients with AN have difficulty in dealing with the social and emotional demands of their everyday lives, and there is a degree of congruence across the three groups of participants, across most of the themes.

Grounded theory

Grounded theory
Qualitative data analysis approach which focuses on generating theory directly from data

Grounded Theory is one of the "branded" qualitative methodologies mentioned in the last section and is, in many ways, similar to thematic analysis. Grounded theory works from the bottom up, through a process of coding data, and progressively identifying categories and relationships between categories, eventually leading to the development of theory. It is important to note that in grounded theory categories and theory are not predetermined before analysis, but emerge directly from the data. In other words, the theory is "grounded" in the data. The point of grounded theory, therefore, is not to test or validate an existing theory, but to generate new context-specific theories which can explain a particular phenomenon.

Another important characteristic of grounded theory is that it is an inductive process, requiring researchers to continuously go back over data and review their analysis. This also means that data collection and analysis are not two distinct phases of research in grounded theory – data analysis tends to occur early on, and data collection and analysis can occur simultaneously. grounded theory can be used with a wide range of data, including those generated by semi-structured interviews, focus groups and diary studies.

Analysing qualitative data using grounded theory

After reading through the data a few times to familiarize yourself, analysing qualitative data using grounded theory begins by starting to code the data. Usually this is done line by line, as this encourages you to engage with the material in new ways, and thus ensures the analysis is truly grounded and covers the data in adequate detail. However, other units of analysis can also be used (e.g. sentence, paragraph, page).

Different researchers have different methods for coding data in grounded theory, but one of the more common approaches is to start with an open coding system, where each unit of analysis (e.g. line) is given a fairly descriptive label. As far as possible, these labels should come from the data themselves and can be words or phrases. Once you have these low-level codes, you should identify the ones that are the most frequent or most important, and go through the data in a more focused manner, looking for similarities and differences. This focused coding process means that you can sift through a large amount of data and begin to synthesize and integrate the data, producing higher level categories. It is these higher level categories which will inform your emerging theory.

Constant comparative analysis
Analytic technique used in grounded theory, involving repeated comparison of categories within and across accounts.

This process of going back and forth through the data making comparisons is called **constant comparative analysis** and is central to grounded theory. You could compare data from different participants, data from the same participant (e.g. within the same interview, from interviews recorded at different times), data with the category criteria, and categories with other categories.

Negative sampling
Analytic technique used in grounded theory involving the search for cases which do not fit the emerging theory.

Remember that you should look for similarities *and* differences. So, as well as building up categories, you should also try to break them down again. To do this, you should focus on differences within individual categories and try to identify any subcategories. You should also undertake **negative sampling** and look for cases that do not fit the emerging categories. In this way, the full detail of the data will not be forgotten, and you will devise a theory that will capture the complexity of the phenomenon in question.

Strauss and Corbin (1990) also recommend that you should use another type of coding, **axial coding**, to identify the dimensions of a category and how different categories are linked. They suggest that, when coding data, the researcher should focus on examples of "process" and "change" in the data. For example, the researcher may want to consider the specific context in which a category is based.

Axial coding
Coding technique used in grounded theory which focuses on the dimensions of categories.

It is essential that you keep a written record during analysis. In grounded theory, you should write memos, which give details of your categories and their components. Not only does this form a useful paper trail of your thoughts and decisions, but it also helps you with the development of theory as memo-writing encourages you to clarify your thinking and engage with the categories in new ways. A memo should include a clear definition of a category, give details on any subcategories, as well as reasoning and justification for decisions. You can also add details on any comparisons or links, ideas for areas to follow up in your reading on the topic, and any gaps in the analysis. Do not forget to add raw data and a date either. You should not worry too much about how the memo looks or is written – it is meant only for you and you can always edit it later. The important thing is to get your ideas down as quickly and clearly as possible.

As the analysis proceeds and you progressively develop your categories, you should continue collecting further data. This process of collecting more data in light of the emerging categories from data analysis is called **theoretical sampling**. The point of this is not to just check whether you can generalize your theory or whether you can replicate the analysis. Instead, you are collecting more data to help with the development of the theory. You may specifically go about collecting data which you think may help you to elaborate or challenge the theory. Perhaps you have identified a key category which you think needs more data, or maybe there is a gap in the analysis that needs addressing. However, sometimes it may not be practicable to use theoretical sampling, for example, when using existing data or when time and resources are limited. In this instance, you can use an abbreviated version of grounded theory and apply the coding procedures to the data without sampling further data. The full version of grounded theory should be the first option where possible, as this allows for a broader and more refined analysis, and means that you move constantly between data and memo-writing, and, consequently, your memos become more analytic and precise.

Theoretical sampling
The collection of new data to refine emerging theories in grounded theory analysis.

The ultimate goal of grounded theory is **theoretical saturation**, which is the point where collecting and coding new data does not add anything new: the categories and subcategories you have identified appear to account for the majority of the data. Clearly, this can be very difficult to achieve and is seen more as an ideal goal, rather than a reality. Nevertheless, by this stage you should be clear about the categories and subcategories which form the theory, the relationships between them, and the evidence to support them.

Theoretical saturation
The end point of grounded theory; occurs when the categories that have been coded account for all the data.

Analysis continues during the writing-up of your findings. The process of presenting your categories, the relationships between them and your logic behind the analysis, should help you to refine your conceptual analysis even further. Only at this stage should you go to the relevant literature and see how your work fits in.

Critique of grounded theory

Although we have presented a model of grounded theory, you should be aware that is there is disagreement between researchers about the precise details of analysis. One obvious area for differences of opinion is on how best to code the data, and some researchers feel that grounded theory is too prescriptive. This had led to the development of different coding paradigms.

Another issue related to grounded theory concerns epistemology and the nature of knowledge. For instance, the language of grounded theory discusses theory and categories as "emerging" from the data, suggesting that the researcher is merely finding something that is already there. This positivist approach to knowledge has been challenged by other researchers who say that we cannot ignore the role of the researcher. These researchers (e.g. Charmaz, 1990) have developed social constructionist versions of grounded theory which assume that categories and theories are constructed by the researchers interacting with the data, rather than merely arising out of the data.

In the Know

Example of Grounded Theory in real-life research
Abrams and Curran (2009) used grounded theory to examine understanding of the symptoms of post-partum depression (PPD) in low-income mothers, who are more likely to experience this disorder. They interviewed 19 low-income mothers about their own experiences of PPD and adopted a more constructionist version of grounded theory for analysis, since the focus was on how mothers constructed and understood their experiences of PPD.

Five main categories arose from the data, each made up of a number of properties:

1 ambivalence (composed of "I wasn't prepared for this baby", "I didn't want any more children");

2 caregiving overload ("Please stop crying", "I need a break", "I can't do this any more");

3 juggling ("No time to breathe", "Everyone depends on me", "Navigating the maze");

4 mothering alone ("I really don't have any help", "My baby has no father");

5 real-life worry ("I don't have the money", "Will my baby be OK?", "It's not safe here").

You will notice that many of the properties look as though they have come directly from a transcript – this suggests that the themes have clearly emerged from the data and were not driven by previous theory.

Overall, Abrams and Curran found that the main experience for these mothers was that mothering is overwhelming, and that many of the symptoms associated with PPD were related to the stresses and demands placed upon this low-income group.

Interpretative Phenomenological Analysis (IPA)
Qualitative data analysis approach which focuses on how individuals experience and make sense of the world.

Interpretative Phenomenological Analysis

Interpretative Phenomenological Analysis (IPA) aims to explore how individuals experience and make sense of the world, and is a popular qualitative methodology, particularly in health psychology and related fields. Like grounded theory, it is an inductive, bottom-up method of analysis, but here the focus is on what experiences, events and states mean to individuals.

Interpretative Phenomenological Analysis is based heavily on phenomenology, a branch of philosophy which emphasizes the individual's own perspective of the world. However, IPA acknowledges that it is impossible to gain complete access to and understanding of the "insider's perspective", and recognizes the fact that the researcher is making his or her own interpretation in the analysis (hence *Interpretative* Phenomenological Analysis). IPA therefore can be thought of as "the researcher . . . trying to make sense of the participants trying to make sense of their world" (Smith & Osborn, 2003, p. 51).

IPA is typically used with **semi-structured interviews** conducted on a small, homogeneous sample. In contrast to much other research, where researchers attempt to have a representative or random sample, IPA tries to have a sample which is closely defined. The data are then subjected to a case-by-case analysis. You should note that there is no single definitive way of doing IPA, but what is presented here should give you a fair indication of what to expect.

ch. 11
pp.201–207

Analysing qualitative data using IPA

The first stage in analysis using IPA is to make notes. You should look at the first interview transcript and read it through several times to ensure you are fully familiar. As you reread the transcript, note anything interesting or relevant. You could do this by writing notes in the left-hand margin of the transcript next to the appropriate line, or you could highlight the interesting words or phrases and write comments on these somewhere else. In contrast to Grounded Theory, there is no specific unit of analysis, so you do not need to write a comment for every line for example. Equally, there are no hard-and-fast rules about what your comments will consist of – you may want to summarize or paraphrase data; make notes of connections, similarities and differences; or note idiosyncrasies or unusual phrases or words.

Once you have commented on the transcript, you should return to the beginning and write down theme titles (e.g. in the right-hand margin or in a computer file). The theme titles should be at a higher, more abstract level than the comments and should make more use of psychological terminology. The titles should be concise, but should at the same time still capture the essence of the data, and this can be quite a difficult thing to achieve. You may well find that you end up using the same theme title several times throughout your transcript, and this is fine.

The next stage in analysis is to connect the themes and identify a structure. (Thus, this stage is quite similar to thematic analysis.) To do this, list all the emergent theme titles, and try to find connections and links between them. You may find that some themes cluster together quite naturally and others may suggest a hierarchical relationship. You should then list the theme titles again, but re-order them according to your new clusters and groupings.

Next, you should go back to the data and check that your themes and connections actually work for the data. You may find that some themes need to be dropped at this stage. You should make a note of any phrases or extracts which fit your themes, and produce a table of themes. In this table, the themes should be in a coherent order, and should consist of theme titles along with any underlying sub-themes. You should also provide an identifier for evidence for each theme and subtheme. For example, 1.16 would indicate page 1, line 16 as an appropriate piece of evidence (Table 22.1).

Having completed this process for the first transcript, you can then move on to do the same for the next transcript. You can either start to code the second transcript using the themes that

Table 22.1 Example of table of themes from IPA study looking at experiences of moving to a new city for work or study

Emergent themes	Page reference (page.line)	Example quote
1. Positive emotions		
a. Excitement	1.21	"excited"
b. Anticipation	3.12	"looking forward to it"
2. Negative emotions		
a. Scared	1.20	"a bit frightened and scared"
b. Lost	1.6	"felt like I didn't know anybody . . . felt a bit lost"
c. Uncertainty	4.5	"didn't know what to expect"
3. Change and development		
a. A new start	5.4	"a fresh start"
b. New friends	6.8	"meet new people and make new friends"
c. Change of environment	4.20	"a new city, first time away from home"
d. Independence	5.10	"independent"

emerged from analysis of the first transcript, or you can start from the beginning all over again. Either way, you need to be careful that you can identify recurring themes as well as identifying new themes in the new transcript.

After you have analysed all of the transcripts, you will have a final table of themes, which summarizes the themes and evidence for the whole data-set. You may decide to cut down the number of themes further, by identifying themes that occur consistently through the data. As a general rule of thumb, if more than half of the participants report a theme, it can be considered to be recurrent.

Your analysis will continue as you write up your findings. You should present your themes (or recurrent themes) in a coherent way, providing a clear narrative of your themes, what they mean, what evidence supports them, and what this tells us about how individuals experience their world.

Critique of IPA

Interpretative Phenomenological Analysis is a useful technique for examining people's lives and is suitable for a variety of research topics. However, one criticism is that is takes a realist perspective – it assumes that the data used in analysis describe reality and can tell us about how individuals actually experience and make meaning of the world. In contrast, some would question whether individuals have the necessary skill in language to convey this level of meaning. Another criticism of IPA is that although it recognizes the active role of the researcher, it does not specify how this should be used in analysis. Finally, some researchers believe that IPA is useful for describing people's lives, but lacks explanatory power.

In the Know

Example of IPA from real-life research
Green et al. (2009) used IPA to analyse data from 10 interviews with members of a slimming club about their experiences of dieting and dieting failure. They identified five main themes: dieting mode (reflecting the idea of participants adopting a particular mindset or mode when dieting); multi-me (internal battle and multiple selves); not me (factors seemingly outwith participants' control, such as biological conditions and addiction); modern life (the pace of modern life, lack of time, influence of marketing); and challenges of emotional and social eating (using eating to regulate emotions). The range of themes tells us that there is a range of explanations for dieting failure, and that there may be no one easy solution for the problem.

Discourse analysis

The main focus of **discourse analysis** is discourse itself – that is to say all forms of text and speech. The discourse may be pre-existing or collected specifically for the research but, either way, the analysis centres on the content and organization of the discourse. In contrast to some of the qualitative approaches we have considered, discourse analysis does not accept that language can directly inform us about internal states and describe reality. Instead, it views language as being constructive – it constructs social reality and is used to achieve certain social objectives. People use discourse to do specific things and this all exists within a social context. Consequently, the meaning of a fairly neutral-sounding phrase such as "I missed the bus" depends on the social context. It may used as an excuse for being late for an appointment, to blame someone who stopped you from getting the bus on time, or as an implicit request for a friend to give you a lift in their car next time.

Discourse analysis is not a method that can be used "off the shelf" (Gill, 1996) as it requires quite a fundamental shift in epistemological position and there is no single "how to" guide. It is recommended that discourse analysis should not be attempted without first being familiar with its theoretical framework. So although we will give you a flavour of discourse analysis here, if you are serious about using it, you really should do a lot more further reading around the topic (e.g. Gill, 1996; Willig, 2001).

Willig (2008) identifies two main types of discourse analysis: **Discursive Psychology** and **Foucauldian discourse analysis**. In Discursive Psychology the focus is on how people use discourse to achieve certain objectives in social contexts, whereas in Foucauldian discourse analysis (named after Michel Foucault), the focus is more on the subjects and objects that are constructed by discourse, and how these constructions relate to subjectivity, power relations and a feeling of self.

> **Discourse analysis**
> Qualitative data analysis approach which focuses on discourse and how language constructs social reality.

> **Discursive Psychology**
> Form of discourse analysis which focuses on how people use discourse to achieve certain interpersonal objectives.

> **Foucauldian discourse analysis**
> Form of discourse analysis which focuses on how discourse constructs subjects and objects.

Analysing qualitative data using Discursive Psychology discourse analysis

The starting point for analysis in Discursive Psychology is the collection of data. This is usually in the form of naturally occurring text and speech, such as natural conversations, although you may collect data for analysis in the form of interviews or focus groups. The data should then be transcribed carefully, including non-linguistic features such as speech errors, pauses, emphasis and changes in volume, which could affect the meaning of what is being said. Note that this type of transcription can be particularly time-consuming.

The data are then ready for analysis. This first stage is immersing yourself in the text through careful reading and rereading of the transcripts. This is followed by the process of coding, or selecting the material which will be used for analysis. You should go through the transcripts highlighting anything that is relevant to the research question, even if it is only loosely related. Remember that the topic of interest may not always be explicit, so be aware that you need to look "beneath the surface".

Having coded the material, the next stage is analysing it. Unlike some other qualitative approaches in which you are trying to summarize or condense, analysis in Discursive Psychology requires you to focus on the detail in the text. Potter and Wetherell (1987, p. 168) suggest that during this stage you ask yourself: "Why am I reading this passage in this way? What features produce this reading?" Gill (1996) recommends that you look for patterns in the data in terms of differences and consistency both within and between different accounts. You may identify what are called **interpretative repertoires**, or consistent ways of saying something. For example, you may focus on favoured metaphors and figures of speech, or particular grammatical or stylistic features – why have they been used? What does this tell us? You should also think about the context in which the discourse is taking place and this will tell you something about its function. Remember to keep detailed notes as you go through the analysis.

Interpretative repertoires Consistent ways of saying something identified in discourse analysis.

By now, you should have formulated some ideas about the functions of certain features in the text, and it is time to go back to the data to check that the material supports your ideas. This analysis is then refined further when you write it up. You may decide to organize your discussion according to interpretative repertoires you have identified or perhaps to the different functions and strategies uncovered in your analysis.

Foucauldian discourse analysis

Whereas Discursive Psychology focuses specifically on text and speech, Foucauldian discourse analysis can be used with a very wide range of materials. Indeed, any symbolic system (e.g. sign language, advertisements, and even gardens and cities) can be analysed, although text does seem to be the most common type of data. There is little consistency in how to do Foucauldian discourse analysis and, as it requires you to be thoroughly grounded in the appropriate philosophy to even understand any available guidelines, we will not go into too much detail here. However, essentially this type of analysis involves going through the data looking for instances of the "discursive object" of interest and thinking about the different ways in which the discursive object can be constructed in the discourse. How these different constructions relate to wider existing discourses is considered, along with what the constructions tell us about the function of these constructions, the context in which they are placed and how this relates to subjective experience.

Critique of discourse analysis

As you may have noticed, parts of discourse analysis seem a bit vague, and this lack of detail and consistency in approach can be considered a criticism. It mystifies the approach and can make it seem elitist (see Braun & Clarke, 2006). However, it could be said that having strict guidelines goes against the principles of discourse analysis. Some researchers disagree with the radical epistemological stance of discourse analysis and believe that, although language is important, it cannot account for everything. If you intend to adopt discourse analysis as a methodology, you need to consider if you are willing to sign up to its particular theoretical framework as, rather than being a simple method of analysis, it represents a different way of thinking.

In the Know

Examples of discourse analysis in real-life research
Riley et al. (2009) used discourse analysis to analyse data from pro-anorexia and anorexia-recovery website discussion forums, focusing on body-talk (i.e. text communication about bodies and experiences related to the body). They collected over 200 posts to the discussion forums and coded the data for references to the body. Three different types of body-talk were identified: "descriptions of the body", "descriptions of doing something with the body" and "bodily experiences and sensations". As an illustration, consider the first of these – "descriptions of the body". Riley et al. found that both types of site included descriptions of forum members' bodies in discussion posts. They argue that these descriptions functioned to portray forum members as appropriate members of such a website, as well as constructing an idea of the ideal body size – small for the pro-anorexia sites and small but healthy for the recovery sites. In other words, Riley et al. were not merely focusing on what was being written about the body, but why and what function that serves.

Johnson et al. (2004) conducted a study which also looked at discourse on the body, but this time in pregnant mothers and using Foucauldian discourse analysis. (They also used IPA as part of their analysis.) They interviewed six first-time mothers during the latter stages of their pregnancy about bodily changes associated with pregnancy. In their analysis they identified three discursive constructions (or objects): "pregnancy-as-transgressing-the-idealized-female-body", "pregnancy-as-legitimizing-transgression" and "pregnancy-as-transgressing-the-usual-boundaries". These constructions were related to a wider discourse of femininity, with a focus on how women are valued in terms of their looks and their reproductive function. For example, the pregnant women described their body using negative terms (e.g. "fat", "bloated"), which reflects the notion of the thin-ideal female body. Johnson et al. also examined how these discursive constructions were used in other contexts (e.g. women's pregnant bodies described in negative terms by friends and family). They concluded that the discursive constructions were often difficult to deal with and were likely to result in negative experiences.

Evaluating qualitative research

When considering quality in quantitative research, we talk about reliability and validity. These concepts can be applied to quantitative analysis of qualitative data in content analysis, but in qualitative analysis these concepts are almost irrelevant as they make the assumption that there is a "correct" reality to which we are aspiring. As you will have seen, some qualitative approaches do not accept this epistemological viewpoint. This then leaves the question – how then do you evaluate the quality of qualitative analysis?

One way is to ask whether the analysis is coherent and consistent. The analysis should be presented in a logical manner, which makes it clear to the reader how the analysis was done, what the main findings were, and how a theoretical framework is integrated into the analysis.

Good qualitative research should also be clearly supported by the data. Analytic themes and categories should fit the data and there should be sufficient examples of evidence. Additionally, the researcher should report a clear rationale for how and why they arrived at the labels and categories they have used. This is aided by keeping good notes and memos during analysis.

Triangulation

The process of assessing the outcome of a piece of research by viewing it from a number of differing perspectives. If the perspectives converge on the same conclusion, "triangulation" can be said to have occurred.

Triangulation is another way in which you can evaluate the quality of qualitative research. We covered this briefly in Chapter 10, but, to recap, this is when you use different methods, sources of information or even researchers to investigate the same topic. By combining these different perspectives, potential bias, problems or gaps in coverage associated with a particular method, researcher or source of data will be limited, thus producing a richer and potentially more valid analysis.

Another idea to consider is going back to participants and asking them to validate the analysis and the interpretation of their responses. This could be done early on in the analysis or even as the analysis being written up. Although this can be very useful, there is the question of power relationships with the participant and researcher, and what should be done if there are disagreements.

Some approaches, such as grounded theory, recommend that you try to find examples of negative cases, which do not appear to fit an emerging theory, thus requiring the theory to be amended and refined. However, Coolican (2008) notes that it is problematic to use an analytic process *and* then as a method of checking quality at a later stage. Other qualitative approaches, such as IPA, even allow researchers to eliminate data which do not fit the emerging analysis.

Other criteria relate to the researcher. For example, they should feel that they have clarified or learned something new about the topic of interest. Elliott et al. (1999) refer to this as a feeling of "resonance". But perhaps one of the most important criteria is reflexivity – the researcher should acknowledge the part that they have played in the analysis and recognize how their subjectivity has influenced the analysis. For this reason, it is quite common to see a reflexive account included in **qualitative research reports**, where the researcher discusses these sorts of issues.

ch. 25
pp.634–635

Qualitative data analysis: a final thought

Now that you have read through this chapter, we hope that you will see that qualitative data analysis is not necessarily an easier option compared to statistics. To do qualitative data analysis well takes time – to become familiar with epistemological or theoretical frameworks, to collect and transcribe data, to immerse oneself in the data, to code the data, to analyse data, to develop the skills required for analysis, and to write up the analysis. The methods we discussed cannot be learned by merely reading through short sections in a textbook – you need to read widely and get out there and have a go for yourself.

Summary

In this chapter you were introduced to some of the main ways in which researchers analyse qualitative data. Content analysis is used to convert qualitative data into quantitative data suitable for analysis. A wide range of data can be used for content analysis, including verbal protocols from "think aloud" studies. Thematic analysis involves the identification and analysis of patterns or themes across sets of data, and is a flexible technique. However, it has been criticized for its lack of theoretical framework and tends to have less kudos than some other qualitative methods. Grounded theory focuses on developing theory that emerges directly from the data. The full version of grounded theory requires simultaneous coding of categories and collection of data, producing a broad and refined analysis. Interpretative Phenomenological Analysis is another bottom-up, data-driven form of analysis, but here the focus is on trying to analyse how individuals understand and make sense of the world. Discourse analysis is one of the more radical qualitative approaches and is based on the assumption that language is used to construct reality. Discursive Psychology emphasizes how people use discourse to achieve certain interpersonal objectives, whereas Foucauldian discourse analysis focuses on how objects and subjects are constructed through discourse. Finally, criteria for evaluating qualitative research were discussed, including coherence, good data fit, triangulation and reflexivity.

Questions

1 What factors should you consider when deciding on data for use in content analysis?
2 What are the main advantages and disadvantages of thematic analysis?
3 What is the general aim of grounded theory?
4 What are the main similarities and differences between grounded theory and Interpretative Phenomenological Analysis?
5 What type of research questions can be addressed using Interpretative Phenomenological Analysis?
6 Describe the epistemological position adopted by discourse analysis. How does this influence analysis?
7 What are the main ways in which qualitative analysis methods can be evaluated?

Activities

1 Select a magazine article on a topic of your choice and analyse the data using both content analysis and thematic analysis. Think carefully about how the two types of analysis differ and what type of research questions could be addressed.
2 Search the literature for examples of journal articles which use the approaches discussed in this chapter. Make notes on how the analysis is presented and written up. Using the different criteria for evaluating qualitative analysis, evaluate the analysis in each of the articles you have selected.

SECTION 4

The Research Process in Context

Chapter 23

Planning Research

OVERVIEW

Undertaking a research project involves careful planning. There are many things that have to be planned in advance. This chapter will start with the difficult question "how do we get ideas for research?" and will move on to offer advice and tips on the practical aspects of research, from conducting literature searches and critically reading articles to conducting your data collection and dealing with participants and data.

OBJECTIVES

After studying this chapter and working through the exercises, you should be able to:

- State where research ideas might come from
- Give an account of what constitutes a good research question
- Identity what things must be considered at the start of any research project, both conceptually and practically
- Conduct a literature search using both academic databases and other sources
- Critically evaluate research articles
- Show an awareness of the practical aspects of planning and carrying out research

All I need now is an idea . . .

Getting a good idea for a research project is not as easy as it sounds, and there are no hard-and-fast rules for coming up with one. It's not easy to say where good ideas come from. Many people are capable of coming up with worthwhile ideas but find it difficult to verbalize the process by which they are generated. Cartoonists know this – they show a brilliant idea as a lightbulb flashing over a person's head. But how do we switch that lightbulb on? Let's consider five sources of ideas: common sense, observation of the world around us, theories, previous research and real-world problems.

Common sense

Many people say that psychology is "just common sense". Sometimes this is true and sometimes it is not, but we can sometimes get inspiration from things that we suppose are true. Do "opposites attract" or do "birds of a feather flock together"? Is a "picture worth a thousand words"? Asking questions like these can lead to research programmes studying attraction, social groupings and the role of visual images in learning and memory.

Testing a common-sense idea can be valuable because such notions don't always turn out to be correct, or research may show that the real world is much more complicated than our common-sense ideas would have it. For example, pictures can help people remember things under certain circumstances, but sometimes pictures actually make learning worse (see Levin, 1983). Conducting research to test common-sense ideas often forces us to go beyond a common-sense theory of behaviour, which in itself is useful to know.

The world around us

If you have chosen to study psychology, then you have probably been paying close attention to how people behave in the world around you. The world around us is a rich source of material for investigation. Observations of personal and social events can provide psychologists with many ideas for research, and the curiosity that is sparked by your observations and experiences can lead you to ask questions about all sorts of phenomena. It is this type of curiosity that drives many students to engage in their first research project.

In the Know

Getting inspired by the world around you
When he was a student, psychologist Michael Lynn worked as a waiter and depended on tips from customers to supplement his wages. The experience sparked an interest that fuelled an academic career (Crawford, 2000). For many years, Lynn studied tipping behaviour in restaurants and hotels in the USA and in other countries. He looked at factors that increase the tips that people give, such as posture, touching and what phrases customers might see on their bill. Lynn's research has had an impact on the hotel and restaurant industry. If you have ever worked in restaurants, you have undoubtedly formed many of your own hypotheses about tipping behaviour. Lynn went one step further and took a scientific approach to testing his ideas. His research illustrates that taking a scientific approach to a problem can lead to new discoveries and important applications.

We should also mention the role of *serendipity* – sometimes the most interesting discoveries are the result of accident or sheer luck. Ivan Pavlov is best known for discovering what is called classical conditioning – a neutral stimulus (such as a tone), if paired repeatedly with an unconditioned stimulus (food) that produces a reflex response (salivation), will eventually produce the response when presented alone. But Pavlov didn't set out to discover classical conditioning. Instead, he was studying the digestive system in dogs by measuring their salivation when given food. He accidentally discovered that the dogs were salivating prior to the actual feeding, and then studied the ways that the stimuli preceding the feeding could produce a salivation response.

Theories

ch. 2
pp.28–36

We have already mentioned theories in Chapter 2. **Theories** serve two important functions in increasing our understanding of behaviour. First, theories *organize and explain* a variety of specific facts or descriptions of behaviour. These facts and descriptions are not very meaningful by themselves, and so we need theories to impose a framework on them, which allows us to make sense of them as a whole. This framework makes the world more comprehensible by providing a few abstract concepts around which we can organize and explain a variety of behaviours.

Theories also *generate new knowledge*. Psychological theories do this by making predictions about new aspects of behaviour or new psychological phenomena – they guide our observations of the world. A good theory should generate hypotheses, and the researcher conducts studies to see whether these hypotheses are correct. If the studies confirm the hypotheses, the theory is supported. As more and more evidence accumulates that is consistent with the theory, we become more confident that the theory is correct.

Theory
A logically organized set of propositions (claims, statements, assertions) that serves to define events (concepts), describe relationships among these events and explain the occurrence of these events.

Previous research

Another source of ideas is research that has already been done. Science is cumulative and you will need to know what has been found in the past if you're ever going to be able to make your own contribution. Becoming familiar with a body of research on a topic is perhaps the best way to generate ideas for new research. The more you know about a research area, the easier it will be to identify what gaps there are in knowledge that require further research.

Because the results of research are published, researchers can use the body of past literature on a topic to continually refine and expand our knowledge. Just about every study raises further questions that can be addressed in future research. The research may lead to an attempt to apply the findings in a different setting, to study the topic with a different sample or to use a different methodology to replicate the results.

In addition, as you become familiar with the research literature on a topic, you may see inconsistencies in research results that need to be investigated, or you may want to study alternative explanations for the results. Sometimes you might just flat out disagree with the conclusions that a researcher has drawn, the method that they have employed or the basic premise from which they started. In these cases you can design a study that will see whether your suspicions are justified. Also, what you know about one research area often can be successfully applied to another research area, and it is often useful to look at one area of research from the perspective of someone familiar with another area.

In the Know

Doing new research based on potentially flawed previous research – facilitated communication in autism
Childhood autism is characterized by a number of symptoms including severe impairments in language and communication ability. Recently, parents and care providers have been encouraged by a technique called "facilitated communication" that apparently allows an autistic child to communicate with others by pressing keys on a keyboard showing letters and other symbols. A facilitator holds the child's hand to facilitate the child's ability to determine which key to press. With this technique, many autistic children begin communicating their thoughts and feelings and answer questions posed to them. Most people who see facilitated communication in action regard the technique as a miraculous breakthrough.

The conclusion that facilitated communication is effective is based on a comparison of the autistic child's ability to communicate with and without the facilitator. The difference is impressive to most observers. Scientists, however, are sceptical by nature. They examine all evidence carefully and ask whether claims are justified. In the case of facilitated communication, Montee et al. (1995) noted that the facilitator may be unintentionally guiding the child's fingers to type meaningful sentences. In other words, the facilitator, and not the autistic individual, is controlling the communication. Montee et al. conducted a study to test this idea. In one condition, both the facilitator and the autistic child were shown a picture, and the child was asked to indicate what was shown in the picture by typing a response with the facilitator. This was done on a number of trials. In another condition, only the child saw the pictures. In a third condition, the child and facilitator were shown different pictures (but the facilitator was unaware of this fact). Consistent with the hypothesis that the facilitator is controlling the child's responses, the pictures were correctly identified only in the condition in which both saw the same pictures. Moreover, when the child and facilitator viewed different pictures, the child never made the correct response, and usually the picture the facilitator had seen was the one identified.

Real-world problems

Research is also stimulated by practical problems that can have immediate applications. Groups of city planners and citizens might survey bicycle riders to determine the most desirable route for a city bicycle path, for example. On a larger scale, researchers have guided public policy by conducting research on the effects of exposure to pornographic materials or violent video games, as well as other social and health issues. Doing this type of research is an example of the "applied" research that we mentioned in Chapter 2.

ch. 2 p.27

Developing a good research question

Having a good idea for research is not enough. You may be able to come up with the most creative and unique research question based on experience, theory, or real-world problems, but you must also translate your idea into a good research. If you do not do this, then your good idea will forever remain just that – an idea. This section describes how to identify good research questions, and suggests what kinds of questions are likely to be important.

Asking answerable questions

The first step in developing a workable research project is to ask the kind of question that can be answered by using the scientific method. This sounds obvious, but it's worthwhile getting into the habit of asking yourself whether any particular question that you might ask is actually answerable. Not all questions are, and we mentioned some of them in **Chapter 2**. Here are a few more unanswerable questions; why is there suffering in the world? Is stem-cell research morally acceptable? What makes a work of art "beautiful"?[1] We have said it a few times already in this book, but students sometimes find a question that is definitely interesting, but which is very difficult to actually answer. Linked to this is the importance of asking empirical questions.

ch. 2
Table 2.2

Asking empirical questions

The questions above are not answerable by scientific means because the answers cannot be obtained through objective observation. If you are intending to do quantitative research then you must be sure that your questions are empirical. To be empirical, an observation must be as objective as possible, be made under precisely defined conditions, must be reproducible when those same conditions are present again, and must be confirmable by others. Here are some examples of **empirical questions**:

> **Empirical question**
> A question that can be answered through objective observation.

- Do males and females cope differently with terrorism?
- Do men and women prefer different characteristics in potential mates?
- Does a deprived early environment result in lower intelligence?
- Is punishment an effective tool in socializing children?

All these questions can be answered through well-designed and carefully conducted research. Unlike the first set of questions above, the second set identifies variables that can be defined in terms of observable characteristics. For example, the question of whether males and females cope differently with terrorism asks about the relationship between two observable variables: gender and coping skills (although what is meant by "terrorism" in this context would have to be carefully defined).

Some questions seem to be empirical but are formulated too broadly to make appropriate observations. Consider the following example of such a question: do children who are raised in a permissive atmosphere lack self-discipline as adults? Before this question can be answered, a number of preliminary questions must be addressed. What exactly is a permissive atmosphere? How do we measure it? Exactly what does it mean to lack self-discipline, and how do we determine when self-discipline is present or absent? Until you can specify exactly what these terms mean and how to measure the variables they represent, you cannot answer the original question. Again, we have covered this already – in the section in Chapter 3 on "**Constructs and operational definitions**".

ch. 3
p.49

---

1 It is important to distinguish questions like this from other similar questions that might be amenable to qualitative research. For example, we might be able to do research on what people view as "beautiful" or what people's views are on stem-cell research. These are subtly different questions, however, because they do not actually get at the inherent nature of "beauty" or the absolute moral status of stem-cell research. Rather they are questions about people's subjective opinions on these things, rather than the things themselves.

Questions for qualitative research

Qualitative research questions do not always have to be empirical in the same way that quantitative questions do. We mentioned in Chapter 10 that many **qualitative approaches** to research do not subscribe to empiricism and so the criteria that we would normally use to determine quantitative hypotheses do not apply. Instead, research questions are formulated that might address the way individuals make sense of their world or that might attempt to describe the way people behave in situations. Qualitative research questions are often discursive in nature, meaning that the focus will either be on the way that the participant under study verbalizes his or her understanding, or on the way the researcher interprets what is being studied. As such, qualitative research questions do not usually concern themselves with the problems of finding out about "objective reality" in the way that quantitative empirical methods would.

Asking important questions

Whatever question you decide to address in your research should also be of some importance. Researching a question imposes demands on your time, financial resources and the institution's available space. Researching a question makes demands on the available population of human participants or animal subjects. These resources should not be expended to answer trivial questions. Whether a question is important is often difficult to determine. In the past, valuable information has occasionally been obtained in the course of answering an apparently mundane question. Some questions that at one time seemed terribly important to answer now appear trivial. However, some rough guidelines will help in identifying important questions.

Important questions

A question is probably important if answering it will clarify relationships among variables known to affect the behavioural/psychological system under study. For example, knowing that memory tends to deteriorate with time since learning, you would want to establish the rate of deterioration as a function of time. You would want to identify how the amount of initial practice, over-learning, previous learning, activity during the retention interval, and other such factors interact to determine the rate of forgetting under specified conditions.

A question is probably important if the answer can support only one of several competing models or theoretical views. As noted in **Chapter 2**, developing and testing such questions is at the heart of the scientific method. The answers to such questions allow you to "home in" on a proper interpretation of the data. On the negative side, if the theories under test are later discarded, research designed to test the theories may become irrelevant unless the findings demonstrate clearly interpretable empirical relationships that must be accounted for by any future theory that might come along.

A question is probably important if its answer leads to obvious practical application. (However, the lack of obvious practical application does not automatically mean that the question is unimportant!) Much research has been conducted to identify working conditions that maximize productivity and job satisfaction or to screen drugs for potential effectiveness in controlling psychosis. Few would argue that the answers to these problems are unimportant.

Unimportant questions

In contrast, a question is probably unimportant if its answer is already firmly established, meaning that the results have been replicated (duplicated) by different scientists and that the scientists agree that the finding does occur under the stated conditions. Unless serious deficiencies are identified in the methods used to establish those answers, performing the research again is likely to be a waste of time.

A question is probably unimportant if the variables under scrutiny are known to have small effects on the behaviour of interest and if these effects are of no theoretical interest. A question is also probably unimportant if there is no *a priori* reason to believe that the variables in question are causally related. Research aimed at determining whether the temperature of a room affects memory recall for faces may turn out to have surprising and useful results. However, without a reason to expect a relationship in the first place, such research would amount to a "fishing expedition" (when researchers conduct research without any real justification, to "fish" for effects) that would be unlikely to pay off. The time would be better spent pursuing more promising leads.

When you have identified your research idea, the next step is to develop it to the point at which you can specify testable hypotheses and define the specific methods to be used to test these hypotheses. This is the stage at which you have to give serious thought to what it is you are going to do, and how you are going to do it.

Thinking about your research

We cannot stress how important it is to think about the design of your study as early as possible in the research process. In fact, you should try to get into the habit of always repeating the mantra "how am I going to do this?" whenever you're coming up with ideas for research or whenever you are developing research questions. The simple reason you should do this is so you do not end up wasting lots of time on an idea that is impossible to turn into a tangible piece of research. There is nothing more frustrating than realizing that you have been wasting your time. To prevent this, you need to be thinking about how you might operationalize your constructs. Once you manage to **operationally define** your constructs (which, remember, means specifying what they are and how you are going to measure them) you then need to think about whether you can actually make those measurements. Do you have the measurement tools at your disposal? Most of the time, this will be a practical matter; there is no point in pursuing research that requires a brain-scanner if you do not have access to a brain scanner. On many occasions, you will find yourself answering the question "how will I measure this?" by answering "with a questionnaire". This can present its own problems. First, is there already a questionnaire that has been used in the past to measure the thing that you are interested in? If there is, do you have access to it? Not all questionnaires and measurement scales are in the public domain. Sometimes they will be published as part of a journal article describing that area of research. If that is the case, then you will have to get **access to the article**. In other cases (specifically when you want to measure personality or intelligence) the questionnaire or measurement scale will be under copyright and you (or, more likely, your institution) will have to pay to use it. In these instances, you will have to see whether your institution owns the questionnaire that you wish to use, and

ch. 3
p.49

p.582

whether you are entitled to use it in your research. If not, then you will have to see whether or not your institution would be willing to buy it for you (and these instruments can sometimes be quite expensive). If they agree to this, you will have to order it from the publisher. If they do not agree, you will have to come up with an alternative measurement instrument. It is sometimes possible to create your own, but unless you are experienced in doing this, it can often be more work than it is worth, especially if it is something that will require to be tested for its validity and reliability, etc. This is an issue that often trips up students, so you should think about the measurement instruments you think you might use quite early in the process, because it can be quite time-consuming tracking down materials that aren't immediately available.

Which design? Which analysis?

We have said this so many times that we are at risk of boring ourselves as well as you, but you do need to spend some time thinking about the design of your study, and this should happen very early in the whole process. The reason for this is that knowing what design you will be using will often make decisions further down the line easier. At the same time (yes, the *same time*) as you decide on your design, you should also decide upon your method of analysis. Design and analysis go hand in hand, but too often people are frightened of the analysis, which causes them to put it off until later. Designing a study without thinking about how the data are to be analysed is a recipe for disaster, because you run the risk of getting to the end of your study, having all of your data in front of you and not having a clue what to do with any of it. If you are extremely unlucky, you might find that the data you have collected are unable to be analysed in any meaningful way, or could have been collected in a form that was more amenable to a more appropriate form of analysis. This is easily avoided by making decisions on the design and the analysis at the same time. If you are apprehensive about statistics, *do not* put thinking about the analysis off until you've collected the data, because this will only make things worse. It seems counter-intuitive, but thinking about the analysis early will make the whole thing less painful rather than more.

Quantitative or qualitative?

Another early decision you should make is whether to do qualitative or quantitative research. In most cases, this decision should be fairly easy to make and will be linked to the question that you have asked and how you plan to measure the constructs that you are interested in. If you choose to do a qualitative study, then many of the same rules apply as when you undertake a quantitative one. You will have to have a well-defined research question and a clear idea of what your aims are. You will have to think about the type of data you want to gather and how you plan to analyse this data. Do not be fooled into thinking that qualitative research is easier. When undertaking research, many students think that doing qualitative research is a good way of avoiding having to do statistics. In many ways it is even more time-consuming and the analysis, although of a different sort to statistical quantitative analyses, can be equally as difficult to do. The best advice we can offer is that your design should be appropriate to the research question. There is nothing to stop you adopting a mixed-method approach and using both qualitative and quantitative methods, if the phenomenon lends itself to being studied using each type of approach. If you have a full and thorough understanding of your area, then it should be clear what the most appropriate method is to answer the question that you have set. And how do you get a full and thorough understanding of your area? You need to become familiar with the literature . . .

Searching the literature

Before conducting any research project, an investigator must have a thorough knowledge of previous research findings. Even if the basic idea has been formulated, a review of past studies will help the researcher clarify the idea and design the study. It is therefore important to know how to search the literature on a topic and how to read research reports in professional journals.

Why do a literature search?

Scientists do not conduct a research project as soon as they get an idea. One reason is that someone else may have already had the same idea and already published on it. Another reason is that reading the literature may improve the original idea. **Literature searches** also show who else is interested in similar ideas, and they reveal the history of research about the topic.

> **Literature search**
> An organized and thorough search of all the literature published on a topic.

The answer may already be known

By consulting the literature, scientists may find the answer to their research question without having to conduct their own research project. An important feature of science is publishing research findings, which allows future researchers to build on what has been done before.

Your own research will be improved

By reading the literature, scientists refine and sharpen their ideas. By knowing the research others have published, they can design better and more important research projects. Previous projects often provide examples of materials, control procedures, statistical tests and background information that are helpful to your research.

Connects you to the research community

Reading the literature is also an avenue to the worldwide community of those interested in the same topic. As part of your project, you can explore and enter that community. Technology (primarily the Internet) has made the process of joining scientific communities easier than ever, and has removed many geographical barriers. It is exciting to find others who are interested in the same ideas that you are.

Shows the history of topics

By reading the literature, scientists learn the history of their topic. A literature search tells them how popular a topic is, when research on that topic began and how the topic developed. They also can determine how their own research question fits into that history.

Replicates previous work

ch. 2
p.26

As noted in Chapter 2, science is a self-correcting system. The mechanism that fixes science's errors is **replication**. When scientists replicate the work of others, they intentionally repeat the original work. If they obtain the same (or broadly similar) results found by the original researcher, confidence in the original conclusions increases. Sometimes, however, the original results are not obtained when replication is attempted. In those cases, confidence in the original conclusions is suspended. The discrepancy between the original work and its replication usually produces further research that may resolve the discrepancy. Conducting a replication is a worthwhile research project for beginners, both for reasons of training and scientific confirmation.

Journals

If you have wandered through the periodicals section of your library, you will probably have noticed the enormous number of journals. In these journals, researchers publish the results of their investigations. After a research project has been completed, the study is written as a report, which then may be submitted to the editor of an appropriate journal. The editor sends the report out to other scientists in the same field and asks them to review it. Once the editor has the reviews, a decision can then be made on whether the report is acceptable for publication. This is the process of *peer review*. Because each journal has a limited amount of space and receives many more papers than it has room to publish, most papers are rejected.

Most psychology journals specialize in one or two areas of human or animal behaviour. Even so, the number of journals in many areas is so large that it is almost impossible for anyone to read them all. That is why you need to do a careful search to find out where the most important information relating to your topic has been published.

Doing a PsycINFO search

PsycINFO
A database of abstracts from journal articles and book chapters relevant to psychology and related fields.

PsycINFO is a search engine that allows you to look for articles that have been published in a particular area, on a particular topic or by particular authors. It is similar to Internet search engines, but instead of trawling the Internet, it trawls a huge database of published articles. All of the major journals are included, as well as many other journals, meaning that you can search through thousands of articles at the click of a button.

The exact "look and feel" of the system you will use to search PsycINFO will depend on your computer system. Figure 23.1 shows a "generic" display; your PsycINFO screen will have its own appearance. You need to enter the term or phrase that you want to search for. In most simple searches, such as the one shown, you have some other options. For example, you can limit your search to articles that have a specific word or phrase in the title.

Your most important task is to specify the search terms that you want the computer to use to do the search. These are typed into an input box. Searching databases like PsycINFO is a skill and you will usually have to do a number of different searches using different terms and combinations of terms. The problem that everyone has who searches academic databases is the sheer number of "hits" that you get. You have to know what search terms are going to give you the best chance of finding articles that are directly relevant to your research. So how do you know which

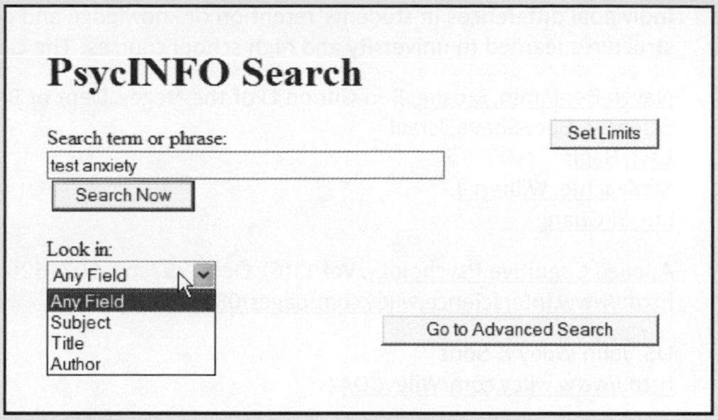

Figure 23.1 Example of a PsycINFO user screen

words to type in the input box? Most commonly, you will want to use standard psychological terms. The **Thesaurus of Psychological Index Terms** lists all the standard terms that are used to index the abstracts, and it can be accessed directly with most PsycINFO systems. Suppose you are interested in the topic of test anxiety (the anxiety that prevents some people from performing well in a test of their abilities or their knowledge). It turns out that both *test* and *anxiety* are major descriptors in the thesaurus. If you look under *anxiety* you will see all of the related terms including *separation anxiety*, *social anxiety* and *test anxiety*. While using the thesaurus, you can select any term and then request a search of that term. However, let's assume that you are using a standard search window as in Figure 23.1. When you click on the button to start the search, the results of the search will be displayed.

Figure 23.2 is the output of one of the articles found with a search on test anxiety. The exact appearance of the output that you receive will depend on the computer system you are using as well as the information that you choose to display. The default output includes citation information that you will need (title of the article, who the authors were, name and volume number of the journal and the page numbers of the article) along with the abstract (a short summary of the article). We chose to display a bit more information to illustrate how information is organized in the database. Notice that the output is organized into "fields" of information. The full name and abbreviation of each field is included here. You will almost always want to see the title (abbreviated as TI), author (AU), source (SO – basically the title of the journal or book that the article is in) and abstract (AB).

When you do the search, some fields will appear as clickable hyperlinks to lead you to other information in your library database or to other websites. Systems are continually being upgraded to enable users to more easily obtain full-text access to the articles and find other articles on similar topics. The *Digital Object Identifier* (DOI) field is helpful in finding electronic copies of the article.

When you do a simple search with a single word or a phrase such as *test anxiety*, the default search will find articles that have that word or phrase anywhere in any of the fields listed. Often you will find that this produces far too many articles, including articles that are not directly relevant to your interests. One way to narrow the search is to limit it to certain fields. The simple

Thesaurus of Psychological Index Terms
A thesaurus that is used to help narrow or broaden a search of the psychological literature.

Title: Individual differences in students' retention of knowledge and conceptual
                    structures learned in university and high school courses: The case of test anxiety.

Author(s):   Naveh-Benjamin, Moshe, Ben-Gurion U of the Negev, Dept of Behavioural
                    Sciences, Beer-Sheva, Israel
                    Lavi, Hagit
                    McKeachie, Wilbert J.
                    Lin, Yi-Guang

Source: Applied Cognitive Psychology, Vol 11(6), Dec 1997. pp. 507–526.
Journal URL: http://www.interscience.wiley.com/pages/0888-4080/

Publisher: US: John Wiley & Sons
Publisher URL: http://www.wiley.com/WileyCDA/

Abstract: Examined individual differences in students' retention of knowledge several years
                    after studying academic material. Assessment of retention of materials as
                    a function of students' *test anxiety* can allow one to evaluate whether high
                    test-anxious students' original deficient academic performance and organization
                    of the materials are due to a retrieval deficit or a deficit in learning and
                    knowledge organization. In 2 studies, 210 American students (Study 1) and
                    258 Israeli students (aged 17–27 yrs; Study 2) with different *test-anxiety* levels
                    completed tasks that enabled us to evaluate both students' levels of knowledge
                    and their cognitive organization of the materials. The tasks were administered
                    either at the end of the course, or at different retention intervals up to 7 yrs after
                    the end of learning. Results indicated that whereas high *test*-anxious students
                    tested worse at the end of the courses than other students on *tests* of knowledge
                    and cognitive organization, high *test*-anxious students tested at various retention
                    intervals after the courses performed as well as other students. The theoretical
                    and practical implications of these results are discussed. (PsycINFO Database
                    Record © 2004 APA, all rights reserved)

Digital Object Indentifier: 10.1002/(SICI)1099-0720(199712)11:6<507::AID-ACP482>3.3.CO;2-7

Keywords: test anxiety & individual differences in retention of knowledge & conceptual
                    structures learned in university & high school courses, US & Israeli students

Subjects: *Individual Differences; *Retention; *Test Anxiety; College Students; High School
                    Students

Population: Human
Male
Female

Age Group: Adulthood (18 yrs & older)

Form/Content Type: Empirical Study

Publication Type: Peer Reviewed Journal; Print

Database: PsycINFO

View Links: Check for Full Text & More

Figure 23.2 Article found with a search on test anxiety

search screen (see Figure 23.1) may allow you to limit the search so that the search looks for your search term in only one field, such as the title of the article. Also note in Figure 23.1 that there is a "Set Limits" option. This allows you to easily specify that the search should find only journal articles (not books or dissertations) or include articles that report studies on participants from certain age groups.

Top tips for searching

Most PsycINFO systems also have advanced search screens that enable you to use the Boolean operators AND and OR and NOT. Suppose you want to restrict the *test anxiety in TITLE* search to college students only. You can do this by asking for *(test anxiety in TITLE) AND (college students)*. The AND forces both conditions to be true for an article to be included in the list of results. The parentheses are used to separate different parts of your search specification and are useful when your searches become increasingly complicated.

The OR operation is used to expand a search that is too narrow. Suppose you want to find articles that discuss romantic relationships on the Internet. I (SW) just searched for *Internet AND romance* and found 24 articles; changing the specification to *Internet AND (romance OR dating OR love OR attraction)* yielded 101 articles. Articles that have the term *Internet* and *any* of the other terms specified were included in the second search.

The NOT operation will exclude terms that you specify. The NOT operation is used when you anticipate that the search criteria will result in irrelevant articles being found. In the Internet example, it is possible that the term *attraction* will find research on Internet job interviews in which attraction to a particular job or job candidate is described. To exclude the term *job* from the results of the search, the following adjustment can be made: *Internet AND (romance OR dating OR love OR attraction) NOT job*. When this search was conducted, I (SW) found 92 abstracts instead of the 101 obtained previously.

Another helpful search tool is the "wildcard" asterisk (*). The asterisk stands for any set of letters in a word and so it can expand your search. Consider the word *romance* in the search above – by using *roman**, the search will expand to include both *romance* and *romantic*. The wildcard can be very useful with the term *child** to find *child, children, childhood* and so on. You have to be careful when doing this, however; the *roman** search would also find *Romania* and *romanticism*! In this case, it might be more efficient to simply add *OR romantic* to the search. These search strategies are summarized in Figure 23.3.

Strategy 1:   Use fields such as TI and AU.
    Example: *(divorce) in TI* requires that a term appear in the title.
Strategy 2:   Use AND to limit search.
    Example: *divorce AND child* requires both terms to be included.
Strategy 3:   Use OR to expand search.
    Example: *divorce OR breakup* includes both terms.
Strategy 4:   Use NOT to exclude search terms.
    Example: *shyness NOT therapy* excludes any shyness articles that have the term *therapy*.
Strategy 5:   Use the wildcard asterisk (*).
    Example: *child** finds any word that begins with *child* (childhood, child's, etc.).

Figure 23.3 Some PsycINFO search strategies

It is a good idea to give careful thought to your search terms. Consider the case of a student who decided to do a paper on the topic of "road rage". She wanted to know what might cause drivers to become so angry at other drivers that they will become physically aggressive. A search on the term *road rage* led to a number of interesting articles. However, when looking at the output from the search she noticed that the major descriptors included *driving behaviour* and *anger* but not *road rage*. She soon realized that she had found only articles that included the term *road rage* in the title or abstract. This term has become popular in the media and in everyday life, but it may not be used in all scientific studies of the topic. She then expanded the search to include *driving AND anger* and also *dangerous driving*. The new search gave her many articles that were not found in the original search.

When you complete your search, you can print the results. When you print, you can choose which of the fields to display. You probably will not need all the fields shown in the previous example. Many researchers prefer to save the results of the search on a disc or email it to themselves. The information can then be used with other programs such as a word processor or a citation manager.

Science Citation Index and Social Sciences Citation Index

Science Citation Index (SCI)
A database of scientific and technical journal articles which provides information on citation (e.g. how many times an article has been cited by others, which later articles have cited a particular earlier article).

Social Sciences Citation Index (SSCI)
A database of social and behavioural sciences journal articles which provides information on citation (e.g. how many times an article has been cited by others, which later articles have cited a particular earlier article).

Two related search resources are the **Science Citation Index (SCI)** and the **Social Sciences Citation Index (SSCI)**. Both allow you to search through citation information such as the name of the author or article title. The SCI includes disciplines such as biology, chemistry, biomedicine and pharmacology, whereas the SSCI includes social and behavioural sciences such as sociology and criminal justice. The most important feature of both resources is the ability to use the "key article" method. Here you need to first identify a "key article" on your topic, usually one published some time in the past that is particularly relevant to your interests. You can then search for subsequent articles that cited the key article. This search will give you a bibliography of articles relevant to your topic. To provide an example of this process, we chose the following article:

Wells, G.L. & Bradfield, A.L. (1999). Distortions in eyewitnesses' recollections: can the postidentification feedback effect be moderated? *Psychological Science*, *10*, 138–44.

When we did an article search using the SSCI, we found 26 articles that had cited the Wells and Bradfield paper since it was published in 1999. Here is one of them:

Ghetti, S., Qin, J. & G.S. Goodman (2002). False memories in children and adults: age, distinctiveness, and subjective experience, *Developmental Psychology*, *38*, 705–18.

We will now want to become familiar with this article as well as the others on the list. It may then turn out that one or more of the articles might become new "key articles" for further searches. It is also possible to specify a "key person" in order to find all articles written by or citing a particular person after a given date.

Other electronic search resources

Your library may or may not have access to PsycINFO or the SCI/SSCI databases. The number of information databases that a library may purchase today is enormous; budget and other considerations will determine which ones are available to you. You will need to take advantage of instructional materials that your library provides to help you learn how to best search for information available through your library. Other major databases include FirstSearch, Sociological Abstracts, MEDLINE, and ERIC (Educational Resources Information Centre). In addition, services such as Lexis-Nexis and Factiva allow you to search general media resources such as newspapers. A reference librarian can help you use these and other resources available to you.

Some of the information resources available provide the full text of articles in the database, whereas others provide only abstract or citation information. For example, the American Psychological Association (APA) has developed a database of full-text articles called PsycARTICLES (http://www.apa.org/psycarticles/). The articles in this database all come from journals published by the APA. Other full-text article databases draw from different sources. Sometimes it is tempting to limit yourself to full-text services because it is so easy to obtain the complete article. A problem with this strategy is that you limit yourself to only those journals that are in the full-text database. It is usually a good idea to widen your search so that you are more likely to find the articles of greatest relevance to your topic. Even if the full text of the article is not available electronically, you may be able to obtain it from another library source.

Internet searches

The most widely available information resource is the wealth of material that is freely available on the Internet. Services such as Yahoo!, Google and About allow you to search through a variety of materials stored on the Internet. The Internet is a wonderful source of information; any given search may help you find websites devoted to your topic, articles that people have made available to others, book reviews and even online discussions. Although it is incredibly easy to search (just type something in a dialogue box and hit the Enter key), you can improve the quality of your searches by learning: (1) the differences in the way each service finds and stores information, (2) advanced search rules including how to make searches more narrow and how to find exact phrases, and (3) ways to critically evaluate the quality of the information that you find. You also need to make sure that you carefully record the search service and search terms you used, the dates of your search and the exact location of any websites that you will be using in your research; this information will be useful as you provide documentation in the papers that you prepare.

Scholar.google.com

The Google search service has developed a specialized scholarly search engine that can be accessed at http://scholar.google.com. When you do a scholar search, you find papers and books from scholarly journals, universities and academic book publishers.

Evaluating Web information

One downside to the Internet is that there is a lot of rubbish on it. Not all claims made on the Internet will be scientifically valid and not all web pages will give you trustworthy information.

You need to be sure that the results of any Internet search that you do for the purposes of your research are of an acceptable standard. Some of the most important things to look for are listed below.

- Is the site associated with a major educational institution or research organization? A site sponsored by a single individual or an organization with a clear bias should be viewed with scepticism.
- Is information provided on the people who are responsible for the site? Can you check on the credentials of these individuals?
- Is the information current?
- Do links from the site lead to legitimate organizations?

Reading a research report

So, you have came up with a good idea and you've meticulously searched for articles relating to it. The next part of the process is to get the articles and read them (obviously). In this section, we discuss the things you should be looking for in any research reports that you read. The information contained in the report reflects the purposes for which it was written. These purposes include (1) arguing the need for doing the research, (2) showing how the research addresses that need, (3) clearly describing the methods used so that others can duplicate them, (4) presenting the findings of the research and (5) integrating the findings with previous knowledge, including previous research findings and theories.

Obtaining a copy

After identifying relevant research reports, your next step is to obtain copies. Many libraries now subscribe to services that provide full-text articles online (e.g. through EBSCOhost, JSTOR or PsycARTICLES). You should contact your library to see which, if any, of these services are available. If these services are available, you can directly access html or .pdf versions of articles on your computer. If your library does not subscribe to these services, you will have to obtain your copy by using the hardbound journals stocked by your library.

Your library will have a list of all periodicals (including scientific journals) found on its shelves; this list is usually accessible electronically and is normally linked with the general database system that you would use to search for books. Libraries without computerized systems most likely have a *Serials Index* that includes the call number assigned to each journal. Use the call number to find the journal, just as you would to locate a book. If your library does *not* subscribe to that journal, you may still be able to obtain a copy of the article you want by submitting a request for interlibrary loan (see your librarian for advice on how to do this). Getting articles via interlibrary loan has become faster with the advent of the Internet: articles can usually be emailed to you. However, the library may not always use these electronic methods, and in some instances it can take several days or weeks to get your article via interlibrary loan.

If you do find the article in the library, have a quick read over the abstract and the introduction to see if it is indeed relevant to your research. If it is relevant, photocopy the article for future reference. Making a copy is legal, even if the article is copyrighted, as long as the copy is for personal use in your research.

Reading critically

When reading a journal article, think of yourself as a consumer of research. Apply the same skills to deciding whether you are going to "buy" a piece of research as you would when deciding whether to buy any other product. Critically reading and analysing research literature (or any source of information) involves two steps: an initial appraisal and a careful analysis of content.

The *initial* appraisal involves evaluating the following (Cornell University Library, 2000): the author, date of publication, edition or revision, publisher and title of the journal. When evaluating the author, you should look at his or her credentials, including institutional affiliation and past experience in the area. It is important to consider the author and the author's institutional affiliation because not all research findings are reported in scholarly journals. Some research is disseminated through "research centres" and other organizations. By evaluating the author and the institution, you can make an assessment of any potential biases. For example, a study that comes from an organization with a political agenda may not present facts in a correct or unbiased fashion. The main author of a research report from such an organization might not even be academically qualified or trained to conduct research and correctly interpret findings. One way you can check on the author is to see if the author's work has been cited by others in the same area. Important works by respected authors are often cited by other researchers. If you do not find these things, it does not always mean that the research is not of value. New researchers or young researchers might not have published widely or might not have been extensively cited. In these cases, you should consider the journal that the article was published in as well as using your own judgement about its quality once you have read it.

You should also look at the date of the publication to see if the source is current or potentially out of date. In some areas (e.g. neuroscience), new discoveries are made almost daily and may make older research out of date and obsolete. Try to find the most up-to-date sources that you can. When evaluating a book, determine if the copy you have is the most recent edition. If it is not, find the most recent edition because it will have been updated with the most current information available at the date of publication. Also, note the publisher for both books and journals. Some books are published by companies (sometimes called "vanity presses") that require authors to pay for publication of their works. Books published in this way may not undergo a careful scholarly review prior to publication. Generally, books published by university publishers will be scholarly, as will books published by well-recognized publishing houses (e.g. Lawrence Erlbaum Associates; McGraw-Hill Education). Although this is no guarantee of quality, a book from a reputable publisher will usually be of high quality. The same goes for journals. As indicated earlier, some journals are peer reviewed and some are not. You should try to use peer-reviewed journals whenever possible. Finally, look at the title of the publication that you are thinking of using. This will help you determine if the publication is scholarly or not. There is no hard and fast rule of thumb to tell you if a publication is scholarly, but you will quickly get an idea of what the respected journals in the field are.

Evaluating the content of an article published in a scholarly psychological journal involves a careful reading and analysis of the different parts of the article. In the next sections, we explore how to critically analyse each section of an APA-style journal article.

Evaluating the Introduction

ch. 25
pp.621 – 638

When reading the Introduction to a **research report**, determine whether or not the author has adequately reviewed the relevant literature. Were any important papers neglected? Does the author support any assertions with reference citations? In addition, ask yourself the following:

1 Has the author correctly represented the results from previous research? Sometimes when authors summarize previous research, they make errors or select only findings consistent with their ideas. It is often the case that authors have a theoretical orientation that may bias their summary of existing research findings. If you are suspicious, look up the original articles and evaluate them for yourself. Also, you should determine if the author has cited the most up-to-date materials. Reliance on older material may not give you an accurate picture of the current research or theory in an area.

2 Does the author clearly state the purposes of the study and the nature of the problem under study?

3 Do the hypotheses logically follow from the discussion in the introduction?

4 Are the hypotheses clearly stated and, more important, are they testable?

Evaluating the Method section

The Method section describes precisely how the study was carried out. You might think of this section as a "cookbook", or a set of directions, for conducting the study. When reading the method section of an article, evaluate the following:

1 Who served as participants in the study? How were the participants selected (randomly, through a subject pool, etc.)? Were the participants all of one race, gender or ethnic background? If so, this could limit the generality of the results (the degree to which the results apply beyond the parameters of the study). For example, if only male participants were used, a legitimate question is whether the results would apply as well to females. Also, look at the size of the sample. Were enough participants included to allow an adequate test of any hypotheses stated in the introduction?

2 Does the design of the study allow an adequate test of the hypotheses or the research question stated in the introduction? For example, do the variables included allow an adequate test of the hypotheses? Is information provided about the reliability and validity of any measures used?

3 Are there any flaws in materials or procedures used that might affect the validity of the study? A good way to assess this is to outline the design of the study and evaluate it against the stated purpose of the study.

Evaluating the Results section

When evaluating the Results section, look for the following:

1 Which effects are statistically significant? Note which effects were significant and whether those effects are consistent with the hypotheses stated in the introduction.

2 Are the differences reported large or small? Look at the means (or other measures of central tendency) being compared and note how much difference emerged. You may find that, although an effect is significant, it is small.

3 Were the appropriate statistics used?

4 Do the text, tables and figures match? Sometimes errors occur in the preparation of tables and figures, so be sure to check for accuracy. Also, check to see if the author's description of the relationships depicted in any tables or figures matches what is shown. If statistics are not reported, determine whether the author has correctly described the relationships among the variables and has indicated how reliability was assessed.

5 If the study is qualitative in nature, you will need to assess whether the form of analysis was appropriate for the research question that the study was addressing. Were the basic tenets of the qualitative analysis followed and did the analyses appear meticulous?

Evaluating the Discussion section

In the Discussion section, you will find the author's interpretations of the results reported. The Discussion section usually begins with a summary of the major findings of the study, followed by the author's interpretations of the data and a synthesis of the findings with previous research and theory. You also may find a discussion of any limitations of the study. When evaluating the Discussion section, here are a few things to look for:

1 Do the author's conclusions follow from the results reported? Sometimes authors overstep the bounds of the results and draw unwarranted conclusions.

2 Does the author offer speculations concerning the results? In the discussion section, the author is free to speculate on the meaning of the results and on any applications. Carefully evaluate the discussion section and separate the author's speculations from conclusions that are actually supported directly by the results. Evaluate whether the author strays too far from the data when speculating about the implications of the results.

3 How well do the findings of the study mesh with previous research and existing theory? Are the results consistent with previous research, or are they unique? If the study is the only one that has found a certain effect (if other research has failed to find the effect or found just the opposite effect), be sceptical about the results.

4 Does the author point the way to directions for future research in the area? That is, does the author indicate other variables that might affect the behaviour studied and suggest new studies to test the effects of these variables?

References

The final section of an article is usually the **reference section** (a few articles include appendices as well) in which the author lists all the references cited in the body of the paper. Complete references are provided. You can use these to find other research on your topic.

ch. 25 pp.629–634

Developing hypotheses

All the library research and critical reading that you have done has now put you on the threshold of the next major step in the research process: developing your idea into a testable **hypothesis**. This hypothesis, as we pointed out in Chapter 4, will be a tentative statement relating two (or more) variables that you are interested in

ch. 4 p.77

Hypothesis
A tentative statement, subject to empirical test, about the expected relationship between variables.

studying. Your hypothesis should flow logically from the sources of information used to develop your research question. That is, given what you already know from previous research (either your own or what you read in the journals), you should be able to make a tentative statement about how your variables of interest relate to one another. You will probably have formed a tentative hypothesis at the same time as you established your research question (which is a more general statement), and your hypothesis may or may not have changed as a result of your review of the literature. Either way, it is useful to revisit your hypothesis after you have read the literature to see whether it still makes sense and postulates a meaningful relationship between variables.

Hypothesis development is an important step in the research process because it will drive your later decisions concerning the variables to be manipulated and measured in your study. Because a poorly conceptualized research hypothesis may lead to invalid results, take considerable care when stating your hypothesis.

If your research is qualitative, then you will not normally have a hypothesis (as most qualitative techniques do not make any assertions about the relationship between variables). If this is the case, then a well-formed research question will be what you use to guide your research.

Preparing to start your research

You have got your idea. It is answerable, it is testable and it is important. You have searched the literature, gathered relevant articles, and read them all carefully and critically. You have developed a hypothesis and you have designed a study to test it. You have sent a proposal to an **ethics** committee and it has been given the go-ahead. You are now ready, at long last, to conduct your study and collect your data. You are entitled to feel a little excited at this point.

ch. 24

Prepare to collect data

Collecting data is one of the most important parts of any research project. The logistics of data collection include recruiting participants, scheduling data collection times, treating participants appropriately, and handling and storing the collected data. Most of the logistical issues should have been anticipated during the planning phase of research. However, no one can anticipate all possible logistical issues. One way to detect them is by conducting a pilot study.

Pilot studies

A *pilot study* is a brief and limited version of the planned research. The goal of a pilot study is to refine the procedures of the research project. Pilot studies are used as test runs to make sure everything is likely to run smoothly once the main study gets under way, and to iron out any potential problems before the actual data are collected. A secondary goal is to determine if the planned statistical analyses are going to work. Problems that show up in the pilot study are fixed by changing the data collection procedures or the statistical analyses. For example, a student researcher studying rats' maze-navigating abilities built a maze for rats that had vertical, sliding doors that prevented rats from retracing their steps. Before she collected data, however, she conducted a pilot study with two rats. She soon discovered a major problem: she had not accounted for the rats' tails! The problem was that the doors descended all the way to the floor and struck the rats' tails. Rather quickly, the two rats in the pilot study refused to enter new sections of the maze. She solved the problem by installing small wooden blocks at the bottom of the slides so that the doors no longer struck the rats' tails. A second pilot study with two more rats confirmed the success of her solution. The doors did not hit the rats' tails and they readily entered the next section of the maze. Obviously this was important to rectify early because if she had not realized this problem, then the study might have failed entirely. Rats that were fearful of entering the next section of the maze would have been very slow learners.

Collecting data

Collecting data is exciting, especially if you conceived and designed the project yourself. There are a few things you need to consider when you are about to embark on the data collecting process.

Recruiting participants

In psychological research, people are a valuable commodity. You will have to find enough people to take part in your study, and you will have to recruit them in some way. We have already covered **sampling techniques** in Chapter 9, but there are also many practical considerations when recruiting participants. Whatever sampling method you decide to use, you will have to have a recruitment strategy that is practical and manageable. This might mean putting posters up around campus or around the local community, or it might mean sending out an email to multiple recipients from your target population, or it might mean standing on a street corner asking every tenth passer-by. Be realistic when deciding how to sample and be aware of the time constraints that you are under. Try not to overestimate how many participants you are likely to be able to recruit in the time that you have got, and be sensible in the number of participants you schedule in a single day. A pilot study can often help you in estimating how many participants you can realistically test in a given period of time. If you are sending out surveys, be aware that not everyone will return them. You should always send out more surveys than you expect to get back.

ch. 9

Scheduling participants

There are many ways to collect data from participants. If you are collecting observational data from animals or humans, you may not actually meet or interact with them. If you are conducting research with animals in a laboratory setting, you must follow established guidelines for handling them. If you are collecting data from human participants face to face, you must be practised and ready. If you meet them one by one and collect data, you will have prepared a place to meet, set a time for them to arrive and will have all your materials ready. If you meet them as a group in a place where they normally meet (such as at a classroom or in their hall of residence) you will take whatever you need with you. There are so many ways to collect data from human participants face to face that the best we can do is give you some general guidelines:

1   *Be ready to collect data.* It sounds like something we should not need to tell you, but we will tell you anyway (with apologies if it appears condescending). You need to be ready to collect your data. The more prepared you are, the more smoothly the whole process will run. Do you need to schedule or reserve a room for data collection? Should you post a sign outside the door to prevent interruptions? Do you have all the materials you will need for data collection? Do you have spare pens/pencils if your participants will be filling in questionnaires or other forms? In short, before you can collect data, you must be ready for your participants before they arrive.

2   *Be on time.* If you have scheduled arrival times for participants, be there before the appointed time. Arriving late is a sign of disrespect; furthermore, participants will not take you or your study seriously. Help participants be there at the appointed time. Sometimes a reminder call or email the night before will help, and for these to be successful you will have to be well organized to have a system in place that allows you to make these calls or send these emails to the right people at the right time.

3   *Treat all participants the same.* All of your participants must be treated alike. Your research design should include procedures that help you treat all the participants the same. For instance, if all participants receive complex instructions before providing data, you should ensure that all participants get exactly the same instructions. A simple way to accomplish this is to read written instructions (instead of telling them relevant information as it comes to mind). Another way is to videotape a presentation of the instructions and play the tape for each participant. Similarly, instructions may be presented on a computer screen. Of course, treating all participants in the same way means more than just providing instructions. All details of the research and all interactions with participants should be the same within each treatment condition (unless, of course, you are explicitly studying the effects of treating your participants differently, in which case you need to be sure to treat everyone in the same group equally). Our best advice is to respect your participants and to convey this respect to them.

ch. 24
pp.600–601

4   *Keep data confidential.* Maintaining the participants' privacy is a major ethical issue; privacy is one of the general principles of the *Ethics Code*. Psychologists do not violate privacy or confidentiality. At times, maintaining privacy requires a deliberate effort. For example, two friends might serve as participants in your research project. One might ask you about the data you collected from the other. As a researcher, you cannot reveal that information. To do so would be a breach of ethics on your part. The solution to this problem is to prepare ahead of time. Practise saying, "I'm sorry, but for ethical reasons I can't tell you that information." Of course, you cannot reveal data to anyone else either. That includes parents, relatives, school officials and others. You may reveal individual data to other researchers, provided they have a research-based reason to know and they agree to maintain confidentiality. However, you may not reveal individual data to other researchers who want to know for non-research reasons. For example, if a fellow student finds a participant attractive and wants to know information about the participant that was obtained as part of your research, you must not reveal those data. You may, of course, reveal averaged data to anyone as long as individual participants' scores cannot be identified.

In the Know

As an example of why confidentiality is important, consider the following scenario. Three student researchers conducted a study on self-esteem. Later, one of the men took a human sexuality class and learned that there is a high inverse correlation between self-esteem and sexuality in college females (Walker-Hill, 2000). He retrieved the data that he and his fellow students had collected so he could identify female participants with low self-esteem to ask out for a date. We hope that you can see that this is a very unethical thing to do. Using the data collected for such a personal purpose is a serious violation of confidentiality. Furthermore, such behaviour could result in consequences such as suspension or expulsion from university.

Project etiquette and responsibilities

After the data are collected, there are a number of things yet to do. Some are required by the *Ethics Code*, and others ensure that future research by other psychologists will continue to be well received:

1 *Communicate with participants.* Throughout the research process, communication with participants is important. In the early stages of research, communication is necessary to recruit participants and to get them to the research site. During the data collection phase, participants must know exactly what is being asked of them. After data collection, researchers still have communication responsibilities to their participants. Most research involving human participants requires that participants be debriefed or at least be given an opportunity to be debriefed.

2 *Debrief participants.* As outlined in the next chapter, participants must be debriefed. Debriefing is a reciprocal process. The researchers obtained data because participants volunteered to participate. The participants are entitled to know their own performance. How debriefing is accomplished is up to the researchers. In every case, however, researchers should reveal any deceptions in the research. They should ask if the participants have any questions about the research and answer them. If the data are not yet known or analysed, researchers should tell participants how they may obtain that information later, which might be by postal mail, email or posted on a web page. Researchers' responsibilities to their participants do not end when data collection ends.

ch. 24
p.604

3 *Handle and store data.* All materials used in data collection and the data themselves should be kept and stored. Hard copy and software files used to analyse the data should also be kept. Ideally, these materials should be available to you and others for years. As a practical matter, research materials should be kept for at least 5 years. Materials that lead to published research should be kept for 10 years. In most cases, the person responsible for these research materials should be the first author or the principal investigator. Often, in the case of student research, the instructor supervising the research keeps the materials. The rules of confidentiality still apply, so data storage must be secure. Only the original researchers should have access to these records.

Analysing data

As we have emphasized throughout this book, you should select statistical tests you will use *before* the data are collected or as part of the prospectus. Not doing so can lead to serious trouble. For example, if an analysis of variance (ANOVA) was selected for the statistical analysis but the data collected were yes–no responses, the data and the analysis are mismatched. ANOVAs require **interval or ratio data**. Yes–no data are frequency counts of categorical data and should be analysed with a **chi-square** test or other non-parametric statistic.

ch. 4
p.66

ch.20
pp.502–5
& 513–5

Using the data actually collected is the key to a proper analysis. What we mean is that you must be careful in transferring data from the collection format to the analysis method. Most data analysis is conducted with computer-based statistical software such as SPSS. Be sure you transfer the data accurately from data collection forms to the software input. You may have collected the data perfectly, but if you make mistakes inputting the data to the statistical software, your research will become invalid.

Prepare data

Before raw data are entered into a statistics program, they should be organized. The details of this organization will vary depending on the type of research conducted, but the general suggestions we give below usually apply. These suggestions also make data entry, which is a tedious process at best, a little easier.

Raw data collected during research take many forms. For example, returned questionnaires constitute raw data. In a naturalistic observation study, the raw data may be tally marks that indicate the different behaviours observed. A data file in a computer program could be the raw data. Regardless of the form of the raw data, the first task in data analysis is to convert it into a form that will allow you to analyse it using whatever form of analysis you have decided is most appropriate.

You should conduct a preliminary check of the data before conducting any analyses. An easy method is to compute descriptive statistics for all variables using your statistics software. Look at the ranges. Do any of the variables show an impossible range? For example, if a variable has Likert scale values of 1 to 5 and the range for that variable is 1 to 50, you know you have at least one error. Find the error and correct it. Re-compute the descriptive statistics until all easy-to-detect errors are corrected.

Graph data

Examine your scores by graphing them. How do your data look? Are there obvious variations between groups? Do the graphed means correspond to the calculated means? A good graph presents your data visually and succinctly; it allows you to see the data all at once.

Most graphs are created with statistical software packages that include three-dimensional tools and shading. Be careful. Those tools can lead to graphical overkill and actually make your graph less understandable. Avoid the temptation to add computer-graphic elements such as shading and colour. Here are some rules to follow for making graphs that are based on the recommendations of Pittenger (1995) and Cleveland and McGill (1985):

- It is tempting to crowd as much data as possible on one graph. Better to make more graphs, each with its own story to tell. A simple graph depicting one dependent variable is clearer than a graph that shows multiple dependent variables.

- Line graphs are the easiest to read and to interpret. However, line graphs are not appropriate for categorical, qualitative or dichotomous data. Use bar graphs instead.

- Use pie charts sparingly because they require that users interpret both angles and areas displayed, a more difficult task than interpreting the two-dimensional position of a point in a scatterplot (Pittenger, 1995). However, flat pie charts are useful for conveying information about proportions and can be very clear.

After preparing your graphs, show them to friends and colleagues. What kind of response do you get? If they ooh and ahh at your graphed data, it often means that they understood what your graph means (unless, of course, your friends and colleagues are the type of people who ooh and ahh at everything, in which case you should just ask them if they understand it).

Interpret data

Data do not speak for themselves. It is the researcher who speaks for the data. Data interpretation is a complex process, not just a single step near the end of data analysis. The task is to tell a story that the data support. Recall how you became interested in the research topic in the first place. Reread the literature about your topic. Look at your graphs and your results. What kind of story do they support? Can you tell the story aloud or in writing? Let's look at some specific steps in data interpretation:

1 *Compare results to hypotheses.* Have another look at your hypotheses (if you are doing the kind of study that demands hypotheses). How did those hypotheses fare? Were you able to reject any null hypotheses? If yes, what are the alternative hypotheses? If none was rejected, what does that mean? These are the types of questions you should ask as you begin to interpret your data.

2 *Separate statistically significant results from non-significant results.* For research using significance tests, separate statistically significant results from non-significant results. For the significant results, the null hypothesis is rejected. The story the data support must be made with the significant results.

3 *Order correlations.* In correlational research, order the correlations numerically from high to low (meaning from +1.00 to −1.00). Keep in mind that the sign of the correlation indicates the direction of the relationship only. Now look at the absolute value of the correlations (the numerical part only). Pay close attention to the strength of the correlation. Even if it is significant, does the correlation coefficient suggest a strong association? Also, be sure to interpret the sign of the correlation correctly!

4 *Tell a story.* Regardless of the topic area or design, data interpretation is the climax of research. All of the effort expended during the research is directed towards the goal of interpreting the data obtained. In the next two sections, we give you more help with interpretation as we discuss writing the report of your research. Does the story that the results suggest match the story that you expected to be telling at the end of the research?

... and then

At this point you are ready to present your findings to the world, which we tell you how to do in the next chapter.

Questions

1 How can experience help you come up with research ideas?
2 In what two ways can a theory help you develop research ideas?
3 How can applied issues suggest research ideas to you?
4 What are the characteristics of a "good research question"?
5 Why should you conduct a literature review before you begin to design your study?
6 What is PsycINFO and how is it used to conduct a literature search?
7 What initial appraisals should you make of an article that you are going to read?
8 Why is it important to read a research report critically?
9 How can you broaden or narrow a PsycINFO search?

Activities

1 Think of at least five "common-sense" sayings about behaviour (e.g. "Like father, like son"; "Absence makes the heart grow fonder"). For each, develop a hypothesis that is suggested by the saying.

2 Choose one of the hypotheses formulated in question 1 above and develop a strategy for finding research on the topic using the computer database in your library. What key words would you use, and how might you make your search better and more likely to give you relevant articles? Conduct the search and find five key articles that you would have to consult before progressing with this research.

Ethics in Psychological Research

- Show an appreciation of the specific ethical challenges involved when conducting research on the Internet or with animal subjects

- Appreciate the importance of integrity in research and understand what this constitutes

- Assess research designs from an ethics perspective

- Conduct ethical and responsible psychological research

Introduction to ethics[1]

The best way to start a chapter on ethics is with a couple of famous examples from psychology's past. As you read them, think about how you might have felt if you were participating in them. In particular, think about the ethics involved, and whether you consider it right to put people through these experiences for the sake of a psychology study.

Shocking psychology

Picture this: it is the early 1960s and you are a student at Yale University in the USA. You volunteer to participate in an experiment on learning and teaching. Another student volunteer arrives at the laboratory at the same time. You are asked to pick a slip of paper from a hat, and this decides that you will be a "teacher" and your fellow student the "learner". The learner is taken to a nearby room, but you can still hear him easily.

As teacher, you sit in front of an instrument panel with many switches (Figure 24.1). Your task is to ask the learner questions. If the learner gets an answer wrong, you have to flip a switch that delivers an electric shock. Each switch is labelled with a voltage: the lowest is 15 volts and the highest is 450 volts. Beneath the switches are warnings that range from "Mild shock" on the left to "Danger: severe shock" on the right. Switches above 400 volts are also accompanied by a red "XXX" sign. The experimenter senses your concern and tells you not to worry. To show you what it is like, he gives you the 15-volt shock that is delivered by the first switch. It is not very painful. The experimenter then instructs you to administer a shock to the learner for each incorrect answer. Every time the learner gets another answer wrong, you are instructed to increase the level of shock given to him.

The experiment starts and, after a few trials, the learner makes his first mistakes. You administer the punishment, and he does not seem to mind the pain from the lower-voltage shocks. Later, however, as more and more mistakes are made, he begins to complain. When you flip the switch labelled 180 volts, he shouts that he can no longer stand the pain. You look at the experimenter nearby, but he tells you to continue. Reluctantly, you go on. When you flip the switch labelled 270 volts, the learner screams in agony. You look at the experimenter again; he says you must continue. Soon afterwards, the learner stops answering your questions. The silence worries you.

---

1   To access the ethical guidelines of the American Psychological Association, visit http://www.apa.org/ethics/. For the British Psychological Society's ethical code, visit http://www.bps.org.uk/the-society/code-of-conduct/code-of-conduct_home.cfm.

Figure 24.1 Milgram's apparatus

You do not know what to do when the learner does not respond. The experimenter tells you to treat no response as an error and to deliver the appropriate shock. Finally, you get to the last switch and pull it. The study is over at last. You feel drained and exhausted. You also feel lucky; if you had not chosen that piece of paper from the hat, it could have been you being shocked in that room.

Playing at prisons

Another example: it is 1971 at Stanford University in the USA and you volunteer to participate in a two-week prison simulation study for $15 per day. (Today, the equivalent amount is about $75, or about £50). You and 24 other volunteers are chosen because you have no criminal record, no medical or psychological problems and no history of drug abuse. For two weeks, you are to serve as either a prisoner or as a guard. Whether you play the role of prisoner or guard is decided by the toss of a coin at the beginning of the study. You call "heads" and find that this means you are to serve as a prisoner. On a Sunday afternoon and in full view of your neighbours, the local police come to your home and arrest you, charge you with armed robbery and burglary, advise you of your legal rights, handcuff you, and take you to the local jail with lights flashing and sirens blaring (see Figure 24.2). You are arrested, finger-printed, blindfolded and put into a holding cell. From the holding cell you are moved to "prison". The prison is in the basement of the Stanford psychology building, where three rooms have been converted into makeshift cells. Each cell has three basic camp-beds and real bars instead of a door. The hall is the prison's "yard" and a small cupboard serves as the "hole", which is used to discipline unruly prisoners. There is a bathroom. The walls are bare and there are no clocks.

You are assigned a number, and you are called by it instead of your name during the study. You are stripped naked and sprayed for lice and bacteria. You wear a smock, rubber sandals and a cap made from women's nylon tights (to simulate having your head shaved). No underwear is issued. A heavy piece of chain is padlocked to your right ankle. The guards (fellow students, remember, allocated on the basis of a coin toss) wear khaki uniforms and sunglasses. They carry

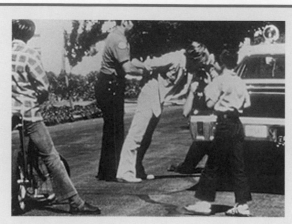

Figure 24.2 Arrest of a "prisoner"

clubs and whistles and are untrained. You are one of nine prisoners. There are nine guards, three per shift, with three shifts per day. When the guards are not on duty, they are free to go anywhere they please. They, too, are paid $15 daily.

The first day is uneventful until 2.30 a.m. when the guards conduct a prisoner count, forcing the inmates to stand in the yard. On the morning of the second day, the prisoners riot during the guards' shift change. Prisoners remove their caps, barricade the barred doors with beds, and tear off their identification numbers. The other guards are called in and all nine move against the prisoners using fire extinguishers. The guards lock the leaders of the rebellion in the hole. The prisoners who participated least are placed in a new special privileges cell, given back their beds and uniforms, and fed better food. Twelve hours later, however, the guards move some leaders of the rebellion into the special privileges cell and move some of the others to the regular cells. The action breaks the prisoners' solidarity and intensifies the differences between prisoners and guards.

According to plan, parents and friends visit for 10 minutes on the third day. Before the visit, the guards clean the prison and issue fresh uniforms. All visitors are forced to register and then made to wait 30 minutes. During the visit, a guard is always present. After the visit, the guards hear a rumour about a mass-escape attempt that is to be aided by students on the outside. The guards respond by temporarily moving all prisoners, blindfolded and chained together, to a fifth-floor storage room. The rumour proves false. Over the next two days, the guards become more dominant as the prisoners become meeker and more disorganized.

After five days, prisoners, guards, staff and visitors had fallen into the experiment completely. Dr Phillip Zimbardo, head of the project, reported that he felt more like a warden than a research psychologist. When his fiancée (also a social psychologist) visited and protested vigorously, he decided it was time to halt the experiment (Zimbardo, 1973). On the sixth day, all of the participants attended two encounter sessions (a two-way debriefing session encompassing information and emotions): one for the prisoners, one for the guards, and one for prisoners and guards together. All of the prisoners were glad that the experiment was over, but most of the guards were not.

What are ethics? Why be ethical?

Ethics is a branch of philosophy concerned with the way in which we formulate codes and principles of moral behaviour. Moral conduct has been important throughout human history and has been a topic for reflection ever since humans started reflecting upon themselves and their place in the world. At a general level, moral philosophers raise critical questions about the nature of morality, what form it takes, how we should define it and how we can construct principles to live by. Although the terms "morals" and "ethics" are often used to mean the same thing, there is a subtle difference between them. Morals are personally defined. Morals are things that relate to your own character – your "moral values". Generally, your morals do not change much (although they sometimes do). Ethics are related to the system in which we live. Each group that an individual belongs to, whether it is a country or a psychological society, will have basic ethical principles, and these ethical principles exist for the good of the system as a whole. You would expect there to be large overlaps between morals and ethics, and there are. However, the two can sometimes clash. For example, abortion is legal in many countries, and therefore it is medically ethical. Despite this, there are many people (including people in the medical profession) whose morals tell them that abortion is a bad thing. In psychology, your morals might tell you that physically punishing small children (e.g. smacking them) is morally wrong. However, if you are involved in a psychology study on parents who hit their children, you have ethical responsibilities in the way in which you treat these people, despite what you might think of their actions.

Why be ethical? This is a big question. In the context of psychology, ethical principles have been formulated to avoid harm. Psychologists have a responsibility to protect anyone with whom they come into contact (and also to protect themselves), and **ethical guidelines** are produced by professional bodies to ensure that this is the case. The guidelines are devised in line with current thinking and may be amended appropriately according to the current cultural and technological climate, as long as the basic principles of protection are adhered to. We would hope that wishing to avoid harm to others was part of most people's moral codes (especially those people wishing to be involved in psychology), and that is why we must be ethical and why we must pay attention to ethical codes of conduct. There will, however, be occasions on which an ethical principle might clash with personal conscience, such as the two examples described above. This is an extremely delicate issue and there is no easy or simple way of dealing with it. However, many professional bodies' guidelines (see following section) encourage individuals to use the ethical principles as a guide to thinking about ethical problems, rather than a set of strict rules that must never be broken.

> **Ethical guidelines**
> General principles and rules of ethical behaviour.

That said, the formulation of the British Psychological Society's code of conduct is based on Immanuel Kant's categorical imperative, which states that one must act "on such maxims as you could will to become universal law", which is also formulated as "treat humanity in your own person and that of others always as an end and never only as a means". In other words, "treat people as you would wish to be treated yourself". This will not get rid of all possible clashes between personal morals and ethical guidelines, but it is a foundation from which to think about your behaviour as a psychologist. We hope that there are not too many instances in which your morals conflict with professional ethical principles. If it does happen, we recommend seeking advice from others who are conversant with the ethics system within which you are working. The rest of this chapter will introduce you to the main ethical issues that psychologists face.

Fundamental ethical principles

Good science requires good scientists. Scientists in any discipline must be professional and competent, maintaining high levels of integrity in their research, practice and applications. There are many reasons why this is important. Scientific advances often come with profound ethical questions. Is embryonic stem-cell research ethical? Is research on animals justified if it advances our ability to alleviate human suffering? Are there things that scientists just should not study because doing so would be detrimental to society? These are all "big" questions, but each individual scientist and each individual psychologist also has to think carefully about the ethical implications involved in what they do.

Diener and Crandall (1978) identify several specific responsibilities that scientists should adhere to. According to these authors, scientists should:

- carry out research in a competent manner
- report results accurately
- manage research resources honestly
- fairly acknowledge, in scientific communications, the individuals who have contributed their ideas or their time and effort
- consider the consequences to society of any research endeavour
- speak out publicly on societal concerns related to a scientist's knowledge and expertise.

In striving to meet these obligations, individual scientists face challenging and sometimes ambiguous ethical issues and questions. Because psychologists work with humans (all kinds of humans – babies, children, adults, people with psychological problems and so on) as well as animals, they are faced with their own specific ethical issues. Many countries have an organization that oversees the practice of psychology, and these organizations usually have guidelines on ethics that anyone involved in psychology can consult. In the UK, this professional body is the British Psychological Society (BPS), while in America it is the American Psychological Association (APA). In some countries there are also governmental regulations, but for the purposes of this chapter, we will use the BPS regulations as a model. Most ethical guidelines are derived from the same basic principles, so do not massively differ from each other. The BPS "Code of Conduct and Ethical Guidelines" can be found at http://www.bps.org.uk/the-society/code-of-conduct/. The code of conduct applies to all psychologists, whether working in a research setting or private practice, and it is based on four ethical principles (Box 24.1). In addition to this, universities and institutions in which research takes place will have their own ethics panels that will review the ethics of each research project that is proposed to be carried out within the institution. These ethics panels will be well versed in the ethical principles of the professional body and will be knowledgeable about any local or national issues that will be pertinent to each individual study.

The BPS also publishes other sets of guidelines that specifically address issues relating to conducting research with humans and with animals, and a further set of recommendations for conducting research on the Internet. Let's see how we can apply these principles in the research that we undertake. To do this, we will consider some of the main ethical issues that research psychologists are faced with.

In the Know

Four ethical principles for psychologists

Respect
"Psychologists value the dignity and worth of all persons, with sensitivity to the dynamics of perceived authority or influence over clients, and with particular regard to people's rights including those of privacy and self-determination." (BPS, 2009, p. 10)

Competence
"Psychologists value the continuing development and maintenance of high standards of competence in their professional work, and the importance of preserving their ability to function optimally within the recognised limits of their knowledge, skill, training, education, and experience." (BPS, 2009, p. 15)

Responsibility
"Psychologists value their responsibilities to clients, to the general public, and to the profession and science of Psychology, including the avoidance of harm and the prevention of misuse or abuse of their contributions to society." (BPS, 2009, p. 18)

Integrity
"Psychologists value honesty, accuracy, clarity, and fairness in their interactions with all persons, and seek to promote integrity in all facets of their scientific and professional endeavours." (BPS, 2009, p. 21)

Ethics in psychological research with humans

Respect for participants

The most general (and hopefully obvious) ethical point concerns the way you treat your participants. This is reflected in the slow transition from referring to the people who take part in psychology research as "subjects" to referring to them as "participants", which is considered to be a more respectful term. It also means that we must respect the diversity of people and their right to **privacy** and confidentiality. As the BPS guidelines point out, psychologists owe the people who take part in their studies a great deal of gratitude, and they should be treated with consideration and respect at all times. Specifically, this means ensuring their well-being.

Privacy
Right of individuals to decide how information about them is to be communicated to others.

Physical harm

A research psychologist must always remember that he or she has a duty of care towards any participant who is giving up time in order to take part in a study. This duty of care requires the researcher to ensure that participants are protected from any undue **risks** that might be associated with taking part in the research. To suggest that all participants must be under "no risk" whatsoever would be naive, because life is unpredictable and there are always risks present when we go about our daily business. Instead, the BPS stipulates that researchers should ensure that the participant is not put under any

Risk
The possibility of harm, both physical and mental.

undue risk, beyond that which would normally be expected in their everyday lives. So, if you want to do research on the immediate psychological effects of sky-diving or rock-climbing, you would study sky-divers or rock-climbers, provided that you do not ask them to do anything above and beyond what they would normally do when undertaking those activities.

It is not always straightforward, however. Many medical procedures might be considered as being harmful to the participants – for example, administering a drug such as alcohol or caffeine, or depriving people of sleep for an extended period of time. The risks in such procedures require that great care be taken to make them ethically acceptable. The researcher must be sure (and be able to convince others) that the benefits of the research outweigh the potential costs.

Psychological stress

As well as considering the risk of physical harm in our research, we must also think about the risk of psychological and emotional distress. This can sometimes be a grey area. It almost goes without saying that we should not risk physically harming our participants, but how can we be sure about what is likely to count as being psychologically stressful?

For example, participants might be told that they will receive some extremely intense electric shocks. They never actually receive the shocks because it is the fear or anxiety caused by the expectation during the waiting period that the researcher is interested in. Schachter (1959) employed a procedure like this, and showed that the anxiety produced a desire in participants who expected to be shocked to interact with others during the waiting period.

In another procedure that produces psychological stress, participants are given unfavourable feedback about their personalities or abilities. Researchers interested in self-esteem have typically given a subject a bogus test of personality or ability. The test is followed by an evaluation that lowers self-esteem by indicating that the participant has an unfavourable personality trait or a low ability score.

Asking people about traumatic or unpleasant events in their lives might also cause stress for some participants. Thus, research that asks people to think about the death of a parent, spouse or friend, or their memories of living through a disaster, could trigger a stressful reaction.

p.604

When stress is possible, it must be asked whether all safeguards have been taken to help participants deal with the stress. Usually there is a "**debriefing**" session following the study that is designed in part to address any potential problems that may arise during the research. Where possible, participants should be as fully informed as possible and explicitly consent to their participation on the basis of the information provided to them.

Privacy and confidentiality

Another potential risk is the loss of expected privacy and **confidentiality**. Researchers must take care to respect and protect the privacy of their participants. At a minimum, researchers should protect privacy by keeping all data locked in a secure place. Confidentiality becomes particularly important when studying topics such as sexual behaviour, divorce, family violence or drug abuse; in these cases, researchers may need to ask people very sensitive questions about their private lives and it is extremely important that responses to such questions be confidential. In most cases, the researcher should

Confidentiality
Requirement to keep research data about individual participants private.

ensure that the responses are completely anonymous – there should be no way to connect any person's identity with the data. This happens, for example, when questionnaires are administered to groups of people and no information is requested that could be used to identify an individual (such as name, National Insurance number or phone number). In other cases, such as a personal interview in which the identity of the person might be known, the researcher must carefully plan ways of coding data, storing data and explaining the procedures to participants so that there is no question concerning the confidentiality of responses.

In some research, there is a real need to be able to identify individual participants. This occurs when individuals are studied on multiple occasions over time, or when personal feedback, such as a test score, must be given. In such cases, the researcher should develop a way to identify the individuals but to separate the information about their identity from the actual data itself. Thus, if questionnaires or the computerized data files were seen by anyone, the data could not be linked to specific individuals.

Another privacy issue concerns concealed observation of behaviour. In some studies, researchers make observations of behaviour in public places. Observing people in shopping malls or in their cars does not seem to present any major ethical problems. The general rule in these situations is that it is fine to observe people unobtrusively in situations in which they would reasonably expect their behaviour to be seen by strangers. However, what if a researcher wishes to observe behaviour in more private settings or in ways that may violate individuals' privacy? For example, would it be ethical to rummage through people's rubbish or watch them in public toilets?

In the Know

In one study, Middlemist et al. (1976) measured the time to onset of urination and the duration of urination of males in toilets at a college. The purpose of the research was to study the effect of personal space on a measure of physiological arousal (urination times). The students were observed while alone or with a confederate of the experimenter, who stood at the next stall or a more distant stall in the restroom. The presence and closeness of the confederate did have the effect of delaying urination and shortening the duration of urination. In many ways, this is an interesting study; also, the situation is one that males experience on a regular basis. However, one can question whether the invasion of privacy was justified (Koocher, 1977). The researchers can, in turn, argue that through pilot studies and discussions with potential participants they determined that ethical problems with the study were minimal (Middlemist et al., 1977). Middlemist et al. employed a method for determining whether a procedure is ethical that was first proposed by Berscheid et al. (1973). Role-playing is used to gather evidence about participants' perceptions of a potential experiment. If the role-playing participants indicate that they would participate in the experiment, at least one objection to deception has been addressed.

Informed consent

Participants must consent to taking part in a research study, and in most cases, this consent will be informed (i.e. informed consent). What this means is that the researcher is ethically obligated to provide each participant with enough information about the research so that they can make an informed decision about whether or

Informed consent
Agreement, usually written, to participate in a study after being informed of the consequences of participation.

not they wish to take part. The information provided to the participant must be detailed enough to allow them to make a decision, and must include information about the research that might reasonably be expected to influence their willingness to participate. If the researcher wishes to take audio/video/photographic recordings of participants, then this must be brought to the attention of the participants and their consent obtained. Except for situations in which informed consent may be dispensed with (described below), psychologists *must* inform participants:

- of the purpose, duration and procedures of the study
- that they may decline to participate or withdraw from the research without having to give a reason (including withdrawal retrospectively with the requirement that their data, including any recordings, be destroyed)
- of any risks, discomfort or adverse effects related to the research
- of any possible benefits related to the research
- about any limits of confidentiality of the research
- of any incentives, such as money or grades, for research participation
- of their rights and whom to contact for answers to questions about the research.

Figure 24.3 shows a sample informed consent form that was used in a student project which was designed to determine if there was a relationship between personality traits and self-inflicted wounds. Informed consent forms like this one are used routinely to document that informed consent was obtained. A research project is unethical if the principles of informed consent are not followed. However, there are occasions when you need not provide informed consent.

Consent Form

For this study, the researcher cannot give you information about its purpose until after the study is finished. If you would like, the researcher will email you a description and the results when the study is completed.

This survey may ask you personal details about your life. However, there will be no way to link the information you provide to your name. In addition, any information about your participation will be kept confidential.

Please complete this survey honestly. If at any time you feel uncomfortable, you are free to withdraw from the study and none of your information will be used in the results. There is no penalty for withdrawing, but you are encouraged to complete the survey for the sake of the study.

By signing this form you agree not to discuss this survey with others until the researcher has contacted you. If you discuss this survey with others who complete it at a later date, it may influence their responses. By signing, you are agreeing to complete this survey honestly and accurately.

Thank you for participating. If you have any questions please ask one of the researchers or you may contact Jaz Mundo by phone (•••–•••) or email (address.ac.uk) or Dr Wilson by phone (•••–•).

_____   _____
Signature   Date

_____
Email address

Figure 24.3 Sample consent form

Dispensing with informed consent

In certain situations, the researcher does *not* have to obtain informed consent. These are normally observational studies in which participants are being observed in a naturalistic setting. If, for example, you want to observe the number of same-sex and mixed-sex groups in your library, you probably do not need to stand on a table and announce your presence before gaining the consent of everyone who happens to be in the library at that time. If you are looking at the way people describe themselves on an online dating service, you probably do not need to contact each person to get their permission. In these cases, the researcher must be sure that the research cannot reasonably be assumed to cause distress or harm. As always in these situations, the participant's confidentiality must be protected, so issues of anonymity still apply. When doing research like this, the general rule to follow is that, if information is in the public domain, or if an individual is in a public place where he or she might reasonably expect to be observed by strangers, then you do not need to obtain explicit consent, *as long* as the research is otherwise ethical and all other ethical principles are adhered to. Whether or not informed consent is required, participants are always free to withdraw from research participation.

Autonomy issues

Informed consent seems simple enough, but it is not always straightforward. What happens when the participants may lack the ability to make a free and informed decision to voluntarily participate (i.e. lack **autonomy**)? Special populations such as young children, patients in psychiatric hospitals or adults with cognitive impairments require the researcher to take special precautions. Whenever young children or individuals with impairments are asked to participate, consent from them must be obtained wherever possible, as well as consent from the participant's parent or guardian (**dual consent**). If a participant cannot provide consent or has an impairment in communication or understanding that prevents them being able to consent, then a written consent form signed by a parent or guardian who is in a position to understand the participant's reaction must be obtained (**dual consent by proxy**). In cases such as this, it is also advisable for the researcher to seek approval from a disinterested adviser who is familiar with ethical issues in research.

All researchers should be sensitive to the specific circumstances under which they are conducting the research, and how these circumstances might impinge upon the participants' ability to provide consent. For example, detained individuals (such as those in prisons or in juvenile care) might feel obliged or under pressure to take part, so the researcher must ensure that any consent that is given is free from coercion of any sort and represents a free choice on the part of the individual. Researchers must also be sensitive to the role that they play and the authority they might be seen to have by those that they are asking to participate, and ensure that this does not influence the decision in an undue way.

Deception

One of the most common topics to come up whenever the ethics of psychology research is discussed is that of **deception**. Lying to people is generally considered bad, but in

Autonomy
Principle that individuals in research investigations are capable of making a decision of whether to participate.

Dual consent
Principle that consent should be sought from potential participants and their parent/guardian, when the participant is unable to make a free and informed decision about giving consent (usually children and people with impairments).

Dual consent by proxy
Principle that consent should be sought from the parent/guardian of a potential participant, when the participant cannot provide consent or cannot communicate this.

Deception
Deliberately misleading participants about any aspect of the research.

everyday life, there is a common notion of "white lies" – lies that do not hurt anyone. Is there such a thing as a white lie in psychology? The answer is "yes" – within strict boundaries.

Why would psychology researchers deceive their participants? As acknowledged in the BPS guidelines, "since there are very many psychological processes that are modifiable by individuals if they are aware that they are being studied, the statement of the research hypothesis in advance of the collection of data would make much psychological research impossible"; and "there is a distinction between withholding some of the details of the hypothesis under test and deliberately falsely informing the participants of the purpose of the research, especially if the information given implied a more benign topic of study than was in fact the case"[2]. In other words, if you told people exactly what you were studying in every piece of research that you did, then it becomes likely that their behaviour or their responses would change as a result of this knowledge. That would make the research pointless, so researchers must necessarily prevent participants from knowing aspects of the research that are likely to alter the psychological phenomena under study. In situations like this, the deception might be omission of the information that is likely to alter the phenomena under study. It might not be an outright lie, but it is deception nonetheless. This is not to say that psychologists have permission to deceive their participants at every turn. The BPS suggests that deception should be avoided where possible, and where it is employed, it should not be of the type that is likely to cause the participants to object to the deception, to be angry at the deception, or to feel discomfort or distress as a result of the deception.

Debriefing

Debriefing
Explaining to participants the nature, results and conclusions of the research they participated in and correcting any misconceptions.

Debriefing occurs after the completion of the study. It is an opportunity for the researcher to deal with issues of withholding information, deception and any potential harmful effects of participation, although debriefing participants after they have participated should not be seen as a way of making amends for any form of unjustified deception. If participants were deceived in any way, the researcher needs to explain why the deception was necessary. This can sometimes be done verbally while at the same time giving the participants an opportunity to discuss the study with the researcher. It can also be done by handing out information and debriefing sheets, outlining the nature of the research and any issues that the researcher feels the participant ought to know about. The researcher should consider what the most appropriate form of debriefing is, given the nature of the research that he or she is conducting. Sometimes the debriefing can happen immediately after the participant has completed his or her tasks; sometimes the researcher might not immediately debrief (for example, in case "word gets out" among others who are likely to take part in the study) and will debrief all participants at the end of the research.

If the research altered a participant's physical or psychological state in some way – as in a study that produces stress – the researcher must make sure that the participant has "calmed down" or has returned to pre-study levels and is comfortable about having participated. If there is a need for the participant to receive additional information or to speak with someone else about the study, the researcher should provide access to these resources. The participants should

---

2   The guidelines from which these quotes are taken can be accessed at http://www.bps.org.uk/the-society/code-of-conduct/ethical-principles-for-conducting-research-with-human-participants.cfm.

leave the experiment without any ill feelings towards the field of psychology, and they may even leave with some new insight into their own behaviour or personality.

Debriefing provides an opportunity for the researcher to explain the purpose of the study and tell participants what kinds of results are expected, as well as discussing any practical implications of the research. In some cases, researchers may contact participants later to inform them of the actual results of the study. Thus, debriefing has both an educational and an ethical purpose as it provides an opportunity for participants to learn more about research in general. For instance, participants can learn that their individual performance in a study is not a direct measure of their abilities. How well they perform on a memory test, for instance, is affected by how good a memory they have, but their performance is also affected by factors such as what the researcher asks them to remember and how they are tested (these things would be *independent variables*).

Debriefing also helps researchers learn how participants viewed the procedures in the study. A researcher may want to find out whether participants perceived a particular experimental procedure in the way the investigator intended (Blanck et al., 1992). For example, a study of how people respond to failure may include tasks that are impossible to complete. If participants do not judge their performance as a failure, however, the researcher's hypothesis cannot be tested. Debriefing allows the investigator to find out whether participants perceived that they had failed at the tasks or whether they perceived that they had no chance to succeed.

Additionally, debriefing can help inform researchers because it can help them plan future research, both by providing ideas for new research studies and by helping the researcher identify any potential problems with the procedures of the current study. Debriefing, in other words, can provide clues to the reasons for participants' performance, which may help researchers interpret the results of the study and can sometimes allow participants to report on any errors they may have detected in experimental materials – for instance, missing information or ambiguous instructions. So, debriefing is not only good practice and necessary whenever any element of deception has been used, it is also useful for the researcher in informing them about the experience of their participants.

Ethics in Internet research

The Internet has opened up a whole new venue for conducting scientific research, and psychology is no exception. Researchers from around the world often collaborate on scientific projects, and can now quickly and easily exchange ideas and findings with one another via the Internet. Vast quantities of archival information are accessible though government-sponsored Internet sites (e.g. census information). In the last decades of the twentieth century, researchers began to collect data from human participants via the World Wide Web and there is the potential to include millions of people in one study! Types of psychological research on the Internet include simple observation (e.g. recording "behaviour" in chat rooms), surveys (questionnaires, including personality tests) and experiments involving manipulated variables.

Although the Internet offers many opportunities for psychologists, it also raises many ethical concerns. Can we apply traditional ethical guidelines developed for traditional offline research to research conducted on the Internet? In most cases, ethical guidelines transfer quite well and they should be adhered to whether the research is conducted online or offline. For example, some Internet research involves a potential participant going to a website and choosing a study to participate in. As in an offline study, the participants will be given a full description of the study, an informed-consent form, and an opportunity to withdraw from the study. They will also receive details of how to obtain follow-up information. Although this kind of research is largely similar to offline research, the fact that the researcher has no contact with the participants as they take part might be seen as problematic, because the researcher cannot monitor the participant and the progress of the study, taking action if anything goes wrong or the participant becomes distressed in any way. Because of the separation between researcher and participant, special consideration must be given to the nature of the task that online participants are asked to do and the stimuli that are used as part of the research.

There are some forms of Internet research that raise a host of issues that are not covered particularly well in traditional ethical guidelines. Research that makes use of existing chat rooms, online communities, email groups or list servers falls into this category. For example, if you were to enter a chat room to study the interactions among the participants, several ethical issues arise. First, how do you obtain informed consent from the chat room participants? Do you need to? Is this the equivalent to an observational study conducted in a public library (for example)? Second, how do you protect the privacy and confidentiality of research participants online? Should participants who agree to remain in the chat room be assigned pseudonyms to protect their identities?

Informed consent on the Internet

Gaining informed consent for Internet research would seem a simple matter: just have willing participants sign an electronic version of a consent form after having read accompanying information about the study they are consenting to. However, this procedure, which works well in other contexts, may not work well when doing Internet research. For one thing, how many of us check the "I agree" box on web pages without properly reading the information that we are agreeing to? I know I do. If a participant does this without reading the information given to them, then this is not "informed" consent (and it is probably the case that they are more likely to do this online than when presented with a sheet of paper by the researcher and asked to read it). Researchers conducting research on the Internet should be aware of the fact that this is likely to be the case for at least some participants, and should consider the potential implications of participation without having fully read the relevant information. If the researcher thinks that this would be problematic, then a decision has to be made about alternative safeguards or alternative data-collection methods.

A further concern arises when the research is conducted on young children or adults with impairments. As **outlined previously**, the standard procedure is to seek consent from a parent or guardian who is in a position to know the reaction of the individual. This form of consent is difficult to obtain when the researcher is present (e.g. how exactly does the researcher know that the adult is in a suitable position to provide consent?) and becomes even more problematic if done online, when the researcher is not present. There is no easy answer to this, and researchers are advised to proceed with caution and seek the advice of other researchers who are not part of the project.

Yet another potential problem concerns the researcher's inability to confirm the identity of online participants. If someone checks a box saying "I am over 18" because the research specifically requires (perhaps for ethical reasons) that only over-18s can participate, then there is no way of verifying whether this person is actually over 18. If the research demands that specific information about the individual must be accurate, then the researcher must consider the possibility that the Internet might not be an appropriate way of collecting such data, given the difficulties involved in verifying the identity of potential participants.

Chat rooms

There are other ethical issues when Internet chat rooms are used. For example, if a researcher enters a chat room with the intention of collecting data, should other members of that chat room be asked to consent? Is a chat room a public or a private forum? Are interactions in chat rooms comparable to interactions in public places? If the researcher decides that consent should be obtained, what happens if one or more people in the chat room do not give consent? Robert Jones (1994) questions whether it is ethical to exclude individuals from a chat room if they refuse to take part in the research study (especially if it is one that people join to get help for some condition). One solution would be to allow everyone to participate but exclude responses from those who refuse to be in the study. Jones, however, questions whether this is feasible, and whether it is possible to ensure the anonymity and privacy of non-participants.

How might chat room participants respond to being part of a research study? Hudson and Bruckman (2004) investigated this question, and the results were not pretty. Hudson and Bruckman entered over 500 chat rooms under one of four conditions. In the first condition, they did not identify themselves as researchers conducting a study. In the second condition, they entered the chat room and identified themselves as researchers studying language use in chat room discussions. In the third condition, they entered the chat room, identified themselves as researchers, and gave chat room participants the option of privately opting out of the study. The fourth condition was identical to the third except that chat room participants were given an opportunity to privately opt into the study.

What these researchers found was that they were more likely to be kicked out of a chat room when they identified themselves as researchers. It did not matter which introduction they used. Additionally, they found that they were more likely to be kicked out of small chat rooms than large ones. Hudson and Bruckman (2004) note that for every increase of 13 chat room members, the likelihood of being kicked out was halved. As the number of moderators in a chat room increased, so did the likelihood of being kicked out. Hudson and Bruckman's results indicate that, in general, chat room members do not take kindly to being studied. This can pose serious problems for Internet researchers who must obtain informed consent from potential research participants.

Privacy and confidentiality on the Internet

The Internet, by its nature, is a very public medium, and this poses a serious threat to the privacy of Internet research participants. Although the Internet is public, the distinction is sometimes blurred because Internet use often happens within people's private homes, and sometimes postings that people think are private are later made publicly available. Researchers should be sensitive to such issues as much as possible.

Pittenger (2003) states that concerns about privacy and confidentiality on the Internet are twofold. The first concern is a technical one and refers to the protections that are available in the software programs used by researchers. These programs vary in their ability to secure unauthorized access by computer hackers. You must be reasonably sure that hackers will not gain access to participants' responses. Additionally, if data are housed on a publicly owned computer, the data may be vulnerable to exposure by existing freedom of information laws. You are ethically bound to protect the confidentiality of participants' responses as fully as possible. This can be done with appropriate hardware and software, and by keeping data stored on a portable storage device like a CD-ROM or memory stick. Of course, you should inform potential participants of the possibility of data disclosure, and if the risk of disclosure significantly compromises the ethics of the research, then the researcher should consider an alternative means of collecting data.

Related to this is the issue of quoting material from discussion boards. If the material is quoted verbatim, then the possibility arises that it is traceable back to the individual, through search engines. If the individual has consented to being quoted, then this becomes less of an issue, but if this is not the case, then the researcher should exercise caution and consider paraphrasing the material or using some other method of coding the material to protect anonymity.

A second concern is over the ethical responsibilities of researchers who become involved in online groups (e.g. chat rooms and communities) without identifying themselves as researchers. You, as the researcher, must be mindful of whether the group that you are studying is a public or private group. Entering a private group poses special ethical concerns for your research. Research on participants in public groups may pose fewer concerns. Pittenger argues that there are three arguments for considering the Internet equivalent to a public place like a shopping mall:

1 Internet use is now so common that users should understand that it does not afford privacy.

2 A person can easily maintain anonymity by using a pseudonym that cannot be traced back to reveal the user's identity.

3 The exchange of information in open, public Internet forums does not fall under the heading of research that requires informed consent and can legitimately be studied as long as there is no potential harm to participants.

Of course, such arguments would not apply to forums or groups that are advertised as being "confidential" or as having limited access. Internet groups that are created for people with medical conditions (e.g. AIDS) or other afflictions (e.g. alcoholism) often include these provisions. Doing research on such groups would require a more strict research protocol, including full disclosure and informed consent.

Alternatively, one might also argue that not all postings to chat rooms or discussion boards are automatically public, so the researcher should employ discretion, respect the participants' expectations of privacy, and consider the nature of the research and the potential implications of observing postings.

With this in mind, Pittenger (2003) suggests the following guidelines for ethical research on Internet groups:

1 Learn about and respect the rules of the Internet group that you are going to study. Find out if the group is an open, public one or if it is a closed, private one.

2 Edit any data collected. Comb through the data that you collect and eliminate any names or pseudonyms that may lead to participant identification. You should also eliminate any references to the name of the group being studied.

3 Use multiple groups. You might consider studying several groups devoted to the same topic or issue (e.g. several groups for alcoholics). In addition to increasing the generality of your results, this technique adds another layer of protection to participant privacy.

Deception and debriefing on the Internet

Both the British Psychological Society and the American Psychological Association permit deception in research under certain conditions. With Internet research, the guiding principles are the same as in any other form of research. Particular consideration must be given to research in which the researcher poses as a member of a chat room and does not reveal that the interactions are being observed. Again, the guidelines covering observation in public places also apply in circumstances such as these, but thought must be given to whether the chat room can reasonably be considered a public place.

When deception is used, you have an obligation to debrief your participants. Debriefing may be more difficult in Internet research. If, for example, participants decide that they have had enough before the end of a session or the entire study, it may be difficult to track them down for debriefing. One way around this may be to have a "Quit" button onscreen that participants can click on when they decide to withdraw. Clicking the button would take them to a debriefing page, although there is no way of ensuring that participants will click the "Quit" button rather than just closing their browsers. Another way might be to create a separate Internet group or "enclave" where participants can go for debriefing, although there is still an issue about the individuals who take part but do not visit a debriefing page.

Debriefing will usually take the form of an information page that is displayed when the participant has completed his or her task. If the research is considered to necessitate it, an alternative method of feedback and/or debriefing should be considered, e.g. telephone debriefing or some other means of post-session contact. All participants should be given the contact details of the researcher in case they have further questions regarding the study.

Research with animals[3]

Research on animals is a topic that often stirs passionate debate. Psychologists have used animals in the past, and continue to use animals for certain types of study. Regardless of whether you think this is right or wrong, everyone can agree that there must be strict regulations on any animal research that is being done. Animals are used for a variety of reasons. The researcher can carefully control the environmental conditions of the animals, study the same animals over a long period, and monitor their behaviour 24 hours a day if necessary. Animals are also used to test the effects of drugs, and to study physiological and genetic mechanisms underlying behaviour. Animals are also increasingly used in various forms of therapy.

---

3 For the BPS guidelines on working with animals, visit http://www.bps.org.uk/the-society/code-of-conduct/guidelines-for-psychologists-working-with-animals.cfm. For the APA guidelines, visit http://www.apa.org/science/anguide.html.

Scientists argue that animal research benefits humans and point to many discoveries that would not have been possible without animal research (Carroll and Overmier, 2001; Miller, 1985). Plous (1996a, 1996b) conducted a national survey of attitudes towards the use of animals in research and education among psychologists and psychology students. The attitudes of both psychologists and students were quite similar. In general, there is support for animal research: 72 per cent of the students support such research, 18 per cent oppose it, and 10 per cent are unsure (the psychologists "strongly" support animal research more than the students, however). In addition, 68 per cent believe that animal research is necessary for progress in psychology. Still, there is some ambivalence and uncertainty about the use of animals: when asked whether animals in psychological research are treated humanely, 12 per cent of the students said "no" and 44 per cent were "unsure". In addition, research involving rats or pigeons was viewed more positively than research with dogs or primates unless the research is strictly observational. Finally, females have less positive views towards animal research than males.

Animal research is indeed important and will continue to be used to study many types of research questions. It is crucial to recognize that strict laws and ethical guidelines govern all work that psychologists do that involves animals. Such regulations deal with the need for proper housing, feeding, cleanliness and health care. They specify that the research must avoid any cruelty in the form of unnecessary pain caused to the animal.

In most countries, the use of animals in research is regulated by law. In the UK, the Animals (Scientific Procedures) Act of 1986 covers the use of animals in research, while in the USA, any institution conducting animal research must have an Institutional Animal Care and Use Committee (IACUC) comprising at least one scientist, one veterinarian and one member of the community. The IACUC reviews all animal research procedures and ensures that all federal regulations are adhered to.

Before you begin conducting your research using animal subjects, you should familiarize yourself with the principles for the care and use of animals, and design your research accordingly. Before you can conduct your study, you will have to submit a research proposal to an appropriate ethics panel, describing what animals you plan to use in your research and how, and justifying your decisions concerning the species and number of animals to be used and specifics of your procedure. Only when your proposal has been formally approved will you be permitted to obtain your animals.

If you are doing animal research, keep in mind that ethical treatment of animals is in your best interest as a researcher. Ample evidence shows that mistreatment of animals (such as rough handling or housing them under stressful conditions) leads to physiological changes (e.g. housing animals under crowded conditions leads to changes in the adrenal glands). These physiological changes may interact with your experimental manipulations, perhaps damaging the external validity of your results. Proper care and handling of your subjects helps you obtain reliable and generalizable results. Thus, as well as being morally and ethically important, it is also to your benefit as a researcher to treat animals properly.

Cost–benefit assessment: should the research be done?

Even though a study is designed to conform to ethical standards for the use of animal subjects – giving proper care and housing, avoiding unnecessary pain or hardship, and so on – this does not automatically mean that the study should be done. Your decision to go ahead with the study should be based on a critical evaluation of the cost of the study to the subjects weighed against its potential benefits, otherwise known as the cost–benefit ratio. Cost to the subjects includes such factors as the stressfulness of the procedures and the likely degree of discomfort or suffering that the subjects may experience as a result of the study. The potential benefits might include the study's possible contribution to knowledge about the determinants of behaviour, its ability to discriminate among competing theoretical views, or its possible applied value in the real world.

Conducting an unbiased evaluation is not easy. Having designed the study, you have a certain vested interest in carrying it out and must be aware that you are likely to be biased in your judgement of the benefits of the research. Yet if you reject a study because its potential findings do not have obvious practical application, you may be tossing out research that would have provided key insights necessary for the development of such applications. The history of science is littered with research findings whose immense value was not recognized at the time they were announced.

Despite these difficulties, in most cases it is possible to come up with a reasonable assessment of the potential cost–benefit ratio of your study. For example, imagine you have designed a study to evaluate the anti-anxiety effect of a certain drug. You have no particular reason to believe that it has any effect on anxiety; in fact, its chemical structure argues against such an effect. However, you have a sample of the drug, and you are curious. Your subjects (rats) will have to endure a procedure involving water deprivation and exposure to foot shock in order for you to assess the effect of the drug. Given that the cost in stress and discomfort to the rats is not balanced against any credible rationale for conducting the study, you should shelve the study.

Integrity in research

So far in this chapter, we have made a case for you to treat your human participants or animal subjects ethically and in a manner consistent with all relevant professional and government regulations. However, you should understand that your responsibility to be an ethical researcher does not end with how you treat your participants or subjects. You, as a researcher, also have an obligation to treat your sciences ethically and with integrity.

Fraudulent or otherwise dishonest research practices can erode the public's confidence in scientific findings. It can also lead to potentially harmful outcomes for large groups of people. For example, fraudulent breast cancer research done in the 1990s suggested that the less radical lumpectomy (where only the tumour and surrounding tissue are removed) was just as effective as the more radical mastectomy (where an entire breast and surrounding tissue are removed). It turned out that the researcher, Dr Roger Poisson, a noted cancer researcher, admitted that he had falsified his data concerning clinical tests of the two surgical procedures. He had allowed women into his research who were in more advanced stages of cancer than were to be permitted in the study, and he had not reported on the progress of women who had died. He kept two sets of files on his research, one false and one truthful. As a result of Poisson's unethical conduct, confidence in the lumpectomy versus mastectomy research was shaken. It also called into question the honesty of the entire scientific community. The public could no longer be sure that the results coming out of research laboratories could be trusted.

This example illustrates how the process of science can be subverted by a dishonest scientist. Expectations of a researcher also can affect the outcome of a study. The case of Poisson and the impact of researcher expectations reveal an important truth about research in the social and behavioural sciences: it is a very human affair. The research process benefits from all the good qualities of human researchers: ingenuity, dedication, hard work, a desire to discover the truth, and so on. However, as in any human endeavour, the more negative qualities of human researchers also may creep into the research process: ambition, self-promotion, ego, securing and keeping a job, and obtaining scarce grant money.

What is research fraud?

Research fraud
Occurs when a researcher intentionally produces research which is inaccurate or untruthful (e.g. through falsification or manipulation of data, by claiming another's work as their own).

Fraud in research takes a variety of forms. Perhaps the most pernicious, albeit rare, form of **research fraud** is the outright fabrication of data (Broad and Wade, 1983). A scientist may fabricate an entire set of data based on an experiment that might never have been run, or replace actual data with false data. Other forms of fraud in research include altering data to make them "look better" or to fit with a theory, selecting only the best data for publication, and publishing stolen or plagiarized work (Broad and Wade, 1983). Altering or otherwise manipulating data in order to achieve statistical significance (e.g. selectively dropping data from an analysis) also would constitute research fraud.

Research fraud can occur if scientists sabotage each other's work. Claiming credit for work done by others also could be considered fraud. If, for example, a student conceptualizes, designs and carries out a study and a professor takes senior author status on the publication, then that would be considered fraud. It is also dishonest to attach your name to research that you had little to do with, just to pad your CV. Some articles may have as many as 10 or more authors. Each of the junior authors may have had some minor input (such as suggesting that Wistar rats be used rather than Long–Evans rats). However, that minor input may not warrant authorship credit. Finally, plagiarism, in which a researcher uses another person's work or ideas without proper acknowledgment, is also a form of research fraud.

The perils of plagiarism

Plagiarism
Using someone else's words or ideas – intentionally or unintentionally – without properly citing the source.

Plagiarism is using the written or other intellectual work of someone else and claiming it as your own. Sometimes, "claiming it as your own" can mean simply reproducing another person's material without duly acknowledging them. Plagiarism is a serious ethical breach. One problem in academic institutions is that many students do not know what constitutes plagiarism, nor do faculties always provide a clear definition (Murray, 2002).

Martin (1994) identifies four types of plagiarism of interest to students:

1 word-for-word plagiarism
2 paraphrasing plagiarism
3 plagiarism of secondary sources
4 plagiarism of ideas.

You can prevent these types of plagiarism in your work by knowing that they are wrong and actively avoiding them. Certainly, plagiarism caused by carelessness or incompetence is curable by skill building. For example, many students do not realize that cutting and pasting from the Web without acknowledging the original author is plagiarism. In response, many university lecturers now use software tools that detect plagiarism from Web sources.

Why are we so concerned about plagiarism? One reason is that we want to teach correct scientific procedures. Properly acknowledging the work of fellow scientists is important not only as a basic procedural characteristic of science but also as a safeguard for science itself. Science suffers when research results are plagiarized. Healthy science requires that all people trust scientific results. Another reason is to protect the scientists who think up research ideas, conduct studies and publish data. They are valuable to society. Plagiarizers threaten scientific procedures, public confidence in science, and scientists' livelihoods. So, learn what plagiarism is and how to avoid it. Cite previous scientific work properly.

The prevalence of research fraud

At one time, the editor of *Science* stated that 99.9999 per cent of scientific papers are truthful and accurate (Bell, 1992). The US Office of Research Integrity (2006) found fraud in eight out of 22 cases that it closed (three cases of data falsification, two cases of fabrication, two cases of fabrication and falsification, and one case of plagiarism). A survey by Geggie (2001) of medical consultants in England found that 55.7 per cent of respondents reported witnessing at first hand some form of research misconduct. Additionally, 5.7 per cent reported engaging in misconduct themselves, and 18 per cent indicated that they would consider engaging in misconduct in the future or were unsure about whether they would engage in research misconduct.

Critics suggest that it is not possible to exactly quantify research fraud (Bell, 1992). For one thing, fraud may not be reported, even if it is detected. In one survey (cited in Bell, 1992), many researchers who suspected that a colleague was falsifying data did not report it. Fraud may also go unreported because the liabilities associated with "whistle-blowing" can be quite severe. Whistle-blowers may be vilified, their credibility is called into question, and they may, perhaps, even be fired for "doing the right thing". Thus, the relatively few celebrated cases of fraud reported may be only the tip of the iceberg.

Regardless of how low the actual rate of fraud in science turns out to be, even a few cases can have a damaging effect on the credibility of science and scientists (Broad and Wade, 1983). Fraud in research undermines the credibility of science and undermines the public's confidence in the results that flow from scientific research. In the long run, this works to the detriment of individuals and of society.

How can we explain research fraud?

Why would a scientist perpetrate a fraud? There are many reasons. Fraud may be perpetrated for personal recognition. Publishing an article in a prestigious journal is a boost to one's self-esteem. Personal pressure for such self-esteem and recognition from others can motivate a person to falsify data or commit some other form of research fraud.

The pursuit of money is a major factor in fraudulent research (Bell, 1992). Doing research on a large scale takes quite a bit of money, and researchers are generally not wealthy and cannot fund their own research. Nor can financially strapped universities or hospitals provide the level of funding needed for many research projects. Consequently, researchers must look to funding agencies with budgets that are typically limited with respect to the number of applications that can be accepted for funding. Consequently, competition for research funding becomes intense. In addition, it is generally easier to obtain grant money if you have a good track record of publications. The pressure for obtaining scarce grant money can lead a person to falsify data in order to "produce" and be in a good position to get more funding. Moreover, at some universities, obtaining grants is used as an index of a researcher's worth and may even be the difference between keeping or losing a job. This can add additional pressure towards committing research fraud.

Dealing with research fraud

Peer review
Formal process in which scientists judge colleagues' work submitted for publication or funding.

Bell (1992) points out that science has three general methods for guarding against research fraud: the grant review process, the **peer review** process for publication, and replication of results. Bell points out that, unfortunately, none of these is effective in detecting fraud. Editors may be disinclined to publish papers that are critical of other researchers, let alone that make accusations of fraud (Bell, 1992). In addition, replication of experiments is expensive and time-consuming and unlikely to occur across labs (Bell, 1992). Even if a finding cannot be replicated, that does not necessarily mean fraud has occurred.

Probably the best guard against fraud in science is to imbue researchers during the training process with the idea that ethical research means being honest. This process should begin as early as possible. Steinberg (2002) suggests that teaching about research fraud should begin in psychology students' research methods courses. She recommends that students be presented with cases of research fraud. Those cases should be discussed and evaluated carefully. Students should learn the implications of research fraud for researchers themselves, their field of study and the credibility of science (Steinberg, 2002). The short-term consequences (loss of a job, expulsion from school, etc.) and long-term consequences (harm to innocent individuals because of false results, damage to the credibility of science, etc.) should be communicated clearly to researchers during their education and training.

Assessing Milgram and Zimbardo

Let's return to the two studies described at the beginning of this chapter. By examining them in chronological order, we show how ethics codes for psychological research emerged and developed over time.

Milgram's shocking obedience experiment

Given the ethical issues that we have discussed in this chapter, it should be obvious why Milgram's study caused so much controversy. Criticism of the ethics of Milgram's (1963) obedience study began shortly after he published his results. The criticism focused on his treatment of the participants (Baumrind, 1964). Baumrind argued that Milgram had caused so much anxiety in his participants that some were permanently harmed. She predicted that future research involving deception would not be effective because participants would know about Milgram's study and would behave differently because of that knowledge. In other words, participants would no longer trust psychologists. Milgram (1964) responded by noting that his debriefing procedure, combined with psychiatric referrals where necessary, removed any effects of his anxiety-producing procedure. Furthermore, he pointed out that only a few participants believed that they had been harmed when they were asked after the study was completed. Milgram believed that he was acting properly as a psychologist. All of his actions fell within the normal social role of a research psychologist at the time. Psychology in the 1960s was unaware of the unique relationship between researcher and participant. Later, when researchers realized that participants were likely to suspend their normal cautions in research situations, it became the responsibility of researchers to protect their participants. As a result of this realization, ethical standards for research changed. Milgram's research stimulated a concern for how research psychologists and participants should interact. Today's requirement that participants be free to withdraw from a study stems partially from Milgram's obedience studies.

Zimbardo's prison

When Zimbardo (1973) suspended his famous prison study, he was acting ethically within the new and evolved ethical context created by Milgram's work. Institutional ethics boards had been established at some universities as a result of earlier studies such as Milgram's. Zimbardo obtained permission from the Stanford ethics panel to conduct the prison study. Unfortunately, the prison study worked all too well, sucking both participants and researchers into uncertainty as to what was research and what was real life. When Zimbardo began to fear for the welfare of his participants, he cancelled the remainder of the study. Retrospectively, Zimbardo stated that he should have called off the experiment sooner (O'Toole, 1997).

Neither Milgram's nor Zimbardo's studies would be approved by an ethics panel today. Neither study obtained informed consent from the participants, which would be required now. Also, both studies required participants to remain throughout the study and only excused participants after the most vigorous protests on their part. Today participants would be allowed to withdraw from the study at any time they wished. Ethics is a dynamic process and ethical standards will continue to change.

Ethics and you

Concerns about ethical practices have been around since the beginning of recorded history, and are an issue in everything we do, including research. Fully fledged psychological researchers usually become so familiar with the ethical standards discussed in this chapter that such issues become second nature to them, and thinking about ethics is a natural part of thinking about research. You may be conducting your first research project soon. The basic ethical responsibilities that we have discussed should be at the forefront of your mind when thinking about the design of your study. Things like confidentiality, informed consent, dispensing with informed consent, deception, debriefing, reporting data and plagiarism should all be considered along with the more practical issues concerning research design and what analyses are most appropriate. Practise these ethical responsibilities now as part of your transition to becoming a more fully trained scientist.

The line between ethical and unethical research is not always clear and that line may change over time. Good scientists take risks, but they take them only after carefully considering alternatives and consequences. They know that they should not take risks to answer trivial questions. They also depend on their peers beforehand, using consultations and ethics panels as tools to help prevent ethical problems before they occur. In today's scientific research, ethical decisions are woven into the fabric, not stitched on later. Refer to this chapter often as you conduct research, and let the ethics code guide you as you undertake your research activities.

Summary

Ethics are a critical part of all psychologists' lives and this chapter has introduced you to the basic underlying principles that we all must think carefully about. Behaving ethically serves to ensure the safety of everyone who is involved in psychological research and practice. The BPS builds its ethical principles from the foundation of Kant's moral imperative, and emphasizes four key features of ethical practice: respect, competence, responsibility and integrity. Psychologists who work with humans must ensure that they behave in a manner that prevents both physical and psychological harm, while maintaining privacy and confidentiality. Informed consent and debriefing are also important components of working with other people. Research with animals has its own set of issues, including the way the animals are treated and whether the research is necessary in the first place. Another ethical obligation for psychologists (and scientists in general) is to act with integrity. Issues surrounding this include plagiarism and research fraud.

Questions

1 Why is informed consent an ethical principle? What are the potential problems with obtaining fully informed consent?

2 What constitutes fraud, what are some reasons for its occurrence and why doesn't it occur more frequently?

3 What are the four main principles of ethical conduct that form the basis of the BPS code of ethics?

4 What are the main ethical issues raised by using children as research participants?

5 What special ethical concerns face you if you conduct your research on the Internet?

6 What are the issues surrounding obtaining informed consent in Internet research?

7 What are the issues surrounding privacy and confidentiality in Internet research?

8 What steps can be taken to protect Internet participants' privacy?

9 What special issues are presented by using deception in Internet research?

10 Match the concept with the responsibility.

1 Confidentiality	a. Explaining the risks and benefits of participating in a research project.
2 Debriefing	b. Allowing participants to exit the research situation at any time.
3 Plagiarism	c. Informing participants of the nature of the study and its results.
4 Reporting results	d. Keeping information and scores of participants secure.
5 Informed consent	e. Not modifying data from a study.
6 Permitting participants to withdraw	f. Not using another's words or ideas without acknowledgment.

11 Why is deception such a difficult ethical issue in psychological research? Under what circumstances is deception justified?

12 What was it about Zimbardo's prison experiment that made it so controversial from an ethical perspective?

✪ Activities

1 Assess the risks for the following research activities (answers below). Can you explain the basis for your answers?

Read the following research scenarios and assess the risk to participants by placing a check mark in the appropriate column.	No risk	Minimal risk	Greater than minimal risk
(a) Researchers conducted a study on a college campus examining the physical attractiveness level among peer groups by taking pictures of varied groups of students and then asking others at another college to rate the attractiveness levels of each student in each group.			
(b) A group of researchers plan to measure differences in depth perception accuracy with and without perceptual cues. In one condition participants could use both eyes and in another condition one eye was covered with an eye patch.			

▶ (c) Researchers conducted an anonymous survey on attitudes towards gun control among shoppers at a local mall.

(d) A developmental psychologist asked college student participants to play a video game. They were randomly assigned to play either a violent or non-violent game, and the differences in their blood pressure before and after playing the game were measured.

2 Have a look at the following research proposal. If you were sitting on an ethics panel that was presented with these proposals, what would you ask the researcher and what would your recommendations be? You will have to decide whether specific ethical standards have been violated and make recommendations regarding the proposed research, including the most basic recommendation of whether the investigator should be allowed to proceed. You will have to decide whether you would approve carrying out the study at your institution in its present form, whether modification should be made before approval, or whether the proposal should not be approved. (An actual research proposal submitted to an ethics panel would include more detail than we present here.)

Rationale Psychological conformity occurs when people accept the opinions or judgements of others in the absence of significant reasons to do so or in the face of evidence to the contrary. Previous research has investigated the conditions under which conformity is likely to occur and has shown, for example, that conformity increases when people anticipate unpleasant events (e.g. shock) and when the pressure to conform comes from individuals with whom the individuals identify. The proposed research examines psychological conformity in the context of discussions about alcohol consumption among teenage students. The goal of the research is to identify factors that contribute to students' willingness to attend social events where alcohol is served to minors and to allow obviously intoxicated persons to drive an automobile. This research seeks to investigate conformity in a natural setting and in circumstances where unpleasant events (e.g. legal penalties, school suspension, injury or even death) can be avoided by not conforming to peer pressure.

Method The research will involve 36 high school students between the ages of 16 and 18 who have volunteered to participate in a research project investigating "beliefs and attitudes of today's high school students". Participants will be assigned to four-person discussion groups. Each person in the group will be given the same 20 questions to answer; however, they will be asked to discuss each question with members of the group before writing down their answers. Four of the 20 questions deal with alcohol consumption by teenagers and with possible actions that might be taken to reduce teenage drinking and driving. One member of the group will be appointed discussion leader by the principal investigator. Unknown to the participants, they will be assigned randomly to three different groups. In each group, there will be either 0, 1 or 2 students who are actually working for the principal investigator. Each of these "confederates" has received prior instructions from the investigator regarding what to say during the group discussion of the critical questions about teenage drinking. [The use of confederates in psychological research is discussed in Chapter 4.] Specifically, confederates have been asked to follow a script which presents the argument that the majority of people who reach the legal driving age (16), and all individuals who are old enough (18) to vote in national elections and serve in the armed forces, are old enough to make their own decisions about drinking alcohol; moreover, because it is up to each individual to make this decision, other individuals do not have the right to intervene if someone under the legal age chooses to drink alcohol. Each of the confederates "admits" to drinking alcohol on at least two previous occasions. Thus, the experimental manipulation involves either 0, 1 or 2 persons in the four-person groups suggesting they do not believe students have a responsibility to avoid situations where alcohol is served to minors or to intervene when someone chooses to drink and drive. The effect of this argument on the written answers given by the actual participants in this experiment will be evaluated. Moreover, audiotapes of the sessions will be made without participants' knowledge, and the contents of these audiotapes will be analysed. Following the experiment, the nature of the deception and the reasons for making audiotapes of the discussions will be explained to the participants.

Chapter 5

Communicating and Reporting Research – Reports, Presentations and Posters

OVERVIEW

In this chapter you will learn about the ways in which research findings can be communicated to different audiences. We will focus on writing research reports and journal articles as this is probably the most common way in which you will report your own research. Referencing will also be discussed, along with presenting your findings in the form of oral and poster presentations.

OBJECTIVES

After studying this chapter and working through the exercises, you should be able to:

- Write a research report using the appropriate format
- Identify the different sections of a research report and describe what information the sections should contain

- Construct a reference list in APA style and cite sources correctly in text
- Describe how to report research findings in a oral presentation
- Describe how to report research findings in a poster presentation

Communicating and reporting research

Communicating and reporting your research findings is the final, and most important, part of the research process. It is only by this reporting that science can progress. Others need to know the questions you have asked, the methods you used and the answers you found. This is vital not only for progress of knowledge, but also to assess the reliability of your findings and conclusions – it allows others to attempt to replicate and extend your findings.

The main ways in which research is communicated is through research reports, journal articles, oral presentations and poster presentations. We will look at the main guidelines covering these methods of communication. However, if you are preparing a report or presentation for assessment, please refer to the guidelines provided by your tutor as there may be some minor, but important, differences.

As you prepare any report or presentation, you should think about the audience and the purpose of the work. Usually, you need to tell the audience what you did, why you did it, what you found and what this means.

Even if you do not plan on continuing with a career in psychological research, the skills discussed in this chapter are relevant to many occupations, particularly those at managerial or technical level. The ability to organize facts and draw conclusions, and present these clearly and logically in a report or presentation is important in a variety of careers, so it is worth paying attention to it now.

Reports and journal articles

Research reports and journal articles tend to follow a similar format. This means that the author knows where things should go and the reader can find the relevant information quickly. Although there are no definitive rules about the format, quantitative research reports usually consist of the following sections:

- Title
- Abstract
- Introduction
- Method
- Results
- Discussion
- References

The information discussed here is only a general guide – if your tutor has given you specific instructions about the format of a report, please follow that guidance.

Title

The title of an article or report is the first thing that grabs attention, so it is important that you produce a title that is concise but informative. It should give the reader an indication of the main problem under investigation, as well as the variables of interest. For example, the following titles are both short and informative:

Effect of anxiety on mathematical problem solving

Memory for faces among elderly and young adults

Sometimes having a colon in the title will help to convey the nature of your research or even add a bit of "flair" to your title, as in:

Cognitive responses in persuasion: Affective and evaluative

Determinants comparing the tortoise and the hare: Gender differences and experience in dynamic spatial reasoning tasks

You could always make the title the question that the research addresses. For example:

Do rewards in the classroom undermine intrinsic motivation?

Does occupational stereotyping still exist?

However, beware of trying to be too clever or humorous with your titles – this is not always appreciated!

Another thing to consider if you are writing an article for publication is that you should use words and phrases that are likely to be used in computer **literature searches**. Do not limit yourself by using obscure words or by being too cryptic – think about which terms people are likely to use when they search for literature on your topic of interest.

ch. 23
pp.575–582

Abstract

Abstract
Short summary of the contents of a research report or journal article.

The **abstract** appears at the beginning of a report. However, it is *not* an introduction, but a summary of the entire research report. It should be concise, usually between 100 and 120 words, and is only very rarely over 200 words – check the guidelines for the particular report/article you are writing. The abstract should summarize the key points of your report: the problem under investigation; the nature of the participants; a description of the equipment/materials and procedure; your main findings, including significance level;[1] any implications or applications of the findings; and a conclusion. A sentence or two on

---

1   The American Psychological Association (2010) recommends that you report significance levels in your abstract. However, some researchers would advise against including numbers in the abstract, and would say that they should be included only if there is something special or unusual about them. If you are unsure, consult your tutor.

each of these points is usually sufficient. You may often see statements such as "the implications of the study are discussed" in abstracts, but they are pretty pointless as they tell the reader nothing. Avoid this if possible.

As well as being concise, the abstract should be accurate, coherent and readable, and should not contain anything that is not already in the report. It should also be self-contained – all the information required to understand the abstract should be in the abstract. This means that if you use any abbreviations or unique terms in the abstract, they should be defined clearly.

Just because the abstract appears at the beginning of a report does not mean that you should write it first. In fact, you are advised to write it last, as it is much easier to write a summary of something once it is written.

But what is the point of having a summary, which is written last, at the beginning of a report? Imagine you were searching for articles to use in an assignment and had to read through each article in its entirety in order to determine whether it was relevant or not – very time-consuming and frustrating! However, you can read through an abstract and very quickly get an idea of what the study is about and whether you want to read the full article. An abstract also makes the content of the article easier to comprehend as you have already got a basic idea of the aims and nature of the study before reading it in detail. In published articles, people are much more likely to read an abstract than the full article, so it is important that you make a good job of it and get people interested in your research.

Introduction

> **Introduction**
> The first main section of a research report or journal article, which includes the rationale for the study, a literature review, and usually a statement of the aims or hypotheses for the research.

The aim of the **Introduction** section is to introduce the topic of interest, put it in context by reviewing previous literature, and discuss the rationale and predictions for the current study. The best approach to take is to go from general at the beginning of the Introduction to specific at the end (see Figure 25.1). The Introduction usually consists of the following parts:

- An introduction to the general issue being investigated – why is it important, interesting or relevant?

- A literature review – a brief review of previous research and theories related to the topic of interest. This does not need to be a definitive, all-encompassing review – you can assume that the reader has some level of knowledge – but it should at least cover the main issues and bring the reader up to date.

- A statement of the problem to be addressed by the research, identified as a gap in knowledge or an area of debate in the literature.

- A statement of the aim(s) of the research.

- A *brief* description of the research strategy, which identifies how the method used is appropriate to the research topic.

- A description of any predictions about the outcome and/or hypotheses.

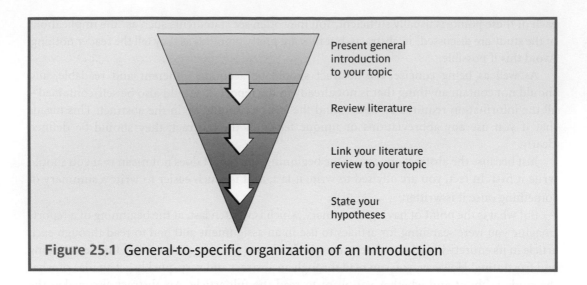

Figure 25.1 General-to-specific organization of an Introduction

The last part in particular is important as this is where you tell the reader what you will be testing in your analyses. Students are often asked to write hypotheses in their reports, although you may choose to write more general research questions. For your own reports, please follow the guidance given by your tutor.

Hopefully, by the end of the Introduction the reader should understand the rationale for your research and the hypotheses/predictions should make complete sense.

Method

Method
Section of a research report or journal article in which the methods used in the study are described in detail.

In the **Method** section you tell the reader how the study was conducted. A good rule of thumb to use when writing this section is that there should be enough detail for someone to replicate the study. In order to improve organization and readability, the Method section is usually divided into subsections. The four most commonly used subsections are: Design, Participants, Materials and Procedure. However, there is flexibility – for example, you can combine subsections if it is more appropriate (e.g. Materials and Procedure are often combined when the procedure is simple).

The Method section is fairly straightforward to write – you are just telling the reader about what you did. As a result, this is often the easiest section to write first.

Design
Subsection of the Method section of a research report or journal article that provides an overview of the research design and variables.

Design

The **Design** subsection is used to give the reader an overview of the research design being used. You should include details such as:

- whether the study was experimental or non-experimental (e.g. correlational)
- if experimental, whether the study was between subjects, within-subjects (repeated measures) or mixed design

- details on the independent variable(s) (or factors) and number of conditions/levels; for example if you were using a between-subjects design, you could say how many groups there were and what the purpose of each group was (e.g. was one group a control group?)
- details on the dependent variable(s)
- other relevant design issues (e.g. counterbalancing).

The Design subsection is notoriously difficult to get right. It should provide the basic framework of your study and should be written in one or two concise sentences.

A simple design might be something like "Current mood was measured in two conditions (after 30 minutes exercise, after 30 minutes completing reading) using a between-subjects design." Note that this does not say "the independent variable was . . . the dependent variable was . . .". Instead, it integrates all that information into one concise sentence.

Another example might be "A repeated measures design was employed in which participants were asked to rate familiarity of previously seen words in each of three 'word-type' conditions: nouns, adjectives and adverbs. Order of presentation was randomized."

Do not go into details about the procedure or materials. Just give the basic structure of the experiment, and move on. If in doubt, read the Design subsection in other research papers and you will get an idea of how they should be structured.

The Design subsection is not always included in some reports or articles that you may come across. However, writing it can be very useful, particularly in experimental research, as it forces you to think clearly about your design – vital for analysis – as well as providing a useful overview for readers.

Participants

In the **Participants** subsection you should include details on the nature and size of the sample. In order for someone to replicate your research, they need to know who took part. You may choose to report details such as:

Participants
Subsection of the Method section of a research report or journal article used to describe the number and nature of the sample.

- number of participants
- relevant demographic information (e.g. gender, age, ethnicity)
- how participants were recruited/selected (be careful if you say your participants were randomly sampled – were they really?)
- any inclusion/exclusion criteria for selection
- how participants were assigned to any conditions or groups
- if participants were rewarded in some way (e.g. with payment or course credit) for taking part
- any other personal characteristics relevant to the research (e.g. handedness, degree subject, year of study, socio-economic class).

Remember that "participants" is the preferred term for describing those people who took part in your research; "subjects" should be used only when your research involved animals. If you are conducting research involving animals, then you should give details on factors such as number, sex, age, weight, physical condition, care and housing.

Materials/Apparatus

Materials/Apparatus
Subsection of the
Method section of
a research report or
journal article that
describes the
materials and
apparatus used in
the study.

The next subsection of the Method section is used to provide details of the test materials and equipment that you used in your research. This is called **Materials** if you used mainly written material, but you may choose to use the heading **Apparatus** if you primarily used technical equipment when measuring behaviour (check the specific guidelines for the report or article you are writing for guidance on which heading to use). This subsection should *not* be written in the style of a shopping list, but should be in proper sentences and paragraphs. Check the Materials section of published articles to get an idea.

You need to provide adequate detail on your materials, while also at the same time thinking about what is relevant and appropriate to the research in question. For example, if you were conducting a perception experiment, you may want to provide quite a lot of detail on the monitor screen being used (e.g. manufacturer, model number, size, refresh rate). However, if the monitor was just being used for presenting instructions for participants, say, in a social psychology experiment, such detail may not be necessary.

Be sure that you go into adequate depth so that someone could replicate the study, but avoid the temptation to describe *everything* – we do not really need to know who manufactured the pen used to write answers in a test! You can usually assume that the reader will have a basic level of familiarity with psychological research, so be careful you do not patronize them. Many readers will already be familiar with widely used standardized tests, for example, so you can usually afford to just give the name of the test and the version. You should also provide a reference to the test manual or article in which the test originally appeared so that readers can follow it up if they require more information.

In some cases, though, particularly when you are dealing with unfamiliar or new materials such as a new questionnaire or a word list, you may need to go into more detail. However, space is limited and you may not be able to fit in the whole questionnaire or word list. Instead, you can get around this by giving an overview of the materials in the Materials section, possibly with a few examples of items, and then refer the reader to an Appendix – a section at the back of a report which can be used for additional information. It is also quite common in published research for readers to be directed to a website or to the author for further information.

Procedure

Procedure
Subsection of the
Method section of
a research report or
journal article that
provides a detailed
description of the
procedures used in
the study.

The aim of the **Procedure** subsection is to tell the reader what happened to each participant during testing. For example, how were materials presented to participants, what instructions and information were given to them, what different conditions were participants exposed to? You should describe to the reader how the session progressed.

As with the rest of the Method section, there should be enough detail to allow for replication. So, if you had standardized instructions, you should probably provide those here (or in an Appendix).

Sometimes you will find the Materials and Procedure subsections combined. This usually occurs when the study involves the simple completion of a number of tests or materials which would be described fully in the Materials, so having a separate Procedure would be a bit redundant.

Results

The **Results** section is where you present your data and analyses. You should *not* try to interpret or explain your results here – leave that for the Discussion. Instead, present your results and take the reader through them in a logical, clear and objective manner. The reader should not be left to their own devices to make sense of tables and graphs – the Results section should be in the form of a *written* narrative and is not just a collection of tables and graphs.

> **Results**
> Section of a research report or journal article that summarizes and analyses data and statistics.

What you include should be *relevant* – it is no good throwing in every table and graph from your SPSS output, hoping that the reader will work out for themselves what is important. You need to be selective. It is not usual to include raw (unanalysed) data or individual cases unless your study was focused on individuals (e.g. case study), so any data you present should be a summary.

In a quantitative report, you should include both descriptive and inferential statistics. **Descriptive statistics** such as the mean, median, standard deviation or frequencies are used to summarize data (see Chapter 14) and are needed in a report to put everything in context and to "set the scene" for your later analysis. You should therefore present descriptive statistics before moving on to the statistical analysis to which they refer. If you are dealing with nominal data you should provide frequencies, but for other types of data you should present a measure of central tendency and a measure of spread. Although the most commonly reported descriptive statistics are the mean and standard deviation, remember that other measures (e.g. median) may be more appropriate if your data are ordinal or you have outliers.

> ch. 14

Tables and figures are useful ways of presenting descriptive statistics or summarizing other information in your Results section. They can also appear in other sections of a report, but are most commonly found here. A table is simply numerical data in table form, whereas a figure refers to a graph, chart, photograph or drawing. Tables and figures should be able to stand by themselves, so all the necessary information for understanding should be with the table or figure and not hidden in the text. Imagine that you cut out a table or figure from a report and gave it to someone – would they be able to make sense of it by itself? It is therefore essential that you provide tables and figures with full titles – headings such as "Table 1" do not tell us anything. Columns and rows in tables, and axes in graphs, should be properly labelled as well. If you are planning on copying output from SPSS ensure that you check that the variable names make sense and that any labels are meaningful – all too often we see variables called "VAR00001" or groups labelled simply as "1" and "2" without any further explanation. You are therefore strongly recommended to edit any SPSS output before presenting it in a report, or preferably just create your own tables and graphs within your word-processing package.[2]

---

2 On many occasions, markers who see a report with unedited SPSS output that has been copy-pasted in are immediately tipped off that the student might not truly understand what the data mean. Look at published research reports. They rarely, if ever, include unedited output from statistical packages. Avoid doing this if at all possible.

As the point of the Results section is to take the reader through the data and analysis, you should refer to the tables and figures in your text before presenting them. Introduce the reader to the table or figure in your text (remember to number them, e.g. Table 1.1, Figure 1.1) and describe what it shows. You should avoid repeating yourself, so if you are presenting means in your text, for instance, there is no reason to present them in a table and a graph as well. Also watch that you do not try to make your tables and figures too flashy – simple works best here.

Once you have presented descriptive statistics, you should move on to your inferential statistics. You should describe which statistical test you used and which specific data were analysed, before stating the outcome of your analysis and reporting the statistics in the appropriate manner. This means that you will need to give the values of the test statistic (e.g. t, F, χ^2), degrees of freedom (df) or N, and significance (p); you are also strongly recommended to report the effect size where appropriate. We have already discussed the ways to report the results of different statistical tests in previous chapters, so please refer to the guidelines appropriate for your analysis. It is now preferred to report precise p-values (e.g. $p = .024$ rather than $p < .05$), so you should state what your alpha level is (usually .05) before you report any **inferential statistical** analyses. If you are reporting precise p-values, note that you should *not* write "$p = .000$", even though ".000" may appear in SPSS output – you can never have a probability of exactly 0 in statistics. What has happened is that SPSS has rounded down the p-value to three decimal places; you should therefore report such a result as $p < .001$ or $p < .0005$.

chs 16–21

Discussion

Discussion
Section of a research
report or journal
article that evaluates
and interprets results.

The final main section of a report is the **Discussion**; this is where you interpret your results and relate your findings to previous research. You should note that the structure of the Discussion reverses that of the Introduction: rather than moving from general to specific, it moves from the specific research findings to more general implications (see Figure 25.2).

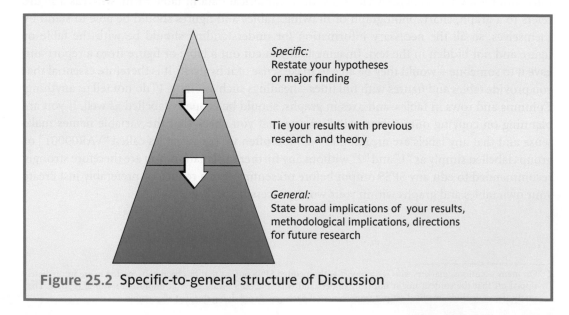

Specific:
Restate your hypotheses
or major finding

Tie your results with previous
research and theory

General:
State broad implications of your results,
methodological implications, directions
for future research

Figure 25.2 Specific-to-general structure of Discussion

It is common to start the Discussion with a reminder of the main aim of the research or the main hypotheses, before discussing whether the results support these hypotheses. Next, you should relate the current findings to the previous research and theory discussed in your Introduction, and try to explain your findings. If your results are consistent with the previous research, you should discuss the implications of this; if the results are not consistent with previous research, you should discuss why this may have occurred and what this may mean in terms of theory.

The next part of the Discussion consists of an evaluation of the current research. Are there any alternative explanations for your findings (e.g. confounding variables)? Were there any problems with the method that could have affected the results? Do not get carried away, though – this is not the place to completely write off your research. If it was so bad in the first place, why did you bother?

This evaluation leads on to a discussion of ideas for improvements to the method and ideas for future research. For example, if you identified a potential confounding variable, you could measure that variable in a future study to see if it really was having an effect. You should suggest ways to address any problems you identified with the current research. You may think of other ways in which you could alter the method, perhaps by using different stimuli or measures, or extending the current method to a different context.

You should finish off the Discussion with a conclusion in which you summarize the main implications of your findings. This should hopefully tie in with the beginning of the Introduction, where you explained why it was important to study the topic.

References

The **References list** should include every book, journal article or other source of information that you cited in your report. There is a specific way in which you should cite your references within the report itself and in the References list, and it is important that you get this right. If you use the work of someone else but do not credit them in your References – either intentionally or unintentionally – this is **plagiarism** and it can have serious consequences. It is therefore essential that you pay attention to how to reference correctly. The rules for referencing are clear, so there is really no reason to get it wrong.

> **References list**
> An alphabetical list of all of the sources cited within a body of text.
>
> **Plagiarism**
> Using someone else's words or ideas – intentionally or unintentionally – without properly citing the source.

The most commonly used referencing system in psychology is the APA reference style, although some tutors may ask you to use Harvard, of which APA style is a variation. Both systems of referencing involve giving the surname(s) of the author(s) and the date of publication when citing within the body of the report, and then giving the full corresponding citation in the References list. We will now provide you with an overview of APA reference style, which is suitable for most psychological journal articles. However, you should double-check with your tutor which referencing format they expect from you.

Citation within the body of the report

As already stated, when citing a source of information within a report or article, you should give the author name(s) and year of publication. The format depends on whether the author names are part of the narrative (i.e. in the sentence proper) or if they are in parentheses (brackets).

One author: when the author's name is part of the narrative, include the publication date in parentheses immediately after the name:

Markman (1991) found that marital discord can lead to constructive resolution of conflict.

When the author's name is not part of the narrative, the name and date are cited in parentheses at the end of an introductory phrase or at the end of the sentence:

In one study (Markman, 1991), couples learned to discuss . . .

Couples have lower rates of divorce and marital violence after problem-solving intervention (Markman, 1991).

Two authors: when the source has two authors, both names are included in each citation. The only thing you have to watch is that you should use "and" between the names when part of the sentence, and "&" when in parentheses.

Harris and Marmer (1996) reported that fathers in poor families are less involved with their adolescent children than fathers in non-poor families.

Fathers in poor families are less likely to spend time with their adolescent children than fathers in non-poor families (Harris & Marmer, 1996).

Three to five authors. When a source has three to five authors, *all* author names are cited the *first time* the reference occurs. Thereafter, you cite the first author's surname followed by the abbreviation et al. ("and others") along with the publication date. The abbreviation may be used in narrative and parenthetical citations:

First citation

Abernathy, Massad, and Romano-Dwyer (1995) reported that female adolescents with low self-esteem are more likely to smoke than their peers with high self-esteem.

Research suggests that low self-esteem is one reason teenage girls are motivated to smoke (Abernathy, Massad, & Romano-Dwyer, 1995).

Subsequent citations

Abernathy et al. (1995) also examined the relationship between smoking and self-esteem in adolescent males.

For males, there is no relationship between smoking and self-esteem, suggesting gender-specific motivations for initiating smoking in adolescence (Abernathy et al., 1995).

Another question about subsequent citations is whether to include the publication date each time a source is referenced. Within a paragraph, you do *not* need to include the year in subsequent citations as long as the study cannot be confused with other studies cited in your report.

Citation within a paragraph

> In a recent study of video games, Anderson and Dill (2000) claim that . . .
>
> Anderson and Dill also reported that . . .

When subsequent citations are in another paragraph or in another section of the report, the publication date should be included.

Six or more authors: occasionally you will reference a report with six or more authors. In this case, use the abbreviation et al. after the first author's last name in *every* citation. Although you would not list all author names in the text, the citation in the references section of the report should include the names of the first six authors followed by et al. for additional authors.

Multiple works: a convenient way to cite several studies on the same topic or several studies with similar findings is to reference them as a series within the same parentheses. When two or more works are by the same author(s), report them in order of year of publication, using commas to separate citations:

> Buss (1988, 1989) found . . .
>
> Past research (Buss, 1988, 1989) indicates . . .

When two or more works by different authors are cited within the same parentheses, arrange them in alphabetical order and separate citations by semicolons:

> Investigations of families in economic distress consistently report that girls react with internalization problems whereas boys respond with externalization problems (Conger, Ge, Elder, Lorenz, & Simons, 1994; Flanagan & Eccles, 1993; Lempers, Clark-Lempers, & Simons, 1989).

Reference list style

The APA *Publication Manual* (2010) provides examples of 95 different reference formats for journal articles, books, book chapters, technical reports, convention presentations, dissertations, web pages and videos, among many others. We will only cover the main types of references here; you should consult the APA manual for further information. The general format for a reference list is as follows:

1 The references are listed in alphabetical order by the first author's last name. Do not categorize references by type (i.e. books, journal articles, and so on).

2 Elements of a reference (authors' names, article title, publication data) are separated by full stops.

The first line of each reference is typed flush to the left margin; subsequent lines are indented. This is called a "hanging indent" and would appear like this:

> Davis, J. L., & Rusbult, C. E. (2001). Attitude alignment in close relationships. *Journal of Personality and Social Psychology, 81*, 65–84.

Journal articles: For a journal article, you should give details of the author(s), date of publication, article title, journal name, volume and pages. Sometimes you may need to provide the issue number of a journal article, but this is necessary only when each issue of a volume begins with page 1 rather than continuing its page numbering throughout the volume. The general format for referencing a journal article in APA style is:

> Surname 1, initials., Surname 2, initials., & Surname 3, initials. (Year of publication). Article title. *Journal title, volume number* (issue number), start page number–end page number. doi:xx. xxxxxxxxxx

Note that both the name of the journal and the volume number are italicized in APA style, and only the first letter of the first word of the article title is capitalized (unless there a proper nouns such as names of countries or people, or after a colon or question mark). A recent addition to the referencing format is the DOI (digital object identifier), which is a unique code assigned to every article published online. If you know the DOI for an article, you can locate it on the Internet (provided you have access to that journal). The DOI can be found on the front page of most recently published articles. If your article does not have a DOI, APA format recommends that you include the homepage for the journal instead (not the database or search engine you used to find it). Here are some examples.

One author – no issue number

> Stokes, P. D. (2009). Using constraints to create novelty: A case study. *Psychology of Aesthetics, Creativity, and the Arts, 3*, 174–180. doi: 10.1037/a0014970

Two authors – use of issue number

> Saunders, J., Fernandes, M., & Kosnes, L. (2009). Retrieval-induced forgetting and mental imagery. *Memory & Cognition, 37* (6), 819–828. doi: 10.3758/MC.37.6.819

Books. When citing a book, you should include details of the author(s), date of publication, book title, publisher and place of publication. The general format is:

> Surname 1, initials., Surname 2, initials., & Surname 3, initials. (Year of publication). *Book title*. City or town of publication: Publisher.

Note that the book title is italicized and only the first word of the title has a capital letter. If the city of publication is not well known, you should provide details of the county or state; for US towns and cities, you can use the two-letter state abbreviation (e.g. AZ, NY, TX). If the book is edited and has different authors for each chapter, be sure to make it clear that the named author is the editor (Ed.)

One-author book

> Uba, L. (1994). *Asian Americans: Personality patterns, identity, and mental health*. New York: The Guilford Press.

One-author book – second or later edition

> McAdoo, H. P. (1988). *Black families* (2nd ed.). Newbury Park, CA: Sage.

Edited book

> Huston, A. H. (Ed.). (1991). *Children in poverty: Child development and public policy.* New York: Cambridge University Press.

Chapters from edited books. If you cite a chapter from an edited book, the reference should begin with the names of the authors of the *chapter*, not the book. You should then give the date, chapter title, name(s) of the editor(s), book title, page numbers for the chapter, and publication information. The general format is:

> Surname 1, Initials., Surname 2, Initials., & Surname 3, Initials. (Year of publication). Chapter title. In Initials., Surname (Ed.), *Book title* (pp. start page number-end page number). City or town of publication: Publisher.

Note that the book title should be italicized; "pp." refers to pages, "p." refers to a single page. Here are some examples.

One editor

> Brown, A. L., & Campione, J. C. (1994). Guided discovery in a community of learners. In K. McGilly (Ed.), *Classroom lessons: Integrating cognitive theory and classroom practice* (pp. 229–270). Cambridge, MA: MIT Press.

Two editors

> Bates, J., Bayles, K., Bennett, D., Ridge, B., & Brown, M. (1991). Origins of externalizing behaviour problems at eight years of age. In D. Pepler & K. Rubin (Eds.), *The development and treatment of childhood aggression* (pp. 93–120). Hillsdale, NJ: Erlbaum.

Chapter from book in multivolume series

> Kagan, J. (1992). Temperamental contributions to emotion and social behavior. In M. S. Clark (Ed.), *Review of personality and social psychology: Vol. 14. Emotion and social behavior* (pp. 99–118). Newbury Park, CA: Sage.

Secondary sources. Sometimes you need to cite an article, book or book chapter that you read about somewhere else. Although you should always try to read the primary source, sometimes you may have to cite a secondary source instead, particularly if you are dealing with an old or obscure original source. If you use secondary citations you should always be aware that what you are reading are not the original words and that what the author(s) of the secondary source writes may not be entirely faithful to the original source. The underlying principle when citing secondary sources in APA style is that you need to make it clear to the reader when you used a secondary source, and you should reference the secondary source (but not the primary source) in your References list. This way, the References list should be a list of the sources you have actually read and cited in your report. In the following example, an article by Conway and Pleydell-Pearce was written about in a book by Woll:

> Conway and Pleydell-Pearce (as cited in Woll, 2002) suggested that autobiographical memory . . .

In the References list, simply provide the reference for the *secondary* source you used (in this case, the Woll citation):

> Woll, S. B. (2002). *Everyday thinking: Memory, reasoning, and judgment in the real world.* Mahwah, NJ: Erlbaum.

Electronic sources

We have already mentioned using the DOI when referencing journal articles. When citing other Internet-based resources, the APA (2010) recommends that you follow the same format as for the equivalent fixed-media sources, adding in sufficient information for someone to retrieve the electronic source. This means that you should add in the full URL (i.e. Internet address) to the source (not the database or search engine used to find it) or, preferably, the DOI. Note that you are not required to give the date of retrieval unless the source is likely to change frequently (e.g. Wikipedia). This is a change from the previous version of APA format.

Qualitative research reports

The format we have been describing so far relates to quantitative research and cannot be so easily applied to qualitative research. For example, the objective, scientific approach to describing research findings is not appropriate for qualitative research, and some would argue that there is no such thing as "results" in qualitative research (Parker, 2005). And just as there is no one agreed method of qualitative analysis, there is no one definitive format for a qualitative report. Having said that, though, here are some notes on sections you may see in a qualitative report:

- *Abstract*: similar to that for quantitative research, but usually discusses the particular methodology and type of analysis in more depth.

- *Introduction*: this usually has a general-to-specific structure, similar to that of a quantitative report; there should be a literature review before moving on to the aims of the research. You will probably need to discuss why you have chosen a particular qualitative methodology. It is unlikely that you will specify hypotheses as these are not always appropriate for qualitative research.

- *Method*: this does not need to have distinct subsections as in a quantitative report, but you may choose to use headings to help organize material. What you include will depend on the nature of the research but you could provide details on such things as: the general design, who took part in the research and how access was gained, who the researcher is, the location and timing of the study, the procedure used to elicit data, how data were recorded and transcribed, and any ethical issues.

Analysis
Section of a qualitative research report or journal article that states what was found with evidence.

- **Analysis**: state what was found and provide evidence, usually in the form of quotes.

- *Discussion*: this is often combined into one section with the Analysis, but can also be separate. You should remind the reader of the aim of the research, summarize the findings, relate them to previous research and theory, and discuss the implications.

- **Reflexive analysis**: this may form part of your Discussion or may be a separate section. It is vital that you evaluate your own role in the qualitative analytic process and identify how that may have influenced your findings. You should also evaluate the design and suggest improvements or ideas for future research.

- *References*: as with quantitative reports, you must give full references for all sources cited in your report.

- *Appendices*: these are commonly used in qualitative research reports, often for transcripts, interview schedules, etc.

> **Reflexive analysis**
> Section of a qualitative research report or journal article that contains an evaluation of the research and the researcher's own role in the analytic process.

Guidance on writing

Now that you have a clear idea of the format of a research report and how to reference correctly, all you have to worry about is actually writing the report! Here are some suggestions to help you with your writing.

Know your audience

Think carefully about who your audience will be, and tailor your writing accordingly. For example, if you are writing up a research report as part of an assessment for your degree, your audience will be the tutor and any other markers.

Identify your purpose

The main point of writing a research report or journal article is to describe what you have done and what you have found, and also to convince the reader that your interpretation of the results is appropriate. So, when you are writing your research report, think of it as a way of selling and promoting your research.

Writing style

As a general rule, you should write in the active voice (subject-verb-object construction, e.g. "Participants completed a questionnaire . . .") rather than the passive voice (object-verb-subject, e.g. "A questionnaire was given to participants to complete . . ."). Traditionally, authors were encouraged to write in the third person rather than use personal pronouns such as "I" or "we". However, it is becoming more common for personal pronouns to be used in psychological reports and is positively encouraged in qualitative research. You should check, though, with your tutor to see what their preference is.

Presentation

You should spend some time thinking about how your report will be presented. In terms of font, the APA recommends that you use a serif font such as Times New Roman or Courier for the body of the report, and a sans serif font such as Arial for any figures. Text should be font size 12 and double-spaced. Headings should be used throughout; numbered headings can be particularly useful. Do not forget page numbers either! Remember to check with your own tutors to see if they have any preferences for presentation.

Write clearly

Avoid ambiguity and try to make your writing as clear as possible. This means that you should be concise. Do not try to use complicated or wordy language – short words and sentences are much easier to read and understand. Be ruthless in your editing and avoid needless jargon, repetition or words that do not add anything. Clarity can also be achieved by being precise and selecting the right word for what you want to say. Table 25.1 shows some commonly misused words – you should study them carefully!

Another aspect of clarity in expression is being grammatically correct. While we cannot cover the intricacies of grammar here, you really need to pay attention to it in your writing. For example, "data" is the plural form of "datum" (see Table 25.1), so you should write "The data were analysed . . ." rather than "The data was analysed . . .". Grammar checkers in word-processing packages can help, but they do not pick up everything.

You can improve the clarity of expression even further by using transition words and phrases between paragraphs and sentences, which act as signposts for the reader to indicate the flow of your argument. For example, you can show contrast by using words and phrases such as: "in contrast", "however", "on the other hand", "nevertheless" and "conversely". Agreement or similarity can be indicated through words and phrases such as: "likewise", "similarly", "in addition", "furthermore" and "moreover". Some useful words and phrases suggest implications, for instance: "therefore", "thus" and "in conclusion". All of these phrases are very useful when used sparingly – if overdone, they can interrupt the flow of your writing.

Table 25.1 Commonly misused words

Words	True meanings and comments
affect/effect	*affect:* to influence
	effect: the result of; to implement
accept/except	*accept:* to take willingly
	except: excluding; to exclude
among/between	*among:* used when you refer to more than two
	between: used when you refer to only two
amount/number	*amount:* refers to quantity
	number: refers to countable elements

analysis/analyses	*analysis:* singular form
	analyses: plural form
cite/site	*cite:* make reference to
	site: location
datum/data	*datum:* singular form
	data: plural form
every one/everyone	*every one:* each one
	everyone: everybody
few/little	*few:* refers to number
	little: refers to amount
hypothesis/hypotheses	*hypothesis:* singular form
	hypotheses: plural form
its/it's	*its:* possessive pronoun
	it's: contraction of "it is"
many/much	*many:* refers to countable elements
	much: refers to quantity
phenomenon/phenomena	*phenomenon:* singular form
	phenomena: plural form
principle/principal	*principle:* strongly held belief
	principal: foremost
than/then	*than:* conjunction used when making a comparison
	then: refers to the past in time
that/which	*that:* used to specify a crucial aspect of something: "the study that was conducted by Smith (1984)"
	which: used to offer a qualification that is not crucial to something: "the study, which was published in 1984"
	(*which* is usually preceded by a comma; *that* takes no comma)
there/their/they're	*there:* refers to a place
	their: possessive pronoun
	they're: contraction of "they are"
whose/who's	*whose:* the possessive of "who"
	who's: contraction of "who is"
your/you're	*your:* possessive pronoun
	you're: contraction of "you are"

Source: compiled from Crews (1980); Hall (1979); Leggett et al. (1978); Strunk and White (1979).

Avoid biased language

You should try to be as fair and unbiased as possible when writing about other people in your reports. For example, when describing humans in general, it is better to use "men and women" as opposed to "man". You should avoid labelling people, for instance: "the elderly", "the schizophrenics", as this categorizes people as if they were objects. Therefore, the APA recommends that you use "elderly people" or "schizophrenic patients" instead. Any descriptions of people should be at an appropriate level of specificity, so if you were describing ethnic groups, it is better to use terms such as Chinese or French rather than Asian or European. Another way in which bias in language can be avoided is by referring to those people who took part in your research in a way that acknowledges their participation: "Participants completed the memory test" is therefore preferred to "The memory test was given to the participants."

Plagiarism and lazy writing

Lazy writing
Using too much quoted material (albeit correctly cited) in written work.

We have already discussed plagiarism in relation to referencing, but it is essential that you realize that using someone else's words without credit is plagiarism, whether it's intentional or not. This does not mean to say that using someone else's words and citing them correctly is acceptable either. This is referred to as **lazy writing** (Rosnow & Rosnow, 1986) and should be avoided. Quoted material should be used sparingly, if at all – it is much better to put things into your own words (paraphrasing) rather than having quote after quote. Using your own words demonstrates to your tutor that you have understood the material and can use it effectively. If you are concerned about the originality of your report, plagiarism detection services such as Turnitin can be very useful.

Publishing your report

You may decide to put a research report forward for publication in a journal. You are recommended to consult with your tutor before sending a research report to a journal. Before you submit anything, you need to identify a suitable journal, which publishes research in your topic area. You should check the guidelines for submission and follow them very carefully – your article will not be considered if it is in an inappropriate format. Remember that most, but not all, psychology journals follow the APA format and some use different referencing systems. The APA manual (2010) provides detailed instructions for preparing a manuscript for publication and is well worth looking at carefully.

Once the manuscript is ready, you should submit it to the journal, where it will usually be looked at by an editor. They will decide whether it should be considered for publication or not. If they think it may be suitable, the article will be sent out to reviewers who will make comments and a recommendation to the editor. The article may be accepted as it stands, may be accepted with minor modifications or it may be rejected. If you are lucky and the article is accepted, you then have to make any amendments and prepare the article for final publication. As you can imagine, this whole process can take a long time – it is common for it to take well over a year between submitting a manuscript and getting it published – so you will need to be patient and persistent.

Other ways of communicating research findings

Although research reports and journal articles are the most common way in which research is reported, you may also communicate research findings in oral or poster presentations.

Oral presentations

Oral presentations of research findings are common at conferences, research seminars and even in class. The main thing to bear in mind is that what works in writing does not necessarily work in oral presentations. People tend to use much longer and more complex sentences when writing than when speaking, so if you just read out a research report, the audience will very quickly lose interest. Reading a "script" is not a good idea either – the best option is to use key words or phrases as reminders. This means that your speech will be natural, plus you will not spend all of your time looking down at your script and can engage with the audience more.

> **Oral presentation**
> Method of communicating research findings by speaking in front of an audience.

You need to think about other ways in which you can keep the audience's interest in your presentation. Visual aids such as presentation slides and/or handouts can be extremely useful. Imagine if an audience member lost attention for a moment – if there was no visual aid it would be very difficult to get "back on track" with the presentation. Instead, a visual aid can provide a helpful skeleton of the presentation, making it easy to catch up on any missed content.

Similarly, it is a good idea to make it clear to the audience at the beginning of the presentation what you are going to speak about. Do not expect people to remember something you have said only once, so you should consider repeating and emphasizing the key parts of your presentation. You are normally given a strict time limit for an oral presentation so it is important to focus on the big picture and getting the main message across. Do not go into too much detail on methods and procedure, you can probably be quite concise when discussing previous literature, and it is sensible to cut down on jargon, particularly for a non-psychology audience. If necessary, you can put extra detail on a handout.

You should prepare thoroughly for an oral presentation. Practice is essential in order to determine if your presentation fits the time limit as well. It also means that you will know what you are going to say and will have identified any potential areas of difficulty. It is helpful to practise in front of a small audience, who can tell you if there are any parts that are confusing, unnecessary or need more detail.

Although you may be well prepared and ready for your presentation, be aware that technical difficulties can occur at any time, particularly if you are using a computer to present slides. Try to second-guess any potential problems that may occur. For example, what would you do if the projector did not work? You may need to bring along handouts. And what if your file does not work? Make back-up copies on different media (e.g. CD, USB stick, email attachment). If you can, check out the room in which you will be presenting before the day of the presentation, look at the room layout and the computer and determine whether you will need to amend your presentation accordingly. On the day of the presentation itself, get to the room early so that you can get set up and sort out any technical problems.

The motto for oral presentations, therefore, is: be prepared . . . and practise lots!

Poster presentations

Poster presentation
Method of communicating research findings by presenting them in the form of a poster and discussing research with viewers of the poster.

Another way in which you can present research findings is in a **poster presentation**. This is common in conferences and you may be asked to do it as part of your degree. Giving a poster presentation usually entails putting up a poster on your research, standing by it, waiting for viewers and being prepared to answers any questions that viewers may have. This interaction with your audience is one of the main benefits of a poster presentation. You should have a copy of the poster or of the research report on which it was based, for any interested viewers.

As with oral presentations, what works in writing does not necessarily work in poster presentations. A poster should most definitely not be a research report printed out large and stuck on the wall. Posters should be visually pleasing and should convey the main message quickly and from a distance.

Different conferences or tutors will give you different guidelines for the format of your poster. However, the APA recommends that you use a minimum font size of 72 point for a title and 27 point for other text. Space is limited in a poster, so your text needs to be concise and clear, and should include only the key points. Feel free to use bullet points rather than sentences and paragraphs – whatever gets the message across quickly. Figures (i.e. graphs, charts, diagrams) are another useful way of summarizing lots of information and add visual interest to your poster. Colour could also be used to make your poster more attractive and is helpful to highlight key points.

Your poster could consist of a series of separate pages or a single large poster, and there is a range of layouts that you can use; Figures 25.3 and 25.4 present just a few. The easiest option is to divide the content into the main sections found in a research report. Make the flow of the sections clear – should people read the sections up and down, or from left to right? Having headings and/or numbered sections would therefore be helpful. There may be specific guidelines for layout for a particular conference, so be sure to check these.

Bear in mind that producing a poster can be time-consuming, particularly if you want to create a large single poster that needs professional printing. Designing the poster can take a long time and it can be frustrating if you are not familiar with the software you are using. Make sure that you check the format preferred by the printers – you do not want to produce a poster in a file format that cannot be printed easily. And do not forget that printing takes time – printers are often busy and cannot always print your poster immediately – so make sure you take this into account and do not leave everything to the last minute. Having a poster printed professionally can also be expensive, so it is worth shopping around to find the cheapest deal.

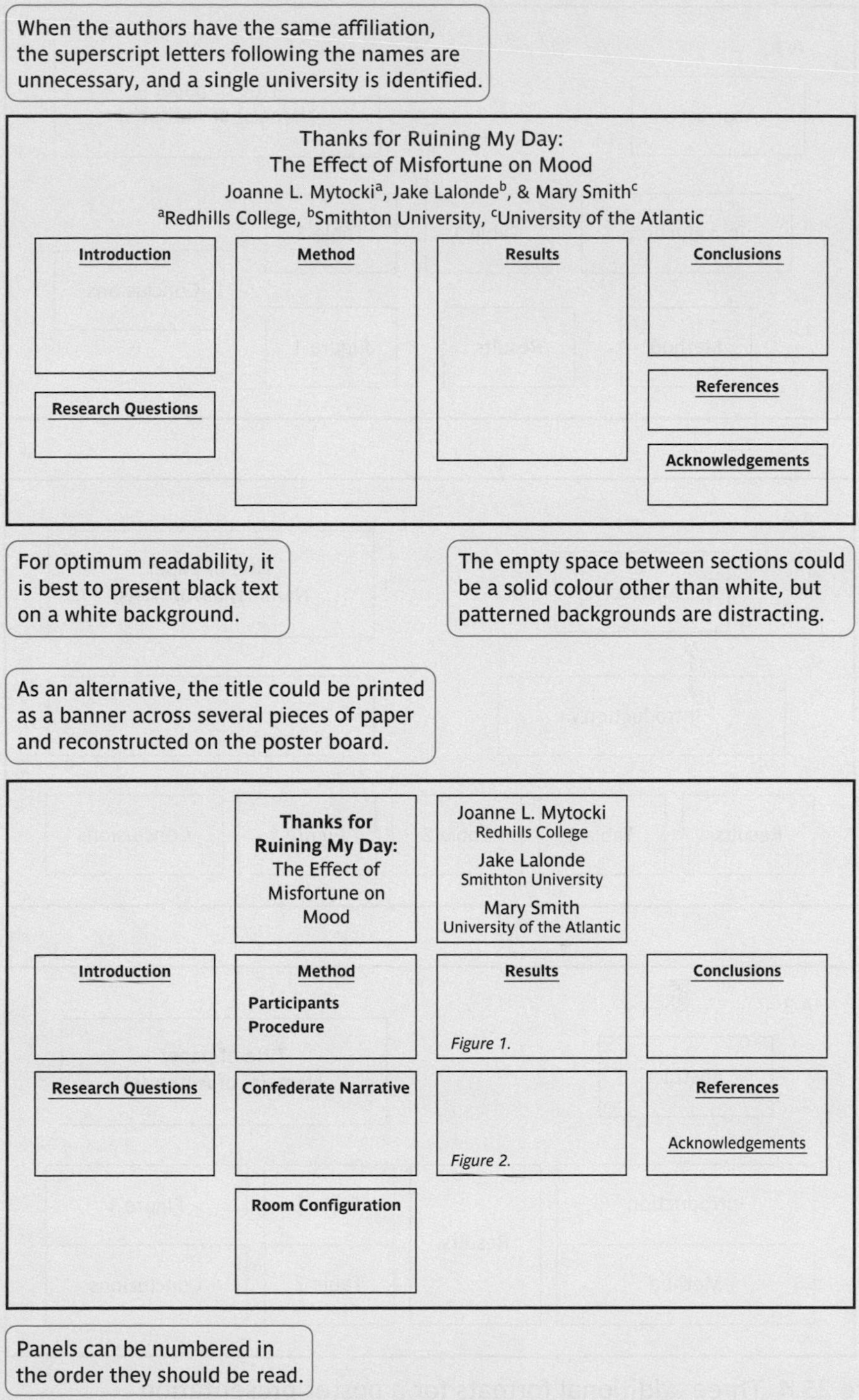

When the authors have the same affiliation, the superscript letters following the names are unnecessary, and a single university is identified.

Thanks for Ruining My Day:
The Effect of Misfortune on Mood
Joanne L. Mytocki[a], Jake Lalonde[b], & Mary Smith[c]
[a]Redhills College, [b]Smithton University, [c]University of the Atlantic

Introduction

Research Questions

Method

Results

Conclusions

References

Acknowledgements

For optimum readability, it is best to present black text on a white background.

The empty space between sections could be a solid colour other than white, but patterned backgrounds are distracting.

As an alternative, the title could be printed as a banner across several pieces of paper and reconstructed on the poster board.

Thanks for Ruining My Day:
The Effect of Misfortune on Mood

Joanne L. Mytocki
Redhills College

Jake Lalonde
Smithton University

Mary Smith
University of the Atlantic

Introduction

Research Questions

Method
Participants
Procedure

Confederate Narrative

Room Configuration

Results

Figure 1.

Figure 2.

Conclusions

References

Acknowledgements

Panels can be numbered in the order they should be read.

Figure 25.3 Standard layout for a poster presentation

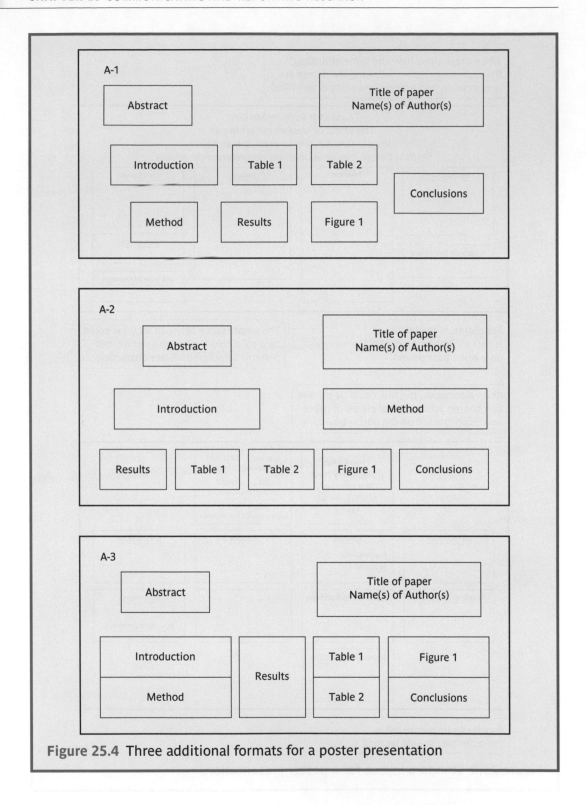

Figure 25.4 Three additional formats for a poster presentation

Summary

In this chapter we discussed the main ways in which research findings can be communicated. Research reports and journal articles are the most common method of reporting research findings and usually consist of the following sections: Abstract, Introduction, Method (with subsections: Design, Participants, Materials/Apparatus, Procedure), Results, Discussion and References. Qualitative research reports and journal articles do not follow the same format, but often include Analysis and Reflexive analysis sections. Regardless of the type of report, you should pay particular attention to how you reference sources of information and make an effort to use your own words, which should be clear and concise. Research findings can also be communicated via oral presentations and poster presentations. What works in written reports does not necessarily work for presentations. You should think about the audience and the purpose of the presentation. Oral presentations should engage the audience and highlight key points; visual aids are extremely helpful, and preparation and practice are essential. Poster presentations should be attractive and convey the main message quickly and from a distance. Bullet points, colour and figures are effective ways of emphasizing key points and getting the main findings across concisely. However you communicate your research, be sure to check any guidelines specific to your work before beginning.

Questions

1 What is an abstract, and why is it so important?

2 What information is included in the Introduction? How is the Introduction organized?

3 What information would you expect to find in the Method section? Describe the various subsections of the Method section.

4 What would you expect to find in the Results section of a research report?

5 How is the Discussion organized, and what would you expect to find in the Discussion section?

6 What section of a research report should you write first? Why?

7 How does a qualitative research report or journal article differ from a quantitative report or article?

8 What is included in the reference list of an APA-style research report or journal article? Describe how a typical journal reference is formatted.

9 What can you do in an oral presentation to engage the audience?

10 What factors should you bear in mind when producing a poster?

Activities

1 Find an interesting journal article that is published in a well-respected journal. Read it thoroughly, but leave the abstract for now.

   (a) Write your own abstract for the article – how does it differ from the real abstract for the article?

   (b) Now go through the article again and make notes on whether it follows the guidelines and format discussed in this chapter. If there are any differences, why may this be the case?

   (c) If you were to present the research in this article in a 10-minute oral presentation, what information would you include? Have a go at producing a 10-minute presentation and have a trial run.

   (d) If you were to present the research in a poster, how would you lay out the material? Sketch an outline of the poster, including any figures or use of colour.

2 Find an example of a journal article, a book, a chapter in an edited book and an online document, and write up the entry for each of these in a references list in APA style.

Appendix A: Areas Under the Normal Curve

Table A. Areas under the right half (positive z-scores) of the standard normal curve ($\mu = 0, \sigma = 1$)

(A) z	(B) Area between mean and z	(C) Area beyond z	(A) z	(B) Area between mean and z	(C) Area beyond z	(A) z	(B) Area between mean and z	(C) Area beyond z
0.00	00.00	50.00	0.23	09.10	40.90	0.46	17.72	32.28
0.01	00.40	49.60	0.24	09.48	40.52	0.47	18.08	31.92
0.02	00.80	49.20	0.25	09.87	40.13	0.48	18.44	31.56
0.03	01.20	48.80	0.26	10.26	39.74	0.49	18.79	31.21
0.04	01.60	48.40	0.27	10.64	39.36	0.50	19.15	30.85
0.05	01.99	48.01	0.28	11.03	38.97	0.51	19.50	30.50
0.06	02.39	47.61	0.29	11.41	38.59	0.52	19.85	30.15
0.07	02.79	47.21	0.30	11.79	38.21	0.53	20.19	29.81
0.08	03.19	46.81	0.31	12.17	37.83	0.54	20.54	29.46
0.09	03.59	46.41	0.32	12.55	37.45	0.55	20.88	29.12
0.10	03.98	46.02	0.33	12.93	37.07	0.56	21.23	28.77
0.11	04.38	45.62	0.34	13.31	36.69	0.57	21.57	28.43
0.12	04.78	45.22	0.35	13.68	36.32	0.58	21.90	28.10
0.13	05.17	44.83	0.36	14.06	35.94	0.59	22.24	27.76
0.14	05.57	44.43	0.37	14.43	35.57	0.60	22.57	27.43
0.15	05.96	44.04	0.38	14.80	35.20	0.61	22.91	27.09
0.16	06.36	43.64	0.39	15.17	34.83	0.62	23.24	26.76
0.17	06.75	43.25	0.40	15.54	34.46	0.63	23.57	26.43
0.18	07.14	42.86	0.41	15.91	34.09	0.64	23.89	26.11
0.19	07.53	42.47	0.42	16.28	33.72	0.65	24.22	25.78
0.20	07.93	42.07	0.43	16.64	33.36	0.66	24.54	25.46
0.21	08.32	41.68	0.44	17.00	33.00	0.67	24.86	25.14
0.22	08.71	41.29	0.45	17.36	32.64	0.68	25.17	24.83

(A) z	(B) Area between mean and z	(C) Area beyond z	(A) z	(B) Area between mean and z	(C) Area beyond z	(A) z	(B) Area between mean and z	(C) Area beyond z
0.69	25.49	24.51	1.02	34.61	15.39	1.35	41.15	08.85
0.70	25.80	24.20	1.03	34.85	15.15	1.36	41.31	08.69
0.71	26.11	23.89	1.04	35.08	14.92	1.37	41.47	08.53
0.72	26.42	23.58	1.05	35.31	14.69	1.38	41.62	08.38
0.73	26.73	23.27	1.06	35.54	14.46	1.39	41.77	08.23
0.74	27.04	22.96	1.07	35.77	14.23	1.40	41.92	08.08
0.75	27.34	22.66	1.08	35.99	14.01	1.41	42.07	07.93
0.76	27.64	22.36	1.09	36.21	13.79	1.42	42.22	07.78
0.77	27.94	22.06	1.10	36.43	13.57	1.43	42.36	07.64
0.78	28.23	21.77	1.11	36.65	13.35	1.44	42.51	07.49
0.79	28.52	21.48	1.12	36.86	13.14	1.45	42.65	07.35
0.80	28.81	21.19	1.13	37.08	12.92	1.46	42.79	07.21
0.81	29.10	20.90	1.14	37.29	12.71	1.47	42.92	07.08
0.82	29.39	20.61	1.15	37.49	12.51	1.48	43.06	06.94
0.83	29.67	20.33	1.16	37.70	12.30	1.49	43.19	06.81
0.84	29.95	20.05	1.17	37.90	12.10	1.50	43.22	06.68
0.85	30.23	19.77	1.18	38.10	11.90	1.51	43.45	06.55
0.86	30.51	19.49	1.19	38.30	11.70	1.52	43.57	06.43
0.87	30.78	19.22	1.20	38.49	11.51	1.53	43.70	06.30
0.88	31.06	18.94	1.21	38.69	11.31	1.54	43.82	06.18
0.89	31.33	18.67	1.22	38.88	11.12	1.55	43.94	06.06
0.90	31.59	18.41	1.23	39.07	10.93	1.56	44.06	05.94
0.91	31.86	18.14	1.24	39.25	10.75	1.57	44.18	05.82
0.92	32.12	17.88	1.25	39.44	10.56	1.58	44.29	05.71
0.93	32.38	17.62	1.26	39.62	10.38	1.59	44.41	05.59
0.94	32.64	17.36	1.27	39.80	10.20	1.60	44.52	05.48
0.95	32.89	17.11	1.28	39.97	10.03	1.61	44.63	05.37
0.96	33.15	16.85	1.29	40.15	09.85	1.62	44.74	05.26
0.97	33.40	16.60	1.30	40.32	09.68	1.63	44.84	05.16
0.98	33.65	16.35	1.31	40.49	09.51	1.64	44.95	05.05
0.99	33.89	16.11	1.32	40.66	09.34	1.65	45.05	04.95
1.00	34.13	15.87	1.33	40.82	09.18	1.66	45.15	04.85
1.01	34.38	15.62	1.34	40.99	09.01	1.67	45.25	04.75

(A) z	(B) Area between mean and z	(C) Area beyond z	(A) z	(B) Area between mean and z	(C) Area beyond z	(A) z	(B) Area between mean and z	(C) Area beyond z
1.68	45.35	04.65	2.01	47.78	02.22	2.34	49.04	00.96
1.69	45.45	04.55	2.02	47.83	02.17	2.35	49.06	00.94
1.70	45.54	04.46	2.03	47.88	02.12	2.36	49.09	00.91
1.71	45.64	04.36	2.04	47.93	02.07	2.37	49.11	00.89
1.72	45.73	04.27	2.05	47.98	02.02	2.38	49.13	00.87
1.73	45.82	04.18	2.06	48.03	01.97	2.39	49.16	00.84
1.74	45.91	04.09	2.07	48.08	01.92	2.40	49.18	00.82
1.75	45.99	04.01	2.08	48.12	01.83	2.41	49.20	00.80
1.76	46.08	03.92	2.09	48.17	01.83	2.42	49.22	00.78
1.77	46.16	03.84	2.10	48.21	01.79	2.43	49.25	00.75
1.78	46.25	03.75	2.11	48.26	01.74	2.44	49.27	00.73
1.79	46.33	03.67	2.12	48.30	01.70	2.45	49.29	00.71
1.80	46.41	03.59	2.13	48.34	01.66	2.46	49.31	00.69
1.81	46.49	03.51	2.14	48.38	01.62	2.47	49.32	00.68
1.82	46.56	03.44	2.15	48.42	01.58	2.48	49.34	00.66
1.83	46.64	03.36	2.16	48.46	01.54	2.49	49.36	00.64
1.84	46.71	03.29	2.17	48.50	01.50	2.50	49.38	00.62
1.85	46.78	03.22	2.18	48.54	01.46	2.51	49.40	00.60
1.86	46.86	03.14	2.19	48.57	01.43	2.52	49.41	00.59
1.87	46.93	03.07	2.20	48.61	01.39	2.53	49.43	00.57
1.88	46.99	03.01	2.21	48.64	01.36	2.54	49.45	00.55
1.89	47.06	02.94	2.22	48.68	01.32	2.55	49.46	00.54
1.90	47.13	02.87	2.23	48.71	01.29	2.56	49.48	00.52
1.91	47.19	02.81	2.24	48.75	01.25	2.57	49.49	00.51
1.92	47.26	02.74	2.25	48.78	01.22	2.58	49.51	00.49
1.93	47.32	02.68	2.26	48.81	01.19	2.59	49.52	00.48
1.94	47.38	02.62	2.27	48.84	01.16	2.60	49.53	00.47
1.95	47.44	02.56	2.28	48.87	01.13	2.61	49.55	00.45
1.96	47.50	02.50	2.29	48.90	01.10	2.62	49.56	00.44
1.97	47.56	02.44	2.30	48.93	01.07	2.63	49.57	00.43
1.98	47.61	02.39	2.31	48.96	01.04	2.64	49.59	00.41
1.99	47.67	02.23	2.32	48.98	01.02	2.65	49.60	00.40
2.00	47.72	02.28	2.33	49.01	00.99	2.66	49.61	00.39

(A) z	(B) Area between mean and z	(C) Area beyond z	(A) z	(B) Area between mean and z	(C) Area beyond z	(A) z	(B) Area between mean and z	(C) Area beyond z
2.67	49.62	00.38	2.90	49.81	00.19	3.13	49.91	00.09
2.68	49.63	00.37	2.91	49.82	00.18	3.14	49.92	00.08
2.69	49.64	00.36	2.92	49.82	00.18	3.15	49.92	00.08
2.70	49.65	00.35	2.93	49.83	00.17	3.16	49.92	00.08
2.71	49.66	00.34	2.94	49.84	00.16	3.17	49.92	00.08
2.72	49.67	00.33	2.95	49.84	00.16	3.18	49.93	00.07
2.73	49.68	00.32	2.96	49.85	00.15	3.19	49.93	00.07
2.74	49.69	00.31	2.97	49.85	00.15	3.20	49.93	00.07
2.75	49.70	00.30	2.98	49.86	00.14	3.21	49.93	00.07
2.76	49.71	00.29	2.99	49.86	00.14	3.22	49.94	00.06
2.77	49.72	00.28	3.00	49.87	00.13	3.23	49.94	00.06
2.78	49.73	00.27	3.01	49.87	00.13	3.24	49.94	00.06
2.79	49.74	00.26	3.02	49.87	00.13	3.25	49.94	00.06
2.80	49.74	00.26	3.03	49.88	00.12	3.30	49.95	00.05
2.81	49.75	00.25	3.04	49.88	00.12	3.35	49.96	00.04
2.82	49.76	00.24	3.05	49.89	00.11	3.40	49.97	00.03
2.83	49.77	00.23	3.06	49.89	00.11	3.45	49.97	00.03
2.84	49.77	00.23	3.07	49.89	00.11	3.50	49.98	00.02
2.85	49.78	00.22	3.08	49.90	00.10	3.60	49.98	00.02
2.86	49.79	00.21	3.09	49.90	00.10	3.70	49.99	00.01
2.87	49.79	00.21	3.10	49.90	00.10	3.80	49.99	00.01
2.88	49.80	00.20	3.11	49.91	00.09	3.90	49.995	00.005
2.89	49.81	00.19	3.12	49.91	00.09	4.00	49.997	00.003

Source: This table is from *Fundamentals of Behavioral Statistics* (3rd ed.), by R.P. Runyon, & A. Haber, 1976, Addison-Wesley, pp. 377–379. Copyright © 1976 by Addison-Wesley. Reprinted with permission of The McGraw-Hill Companies.

Appendix B: Critical Values of Chi-square

Degrees of freedom	Probability level		
	.10	.05	.01
1	2.706	3.841	6.635
2	4.605	5.991	9.210
3	6.251	7.815	11.345
4	7.779	9.488	13.277
5	9.236	11.070	15.086
6	10.645	12.592	16.812
7	12.017	14.067	18.475
8	13.362	15.507	20.090
9	14.684	16.919	21.666
10	15.987	18.307	23.209
11	17.275	19.675	24.725
12	18.549	21.026	26.217
13	19.812	22.362	27.688
14	21.064	23.685	29.141
15	22.307	24.996	30.578
16	23.542	26.296	32.000
17	24.769	27.587	33.409
18	25.989	28.869	34.805
19	27.204	30.144	36.191
20	28.412	31.410	37.566

Source: Table adapted from Fisher, R.H., & Yates, F. (1963) *Statistical Tables for Biological, Agricultural, and Medical Research* (6th ed.), London: Longman. Reprinted by permission.

Appendix C: Critical Values of *t*

	Significance level*			
	.05	.025	.01	.005
df	.10	.05	.02	.01
1	6.314	12.706	31.821	63.657
2	2.920	4.303	6.965	9.925
3	2.353	3.182	4.541	5.841
4	2.132	2.776	3.747	4.604
5	2.015	2.571	3.365	4.032
6	1.943	2.447	3.143	3.707
7	1.895	2.365	2.998	3.499
8	1.860	2.306	2.896	3.355
9	1.833	2.262	2.821	3.250
10	1.812	2.228	2.764	3.169
11	1.796	2.201	2.718	3.106
12	1.782	2.179	2.681	3.055
13	1.771	2.160	2.650	3.012
14	1.761	2.145	2.624	2.977
15	1.753	2.131	2.602	2.947
16	1.746	2.120	2.583	2.921
17	1.740	2.110	2.567	2.898
18	1.734	2.101	2.552	2.878
19	1.729	2.093	2.539	2.861
20	1.725	2.086	2.528	2.845
21	1.721	2.080	2.518	2.831
22	1.717	2.074	2.508	2.819
23	1.714	2.069	2.500	2.807
24	1.711	2.064	2.492	2.797
25	1.708	2.060	2.485	2.787
26	1.706	2.056	2.479	2.779

	Significance level*			
	.05	.025	.01	.005
df	.10	.05	.02	.01
27	1.703	2.052	2.473	2.771
28	1.701	2.048	2.467	2.763
29	1.699	2.045	2.462	2.756
30	1.697	2.042	2.457	2.750
40	1.684	2.021	2.423	2.704
60	1.671	2.000	2.390	2.660
120	1.658	1.980	2.358	2.617
	1.645	1.960	2.326	2.576

Note: *Use the top significance level when you have predicted a specific directional difference (a one-tailed test; e.g., Group 1 will be greater than Group 2). Use the bottom significance level when you have predicted only that Group 1 will differ from Group 2 without specifying the direction of the difference (a two-tailed test).

Appendix D: Critical Values of F

df for denominator (error)	sig level	df for numerator (systematic)											
		1	2	3	4	5	6	7	8	9	10	11	12
1	.10	39.9	49.5	53.6	55.8	57.2	58.2	58.9	59.4	59.9	60.2	60.5	60.7
	.05	161	200	216	225	230	234	237	239	241	242	243	244
2	.10	8.53	9.00	9.16	9.24	9.29	9.33	9.35	9.37	9.38	9.39	9.40	9.41
	.05	18.5	19.0	19.2	19.2	19.3	19.3	19.4	19.4	19.4	19.4	19.4	19.4
	.01	98.5	99.0	99.2	99.2	99.3	99.3	99.4	99.4	99.4	99.4	99.4	99.4
3	.10	5.54	5.46	5.39	5.34	5.31	5.28	5.27	5.25	5.24	5.23	5.22	5.22
	.05	10.1	9.55	9.28	9.12	9.01	8.94	8.89	8.85	8.81	8.79	8.76	8.74
	.01	34.1	30.8	29.5	28.7	28.2	27.9	27.7	27.5	27.3	27.2	27.1	27.1
4	.10	4.54	4.32	4.19	4.11	4.05	4.01	3.98	3.95	3.94	3.92	3.91	3.90
	.05	7.71	6.94	6.59	6.39	6.26	6.16	6.09	6.04	6.00	5.96	5.94	5.91
	.01	21.2	18.0	16.7	16.0	15.5	15.2	15.0	14.8	14.7	14.5	14.4	14.4
5	.10	4.06	3.78	3.62	3.52	3.45	3.40	3.37	3.34	3.32	3.30	3.28	3.27
	.05	6.61	5.79	5.41	5.19	5.05	4.95	4.88	4.82	4.77	4.74	4.71	4.68
	.01	16.3	13.3	12.1	11.4	11.0	10.7	10.5	10.3	10.2	10.1	9.96	9.89
6	.10	3.78	3.46	3.29	3.18	3.11	3.05	3.01	2.98	2.96	2.94	2.92	2.90
	.05	5.99	5.14	4.76	4.53	4.39	4.28	4.21	4.15	4.10	4.06	4.03	4.00
	.01	13.7	10.9	9.78	9.15	8.75	8.47	8.26	8.10	7.98	7.87	7.79	7.72
7	.10	3.59	3.26	3.07	2.96	2.88	2.83	2.78	2.75	2.72	2.70	2.68	2.67
	.05	5.59	4.74	4.35	4.12	3.97	3.87	3.79	3.73	3.68	3.64	3.60	3.57
	.01	12.2	9.55	8.45	7.85	7.46	7.19	6.99	6.84	6.72	6.62	6.54	6.47
8	.10	3.46	3.11	2.92	2.81	2.73	2.67	2.62	2.59	2.56	2.54	2.52	2.50
	.05	5.32	4.46	4.07	3.84	3.69	3.58	3.50	3.44	3.39	3.35	3.31	3.28
	.01	11.3	8.65	7.59	7.01	6.63	6.37	6.18	6.03	5.91	5.81	5.73	5.67
9	.10	3.36	3.01	2.81	2.69	2.61	2.55	2.51	2.47	2.44	2.42	2.40	2.38
	.05	5.12	4.26	3.86	3.63	3.48	3.37	3.29	3.23	3.18	3.14	3.10	3.07
	.01	10.6	8.02	6.99	6.42	6.06	5.80	5.61	5.47	5.35	5.26	5.18	5.11
10	.10	3.29	2.92	2.73	2.61	2.52	2.46	2.41	2.38	2.35	2.32	2.30	2.28
	.05	4.96	4.10	3.71	3.48	3.33	3.22	3.14	3.07	3.02	2.98	2.94	2.91
	.01	10.0	7.56	6.55	5.99	5.64	5.39	5.20	5.06	4.94	4.85	4.77	4.71

df for denominator (error)	sig level	\multicolumn{12}{c}{*df* for numerator (systematic)}
		1	2	3	4	5	6	7	8	9	10	11	12
11	.10	3.23	2.86	2.66	2.54	2.45	2.39	2.34	2.30	2.27	2.25	2.23	2.21
	.05	4.84	3.98	3.59	3.36	3.20	3.09	3.01	2.95	2.90	2.85	2.82	2.79
	.01	9.65	7.21	6.22	5.67	5.32	5.07	4.89	4.74	4.63	4.54	4.46	4.40
12	.10	3.18	2.81	2.61	2.48	2.39	2.33	2.28	2.24	2.21	2.19	2.17	2.15
	.05	4.75	3.89	3.49	3.26	3.11	3.00	2.91	2.85	2.80	2.75	2.72	2.69
	.01	9.33	6.93	5.95	5.41	5.06	4.82	4.64	4.50	4.39	4.30	4.22	4.16
13	.10	3.14	2.76	2.56	2.43	2.35	2.28	2.23	2.20	2.16	2.14	2.12	2.10
	.05	4.67	3.81	3.41	3.18	3.03	2.92	2.83	2.77	2.71	2.67	2.63	2.60
	.01	9.07	6.70	5.74	5.21	4.86	4.62	4.44	4.30	4.19	4.10	4.02	3.96
14	.10	3.10	2.73	2.52	2.39	2.31	2.24	2.19	2.15	2.12	2.10	2.08	2.05
	.05	4.60	3.74	3.34	3.11	2.96	2.85	2.76	2.70	2.65	2.60	2.57	2.53
	.01	8.86	6.51	5.56	5.04	4.69	4.46	4.28	4.14	4.03	3.94	3.86	3.80
15	.10	3.07	2.70	2.49	2.36	2.27	2.21	2.16	2.12	2.09	2.06	2.04	2.02
	.05	4.54	3.68	3.29	3.06	2.90	2.79	2.71	2.64	2.59	2.54	2.51	2.48
	.01	8.68	6.36	5.42	4.89	4.56	4.32	4.14	4.00	3.89	3.80	3.73	3.67
16	.10	3.05	2.67	2.46	2.33	2.24	2.18	2.13	2.09	2.06	2.03	2.01	1.99
	.05	4.49	3.63	3.24	3.01	2.85	2.74	2.66	2.59	2.54	2.49	2.46	2.42
	.01	8.53	6.23	5.29	4.77	4.44	4.20	4.03	3.89	3.78	3.69	3.62	3.55
17	.10	3.03	2.64	2.44	2.31	2.22	2.15	2.10	2.06	2.03	2.00	1.98	1.96
	.05	4.45	3.59	3.20	2.96	2.81	2.70	2.61	2.55	2.49	2.45	2.41	2.38
	.01	8.40	6.11	5.18	4.67	4.34	4.10	3.93	3.79	3.68	3.59	3.52	3.46
18	.10	3.01	2.62	2.42	2.29	2.20	2.13	2.08	2.04	2.00	1.98	1.96	1.93
	.05	4.41	3.55	3.16	2.93	2.77	2.66	2.58	2.51	2.46	2.41	2.37	2.34
	.01	8.29	6.01	5.09	4.58	4.25	4.01	3.84	3.71	3.60	3.51	3.43	3.37
19	.10	2.99	2.61	2.40	2.27	2.18	2.11	2.06	2.02	1.98	1.96	1.94	1.91
	.05	4.38	3.52	3.13	2.90	2.74	2.63	2.54	2.48	2.42	2.38	2.34	2.31
	.01	8.18	5.93	5.01	4.50	4.17	3.94	3.77	3.63	3.52	3.43	3.36	3.30
20	.10	2.97	2.59	2.38	2.25	2.16	2.09	2.04	2.00	1.96	1.94	1.92	1.89
	.05	4.35	3.49	3.10	2.87	2.71	2.60	2.51	2.45	2.39	2.35	2.31	2.28
	.01	8.10	5.85	4.94	4.43	4.10	3.87	3.70	3.56	3.46	3.37	3.29	3.23

df for denominator (error)	sig level	*df* for numerator (systematic)											
		1	2	3	4	5	6	7	8	9	10	11	12
22	.10	2.95	2.56	2.35	2.22	2.13	2.06	2.01	1.97	1.93	1.90	1.88	1.86
	.05	4.30	3.44	3.05	2.82	2.66	2.55	2.46	2.40	2.34	2.30	2.26	2.23
	.01	7.95	5.72	4.82	4.31	3.99	3.76	3.59	3.45	3.35	3.26	3.18	3.12
24	.10	2.93	2.54	2.33	2.19	2.10	2.04	1.98	1.94	1.91	1.88	1.85	1.83
	.05	4.26	3.40	3.01	2.78	2.62	2.51	2.42	2.36	2.30	2.25	2.21	2.18
	.01	7.82	5.61	4.72	4.22	3.90	3.67	3.50	3.36	3.26	3.17	3.09	3.03
26	.10	2.91	2.52	2.31	2.17	2.08	2.01	1.96	1.92	1.88	1.86	1.84	1.81
	.05	4.23	3.37	2.98	2.74	2.59	2.47	2.39	2.32	2.27	2.22	2.18	2.15
	.01	7.72	5.53	4.64	4.14	3.82	3.59	3.42	3.29	3.18	3.09	3.02	2.96
28	.10	2.89	2.50	2.29	2.16	2.06	2.00	1.94	1.90	1.87	1.84	1.81	1.79
	.05	4.20	3.34	2.95	2.71	2.56	2.45	2.36	2.29	2.24	2.19	2.15	2.12
	.01	7.64	5.45	4.57	4.07	3.75	3.53	3.36	3.23	3.12	3.03	2.96	2.90
30	.10	2.88	2.49	2.28	2.14	2.05	1.98	1.93	1.88	1.85	1.82	1.79	1.77
	.05	4.17	3.32	2.92	2.69	2.53	2.42	2.33	2.27	2.21	2.16	2.13	2.09
	.01	7.56	5.39	4.51	4.02	3.70	3.47	3.30	3.17	3.07	2.98	2.91	2.84
40	.10	2.84	2.44	2.23	2.09	2.00	1.93	1.87	1.83	1.79	1.76	1.73	1.71
	.05	4.08	3.23	2.84	2.61	2.45	2.34	2.25	2.18	2.12	2.08	2.04	2.00
	.01	7.31	5.18	4.31	3.83	3.51	3.29	3.12	2.99	2.89	2.80	2.73	2.66
60	.10	2.79	2.39	2.18	2.04	1.95	1.87	1.82	1.77	1.74	1.71	1.68	1.66
	.05	4.00	3.15	2.76	2.53	2.37	2.25	2.17	2.10	2.04	1.99	1.95	1.92
	.01	7.08	4.98	4.13	3.65	3.34	3.12	2.95	2.82	2.72	2.63	2.56	2.50
120	.10	2.75	2.35	2.13	1.99	1.90	1.82	1.77	1.72	1.68	1.65	1.62	1.60
	.05	3.92	3.07	2.68	2.45	2.29	2.17	2.09	2.02	1.96	1.91	1.87	1.83
	.01	6.85	4.79	3.95	3.48	3.17	2.96	2.79	2.66	2.56	2.47	2.40	2.34
200	.10	2.73	2.33	2.11	1.97	1.88	1.80	1.75	1.70	1.66	1.63	1.60	1.57
	.05	3.89	3.04	2.65	2.42	2.26	2.14	2.06	1.98	1.93	1.88	1.84	1.80
	.01	6.76	4.71	3.88	3.41	3.11	2.89	2.73	2.60	2.50	2.41	2.34	2.27
	.10	2.71	2.30	2.08	1.94	1.85	1.77	1.72	1.67	1.63	1.60	1.57	1.55
	.05	3.84	3.00	2.60	2.37	2.21	2.10	2.01	1.94	1.88	1.83	1.79	1.75
	.01	6.63	4.61	3.78	3.32	3.02	2.80	2.64	2.51	2.41	2.32	2.25	2.18

Appendix E: Critical Values of r (Pearson Product–Moment Correlation Coefficient)

df	Level of significance for two-tailed test*		
	.10	.05	.01
1	.988	.997	.9999
2	.900	.950	.990
3	.805	.878	.959
4	.729	.811	.917
5	.669	.754	.874
6	.622	.707	.834
7	.582	.666	.798
8	.549	.632	.765
9	.521	.602	.735
10	.497	.576	.708
11	.476	.553	.684
12	.458	.532	.661
13	.441	.514	.641
14	.426	.497	.623
15	.412	.482	.606
16	.400	.468	.590
17	.389	.456	.575
18	.378	.444	.561
19	.369	.433	.549
20	.360	.423	.537
25	.323	.381	.487
30	.296	.349	.449
35	.275	.325	.418

df	Level of significance for two-tailed test*		
	.10	.05	.01
40	.257	.304	.393
45	.243	.288	.372
50	.231	.273	.354
60	.211	.250	.325
70	.195	.232	.303
80	.183	.217	.283
90	.173	.205	.267
100	.164	.195	.254

Note: *The significance level is halved for a one-tailed test.

									$p < .05$ (Two-tailed test)										
										n									
m	1	2	3	4	5	6	7	8	9	10	11	12	13	14	15	16	17	18	19	20
1	—																			
2	—	—																		
3	—	—	—																	
4	—	—	—	0																
5	—	—	0	1	2															
6	—	—	1	2	3	5														
7	—	—	1	3	5	6	8													
8	—	0	2	4	6	8	10	13												
9	—	0	2	4	7	10	12	15	17											
10	—	0	3	5	8	11	14	17	20	23										
11	—	0	3	6	9	13	16	19	23	26	30									
12	—	1	4	7	11	14	18	22	26	29	33	37								
13	—	1	4	8	12	16	20	24	28	33	37	41	45							
14	—	1	5	9	13	17	22	26	31	36	40	45	50	55						
15	—	1	5	10	14	19	24	29	34	39	44	49	54	59	64					
16	—	1	6	11	15	21	26	31	37	42	47	53	59	64	70	75				
17	—	2	6	11	17	22	28	34	39	45	51	57	63	69	75	81	87			
18	—	2	7	12	18	24	30	36	42	48	55	61	67	74	80	86	93	99		
19	—	2	7	13	19	25	32	38	45	52	58	65	72	78	85	92	99	106	113	
20	—	2	8	14	20	27	34	41	48	55	62	69	76	83	90	98	105	112	119	127
21	—	3	8	15	22	29	36	43	50	58	65	73	80	88	96	103	111	119	126	134
22	—	3	9	16	23	30	38	45	53	61	69	77	85	93	101	109	117	125	133	141
23	—	3	9	17	24	32	40	48	56	64	73	81	89	98	106	115	123	132	140	149
24	—	3	10	17	25	33	42	50	59	67	76	85	94	102	111	120	129	138	147	156

	\multicolumn{20}{c	}{*p* < .05 (Two-tailed test)}
	\multicolumn{20}{c	}{*n*}
m	1	2	3	4	5	6	7	8	9	10	11	12	13	14	15	16	17	18	19	20
25	—	3	10	18	27	35	44	53	62	71	80	89	98	107	117	126	135	145	154	163
26	—	4	11	19	28	37	46	55	64	74	83	93	102	112	122	132	141	151	161	171
27	—	4	11	20	29	38	48	57	67	77	87	97	107	117	127	137	147	158	168	178
28	—	4	12	21	30	40	50	60	70	80	90	101	111	122	132	143	154	164	175	186
29	—	4	13	22	32	42	52	62	73	83	94	105	116	127	138	149	160	171	182	193
30	—	5	13	23	33	43	54	65	76	87	98	109	120	131	143	154	166	177	189	200
31	—	5	14	24	34	45	56	67	78	90	101	113	125	136	148	160	172	184	196	208
32	—	5	14	24	35	46	58	69	81	93	105	117	129	141	153	166	178	190	203	215
33	—	5	15	25	37	48	60	72	84	96	108	121	133	146	159	171	184	197	210	222
34	—	5	15	26	38	50	62	74	87	99	112	125	138	151	164	177	190	203	217	230
35	—	6	16	27	39	51	64	77	89	103	116	129	142	156	169	183	196	210	224	237
36	—	6	16	28	40	53	66	79	92	106	119	133	147	161	174	188	202	216	231	245
37	—	6	17	29	41	55	68	81	95	109	123	137	151	165	180	194	209	223	238	252
38	—	6	17	30	43	56	70	84	98	112	127	141	156	170	185	200	215	230	245	259
39	0	7	18	31	44	58	72	86	101	115	130	145	160	175	190	206	221	236	252	267
40	0	7	18	31	45	59	74	89	103	119	134	149	165	180	196	211	227	243	258	274

Source: reprinted from R.C. Milton (1964) An extended table of critical values for the Mann–Whitney (Wilcoxon) two-sample statistic, *Journal of the American Statistical Association, 59*, 925–934.

Appendix F(b): Critical Values of the Mann–Whitney *U* Test

									p < .01 (Two-tailed test)										
									n											
m	1	2	3	4	5	6	7	8	9	10	11	12	13	14	15	16	17	18	19	20
1	—																			
2	—	—																		
3	—	—	—																	
4	—	—	—	—																
5	—	—	—	—	0															
6	—	—	—	0	1	2														
7	—	—	—	0	1	3	4													
8	—	—	—	1	2	4	6	7												
9	—	—	0	1	3	5	7	9	11											
10	—	—	0	2	4	6	9	11	13	16										
11	—	—	0	2	5	7	10	13	16	18	21									
12	—	—	1	3	6	9	12	15	18	21	24	27								
13	—	—	1	3	7	10	13	17	20	24	27	31	34							
14	—	—	1	4	7	11	15	18	22	26	30	34	38	42						
15	—	—	2	5	8	12	16	20	24	29	33	37	42	46	51					
16	—	—	2	5	9	13	18	22	27	31	36	41	45	50	55	60				
17	—	—	2	6	10	15	19	24	29	34	39	44	49	54	60	65	70			
18	—	—	2	6	11	16	21	26	31	37	42	47	53	58	64	70	75	81		
19	—	0	3	7	12	17	22	28	33	39	45	51	57	63	69	74	81	87	93	
20	—	0	3	8	13	18	24	30	36	42	48	54	60	67	73	79	86	92	99	105
21	—	0	3	8	14	19	25	32	38	44	51	58	64	71	78	84	91	98	105	112
22	—	0	4	9	14	21	27	34	40	47	54	61	68	75	82	89	96	104	111	118
23	—	0	4	9	15	22	29	35	43	50	57	64	72	79	87	94	102	109	117	125
24	—	0	4	10	16	23	30	37	45	52	60	68	75	83	91	99	107	115	123	131

										$p < .01$ (Two-tailed test)										
											n									
m	1	2	3	4	5	6	7	8	9	10	11	12	13	14	15	16	17	18	19	20
25	—	0	5	10	17	24	32	39	47	55	63	71	79	87	96	104	112	121	129	138
26	—	0	5	11	18	25	33	41	49	58	66	74	83	92	100	109	118	127	135	144
27	—	1	5	12	19	27	35	43	52	60	69	78	87	96	105	114	123	132	142	151
28	—	1	5	12	20	28	36	45	54	63	72	81	91	100	109	119	128	138	148	157
29	—	1	6	13	21	29	38	47	56	66	75	85	94	104	114	124	134	144	154	164
30	—	1	6	13	22	30	40	49	58	68	78	88	98	108	119	129	139	150	160	170
31	—	1	6	14	22	32	41	51	61	71	81	92	102	113	123	134	145	155	166	177
32	—	1	7	14	23	33	43	53	63	74	84	95	106	117	128	139	150	161	172	184
33	—	1	7	15	24	34	44	55	65	76	87	98	110	121	132	144	155	167	179	190
34	—	1	7	16	25	35	46	57	68	79	90	102	113	125	137	149	161	173	185	197
35	—	1	8	16	26	37	47	59	70	82	93	105	117	129	142	154	166	179	191	203
36	—	1	8	17	27	38	49	60	72	84	96	109	121	134	146	159	172	184	197	210
37	—	1	8	17	28	39	51	62	75	87	99	112	125	138	151	164	177	190	203	217
38	—	1	9	18	29	40	52	64	77	90	102	116	129	142	155	169	182	196	210	223
39	—	2	9	19	30	41	54	66	79	92	106	119	133	146	160	174	188	202	216	230
40	—	2	9	19	31	43	55	68	81	95	109	122	136	150	165	179	193	208	222	237

Source: reprinted from R.C. Milton (1964) An extended table of critical values for the Mann–Whitney (Wilcoxon) two-sample statistic, *Journal of the American Statistical Association, 59,* 925–934.

References

Abernathy, T. J., Massad, L., & Romano-Dwyer, L. (1995). The relationship between smoking and self-esteem. *Adolescence, 30,* 899–907.

Abrams, L., & Curran, L. (2009). "And you're telling me not to stress?" A grounded theory study of postpartum depression symptoms among low-income mothers. *Psychology of Women Quarterly, 33* (3), 351–362.

Altmann, J. (1974). Observational study of behavior: Sampling methods. *Behavior, 48,* 1–41.

American Psychological Association (APA). (2001). *Publication manual* (5th ed.). Washington, DC: Author.

American Psychological Association (APA). (2010). *Publication manual of the American Psychological Association* (6th ed.). Washington, DC: Author.

Anastasi, A. (1976). *Psychological testing* (4th ed.). New York: Macmillan.

Anderson, C. A., & Anderson, D. C. (1984). Ambient temperature and violent crime: Test of the linear and curvilinear hypotheses. *Journal of Personality and Social Psychology, 46,* 91–97.

Anderson, C. A., & Dill, K. E. (2000). Video games and aggressive thoughts, feelings, and behavior in the laboratory and in life. *Journal of Personality and Social Psychology, 78,* 772–790.

Anderson, J. R. (1990). *The adaptive character of thought.* Hillsdale, NJ: Erlbaum.

Anderson, J. R. (1993). *Rules of the mind.* Hillsdale, NJ: Erlbaum.

Anderson, J. R., & Milson, J. R. (1989). Human memory: An adaptive perspective. *Psychological Review, 96,* 703–719.

Asher, H. B. (1976). Causal modeling. Sage University paper series on quantitative applications in the social sciences (Series No. 07003). Beverly Hills, CA: Sage.

Banister, P., Burman, E., Parker, I., Taylor, M., & Tindall, C. (1994). *Qualitative methods in psychology: A research guide.* London: Open University Press.

Barton, E. M., Baltes, M. M., & Orzech, M. J. (1980). Etiology of dependence in older nursing home residents during morning care: the role of staff behavior. *Journal of Personality and Social Psychology, 38,* 423–431.

Basch, C. E. (1987). Focus group interview: An underutilized research technique for improving theory and practice in health education. *Health Education Quarterly, 14,* 411–448.

Bates, J., Bayles, K., Bennett, D., Ridge, B., & Brown, M. (1991). Origins of externalizing behavior problems at eight years of age. In D. Pepler & K. Rubin (Eds.), *The development and treatment of childhood aggression* (pp. 93–120). Hillsdale, NJ: Erlbaum.

Baumrind, D. (1985). Research using intentional deception: Ethical issues revisited. *American Psychologist, 40,* 165–174.

Beck, A. T., Steer, R. A., & Garbin, M. G. (1988). Psychometric properties of the Beck Depression Inventory: Twenty-five years of evaluation. *Clinical Psychology Review, 8,* 88–100.

Bell, R. (1992). *Impure science: Fraud, compromise and political influence in scientific research.* New York: Wiley.

Bennett, S., & Bowers, D. (1976). *An Introduction to multivariate techniques for social and behavioural sciences.* New York: Wiley.

Berg, B. L. (2007). *Qualitative research methods for the social sciences.* London: Pearson.

Bernstein, D. M., Laney, C., Morris, E. K., & Loftus, E. F. (2005). False memories about food can lead to food avoidance. *Social Cognition, 23*, 11–34.

Berscheid, E., Baron, R. S., Dermer, M., & Libman, M. (1973). Anticipating informed consent: An empirical approach. *American Psychologist, 28*, 913–925.

Bingham, W., & Moore, B. V. (1959). *How to interview* (4th ed.). New York: Harper and Bros.

Blanchard, F. A., Crandall, C. S., Brigham, J. C., & Vaughn, L. A. (1994). Condemning and condoning racism: A social context approach to interracial settings. *Journal of Applied Psychology, 79*, 993–997.

Blanck, P. D., Bellack, A. S., Rosnow, R. L., Rotheram-Borus, M. J., & Schooler, N. R. (1992). Scientific rewards and conflicts of ethical choices in human subjects research. *American Psychologist, 47*, 959–965.

Bordens, K. S., & Abbott, B. B. (2008). *Research design and methods: A process approach.* London: McGraw-Hill International.

Bortnik, K., Henderson, L., & Zimbardo, P. (2002). *The Shy Q, a measure of chronic shyness: Associations with interpersonal motives and interpersonal values.* Retrieved from http://www.shyness.com/documents/2002/SITAR2002poster_handout.pdf.

Braun, V., & Clarke, V. (2006). Using thematic analysis in psychology. *Qualitative Research in Psychology, 3* (2), 77–101.

Bray, J. H., & Maxwell, S. E. (1982). Analyzing and interpreting significant MANOVAs. *Review of Educational Research, 52*, 340–367.

British Psychology Association. (2009). Ethical guidelines. Retrieved from http://www.bps.org.uk/the-society/code-of-conduct/.

Broad, W., & Wade, N. (1983). *Betrayers of the truth.* New York: Simon & Schuster.

Broca, P. (1861). Remarques sur le siège de la faculté du langage articule, suivies d'une observation d'aphémie. *Bulletin et Mémoires de la Société Anatomique de Paris, 2*, 330–357.

Brown, A. L., & Campione, J. C. (1994). Guided discovery in a community of learners. In K. McGilly (Ed.), *Classroom lessons: Integrating cognitive theory and classroom practice* (pp. 229–270). Cambridge, MA: MIT Press.

Brown, R., & Kulik, J. (1977). Flashbulb memories. *Cognition, 5*, 73–99.

Burman, E. (1994). Interviewing. In P. Banister, E. Burman, I. Parker, M. Taylor & C. Tindall (Eds.), *Qualitative methods in psychology: A research guide.* Buckingham: Open University Press.

Burman, E. (2008). Developmental psychology. In C. Willig & W. Stainton-Rogers (Eds.), *The Sage handbook of qualitative research in psychology* (pp. 407–429). London: Sage Publications.

Burr, V. (1995). *An Introduction to Social Constructionism.* London: Routledge.

Buss, D.M. (1988). The evolution of human intrasexual competition: Tactics of mate attraction. *Journal of Personality and Social Psychology, 54*, 616–628.

Buss, D. M. (1989). Sex differences in human mate preferences: Evolutionary hypotheses tested in 37 cultures. *Behavioral and Brain Sciences, 12*, 1–49.

Buss, D. M. (2009). *Evolutionary psychology: The new science of the mind* (3 ed.). London: Allyn & Bacon.

Campbell, D. T., & Stanley, J. C. (1966). *Experimental and quasi-experimental designs for research.* Chicago: Rand McNally.

Candland, D. K. (1993). *Feral children and clever animals.* Oxford: Oxford University Press.

Carroll, M. E., & Overmier, J. B. (Eds.). (2001). *Animal research and human health: Advancing human welfare through behavioral science.* Washington, DC: American Psychological Association.

Carroll, R. T. (2006). Pseudoscience. Retrieved from http://skepdic.com/pseudosc.html.

Cavan, S. (1966). *Liquor license: An ethnography of bar behavior.* Chicago: Aldine.

Chaiken, S., & Pliner, P. (1987). Women, but not men, are what they eat: The effect of meal size and gender on perceived femininity and masculinity. *Personality and Social Psychology Bulletin, 13,* 166–176.

Chalmers, A. F. (2004). *What is this thing called science?* Buckingham: Open University Press.

Chamberlain, K., & Murray, M. (2008). Health psychology. In C. Willig & W. Stainton-Rogers (Eds.), *The Sage handbook of qualitative research in psychology* (pp. 390–406). London: Sage Publications.

Chambers, J. H., & Ascione, F. R. (1987). The effects of prosocial and aggressive videogames on children's donating and helping. *Journal of Genetic Psychology, 148,* 499–505.

Charmaz, K. (1990). "Discovering" chronic illness: using grounded theory. *Social Science and Medicine, 30,* 1161–1172.

Cialdini, R. B. (1988). *Influence: Science and practice* (2nd ed.). Glenview, IL: Scott, Foresman.

Cleveland, W. S., & McGill, R. (1985). Graphical perception and graphical methods for analyzing scientific data. *Science, 229,* 828–833.

Cohen, J. (1969). *r*: A profile similarity coefficient invariant over variable reflection. *Psychological Bulletin, 71,* 281–284.

Cohen, J. (1988). *Statistical power analysis for the behavioral sciences* (2nd ed.). Hillsdale, NJ: Erlbaum.

Cohen, R. J., & Swerdlik, M. E. (2005). *Psychological testing and assessment: An introduction to tests and measures* (6th ed.). London: McGraw-Hill.

Coker, R. (2007). Distinguishing science from pseudoscience. Retrieved from https://webspace.utexas.edu/cokerwr/www/index.html/distinguish.htm.

Coles, P. (1999). *Einstein and the total eclipse.* Cambridge: Icon Books.

Conger, R. D., Ge, X., Elder, G. H., Jr., Lorenz, F. O., & Simons, R. L. (1994). Economic stress, coercive family process, and developmental problems of adolescents, *Child Development, 65,* 541–561.

Converse, J. M., & Presser, S. (1986). *Survey questions: Handcrafting the standardized questionnaire.* Newbury Park, CA: Sage.

Coolican, H. (2001). *Research methods and statistics for psychology* (3rd ed.). London: Hodder & Stoughton.

Coolican, H. (2008). *Research methods and statistics for psychology* (5th ed.). London: Hodder & Stoughton.

Cooperman, E. (1980). Voluntary subjects' participation in research: Cognitive style as a possible biasing factor. *Perceptual and Motor Skills, 50,* 542.

Cordaro, L., & Ison, J. R. (1963). Psychology of the scientist: X. Observer bias in classical conditioning of the planarian. *Psychological Reports, 13,* 787–789.

Cornell University Library. (2009). *Distinguishing scholarly journals from other periodicals.* Retrieved from http://www.library.cornell.edu/olinuris/ref/research/skill20.html.

Couvalis, G. (1999). *The philosophy of science: Science and objectivity.* London: Sage Publications.

Cozby, P. (2007). *Methods in behavioral research* (9th ed.). London: McGraw-Hill.

Crawford, F. (2000). Researcher in consumer behavior looks at attitudes of gratitude that affect gratuities. *Cornell Chronicle.* Retrieved from http://www.news.cornell.edu/Chronicle/00/8.17.00/Lynn-tipping.html.

Crews, F. (1980). *The Random House handbook* (3rd ed.). New York: Random House.

Curtiss, S. R. (1977). *Genie: A psycholinguistic study of a modern-day "wild child."* New York: Academic Press.

Darwin, C. (1859). *On the origin of species.* London: Murray.

Davis, J. L., & Rusbult, C. E. (2001). Attitude alignment in close relationships. *Journal of Personality and Social Psychology, 81,* 65–84.

de Blois, S. T., Novak, M. A., & Bond, M. (1998). Object permanence in orangutans (Pongo pygmaeus) and squirrel monkeys (Saimiri sciureus). *Journal of Comparative Psychology, 112,* 137–152.

Dickie, J. R. (1987). Interrelationships within the mother-father-infant triad. In P. W. Berman & F. A. Pedersen (Eds.), *Men's transitions to parenthood: Longitudinal studies of early family experience* (pp. 113–143). Hillsdale, NJ: Erlbaum.

Diener, E., & Crandall, R. (1978). *Ethics in social and behavioral research.* Chicago: The University of Chicago Press.

Diener, E., Emmons, R. A., Larsen, R. J., & Griffin, S. (1985). The Satisfaction With Life Scale. *Journal of Personality Assessment, 49,* 71–75.

Dillman, D. A. (2000). *Mail and Internet surveys: The tailored design method* (2nd ed.). New York: Wiley.

Dolan, C. A., Sherwood, A., & Light, K. C. (1992). Cognitive coping strategies and blood pressure responses to real-life stress in healthy young men. *Health Psychology, 11,* 233–240.

Eagly, A. M., & Wood, W. (1999). The origins of sex differences in human behavior: Evolved dispositions versus social roles. *American Psychologist, 54,* 408–423.

Elliott, R., Fischer, C. T., & Rennie, D. L. (1999). Evolving guidelines for publication of qualitative research studies in psychology and related fields. *British Journal of Clinical Psychology, 38,* 215–229.

Elms, A. C. (1994). *Uncovering lives: The uneasy alliance of biography and psychology.* Oxford: Oxford University Press.

Estes, W. K. (1997). On the communication of information by displays of standard errors and confidence intervals. *Psychonomic Bulletin & Review, 4,* 330–341.

Feild, H. S., & Barnett, N. J. (1978). Students vs. "real" people as jurors. *Journal of Social Psychology, 104,* 287–293.

Festinger, L., Riecken, H., & Schachter, S. (1956). *When prophecy fails.* Minneapolis: University of Minnesota Press.

Field, A. (2009). *Discovering statistics using SPSS.* London: Sage Publications.

Fischer, K., Schoeneman, T. J., & Rubanowitz, D. E. (1987). Attributions in the advice columns: II. The dimensionality of actors' and observers' explanations of interpersonal problems. *Personality and Social Psychology Bulletin, 13,* 458–466.

Fisher, R. A., & Yates, F. (1963). *Statistical tables for biological, agricultural and medical research* (6th ed.). London: Longman.

Flanagan, C. A., & Eccles, J. S. (1993). Changes in parents' work status and adolescents' adjustment at school. *Child Development, 64,* 246–257.

Fossey, D. (1981). Imperiled giants of the forest. *National Geographic, 159,* 501–523.

Fossey, D. (1983). *Gorillas in the mist.* Boston: Houghton-Mifflin.

Frick, R. W. (1995). Accepting the null hypothesis. *Memory and Cognition, 25,* 132–138.

Garson, D. G. (2009). *Structural equation modeling.* Retrieved from http://faculty.chass.ncsu.edu/garson/PA765/structur.htm.

Gaulin, S. J. C., & McBurney, D. (2000). *Psychology: An evolutionary approach.* Upper Saddle River, NJ: Prentice-Hall.

Geggie, D. (2001). A survey of newly appointed consultants' attitudes towards fraud in research. *Journal of Medical Ethics, 27,* 344–346.

Geller, E. S., Russ, N.W., & Altomari, M. G. (1986). Naturalistic observations of beer drinking among college students. *Journal of Applied Behavior Analysis, 19,* 391–396.

Ghetti, S., Qin, J. J., & Goodman, G. S. (2002). False memories in children and adults: Age, distinctiveness, and subjective experience. *Developmental Psychology*, *38*, 705–718.

Gilhooly, K., & Green, C. (1996). Protocol analysis: theoretical background. In J. T. E. Richardson (Ed.), *Handbook of qualitative research methods for psychology and the social sciences* (pp. 43–74). Leicester: BPS Books.

Gill, R. (1996). Discourse analysis: Methodological aspects. In J. E. Richardson (Ed.), *Handbook of qualitative research methods for psychology and the social sciences*. Leicester: British Psychological Society.

Gilovich, T., Vallone, R. & Tversky, A. (1985). The hot hand in basketball: On the misperception of random sequences. *Cognitive Psychology*, *17*, 296–314.

Glaser, J., Dixit, J., & Green, D. P. (2002). Studying hate crime with the Internet: What makes racists advocate racial violence? *Journal of Social Issues*, *58*, 177–193.

Godden, D. R., & Baddeley, A. D. (1975). Context-dependent memory in two natural environments: On land and underwater. *British Journal of Psychology*, *66* (3), 325–331.

Gormly, E. (2004). Peering beneath the veil: An ethnographic content analysis of Islam as portrayed on The 700 Club following the September 11th attacks. *Journal of Media and Religion*, *3* (4), 219–238.

Gosling, S. D., Vazire, S., Srivastava, S., & John, O. P. (2004). Should we trust Web-based studies? A comparative analysis of six preconceptions about Internet questionnaires. *American Psychologist*, *59*, 93–104.

Graesser, A. C., Kennedy, T., Wiemer-Hastings, P., & Ottati, V. (1999). The use of computational cognitive methods to improve questions on surveys and questionnaires. In M. G. Sirkin, D. J. Hermann, S. Schechter, N. Schwarz, J. M. Tanur, & R. Tourangeau (Eds.), *Cognition and survey methods research* (pp. 199–216). New York: Wiley.

Gravetter, F. J., & Wallnau, L. B. (2007). *Statistics for the behavioral sciences* (7th ed.). Belmont, CA: Wadsworth.

Green, A., Larkin, M., & Sullivan, V. (2009). "Oh stuff it!" The experience and explanation of diet failure: An exploration using Interpretative Phenomenological Analysis. *Journal of Health Psychology*, *14* (7), 997–1008.

Green, C., & Gilhooly, K. J. (1996). Protocol analysis: Practical implementation. In J. Richardson (Ed.), *Handbook of qualitative research methods for psychology and the social sciences* (pp. 55–74). Leicester: BPS Books, Leicester.

Greenfield, D. N. (1999). *Nature of Internet addiction: Psychological factors in compulsive Internet use.* Paper presented at the meeting of the American Psychological Association, Boston, MA.

Guillaume, L., & Bath, P. A. (2008). A content analysis of mass media sources in relation to the MMR vaccine scare. *Health Informatics Journal*, *14* (4), 323–334.

Haack, S. (2007). *Defending science: Between scientism and cynicism.* New York: Prometheus Books.

Hall, D. (1979). *Writing well.* Boston: Little, Brown.

Haraway, D. (1988). Situated knowledges: The science question in feminism and the privilege of partial perspective. *Feminist Studies*, *14*, 579–599.

Harding, S. (Ed.). (1987). *Whose science? Whose knowledge?* New York: Cornell University Press.

Harding, S. (1991). *Whose science? Whose knowledge? Thinking from women's lives.* Buckingham: Open University Press.

Harlow, H. F., & Harlow, M. K. (1966). Learning to love. *American Scientist*, *54*, 244–272.

Harris, K. M., & Marmer, J. K. (1996). Poverty, paternal involvement, and adolescent well-being. *Journal of Family Issues*, *17*, 614–640.

Hartup, W. W. (1974). Aggression in childhood: Development perspectives. *American Psychologist*, *29*, 336–341.

Hemphill, J. F. (2003). Interpreting the magnitudes of correlation coefficients. *American Psychologist*, *58*, 78–79.

Hepworth, J. (1999). *The social construction of anorexia nervosa*. London: Sage.

Hershberger, S. L., Marcoulides, G. A., & Parramore, M. M. (2003). Structural equation modeling: An introduction. Retrieved from www.loc.gov/catdir/samples/cam033/2002035067.pdf.

Hess, D. W., Marwitz, J., & Kreutzer, J. (2003). Neuropsychological impairments in SCI. *Rehabilitation Psychology*, *48* (3), 151–156.

Hippler, H. J., & Schwarz, N. (1987). Response effects in surveys. In H. J. Hippler, N. Schwarz, & S. Sudman (Eds.), *Social information processing and survey methodology* (pp. 102–122). New York: Springer-Verlag.

Hogan, T. P., & Evalenko, K. (2006). The elusive definition of outliers in introductory statistics textbooks for behavioral sciences. *Teaching of Psychology*, *33*, 252–256.

Horowitz, I. A. (1969). The effects of volunteering, fear arousal, and number of communications on attitude change. *Journal of Personality and Social Psychology*, *11*, 34–37.

Howell, D. C. (2002). *Statistical methods for psychology* (5th ed.). London: Wadsworth.

Howell, D. C. (2007). *Fundamental statistics for the behavioral sciences*. London: Wadsworth.

Huck, S. W., & Sandler, H. M. (1979). *Rival hypotheses: Alternative explanations of data based conclusions*. New York: Harper & Row.

Hudson, J. M., & Bruckman, A. (2004). "Go away": Participant objections to being studied and the ethics of chatroom research. *The Information Society*, *20*, 127–139.

Hunter, J. E. (1987). Multiple dependent variables in program evaluation. In M. M. Mark & R. L. Shotland (Eds.), *Multiple methods*. San Francisco: Jossey-Bass.

Hunter, J. E., & Gerbing, D. W. (1982). Unidimensional measurement, second-order factor analysis and causal models. *Research in Organizational Behavior*, *4*, 267–320.

Huston, A. H. (Ed.). (1991). *Children in poverty: Child development and public policy*. New York: Cambridge University Press.

Jackson, S. M., & Cram, F. (2003). Disrupting the sexual double standard: young women's talk about heterosexuality. *British Journal of Social Psychology*, *42* (1), 113–127.

Jaffee, S., & Hyde, J. S. (2000). Gender differences in moral orientation: A meta-analysis. *Psychological Bulletin*, *126*, 703–726.

James, J. M., & Bolstein, R. (1990). The effect of monetary incentives and follow-up mailings on the response rate and response quality in mail surveys. *Public Opinion Quarterly*, *54*, 346–361.

Johnson, S., Burrows, A., & Williamson, I. (2004). Does my bump look big in this? The meaning of bodily changes for first time mothers-to-be. *Journal of Health Psychology*, *9* (3), 361–374.

Jones, R. A. (1994). The ethics of research in cyberspace. *Internet Research*, *4*, 30–35.

Judd, C. M., Smith, E. R., & Kidder, L. H. (1991). *Research methods in social relations* (6th ed.). Fort Worth, TX: Holt, Rinehart & Winston.

Kagan, J. (1992). Temperamental contributions to emotion and social behavior. In M. S. Clark (Ed.), *Review of personality and social psychology: Vol. 14. Emotion and social behavior* (pp. 99–118). Newbury Park, CA: Sage.

Kagan, J., Reznick, J. S., & Snidman, N. (1988). Biological bases of childhood shyness. *Science*, *240*, 167–171.

Kanuk, L., & Berenson, C. (1975). Mail surveys and response rates: A literature review. *Journal of Marketing Research*, *12*, 440–453.

Kardes, F. (1996). In defense of experimental consumer psychology. *Journal of Consumer Psychology*, *5*, 279–296.

Keppel, G. (1982). *Design and analysis: A researcher's handbook* (2nd ed.). Englewood Cliffs, NJ: Prentice Hall.

Keppel, G. (1991). *Design and analysis: A researcher's handbook* (3rd ed.). Englewood Cliffs, NJ: Prentice-Hall.

Kinnear, P. R., & Gray, C. D. (2010). *IBM SPSS Statistics 18 made simple.* London: Psychology Press.

Kirkham, G. L. (1975). Doc cop. *Human Behavior, 4*, 16–23.

Koocher, G. P. (1977). Bathroom behaviour and human dignity. *Journal of Personality and Social Psychology, 72*, 1245–1267.

Korr, J. L. (2008). Healthy cartoons. A content analysis of foods in children's animated television programs. *Food, Culture & Society, 11* (4), 449–462.

Kuhn, T. (1962). *The structure of scientific revolutions.* Chicago: University of Chicago Press.

Kyriacou, O., Easter, A., & Tchanturia, K. (2009) Comparing views of patients, parents, and clinicians on emotions in anorexia: A qualitative study. *Journal of Health Psychology, 14*, 843–854.

LaFrance, M., & Mayo, C. (1976). Racial differences in gaze behavior during conversations: Two systematic observational studies. *Journal of Personality and Social Psychology, 33*, 547–552.

Larson, R. W., Richards, M. H., Moneta, G., Holmbeck, G., & Ducket, E. (1996). Changes in adolescents daily interactions with their families from ages 10 to 18: disengagement and transformation. *Developmental Psychology, 32*, 744–754.

Latané, B., & Darley, J. M. (1970). *The unresponsive bystander: Why doesn't he help?* New York: Appleton-Century-Crofts.

Leggett, G., Mead, C. D., & Charvat, W. (1978). *Prentice Hall handbook for writers* (7th ed.). Englewood Cliffs, NJ: Prentice Hall.

Lempers, J. D., Clark-Lempers, D., & Simons, R. L. (1989). Economic hardship, parenting, and distress in adolescence. *Child Development, 60*, 25–39.

Levin, J. R. (1983). Pictorial strategies for school learning: Practical illustrations. In M. Pressley & J. R. Levin (Eds.), *Cognitive strategy research: Educational applications* (pp. 213–238). New York: Springer-Verlag.

Likert, R. A. (1932). A technique for the measurement of attitudes. *Archives of Psychology, 140* (55), 174–175.

Lillenfeld, S. O. (2005). The 10 commandments of helping students distinguish science from pseudoscience in psychology. *APS Observer, 18*. Retrieved from http://www.psychologicalscience.org/observer/getArticle.cfm?id=1843.

Loftus, E. (1979). *Eyewitness testimony.* Cambridge, MA: Harvard University Press.

Loftus, E. F., & Burns, T. E. (1982). Mental shock can produce retrograde amnesia. *Memory & Cognition, 10*, 318–323.

Luria, A. R. (1968). *The mind of a mnemonist.* New York: Basic Books.

Lyubomirsky, S. (1999). A measure of subjective happiness: Preliminary reliability and construct validity. *Social Indicators Research, 46*, 137–155.

Markman, H. J. (1991). Backwards into the future of couples' therapy and couples' therapy research: A comment on Jacobson. *Journal of Family Psychology, 4*, 416–425.

Martin, B. (1994). Plagiarism: a misplaced emphasis. *Journal of Information Ethics, 3*, 36–47.

Martino, S. C., Collins, R. L., Kanouse, D. E., Elliott, M., & Berry, S. H. (2005). Social cognitive processes mediating the relationship between exposure to television's sexual content and adolescents' sexual behavior. *Journal of Personality and Social Psychology, 89*, 914–924.

Matthews, R. (2001). Storks deliver babies p = 0.008. *Teaching Statistics, 22* (2), 36–38.

Mautner, G. (2008). Analyzing newspapers, magazines and other print media. In R. Wodak & M. Krzyzanowski (Eds.), *Qualitative discourse analysis in the social sciences* (pp. 30–53). London: Palgrave Macmillan.

McAdoo, H. P. (1988). *Black families* (2nd ed.). Newbury Park, CA: Sage.

McKinlay, A., & McVittie, C. (2008). *Social psychology and discourse.* London: Wiley-Blackwell.

McNemar, Q. (1946). Opinion-attitude methodology. *Psychological Bulletin, 43,* 289–374.

Meier, B. P., Robinson, M. D., & Clore, G. L. (2004). Why good guys wear white: Automatic inferences about stimulus valence based on brightness. *Psychological Science, 15,* 82–87.

Merriam-Webster's Collegiate Dictionary 11th Edition. (2004). Massachusetts: Merriam-Webster.

Merrick, E. (1999). An exploration of quality in qualitative. Are "reliability" and "validity" relevant? In M. Kopala & L. A. Suzuki (Eds.), *Using qualitative methods in psychology* (pp. 25–48). London: Sage Publications.

Mesquita, B., Frijda, N. H., & Scherer, K. R. (1997). Culture and emotion. In P. Dasen & T. S. Saraswathi (Eds.), *Handbook of Cross-Cultural Psychology. Basic Processes and Human Development* (vol. 2, pp. 255–297). Boston: Allyn & Bacon.

Michael, R. T., Gagnon, J. H., Laumann, E. O., & Kolata, G. (1994). *Sex in America: A definitive survey.* Boston: Little, Brown.

Middlemist, R. D., Knowles, E. S., & Matter, C. F. (1976). Personal space invasion in the lavatory: Suggestive evidence for arousal. *Journal of Personality and Social Psychology, 33,* 541–546.

Middlemist, R. D., Knowles, E. S., & Matter, C. F. (1977). What to do and what to report: A reply to Koocher. *Journal of Personality and Social Psychology, 35,* 122–124.

Milgram, S. (1963). Behavioral study of obedience. *Journal of Abnormal and Social Psychology, 67,* 371–378.

Milgram, S. (1964). Issues in the study of obedience: A reply to Baumrind. *American Psychologist, 19,* 848–852.

Milgram, S., Liberty, H. J., Toledo, R., & Wackenhut, J. (1986). Response to intrusion into waiting lines. *Journal of Personality and Social Psychology, 51,* 683–689.

Miller, J. M., & Peden, B. F. (2003). Complexity and degree of tempo modulation as factors in productivity. *Psi Chi Journal of Undergraduate Research, 8,* 21–27.

Miller, N. E. (1985). The value of behavioral research on animals. *American Psychologist, 40,* 423–440.

Milton, R. C. (1964). An extended table of critical values for the Mann–Whitney (Wilcoxon) two-sample statistic, *Journal of the American Statistical Association, 59,* 925–934.

Montee, B. B., Miltenberger, R. G., & Wittrock, D. (1995). An experimental analysis of facilitated communication. *Journal of Applied Behavior Analysis, 28,* 189–200.

Mook, D. G. (1983). In defense of external invalidity. *American Psychologist, 38,* 379–387.

Morgan, D. L. (1997). *Focus groups as qualitative research* (2nd ed.). Newbury Park, CA: Sage Publications.

Murray, B. (2002). Research fraud needn't happen at all. *APA Monitor, 33* (2). Retrieved from http://www.apa.org/monitor/feb02/fraud.html.

National Commission for the Protection of Human Subjects of Biomedical and Behavioral Research. (April 18, 1979). *The Belmont Report: Ethical principles and guidelines for the protection of human subjects of research.* Retrieved, from http://ohsr.od.nih.gov/mpa/belmont.php3.

Newsweek. (1973). March 12, p. 49.

O'Connor, D. B., & Ferguson, E. (2008). Studying the natural history of behaviour. *The Psychologist, 21* (12), 1034–1036.

O'Toole, K. (1997, January 8). The Stanford prison experiment: Still powerful after all these years. *Stanford News*, p. 30.

Ogloff, J. R. P., & Vidmar, N. (1994). The impact of pretrial publicity on jurors: A study to compare the relative effects of television and print media in a child sex abuse case. *Law and Human Behavior*, *18*, 507–525.

Orne, M. T. (1962). On the social psychology of the psychological experiment: With particular reference to demand characteristics and their implications. *American Psychologist*, *17*, 776–783.

Osgood, C. E., Suci, G. J., & Tannenbaum, P. H. (1957). *The measurement of meaning*. Urbana: University of Illinois Press.

Pallant, J. (2010). *SPSS Survival Manual* (4th ed.). London: Open University Press.

Park, C. L., Armeli, S., & Tennen, H. (2004). Appraisal-coping goodness of fit: A daily Internet study. *Personality and Social Psychology Bulletin*, *30*, 558–569.

Parker, I. (2005) *Qualitative psychology: introducing radical research*. London: Open University Press.

Parry, H. J., & Crossley, H. M. (1950). Validity of responses to survey questions. *Public Opinion Quarterly*, *14*, 61–80.

Pew Global Attitudes Project. (2006). The great divide: How Westerners and Muslims view each other. Retrieved from http://pewglobal.org/reports/display.php?PageID=830.

Pishkin, V., & Shurley, J. T. (1983). Electrophysiological parameters in anxiety and failure: Evaluation of doxepin and hydroxyzine. *Bulletin of the Psychonomic Society*, *21*, 21–23.

Pittenger, D. J. (1995). Teaching students about graphs. *Teaching of Psychology*, *22*, 125–128.

Pittenger, D. J. (2003). Internet research: An opportunity to revisit classic ethical problems in behavioral research. *Ethics and Behavior*, *13*, 45–60.

Plous, S. (1996a). Attitudes toward the use of animals in psychological research and education: Results from a national survey of psychologists. *American Psychologist*, *51*, 1167–1180.

Plous, S. (1996b). Attitudes toward the use of animals in psychological research and education: results from a national survey of psychology majors. *Psychological Science*, *7*, 352–363.

Potter, J., & Wetherell, M. (1987). *Discourse and social psychology: Beyond attitudes and behaviour*. London: Sage.

Povinelli, D. J., & Bering, J. M. (2002). The mentality of apes revisited. *Current Directions in Psychological Science*, *11*, 115–119.

Richardson, J. (1996) *The handbook of qualitative research methods for psychologists and the social sciences*. London: Wiley-Blackwell.

Richardson, J. E. (2006). *Analysing newspapers: An approach from critical discourse analysis*. London: Palgrave Macmillan.

Riley, S., Rodham, K., & Gavin, J. (2009). Doing weight: Pro-ana and recovery identities in cyberspace, *Journal of Community & Applied Social Psychology*, *19*, 348–359.

Robinson, J. P., Athanasiou, R., & Head, K. B. (1969). *Measures of occupational attitudes and occupational characteristics*. Ann Arbor, MI: Institute for Social Research.

Robinson, J. P., Rusk, J. G., & Head, K. B. (1968). *Measures of political attitudes*. Ann Arbor, MI: Institute for Social Research.

Robinson, J. P., Shaver, P. R., & Wrightsman, L. S. (1991). *Measures of personality and social psychological attitudes* (Vol. 1). San Diego, CA: Academic Press.

Roediger, R. (2004). What should they be called? *Observer*. Retrieved from http://www.psychologicalscience.org/observer/getArticle.cfm?id=1549.

Rogers, T. B. (1995). *The psychological testing enterprise: An introduction*. Pacific Grove, CA: Brooks/Cole.

Rosenblatt, P. C., & Cozby, P. C. (1972). Courtship patterns associated with freedom of choice of spouse. *Journal of Marriage and the Family, 34,* 689–695.

Rosenhan, D. (1973). On being sane in insane places. *Science, 179,* 250–258.

Rosenthal, R. (1966). *Experimenter effects in behavioral research.* New York: Appleton-Century-Crofts.

Rosenthal, R. (1976). *Experimenter effects in behavioral research* (enlarged ed.). New York: Irvington.

Rosenthal, R., & Rosnow, R. L. (1975). *The volunteer subject.* New York: Wiley.

Rosenthal, R., & Rosnow, R. L. (1991). *Essentials of behavioral research: Methods and data analysis* (2nd ed.). New York: McGraw-Hill.

Rosnow, R. L., & Rosenthal, R. (1989). Statistical procedures and the justification of knowledge in psychological science. *American Psychologist, 44,* 1276–1284.

Rosnow, R. L., & Rosnow, M. (1986). *Writing psychology papers.* Monterey, CA: Brooks/Cole.

Runyon, R. P., & Haber, A. H. (1976). *Fundamentals of behavioral statistics* (3rd ed.). Reading, MA: McGraw-Hill.

Russell, D., Peplau, L. A., & Cutrona, C. E. (1980). The revised UCLA Loneliness Scale: Concurrent and discriminant validity. *Journal of Personality and Social Psychology, 39,* 472–480.

Saunders, D. R. (1980). Definition of Stroop interference in volunteers and non-volunteers. *Perceptual and Motor Skills, 51,* 343–354.

Saunders, J., Fernandes, M., & Kosnes, L. (2009). Retrieval-induced forgetting and mental imagery. *Memory & Cognition, 37* (6), 819–828. doi: 10.3758/MC.37.6.819.

Schachter, S. (1959). *The psychology of affiliation.* Stanford, CA: Stanford University Press.

Schoeneman, T. J., & Rubanowitz, D. E. (1985). Attributions in the advice columns: Actors and observers, causes and reasons. *Personality and Social Psychology Bulletin, 11,* 315–325.

Schuman, H., Presser, S., & Ludwig, J. (1981). Context effects of survey responses to questions about abortion. *Public Opinion Quarterly, 45,* 216–223.

Schwarz, N. (1999). Self-reports: How the questions shape the answers. *American Psychologist, 54,* 93–105.

Shaffer, D. (1985). *Developmental psychology: Theory, research, and applications.* Monterey, CA: Brooks/Cole.

Shaughnessy, J. J., Zechmeister, E. B. & Zechmeister, J. S. (2006) *Research Methods in Psychology* (7th ed.). London: McGraw-Hill.

Shin, Y. H. (1999). The effects of a walking exercise program on physical function and emotional state of elderly Korean women. *Public Health Nursing, 16,* 146–154.

Shohat, M., & Musch, J. (2003). Online auctions as a research tool: A field experiment on ethnic discrimination. *Swiss Journal of Psychology, 62,* 139–145.

Simons, D. J., & Levin, D. T. (1998). Failure to detect changes to people during a real world interaction. *Psychonomic Bulletin and Review, 5,* 644–649.

Skitka, L. J., & Sargis, E. G. (2005). Social psychological research and the Internet: The promise and the perils of a new methodological frontier. In Y. Amichai-Hamburger (Ed.), *The social net: The social psychology of the Internet* (pp. 1–26). Oxford: Oxford University Press.

Smith, J. A. (2003) *Qualitative psychology: A practical guide to research methods.* London: Sage.

Smith, J. A., & Osborn, M. (2003) Interpretative phenomenological analysis. In J. A. Smith (Ed.), *Qualitative psychology.* London: Sage.

Smith, J. K., & Hodkinson, P. (2005). "Relativism, Criteria and Politics" in N. Denzin & Y. Lincoln (Eds.), *The Sage handbook of qualitative research* (3rd ed.), (pp. 915–932). London: Sage.

Smith, P. K., & Lewis, K. (1985). Rough-and-tumble play, fighting, and chasing in nursery school children. *Ethology and Sociobiology, 6,* 175–181.

Smith, V. L., & Ellsworth, P. C. (1987). The social psychology of eyewitness accuracy: Misleading questions and communicator expertise. *Journal of Applied Psychology, 72,* 294–300.

Smith, T. W. (1981). Qualifications to generalized absolutes: "Approval of hitting" questions on the GSS. *Public Opinion Quarterly, 45,* 224–230.

Sokal, A., & Bricmont, J. (2003). *Intellectual Impostures.* London: Profile Books.

Spatz, C., & Kardas, E. (2008). *Research methods: Ideas, technique & reports.* London: McGraw-Hill.

Spitz, R. A. (1965). *The first year of life.* New York: International Universities Press.

Spitzer, R. L. (1976). More on pseudoscience in science and the case for psychiatric diagnosis. *Archives of General Psychiatry, 33,* 459–470.

Steinberg, J. A. (2002). Misconduct of others: Prevention techniques for researchers. *American Psychological Society Observer.* Retrieved from http://www.psychologicalscience.org/observer /0102/misconduct.html.

Sternberg, R. J. (1986). A triangular theory of love. *Psychological Review, 93,* 119–135.

Sternberg, R. J., & Grigorenko, E. L. (2001). Unified psychology. *American Psychologist, 56,* 1069–1079.

Stevenson, M. R. (1995). Is this the definitive sex survey? *Journal of Sex Research, 32,* 77–91.

Stokes, P. D. (2009). Using constraints to create novelty: A case study. *Psychology of Aesthetics, Creativity, and the Arts, 3,* 174–180. doi: 10.1037/a0014970.

Stone, V. E., Cosmides, L., Tooby, J., Kroll, N., & Knight, R. T. (2002). Selective impairment of reasoning about social exchange in a patient with bilateral limbic system damage. *Proceedings of the National Academy of Sciences, 99* (17), 11531–11536. Retrieved from http://www.pnas.org/cgi/content/full/99/17/11531.

Strauss, A., & Corbin, J. (1990). *Basics of qualitative research: Grounded theory procedures and techniques.* London: Sage Publications.

Streiner, D. L. (2006). Building a better model: An introduction to structural equation modeling. *Canadian Journal of Psychiatry, 51,* 317–324.

Strunk, W., & White, E. B. (1979). *The elements of style* (3rd ed.). New York: Macmillan.

Tabachnick, B. G., & Fidell, L. S. (2001). *Using multivariate statistics* (4th ed.). London: Allyn & Bacon.

Tabachnick, B. G., & Fidell, L. S. (2007). *Using multivariate statistics* (5th ed.). London: Allyn & Bacon.

Tanford, S. L. (1984). *Decision making processes in joined criminal trials.* Unpublished doctoral dissertation, University of Wisconsin, Madison.

Tassinary, L. G., & Hansen, K. A. (1998). A critical test of the waist-to-hip-ratio hypothesis of female physical attractiveness. *Psychological Science, 9,* 150–155.

Tatsuoka, M. M. (1971). *Multivariate analysis: Techniques for educational and psychological research.* New York: Wiley.

Thorndike, E. (1932). *The fundamentals of learning.* New York: Teachers College Press.

Tukey, J. W. (1972). Some graphic and semigraphic displays. In T. A. Bancroft (Ed.), *Statistical Papers in Honor of George W. Snedecor* (pp. 293–316). Ames: Iowa State University Press.

Tukey, J. W. (1977). *Exploratory data analysis.* Reading, MA: Addison-Wesley.

Uba, L. (1994). *Asian Americans: Personality patterns, identity, and mental health.* New York: The Guilford Press.

Underwood, B. J., & Shaughnessy, J. J. (1975). *Experimentation in psychology.* New York: Wiley.

US Office of Research Integrity. (2006). Office of Research Integrity: 2005 annual report. Retrieved from http://ori.dhhs.gov/documents/annual_reports/ori_annual_report_2005.pdf.

van Gelder, L. (1996, June 19). Thomas Juhn, 73; devised science paradigm. *New York Times*, p. B7.

Walker-Hill, R. (2000). An analysis of the relationship of human sexuality knowledge, self-esteem, and body image to sexual satisfaction in college and university students. Dissertation, University of Tennessee, Knoxville.

Warner, J. L., Berman, J. J., Weyant, J. M., & Ciarlo, J. A. (1983). Assessing mental health program effectiveness: A comparison of three client follow-up methods. *Evaluation Review, 7,* 635–658.

Watson, J. B. (1913). Psychology as the behaviorist views it. *Psychological Review, 20,* 158–177.

Webb, E. J., Campbell, D. T., Schwartz, R. D., Sechrest, L., & Grove, J. B. (1981). *Non-reactive measures in the social sciences* (2nd ed.). Boston: Houghton-Mifflin.

Weiner, B. (1975). "On being sane in insane places": A process (attributional) analysis and critique. *Journal of Abnormal Psychology, 84,* 433–441.

Wells, G. L., & Bradfield, A. L. (1999). Distortions in eyewitnesses' recollections: Can the post-identification feedback effect be moderated? *Psychological Science, 10,* 138–144.

Willig, C. (2001). *Introducing qualitative research in psychology: Adventures in theory and method.* London: Open University Press.

Willig, C. (2008). *Introducing qualitative research methods in psychology* (2nd ed.). London: Open University Press.

Willig, C., & Stainton-Rogers, W. (Eds.). (2008). *The Sage handbook of qualitative research in psychology.* London: Sage Publications.

Woll, S. B. (2002). *Everyday thinking: Memory, reasoning, and judgment in the real world.* Mahwah, NJ: Erlbaum.

Yacker, N., & Weinberg, S. L. (1990). Care and justice moral orientation: A scale for its assessment. *Journal of Personality Assessment, 55,* 18–27.

Yin, R. K. (1994). *Case study research: Design and methods.* Newbury Park, CA: Sage.

Zimbardo, P. G. (1973). The psychological power and pathology of imprisonment. In E. Aronson & R. Helmreich (Eds.), *Social psychology.* New York: Van Nostrand.

Zuckerman, M. (1979). *Sensation seeking: Beyond the optimal level of arousal.* Hillsdale, NJ: Erlbaum.

Glossary

A

A *priori* comparisons Also called planned comparisons; hypothesis-directed statistical tests used to compare differences between two conditions when a significant ANOVA has been obtained; the comparisons to be made are determined before any analysis has been conducted.

Abstract Short summary of the contents of a research report or journal article.

Adjusted R-square Measure of amount of variance in criterion variable predicted by multiple regression equation.

Alpha The probability value that is the criterion for rejecting the null hypothesis; usually .05.

Alternative hypothesis The hypothesis that there is an effect in the population (e.g. difference between means, relationship between variables); the opposite of the null hypothesis.

Analysis Section of a qualitative research report or journal article that states what was found with evidence.

Analysis of covariance (ANCOVA) Statistical technique which compares means on a dependent variable, once the influence of covariates has been controlled for.

Analysis of variance (ANOVA) Set of parametric inferential statistical tests used to test for differences between more than two means by comparing variances between and within groups.

Applied research Research carried out to investigate a real-world problem.

Archival research Analysis of existing records or documents that were obtained from archives (e.g. statistical records, survey archives, written records).

Autonomy Principle that individuals in research investigations are capable of making a decision of whether to participate.

Axial coding Coding technique used in grounded theory which focuses on the dimensions of categories.

B

Bar graph A graph of the frequency, percentage or means of different categories.

Basic research Research carried out primarily to test a theory or empirical issues.

Behaviourism A school of thought in psychology which holds that the only valid unit of measurement in psychology is observable behaviours.

Belief-based explanations/ method of tenacity An explanation for behaviour that is accepted without evidence because it comes from a trusted source or fits within a larger framework of belief.

Beta weight Standardized regression weight used to interpret the results of a linear regression analysis. A beta weight can be interpreted as a partial correlation coefficient.

Between-groups variance The variability of each group mean from the grand mean; attributed to effects of independent variable, plus measurement error and individual differences; also known as systematic variance.

Between-subjects design An experimental design in which independent groups of participants take part in each condition.

Between-subjects factorial ANOVA NHST method used to analyse data from a between-subjects factorial design.

Between-subjects factorial design Factorial design in which every factor is a between-subjects variable; a different group takes part in each condition.

Biased sample A sample that is not representative of the population it is supposed to represent.

Biased selection A threat to internal validity in which groups of participants are not equivalent prior to treatment.

Binary logistic regression Logistic regression in which outcome variable is dichotomous.

Binomial test Non-parametric statistical test used to compare proportions in a dichotomous (two-category) variable.

Biserial correlation Correlation technique used to test for relationship between an artificially dichotomous variable and a continuous variable.

Bonferroni method Method of controlling familywise Type I error rates by dividing alpha level by the number of comparisons to be made.

Boxplot A graph that shows a distribution's range, interquartile range, median and sometimes other statistics.

C

Case study A detailed description of one individual case (usually a person) that represents an instance that is rare or of particular interest to the researcher.

Central tendency Descriptive statistics that indicate a typical or representative score. Examples are mean, median and mode.

Chi-square test of association Non-parametric statistical test used to analyse associations between two nominal variables.

Chi-square test of goodness-of-fit Non-parametric statistical test used to compare proportions of cases in categories of a single nominal variable with proportions expected under null hypothesis.

Closed-ended questions Questions in a survey that have a discrete number of responses for the respondent to select from.

Cluster sampling A probability sampling technique that identifies clusters of individuals and then randomly samples an appropriate number of clusters. Every member of the selected cluster is entered into the sample.

Coding system A method for data reduction in which units of behaviour or particular events are identified and categorized according to specific criteria.

Coefficient of determination Measure of strength of a relationship; describes amount

of variance explained; denoted by r^2.

Cohen's *d* An effect size measure suitable for *t*-tests.

Cohort-sequential design Developmental design that combines features from cross-sectional and longitudinal designs in order to evaluate the contribution of "generation effects".

Concept An abstract idea or unit of knowledge that refers to something in the external world and can be conveyed to others in a meaningful way.

Concurrent validity Determined by assessing the relationship between the measure and a concurrent criterion behaviour.

Confidence interval Range of scores that is expected with a specified degree of confidence to capture a parameter (population value).

Confidentiality Requirement to keep research data about individual participants private.

Confirmational strategy A strategy for testing a theory that involves finding evidence that confirms what is already believed.

Confirmatory factor analysis Factor analysis technique in which the goal is to test theory and confirm predictions.

Confounding Occurs when the independent variable of interest systematically covaries with a second, unintended independent variable.

Constant comparative analysis Analytic technique used in grounded theory, involving repeated comparison of categories within and across accounts.

Construct A concept or idea used in psychological theories to explain behaviour or mental processes; examples include

aggression, depression, intelligence, memory and personality.

Construct validity The degree to which a measurement device accurately measures the theoretical construct it is designed to measure.

Content analysis Qualitative data analysis approach which converts qualitative data into categories which can then be quantified.

Control The act of reducing unwanted effects in an experiment by incorporating techniques that reduce them as much as possible.

Convenience sampling A method of sampling that involves recruiting participants at the researcher's convenience. Also known as "haphazard" sampling.

Convergent validity A measure is assessed by how closely it is associated with other measures of the same construct.

Correlation When scores on one variable covary with scores on another.

Correlation coefficient A statistic which indicates the degree of covariation between two variables; ranges between −1.00 and +1.00.

Correlational method A method that looks for relationships between factors.

Counterbalancing A technique that orders the levels of an extraneous variable so that their effects balance out over the different levels of the independent variable.

Covariate designs Designs in which a variable that is known to correlate with the dependent variable is measured and its effect "subtracted out".

Cramér's V Measure of strength of association between two nominal variables; suitable for any size of contingency table.

Criterion variable An outcome variable that provides an indicator of a psychological construct, against which scores on other measures can be validated.

Criterion-oriented validity Determined by the degree to which the test correlates with another (criterion) variable.

Cronbach's alpha An indicator of internal consistency reliability assessed by examining the average correlation of each item (question) in a measure with every other question.

Cross-sectional design A developmental design in which the researcher recruits a "cross-section" (often related to age) of the population available at the time of the research.

D

Debriefing Explaining to participants the nature, results and conclusions of the research they participated in and correcting any misconceptions.

Deception Deliberately misleading participants about any aspect of the research.

Deductive reasoning Reasoning that goes from the general to the specific (i.e. from general statements to specific observations); forms the foundation of the rational method of enquiry.

Degrees of freedom The number of observations free to vary; related to sample size.

Demand characteristics Cues and other information used by participants to guide their behaviour in a psychological study, often leading participants to do what they believe the observer

(experimenter) expects them to do.

Dependent variable The outcome variable measured in a study; it is expected to change as a result of changes in the independent variable.

Descriptive statistics Numbers or graphs that summarise a set of sample data.

Design Subsection of the method section of a research report or journal article that provides an overview of the research design and variables.

Developmental design Research design in which participant age is used as a quasi-independent variable.

Diary studies A method of qualitative data collection in which individuals keep diaries related to experiences or events of interest over an extended period of time.

Disconfirmational strategy A method of testing a theory that involves conducting research to provide evidence that disconfirms the predictions made by the theory.

Discourse analysis Qualitative data analysis approach which focuses on discourse and how language constructs social reality.

Discriminant analysis Multivariate statistical technique used when you have multiple predictor variables and a categorical criterion variable.

Discriminant function A combination of predictor variables, presented in the form of a linear equation.

Discriminant function analysis Multivariate statistical technique which allows you to distinguish between groups based on sets of variables.

Discriminant validity Determined by the degree to which the measure is distinct from other measures, thus demonstrating that the initial measure is tapping into something distinct.

Discursive Psychology Form of discourse analysis which focuses on how people use discourse to achieve certain interpersonal objectives.

Discussion Section of a research report or journal article that evaluates and interprets results.

Double-blind procedure A way of controlling for expectancy effects in both participants and observers in which all parties directly involved in the administration of treatments are unaware of who is receiving the placebo treatment and who is not.

Dual consent Principle that consent should be sought from potential participants and their parent/guardian, when the participant is unable to make a free and informed decision about giving consent (usually children and people with impairments).

Dual consent by proxy Principle that consent should be sought from the parent/guardian of a potential participant, when the participant cannot provide consent or cannot communicate this.

Dynamic processes Memory, mood, judgement, etc.

E

Ecological validity How much a particular method of research resembles "real life" in the context of the research.

Effect size A measure of the size of a treatment effect or strength of association; unaffected by sample size.

Empirical question A question that can be answered through objective observation.

Empiricism Philosophical and scientific approach to knowledge that uses unbiased observation to discover truths about the world.

Endogenous variable An internal variable in a path analysis model, changes in which are caused by other variables.

Epistemology A branch of philosophy that deals with the nature and origins of knowledge.

Error Anything that might influence your dependent variable that is beyond the control of the investigator. Also known as "extraneous" or "confounding" variables.

Eta squared (η^2) Effect size measure for ANOVA; indicates amount of variance in dependent variable that is attributable to independent variable.

Ethical guidelines General principles and rules of ethical behaviour.

Event sampling A technique to sample infrequent or formally scheduled behaviour. It involves selecting specific events to be observed which must meet predetermined criteria.

Exogenous variable A variable which begins a causal sequence in path analysis.

Expectancy effects When a researcher's preconceived ideas about how participants should behave are subtly communicated to participants and, in turn, affect the participants' behaviour.

Expected frequencies Frequencies expected if the null hypothesis were true; may reflect no preference or no difference from a comparison population.

Experimental method A well-controlled form of research that looks for cause–effect relationships.

Experimenter effects When the behaviour of the researcher influences the results of a study (e.g. through expectancy effects or uneven treatment of participants across conditions).

Exploratory data analysis Approach to analysing data that includes examining boxplots, stem-and-leaf plots, and histograms, to gain an insight into the data prior to statistical analysis.

Exploratory factor analysis Factor analysis technique in which there is no *a priori* reason to predict which variables will cluster together.

External validity The extent to which the results of a research study can be generalized beyond the limits of the study sample, to different populations, settings and conditions.

Extraneous variable Any variable that is not systematically manipulated in an experiment but that still may affect the behaviour being observed.

Extreme score A score that lies towards the extremes of a distribution; sometimes defined as lying more than $3 \times$ interquartile range from the other scores.

F

Face-to-face interview Method of administering a questionnaire that involves face-to-face interaction with the participant.

Face validity The degree to which a measurement device appears to accurately measure a variable.

Factor (1) Another name for independent variable, commonly used when discussing factorial designs.

Factor (2) An underlying dimension that cannot be measured directly, but which can be identified during factor analysis.

Factor analysis Multivariate statistical technique used to identify underlying dimensions based on correlations between variables.

Factor loading The correlation between a variable and an underlying factor.

Factorial design Research design that has more than one independent variable; every level of one independent variable is combined with every level of every other independent variable.

Falsifiability Karl Popper's criterion for deciding the worth of a scientific theory. Falsifiable theories allow their predictions to be tested.

Familywise error rate The likelihood of making a Type I error across a number of comparisons; increases as number of comparisons increase.

Field experiment A method of observation that closely resembles experimental methods, with the exception that the studies are conducted in a more natural setting than the laboratory.

Focus group A small group of participants interact with each other and an interviewer who poses questions.

Foucauldian discourse analysis Form of discourse analysis which focuses on how discourse constructs subjects and objects.

Frequency distribution Arrangement of scores or categories with the frequency of each score or category shown.

Frequency polygon A frequency distribution graph of a continuous variable with frequency points connected by lines.

Friedman test Non-parametric equivalent of one-way within-subjects ANOVA; compares differences in scores from two or more conditions from the same group of participants.

F-statistic The test statistic calculated when using ANOVA; the ratio of the between-groups variance to the within-groups variance.

Functional explanation Functional explanations explain *what things do*.

G

Generation effects A confounding variable relating to differences that exist due to the generation of participants.

Graphic rating scale A rating scale in which respondents indicate their response with a mark on a continuous line, which can then be measured.

Grounded theory Qualitative data analysis approach which focuses on generating theory directly from data.

H

Haphazard (convenience) sampling A sampling method in which participants were selected in a haphazard manner, usually on the basis of availability, and not with regard to having a representative sample of the population.

Heteroscedasticity Occurs when degree of variation in scores in one variable is not the same across the full range of scores

of another variable (e.g. in regression, degree of variation in residuals would increase or decrease consistently across the full range of predictor variable scores).

Hierarchical regression Multiple regression method in which the order in which variables are entered into the equation is determined by the researcher, usually based on theory or previous research.

High-frequency scale A rating scale in which the response options for frequency of behaviour represent high frequencies.

Histogram A graph of frequencies of a continuous variable constructed with contiguous (touching) vertical bars.

History A threat to internal validity in which the occurrence of an event other than the treatment produces changes in the research participants' behaviour.

Homogeneity of variance The parametric assumption that variances of two samples are similar.

Homoscedasticity An assumption of regression and multivariate statistics; occurs when scores on one variable have the same degree of variation across the full range of scores on another variable (e.g. in regression, residuals would have a similar degree of variation across the full range of predictor variable scores).

Hypothesis 1. A tentative explanation for something. 2. A statement about what might be observed in a study.

I

Independent variable Variable whose values are manipulated

by the researcher; it is expected to have an effect on the dependent variable.

Independent-samples t-test Parametric statistical test used to compare means from two separate samples.

Inductive reasoning Reasoning that uses observations as a basis for forming general principles.

Inferential statistics Set of methods used to reach conclusions about populations based on samples and probability.

Informed consent Agreement, usually written, to participate in a study after being informed of the consequences of participation.

Interaction The differing effect of one factor on the dependent variable, depending on the particular level of another factor.

Internal consistency Reliability assessed with data collected at one point in time with multiple individual measures of a psychological construct (e.g. multiple questions on a questionnaire). A measure is reliable when the multiple measures provide similar results.

Internal validity The ability of your method to adequately test the hypothesis it was designed to test.

Internet survey A survey in which the questionnaire is administered electronically via the Internet.

Inter-observer reliability The extent to which two or more observers assessing the same behaviour or event agree about the relevant details.

Interpretation and meaning The basis of the majority of qualitative research is an interpretation of experience (both the participants' and the researcher's) and the meaning that is attached to the experience.

Interpretative Phenomenological Analysis (IPA) Qualitative data analysis approach which focuses on how individuals experience and make sense of the world.

Interpretative repertoires Consistent ways of saying something identified in discourse analysis.

Interquartile range A range of scores that captures the 50 per cent of a distribution that is between the 25th and 75th percentiles.

Interrater reliability Method of detecting inconsistent measuring by comparing observations of two independent observers.

Interrupted time series design A variation of the time series design in which changes in behaviour are charted as a function of time before and after some naturally occurring event.

Interval scale Measurement scale in which numbers indicate rank order, but equal differences between numbers do not indicate equal differences between the thing measured.

Interview A one-to-one discussion with a participant on a specified topic.

Interview schedule A list of pre-prepared questions or discussion topics for use by an interviewer.

Interviewer bias Intentional or unintentional influence exerted by an interviewer in such a way that the actual or interpreted behaviour of respondents is consistent with the interviewer's expectations.

Introduction The first main section of a research report or journal article, which includes the rationale for the study, a literature review, and usually a statement of the aims or hypotheses for the research.

Introspection A method by which the researcher pays attention to his or her own psychological processes while engaged in a task.

Item–total correlation The correlation between the score on one item of a measurement device and the overall total score.

K

Kendall's tau Non-parametric correlation technique used in same way as Spearman correlation, but recommended for small samples and tied ranks; denoted by τ.

Kruskal-Wallis test Non-parametric equivalent of one-way between-subjects ANOVA; used to compare differences in scores for two or more groups.

L

Language The fundamental "unit of analysis" for qualitative research. Language is considered a vehicle to convey interpretation and meaning.

Latent variable Variables in a structural equation model which cannot be observed or measured directly.

Lazy writing Using too much quoted material (albeit correctly cited) in written work.

Level A condition in an independent variable (factor).

Level of significance (alpha) The probability value that is the criterion for rejecting the null hypothesis; usually .05.

Line graph A graph that shows the relationship between two variables with points connected by a line.

Linear regression Statistical technique used to make predictions about scores on one variable based on scores on other variable(s).

Literature search An organized and thorough search of all the literature published on a topic.

Logistic regression Multiple regression technique in which outcome variable is categorical.

Loglinear analysis A type of multiway frequency analysis; an extension to the chi-square test of association, considering more than two categorical variables.

Longitudinal design Developmental design in which the researcher measures or observes participants over a specified period of time.

M

Mail survey Method of administering a survey that involves mailing questionnaires to participants.

Main effect In a factorial design, the overall effect of a factor on the dependent variable.

Mann-Whitney *U*-test Non-parametric test used to compare averages from two independent samples; the non-parametric equivalent of the independent-samples *t*-test.

Matched-groups design A between-groups design in which participants in each group are matched on a variable that is thought to correlate with the dependent variable.

Materials/Apparatus Subsection of the Method section of a research report or journal article that describes the materials and apparatus used in the study.

Maturation A threat to internal validity in which naturally occurring change within the individual (associated with the passage of time) may be responsible for the results.

Mauchly's test of sphericity Statistical test used to test the assumption of sphericity.

Mean The arithmetic average; the sum of the scores divided by the number of scores.

Measurement error The degree to which a measurement device deviates from the true score value.

Mechanistic explanation Mechanistic explanations explain *how things work*.

Media sources Sources of data derived from various media (e.g. magazines, television, speeches).

Median The point that divides a set of scores into equal halves; half the scores are above the median and half are below it.

Method (1) A particular approach to answering a research question.

Method (2) Section of a research report or journal article in which the methods used in the study are described in detail.

Method of authority Relying on authoritative sources (e.g. books, journals, scholars) for information.

Mixed design A design that includes both independent groups (between-subjects) and repeated measures (within-subjects).

Mixed factorial ANOVA NHST method used to analyse data from a mixed factorial design.

Mixed factorial design Factorial design in which one or more factors are between-subjects

variables and one or more are within-subjects variable.

Mixed methods Using both qualitative and quantitative methodologies to approach a particular research question.

Mode The score that occurs most frequently.

Monotonic relationship A relationship that goes in one direction, but is not necessarily linear.

Multicollinearity Occurs when variables are highly correlated with each other.

Multi-level designs Experimental designs in which the independent variable has more than two levels (or conditions).

Multinomial logistic regression Logistic regression in which outcome variable consists of more than two categories.

Multiple correlation coefficient The correlation between actual scores and scores predicted using multiple regression equation.

Multiple observation effects A threat to internal validity associated with longitudinal research, in which participants' scores may change for reasons related to repeated testing over time (e.g. practice effects, factors other than participant age).

Multiple R The correlation between the best linear combination of predictor variables entered into a multiple regression analysis and the dependent variable.

Multiple regression Statistical technique used to predict scores on a criterion variable based on scores on several predictor variables.

Multivariate analysis of covariance (MANCOVA) Multivariate statistical technique which compares

difference on multiple dependent variables, once the influence of covariates has been controlled for.

Multivariate analysis of variance (MANOVA) Multivariate statistical technique which is an extension of ANOVA to analyse more than one dependent variable.

Multivariate design A research design in which multiple dependent measures are analysed with a single, multivariate statistical test.

Multivariate outlier A deviant score on a combination of variables from a single source.

Multivariate strategy Research design which involves multiple dependent measures.

Multiway frequency analysis A set of techniques used to analyse nominal data.

N

Narrative records Records intended to provide a more or less faithful reproduction of behaviour as it originally occurred.

Naturalistic observation An observational method that involves the researcher studying behaviour as it occurs "naturally", without any attempt to intervene.

Negative relationship A relationship in which increases in scores on one variable are associated with decreases in scores on another variable.

Negative sampling Analytic technique used in Grounded Theory involving the search for cases which do not fit the emerging theory.

Nominal scale Measurement scale in which numbers or names serve as labels and do not indicate a numerical relationship. Sometimes called "categorical" scale as we put things into categories when using it.

Non-equivalent group design Design in which one group is tested before and after an intervention, while another group serves as a "control" group for whom no intervention is employed.

Non-probability sampling Sampling techniques that do not specify how likely it is that any member of the population may be selected.

Non-random sample A specialized sample of participants used in a study who are not randomly chosen from the population.

Non-recursive model A path analysis model which includes loops.

Non-response bias A problem associated with survey research, caused by some participants not returning the questionnaire, resulting in a biased sample.

Normal curve A mathematically defined, theoretical distribution with a particular bell shape. An empirical distribution of similar shape.

Null hypothesis The hypothesis that there is no effect in the population (e.g. no difference between means, no relationship between variables).

Null hypothesis significance testing An inferential statistics technique that produces accurate probabilities about samples when the null hypothesis is true.

O

Oblique rotation Factor rotation technique which considers factors to be correlated.

Observational method A series of methods that focuses on

systematically observing individuals or groups either in their natural environment or in other situations. Data from observational methods can be quantitative or qualitative.

Observed frequencies Frequencies that have been actually obtained in a sample.

Observer bias Systematic errors in observation often resulting from the observer's expectancies regarding the outcome of a study (i.e. expectancy effects).

Occam's Razor The principle which states that a problem should be stated as simply as possible, with the fewest propositions possible.

One-tailed (directional) hypothesis Alternative hypothesis in which the direction of a difference is specified. Predicts the direction of the effect that you are investigating.

One-way between-subjects ANOVA Parametric inferential statistical test used to compare differences in means from two or more groups in a single factor design.

One-way within-subjects ANOVA Parametric inferential statistical test used to compare means from the same group of participants under two or more conditions; also called repeated measures ANOVA.

Open-ended questions Questions in a survey that allow the respondent to answer freely, either verbally or in writing.

Operational definition A definition of a variable in terms of the operations and procedures used to measure it.

Oral presentation Method of communicating research findings by speaking in front of an audience.

Ordinal scale Measurement scale in which numbers indicate rank order, but equal differences between numbers do not indicate equal differences between the thing measured.

Orthogonal rotation Factor rotation technique which considers factors to be independent.

Outlier A score separated from others and 1.5 (IQR) beyond the 25th or 75th percentile.

P

Paired-samples *t*-test Parametric statistical test used to compare two means from the same sample or from paired or matched samples.

Paradigm A global viewpoint that determines which scientific questions are asked and the methods used to answer them.

Parametric test A statistical test that makes assumptions about the nature of the underlying population (e.g. that scores are normally distributed).

Parsimonious explanation An explanation or theory that explains a relationship using relatively few assumptions.

Partial correlation Correlation technique which tests for the relationship between two variables, while removing the influence of another.

Partial eta squared Effect size measure for ANOVA commonly calculated in statistical computer packages; differs from eta squared only in the denominator of its formula.

Partially open-ended questions Questions in a survey that offer a number of alternatives to choose from, one of which gives the respondent an opportunity to answer with a response that is not one of the pre-selected alternatives.

Participant observation An observational method that involves the researcher studying behaviour as it occurs "naturally", without any attempt to intervene.

Participant variables The natural ways in which participants in experiments differ from each other.

Participants Subsection of the Method section of a research report or journal article used to describe the number and nature of the sample.

Path analysis Application of multiple regression techniques used to test causal models.

Path coefficient Estimate of relationship between variables in path analysis model.

Pearson correlation coefficient Correlation coefficient which describes degree of linear relationship between two interval/ratio variables; denoted by r.

Peer review Formal process in which scientists judge colleagues' work submitted for publication or funding.

Perfect relationship Occurs when changes in scores in one variable are related to perfectly predictable changes in scores in another variable; indicated by correlation coefficient of +1.00 and −1.00.

Phi coefficient Measure of strength of association between two nominal variables; suitable for 2×2 contingency tables.

Pie chart Circular chart which has been divided into sectors according to the proportion or percentage for different categories.

Placebo control A technique for reducing "expectancy effects" in which participants

do not know whether they are given a "genuine" treatment or not.

Plagiarism Using someone else's words or ideas – intentionally or unintentionally – without properly citing the source.

Point-biserial correlation Correlation technique used to test for relationship between a truly dichotomous variable and a continuous variable.

Population An entire group (or entire set of scores) that is of interest to you as a researcher.

Positive relationship A relationship in which increases in scores on one variable are associated with increases in scores on another variable.

Positivism The view that knowledge about reality can be reliably obtained through empirical observations.

Post hoc **comparisons** Statistical tests used to compare all possible differences between two conditions *after* a significant ANOVA has been obtained; usually involve adjustments to control familywise error rate.

Poster presentation Method of communicating research findings by presenting them in the form of a poster and discussing research with viewers of the poster.

Power The probability of correctly rejecting a false null hypothesis.

Practice effect The influence taking part in one condition has on subsequent performance in other conditions.

Predictive validity Determined by assessing the relationship between the measure and some future behaviour associated with the measure.

Pre-test/post-test design An experimental design in which

the dependent variable is measured both before (pre-test) and after (post-test) manipulation of the independent variable.

Principal components analysis Type of factor analysis mainly used to reduce number of variables to summary of components.

Principal factors analysis Type of factor analysis mainly used to confirm empirical or theoretical predictions.

Privacy Right of individuals to decide how information about them is to be communicated to others.

Probability Likelihood of the occurrence of an event or outcome.

Probability sampling A way of sampling from a population that specifies the specific probability that each member has of being picked.

Procedure Subsection of the method section of a research report or journal article that provides a detailed description of the procedures used in the study.

Protocol analysis Qualitative data analysis approach which converts qualitative data into categories which can then be quantified.

Pseudoscience Claims that are made on the basis of evidence that is designed to appear scientific; however, such evidence is not based on the principles of the scientific method.

Psychobiography A type of case study in which a researcher applies psychological theory to explain the life of an individual, usually an important historical figure.

PsycINFO A database of abstracts from journal articles and book chapters relevant to psychology and related fields.

Publish Recording of scientific results, methods, and theories to create a permanent knowledge base of science.

Purposive sampling A sampling technique in which individuals are selected due to them belonging to a pre-defined group. Selection of individuals is not random.

Q

Qualitative method Research characterized by richness of experience and narrative results.

Quantitative method Research characterized by measurement and numerical results.

Quasi-experiment An experiment in which the researcher is not in full control of the independent variable (e.g. when a naturally occurring variable such as gender is used as the IV).

Quasi-experimental design A design that resembles characteristics of a true experiment (e.g. some type of intervention or treatment is used and comparison is provided), but lacks the degree of control that is found in true experiments.

Quasi-independent variable A variable resembling an independent variable in an experiment, but whose levels are not assigned to participants at random (e.g. participant's age).

Quota sampling A non-probability sampling technique involving the researcher having to fill a "quota" of participants that belong to pre-defined subgroups of the population. Similar to stratified sampling with the exception that the selection is not random within each subgroup.

R

Random sample A sample drawn from the population such that every member of the population has an equal opportunity to be included in the sample.

Range The highest score minus the lowest score.

Rating scale A method of recording a respondent's graded response to a question.

Ratio scale Scale of measurement in which the distance between the points on the scale is known and equal, and which has a "true zero" point (meaning that a score of zero indicates that none of the measured property is present).

Rational method Developing explanations through a process of deductive reasoning.

Reactivity When an observed participant changes his or her behaviour as a result of the observer's presence.

Realism The view that there is a real world "out there".

Recursive model A path analysis model which includes no loops.

Reference list An alphabetical list of all of the sources cited within a body of text.

Reflexive analysis Section of a qualitative research report or journal article that contains an evaluation of the research and the researcher's own role in the analytic process.

Reflexivity The practice of reflecting upon a qualitative research process for the purpose of identifying subjective and contextual factors that may have influenced the outcome.

Regression Statistical technique used to make predictions about scores on one variable based on scores of other variable(s).

Rejection region The portion of a sampling distribution which includes samples with probabilities less than alpha.

Relativism A position that suggests all knowledge is relative to the context in which it emerges.

Reliability The consistency or dependability of a measure.

Replication Repeating an experiment with the same procedures or with planned changes in the procedures to confirm the original results.

Representative sample A sample that closely matches the characteristics of the population.

Representativeness How closely your sample resembles the population from which it was selected.

Research fraud Occurs when a researcher intentionally produces research which is inaccurate or untruthful (e.g. through falsification or manipulation of data, by claiming another's work as their own).

Research question The question that a researcher addresses with a given piece of research.

Residual The difference between an actual score and the score that would be predicted based on the regression equation.

Response bias A source of bias in your data caused by participants failing to return completed surveys.

Response rate The percentage of people selected for a sample who actually completed a survey.

Response set A pattern of individual responses to questions on a self-report measure that is not related to the content of the questions.

Results Section of a research report or journal article that summarizes and analyses data and statistics.

Risk The possibility of harm, both physical and mental.

R-square The square of the multiple *R* in a multiple regression analysis. Provides a measure of the amount of variability in the dependent measure accounted for by the best linear combination of predictor variables.

S

Sample A smaller subgroup drawn from the larger population.

Sampling The process of choosing members of a population to be included in a sample.

Sampling distribution Frequency distribution showing means from all possible samples of a given size taken from a population.

Sampling error The deviation between the characteristics of a sample and a population.

Sampling frame The actual population from which the sample will be drawn. Will match the "true" population to a greater or lesser degree depending on the sampling technique.

Scatterplot Graph in which pairs of scores on two variables are represented by separate points.

Science A method of inquiry that uses unbiased empirical observation, public methods, reproducible results and theory to reveal universal truths about the universe.

Science Citation Index (SCI) A database of scientific and technical journal articles which provides information on citation (e.g., how many times an article has been cited by others, which later articles have cited in a particular earlier article).

Scientific explanation A tentative explanation for a phenomenon, based on objective observation and logic, and subject to empirical test.

Scientific method Approach to knowledge that emphasizes empirical rather than intuitive processes, testable hypotheses, systematic and controlled observation of operationally defined phenomena, data collection using accurate and precise instrumentation, valid and reliable measures, and objective reporting of results; scientists tend to be critical and, most importantly, sceptical.

Scientist A person who adopts the methods of science in his or her quest for knowledge.

Selection bias Threat to the representativeness of a sample that occurs when the procedures used to select a sample result in the over- or under-representation of a significant segment of the population.

Semantic differential scale A rating scale which measures responses to words or concepts using scales labelled with two contrasting adjectives.

Semi-partial correlation Multivariate correlational statistic used to examine the relationship between two variables with the effects of a third variable removed from only one of them; also called part correlation.

Semi-structured interview A one-to-one discussion between a researcher and a participant on a specific topic. The researcher has some prepared questions or topics for discussion, but will let the interview develop naturally.

Sign test Non-parametric test used to compare changes in sign (positive versus negative) between two paired conditions; alternative to Wilcoxon Signed Ranks test.

Simple main effect In a factorial design, the effect of one factor at a particular level of another factor.

Simple random sampling The purest form of probability sampling, in which every member of a population has an equal chance of being selected.

Simple (simultaneous) regression Multiple regression method in which all variables are entered into the equation in one step.

Situation sampling A technique to sample behaviour that involves observing the behaviour of interest in as many different locations and under as many different circumstances as possible.

Social constructionism The view that all knowledge is constructed and is a direct result of the society in which it exists.

Social Sciences Citation Index (SSCI) A database of scientific and technical journal articles which provides information on citation (e.g. how many times an article has been cited by others, which later articles have cited a particular earlier article).

Solomon four-group design An expansion of the pre-test–post-test design that includes control groups to evaluate the effects of administering a pre-test on your experimental treatment.

Spearman correlation Measure of strength of a relationship; describes amount of variance explained; denoted by r^2.

Sphericity Also called homogeneity of covariance; an assumption of within-subjects ANOVA; similar to homogeneity of variance, but refers to difference scores.

Split-half reliability Determining reliability by dividing a test in half and correlating the two part scores.

Spread The degree of dispersion or variability of scores in a data-set. Examples of measures of spread include the range, interquartile range, variance and standard deviation.

Stable characteristics Intelligence, personality, certain beliefs, etc.

Standard deviation A measure of spread of scores about the mean, the average deviation from the mean.

Standard error of the mean Standard deviation of the sampling distribution of means.

Statistical regression A threat to internal validity in which participants who have been selected based on extreme scores move closer to the population mean on retesting (also called regression to the mean).

Statistically significant Sample data with a probability less than .05 (5 per cent).

Stem-and-leaf plot A frequency distribution in which scores are split into "stems" and "leaves", simultaneously showing the shape of the distribution and the individual scores.

Stepwise regression Set of multiple regression methods in which the order in which variables are entered into the equation is determined by statistical criteria.

Stratified random sampling A probability sampling technique that identifies relevant "strata" and samples randomly within each of these strata.

Structural equation modelling (SEM) Version of path analysis which allows for existence of latent variables.

Structured observation A type of observational method that looks at a specific quantifiable behaviour in a particular setting. It involves more intervention from the researcher than naturalistic observation, but does not involve as much manipulation as experimental studies.

Subject mortality A reference to participants withdrawing from your study. Subject mortality is a particular problem in longitudinal research, in which researchers use the same participants over a long period of time.

Survey methods A series of methods that ask individuals to respond to questions relating to the phenomena under study. Can be quantitative or qualitative, and can be conducted in a number of mediums.

Survey research Research method in which participants are questioned directly about behaviour and underlying attitudes, beliefs and intentions.

Systematic observation Observations of one or more specific variables, usually made in a precisely defined setting.

T

T-distribution Sampling distribution used to determine probabilities for *t*-tests.

Telephone interview Method of conducting a survey that involves calling participants on the telephone and asking them questions.

Testing effects A threat to internal validity in which taking a pre-test changes behaviour without any effect on the independent variable.

Test–retest reliability Determining reliability by administering a test a second time and comparing the two scores.

Thematic analysis Qualitative data analysis approach which identifies and analyses patterns or themes across data-sets.

Thematic map Diagrammatic representation of the organization and relationships between themes and sub-themes; used in thematic analysis.

Theoretical sampling A method of sampling used in some qualitative research in which additional sampling is undertaken according to how much new theoretical insight it might provide.

Theoretical saturation The end point of grounded theory; occurs when the categories that have been coded account for all the data.

Theories Organize and explain facts; generate new knowledge; can be tested (and falsified); can be modified if needed.

Theory A logically organized set of propositions (claims, statements, assertions) that serves to define events (concepts), describe relationships among these events, and explain the occurrence of these events.

Thesaurus of Psychological Index Terms A thesaurus that

is used to help narrow or broaden a search of the psychological literature.

Third-variable problem A problem that interferes with drawing causal inferences from correlational results. A third, unmeasured variable affects both measured variables, making it appear as though the measured variables are correlated even though they do not influence each other.

Three-way interaction The differing interaction of two factors, depending on the particular level of a third factor.

Time sampling A technique to sample behaviour that involves selecting observations to be made at various time intervals.

Time series design Designs in which observations are made both before and after an intervention or event.

Transcription A detailed written account of the interaction between an interviewer and interviewee.

Triangulation The process of assessing the outcome of a piece of research by viewing it from a number of differing perspectives. If the perspectives converge on the same conclusion, "triangulation" can be said to have occurred.

Two-tailed (non-directional) hypothesis Alternative

hypothesis in which no direction of difference is specified – both directions are covered by the hypothesis. Predicts that there will be some kind of relationship between the variables, but does not state in which direction this will be.

Type I error Rejecting the null hypothesis when it is actually true; the probability of which is equal to alpha.

Type II error Retaining the null hypothesis when it is actually false; the probability of which is called beta.

U

Univariate outlier A deviant score on one variable.

Univariate strategy Research design which involves one dependent variable.

V

Validity The extent to which your measure is measuring what it is supposed to.

Variable Any characteristic that varies in some way. A variable will have two or more values.

Variance The average squared deviation from the mean.

Varimax Popular method of orthogonal rotation.

Volunteerism A threat to internal validity in which factors related to voluntary participation in a study may influence results.

W

Web-based data First person accounts that have been posted on the internet by an individual.

Wilcoxon Signed Ranks test Non-parametric test used to compare two averages from the same sample, or paired or matched samples; the non-parametric equivalent of the paired-samples *t*-test.

Within-groups variance The variability of each score from its group mean; attributed to error in measurement and individual differences; also known as error variance.

Within-subjects design An experimental design in which each participant takes part in *all* conditions of the independent variable.

Within-subjects factorial ANOVA NHST method used to analyse data from a within-subjects factorial design.

Within-subjects factorial design Factorial design in which every factor is a within-subjects variable; the same group takes part under all conditions.

Z

Z-score Standardized score in which raw score is described by how many standard deviations it is from the mean.

Index